AIRPOWER APPLIED

TITLES IN THE SERIES

Airpower Reborn:
The Strategic Concepts of John Warden and John Boyd

The Bridge to Airpower:
Logistics Support for Royal Flying Corps Operations
on the Western Front, 1914–18

THE HISTORY OF MILITARY AVIATION
Paul J. Springer, editor

This series is designed to explore previously ignored facets of the history of airpower. It includes a wide variety of disciplinary approaches, scholarly perspectives, and argumentative styles. Its fundamental goal is to analyze the past, present, and potential future utility of airpower and to enhance our understanding of the changing roles played by aerial assets in the formulation and execution of national military strategies. It encompasses the incredibly diverse roles played by airpower, which include but are not limited to efforts to achieve air superiority; strategic attack; intelligence, surveillance, and reconnaissance missions; airlift operations; close-air support; and more. Of course, airpower does not exist in a vacuum. There are myriad terrestrial support operations required to make airpower functional, and examinations of these missions is also a goal of this series.

In less than a century, airpower developed from flights measured in minutes to the ability to circumnavigate the globe without landing. Airpower has become the military tool of choice for rapid responses to enemy activity, the primary deterrent to aggression by peer competitors, and a key enabler to military missions on the land and sea. This series provides an opportunity to examine many of the key issues associated with its usage in the past and present, and to influence its development for the future.

AIRPOWER APPLIED

U.S., NATO, AND ISRAELI COMBAT EXPERIENCE

Edited by John Andreas Olsen

NAVAL INSTITUTE PRESS
ANNAPOLIS, MARYLAND

Naval Institute Press
291 Wood Road
Annapolis, MD 21402

© 2017 by John Andreas Olsen
All rights reserved. No part of this book may be reproduced or utilized in any form or by any means, electronic or mechanical, including photocopying and recording, or by any information storage and retrieval system, without permission in writing from the publisher.

First Naval Institute Press paperback edition published in 2023.
ISBN: 978-1-55750-102-8 (paperback)

The Library of Congress has cataloged the hardcover edition as follows:
Names: Olsen, John Andreas, date, editor of compilation.
Title: Airpower applied : U.S., NATO, and Israeli combat experience / edited by John Andreas Olsen.
Other titles: U.S., NATO, and Israeli combat experience
Description: Annapolis, Maryland : Naval Institute Press, [2017] | Series: The history of military aviation | Includes bibliographical references and index.
Identifiers: LCCN 2016050143 (print) | LCCN 2016055221 (ebook) | ISBN 9781682470756 (hardcover : alk. paper) | ISBN 9781682470763 (epdf) | ISBN 9781682470763 (epub) | ISBN 9781682470763 (mobi)
Subjects: LCSH: Air power--United States--Case studies. | Air power--Israel--Case studies. | Combined operations (Military science)--Case studies. | Israel. Hel ha-avir. | Israel--History, Military.
Classification: LCC UG633 .A695 2017 (print) | LCC UG633 (ebook) | DDC 358.4/03095694--dc23
LC record available at https://lccn.loc.gov/2016050143

♾ Print editions meet the requirements of ANSI/NISO z39.48-1992 (Permanence of Paper).
Printed in the United States of America.

31 30 29 28 27 26 25 24 23   9 8 7 6 5 4 3 2 1
First printing

Contents

FOREWORD by Lt. Gen. David A. Deptula, USAF (Ret.)	ix
PREFACE	xiii
LIST OF ABBREVIATIONS	xv
INTRODUCTION: Airpower in Action —John Andreas Olsen	1
CHAPTER 1 America as a Military Aerospace Nation: From Pearl Harbor to Desert Storm —Richard P. Hallion	13
CHAPTER 2 American and NATO Airpower Applied: From Deny Flight to Inherent Resolve —Benjamin S. Lambeth	124
CHAPTER 3 Modeling Airpower: The Arab-Israeli Wars of the Twentieth Century —Alan Stephens	217
CHAPTER 4 The Israeli Air Force and Asymmetric Conflicts, 1982–2014 —Raphael Rudnik and Ephraim Segoli	285
CHAPTER 5 The Airpower Profession —John A. Warden III	342
AFTERWORD by Professor Eliot A. Cohen	365
SELECTED BIBLIOGRAPHY	369
EDITOR AND AUTHORS	393
INDEX	397

Foreword

July 21, 2016, marked the ninety-fifth anniversary of Brig. Gen. Billy Mitchell's successful sinking of the battleship *Ostfriesland*. At that time the airplane's utility was largely unproven, and this bold, dramatic demonstration of airpower's potential was a significant event in military history.

The evolution of airpower from that day in 1921 to the present has been difficult, varied, stunning—and controversial. Airpower's capacity to achieve tactical, operational, and strategic goals has expanded at a tremendous rate. Airmen who fly and fight today have at their disposal capabilities their predecessors could not have imagined. Modern airpower, its survivability greatly enhanced by platform speed and low observability, can strike anywhere around the globe—rapidly, in all weather, day or night, and with extreme precision. A single aircraft today equipped with weapons of near-zero-miss distance capability can achieve the same effects that in World War II took thousands of bombs on hundreds of aircraft. Such technological advances have redefined the way in which military leaders can harness airpower.

Airmen have always embraced their ability to rise—literally—above the constraints of terrain and to transcend the restrictions of a horizontal perspective. As airpower extended its reach into space and the technologies of air and space merged in application, a theory of the indivisibility of aerospace power materialized. By the end of the twentieth century, the resulting combination of air and space technologies gave aerospace systems great accuracy and ensured access.

This combination has yielded a concept of operations for achieving control over an enemy's essential systems that is no longer defined simply by levels of destruction. The concept rests on the realization that denying an adversary the ability to operate as it wishes is ultimately at least as important as destroying the forces that the adversary relies on to achieve its aims. Air forces around the world seize on the advantages of operating in air and space, and now cyberspace, to project power. By imposing very specific effects on an adversary through means employed from air and space, airpower can effectively exercise strategic control over the outcome of a conflict. This outcome-driven or effects-based approach has expanded the options for the conduct of warfare beyond the attrition- and annihilation-based models that defined surface warfare for centuries. Airpower can shape, deter, and dissuade so that nations can attain their most important goals while minimizing the need for combat operations. When combat becomes necessary, aerospace capabilities can create a variety of strategic, operational, and tactical effects that yield disproportionate advantages relative to surface warfare without projecting the same degree of vulnerability.

Leading-edge computing and network capabilities have empowered the emergence of information as the dominant factor in warfare. As a result, today we are in the midst of an "information in war revolution"—one in which the speed of information, advances in technology, and the design of organizations are merging to change the way we conduct warfare. As we move further into the twenty-first century, new aerospace capabilities will create a paradigm shift in the role that aircraft play in warfare. Fifth-generation aircraft and those that will succeed them will become sensor-shooter nodes in a distributed network. When integrated with other system "nodes" in every domain—air, space, land, and sea—these assets will coalesce into a "combat cloud": a self-forming, self-healing intelligence, surveillance, reconnaissance (ISR)-strike-maneuver-sustainment complex that has the potential to usher in a new era of warfare. Instead of relying on traditional approaches that mass fighters, bombers, and supporting aircraft into strike packages to attack particular targets, a combat cloud will integrate complementary capabilities into a single, combined "weapons system" that can conduct disaggregated, distributed operations over an entire operational area.

Concurrently, the concept of employment for aircraft is evolving from a stove-piped, parochial service alignment to a loosely federated "joint and combined" construct today, on the way to a highly integrated enterprise collaboratively leveraged through the broad exchange of information. Stated another way, military forces will increasingly attain desired effects through the interaction of multiple systems, each one sharing information and empowering the others to achieve a common purpose. As a result, aircraft previously labeled as "fighters," "bombers," "reconnaissance," "cargo," and so on will play far broader roles than they ever did in the past. Capturing this potential, however, requires military professionals both to think innovatively and to shed anachronistic beliefs that aircraft can only perform single functions and missions. In the second century of airpower, we must untether airpower from the confining categories of "B- . . . ," "A- . . . ," "F- . . . ," "MQ- . . . ," or any other label. Constrained thinking, restrictive categorization schemes, and anachronistic nomenclature undermine the innovation needed.

The evolution of airpower depends on the evolution of technology, and the human imagination and knowledge that enable the invention, development, and application of airpower instruments. As the case studies in this book reveal, airmen from America, Britain, France, Israel, and elsewhere in the world worked tirelessly during the twentieth century to embrace innovation, creativity, and change. *Airpower Applied* chronicles the results of their efforts, demonstrated in conflicts ranging from the Allies' strategic bomber offensive in World War II to today's campaigns against insurgents. However, while airpower has matured to the point that it is now acknowledged as an indispensable element of modern warfare, current practitioners may have become too complacent regarding its potential to determine the outcomes of warfare.

As succeeding generations get further away from the events described in these case studies, the contents of this book will become even more relevant. Today, more than 75 percent of active-duty military personnel entered the military after the events of September 11, 2001, and that percentage increases each day. Since that calamitous date nations have applied airpower primarily in conjunction with counterinsurgency operations. While airpower performs admirably in that role, this means that the vast majority of active-duty airmen have only taken part in operations at the low-intensity end of the spectrum of conflict. Without ever having experienced the challenges posed by more demanding conflict environments, national leaders—both military and political—may become increasingly inclined to accept this most recent combat experience as normal.

Airpower Applied chronicles the dramatic impact that airpower can have on the course of warfare in a range of settings radically different from those familiar to today's active-duty airmen. The case studies in this book illuminate both the intentions of airmen as they applied airpower in a range of conflict environments and the often unanticipated outcomes. Knowledge of such experiences will become ever more important to future generations of decision makers in all services who only have experience in the asymmetric conflicts of the twenty-first century. Combining an understanding of these multiple contexts with their own experience and expertise will enable the airmen of the future to design and deliver airpower options that optimize evolving aerospace capabilities and best exploit the virtues and value of operating in the third dimension.

—Lt. Gen. David A. Deptula, USAF (Ret.)
Dean, The Mitchell Institute for Aerospace Studies

Preface

Airpower Applied presents an assessment of U.S., NATO, and Israeli combat experience spanning the period from World War II and the Israeli War of Independence to the most recent operations against the so-called Islamic State in Iraq and against Hamas in the Gaza Strip. The book uses the historical record to give political decision makers, members of all military services, and general readers a broad understanding of what airpower can achieve as a tool for national policy and international statecraft.

I am grateful to the Swedish Defence University and its Section of Air Operations for sponsoring yet another book, the previous ones being *A History of Air Warfare* (2010), *Global Air Power* (2011), *Air Commanders* (2012), *European Air Power* (2013), and *Airpower Reborn* (2015). I am obliged to my Swedish colleagues and the authors who have contributed their independent analyses over the years. For this latest offering, I owe a special debt of gratitude to Richard P. Hallion, Benjamin S. Lambeth, Raphael Rudnik, Ephraim Segoli, Alan Stephens, and John A. Warden III for carrying out their designated case studies with true professionalism and to Douglas Birkey, Anders Nygren, and Stefan Wilson for valuable support. In addition, I would like to extend my thanks to David A. Deptula for writing the foreword as well as constantly pushing the envelope and encouraging open and frank debate on airpower, and to Eliot A. Cohen for writing the afterword. The Mitchell Institute for Aerospace Studies and the Fisher Institute for Air and Space Strategic Studies have also been very supportive of this project.

I appreciate the first-class efforts that the Naval Institute Press and its publishing team devoted to turning this manuscript into a book, mainly Emily Bakely, Patti Bower, Tom Cutler, Paul J. Springer, and Gary Thompson. I am yet again indebted to Margaret S. MacDonald for her extraordinary editorial counsel; she has been of immense help in all of these publications. Finally, I am especially grateful to my wife, Tine, for her love and unwavering encouragement.

—*John Andreas Olsen*
Oslo, Norway

Abbreviations

AAA	antiaircraft artillery
AAF	Army Air Forces
ABM	antiballistic missile
ADC	Air Defense Command
AEW	airborne early warning
AFAFRICA	AFRICOM's air component
AFB	Air Force base
AFHRA	Air Force Historical Research Agency
AFRICOM	Africa Command
AMRAAM	advanced medium-range air-to-air missile
AOR	area of responsibility
ARCENT	Army Central Command
ARVN	South Vietnamese army
ATO	air tasking order
AWACS	airborne warning and control system
BDA	battle damage assessment
CALCM	conventional air-launched cruise missile
CAOC	Combined Air Operations Center
CAP	combat air patrol
CAS	close-air support
CENTAF	Central Command Air Forces
CENTCOM	Central Command
CFAC	combined force air component
CFACC	combined force air component commander
CIA	Central Intelligence Agency
CINC	commander in chief
CINCCENT	commander in chief, Central Command
CINCEUR	commander in chief, European Command
CINCPAC	commander in chief, Pacific Command
CINCSAC	commander in chief, Strategic Air Command
CJCS	chairman Joint Chiefs of Staff
CJTF	combined joint task force
COIN	counterinsurgency
COMUSMACV	Commander U.S. Military Assistance Command Vietnam
CONUS	continental United States
CPV	Chinese People's Volunteers

Abbreviations

CSAR	combat search and rescue
DMPI	desired mean point of impact
DMZ	demilitarized zone
DoD	Department of Defense
DRV	Democratic Republic of Vietnam
EAF	Egyptian Air Force
ECM	electronic countermeasures
FAC	forward air controller
FEAF	Far East Air Forces
GBAD	ground-based air defense
GDP	gross domestic product
GHQ	general headquarters
GPS	global positioning system
HVAR	high-velocity aerial rocket
IADS	integrated air defense system
IAF	Israeli Air Force
IAI	Israel Aircraft Industries
IDF	Israel Defense Forces
IMI	Israel Military Industries
IQAF	Iraqi Air Force
IRIAF	Islamic Republic of Iran Air Force
ISIL	Islamic State of Iraq and the Levant
ISIS	Islamic State in Iraq and Syria
ISR	intelligence, surveillance, and reconnaissance
JCS	Joint Chiefs of Staff
JDAM	joint direct attack munition
JFACC	joint force air component commander
JFCOM	Joint Forces Command
JSC	Joint Chiefs of Staff
JSTARS	joint surveillance target-attack radar system
JTAC	joint terminal attack controller
JTF	joint task force
KLA	Kosovo Liberation Army
KTO	Kuwaiti theater of operations
LGB	laser-guided bomb
MACV	Military Assistance Command, Vietnam
MARCENT	Marine Corps Central Command
MEZ	missile engagement zone
MLR	main line of resistance
NATO	North Atlantic Treaty Organization

NAVCENT	Naval Forces Central Command
NAVFE	Naval Forces Far East
NKPA	North Korean People's Army
NSC	National Security Council
NV	North Vietnam
OPLAN	operations plan
PACAF	Pacific Air Forces
PACFLT	Pacific Fleet
PACOM	Pacific Command
PAVN	People's Army of Vietnam
PDF	Panamanian Defense Force
PGM	precision-guided munition
PLO	Palestine Liberation Organization
POL	petroleum, oil, and lubricant
RAAF	Royal Australian Air Force
RAF	Royal Air Force
REAF	Royal Egyptian Air Force
RIrAF	Royal Iraqi Air Force
ROE	rules of engagement
RPA	remotely piloted aircraft
RPV	remotely piloted vehicle
SAC	Strategic Air Command
SAM	surface-to-air missile
SEA	Southeast Asia
SEAD	suppression of enemy air defenses
SOCCENT	Special Operations Command Central
SOF	special operations forces
SOW	Special Operations Wing
SyAAF	Syrian Arab Air Force
TAC	Tactical Air Command
TACP	tactical air control parties
TACS	tactical air control system
TACWAR	an analytical tool
TF	Task Force
TFW	Tactical Fighter Wing
TLAM	Tomahawk land-attack missile
TRADOC	U.S. Army Training and Doctrine Command
UAV	unmanned aerial vehicle
UN	United Nations
UNIFIL	United Nations Interim Force in Lebanon

UNSCOM	United Nations Special Commission
UNSCR	United Nations Security Council Resolution
USA	U.S. Army
USAF	U.S. Air Force
USAFE	U.S. Air Forces in Europe
USEUCOM	U.S. European Command
USMC	U.S. Marine Corps
USN	U.S. Navy
USSR	Union of Soviet Socialist Republics
VC	Viet Cong
VNAF	South Vietnam air force
WMD	weapons of mass destruction

INTRODUCTION
Airpower in Action

—John Andreas Olsen

This book showcases the impact of airpower upon the history of warfare, revealing how airpower emerged as a major strategic element during the course of World War II, remained a dominant contributor throughout the Cold War period, and came of age in the second aerospace century. The operational record demonstrates that airpower at times played a preeminent role in war, delivering outcome-determining results, and at other times supported engagements on the ground. Through a critical examination of twenty-nine case studies in which the United States, either alone or in various coalitions, and Israel took part, the book offers perspectives on the political purpose, strategic meaning, and military importance of airpower. The authors of this volume demystify and decode airpower's strategic history by extracting the most useful teachings to help military professionals and political leaders understand what airpower has to offer as a "continuation of politics by other means."

Airpower Applied presents a spectrum of aerospace achievements, limitations, and potential that determines *how* warfare has changed over the last few decades and *why* airpower has become a prominent factor in war. The book emphasizes the significance of connecting the application of airpower to overall national objectives and the truism that even the most robust and capable air weapon can never be more effective than the strategy and policy it is intended to support. By analyzing the operational history of the world's most battle-tested air forces, the case studies explore the political context in which air operations must be assessed.

As a whole, this book intends to encourage military professionals to combine the insights gained from these historical events with their specific fields of expertise, and ultimately to incorporate their enhanced airpower competence into discussions with political decision makers, nongovernmental organizations, and fellow officers of all services. The focus on lessons and prospects allows officers to reflect on their calling and to articulate military principles more effectively in the councils of defense planning. Thus, while the historical chapters are relevant in their own right, the potential lessons must become integral to both the theoretical and applied dimensions of the airpower profession.

"HISTORY AS A MODE OF INQUIRY"

Operational history, "the record of the deployment and use of military forces," may be of interest to many, but it is essential for the military.[1] In a profession where learning on the job can have fatal consequences, officers and enlisted personnel constantly pursue "lessons learned." Military professionals must explore the historical record to identify what succeeded and what failed in the past, and to translate those experiences into principles and "best practices."[2] Historians, for their part, are often skeptical of such deductive reasoning and tend to warn against drawing any overarching conclusions because the specifics of a situation are unique and cannot be repeated or transferred into generic conclusions. Historians would rather provide nuanced questions than absolute answers. The "use and abuse of military history" is a topic in itself, but the difficulty of interpreting the past must not be used as an excuse for ignoring history altogether.[3]

Despite its emphasis on experience, this book does not suggest that history provides ready-made, reliable, and uncontested guidance for future actions, or that it offers a meta-narrative that resolves all uncertainties. Its thesis is more modest: knowledge of operational history helps political leaders and military professionals to make better informed decisions about the use of force. Those who have a good grasp of operational history are more likely to "get the big things right." Applied military history can significantly enhance professional acumen if used as a means for training the mind. It serves as a pedagogical tool for professional development, helping military officers to analyze, evaluate, and interpret evidence and to present their findings in a logical and coherent fashion. According to Eliot A. Cohen,

> As important as the study of history for military strategists is the acquisition of the historical mind—that is, a way of thinking that uses history as a mode of inquiry. . . . The historical mind will detect differences as much as similarities between cases, avoiding false analogies, and look for the key questions to be asking. It will look for continuity but also for more important discontinuities; it will look for linkages between data points, but not be too quick to attribute causation. It is a well-travelled mind that appreciates the variability of people and places, conditions and problems; it avoids overreliance on "lessons learned." For that reason the historical education of civilian and military strategists is more, not less, important in an age of rapid change.[4]

Colin S. Gray follows the same line of reasoning when he insists on developing context: "The principal reason for the unsatisfactory state of airpower theory, airpower history, and knowledge of how to apply airpower most effectively to contemporary security challenges is lack of contextualization."[5] Gray believes that valid generalizations can be made about the strategic value of airpower if they are framed to accommodate the variety of historical strategic experience.

The Cohen and Gray principles of "historical mind," "history as a mode of inquiry," and "contextualization" form the methodological frame for the studies in this book. As these case studies illustrate, there is no single right way to use airpower in all circumstances; every use of force is situational, and any lessons must be qualified accordingly. The authors use this framework to focus on air-operational history and to examine the development, employment, and utility of airpower. They emphasize how continuity and change vie with each other; demonstrate the interplay among the political, strategic, operational, and tactical levels of war; draw attention to how technology, organizations, and concepts influence each other; and emphasize that the political and military implications of aircraft and weapon systems are more important than the technological details. The authors look beyond combat effectiveness to home in on the central characteristic of the air weapon writ large: its ability to achieve strategic effects when applied correctly for the prevailing circumstances. Airpower zealots and detractors alike would benefit from this rounded perspective because, as the proverb states, "there are none so blind as those who will not see."

AMERICAN, NATO, AND ISRAELI AIRPOWER

The selection of case studies reflects that the United States and Israel are in a league of their own when it comes to applying airpower. While the book offers insight into the air wars of the North Atlantic Treaty Organization (NATO)—specifically, Operations Deny Flight, Deliberate Force, Allied Force, and Unified Protector—it concentrates on American and Israeli air campaigns. This approach has the added value of giving the reader insight into how these two vastly different countries performed, learned, and adapted in a range of conflicts.

The United States has since World War II engaged in more military interventions than any other country and remains the world's dominant military power. In most campaigns, the United States operated with allies or as part of a coalition, but—with the exception of Libya in 2011, when the United States "led from behind"—it has always taken the central role, politically and militarily.

All military services operate forms of airpower, here defined as "the ability of a nation to assert its will by projecting military power in, through and from the air domain."[6] U.S. air-operational history presents abundant examples of how the Navy, Army, and Marine Corps have applied airpower and how the air and space dimensions have become one. This study reflects that realization but focuses primarily on the U.S. Air Force, which is purpose-built for mastering the airpower profession specifically.

The Israeli Air Force (IAF), for its part, is not only the leading air force in the Middle East but also one of the most capable air forces in the world. It has managed to bring together all the elements of modern airpower necessary to give it a combat capability unrivaled in the region. Israel has not shied away from using military power: no other country operates with such military readiness and responsiveness. Israel, a country that is smaller and has fewer citizens than New Jersey, also has excellent scientific institutions and a superb computer industry.

The United States and Israel have outstanding pilots, aircrews, equipment, and technology. Their command-and-control structure, logistics, maintenance, intelligence and targeting, and battle management in general are also of high order. The two countries have strong political, economic, and technological ties. There is a link between the Israeli successes in 1967–82 and Western confidence in airpower between 1991 and 2003. Both countries have also struggled to find the best way to combat nonstate actors and to define the role of airpower in counterinsurgency operations for most of the second aerospace century.

Although both the United States and Israel have used airpower frequently to support their overall national strategy, they differ profoundly in terms of geography and the adversaries they must face. Israel has engaged in military confrontation as a matter of self-preservation and survival ever since it gained its independence in 1948, while the United States has engaged abroad as a matter of discretion and choice since World War II. Israel lacks strategic depth and has depended on airpower to hold its own and, indeed, prevail against larger Arab armies. The United States, by contrast, has carried out its wars and campaigns over great distances in an expeditionary manner. Moreover, Israel always operates "alone" while, as noted, the United States operates with allies and partners.

In sum, the studies of U.S. and Israeli combat experiences presented in this book show how and why airpower has become political leaders' preferred military instrument for demonstrating national resolve. Airpower has become a symbol of American and Israeli strength: the supreme form of political muscle and the ultimate trump card. This air-operational history should therefore have significance for any nation that aspires to develop and operate airpower or that seeks to defend against it.

SYNOPSIS

Airpower Applied comprises case studies of twenty-nine air campaigns spanning the period from World War II and the Israeli War of Independence to the most recent operations in Iraq. By comparing and contrasting more than seventy-five years of airpower experience in very different circumstances, readers can gain insight into the military involvements that have shaped present-day thinking on the use of airpower and on warfare.

The book consists of five chapters. The first two focus on U.S. and NATO airpower while the next two focus on Israeli airpower. The closing chapter reflects on the profession of airmen and the qualities needed to direct and use the powerful aerospace capabilities of the twenty-first century.

Chapter 1. America as a Military Aerospace Nation: From Pearl Harbor to Desert Storm

WORLD WAR II (1939–45), BERLIN AIRLIFT (1948–49),
KOREAN WAR (1950–53), VIETNAM WAR (1960–75),
OPERATION EL DORADO CANYON (1986),
OPERATION JUST CAUSE (1989), AND
OPERATIONS DESERT SHIELD AND DESERT STORM (1990–91)

The first chapter explores the evolution of U.S. airpower from World War II to the end of Operation Desert Storm against the backdrop of "hot" and "cold" conflicts, total versus limited war, and the strategic nuclear impasse. Dr. Richard P. Hallion describes the progression of aerospace technology and its impact upon military affairs and capabilities, particularly the gas turbine engine, standoff and precision weapons, and space-based systems for warning, communication, navigation, and weather reporting. The narrative reveals the deep symbiotic relationship between the advent of high-speed electronic data processing and the extraordinary rapidity with which the United States applied computers first to operational analysis and then to real-time data analysis, and finally incorporated them within aircraft, missiles, other weapons, and sensors. The chapter explains how the United States became the first and only aerospace nation.

World War II marked the ascendency of airpower to a level coequal to that of land and sea power. The war's end brought recognition that the world had entered a new era—that of atomic weapons—but also one that would be radically transformed by the new technologies for delivering weapons. The Berlin Airlift then highlighted the value of air mobility forces as a means of crisis response for both humanitarian relief and military presence.

The outbreak of war in Korea caught the United States both in a state of significant drawdown and in transition from the era of the propeller-driven airplane to the era of the turbojet. It introduced the challenge of fighting a coalition air war with limited objectives, restricted targeting, and "off-limits" sanctuaries against "surrogate" opponents at a time when the United States had assumed unprecedented global responsibility for ensuring stability in Europe and had demonstrated that the atomic era had not supplanted the need for conventional airpower.

Hallion devotes most of his analysis to the war in Vietnam, emphasizing that the United States did not wage "one" air war in Southeast Asia. Instead, the conflict included an "in-country" war below the demilitarized zone, a highly constrained "up North" war over North Vietnam itself, and a variety of "out-of-country" wars in Laos and Cambodia. The doctrinal, force-structure, and technological deficiencies highlighted by the Vietnam experience forced major changes in military training and acquisition as well as an altered relationship between political decision makers and the armed forces, with profound implications for the planning and conduct of subsequent conflicts.

The author also examines Operation El Dorado Canyon (limited joint airpower used as a scalpel in a retributive strike against Libya in 1986) and Operation Just Cause (airpower in the Panama intervention in 1989) before ending his narrative with an account of the highly successful Operation Desert Storm. The liberation of Kuwait from Iraqi forces in 1991 marked the beginning of the routine use of precision air attack, reflecting technological developments in weapons and sensors that blended the classic aerospace revolution with the rapidly expanding computer revolution.

Chapter 2. American and NATO Airpower Applied: From Deny Flight to Inherent Resolve

OPERATION DENY FLIGHT (1993), OPERATION DELIBERATE
FORCE (1995), OPERATION DESERT FOX (1998),
OPERATION ALLIED FORCE (1999), OPERATION ENDURING
FREEDOM (2001), OPERATION IRAQI FREEDOM (2003),
OPERATION UNIFIED PROTECTOR (2011), AND
OPERATION INHERENT RESOLVE (2014–16)

The second chapter, written by Dr. Benjamin S. Lambeth, examines eight military campaigns, from the interventions in the Balkans in the 1990s to the continuing U.S. engagement in Iraq. Lambeth argues that since its unprecedentedly decisive role in Operation Desert Storm, U.S. and NATO airpower has prevailed in four widely dissimilar conflicts. Operations Deliberate Force in Bosnia and Herzegovina (1995), Allied Force against Serbia (1999), Enduring Freedom against the Taliban in Afghanistan (2001), and Iraqi Freedom against Saddam Hussein (2003) were air-dominated campaigns that delivered decisive results, in contrast to Operations Deny Flight (1993) and Desert Fox (1998), which had more limited objectives. The author also explains how the years that followed the high-intensity combat phases in Afghanistan and Iraq have been dominated by lower intensity warfare in which land-centric counterinsurgency operations have seen airpower used mainly in a subordinate and supporting role. Only with NATO's war against Libya's Muammar Gaddafi in 2011 and its subsequent effort against the self-proclaimed Islamic State of Iraq and the Levant did airpower again become the main tool of choice.

In examining these eight air campaigns, Lambeth explores the full spectrum of air operations and the various levels of war to highlight successes and failures: even the most successful air campaigns saw significant room for improvement, and the less successful incorporated many commendable elements. The past quarter-century offers an uneven record of airpower performance, but is also the period when U.S. and NATO airpower has steadily matured into a uniquely capable instrument of modern warfare. Lambeth concludes that among the many operational constants that distinguished the conduct of these diverse conflicts, the most prominent were consistently high levels of military professionalism and performance, skilled and adaptive planning and execution, keen attention to avoidance of casualties, and precise delivery of munitions against designated targets around the clock under all weather conditions. Still, the author insists, such combat effectiveness and technological proficiency must be viewed in a wider context; he concludes that airpower can be everything from single-handedly decisive to largely irrelevant to a combat commander's needs, depending on the most pressing challenges of the moment.

The chapter ends with seven overarching lessons: airpower will inevitably be a player in tomorrow's wars; airpower can sometimes achieve campaign goals all by itself; land-force availability will usually make airpower more effective; airpower will not always be preeminent in joint warfare; airpower and ground forces have reversed roles on major air-land warfare; evolved airpower has yet to be fully tested in high-technology combat against a peer adversary; and no air posture, however capable, can compensate for a deficient strategy.

Chapter 3. Modeling Airpower: The Arab-Israeli Wars of the Twentieth Century

THE FIRST ARAB-ISRAELI WAR (1948–49), THE SUEZ WAR (1956),
THE SIX-DAY WAR (1967), THE WAR OF ATTRITION (1969–70),
THE OCTOBER WAR (1973), THE AL-TUWAITHA RAID (1981),
AND THE FIRST LEBANON WAR (1982)

In the third chapter, Dr. Alan Stephens examines seven distinct conflicts that took place in the Middle East between 1948 and 1982. The Arab-Israeli wars of the twentieth century concerned nothing less than national survival. Unconditional defeat was unthinkable for both the Israelis and the Arabs, and this realization provided an implicit subtext for every decision and action. Stephens argues that throughout this period Israel's exploitation of airpower was exceptional, while that of the Arab states and organizations more often than not was inept—a failing that contributed to a succession of military defeats and, therefore, to the Palestinians' continuing inability to achieve statehood.

Stephens explains the Israelis' stellar performance and the incompetence of Israel's Arab opponents by analyzing the protagonists' evolving models of airpower. Israel built its airpower on the foundations of an educated workforce, rigorous standards, advanced technology, a strong economy, and, for the most part, exemplary planning. The addition of strong leadership and a clear strategic vision created an exceptional combat force. The Arab nations, meanwhile, labored under the legacies of colonialism and a socioeconomic system that in many ways resisted intellectual and technological progress. Their inability to construct an effective airpower model was the main reason for their persistent failure on the battlefield. The IAF's model, by contrast, enabled airpower to play a vital role in Israel's survival.

The chapter shows that during the 1948-49 war the IAF was a useful but marginal contributor; by the time of Suez crisis in 1956, it was an essential component of a highly effective joint force; and in 1967, it conducted an airpower master class that stood in strong contrast to the American misuse of airpower in Southeast Asia. The IAF was also central to Israel's comprehensive military victory in the October War (1973), and again demonstrated extraordinary professionalism in the al-Tuwaitha air raid in 1981 and the First Lebanon War in 1982. In explaining how the IAF developed from "almost nothing" in 1948 to a preeminent air arm in 1960s, Stephens focuses on how it was able to operate in all four core airpower roles: control of the air (air superiority), situational awareness (intelligence, surveillance, and reconnaissance), maneuver (mobility), and strike. He also emphasizes efficient command-and-control arrangements, the alpha and omega of any military undertaking. The author offers a wide perspective on Israeli air-operational history by examining it in light of international, regional, and national statecraft and politics; the logistics and economics of airpower; and, most important, the professionalism of the airmen themselves in terms of individual and collective skills, motivation, and courage.

Chapter 4. The Israeli Air Force and Asymmetric Conflicts, 1982-2014

OPERATION ACCOUNTABILITY (1993), OPERATION GRAPES OF WRATH (1996), OPERATION DAYS OF RETURN (2004), SECOND LEBANON WAR (2006), OPERATION CAST LEAD (2008-9), OPERATION PILLAR OF DEFENSE (2012), AND OPERATION PROTECTIVE EDGE (2014)

In the fourth chapter Dr. Raphael Rudnik and Brig. Gen. (res.) Ephraim Segoli describe and analyze the role of the IAF in the seven major military campaigns that Israel conducted between 1993 and 2014 against Hezbollah in Lebanon and Hamas in the Gaza Strip. The authors show that Israel has had to adapt to warfare against quasi-state organizations after the First Lebanon War and demonstrate how airpower has become an integral part of Israel's national security for the full spectrum of conflicts. In these asymmetric wars, where friend and foe operate in densely populated areas, victory and defeat are hard to define and always temporary—a series of phases in a continuous struggle between Israel and its Arab neighbors.

For Israel, the wars between 1948 and 1982 as well as those between 1993 and 2014 have confirmed the crucial importance of airpower as a coercive political-military instrument. In the process Israel's operational doctrine has tried to combine airpower as "a big stick" and as a "scalpel." The Israeli military has debated in depth how to adapt technology, concepts, and organizations to each situation it confronts and has sought to avoid relying on strategies that proved effective in the previous century but under different conditions. For example, while the IAF used to confront conventional forces operating above the ground, Hamas often conducts its current operations in underground locations that are difficult to discover and destroy from the air.

Rudnik and Segoli emphasize that after seven asymmetric conflicts with nonstate actors, the IAF now focuses more on "presence" than on "raids": it has invested in a series of drones that can loiter over an area for a long time, recognizing that "observation capacity, a short sensor-to-shooter cycle, and precision have become the essential factors in the optimal operation of airpower." This continuous aerial presence offers real-time intelligence, increases the probability of striking the intended targets, and decreases the likelihood of collateral damage. Israel has also invested heavily in an extensive air defense system.

Israel's offensive and defensive airpower superiority relative to its opponents still shapes the geopolitics of the Middle East. Rudnik and Segoli conclude that "the centrality and importance of the air dimension in the armed conflicts of the twenty-first century indeed oblige airmen to act as architects of the military system, not just as engineers or builders within it." It has been a process in which Israeli airmen have transitioned from "bombing contractors" in the 1960s and 1970s to "operational architects" of the present, while airpower has become the politicians' instrument of first resort.

Chapter 5. The Airpower Profession

The book closes with reflections on the airpower profession. Col. John A. Warden III, USAF (Ret.), examines the characteristics that distinguish the profession of airpower from the older profession of arms.[7] To this end, he outlines how airpower differs from land and sea power, identifies five special roles and three characteristics for professional mastery, examines the macro events that he believes are likely to occur in the next fifty years, and considers the education appropriate for airpower professionals. He contends that airmen's knowledge must extend far beyond the bounds of airpower itself: airpower professionals must be able to link airpower to national policy, engage with political leaders to ensure they can comprehend the potential contributions of airpower, develop and manage disruptive technology, and acquire the skills necessary to secure support and adequate funding for airpower. His conceptual foundation builds on understanding "the enemy as a system," endgame analyses, direct strategic attack, centers of gravity, and parallel warfare.

Warden suggests that identifying centers of gravity forms an integral part of national policy, and that airpower professionals must "take on the task of teaching strategy to political leaders, who rarely have any familiarity with strategic concepts." He warns against "jointness" when it takes the form of a "committee approach" and instead advocates allocation of authority in proportion to the role each service will play in executing an operation. Given airpower's strategic capabilities, Warden believes that airpower representatives could and should make the case for building plans around an airpower solution when appropriate. He also presents the advantages of a war-winning strategy with "up-front application of substantial forces" rather than serial war or gradual escalation. Finally, he encourages service organizations to provide an atmosphere in which asking "why" and proposing new ideas are "celebrated, not castigated." He encourages air professionals to consider their history and to work to understand strategy and think conceptually.

PROSPECTS

The real value of airpower does not depend on promises of tactical and technological excellence but on airpower's relevance to statecraft proper and its ability to secure strategic and political objectives at a cost acceptable to governments and the public. The future of airpower depends on the ability of its practitioners to connect it to national policy and to view airpower in its political-strategic rather than tactical-technological domains. By using history "as a mode of inquiry" rather than as a source of revealed truth, "historically minded" military professionals can make more informed decisions about the application of force in general and airpower in particular. Ideally, the "contextualization" of airpower will also give political decision makers a better grasp of what this weapon can and cannot accomplish for them and for their nations.[8]

NOTES

1. Michael Howard, "The Use of Military History," *Shedden Papers*, Australian Defence College: Centre for Defence and Strategic Studies (January 22, 2008), 4–5, http://www.defence.gov.au/ADC/Publications/Shedden/2008/Publctns_ShedPaper_050310_TheUseofMilitaryHistory.pdf.
2. See, for example, Benjamin S. Lambeth, "Israel's War in Gaza: A Paradigm of Effective Military Learning and Adaptation," *International Security* 37, no. 2

(Fall 2012): 81–82; and Benjamin S. Lambeth, "Lessons from Modern Warfare: What the Conflicts of the Post–Cold War Years Should Have Taught Us," *Strategic Studies Quarterly* 7, no. 3 (Fall 2013): 28–72.
3. Michael Howard, *The Lessons of History* (New Haven, Conn.: Yale University Press, 1991); and Michael Howard, "The Use and Abuse of Military History," *Journal of the Royal United Services Institute* 107, no. 625 (1962).
4. Eliot A. Cohen, "The Historical Mind and Military Strategy," *Orbis* 49, no. 4 (Fall 2005), 575–88.
5. Colin S. Gray, *Airpower for Strategic Effect* (Maxwell Air Force Base, Ala.: Air University Press, 2012), 21.
6. Royal Australian Air Force, Air Power Development Centre, "The Air Power Manual," *Australian Air Publication AAP 1000-D* (September 2013), 214.
7. For more on John Warden and his ideas and influence, see John A. Warden, "Smart Strategy, Smart Airpower," in John Andreas Olsen, ed., *Airpower Reborn: The Strategic Concepts of John Warden and John Boyd* (Annapolis, Md.: Naval Institute Press, 2015), 93–127; John Andreas Olsen, *John Warden and the Renaissance of American Air Power* (Washington, D.C.: Potomac Books, 2007); and Richard T. Reynolds, *Heart of the Storm: The Genesis of the Air Campaign against Iraq* (Maxwell Air Force Base, Ala.: Air University Press, 1995).
8. Gray, *Airpower for Strategic Effect*, 24.

Chapter 1

AMERICA AS A MILITARY AEROSPACE NATION
From Pearl Harbor to Desert Storm
—*Richard P. Hallion*

This essay explores the evolution of U.S. military airpower from the time of its early adulthood at the beginning of World War II to the end of Operation Desert Storm—the first air and space war—examining seven very different airpower experiences set within the context of global and transnational historical experience of 1939-91. Over the course of this history, American airmen and their leaders repeatedly learned, forgot, and relearned (at a cost) both fundamental truths and lesser nuances of airpower's development, employment, and utility. Indeed, only those who ignored the "Third Dimension" and regarded airpower with skepticism and disfavor were humbled more in the shattering of their expectations and prognostications.

SETTING THE STAGE: AMERICA'S AIRPOWER PROGRESSION FROM KITTY HAWK TO PEARL HARBOR

Before the Wright brothers flew in 1903, the American military had funded a reconnaissance airplane, the "Great Aerodrome" of Smithsonian Institution Secretary Samuel Langley. Seriously flawed, it crashed twice, generating skepticism among military officials. Only the Wrights' routine demonstrations outside Dayton, Ohio, convinced the Signal Corps to acquire a scouting machine capable of carrying two airmen at 40 mph. From this sprang the first Wright Military Flyer of 1908. Though it crashed during trials, its flights convinced the Army to acquire a successor, the 1909 Military Flyer, which became the service's first airplane. Naval interest in aviation spurred Curtiss—the Wrights' great rival—to support shipboard trials. Thereafter the Navy actively pursued development of scouting aircraft that could work with the American battle fleet. Despite this, for a variety of reasons, the United States lagged badly behind Europe in maturing the airplane, and the early lead of the Wrights quickly evaporated after 1909. By 1914 and the outbreak of the Great War, the United States was last among the world's great powers in the size, modernity, and capability of its aviation forces.

World War I was a sobering experience for air enthusiasts. A flawed acquisition process, unclear and at times contradictory leadership and oversight, and a series of unresolved technical problems resulted in failure to meet the needs of Uncle Sam's combat forces. Consequently, American airmen were "entirely dependent" (in the words of Gen. John Pershing) upon French, British, and Italian firms.[1]

America lacked the science-based aeronautical research and development establishment that other leading nations then enjoyed. That need drove creation in 1915 of the National Advisory Committee for Aeronautics (predecessor of the National Aeronautics and Space Administration) and, slightly later, specialized matériel and acquisition bureaus within the Army and Navy such as the Army Air Service's Engineering Division and the U.S. Navy's Bureau of Aeronautics. It also spurred development of specialized civilian academic education and research institutions, particularly the seven major engineering schools sponsored by the Daniel Guggenheim Fund for the Promotion of Aeronautics (1926-30).

Economic stringency and the absence of any perceived threat hobbled developing military aviation over much of the interwar period, as did struggles within each service about the nature and purpose of airpower and how it should fit with their existing models of power projection. Overall, the services progressed significantly in establishing the administrative and force structure they needed; training qualified aircrew, maintainers, and a cadre of future leaders; and choosing particular forms of aircraft and aviation support systems, including, for the Navy, developing aircraft carriers, initially intended to support scouting operations for the battle fleet, with a secondary attack role. One important development was dive-bombing for pinpoint air support and maritime attack. During the Sandino war (1927-33), the Marine Corps employed such attacks to protect towns and outposts, influencing the later evolution of Marine air-ground tactical air support.[2]

Between 1919 and 1933, the United States rapidly advanced in mastering aviation, particularly in civil air transport.[3] As a result, by the mid-1930s, America had a "dual-use" civil-military technology base in propulsion, structures, and aerodynamics. Developing mass civil air transport held profound significance for America's combat operations in World War II in ways not matched by either the Allies or the Axis powers.

Through a combination of influential leaders (most notably the "two Billys"—the Army Air Service's William Mitchell and the Navy's William Moffett), doctrinal pronouncements, individual advocacy and initiative, and various training exercises and war games, the Army Air Service (later Army Air Corps), and the U.S. Navy and Marine Corps developed the basis for their wartime forces to come. Nevertheless, both the Army Air Corps and naval aviation forces were, by any measure, small and relatively elite formations. For that reason, the mass training of civilian pilots begun as war loomed at the end of the 1930s constituted a critical factor in building a force to match the ramping up of aircraft and material production that began after the outbreak of war in 1939.

America's airpower evolution was far from trouble-free. The Navy's early interest in very-long-range large rigid airships produced three costly accidents (one of which claimed the life of Adm. William Moffett) and consumed resources and investment that could have better been spent on carrier and patrol plane development. The Army Air Corps was disastrously unprepared to carry the air mail when asked to do so in 1934 after the Roosevelt administration canceled civil air mail contracts. Ill-trained pilots in ill-equipped and unsuitable aircraft crashed all across the country, leading to a service-wide grounding and eventual return to civilian mail carriers. The only positive result was greater emphasis on training and instrument flying, which made the Army Air Corps the world's most highly trained force in both visual- and blind-flying radio navigation techniques on the eve of World War II.[4]

WORLD WAR II: AIRPOWER IN THE CONTEXT OF TOTAL WAR

The United States entered World War II deficient in doctrine, technology, and force structure. Because the United States had an Army Air Corps rather than an independent air force, over the interwar era the doctrinal pronouncements of the Army Air Corps (which became the Army Air Forces [AAF] in 1941) stressed the subordination of aviation forces to the service's ground commanders.[5] This drove development of "O"-prefixed spotter aircraft and "A"-prefixed attack aircraft, intended for battlefield air operations. "B"-prefixed bombers were intended for interdiction strikes against lines of communications, supply points, and the like. "P"-prefixed (for "pursuit") fighters were intended for defensive operations, including destroying enemy observation, attack, and bomber aircraft and protecting the operations of friendly aircraft. The Army Air Corps made a small investment in aerial resupply, logistical support, and medical evacuation, acquiring military derivatives of American civil air transports (such as the DC-3, which became the C-47). By Pearl Harbor, the AAF had approximately 125 modern transports, the core of a force that would expand almost sixtyfold over the next three years.[6]

The Technical and Industrial Dimensions

Watching the remarkable development of American civil aviation, army and naval airmen increasingly championed applying this design (and performance) revolution to the Air Corps' own force structure, necessarily affecting both doctrine and combat capabilities. Largely through the Air Corps Tactical School (predecessor of today's Air University) at Maxwell Field (now Maxwell Air Force Base [AFB]), they argued vigorously for a more offensive and strategic view of airpower, exemplified by the drive to produce long-range bombers capable of striking at any enemy threatening American possessions or the homeland, or striking deep into the heart of an enemy nation against its leadership, means of production, and war-making capacity. At great effort, they succeeded in forming a so-called GHQ Air Force that served a vital nurturing function for America's wartime strategic bomber force.[7]

While the Navy and Army made commendable progress in two major aircraft types—maritime patrol planes and long-range bombers, typified by the PBY Catalina and B-17 Flying Fortress—progress on other types was less satisfactory. At the time of the Blitzkrieg in 1939, both the Army Air Corps and naval aviation were forces in transition. The Army Air Corps was transitioning from early monoplane fighters such as the P-26, P-35, and P-36 to the P-38, P-39, and P-40; the P-47 and P-51 were yet to come. The Navy was still operating mixed biplane and monoplane Carrier Air Groups—Japan, at the time, had all-monoplane Carrier Air Groups—but was transitioning into the era of the F4F fighter, SBD scout/dive bomber, and TBD torpedo bomber with the F4U fighter in design (and the F6F, like the Army's P-47 and P-51, still to come). Much as the Air Corps rejected operating in a "support only" role, naval aviators demonstrated using carriers in pairs to achieve maximum effect, operating as a vital strategic and operational striking force with torpedo planes and dive bombers. In this, the U.S. Navy had greater insight and operational boldness than the Royal Navy (which had evolved the first aircraft carriers) though less than the Imperial Japanese Navy, as was sadly evident on the morning of December 7, 1941.

On the eve of Pearl Harbor, the United States possessed tremendous innate productive and training capacity as well as a mastery of relevant military technologies largely reflecting the dual-use civil-military industrial base developed over the previous fifteen years. While each of the major combatants in Europe and Asia at that time—France, Germany, Great Britain, and Japan—had larger aviation workforces than the United States, America's was arguably the most highly trained and most sophisticated in employing mass production techniques. Its productivity exploded, with aircraft production doubling between 1939 and 1940, and doubling again by the end of 1941, when it reached 26,277, of which 19,433 were military airplanes.[8] Between the outbreak of war in Europe and the Japanese attack on Pearl Harbor, the United States began to serve as a major weapons supplier to the Allies; by mid-August 1940 Great Britain had already placed orders for 20,000 American airplanes and 42,000 engines. After

Pearl Harbor the industry expanded further, adding new plants and distributing production among multiple facilities.[9]

Confronting Flawed Doctrinal and Operational Assumptions

Overconfidence, flawed prewar assumptions, and inept leadership caused problems that were largely resolved by the end of 1943. The military services did not profit as much as might be expected from having studied air operations in the Spanish Civil War (1936–39), the Sino-Japanese War (1937–45), and the Battle of Britain (1940). All afforded important lessons that were largely missed, in large measure because these conflicts did not conform to expectations of what planners considered "real" air war.

The Battle of Britain offers a particularly disturbing case of valuable lessons missed, for Air Corps observers were present on scene throughout. While recognizing by mid-September 1940 that the Royal Air Force was winning, the observers tended to dismiss its outcome, one then-planner astonishingly writing afterward that "concrete 'lessons' simply did not materialize."[10] Three missed lessons proved particularly costly: the value of comprehensive radar coverage, the vulnerability of unsupported bombers, and the need for longer-ranging fighters to protect bombers. Missing the first helped ensure the success of Japan's attack at Pearl Harbor.[11] Missing the second and third led to the high bomber loss rates over Germany in the late summer and fall of 1943, pending changes in fighter strategy and introduction of the new long-range P-51.[12]

For America, 1942 constituted a year of holding off the Axis and positioning forces for sustained combat in the Pacific and Europe. The Pearl Harbor attack and the loss of Wake, Guam, and the Philippines shattered prewar illusions of any innate superiority of American airmen over their Japanese counterparts. The Doolittle raid on Tokyo in April 1942 set an important standard for future joint operations as well as demonstrated to the Japanese that the Home Islands were not immune from attack. Hard-won U.S. victories at Coral Sea in May and Midway in June halted Japan's advance, eliminated many of its prewar cadre of trained naval aviators, and rendered easier the establishment of footholds in the Solomons from whence America began its Pacific counteroffensive.[13] Japanese forces landed in the Aleutian Islands, triggering a year-long war in which American and Canadian airmen faced greater challenges from the bitter environmental conditions (including blizzards, fogs, and winds) than from enemy action. In the European theater, the AAF built up both its strategic bombing and fighter forces; not until mid-1943 were American air forces in Great Britain ready to significantly participate in the European air war.[14]

Joint service sea-air-land invasions of the Solomons in August 1942 and North Africa in November 1942 marked the beginnings of two major campaigns: in the Pacific against Japan, and in North Africa against German and Italian forces then already retreating toward Tunisia. The two campaigns had very different but highly significant outcomes. Fighting in the Solomons resulted in establishment of a true joint air command with responsibilities shared among Navy, Marine, and AAF units. Nicknamed the "Cactus Air Force," it secured control of the air over Guadalcanal, extended it more generally over the Solomons, and then used that control to prosecute sea control and anti-access strikes that disrupted and then severed Japanese sea lines of communication, leading to the collapse of Japanese resistance ashore.[15] By early 1943 coalition air operations over the Solomons and over eastern New Guinea had effectively achieved air denial over opposing Japanese forces and Allied airmen were preparing to extend Allied air control more broadly over New Guinea and New Britain.

Air operations in North Africa revealed the bankruptcy of prewar and early wartime air-land operational doctrine, exemplified by FM 1-5, FM 1-10, and FM 31-35, which dictated the control of air forces in support of ground forces. The humiliating defeat of American forces at the Battle of Kasserine in February 1943, where too-restrictive air control procedures had constrained AAF participation, resulted in an immediate review and rewriting of American air doctrine. The new guidance, issued as FM 100-20 "Command and Employment of Air Power," dramatically reshaped and transformed the nature of relations between the AAF and Army ground forces. FM 100-20 famously declared (using upper-case lettering for startling effect) "LAND POWER AND AIR POWER ARE CO-EQUAL AND INTERDEPENDENT FORCES; NEITHER IS AN AUXILIARY OF THE OTHER."[16] It stipulated three sequential air priorities: (1) air superiority, (2) air interdiction, and (3) battlefield air support. For the rest of World War II, FM 100-20 governed the employment of AAF airpower, and its historical legacy has influenced profoundly the postwar U.S. Air Force (USAF) to the present.

The year 1943 was the Allies' year of testing and preparation prior to 1944, the year of great offensives. In the Pacific, the AAF began a comprehensive program of antishipping strikes against Japanese maritime traffic supporting deployed Japanese forces and on supply convoys transporting raw materials from the Dutch East Indies and Southeast Asia to Japan. In the Battle of the Bismarck Sea, a mixed Australian-American attack force sank twelve of sixteen vessels, including all eight transports and four of eight escorting destroyers. It was a signal that Japan, having lost control of the air over the Bismarck Sea, could no longer expect to supply its forces in New Guinea.[17] In the far north 1943 marked the expulsion of Japanese forces from the Aleutians and the beginning of Allied air operations from those islands against the Japanese homeland's northern flank. At sea the U.S. Navy had made good its losses from Pearl Harbor and the fleet actions of 1942 and now fielded new and powerful fleet carriers of the *Essex* class; a superb new carrier fighter, the F6F (which "made" more fighter aces than any other American aircraft of any service); and the TBF, an excellent torpedo bomber. Thus, for the Navy in the Pacific, 1943 constituted a period of "working up" prior to the great island campaigns and fleet battles to come in 1944–45. Informed by Ultra signals intelligence, the Navy and AAF prosecuted an extensive antisubmarine campaign in the Atlantic and Caribbean Sea, using a mix of shore-based, long-range maritime patrol bombers (including those of the AAF) and flying boats coupled with small escort carriers deployed in "Hunter-Killer" teams. Overall, the Allied coalition's antisubmarine air effort effectively won the Battle of the Atlantic in 1943, reducing losses of shipping to levels that, if still unfortunate, were at least tolerable.[18]

In Europe FM 100-20 received its combat test during air operations in the Sicilian campaign, which was also noteworthy for being the first great test of American airborne forces. The latter took heavy losses during the invasion of Sicily from friendly fire, illustrating the need for better command, control, communication, and coordination among joint and combined air, sea, and land forces. The invasion of Italy in September 1943 and the collapse of the Mussolini regime enabled air operations by the 15th Air Force against targets in the Mediterranean theater and across the Alps to Germany, Austria, and various captive nations. Over Germany the 8th Air Force experienced stinging losses in its first deep forays. During the Regensburg-Schweinfurt mission on August 17, 1943, it lost 60 of 346 bombers; Schweinfurt on October 14, 1943, was worse, with 60 lost out of 291. As a consequence, bomber and fighter tactics were reviewed, new leaders—generals Carl Spaatz and James Doolittle—assumed command of the "Mighty Eighth" and its fighter component, fighters were freed from escort and allowed to sweep ahead and to the side of bomber formations to destroy intercepting fighters before they engaged the bombers, and the superlative P-51—having innately long range due to exceptionally streamlined design, jettisonable drop-tanks, and a low-drag wing affording high internal fuel capacity—entered operational service at year's end, complementing the P-38 and P-47.[19]

The Maturation of American Wartime Airpower and Its Implications

The year 1944 marked the beginning of the liberation of captured territories in Europe and the Pacific. In this year of great invasions, airpower played a crucial role. Protected even on strikes deep into Germany by drop-tank-equipped P-38, P-47, and new P-51 long-range fighters, British and American bomber operations in Europe now reached a full and deadly maturity. During "Big Week" (Operation Argument, February 20-25, 1944) the German fighter force was severely mauled by the new tactic of fighter sweeps, never to recover from the combined loss of increasingly scarce aircraft and skilled airmen. As a consequence, in the buildup to the Normandy invasion on June 6, 1944, the Allies enjoyed not merely air superiority but (as Gen. Dwight Eisenhower told his son) air supremacy.[20]

The liberation of France and the Marianas-Philippines campaign in 1944 marked the apotheosis of American land-based and naval airpower during the war. Afterward the Axis had no chance to reverse the decline in its fortunes, and by early 1945 industrial output in both Germany and Japan had come to a halt. In Europe the Nazis' "V"-weapon (cruise and ballistic missile) campaign, the introduction of jet fighters and bombers, and the Bulge offensive in December 1944—the latter undertaken in winter precisely to minimize Allied air attacks—could only slow, not stop, the inexorable Allied advance into Germany, an advance undertaken under the protective cover of American and Allied airpower.[21] In the Pacific, the last-ditch kamikaze campaign, while terribly costly in lives lost and shattered and ships lost or damaged, could likewise do little against the massive joint-service, land-based, and maritime airpower forces deployed against the Home Islands. The dropping of two atomic bombs by B-29 bombers on August 6 and 9, 1945, brought the war to a sobering end, launching the atomic era and an uncertain peace that soon created its own challenges and quandaries.[22]

World War II: Observations, Lessons, and Reflections

World War II taught many and varied airpower lessons, of which these constitute some of the more significant.

Overall, World War II marked the ascendency of airpower to a level coequal to land and sea power. While airpower was not superior to either, neither land forces nor sea forces could function effectively without considering the air dimension, both in its offensive and defensive perspectives. At the operational and tactical levels of warfare, air attack had overturned traditional notions of what constituted maneuver warfare, Germany's Vice Adm. Friedrich Ruge noting immediately after the Normandy invasion that American and British airmen had effectively transformed what constituted "modern type of warfare" by "turning the flank not from the side but from above."[23] Indeed, one can go further and state that, by early 1943, Britain and the United States had established what effectively constituted a new "Anglo-American" form of warfare, joining traditional surface forces to powerful, robust, and land- and sea-based aviation forces. These forces had the ability to strike with unprecedented power across the levels of warfare, from tactical through strategic, and with power ranging from that of a machine gun through 4,000-pound bombs. In 1945 that would rise into the kilotons with the atomic bomb.

In the aftermath of World War II few argued (and none persuasively) against the establishment of an independent United States Air Force. The most important justification for that transformation was arguably not America's own wartime experience (impressive though it had been) but, rather, Great Britain's. British airmen validated the concept of an independent Royal Air Force by their victory in the Battle of Britain. While this battle was at once more complex and nuanced than simply an "airpower victory," it was nevertheless undeniably a victory made possible by airpower, as was plainly evident to the British citizens in southeastern England during the late summer and fall of 1940. Britain arguably would have lost the battle had it not established an independent air force in 1918. It is impossible to imagine the British Army supporting and funding development of the integrated radar- and telecommunications-based air defense network along Britain's eastern and southern coast that did so much to save Britain in 1940, let alone establishing Fighter Command with its expensive high-performance aircraft.

After the war, with the tremendous record of the virtually independent AAF around the globe, it was inconceivable that this post–FM 100-20 genie could be put back in a pre-1943 doctrinal "air in support of" bottle. The same was true of the Navy. The days of a battleship-centric force relying on aircraft for "scouting" and fleet protection while seeking the climax of big-gun, battle-line surface combat were over. The airplane and the submarine, the two great progenitors of twentieth-century three-dimensional warfare, had generated a transformation so powerful that it effectively rendered traditional naval surface maneuver forces both dependent upon them and subject to them.

The war highlighted as well the value of air mobility, resupply, transport, and logistical support. In this respect, America possessed more robust air transport forces at the beginning of the war than other combatants, a reflection of the tremendous investment made in the interwar period in civil air transport design. The most emblematic transport aircraft of the war, the Douglas C-47, was a militarized civilian airliner, the DC-3. The United States built upon its prewar accomplishment to develop more capable (i.e., higher capacity and longer range) aircraft such as the C-46 and C-54 (civil DC-4). It likewise became the major supplier of transport aircraft (such as the C-45, C-47, and C-54) to the Allied powers. By 1945 more than two hundred flights per week were crossing the North Atlantic, and within just months after the end of the war "demobilized" transports were appearing in civil service, together with literally thousands of C-47s.

Finally, the war demonstrated that airpower forces required the same extensive investment in science, technology, and industry that had previously characterized the rise of navies (and to a far lesser extent armies), and that they needed to operate according to sound doctrinal principles rooted in a thorough understanding of modern war. Powers that might otherwise have fared far better against their opponents—France, Italy, Japan, and, ultimately, Nazi Germany itself—had been undone by failures to develop comprehensive balanced strengths across all these areas. While all four of these nations had produced some remarkable aircraft, various failures in research and development, acquisition, production, operational concepts, and (common to all four countries) air doctrine led to disaster against enemies that, in some cases, possessed only slight but still critical advantages in these same areas over them.

THE BERLIN AIRLIFT: AIRPOWER FOR HUMANITARIAN RELIEF AND STRATEGIC ADVANTAGE

The war's end brought a recognition that the world had entered a new and dangerous era—that of atomic weapons—but also one that would be radically transformed by the new technologies of the jet engine, advanced avionics, rocketry, and high-speed flight. Public acceptance and recognition of the value of airpower, aviation, and aviation leaders reached its peak at war's end, never again to be matched.[24] Thus, it is not surprising that the wartime accomplishments of the AAF, the endorsement of revered wartime figures such as Gen. Dwight Eisenhower, and the perception that America was entering an "Air Age" stimulated establishment of the independent USAF in September 1947. In less than a year, that force faced its first great test, again in the skies over Germany, but this time in missions of humanitarian assistance, not destruction.

On June 24, 1948, the Soviet Union imposed a blockade on the city of Berlin, leaving only one possible avenue of access: the sky. The blockade caught the West largely unprepared. It came three months after the seminal "Key West Agreement" whereby Secretary of Defense James Forrestal had overseen the delineation of the services' roles and missions. The agreement gave the USAF responsibility for continental air defense; gaining and maintaining air supremacy; undertaking strategic air attack; establishing forces to support joint warfare, including amphibious assault, airborne operations, and battlefield air support; and furnishing transport and logistical support to joint forces.[25] It was not expected that its airlift responsibilities would incorporate the preservation of a large urban civilian population held hostage by surrounding hostile forces.

In fact, the U.S. Air Forces in Europe (USAFE) was surprisingly small and ill equipped for the immediate needs of any resupply effort, having shrunk dramatically following the end of World War II. The AAF had ended the war with an airlift fleet of 3,700 aircraft, flown and maintained by nearly 210,000 military personnel, supported by nearly 105,000 civilians, and operating over an 180,000-mile route network: every thirteen minutes, an American airlifter crossed the North Atlantic.[26] Then, in the war's immediate aftermath, many of its transports and their crews—particularly the twin-engine C-47 and four-engine C-54 and C-69—returned to civilian life, forming the nucleus of an expanded American airline system that flew its first intercontinental revenue flights just months after the end of the war. Thus, by the spring of 1948, the USAFE had only 104 transports—102 twin-engine low-capacity C-47s and 2 four-engine medium capacity C-54s.[27]

When the crisis erupted, the commander of the Wiesbaden military post, Brig. Gen. Joseph Smith, became de facto commander of the so-called Airlift Task Force. Within two days he organized an emergency airlift of eighty tons of flour, medicine, and milk plus other critical high-priority cargo delivered by thirty-two C-47s. Very quickly Smith realized both that his forces were insufficient and that he needed an organized, process-driven airlift operation. His staff established a flow-path from the West to Berlin, with aircraft separated both by five-hundred-feet altitude separations and three-minute flight spacings, from five thousand to seven thousand feet. In this scheme, four-engine large-capacity C-54s had precedence over smaller C-46s and C-47s.

Further analysis by air transport experts in the Continental United States (CONUS) indicated that very high sustainment levels could be reached, but only for a brief time: the aircraft would eventually encounter such maintenance issues that the airlift would peak and then decline to a halt. Further, with bad weather, flights would have to be curtailed. The solution was to improve in-theater maintenance and all-weather operations. Achieving the former proved easier than first thought, for Germany had large numbers of expert aircraft mechanics who could assist coalition airmen in maintaining their airplanes. As well, technical advances in the development of radar-cued, all-weather, blind-flying approach and landing techniques, particularly the "talk-down" ground-controlled approach, promised to ease the problems of bad weather and winter flying, confounding Soviet expectations that the airlift would come to a swift and disorganized halt.[28]

The Berlin Airlift turned largely around the personality of one individual, Maj. Gen. William H. Tunner. Then deputy commander of the newly formed Military Air Transport Service, forerunner of the present-day Air Mobility Command, Tunner had organized the immensely successful airlift from India to China across the Himalayan "Hump," and he arrived in Germany at the beginning of August to supervise the airlift operation. Tunner got along agreeably with Lt. Gen. Curtis E. LeMay, who headed USAFE, but clashed memorably with LeMay's successor, Lt. Gen. John K. Cannon. Despite their differences, Tunner was largely given a free hand to pursue what he believed had to be done. And what Tunner believed was needed most was a regularized, systematized, and rigorously disciplined airlift effort driven by statistical controls measuring and evaluating the performance of every aspect of the operation—flying hours, cargo delivered, sorties, mission capability rates, safety, and so on. He promoted competition between units to drive sortie and tonnage rates, as well as strict flying discipline over rigidly controlled schedules and routes. If for some reason a pilot missed his approach, he abandoned it and returned to base. After landing, crews stayed in their aircraft as they were unloaded (which typically took five minutes). On April 16, 1949, the airlift's peak day, C-54s and other aircraft of what was now a joint and combined force Combined Airlift Task Force teamed to deliver the equivalent of twelve fifty-car coal trains—a total of 12,941 tons of food, coal, and critical supplies.[29]

The ultimate success of the airlift, and its rhythm of near-constant operations, has obscured that initial air operations were characterized by such confusion, lack of effective command and control, and disorganization that they accomplished little except signaling to the Soviets that the West possessed the resolve to resist their attempts at coercion. Weather posed a critical challenge that cost aircraft and lives. Fortunately, the rapid advance of radar capable of furnishing precise spatial location, coupled with ground control stations, enabled transports to be positioned and guided along the major flight tracks into the Berlin terminal area, "deconflicted" from one another (and prevented from wandering off-corridor into Soviet-controlled airspace), and then guided by ground controllers into precise landings, even in near "zero-zero" flying conditions. Among the many lessons of the Berlin Airlift were the value of combat weather support to air forces and the importance of its integration with air-route traffic control and flying operations to ensure the (relatively) smooth unfolding of planned missions.

The Berlin blockade ended on September 30, 1949, although airlift operations continued to ensure stability of supplies and stocks in case of yet another reversal of Soviet policy. In a total of 277,569 flights, over 500 American and British airlifters had delivered 2,325,509.6 tons of food, coal, and other commodities to Berlin as well as transporting 227,655 passengers in and out of the city. Berlin was a milestone for multiple reasons, particularly for confirming the resolve of the West to confront the Soviet Union. Behind the airlift stood the air forces of the West, ready to intervene if necessary to protect the transports as they went about their work and, indeed, ready if called upon to attack Soviet forces themselves. While the airpower that could have been brought to bear is, by the standards of the present day, relatively minuscule, it was sufficiently decisive at that time to frustrate the hopes of Joseph Stalin.

The Berlin Airlift: Observations, Lessons, and Reflections

The onset of the Berlin crisis and airlift posed a significant challenge in coordinating the actions of Western airpower nations to confront a monolithic opponent at a time when no overall multinational coordinating framework yet existed. Decisions had to be reached in hours, not days, because once the crisis broke out, the "clock was ticking" to the point where Berlin would degenerate into a humanitarian disaster. In this regard it was fortunate that the United States, via its Air Force and naval air transport forces, had established robust air mobility sufficient to meet the challenge of Berlin resupply and that the British had substantial forces to assist.

The airlift was a precursor of a "soft power" approach, where airlift achieved a great and notable strategic success without the use of overt combat force. It also indicated the importance of pointedly backing those forces with robust strategic and tactical airpower to give them the freedom to undertake airlift missions.

The success of the Berlin Airlift—which was a true joint and coalition operation, with participation by various air forces and by civilian contract carriers—demonstrated that airlift had come of age. This included proving that a significant and strategic population center could be supported by air alone and that rapid, responsive—indeed, global—airlift offered a policy option for projecting American influence and presence into a crisis region. If airpower in World War II had been the hard, blunt, pounding hammer of national policy, the Berlin Airlift had highlighted the value of air mobility forces as a means of postwar crisis response for both humanitarian relief and military presence.

The crisis highlighted as well the continuing need for airlift expansion, particularly for special-purpose "workhorse" military airlifters, to avoid the inadequacies of civilian air transport derivatives (useful though many were, both then and in future). While designs derived from the Lockheed Constellation and Douglas DC-6—and, later, the Bristol Britannia, Vickers VC-10, McDonnell-Douglas DC-10, Lockheed L-1011, Airbus family, and Boeing family—would continue to play a significant role in American and allied air forces, the world's air forces would place greater reliance on dedicated airlift designs. These included a string of "Cs," such as the C-119, C-123, C-130 (so ubiquitous as to be the DC-3/C-47/Dakota of the modern era), C-133, C-141, C-5, and C-17, and their NATO equivalents such as the Argosy, Transall, G.222, and (most recently) the A400.

KOREA: AIRPOWER IN THE CONTEXT OF LIMITED WAR

The Korean War is sandwiched uncomfortably between the immensity and decisiveness of World War II and the agonizing discord of the war in Southeast Asia. For this reason it has not often received the attention that it merits. But it was an important conflict and one that offered numerous lessons (if fully appreciated) that constituted glimpses into the future of airpower through the remainder of the Cold War.

For the United States, the Korean War showed how quickly a regional adversary could rise to threaten and even overwhelm a global superpower, for, in 1950, American forces were nearly pushed off the Korean peninsula by an army that had not even existed just five years earlier. Korea was a war that caught America both in a state of significant drawdown and in transition from the era of the propeller-driven airplane to the era of the turbojet. As the war progressed, it highlighted the continuing relevance of lessons observed and doctrine learned from previous conflicts, but it also introduced the challenge of fighting a coalition air war with limited objectives, restricted targeting, and sanctuaries, against "surrogate" opponents. Moreover, it occurred at a time when the United States had assumed unprecedented global responsibility for stability in Europe and the development of a credible nuclear deterrent force/shield.

The Overall Phases and Immediate Challenges of Korean Combat

The Korean War had five distinct phases.[30] The first, lasting from late June until mid-September 1950, was the first invasion phase, with the abrupt North Korean attack and the ineffectual defense of the South. These led to the rapid overrunning of all frontier areas, the seizure of the capital of Seoul, and the surprisingly rapid collapse of resistance down the peninsula until its final consolidation in the southeast of the country (the so-called Pusan Pocket).

The second was the first repulse phase, from mid-September through early December 1950, characterized by the U.S. invasion at Inchon and the liberation of Seoul, the breakout from Naktong, the collapse of North Korean resistance, the linking-up of UN coalition forces, the progression across the 38th Parallel, and the (in retrospect) ill-considered, overextended advance to the Yalu River.

The third phase, lasting from mid-December 1950 through January 1951, was a second invasion phase. It was marked by the intervention of China's People's Liberation Army (though not its air force), a second collapse of resistance (particularly in the west), the evacuation of forces around the Chosin Reservoir complex from Hungnam and of forces in the West from Chinnampo, the withdrawal of UN forces to below the 38th Parallel (with the North's second seizure of Seoul), and the halting of that second invasion across a stabilized front well down the peninsula, from south of Samcheok in the east across to south of Osan in the west.

The fourth phase, from February 1951 through June 1951, encompassed a UN advance past Seoul (liberating it in mid-March for the second and last time in the war), the frustrating of a final Chinese counteroffensive in April 1951, the further advance of UN forces north of the 38th Parallel (for the second time) and establishment of a main line of resistance (MLR) running diagonally from Kosong in the east southwest to Munsan in the west.

The fifth phase, from July 1951 through the armistice in July 1953, featured fighting along an increasingly hardened, entrenched, bunkered MLR that over time more closely resembled the static conditions of World War I. This phase was replete with massive artillery duels and barrages punctuated periodically by mass "human wave" infantry assaults by the communist side. While combat action and tempo during this phase of the war were generally more "predictable" than during the maneuver warfare preceding it, the tempo mirrored to a great degree the state of the armistice talks at Panmunjom. Thus, counterintuitively, as the "peace" talks approached their culminating point, the pace, tempo, and, indeed, ferocity of combat increased sharply, as evidenced in the last weeks and especially days of the war before the armistice was agreed on July 27, 1953.

Effective command and control posed an immediate challenge. The burden of theater command rested upon Gen. Douglas MacArthur, the Supreme Commander for Allied Powers in Japan. Under his command at war's outset were the Far East Air Forces (FEAF) commanded by Lt. Gen. George E. Stratemeyer, and Naval Forces Far East (NAVFE) commanded by Vice Adm. C. Turner Joy. FEAF included the 5th Air Force in Japan and Korea, the 13th Air Force in the Philippines, and the 20th Air Force—the strategic fist in theater—spread across Okinawa, Iwo Jima, and Guam. NAVFE consisted of the Seventh Fleet, with a mix of aircraft carriers, other capital ships and lesser vessels, and submarines, four supporting Fleet Air Wings (patrol planes and amphibious flying boats), and the First Marine Air Wing with a mix of fighter, attack, and reconnaissance aircraft. As the war quickly grew in intensity, NAVFE concentrated its carrier striking forces in Task Force (TF) 77, operating off Korea in the Sea of Japan, and composed of *Essex*-class fleet carriers and a smaller light- and escort-carrier force, with coalition carriers from America, Great Britain, and Australia. Each carrier could launch an average of a hundred sorties per day in summer, and eighty-five sorties per day in winter.

At the beginning of the war, General MacArthur's chief of staff, Maj. Gen. Edward "Ned" Almond, attempted to wrest control over the air war from FEAF and NAVFE. Without regard to existing joint doctrine, he formed a targeting cell even though none of his staff possessed the requisite expertise in targeting. This resulted in wasted missions until MacArthur, who valued good air leadership as a result of his experience with Gen. George Kenney in the Southwest Pacific not quite a decade previously, personally intervened on the side of Stratemeyer and his FEAF. On July 22, 1950, Stratemeyer established a targeting committee of officers from MacArthur's staff, his own FEAF, and Vice Admiral Joy's NAVFE.[31] While this certainly did not resolve all the nuances and uncertainties of command and control—for example, the contentious issue of control of close-air support (CAS) and battlefield air interdiction forces, discussed elsewhere—it did establish an overall operational architecture that generally worked satisfactorily, if not perfectly, throughout the rest of the war.

Halting the enemy advance demonstrated the need for control of the air and the ability to furnish persistent airpower and, for the future, an emphasis upon air refueling for tactical air forces and naval aviation. In phase 1, the UN quickly gained air superiority over the North Korean People's Army (NKPA) Air Force. Having achieved this, the UN coalition—initially the American USAF, U.S. Navy (USN), and U.S. Marine Corps (USMC); the Fleet Air Arm of the Royal Navy; and 77 Squadron of the Royal Australian Air Force (RAAF)—should have been free to prosecute both deep and close attacks against advancing North Korean columns. But the coalition faced a daunting problem: defending South Korean forces had collapsed so rapidly that North Korean forces were able to overrun most of the country's airfields as well as all of those capable of supporting jet aircraft operations. Thus, effectively, the North Korean attackers obviated land-based—that is, South Korean–based—airpower, forcing most UN coalition aircraft (including low-endurance jet fighters) to operate from Japan. The distance from Japanese bases to the Korean battlefront limited jet fighters to carrying very small payloads, typically two 250-pound (or even just 100-pound) bombs, or perhaps four air-to-ground 5-inch high-velocity aerial rockets (HVARs). In addition, the high fuel consumption of early jet aircraft meant that sometimes they would arrive over the target area with as little as two minutes of time to acquire a target, attack it, and then turn for home. Over a seventeen-day period, one USAF F-80 Shooting Star squadron based in Japan dropped only a total of 7,500 pounds of bombs—an average of just 441 pounds of bombs per day for the entire squadron.[32]

Thus, ironically, although well into the "jet age," the Air Force's highest initial priority was shipping large quantities of propeller-driven fighter aircraft to Japan. The carrier USS *Boxer* ferried 145 F-51 Mustangs across the Pacific, arriving on July 23, 1950. FEAF subsequently converted three of its four F-80 jet fighter groups back to the piston-powered F-51s. (Maj. Gen. Edward "Ted" Timberlake, the vice commander of the 5th Air Force, considered that one F-51 operating from Korea was worth four F-80s operating from Japan[33]). But the F-51 was a liquid-cooled design and thus particularly vulnerable to automatic weapons fire and light flak. The Air Force soon paid a steep price for having replaced its superlative radial-engine-powered and highly survivable F-47 with the more alluring, if far more vulnerable, F-51.[34]

Naval airpower was of particular value in this pre-air-refueling era, given its proximity to the battle area, sometimes just dozens, rather than hundreds, of miles away. The USN, USMC, and the Fleet Arm of the Royal Navy possessed a range of fighter and attack aircraft (the jet F9F and propeller-driven F4U, AD, and Britain's Seafire and Firefly) that could undertake interdiction and CAS sorties on a routine, persistent basis against North Korean forces, complementing the efforts of the larger and longer range B-26 light bombers and B-29 medium bombers based in Japan.[35] In a typical day of naval support missions, eight F4Us and eight ADs launched every three hours. F4Us routinely carried eight HVARs, two 150-gallon napalm tanks, and 800 rounds of 20 mm ammunition; ADs loaded up to twelve 250-pound fragmentation bombs, three 150-gallon napalm tanks, and 400 rounds of 20 mm ammunition, sometimes with two 1,000-pound bombs in place of napalm, or with twelve HVARs (or a shaped-charge variant, the antitank aerial rocket), in place of the fragmentation bombs. Napalm proved fearsomely effective against tanks and mechanized transport, with 5th Air Force Tactical Airpower Evaluation battlefield inspectors finding it responsible for nearly 60 percent of all tanks destroyed by UN forces.[36]

Halt-Phase Warfare: The CAS Debate and Relearning the Lessons of World War II

UN coalition airpower in the first phase of the Korean War denied supplies to North Korean forces, heavily attriting them on their advance south, and, combined with resolute ground defense, halting them on the Naktong (as it did during the third phase of the war, when China's entry into the war threatened to once again expel UN forces from the Korean peninsula). Overall, the employment of airpower forces in the war affirmed the equivalence of surface and airpower forces and the three priorities of airpower application rooted in FM 100-20: namely, that land power and airpower were coequal and interdependent, and that the priorities of airpower application were, first, seizure of air control, followed by interdiction of enemy lines of communications and supplies, and then battlefield air support (i.e., CAS and battlefield air interdiction of forces maneuvering within the battlespace).[37]

This success would not have been possible had not coalition fighter and attack pilots seized control of the air by destroying the NKPA Air Force both in the air and on the ground. In August 1950 FEAF had launched a bridge-bombing campaign with B-26 and B-29 bombers. In retrospect, the campaign was more successful than commonly believed, with the service's 22nd Bomb Wing dropping eighteen bridges over three days, and one crew destroying four in a single day.[38] As a consequence of interdiction attacks, NKPA forces began to experience shortages in fuel, ammunition, lubricants, and—most acutely—food. Demoralized by air attacks, many drivers deserted (some NKPA commanders then coerced prisoners to drive the vehicles); consequently, the daily tonnage delivered to NKPA divisions fell by almost 90 percent.[39]

CAS was the most contentious issue of the entire Korean air war, reflecting differing doctrinal concepts of CAS in the Army and Marine Corps as well as the lack of joint operating doctrine, particularly involving command and control.⁴⁰ As phase 1 fighting climaxed along the Naktong before the Pusan Pocket, effective, timely, and devastating CAS was crucial to preventing UN forces from being pushed off the Korean peninsula. Overall, from June 25 through the end of September 1950, the Navy's TF 77 flew 967 CAS sorties; the USMC flew approximately 4,250; and the USAF (with larger numbers of available aircraft) flew 18,409.⁴¹

Exacerbating the problem of furnishing timely CAS and battlefield air interdiction was the erosion of basic skills that had taken place after World War II. As one Korean air-ground pilot recalled, "Things like joint training with efficient equipment that would allow an Air Force pilot and a couple of airmen to integrate with the grunts and put airborne ordnance precisely on army-designated targets had been mostly ignored."⁴²

The Army's view of CAS, adopted by the Air Force as well, encompassed controlled air support either by ground tactical air control parties (TACPs) or airborne forward air controllers (FACs) from the artillery line to the bomb line.⁴³ The Marine view of CAS, accepted by the Navy, likewise encompassed controlled air support by ground Air-Naval Gunfire Liaison Companies and airborne FACs, but from the line of contact to the artillery line. Thus, together, the Army-USAF and USMC-USN systems, when merged, furnished seamless airpower coverage from the line of contact back to the bomb line. Unfortunately, in the rapidly unfolding Korean disaster in the summer of 1950, such doctrinal strictures and procedures had to adjust to the realities of mobile warfare.

In August and September, the specter of impending defeat loomed over the Korean peninsula. Airmen had to compensate for a variety of prewar failures in training, organization, and equipment. Maps were nonexistent, often misleading, and lacked proper jointly recognized grid references. Worst of all was the lack of standardized communication procedures, radio suites, and established communication links between joint-service aircraft, forces on the ground, and forces afloat. Poor on-air discipline and chatter took a further toll, made more serious still by the short time to coordinate strikes from inbound aircraft from Japan, whose pilots were already worried about their lowering fuel states. Fully 30 percent of all Navy CAS sorties in August had to be canceled because pilots were unable to talk to controllers. Other CAS flights abandoned missions to undertake so-called road recce missions, seeking out North Korean vehicles. These were surprisingly effective, one naval aviator recalling years afterward that a flight could expect to destroy "three or four trucks, a bus, and perhaps a locomotive."⁴⁴

Following the Inchon invasion, and anticipating another amphibious landing at Wonsan, MacArthur initially agreed that the USAF 5th Air Force would support the Eighth Army in the west, while the USMC would support X Corps in the east. But the NKPA collapsed so rapidly that Wonsan was taken by land. MacArthur then placed the 1st Marine Air Wing under the 5th Air Force for coordination, but Stratemeyer wisely continued to have the 1st Marine Air Wing exclusively support X Corps. Afterward the Marine Corps' official Korean War history noted that while doctrinal and operational differences between the Army-USAF and USMC-USN CAS systems "were never fully reconciled," nevertheless "the command structure did work."[45]

The rapid collapse of North Korean forces—largely a product of the success of tactical air support during the phase 2 rebound from Inchon and the Pusan Pocket to the Yalu—fed coalition overconfidence that the war would soon end. Echoing the success of the Normandy invasion in 1944, MacArthur's Inchon invasion on September 15, 1950, reflected the successful application of joint and combined land- and sea-based aviation forces to control the air over the battlespace, deny enemy access to and mobility across the battlespace, and augment the invasion fleet's gunfire support with on-call orbiting strike flights that undertook pinpoint CAS strikes in support of the advancing X Corps invasion forces. Concurrent air operations supporting the breakout of the Eighth Army forces within the Pusan Pocket materially assisted its advance against withdrawing NKPA troops, thousands of whom perished from air attacks as they tried to make their way north.

So devastating was the totality of joint-service and coalition airpower that North Korea's communist leader, Kim Il-Sung, and his South Korean equivalent, Pak Hón-Yóng, sent a telegram to Joseph Stalin stating that UN coalition aircraft "totally dominate the air space and perform air raids at the fronts and in the rear day and night . . . by freely destroying railroads and highways, telegraph and telephone communications lines, means of transportation and other facilities, the enemy's air force impedes the provision of supplies to our combat units and bars maneuvers by our troops [as a consequence] units of the People's Army are torn into pieces and cannot receive munitions, armaments and food rations."[46] Indeed, Brig. Gen. Gerald J. Higgins, director of the Army's Air Support Center, reported that prisoner interrogations confirmed "that the impact of UN air efforts in tactical support of UN Ground Forces probably has been the greatest single factor contributing to the overall success of the UN Ground Force scheme of maneuvers."[47]

Far East Command parceled out North Korean airspace into USAF and USN zones. As the UN offensive rolled north, the remaining space still in communist hands shrank to such an extent that UN air commanders complained there was not enough airspace available for efficient air operations. By November war correspondents (exemplified by Hanson Baldwin of the *New York Times*) were reporting the war effectively won—but it was not.[48]

Air Superiority and Its Consequences

On November 1, 1950, six Soviet-piloted MiG-15 sweptwing jets crossed from Manchuria into North Korea, attacking several Air Force aircraft without success, then speeding back to sanctuary across the Yalu. The introduction of the MiG-15—a fighter more advanced than any other then in service over Korea—dramatically transformed the air war, for it meant that coalition fighter pilots no longer enjoyed a qualitative superiority over their foes.[49] Anticipating possible Chinese intervention, Far East Command began bombing Yalu bridges on November 8; MiGs rose to defend them, and an Air Force F-80 pilot claimed one shot down (a Navy pilot shot down another the following day). Unfortunately, by that time approximately 180,000 People's Liberation Army "volunteer" troops (the Chinese People's Volunteers, CPV) had *already* crossed into North Korea under the command of Peng Dehuai. On November 25 they launched a devastating attack upon both the Eighth Army in the west and X Corps in the east. By month's end, UN forces were in retreat, and all talk of war's end ceased.

At the beginning of December Marines at the Chosin and Fusen reservoirs began their own breakout and withdrawal down to Hungnam, from where the Navy would evacuate them later in the month. During the harrowing withdrawal constant air support proved crucially important, as did airborne resupply (even delivery of prefabricated bridge sections to replace a sabotaged bridge at the Funchilin Pass) and aeromedical evacuation.[50]

It was fortunate for the UN forces that the MiG-15 was not used more aggressively, for it could easily have disrupted UN air operations over the various retreating forces, especially those shielding the retreating Marines. Because it was not, throughout the retreat, advancing Chinese forces came under withering air attack, resulting in a series of ever more anguished appeals for air support from Peng. That the MiG was not used to best advantage reflected Stalin himself. While he had promised People's Republic of China foreign minister Zhou Enlai early the previous July that the Soviet air force—the Voenno-Vozdushnye Sily—would protect China in the event of an expanded Korean war, this did not include any blanket promise to intervene over the Korean peninsula. It caused consternation for Mao Zedong and Chinese military leaders, for they had assumed Stalin would furnish far greater support than he did. Stalin authorized only a carefully delineated role for Soviet airmen, emphasizing defensive operations across the Yalu (subsequently dubbed "MiG Alley"), and forbidding any cross-border operations by Soviet-flown bombers and attack aircraft. Instead, he preferred that Mao take a more aggressive stance with his own emerging People's Liberation Army Air Force, something Mao was loath to do, particularly after some early encounters in which his unskilled airmen were very roughly handled by far more experienced American veterans.[51]

It is unlikely the UN could have withdrawn as well as it did if, over the seven uncontested weeks the MiG enjoyed before the arrival of the F-86 Sabre, Soviet airmen had covered the advance of CPV forces, shielding them from routine depredations by UN coalition attack aircraft. By Peng's own account, air attacks robbed his forces of approximately 70 percent of the supplies they required to maintain their offensive. Afterward, CPV and NKPA leaders recognized the difference that the unopposed battlefield air attack had made. A report captured from a CPV study team concluded that, with air superiority, "We could have driven the enemy into the sea and the protracted defensive battles ranging from 25 January to 22 April [1951] should have been avoided."[52] Fully 43 percent of CPV trucks were lost to air attack and artillery, according to Gen. Hong Xuehi, Peng's deputy commander, and Peng wrote bitterly, "Had the Chinese controlled the skies during the early offensive campaigns, the American and British invaders would have already been eliminated from Korea."[53] During subsequent armistice talks, North Korea's chief negotiator, Gen. Nam Il, remarked to his UN counterparts, "I would like to tell you frankly that in fact without direct support of your tactical aerial bombing alone, your ground forces would have been completely unable to hold their present positions."[54]

Under near-constant air attack, the CPV suffered from steadily declining morale, as evidenced in prisoner interrogation reports. "I think it is quite impossible," one captured squad leader said, "that with manpower alone China can defeat the USA, which fights scientifically with the newest weapons of army and aircraft."[55] Fear of air attack was a common theme, some captured soldiers bitterly castigating officers back in Manchuria who had "deceived" CPV troops by telling them to "have no fear of enemy planes" as they could rely on the protection of trenches.[56] Trenches offered at best little protection and none whatsoever against napalm, the war's predominant air support weapon.

The introduction of the first sweptwing F-86As into the Korean War in mid-December 1950 redressed the technological imbalance between opposing fighter forces.[57] Still, at any one time, the number of MiGs greatly exceeded the number of Sabres: in June 1952, for example, the 163 F-86s of the two Sabre fighter wings in Korea faced approximately 1,000 MiGs, an enemy-to-friendly ratio of over 6:1. Despite this, F-86 pilots, exploiting their fighter's better transonic controllability coupled with their own generally better pilot training and experience, were credited with downing 792 MiG-15s for a loss of 78 Sabres, a victory/loss ratio over the MiG of more than 10:1. Thus, frustratingly for Chinese and Korean communist ground forces, the MiGs' presence effectively meant nothing. While it battled far away above the Yalu, along the moving front and, subsequently, the essentially "fixed" MLR, the UN coalition enjoyed total control of the air and thus undertook near-constant air operations against opposing ground forces, from CAS to artillery control to deeper interdiction.

During the war both sides had air sanctuaries immune—at least in theory—from enemy counterattack. For the UN coalition, these included Japan, Okinawa, and the Sea of Japan and Yellow Sea; Manchuria constituted a sanctuary for communist airmen. Far East Command strenuously worked to prevent bombers from breaching Manchurian airspace, for example, by requiring bombers to drop bombs perpendicular to the Yalu bridges (and then only over the North Korean side of the river), rather than along the line of the bridges, even though this made hitting them much more difficult. Rules for fighters were less strenuous, acknowledging a "hot pursuit" freedom if a fighter had been engaged over the Korean side of the line and its attacker then turned toward Manchuria. Unfortunately, over time this evolved into a largely unspoken but tacitly acknowledged practice among many particularly aggressive airmen and fighter leaders to slip across the Yalu, even as far as Mukden (now Shěnyáng), in hopes of destroying MiGs and other aircraft. These incursions did not result in counterincursions against UN sanctuary areas, although this might have reflected the much more difficult challenge communist airmen would have faced attempting to reach them.

Incursions into Soviet airspace were more dangerous, given the global implications. Generally speaking, aside from penetrating reconnaissance flights by Air Force and Marine photoreconnaissance aircraft, the UN Command scrupulously avoided overflying Soviet territory. But accidental incursions took place on at least two occasions (including the strafing of a Soviet fighter base at Sukhaya Rechka, fortunately without apparent Soviet casualties) together with the shoot-down of a Soviet bomber over the Yellow Sea, the Soviet shoot-down of an Air Force electronic reconnaissance aircraft over the Sea of Japan, and a Soviet air attack on the combat air patrol of a TF 77 carrier in international waters south of Vladivostok.

The latter incident was the most serious. On the afternoon of November 18, 1952, seven MiG-15s took off from an airfield near Vladivostok and flew directly toward TF 77, then approximately a hundred miles south-southeast of the port city. They dove upon two F9Fs of the carrier *Oriskany*'s combat air patrol, and in the exceptionally hard-fought dogfight that followed, the courage and superior training of the Navy airmen and the F9F's better gunsight and gun system prevailed. At least four MiGs were shot down for one F9F very seriously damaged. Afterward the Panther pilots were flown to Seoul to brief President-elect Dwight Eisenhower, Adm. Arthur Radford, and Gen. Mark Clark.[58] It is difficult to explain away this attack as anything other than a deliberate attempt to teach some sort of lesson, though its purpose remains unclear. Significantly, Soviet airmen never again approached TF 77.

Interdiction: The Never-Ending Struggle

Despite around-the-clock attacks, UN airmen failed to inflict supply denial upon North Korean and Chinese forces fighting along the MLR once the war of movement stopped in May 1951. As North Korea's generals found to their dismay in the late summer of 1950, and China's generals in the winter and early spring of 1951, an army on the move is particularly vulnerable to air interdiction because it has innately high consumption rates of food, ammunition, and other supplies and is critically dependent upon its transport and logistics. But once fighting enters a stalemate, usage markedly drops, and even if strikes are still productive, sufficient supplies can get through to keep an enemy force functioning at an operationally capable and effective level.

After the repulse of the second invasion of South Korea and the establishment of a relatively stable MLR, Far East Command faced a serious challenge when trying to inflict a level of supply denial on communist forces that would materially degrade their resources and firepower along the MLR. The UN coalition had such airpower available to it by mid-summer 1951 that it could meet the requirements for CAS and battlefield air interdiction at and slightly behind the MLR with relative ease. But interdiction further back presented a much more demanding challenge, particularly in the pre-"smart"-bomb era, when military airpower effectiveness was measured in the number of sorties to destroy a target rather than the number of targets destroyed per sortie. Consequently, in late September 1951 FEAF released the Navy's TF 77 from further responsibility for CAS, except in an emergency: it was more urgently needed for route interdiction. For both FEAF and TF 77, the major challenge for the remainder of the war would be cutting and patrolling supply lines from Manchuria down to the MLR.[59]

From mid-1951 through late 1952 FEAF and NAVFE oversaw three sequential denial operations, each a part of the overall interdiction effort, and each reflecting Far East Command's growing frustration at the inability of its airmen to shut off supply lines to the MLR. These were Operations Strangle I (mid-1951), Strangle II (late 1951), and Saturate (1952).

As the UN coalition increasingly turned to interdiction, North Korean and Chinese air defenders increased the number of antiaircraft guns along supply routes by approximately sixfold and deployed large numbers of light rapid-firing cannon and heavy machine guns. Thus, strike aircraft attacking bridges, road junctures, and railyards and networks took increasingly high losses: fifty-six B-26 bombers alone and hundreds of fighters and attack airplanes. Night operations posed special challenges given the uncertain terrain, lack of night-vision systems, passive defenses such as cable strung between ridges, and the necessity to dive to low altitude to prosecute strafing and napalm attacks against road and rail traffic. The 5th Air Force's director of operations complained of "trading B-26's for trucks in a most uneconomical manner."[60]

Given that most bridges were low-lying in generally flat country, damaged spans and road cuts could be easily replaced by diversions and other "workarounds," often within a few hours at most, thus ensuring that communist forces at the MLR remained relatively well supplied given their reduced usage under effectively stalemate conditions. As the airmen's enthusiastic claims of destroyed trucks and other vehicles soared to thousands per month (largely by mistaking the explosions of their own ordnance for erupting targets), serious doubts—subsequently confirmed—rose regarding their accuracy. Rigorous bombing and strafing trials by Korean combat aircrews demonstrated that even the best crews were only destroying approximately one truck for every fifty bombs they dropped, while only one or two out of every hundred 0.50-caliber machine gun rounds fired at a vehicle actually hit it.[61]

Air Pressure to Armistice

Frustration over the failure to isolate the battlefield drove a search for alternative targets, resulting in strikes from the summer of 1952 onward that targeted hydroelectric dams, key industrial and manufacturing infrastructure, rice production, and forward-based logistical delivery points and storage sites. FEAF and NAVFE turned away from pure interdiction to an "air pressure" strategy, an attempt at what would later be termed a "nodal" joint targeting strategy. In April 1951 TF 77 and 5th Air Force coordinated on a series of four bridge strikes near Pyongyang, and on August 25, 1951, three bomb wings of B-29s from FEAF Bomber Command, escorted by twenty-three Navy fighters, raided Rashin (now Najin), a major northern port and rail terminus just twenty miles from the Soviet frontier.

In January 1952 Brig. Gen. Jacob E. Smart, USAF, became FEAF's deputy for operations. Smart was determined that FEAF and NAVFE work together more productively and within months had overseen preparation of a joint plan to shut down North Korean hydroelectric power generation. It won swift approval from UN commander General Clark.[62]

North Korea had four major hydroelectric generating facilities, the most powerful and most difficult to attack being the Sui-ho Dam and power station on the Yalu, in the middle of MiG Alley. On June 23, 1952, under a protective screen of watchful F-86s, Air Force and Navy attack aircraft shattered its generators and turbines. Simultaneously, Navy, Air Force, and Marine attackers hit the three other generator plants at Chosin, Fusen, and Kyosen, the day's raids in total costing North Korea's grid all of the electricity produced by these four plants, amounting to 90 percent of the country's electric power.[63]

The readily evident success of these strikes encouraged further FEAF-USN-USMC joint operations in the months ahead. Further joint attacks followed, on North Korea's extractive and processing industry: the Sindok lead and zinc mill; a magnesium carbonate plant at Kilchin; a supply center at Changpyong-ni; the Aoji oil refinery; industrial and power plant targets at Munsan and Chongjin; and a rail center at Kowon. The cumulative effect of all of these eliminated, by year's end, essentially all remaining worthwhile industrial or otherwise "developed" targets in North Korea.[64]

The air pressure strikes exacerbated growing divisions between the Soviet, Chinese, and North Korean leadership. Xiaoming Zhang has concluded, "As U.S./U.N. air campaigns were sustained against North Korean industrial facilities throughout the summer and early fall of 1952, the North Koreans began to waver and became increasingly unsteady, and some members of the North Korean leadership began to panic."[65] The only air raids South Korea experienced were by Kim's own airmen, who, flying light biplanes and similar aircraft, made night harassing attacks against South Korean airfields and other targets.

In the fighting from the fall of 1952 through the armistice, the combatants' logistical demands rose sharply. While this meant little to the resource-rich UN coalition, such was not true for the NKPA and CPV, whose frontline supplies represented just a small fraction of those sent from Manchurian supply points southward. In May 1953 Adm. J. J. Clark had flown over UN supply areas and located out-of-reach of communist artillery, taking note of the large amount of matériel lying in plain sight. At once he realized that the NKPA and CPV had to have equally large cached supplies located in sites between the artillery and bomb lines, which, if destroyed, could not be readily replaced. Subsequent photoreconnaissance by carrier-based recce aircraft confirmed his hunch, and in October 1952 TF 77 launched the first of what became known as "Cherokee" strikes in honor of Clark's Native American ancestry. Numerous secondary explosions confirmed the wisdom of the attacks, which continued at the rate of approximately three per day through the end of the war. "The Cherokee strikes really clobbered the enemy," the Eighth Army's James Van Fleet stated after the war, adding, "If followed up by ground action, they might have caused a break-through or caused the enemy to react violently to restore his lines, consuming his reserves of manpower and ammunition until he was exhausted over a period of a week to ten days. Then the ground armies could have been released to produce a war of movement instead of a war of digging in."[66]

Stalin died on March 5, 1953; two weeks later the Soviet Politburo decided to end the war, and, after another week, China's Mao concurred. Fighting sharply increased as both sides sought to gain and hold as much territory as possible before an armistice took effect. As fighting increased, aviators took the air pressure campaign to a new level. On May 13, 1953, Air Force and Marine airmen launched three days of attacks on irrigation dams at Toksan and Chasan, releasing impounded waters that destroyed eight bridges, washed away miles of rail line and roads, ruined miles of newly planted prime rice fields along rivers, and flooded Sunan airfield. Afterward General Clark called the road and rail destruction caused by releasing the waters of the Toksan dam "as effective as weeks of rail interdiction."[67] Shocked, North Korean authorities moved within a week to lower water levels in other dams to prevent their exploitation. Afterward, Kim Il-Sung, already frustrated at Soviet and Chinese unwillingness to expand the air war, at last decided to seek a settlement. Having realized that they could not impose their will upon the other, both sides signed an armistice on July 27, 1953.[68]

Armistice and Reckoning

The Korean air war was far more extensive than is generally appreciated and involved substantial coalition air operations as well as the more publicized joint American air effort. Although numbers are difficult to reconcile, coalition airmen flew 1,170,590 sorties, averaging over 1,000 sorties per day.[69] The airmen of the United States flew 1,096,570 (94 percent) of all these, with other UN airmen flying the remaining 74,020 (6 percent).[70] While deceptively small, the participation of non-USAF coalition air forces was at times of critical importance (and often occurred at tremendous cost as well). For example, the RAAF's 77 Squadron played a crucial role in saving South Korea during the initial communist invasion, as its propeller-driven Mustangs could operate off Korean airstrips (something FEAF's F-80s then could not do), thus enabling them to have both greater endurance and greater payload. But its contribution came at a tremendous cost in aircraft and airmen. During the war, it lost 59 Mustang and Meteor fighters, together with 40 pilots killed, 30 of whom perished in combat.[71]

Ground attack—CAS, battlefield air interdiction, and deep interdiction—accounted for 53 percent of Korean combat sorties. Approximately 80 percent of all combat sorties furnished direct or indirect combat support (live fire; intelligence, surveillance, and reconnaissance; or matériel) to Korea's ground warriors. In contrast, counterair sorties only accounted for 14 percent of coalition combat sorties, and strategic bombing (despite all the publicity surrounding it), little more than one-tenth of 1 percent.

During the war, the USAF lost 787 aircraft to enemy action and 960 in noncombat incidents; the U.S. Navy and Marine Corps lost 567 aircraft in combat and 684 in noncombat incidents. Noncombat losses were thus 55 percent of all losses. Ground fire—primarily light automatic weapons—claimed roughly 90 percent of all combat losses. Slower propeller-driven aircraft were more vulnerable than faster jets as they lacked the power and, consequently, the speed to pull rapidly off-target and climb to safety. A total of 147 American aircraft fell to enemy fighters; in turn, 954 enemy aircraft—792 of which were MiG-15s—fell to USAF and USN-USMC pilots, an overall victory-loss ratio of 6.48:1, comparable to American performance in World War II.

Korea highlighted the need for precision munitions for attacks against hard, densely defended targets, particularly bridges. Bridges were also notorious as "flak traps" because, to achieve the highest probability of destruction, a pilot had to fly down the line of the bridge, along an all-too-predictable flight path. Korea witnessed some use of early precision weapons, though only sporadically. The Air Force employed its 1,000-pound VB-3 Razon (range and azimuth only) with surprisingly encouraging results: of 489 Razons dropped from B-29s, 331 hit their aim points, a 68 percent success rate roughly equivalent to initial laser-guided bomb experience in Southeast Asia.[72] In August–September 1952, Navy testers on board the carrier USS *Boxer* flew bomb-carrying F6F strike drones against bridges, tunnels, and power plants in the Wonsan-Chosin-Chongjin-Hungnam area, scoring one hit, one abort, and four misses. These efforts stimulated postwar development of early precision munitions by the Navy and Air Force.[73]

The Air War in Korea: Observations, Lessons, and Reflections

The foremost lesson of the air war in Korea was illustrating how lack of a coherent foreign policy, unclear regional intentions, ill-considered public pronouncements, and military weakness can encourage a potential aggressor to step over into outright conflict. This constituted the gravest penalty the Truman administration paid for its recklessly rapid military drawdown after World War II. Coalition forces also suffered for the failure to organize, train, and equip military forces in the half-decade after V-J Day for the challenge of conventional war, despite witnessing what was taking place in Eastern Europe, Greece, China, Indochina, and so on. Overall, Korea introduced American political and military decision makers to the uncertain world of limited war for limited objectives—one of surprisingly costly "pop-up" contingencies and conflicts rooted in ideological, nationalist, and ethnic causes. Korea taught that regional competitors, drawing on the support of larger powers, could rise quickly, challenging the ability of the United States to confront them since they only had to be concerned about their own "neighborhood" while the United States had to deal with threats and concerns in multiple regions, perhaps even simultaneously around the globe.

Korea produced only a limited victory but one that arguably was the best that could have been achieved once China entered the war. Had MacArthur and his commanders managed their advance north in a more systematic and cohesive fashion, a settlement might have been reached for an armistice line further north, perhaps from Wonsan in the east across the peninsula, leaving North Korea an independent (if rump) state. While not as satisfactory as the total victory of the Allied powers in World War II, the UN coalition did achieve its basic objective: the preservation of South Korea's independence. There were markedly different economic and industrial circumstances in North Korea compared to, say, Nazi Germany and Imperial Japan. Korea would always be more about operational and tactical-level interdiction and ground attack than about strategic airpower.

Airpower was neither as decisive nor indecisive as advocates and critics claimed in the immediate aftermath of the war. During and after the war many critics took pro- or anti-airpower positions either "proving" that airpower was "decisive" or that it had "failed." The peculiar "limited" circumstances of the Korean War shaped the use of airpower in important ways: it simply could not be employed in the same free-ranging fashion applied in World War II. As much as critics grumbled over sanctuaries and rules of engagement (ROE), the restrictions placed upon airmen in Korea were far less than those imposed in Southeast Asia a decade later. Overall, airpower worked in important ways to prevent the collapse of South Korea and the expulsion of UN forces from the Korean peninsula. It could not be decisive on its own, nor was it expected to be. But thanks to the control of the air that coalition airmen secured, all other tasks in the war were made easier. "Not only did air power save us from disaster," Gen. Matthew Ridgway wrote in 1967, "but without it the mission of the United Nations forces could not have been accomplished."[74] That suffices as a fitting epitaph.

At the war's outset, the lack of effective command and control posed the gravest and most immediate challenge, which, if not resolved, could have proven fatal to the UN coalition effort given the surprise and rapidity of the North Korean assault and unfolding advance. Debates over control of theater air and routine air support revealed the need for well-established and well-considered joint doctrine and demonstrated that prewar doctrinal formulations, however seemingly well rooted in historical experience and prewar service agreements, came apart under wartime pressures. Even as their forces fought in Korea, the Air Force and Army intensified their joint training in air support, troop and cargo delivery, and other mission areas, with the exercises further revealing how differences in the way the two services perceived air command and control over the battle area hindered the kind of smooth integration both sides sought, emphasizing yet again the necessity of paying more than lip service to joint doctrine.[75]

Halting the North Korean advance highlighted the necessity of air control, persistent airpower application, and air refueling. Without control of the air, the UN coalition would not have had the benefits of the persistent airpower that constituted the single greatest factor in bringing two invasions to a halt as well as furnishing routine support across the MLR following its establishment in the late spring of 1951. But the opening of the war also demonstrated the necessity of equipping tactical forces for air refueling, as the North Korean advance, by rapidly seizing airfields, almost succeeded in inflicting air denial upon embattled UN forces.

Halt-phase operations reaffirmed earlier lessons about the roles and missions of airpower and the devastating effect air attack has upon mobile mechanized forces and those bereft of supporting air cover. As evidenced by communications and dissension among North Korean, Chinese, and Soviet authorities as well as by interrogations of captured communist forces of all ranks, air attack severely impacted North Korean (and later Chinese) logistics, combat efficiency, and morale. Again, this reflected badly on the communist air strategy, which emphasized defensive operations over the North Korean heartland rather than undertaking offensive air support of its advancing ground forces. UN battlefield air attack proved effective despite the relatively low leverage of imprecise bombing and strafing characteristics of the pre-precision-sensor and precision-weapon era.

Though seemingly low by the standards of World War II, Korean War loss rates, whether from combat or operationally related causes, were surprisingly high given the oft-cited "limited" nature of the war. Not surprisingly, ground fire and controlled flight into terrain constituted the two greatest dangers facing UN combat airmen operating over Korea. While jet aircraft were less susceptible to loss than slower propeller-driven ones, they were not immune—an ominous signal for the future. The high level of operational (noncombat) losses forced greater emphasis on training and standardization in the post-Korea period. It likewise illustrated how quickly seemingly small but persistent losses could affect force structure, operational tempo, and mission capability, something that would be relearned in Vietnam and illustrated most dramatically during Israel's experience in the 1973 Arab-Israeli War.

Korea accelerated the emergence of the Air Force as a globally deploying and globally ranging force, one that had to have an expeditionary mindset. After the war the service fully embraced air refueling for its tactical aircraft, not just its strategic bombers. Global deployments of fighter forces enabled by aerial refueling became commonplace, particularly during times of crisis, such as over Quemoy and Matsu and Lebanon in 1958.[76] In addition, influenced by its Berlin experience as well as Korea, the Air Force moved rapidly to bring its airlift forces into the gas turbine age, exemplified best, perhaps, by the extraordinarily versatile Lockheed C-130, which replaced the iconic Douglas C-47 as the exemplar of military airlift.

SOUTHEAST ASIA: AIRPOWER IN MULTIPLE AIR WARS

The U.S. Navy and U.S. Air Force followed different paths in evolving their service aviation in the aftermath of the Korean armistice. For the U.S. Navy, Korea constituted an important "wake-up call," highlighting equipment, doctrinal, and operational deficiencies that had to be redressed if the service were to meet the jet age's global power-projection challenges. The carrier, previously a destroyer of fleets with a secondary role as a prosecutor of littoral warfare, was recast primarily as a mobile airfield and tool of crisis response. It was reshaped as well, beginning with the USS *Forrestal* of 1955, the first of the supercarriers. Unlike their smaller *Essex*-class predecessors, the supercarriers adopted three innovations from British practice: angled flight decks (affording a welcome increase in operational safety, particularly for jet aircraft), steam-fed rather than hydraulic catapults, and mirror landing systems. (Later they grew larger still, and with nuclear propulsion reflecting the Rickover revolution.) At over twice the displacement of earlier vessels, they had the size and flight deck area to safely operate the highest performance jet aircraft. The Navy also moved rapidly to replace its "legacy" aircraft dating to World War II, developing the types with which it would fight the war in Southeast Asia a decade later. In particular, the service invested in airborne early warning (AEW), surface-to-air missiles (SAMs), air-to-air missiles (notably, both Sparrow and Sidewinder were Navy-rooted programs), "buddy" air-refueling, "smart" weapons such as Bullpup and Walleye, all-weather day/night attack (with the Grumman A-6), and swing-role air-to-air and air-to-surface strike fighters typified by the McDonnell F-4. Altogether, the Navy was far more capable a decade after the Korean War than in June 1950.[77]

For the Air Force, Korea appeared an unalloyed triumph, particularly the lopsided air war over MiG Alley.[78] Unfortunately, the service's wartime performance bred an unwarranted complacency while the war itself seemed atypical of the future atomic-centric war its leadership envisioned having to fight. They viewed the world largely through the prism of waging and defending against atomic war, exemplified by the introduction of AFM 1-8, a doctrine on strategic air operations issued in May 1954 and consistent with President Eisenhower's "New Look" defense doctrine.[79] In 1955 Eisenhower's National Security Council (NSC) issued NSC 5501, which stated that the United States must "develop and maintain its effective nuclear-air retaliatory power, and must keep that power secure from neutralization or from a Soviet knockout blow."[80] Thus, throughout the 1950s, the Air Force prepared for atomic war, developing long-range bombers, intercontinental ballistic missiles, an early-warning network, and rocket- and missile-armed interceptors. Of its 5,525 Century series fighters, just 1,274—less than a quarter—were fighter-bombers capable of "traditional" conventional air-to-air and air-to-ground operations.[81] Writing in 1968 Gen. Bruce K. Holloway, the Air Force vice chief of staff (and a noted fighter leader), stated: "Between 1954 and 1962, the USAF training curriculum for fighter pilots included little, if any, air-to-air combat. This omission was partly a result of doctrine, which then regarded tactical fighters primarily as a means for delivering nuclear ordnance."[82]

The 1960 election of President John F. Kennedy resulted in a redirection of America's social, civil, military, diplomatic, scientific, and technological priorities. Yet, within just weeks of taking office, the Kennedy administration stumbled badly. On April 17, 1961, 1,400 Central Intelligence Agency (CIA)– and Department of Defense (DoD)–trained Cuban exiles landed at the Bay of Pigs, intent upon ousting Fidel Castro. Planned in the last year of the Eisenhower administration and executed in the first months of Kennedy's, the invasion collapsed into ignominious defeat. Given the small size of the landing force, it is difficult to imagine it could have catalyzed a broader national uprising against the charismatic Castro. But for airmen, it held broader and more disturbing lessons. Although CIA planners had emphasized destroying Castro's air force, the Joint Chiefs, Secretary of State Dean Rusk, and, ultimately, Kennedy himself rejected their recommendations, canceling planned strikes just as the operation got under way. Consequently, the air strikes that did take place achieved far less than hoped. Castro's airmen controlled the skies, and, using their few flyable Sea Fury fighters and armed T-33 trainers, sank two transports (one of which, the *Rio Escondido*, carried the force's ammunition and much of its communications support) and downed several Agency-flown B-26s, killing four American Air National Guard pilots. Short of ammunition and denied air support, the landing force quickly disintegrated into small groups just seeking to escape. The administration now effectively abandoned them; the majority went into captivity— some to their death—even though on-scene naval forces, if authorized, likely could have executed a Dunkirk-like extraction.[83] In the Bay of Pigs one can discern the same fatal pattern of half-heartedness, uncertainty, indecision, political intervention in operational planning, and contradictory command and control all too soon associated with the coming air war in Southeast Asia.

As bruising as the Bay of Pigs had been, and although Cuba would soon enough demand the Kennedy administration's fullest attention in arguably the single most dangerous crisis of the Cold War era, Kennedy and his advisors faced a more complex challenge: the escalation of insurgency across Southeast Asia, largely fomented and supported by the Ho Chi Minh's North Vietnamese government. Prior to his election, Kennedy had roundly criticized Eisenhower's defense policy, which he derided as a choice between "all or nothing at all, world devastation or submission."[84] Thus, upon assuming office, he oversaw redirection of American defense policy and transformation of its national security establishment. Together with his secretary of defense, Robert S. McNamara, he proposed a policy of "graduated pressure" using conventional forces—a policy that would necessitate major changes in training and weapon-system acquisition—to move away from the nuclear-centric 1950s. In June 1961, with Southeast Asia clearly in mind, National Security Advisor McGeorge Bundy directed the services to review the forces they had for unconventional warfare and paramilitary operations, a first step toward determining goals, requirements, and a cohesive strategy for waging such warfare.[85]

For the Army, the Kennedy initiatives triggered formation of a special Army Tactical Mobility Requirements Board, chaired by Lt. Gen. Hamilton Howze, to reshape the Army's air mobility forces. The Howze board subsequently recommended special air assault divisions formed around the capabilities of two then-new turboshaft-powered helicopters, the single-rotor UH-1 (the "Huey," soon to become the iconic symbol of the war in Southeast Asia) and the twin-rotor CH-47, as well as two fixed-wing transport and reconnaissance aircraft, the CV-2 (later redesignated C-7 and transferred to the U.S. Air Force) and the OV-1. The first air assault division, predecessor of the famed 1st Cavalry Division (Air Mobile) in Southeast Asia, formed at Fort Benning late in 1962.[86]

For the Air Force, the Kennedy transformation built upon earlier initiatives and launched new ones. After its Korean experience, the Air Force had established air-refueled Composite Air Strike Forces that could quickly respond to crises, and these featured prominently in the Taiwan Straits, Lebanon, and Berlin crises of the late 1950s and early 1960s. NATO's needs resulted in expansion of USAFE, charged with air defense of the alliance and with prosecution of tactical and strategic nuclear strikes in accordance with NATO doctrine. Closer to home, the Air Force furnished extensive reconnaissance support during the Cuban missile crisis of October 1962, including stratospheric U-2 overflights (one of which was lost to an SA-2 SAM, together with its pilot), low-level RF-101 tactical reconnaissance sorties, and maritime patrol sorties to locate Soviet vessels and enforce the naval blockade imposed against the Cuban regime.

The Air Force soon took a more active role in counterinsurgency warfare. This was in many ways a return to its roots, for as the U.S. Army Air Forces, it had pioneered "Carpetbagger" and "Air Commando" operations in Europe and South Asia during World War II and had participated in many covert actions since supporting conventional forces in Korea and elsewhere. In mid-April 1961 the Air Force launched Project Jungle Jim at Eglin AFB, Florida. Jungle Jim combined training and combat, instructing airmen from foreign air forces, and furnishing Air Force airmen in an oversight role "for supervising the development of unit combat capability in similar type aircraft of friendly foreign nations."[87]

Prequel: The United States and Southeast Asia

In 1961 American airmen went to war in Southeast Asia in tandem with the nation's military services, those of host countries, and representatives the CIA. They flew over most of Southeast Asia, and CIA U-2s overflew North Vietnam. Such region-wide operations demonstrated that, even by the earliest days of America's involvement, the expression "Vietnam war" was little more than a convenient popular shorthand for a much broader conflict in which the two Vietnams then extant constituted the most visible (though hardly only) arenas. Although the conflict ostensibly ended with the collapse of South Vietnam and the denouement of the *Mayaguez* incident in 1975, its reverberations and repercussions subsequently became tragically evident in Pol Pot's Cambodia and the Sino-Vietnamese short war that occurred later in the decade.[88]

Just as the "Vietnam war" was broader than the expression implies, so too was its air war. There was no "one" air war; instead, the combatants carried out a multi-tiered air war consisting of "out-of-country" wars in Laos and Cambodia, an "in-country" war below the demilitarized zone (DMZ), and a highly constrained war over North Vietnam itself.[89] The doctrinal, force-structure, and technological deficiencies highlighted by the Vietnam experience forced major changes in military training and acquisition as well as a changed relationship between political decision makers and the military, with implications for subsequent conflicts. Any discussion of the various "Vietnam air war(s)" must consider time period and location.

Laos and the War to Sever the Ho Chi Minh Trail

Key to regional stability was Laos, running roughly north-south along the western borderlands of both North and South Vietnam. A leftist Laotian insurgency pitted two half-brother princes, centrist Souvanna Phouma and leftist Souphanouvong (known as the "Red Prince") against one other. Laos occupied a position of extreme strategic importance as the multibranched communist supply line—soon known as the "Ho Chi Minh Trail"—ran through it (and Cambodia), bypassing the DMZ and acting as a conduit for North Vietnamese supplies (delivered from the Soviet Union, China, and the Eastern Bloc) and personnel.[90]

In June 1960 the Joint Chiefs of Staff had recommended to the secretary of defense that he secure "support of counter-insurgency operations in Laos and Vietnam."[91] In August 1960 a dissident Laotian officer, Kong Le, overthrew the government and persuaded Souvanna Phouma to assume the mantle of prime minister. North Vietnam and the Soviet Union then responded with military aid. America moved uncertainly back and forth before eventually uneasily supporting an internationally brokered tripartite left-right-center regime headed by Souvanna Phouma. Within it, Kong Le played an often distracting, even disruptive, role as chief of the army before being dismissed in 1966 and going into exile.[92]

In January 1961, on the eve of Kennedy's taking office, Eisenhower warned the young president-elect that if Laos fell, all of Southeast Asia (SEA) could follow, consistent with the then-popular "domino theory" that Ike had first enunciated at a news conference almost a decade earlier, in April 1954.[93] Kennedy concurred, although that he readily accepted Laotian neutralization on July 23, 1962, suggests he either did not fully comprehend or did not fully share Eisenhower's concern over controlling its territory.[94]

The 1954 Geneva Accords prohibited introducing advanced aircraft into the region, so air operations involved older piston-engine designs predating 1954. Thus, America's air war over Laos began in December 1960 with two reconnaissance sorties flown by a C-47 assigned for use by the embassy's air attaché. In early March Kennedy approved a covert air strike, Project Mill Pond, by sixteen CIA and Air Force B-26s targeting Xieng Khouang airfield and Pathet Lao troop concentrations. A special communications-gathering C-47, detailed from Korea to gather information for the upcoming strike, was shot down over the Plain of Jars on March 23—the first American combat aircraft lost in SEA—with the loss of all but one of its crew.[95] After the Bay of Pigs disaster, plans for Mill Pond were abruptly abandoned.

The signing of the 1962 accords, which governed the neutralization of Laos, worked to accelerate North Vietnamese aid to the Viet Cong (VC). Virtually immediately thereafter the pace of communist activities on the trail increased, and with that increase came an increase in the intensity of what was emerging as an intensive, if largely secret, air war.

Laos came to exemplify the jumbled and intersecting chains of command and at times crippling decision-making processes more commonly associated with the air war over North Vietnam. The confusion was exacerbated by successive ambassadors—Leonard Unger, William Sullivan, and G. McMurtrie Godley—who, as the senior Americans in Laos, had responsibility for overseeing all American military operations. In Laos itself, Air Force Raven FACs (flying O-1s and T-28s) and CIA Air America paramilitaries generally preferred the close and streamlined command relationships they enjoyed with the ambassadors and Gen. Vang Pao's Hmong over those with the more cumbersome and slow-to-respond 7th Air Force of the Pacific Air Forces (PACAF) structure. This clearly annoyed higher authorities, one of whom questioned (not without reason) "Lieutenants and Captains running their own air war."[96] "Command relationships with the Ambassador in Laos were complex and difficult," former 7th Air Force commander Gen. William W. Momyer wrote after the war, noting, "In effect the embassy air attaché functioned as an air commander since he could determine 7th Air Force employment through the authority of the

Ambassador."[97] "As long as I was there [1962–64]," Unger recalled, "there was no bombing carried out unless they had explained to me what they intended to do. I had to be satisfied that it was not, in a serious way, going to interfere with things in Laos."[98] Unger was "a most reluctant militarist" (in Sullivan's words), and he passed up some opportunities for potentially productive attacks, encouraging President Lyndon Johnson to restrict U.S. Air Force operations over Laos lest it risk expanding the war.[99]

Unger's successor, William Sullivan, enjoyed being military supremo. "Many a night [I] had to decide whether to order the evacuation of an outpost under attack, to hold on, to reinforce, to call for air support, or to mount a diversionary action to relieve the pressure on the front," he recalled; "It was a far cry from the normal pursuits of the striped-pants set."[100] Though Sullivan took pride in having "only a handful" of casualties among Laos' American military and paramilitary personnel, one blunder led to loss of a radar station, Lima Site 85. Perched on a sheer rock cliff, it furnished positional cuing for strike flights over North Vietnam. It fell to the North Vietnamese Army (PAVN, the People's Army of Vietnam) in 1968 due to a fatal misreading of enemy intent, the ignoring of clear intelligence indicators, and a disturbing complacency.[101]

The Laotian air war escalated significantly in 1964 after the Pathet Lao seized control of the Plain of Jars. The United States accelerated reconnaissance over Laos by Air Force, Navy, and CIA aircraft. In June 1964, following the shoot-down of two Navy airplanes, the Air Force deployed F-100 fighter-bombers from Thailand to Tan Son Nhut, South Vietnam, and on June 9 they attacked Pathet Lao antiaircraft sites near Xieng Khouang. In November VC mortar teams shelled Bien Hoa air base outside Saigon, killing four Americans and destroying or damaging a number of aircraft; in response, the Air Force and Navy launched air strikes into Laos.

Thereafter the air war steadily expanded. Air Force and naval attackers operating over southern Laos on Steel Tiger interdiction attacks or on Barrel Roll strikes over the north now employed a variety of strike aircraft ranging from propeller-driven attack aircraft to jet-propelled "fast movers" and specialized loitering transports-turned-gunships (the latter, in retrospect, the most successful of all interdiction attack systems used over the trail).[102] Altogether, from 1964 through 1967, American airmen averaged roughly 170 strike sorties per day flying against the Ho Chi Minh Trail. Trail sorties escalated sharply after November 1, 1968, which marked the beginning of the Commando Hunt trail interdiction program. From then through the Vientiane agreement signed on February 21, 1973, American airmen flew 401,296 strike sorties over Laos, an average of 265 air strikes every day, almost equaling the combined total of air strikes flown over South *and* North Vietnam across the war, dropping a total of 3 million tons of ordnance over the Ho Chi Minh Trail, though to little effect: only a blocking force actually in place across the trail could have achieved success.[103]

Consequently, despite this massive effort, the Laotian war ended in failure. Over a decade, and with great courage and skill, the airmen and the Hmong staved off the Pathet Lao (and more typically the PAVN), thus saving many villages, hamlets, and strategic locations, but their actions were largely limited by the current state of technology and contemporaneous policy. As in Korea, the trail attacks—over Cambodia as well as Laos—despite destroying thousands of vehicles, could not halt the flow of matériel and supplies. After Sullivan's departure, the war turned toward the conventional, with the PAVN making mass assaults and increasingly using mechanized vehicles, inflicting such heavy casualties on Vang Pao's hard-pressed Hmong that no less than thirty battalions of Thai mercenaries were imported to augment his forces. Meanwhile, Sullivan's successor, G. McMurtrie Godley (as historian Timothy Castle has noted), "clung to the policies of the past and allowed his staff to dictate military requirements to a wholly exasperated 7/13thAF and COMUSMACV [Commander U.S. Military Assistance Command Vietnam]."[104]

In January 1971 South Vietnam and the United States launched an ambitious cross-border assault, Operation Dewey Canyon II/Lam Son 719, to seize Tchepone and cut the trail. Unfortunately, as one Raven recalled, it "turned into a disaster" because of "poor security all around," leadership that "did not face military reality," and inept execution.[105] U.S.-Vietnamese forces suffered approximately 8,400 casualties, including 700 helicopters lost or damaged to light flak and automatic weapons.[106] The 1973 Vientiane agreement (which, by removing all U.S. and Thai military personnel from Laos, brought U.S. air operations to a halt) failed to constrain the PAVN. This, given the chronic ineptness of the Laotian government and its military (excepting Vang Pao's Hmong) and the failure of the U.S. Congress to furnish further aid spelled disaster. In May 1975, following the collapse of South Vietnam the previous month, Souvanna Phouma directed his military to cooperate with the Pathet Lao. On December 2, 1975, Laos became a communist state. That it had lasted as long as it did was a strong tribute to the airmen and Hmong who fought in its defense.[107]

The War over the Two Vietnams: Farm Gate to Pleiku and Flaming Dart

The full panoply of American military might—the aircraft, personnel, formidable logistics enterprise, and massive basing complexes—was most readily evident in the ground and air war fought in South Vietnam and in the skies over North Vietnam. In late 1961 American aviators entered the Vietnam air war. In early October, President Kennedy had ordered the Air Force to deploy a detachment of its Jungle Jim combat crew training program to Vietnam under the project name Farm Gate. Team members arrived at Bien Hoa in November assigned to the Military Assistance Advisory Group. Farm Gate consisted of 155 airmen, 8 T-28 armed trainers, 4 C-47s, and 4 B-26s, the latter delivered slightly later.[108] Its members were ostensibly teaching Vietnamese "students" although, one recalled, "I never logged a single 'training' sortie."[109] Another bluntly wrote, "Training was a façade [and South Vietnam air force (VNAF)] participants knew the back-seat rider requirement was political."[110] A third recalled that VNAF "students" (dubbed "sandbags") were "never allowed anywhere near the controls of the aircraft."[111]

In November the Kennedy administration ordered the deployment of Air Force light assault transports and Army helicopters to increase the mobility of the South Vietnamese army (ARVN). Dispatched under Project Mule Train (ostensibly a "classified training mission"), a squadron of C-123s left Pope AFB for Vietnam in mid-December, arriving at Tan Son Nhut Air Base in early January and immediately flying troop-lift sorties.[112] That same month (responding to a request by South Vietnamese president Ngô Đình Diệm), the Air Force dispatched six C-123s modified as herbicidal sprayers to clear obscuring vegetation away from highways, roads, and trails, beginning Project Ranch Hand.[113] In December four hundred Army troops and thirty-three H-21 helicopters arrived to give the ARVN a modest air assault ability (although the Army soon recognized that the H-21 was both "old and unsuited for this particular mission").[114]

Early air operations over Vietnam and neighboring Laos revealed that the tactical air lessons of World War II and even Korea had been lost. Communication procedures between ground and air forces suffered from lack of equipment, training, and, consequently, basic proficiency. Airmen operated under a convoluted command structure that soon characterized the war as a whole. They lacked reliable maps, photoreconnaissance imagery, and local awareness and had to develop a knowledge base on their own. In one case, inadequate maps led to Farm Gate T-28s accidentally bombing a Cambodian village, generating subsequent ROE that severely constrained operations in the border region.[115]

In short, waging a counterguerrilla air war was essentially new to American airmen. In this effort, airmen had little institutional knowledge to draw upon, except for Air University–sponsored studies of Nazi Germany's counterpartisan campaigns in World War II, the French air campaigns in Indochina and Algeria, and the British experience in Malaya and Kenya. Very quickly they learned to minimize exposure time by flying as low and fast as possible. Dense foliage inhibited view. Absent more lucrative targets, planners ordered attacks on lightly constructed (and thus easily replaced) vine and wood bridges crossing streams and rivers. ("The dumbest missions I've ever flown," one pilot recalled.[116]) More helpful were road patrols by circling T-28s and B-26s "capping" troop convoys and logistics vehicles, preventing the ambush debacles of the first Indochina war, and thus effectively rediscovering the benefits of "on-call cab-rank column cover" sorties such as those that protected American and British armored forces.[117]

Over the summer of 1963 Farm Gate greatly expanded with formation of a special composite Air Commando squadron. Other squadrons soon followed, accompanying the rapid expansion of American involvement in the war.[118] Much as political intrigue and rivalries marred the unity of effort in Laos, Vietnam experienced its own disquiet, ending in the violent coup that overthrew the Diệm regime—a coup undertaken with Kennedy administration connivance—resulting in the death of Diệm and his brother. The civic tranquility its supporters desired never materialized. Instead, through the collapse of Vietnam in 1975, coups and countercoups came to characterize Vietnamese political life, with the United States caught between factions and the North Vietnamese skillfully exploiting South Vietnam's discontents for their own ends.

The abject failure of the ARVN to successfully counter the rapidly blooming insurgency over the 1963 to early 1965 time period signaled what many feared would be the imminent collapse of South Vietnam and changed the role of the United States from an advisory partner to an ally deploying large numbers of its forces. So alarmed was Adm. Harry D. Felt, commander in chief (CINC) of U.S. Pacific Command (CINCPAC of PACOM), that he directed preparation in March 1964 of a three-phase plan for air attacks to reduce North Vietnam's industrial power, military capabilities, and ability to support the VC and Pathet Lao.[119] However, in a meeting between the State Department and Military Assistance Command, Vietnam (MACV) principals in Saigon in May 1964, "no one in the conference showed enthusiasm for taking action," preferring pacification combined with incremental "blows against the North to accelerate the trend against the enemy."[120]

This did not sit well with Adm. U. S. Grant Sharp Jr., who succeeded Felt as CINCPAC. Sharp likewise called for "immediate punitive air strikes against North Vietnam," and after much deliberation among the Joint Chiefs of Staff (JCS), McNamara, and the White House, President Lyndon Johnson authorized retaliatory air strikes known as Operation Pierce Arrow against five torpedo boat bases and a fuel storage area at Vinh. The attacks wrecked eight boats and damaged over twenty others, destroying much of Vinh's fuel storage and distribution as well. But flak claimed two A-4s: one pilot perished, although the second, Lt. (jg) Everett Alvarez Jr., ejected safely, becoming the first captive held in the "Hanoi Hilton."[121] On August 7 Congress passed the Tonkin Gulf Resolution, authorizing the president to take "all necessary measures to repel any armed attack against the forces of the United States and to prevent further aggression."[122]

In response to events in the Tonkin Gulf and passage of the congressional resolution, the DoD bolstered American airpower in Vietnam, ordering deployment of F-102 interceptors, F-100 fighter-bombers, B-57 light jet bombers, and A-1 attack airplanes (the latter acquired from the Navy to give Farm Gate a more powerful punch than available with its T-28s). The thirty B-57s, parked wingtip to wingtip (as at Pearl Harbor over two decades earlier) at Bien Hoa, made a tempting target and, on November 1, 1964, six VC mortar teams shelled them, destroying or damaging twenty (and twelve other USAF and VNAF aircraft as well), killing or wounding seventy-six airmen.[123] Because the attack came just days before the 1964 presidential election, Johnson chose not to act, fearing political consequences.[124] On Christmas Eve, the VC exploded a truck bomb at a Saigon hotel used as an American officers' quarters, killing or injuring dozens of Americans and Vietnamese; again, although American ambassador to South Vietnam Gen. Maxwell Taylor called for retaliation, Lyndon Johnson again chose not to respond. The next month the communist leadership concluded Johnson's reluctance indicated he would neither attack the North nor defend the South.[125]

But even before the Bien Hoa attack, Johnson and his senior advisors had begun tilting inexorably toward attacking the North. Undersecretary of State George Ball had written in October, "We are considering air action against [North Vietnam] as the means to a limited objective—the improvement of our bargaining position with the North Vietnamese," thus telegraphing both the limitations and intent of any future American action.[126] Upon news of the Bien Hoa attack, the JCS—supported by General Taylor; Gen. William Westmoreland, the commander of MACV; and Admiral Sharp (the CINCPAC)—had immediately advocated a Strategic Air Command (SAC)-PACOM air campaign, including bombing Phuc Yen airfield (home to North Vietnam's MiGs), interdiction strikes across Laos and North Vietnam, attacks on industrial sites, and destruction of North Vietnam's petroleum, oil, and lubricant (POL) facilities around Hanoi and Haiphong.[127]

While Johnson and McNamara rejected this, they did favor a program of more limited reprisals pushed by National Security Advisor McGeorge Bundy and his brother William. Then assistant secretary of state for East Asian affairs and chair of an NSC interagency study group considering various options, William Bundy proposed "sustained reprisal," shorthand for "a graduated program of controlled military pressures designed to signal U.S. determination, to boost morale in the South and to increase the cost and strains upon the North."[128] In addition, on December 10 Ambassador Sullivan secured Souvanna Phouma's consent to "armed reconnaissance" sorties along the roads and trails in Laos. The first, flown on December 14 by fourteen F-100 and F-105 fighters (supported by two tankers and two recce aircraft) along Route 8 from North

Vietnam into Laos, marked the beginning of the Barrel Roll program. The Navy flew its first mission on December 17, with A-1s and F-4s from the USS *Ranger*.

Not including Farm Gate or VNAF aircraft, by the end of January 1965 the Air Force, Navy, and Marines possessed significant airpower forces including twenty-eight B-57s, fifty-four F-100s, thirty-six F-105s, twenty-four A-1s, nine A-3s, forty-eight A-4s, forty F-4s, and forty-six F-8s.[129] They were soon put to use: in the predawn dark of February 7, 1965, VC sappers and mortar teams struck Camp Holloway, an airfield and advisory complex at Pleiku, killing or wounding nearly 135 soldiers and destroying or damaging twenty-five aircraft and helicopters.[130] At PACOM, planners had prepared a limited contingency strike plan; Johnson now authorized its implementation under the name Flaming Dart. On February 7–8 Air Force, Navy, and VNAF aircraft struck PAVN installations around Đồng Hới. Undeterred, the VC responded with a second and even more costly attack on an enlisted billet in Quy Nhơn on February 9, triggering a second counterstrike, Flaming Dart II, executed on February 11. Results from the two Flaming Darts were inconclusive, hampered by intermittent bad weather (an occupational hazard), poor coordination, disappointing accuracy, and the loss of five airplanes as well as the death of one pilot and capture of a second.[131]

Rolling Thunder: Johnson and McNamara's Illusory "Air Campaign"

The Pleiku attack transformed the air war, compelling the Johnson administration to lift restrictions on deploying jet aircraft to South Vietnam, bringing what General Momyer called "a long uphill struggle" to a close.[132] Within a week the Johnson team instituted a program of sustained attacks on the North. Although the JCS still advocated prosecuting a comprehensive target strategy (which the new Air Force chief of staff, Gen. John P. McConnell, believed could be fulfilled in just four weeks), Johnson opted on February 13 for "a program of measured and limited air action" approving the deployment of thirty B-52s and thirty KC-135 tankers to Guam and Okinawa, respectively.[133] From this sprang Rolling Thunder, the nation's most unsatisfying and controversial air "campaign," although in reality it was more a series of individual operations born of vain hope that sporadic and unfocused air attacks would generate beneficial political and military results.[134]

Johnson planned to launch Rolling Thunder on February 20, 1965, but a failed coup attempt derailed it for over a week, at which time (on February 28), the American and South Vietnamese governments issued a joint announcement "to open a continuous limited air campaign against the North in order to bring about a negotiated settlement on favorable terms."[135] This gave Hanoi's air defenders adequate warning to mount a strong defense when, on March 2,

104 USAF and 19 VNAF aircraft flew the first Rolling Thunder mission. A mixed force of F-105s and B-57s struck an ammunition depot at Xom Bang, while VNAF A-1s covered by Air Force F-100s hit the naval base at Quảng Khê. While the strike inflicted great damage, it came at the price of three F-105s and two F-100s lost, an ominous portent.[136] On March 15 Task Force 77 launched its first Rolling Thunder strike, with A-1 and A-4 aircraft from the *Hancock* and *Ranger* (capped by eighteen F-4 and F-8 fighters, and with eight other F-8s rocketing and strafing flak sites) attacking an ammunition depot north of Vinh, losing one A-1 and its pilot.[137]

Rolling Thunder mixed illusion and delusion, being neither comprehensive nor coherent, nor serving a well-defined unifying, consistent, and enduring purpose. Before it started William Bundy had argued that any "sustained reprisal" campaign should begin at a "low level," stressing that "the object would not be to 'win' an air war against Hanoi, but rather to influence the course of the struggle in the South," and that naïve intent carried over into Rolling Thunder.[138] It had five goals, of which three were primarily psychological: affecting the will of the North Vietnamese leadership cadre, persuading them to curb their aggression and that of the VC, buttressing the sagging morale of the South's political and military leadership, furnishing a diplomatic "bargaining counter," and reducing infiltration of men and material into the South.[139] In 1969 Secretary of the Air Force Harold Brown acknowledged that, for the Johnson administration, "air power was one of our principal bargaining counters."[140] Undersecretary of State George Ball considered Rolling Thunder "a great bucker-upper for South Vietnam," adding, "That was the whole reason for it."[141]

From its outset, Rolling Thunder lacked the organizational and institutional cohesiveness and the rootedness in sound military strategy found in successful air campaigns. Deficient not only in overall strategy, it also lacked a clearly defined, unifying, and overarching operational command-and-control structure below the PACOM level.[142] But its problems mirrored the larger problems encountered in running a multifaceted joint and combined air war ranging across several countries yet within a single area of responsibility. In a detailed post-Vietnam study of command and control of joint operations, the RAND Corporation concluded that lessons from previous air wars, particularly Korea, had been lost and had to be rediscovered in the 1960s:

> The services and joint commanders had learned little from the Korean experience to enhance joint air operations. Indeed, we would go further: during the early years of U.S. military involvement in Vietnam [1965 to 1968] command and control of tactical air operations were unsatisfactory and would have led to disaster if U.S. forces had faced a capable air opponent. The services

brought their own, mostly unchanged tactical air doctrines into the new conflict; no joint doctrine had been developed in the intervening years. Moreover, new difficulties emerged to bedevil joint air operations. Not only were past mistakes repeated, but new challenges resulted in new mistakes. Consequently, unity of effort was not achieved.[143]

In theater, the North was divided into service-specific "route packages," with MACV in charge of the Route Pack I just north of the DMZ, the Pacific Fleet (PACFLT) responsible for all the coastal regions (Route Packs II through IV and VI-B), and the Air Force in charge of the heartland (Route Packs V and VI-A north to a buffer zone established along the Chinese frontier and west to Laos).[144] This prevented unified effort. Service-centric differences on the use of airpower frustrated air and surface commanders alike (but particularly MACV commander General Westmoreland and 7th Air Force commander Lieutenant General Momyer), and hindered airpower application both in Rolling Thunder and "in-country" operations in South Vietnam.[145]

Efficient and unencumbered operational control was unknown, with multiple chains of command intersecting and overlapping. All, in turn, were influenced by pervasive and ever-present intervention by Washington's political leaders, who used the tools of modern communications to directly involve themselves in day-to-day tactical and operational decision making to a degree unknown in previous wars.

Military commanders in theater certainly lacked the relative freedom of action their predecessors had enjoyed in World War II and even in Korea, largely because of President Johnson's desire to personally micromanage their actions to ensure his own control of events. After the war, shortly before his death, Johnson boasted to biographer Doris Kearns Goodwin that the power to target was the power to control. "I saw our bombs as my political resources for negotiating a peace," he said, adding, "By keeping a lid on all the designated targets, I knew I could keep the control of the war in my own hands."[146] (He also bragged that airmen couldn't "bomb the smallest outhouse . . . without checking with me."[147])

In the place of a centralized joint service and combined forces planning cell like Desert Storm's "Black Hole," headed by any figure holding authorities and responsibilities comparable to those of a modern joint and combined force air component commander working for a theater commander, there was the White House, which sent PACOM an approved target list covering air operations over the following week. The process began with the Joint Staff assembling candidate target folders using information from PACOM, MACV, various service intelligence branches, the CIA, the National Security Agency, and other governmental and even nongovernmental entities. The assemblage was itself haphazard. Neither MACV nor PACOM worked with Air Force and Navy planners to define an overall air strategy and then cohesively assemble a list enabling selection of targets that would fulfill the campaign's intent. These target folders were passed to the JCS, reviewed, and sent to the secretary of defense for consideration. McNamara then passed them to the NSC and the president, who reviewed them for action in White House meetings—typically Tuesday luncheons—attended by Johnson, McNamara, JCS chairman (CJCS) Gen. Earle Wheeler, McGeorge Bundy, and other chosen principals. Discussion focused less on military or strategic advantage than on risks, expectations of collateral casualties, and the need to avoid any actions antagonizing the People's Republic of China and the Soviet Union.[148] After one such meeting, as historian Mark Clodfelter writes, "pilots learned that they had authority to strike moving targets such as convoys and troops, but could not attack highways, railroads, or bridges with no moving traffic."[149]

"In general the success or failure of the air war could be attributed to Washington, and especially to the President and his Secretary of Defense," a 1980 analysis by the BDM Corporation found, stating, "The chain of command for the air war against the DRV [Democratic Republic of Vietnam] ran from 7th Air Force and carrier TF 77 through CINCPAC, then the JCS, and on to the Secretary of Defense, Secretary of State, and the President's National Security Advisor. Final targeting decisions were made at the celebrated 'Tuesday Lunch' meetings [and] a number of high-value targets remained off the target list. By employing airpower in this incremental manner, a fully effective interdiction program could not be achieved."[150]

In 1975, weeks before the collapse of South Vietnam, Walt Rostow asked McNamara to explain the selection process in the Tuesday targeting lunches. The former secretary of defense replied, "The Joint Chiefs of Staff laid out a target system in North Vietnam to maximize the damage to North Vietnam: economic damage, psychological damage, military damage," adding, "My civilian staff and I would receive the recommendations from the Chiefs, examine them, and then submit separate recommendations to the President. *Invariably my recommendations were for lesser bombing than recommended by the Chiefs.*"[151] The Johnson administration later extended the approval process to a biweekly rather than a weekly basis, helping somewhat. Nevertheless, Admiral Sharp recalled in his memoirs, "We were still not permitted the latitude in the field, however, of preparing extended air campaign plans," adding, "The intent was obviously to keep any increase in the intensity of the air war firmly in the hands of the political decision-makers."[152] Such a haphazard, selective, and reactive process could hardly produce good results. As Edward Drea has damningly concluded, "Lacking an integrated and coherent political-military strategic foundation, the air campaign proceeded by fits and starts, sputtering most of the time."[153]

In August 1964 a JCS working group had identified 94 key targets including airfields, railroad and highway bridges, rail yards, rail repair shops, barracks, training centers, military headquarters, ammunition and ordnance depots, petroleum storage, supply depots, telecommunications facilities, ports, bases, chemical plants, iron and steel plants, fertilizer plants, power plants, and main road and rail lines.[154] By the end of 1965 this list had more than doubled, from 94 to 236, increasing both the complexity and urgency for target review and approval. "Nevertheless," PACOM's Sharp wrote, "the targets authorized for attack continued to be selected in Washington by the Secretary of Defense and the White House. Few of these were in the critical northeast quadrant, north of twenty degrees latitude, which contained the Hanoi/Haiphong military complexes and major port facilities, as well as the lines of communication to China."[155] Instead, McNamara continued to emphasize a bombing policy that would "minimize DRV loss of face, optimize interdiction over political costs, be coordinated with other pressures on the DRV, and avoid undue risks of escalation"; when the JCS recommended striking at lucrative targets such as petroleum storage and power plants, McNamara rejected it as a "dangerous escalatory step."[156]

Worse, McNamara—although lacking any relevant experience—made decisions on tactics, techniques, and procedures best left to professional weaponeers and airmen.[157] In one case, when President Johnson asked if Soviet-built SAM sites then under construction in North Vietnam should be attacked, McNamara replied it would require B-52s to bomb Hanoi's airfields. This laughably erroneous pronouncement "promptly diminished Johnson's interest in attacking the SAM sites," one of which, unmolested through completion (and manned by Soviet personnel) promptly shot down an Air Force F-4 on July 24, 1965, the first SAM-loss of the war in SEA.[158]

As a consequence of deficient strategy, bad planning, and questionable execution, Rolling Thunder never fulfilled any of its original goals. Begun to send signals and generate subtle coercion, it evolved into a scattered series of strikes against selected industrial sites, some bridges (which again proved flak magnets responsible for the destruction of dozens of aircraft), some airfields, power generation plants, selected POL facilities, and transportation targets. A 1966 assessment by the CIA concluded that, "despite the increased weight of air attack, North Vietnam continues to increase its support to the insurgency in South Vietnam [and] the North Vietnamese capability to support the war effort has improved."[159] Asked three decades after its onset whether Rolling Thunder had hurt the North, former PAVN staff officer Col. Bùi Tín replied, "If all the bombing had been concentrated at one time, it would have hurt our efforts. But the bombing was expanded in slow stages under Johnson and it didn't worry us. We had plenty of time to prepare alternative routes and facilities."[160]

While strikes on power plants were productive, strikes on bridges and petroleum were not: as in Korea, the North Vietnamese found ways to work around bridge cuts and restored bridges quickly, and attacks on petroleum storage facilities were countered with more dispersed storage and road and sea imports from China and the Soviet Far East. Attacks on transportation proved more useful in that they tied down manpower, and the cost of repairing and restoring damaged or destroyed transport facilities imposed a severe burden on the North Vietnamese government. Moreover, approximately 70,000 troops—fully a fifth of North Vietnam's military—who could have been fighting in Laos or the South were instead assigned to air defense duties. The CIA estimated that doing damage to North Vietnam cost American taxpayers $8.70 for every $1.00 in damage inflicted.[161]

Rolling Thunder exposed critical shortfalls in training, tactics, organization, and equipment that the United States subsequently had to address. Eventual solutions included rediscovering basic fighter air-to-air skills, introducing radar and SAM launch-warning receivers, establishing specialized electronic combat and anti-SAM techniques such as radar-homing missiles (the emergence of the Iron Hand and Wild Weasel programs), improving long-range precision navigation, establishing responsive and heavily armed long-range combat search and rescue, making intelligence more responsive to the needs of combat airmen, and developing more reliable weapons, particularly air-to-air missiles and precision bombs. Not all of these, of course, were completed by the time Rolling Thunder came to an end, and some remain problematic to the present day. Tactics and routes varied little, and revisiting targets served largely to refine and educate Hanoi's air defenders to the point where North Vietnam airspace became increasingly lethal the longer the war went on.

The introduction of MiGs in April 1965 and SA-2 SAMs three months later transformed the air war. MiGs and SAMs could frustrate a strike, whether they scored or not, by forcing the strikers to jettison bombs and fight for their survival. The synergy of SAMs, MiGs, and antiaircraft artillery (AAA)—whereby a pilot avoiding a SAM or MiG might fall victim at lower altitudes to dense barrage antiaircraft fire—caused a sharp ramping up of losses. Ground fire—radar-cued 130 mm and 85 mm AAA firing proximity-fuzed shells, rapid-fire 37 mm and 23 mm light antiaircraft cannon, heavy 12.7 mm machine guns, and even hand-held rifles and small arms—caused 83 percent of all Air Force losses in SEA. SAMs caused only 6 percent, and MiGs a mere 4 percent (7 percent came from other causes, primarily communist sappers attacking airfields in South Vietnam and Thailand).[162]

The Air Force's principal Rolling Thunder attack aircraft, the F-105, suffered 334 combat losses: 22 by MiGs, 32 by SAMs, and 280 to flak, automatic weapons, and small arms. Of its 353 aircrew, 127 were rescued, 25 were killed, 96 were captured, and 105 were missing.[163] By mid-1967 statistical probability held that an F-105 pilot would not survive to complete a hundred-mission tour: he would be shot down early in his tour and, if lucky, would be one of the roughly one in three downed airmen rescued by the Air Force and Navy's extraordinarily courageous helicopter rescue crews. Even so, he could expect that by his sixty-sixth mission he would be shot down *again*, and this time killed or captured.[164] Steadily increasing casualties incurred in attacks on questionable targets for little result fueled a corrosive demoralization and uncertainty that gradually pervaded the daily operations of at least some of the combat forces themselves. In particular, the lack of reliable bomb-damage assessment from persistent overhead imaging systems and the chaotic nature of combat operations encouraged "guesstimation" similar to MACV's obsession over body counts in the ground war.[165]

In June 1967 Israel achieved an extraordinary victory over its Arab rivals. Rooted in the uncompromising and whirlwind air strategy that opened the conflict, its swift triumph stood stark contrast to what was happening over Southeast Asia.[166] In August, desperate to disengage, Johnson proposed ending the bombing if Hanoi would stop infiltrating troops and supplies into the South; playing to win, Hanoi dismissed the offer out of hand.[167] By that time Rolling Thunder's evident failure was hastening McNamara's departure from the Department of Defense. A Senate hearing in August 1967 sharply criticized his decisions.[168] Although he fought back vigorously, he had few defenders, for "three years of Vietnam [had] destroyed his credibility, discredited his policies, and shattered his aura of infallibility."[169] With little option, in November McNamara announced his resignation, leaving office in February 1968. Rolling Thunder lasted another eight months.[170]

Over the length of the Rolling Thunder campaign, American airmen operating in North Vietnamese skies suffered sobering casualties in dead, wounded, missing, and captured. Rolling Thunder cost 171 aircraft in 1965, 318 in 1966, and 321 in 1967.[171] PACOM averaged over $53 million (approximately $388 million in today's dollars) in lost aircraft *per month*, many shot down on questionable strikes, such as attacking individual trucks instead of bombing the depots and truck parks from whence they came.[172] The two principal strike aircraft used over the North—the Air Force F-105 and the Navy/Marine A-4—bore the brunt of these losses. Those airmen who managed to eject often parachuted into a cruel and sometimes fatal captivity. It is a measure of the immense courage they displayed, the abject brutality they endured, and the odious and repellent behavior of their captors that several subsequently received the Medal of Honor.[173]

As Rolling Thunder moved fitfully along, it provoked universal criticism from across the political and policy spectrum: both supporters and critics of the war; military commanders; the airmen tasked to risk their lives fulfilling it; and various military analysts, journalists, and war protestors. The aircrew of Rolling Thunder remain bitter over how the Johnson administration fought its air war "Up North," particularly its targeting strategy and restrictive ROE. "[Of] particular concern to combat flight crews throughout the entire Vietnam War [was] the very RoE under which they had to fly," Adm. James Holloway wrote, adding, "The direction of approach and pullout from bombing attacks were often mandated from Washington.... The sort of micromanagement from Washington that dictated altitudes to be flown and directions of attack could be infuriating to the pilots that had to fly the missions [and] were only one of the many seemingly bureaucratic difficulties that the combatants on our side had to live with."[174]

The In-Country War

Compared to Rolling Thunder, the air support war in the South went generally well. All through the years of the offensive, American airpower, augmented by indigenous VNAF and RAAF units, was plentiful and responsive. The Army and Marines had their own organic aviation forces for battlefield insertion and combat air support, freeing the Air Force to furnish high-capacity tactical airlift, first with C-123 and C-130 transports and later with the C-7 after DoD transferred it from the Army to the Air Force. Like naval airmen in Task Force 77, who flew so-called Alpha strikes with largely self-contained air wings composed of fighter, attack, electronic warfare, tanker, and reconnaissance aircraft, the Marines were likewise characteristically independent, and the justly lauded Marine air-ground team functioned with an unsurprising expertise befitting its reputation. By the end of 1965 Army and Marine helicopters had established themselves firmly as battlefield mobility, observation, fire support, and evacuation systems while the Air Force and Navy were fielding helicopters for combat search and rescue (CSAR) and insertion and support of special operations forces (SOF). Helicopters soon became so ubiquitous that the image most closely associated with Vietnam is the helicopter (specifically the "Huey") disgorging troops on a landing zone.

Vietnam resurrected tactical air support lessons first taught in the Western Desert by Air Vice Marshal Sir Arthur Coningham. These included the importance of radio-equipped TACPs on the ground and in the air, specialized FAC aircraft, and specialized training, tactics development, and operational procedures. The critical requirement, quite simply, was rapid response by air support to a request for help, certainly in time to make a difference on the battleground. In 1962 the Air Force had made suggestions to the VNAF on streamlining air control procedures, one of which was establishing a five-minute limit for approval/disapproval decisions at intermediate command level. As a result, response times compressed from a previous average of nearly fifty minutes to a low of eight minutes. While the services differed about the most desirable command-and-control architecture, the Air Force model of a tactical air control system (TACS) linked to an air operations center eventually prevailed, supported over Army opposition by Admiral Felt at PACOM, particularly following three instances when Army fixed-wing OV-1 observation aircraft, not on the TACS radio net, unsuspectingly entered areas under attack from Farm Gate B-26s and T-28s.[175]

The professional spat between the Army and Air Force over centralized or fragmented air control—and, indeed, over the future of fixed-wing aviation within the U.S. Army—caused some confusion in the minds of the Vietnamese as to the intentions of the two services. One FAC recalled that Vietnamese soldiers wondered "are we here to help them or only to increase the status of our own particular branch of service?"[176] Changes in MACV leadership, particularly the departure of Gen. Paul D. Harkins and his replacement by Westmoreland and the signing of a joint Army–Air Force air-ground coordination agreement in April 1965 stipulating the assignment of TACPs to Army units from battalion-size to field armies, created a workable system. Accompanying these were assignment of more air liaison officers and FACs, an increase in O-1 and other FAC aircraft, and standardization of communication equipment so that airmen and soldiers in contact with the enemy could speak to one another.[177]

ROE posed a serious limitation to effective use of American air support in the early days of the war, primarily because of the requirement that American pilots fly with a Vietnamese air crewman (except under extraordinary circumstances or if working with American Special Forces) and that they strike targets only when under the control of a VNAF FAC. In one case an American Ranger team was ambushed by the VC, and although Farm Gate T-28s were orbiting on scene, they had to jettison their ordnance rather than attack because no VNAF FAC was present. Fortunately, Army helicopters, under no such restriction, were able to defend the Rangers because they were technically authorized to support ground troops, whereas the Farm Gate operation was, at least ostensibly, strictly a training one.[178] At the beginning of January 1965 there were 212 FACs in SEA, 144 of them USAF and 68 VNAF. Although seemingly large, these numbers were still insufficient to meet air support needs and, acting on requests by the CJCS, General Wheeler, following his March 1965 visit to Vietnam, the Air Force added 134 more FAC authorizations and established three more FAC air support squadrons (in addition to the one already existing), increasing the FAC training program run by the Special Air Warfare Center at Hurlburt Field as well.[179]

The clarified support process and increase came just in time, for by then the VC was rapidly expanding and achieving alarming victories. In late December 1964 the VC destroyed two Vietnamese battalions; then came the attack on Pleiku in February, triggering Flaming Dart I and II and Rolling Thunder, followed by the Marine victory over the VC south of Chu Lai in August. In mid-October the VC launched an attack on a Special Forces camp at Plei Me, a Montagnard village in the central highlands, but were beaten back after a sharp ten-day battle in which nearly seven hundred air support sorties played a crucial role in denying the VC a victory they otherwise would have enjoyed. ("I am sure [the airmen] saved the camp," the Special Forces commander of Plei Me stated; "The basic air support was excellent.... Response was very good; the aircraft arrived very quickly. In more than one instance we even had strike aircraft 'stacked up.'"[180]) In the follow-up to Plei Me, the newly arrived "Air Cav" clashed with three PAVN regiments threatening to cut South Vietnam in half, opening the battle of the Ia Drang valley. Lasting fully thirty-five days, it echoed the savagery of the Pacific campaign, and although it ended as an American victory, it signaled the beginning of a long and arduous ground war.[181]

During the fighting that followed, battlefield air support—whether by fixed-wing aircraft, helicopter gunships, or combinations of both—became the mainstay of ground warfare. The beneficial effects of air attack in breaking ambushes and sieges, shielding convoys, covering units on patrol, and supporting troops in direct contact with the VC and PAVN were best measured in the increased confidence of commanders in the field, not in dubious "body counts" of enemy dead.[182] "I learned after a while that my casualties were tremendously decreased if I used the air power and air strikes and used [them] properly," one Army commander recalled.[183] USAF-USN-USMC tactical air sorties devoted to battlefield attack constituted roughly 20 percent of all sorties flown over South Vietnam (airlift sorties were over 50 percent, and reconnaissance approximately 20 percent as well). As ground fighting increased, joint "tacair" sorties rose as well, from not quite 125,000 in 1966 to nearly 170,000 in 1967, then over 205,000 in 1968, the peak year of American air support prior to the beginning of "Vietnamization" of the war following the election of President Richard M. Nixon in 1968.[184]

Army helicopter gunships—first converted UH-1 troop carriers but then, beginning in the summer of 1967, the deadly AH-1 Cobra—furnished vital support during troop insertions and sweeps, particularly in encounters where the VC sought to "hug" their opponents so closely as to prevent attacks by "fast-mover" jet fighters and attack aircraft and by fixed-wing gunships such as the AC-47, AC-119, and AC-130 (all converted airlifters outfitted with multiple cannon and machine guns and special sensor systems).[185] Gunships of all types proved crucially important in major engagements and prolonged battles, never more so than during the siege of Khe Sanh, the Tet rising, and the 1972 North Vietnamese spring invasion.

Located in the far northwest corner of South Vietnam, just east of Laos and immediately south of the DMZ, Khe Sanh was a major Marine base supporting operations along the DMZ and against the Ho Chi Minh Trail. It had a relatively short runway for air supply, was vulnerable to artillery fire, and in both regards thus mirrored the unsustainable "air head" the French had established at Dien Bien Phu. To Gen. Vo Nguyen Giap, Khe Sanh offered the irresistible promise of another Dien Bien Phu. Indeed, if his forces had succeeded in overrunning it, it is not inconceivable—given the political climate within the United States in 1968—that it might have driven the United States toward leaving the war early, particularly with the Tet Offensive occurring near-simultaneously.[186] In September 1967 the PAVN succeeded in cutting all road access into Khe Sanh, forcing it—again like Dien Bien Phu—to rely solely on air supply. The siege opened on January 21, 1968; ten days later the VC launched the Tet Offensive, which, while failing militarily, succeeded as political theater. Whereas Tet came to an end in late February, the siege of Khe Sanh lasted into April before the combination of resolute Marine defenders, on-call artillery support, an intensive and highly successful airlift, and massive joint-service air strikes, including AC-47 and AC-119 gunships and B-52s, broke the siege and enabled a reopening of ground access.

Air Force, Marine, and Navy air attackers dropped an average of near 1,500 tons of bombs per day, guided by Air Force and Marine FACs and tactical air controllers, in an air effort pointedly named Operation Niagara. Overall, they flew 24,449 tactical strike sorties and 2,548 B-52 sorties. During the siege Air Force and Marine airlifters and helicopters delivered just over 17,000 tons of supplies together with 17,238 personnel; the Air Force, Navy, and Marines dropped over 100,000 tons of bombs, nearly 60,000 tons of which were delivered by B-52 strikes. Thanks to precision radar cuing furnished by two different Marine and Air Force radar systems, B-52 strikes occurred as close as a kilometer from friendly forces, and some tactical strikes struck down to 500 feet.[187] This air support, plus artillery, saved Khe Sanh.

Initially, disagreements between the Air Force and Marines on how to control the flow of air assets over Khe Sanh, coupled with poor coordination with SAC, led to situations where airspace was so crowded that some strikes had to be canceled. Westmoreland responded by giving Lieutenant General Momyer, the 7th Air Force commander, full responsibility for the Khe Sanh air effort in mid-February, making it permanent the following month with the designation of 7th Air Force as the single manager for air control. With goodwill on both sides, the service airmen made it work.[188]

The Vietnam experience reaffirmed for airmen the value of tactical airpower over the battlefield and reminded ground commanders of its continuing, even vital, importance. In mid-1967 Maj. Gen. William E. DePuy, then commander of the 1st Infantry Division (and the future head of Army Training and Doctrine Command, TRADOC), said, "This is the way we kill the VC around here. We find them, take two steps back, and let the Air Force kill them. Then we go pick up the bodies."[189] The success of battlefield air support did much to solidify bonds between soldiers and airmen; in 1967 Westmoreland stated that the battlefield air support furnished his forces was "the finest any army could hope to get."[190] After the war 60 percent of the respondents to a postwar Army survey on their Vietnam experience considered Army–Air Force cooperation "outstanding," with only 2 percent rating it "not satisfactory."[191]

If circumstances warranted, arguably the most valuable support aircraft was the B-52, turned from strategic nuclear bomber to counterinsurgency aircraft via pylons and racks permitting it to carry conventional "iron bombs" externally as well as within its cavernous bomb bays. B-52 strikes impressed friend and foe alike. Westmoreland credited the victory at Khe Sanh to "the fire of the B-52s"; various VC and PAVN commanders recalled its attacks left troops "demoralized," "shaking so badly it looked as if they had gone crazy," and "terrifying."[192]

Endgame: Linebacker I and II Lead to an Uncertain and Transitory Peace

In March 1972 North Vietnam invaded the South in a mechanized assault by 14 divisions and 26 regiments, totaling well over 100,000 troops, and including 600 tanks and heavy artillery. It was in every sense a conventional cross-border invasion. The invading force came across the DMZ but also from Laos and Cambodia, posing a diffuse and rapidly unfolding threat. In addition to South Vietnamese forces, the PAVN faced much smaller American ground forces of 95,000, down from the 550,000 peak of 1969 before Vietnamization took effect.[193]

American airpower forces were considerably reduced over the levels that had existed at the time of Rolling Thunder. Thus, in response, the Nixon administration ordered deployment of air and naval forces back to SEA. The Navy furnished six carriers and their air wings while the Air Force increased its fighter, strike aircraft, and gunship strength from nearly 250 to almost 400 and its B-52 force from nearly 140 to over 170. From this came Linebacker (subsequently Linebacker I), which, coupled with heroic resistance on the ground, eventually imposed a crushing defeat upon Giap and the PAVN.[194] Air Force, Navy, and Marine strike aircraft, having suppressed Giap's air defenses, then went after his lines of communication, supply columns, and fielded forces. Fixed-

and rotary-wing aircraft targeted individual armored vehicles with missiles, bombs, and cannon fire. At Kontum—cut off from land access as Khe Sanh had been four years previously—Army attack helicopters, armed with antitank tube-launched, optically tracked, wire-guided missiles, teamed with Air Force F-4s dropping newly developed laser-guided bombs to destroy nearly thirty tanks, assisted by heavily armed AC-119 and AC-130 gunships. B-52s based in Thailand and Guam routinely pounded surrounding PAVN forces both there and outside An Loc, with one Army general judging the B-52 "the most effective weapon we have been able to muster. . . . if [the enemy] does mass his forces, he takes terrible casualties."[195] "I was scared stiff [when] the B-52s were carpet bombing us," recalled PAVN Col. Bùi Tín of his experiences in the 1972 invasion; "The atmosphere was like living through a typhoon with trees crashing down and lightning transforming night into day."[196]

Over the North, due to more realistic ROE and more appropriate targeting (both in reaction to the failure of Rolling Thunder earlier), American airmen were able to exploit the new technology of precision strike (via laser or electro-optically guided smart bombs) to achieve previously unattainable results, including dropping key bridges and thus halting all rail traffic south of Hanoi, shutting down power, and—at last—mining the port of Haiphong, the latter drawing only a "mild protest" from the Soviet Union, North Vietnam's primary military provider.[197] These strikes hindered North Vietnam's efforts to supply its hard-pressed forces in the South, which, now on the move and consuming great quantities of supplies, were vulnerable to interdiction attacks in ways that they had not been previously. Indeed, as Lewis Sorley has noted, the official Vietnamese history of the war frankly states, "Because the enemy had escalated rapidly, was bombarding us massively, and was using many types of new weapons . . . many units and local areas suffered heavy losses. Almost all the important bridges on the railroad and on the road corridors were knocked down. Ground transportation became difficult. Coastal and river transportation were blocked."[198] In June the North Vietnamese offensive collapsed, brought down by strenuous resistance on the ground coupled with 55,803 sorties, of which 17,771 (32 percent) were flown by the VNAF and 38,032 (68 percent) by American airmen. Of the American sorties, 24,079 (63 percent) were USAF, 10,098 (27 percent) were USN, and 3,855 (10 percent) were USMC.[199] Afterward, explaining his defeat, Giap told an interviewer, "The American air force is a very powerful air force. Naturally that air force had an influence on the battlefield. It was a great trump card." Of course, it was a joint and coalition air-land victory, not that of any single service.[200]

Linebacker I confirmed lessons previously learned from the Spanish Civil War, World War II, the Korean War, and the June 1967 Arab-Israeli War about the tremendous stopping power of aviation forces employed against conventional mechanized attackers who could not adequately contest for control of the air. Further, it demonstrated that the modern linkage of precision weapons to fighter-bombers and attack helicopters could tip the scales even against a very powerful assault and compensate for the lack of in-place ground forces to confront an aggressor on the move. But this is not to say that Linebacker I succeeded without considerable risk to airmen. Although Giap's air-denial strategy ultimately failed, his linking of troop-portable SA-7s and light automatic flak endangered such traditional stalwarts as loitering gunships (both fixed and rotary wing), watchful FACs, and A-1 and A-37 attack aircraft. Helicopters proved particularly vulnerable, especially to the newly introduced SA-7. It forced airmen to move to higher altitudes and planners to incorporate more "fast-mover" jet attack aircraft such as the then-ubiquitous joint-service USAF-USN-USMC F-4. From the end of April 1972 through the beginning of September 1972 SA-7s destroyed twenty-six American aircraft, the older and larger SA-2 claiming a further forty-six.[201] In sum, Linebacker I demonstrated the first glimmerings of the even more lethal, missile-rich battlefield air environment experienced by the Israeli air force during the nineteen-day whirlwind of the 1973 Arab-Israeli war.

In December 1972, in the face of Vietnamese intransigence at the Paris peace talks, the Nixon administration ordered a resumption of bombing of the North. Centerpiece of the air campaign was to be heavy, sustained bombing of military targets by B-52s lasting for three days. This reflected the personal desire of President Nixon, who told Secretary of State Henry Kissinger, "Anything less will only make the enemy contemptuous."[202] On December 17 the JCS issued a message to CINCPAC, CINCSAC, and subordinate commanders directing a "three-day maximum effort, repeat maximum effort, of B-52/tacair strikes in the Hanoi/Haiphong areas," though cautioning them to "minimize risk of civilian casualties [by] utilizing LGB [laser-guided] weapons against designated targets [and] avoid damage to third country shipping."[203] Approximately 60 percent of the attacks would target transportation and logistics, with the other 40 percent targeting enemy air defenses; airfields; command, control, and communications; and power plants. It was a daunting prospect, for at that time North Vietnam possessed a robust air defense network manned by highly experienced personnel overseen by Soviet air defense advisors, and the increasing threat forced a ratio of support aircraft to strike aircraft of as much as six or seven to one—greater, even, than fighter-to-bomber ratios in World War II's strategic air offensives against Nazi Germany and Imperial Japan.[204]

This follow-on air campaign was called Linebacker II, and, instead of just three days, it lasted from December 18 through 29, with a brief pause for Christmas. Over eleven days, multiple three-ship cells of B-52s executed 729 night-attack sorties, hitting 34 targets and dropping 15,000 tons of bombs. The B-52s flew with extensive suppression of enemy air defenses (SEAD) support and an F-4 anti-MiG Combat Air Patrol (CAP) but even so took disturbing losses, largely because of serious planning and execution issues within SAC, particularly questionable tactics that negated the B-52s' defensive jamming and enabled the North's SA-2s to successfully target them, especially during turns when mutual interference reduced the effectiveness of their anti-SAM jamming. Overall, fifteen were lost, together with over a dozen other USAF and USN aircraft, for the expenditure of not quite 1,250 SA-2s, 844 of which had been fired at the big "Buffs."[205] Although at 2 percent the B-52's loss rates were hardly those of Ploesti or Schweinfurt decades previously, they nevertheless attracted great attention, if for no other reason than that the B-52 was—and still is today, in the era of the B-2 stealth bomber—the most visible and impressive symbol of American airpower. Indeed, on the night of December 20-21 (the third night of the offensive), SAMs destroyed 6 of 99 B-52s, a 6 percent loss rate, shocking by jet-age standards. Altogether, Linebacker II cost 27 aircraft lost, with 43 crewmen killed or missing, another 41 captured, and 33 recovered.[206]

But at month's end the campaign had achieved its purpose. By postwar strategic bomber standards, the size of the raids, given the payload capacity of the B-52s, was enormous. On December 26, for example, fully 120 B-52s attacked 10 targets around Hanoi within just a few minutes, supported by 114 other aircraft including chaff-droppers, jammers, Wild Weasels, and escorting fighters. Hanoi, running out of SAMs and with its fighters unable to successfully contest for control of the air, capitulated and signaled its renewed willingness to negotiate.[207] "Prior to Linebacker II, the North Vietnamese were intransigent, buying time, refusing even to discuss a formal meeting schedule," a delegate to the Paris peace talks stated later; "After Linebacker II, they were shaken, demoralized, anxious to talk about *anything*," adding, "They finally realized they were at war with a superpower. If there was [NV] bewilderment, it was with our reluctance to use that power earlier."[208] On January 21 a cease-fire went into effect; the parties signed the Paris Peace Accords on January 27, 1973. Slightly over two years later, in the absence of significant airpower following Nixon's resignation after Watergate and America's abandonment of the South, North Vietnam overran South Vietnam in only six weeks, bringing the war to a tragic and bitter close.[209]

Vietnam's Consequences and Lessons: A Retrospective Sampling

The war triggered intensive soul-searching and not a little bitter recrimination within the American military and political establishments. In its aftermath, historians have debated whether intervention was prudent, whether it was a "just" war, and they have debated the responsibility of various parties (president, secretary of defense, JCS, etc.), various strategy options, and myriad other questions. Within the airpower community, debate has continued over whether Rolling Thunder could have worked or whether its deficiencies were those of airpower itself. Again, there is little consensus at the academic and war college level, and controversy reigns unabated.[210]

What is remarkable, however, is the congruence of viewpoint held by the airmen who flew in the war; their views are uniformly negative, even as they are justly proud for having done their duty. While the majority complained only among themselves and determined never to run an air war in such a fashion if given the chance in future, one of their number spoke out at the time in an extraordinarily frank and bitter memoir that gained great attention. Titled *Thud Ridge* (the name of a long distinctive landform rising from the coastal plain to over 2,500 feet northwest of Hanoi) and published in 1969, it was written by Col. Jacksel "Jack" Broughton, one of the war's most charismatic, aggressive, and controversial airmen. Broughton's book captured the unique blend of unwavering courage, steadfastness, cynicism, personal honor, pride, aggressiveness, and resentment of the F-105 force as it fought a politically and militarily constrained air war against an enemy operating under seemingly no constraints whatsoever.[211] *Thud Ridge* is a singularity among American air combat literature, with no other war having produced such a highly critical, even inflammatory self-examination published as the war still raged; this alone an indication of the dissatisfactions American airmen felt over the top-down, run-out-of-theater air war in which they flew, fought, and too often died.

In the years since, others have contributed an equally revealing and often bitter body of memoirs uniformly highly critical of the Washington community's strategic decision making and perceived meddling at the operational and tactical levels of war as well as, occasionally, of their own service leadership.[212] Worse for some were the behaviors that crept into the force and caused veterans of Rolling Thunder—at least those who went on to higher command—to vow never to condone similar practices in future. "All of us in Desert Storm had memories of Vietnam and we were determined not to repeat the mistakes of that war even if it conflicted with the protective agendas of our individual Service doctrines," Gen. Charles Horner recalled, adding, "In Vietnam, answers that did not please Washington or even higher headquarters were unacceptable, so we lied. We and the enemy were the only ones in North Vietnam, so we simply told the headquarters what they wanted to hear. The effect was corrosive. We lost integrity, the only thing that really matters to the military."[213]

Vietnam destroyed the Johnson administration, trigged national protests unseen since the American Civil War a century before, demoralized the American military, and became the reference point for every subsequent conflict.

Many of the most significant lessons of America's long and tragic involvement in SEA relate to issues of grand strategy, the power-sharing aspect of the civil-military relationship, command integrity in the face of questionable leadership, and the impact of disillusion and dissension upon national policy and political outcomes. Indeed, its influence powerfully resonates and echoes into the present day.

Vietnam taught that decision makers contemplating use of force must first define what constitutes "victory"—that is, what is the desired end state?—and, having determined it, then fight to win, authoring and empowering their military chieftains to prosecute the conflict with a minimum of interference from outside the operational theater. While the Johnson administration generally did so in the South, its conduct of the air war over the North, from the time of George Ball's pronouncement on "improvement of our bargaining position" onward, was about persuasion, sending signals, showing resolve, and dissuasion based on the naïve belief that (as Johnson's biographer wrote) "no small power could possibly resist America's sophisticated technology and enormous military strength."[214] But North Vietnam was not impressed: it was fighting to win.[215]

Vietnam revealed that the military services desperately needed institutional and cultural reform. At a more fundamental military level, the officers who served in Vietnam, across all services, worked to transform their services in the years afterward, inculcating greater standards of professional excellence and discipline, better training, improved joint relationships, and more appropriate equipment acquisitions. "Vietnam had one good result," one Army officer remarked after the war, "It's made us question the way things were done."[216] Rightly or wrongly, many professional officers who fought in Vietnam returned from the war with a sense that many senior commanders at the theater level and higher, including the JCS, had placed their personal agendas and prerogatives ahead of the needs of the soldiers, sailors, and airmen in theater and the field. As they subsequently wended their own way through their own military hierarchies, they determined never to treat those serving under their command in similar fashion.[217]

Vietnam exposed critical weaknesses in command and control, from the national command authority down through theater-level and further down to the operational/tactical level of war. The jumbled chain of command from Washington to PACOM to PACAF and PACFLT, and thus to 7th Air Force and TF 77, overlaid by MACV, coupled with the odd ambassadorial-air attaché command-and-control structure of the Laotian air war and the command chain from SAC into theater for control of B-52 "Arclight" missions generated "fog and friction" that worked to hinder the innate speed, flexibility, and responsiveness of airpower. Personal relationships, trust, and "work-arounds" in theater compensated somewhat but could not alter the basically cumbersome and unresponsive nature of an overly complex and at times paralytically bureaucratic system. What was required in the future was a centralized theater-level air command with streamlined command and control between constituent in-theater elements, guided by appropriate doctrine, rigorous procedures, and professional battle staffs.

Vietnam showcased the need for a return to fundamental first principles in military thought and, particularly, for reexamination of the doctrinal underpinnings of the services and their reshaping to meet the war-fighting environment of the 1970s and beyond. In the wake of Vietnam, all military services and allied nations reexamined their basic doctrine and concepts of war-fighting, planning, and operations. After the Vietnam War, stimulated by a resurgent Soviet threat to Europe, NATO established the multinational Tactical Air Working Party that produced two key policy statements on air support and tactical air doctrine.[218] Building on an air-ground partnership between the essentially colocated Army TRADOC and the Air Force's Tactical Air Command (TAC), General Momyer, who had risen to command of TAC, partnered with the Army's brilliant General DePuy to study more closely integrating Army and Air Force battlefield operations. Continued under Gen. Robert Dixon, Momyer's successor, this spawned establishment of the Air-Land Forces Application agency in 1975. Working with both Air Force doctrine and the Army's rewriting of FM 100-5 (its operations manual), this led to operational doctrine for joint battlefield attack, joint suppression of enemy air defenses, and joint attack of second-echelon forces. In 1983, at the instigation of Air Force Chief of Staff Charles Gabriel and Army Chief of Staff Edward "Shy" Meyer, it ultimately generated the now-well-known "31 Initiatives."[219] In basic doctrinal thought, the Air Force (which arguably had the greatest amount of work to do in this area) explored more flexible and adaptable approaches to airpower strategy and application, building upon the ideas in Col. John A. Warden III's seminal text *The Air Campaign*. Out of this climate came the issuance of Secretary of the Air Force Donald Rice's *Global Reach—Global Power*, a position paper that furnished a core strategic planning framework for the Air Force in the 1990s and whose influence continues in the present.[220]

Vietnam showed that changes had to be made in the joint-service research, development, test, and evaluation process to ensure that testing reflected real-world conditions, from a practical effects-on-target standpoint. Experience in the war sadly demonstrated that previous service investment in offensive weapon technologies had been both insufficient and inadequate. In many cases weapons brought into theater—air-to-air missiles and air-to-surface missiles offer classic examples—proved deficient or even dangerous to use, neither performing as expected (for example, the Falcon air-to-air missile) or, as with the

Bullpup air-to-surface missile, exposing the user to prolonged risk from alerted enemy defenses.[221]

Vietnam highlighted the importance of intensive training. Many aircrew and aircraft were lost as a result of inadequate or even nonexistent air-to-air training. Overall, American airmen shot down two hundred North Vietnamese aircraft but lost seventy-six of their own, this overall 2.6:1 victory/loss ratio, when compared to World War II (8:1) and Korea (6:1) being the worst in American air combat history.[222] The establishment of the naval Top Gun program and then the Air Force's development of Red Flag—intended to give aircrews the level of experience attained by flying a dozen or so missions in actual combat—addressed training deficiencies and have become staples of service culture.

Vietnam also highlighted the combat vulnerabilities of aircraft and helicopters as well as operational weaknesses affecting flight safety. The vulnerability of aircraft and helicopter systems to ground fire spurred greater emphasis on aircraft and aircrew/passenger survivability, while operational (i.e., not from direct combat) losses drove greater emphasis on training, procedures, and flight safety generally. From 1961 through 1973, counting both combat and operational losses, the United States lost at least 9,021 aircraft. Of this number, the Army lost 5,448 fixed- and rotary-wing aircraft (60.4 percent), the Air Force lost 2,251 (25 percent), the Navy lost 859 (9.5 percent), and the Marine Corps lost 463 (5.1 percent).[223] Many of these losses had multiple causes, of which (for air-to-air losses) training was an important factor. But many others reflected weaknesses in design, including dangerous handling qualities and performance, inadequate armor, poorly shielded and nonredundant flight-control systems, inadequate instrumentation, and deficient human factors design of cockpit displays and instrumentation and control layouts. Combat aircraft after Vietnam have tended to be safer, more survivable, and more "user friendly."

Vietnam highlighted serious deficiencies in aircraft and weapons. These and the threats posed by new generations of Soviet bloc fighter aircraft and SAM systems dramatically influenced acquisition after the Vietnam War. Well before war's end, combat experience, particularly with fighter aircraft, led to a rediscovered appreciation for the value of aircraft optimized for the military mission they were to fulfill. The so-called superfighters of the 1970s—the F-14, F-15, F-16, and F/A-18—all sprang from this, stimulated as well by the threat posed by new-generation Soviet fighters and SAMs, such as the MiG-23 and MiG-25 (and MiG-29 and Su 27, subsequently). The threat of integrated air defenses built around radars and SAMs—a threat reinforced by the Israeli experience in the 1973 Arab-Israeli war—accelerated development of electronic combat systems to effect both "kinetic" and "soft" kills. In its most radical manifestation, the threat prompted interest in reducing the radar cross-section and, hence, the radar signature ("observables") of aircraft, resulting in an evolutionary path that generated the first "stealth" aircraft.

Finally, Vietnam accelerated development of standoff so-called smart weapons. The high toll exacted by repeat attacks against robust targets (such as bridges and heavy industrial sites) accelerated interest in the development of new precision weapons and precision navigational technologies. This was exemplified within fifteen years of the end of the war by the introduction of newer families of precision-guided munitions (including joint-service cruise missiles), laser-guided bombs, imaging infrared tactical air-to-surface missiles (such as Maverick), and an operational "constellation" of satellites furnishing global positioning.

EL DORADO CANYON: LIMITED JOINT AIRPOWER AS RETRIBUTIVE SCALPEL

In 1969 Muammar Gaddafi, a young pan-Arab nationalist officer heading a group of like-minded Libyan military personnel, overthrew King Idris, an unpopular autocrat, while the latter was out of country. Consolidating his power over the next decade while benefiting from high oil revenues, Gaddafi became ever more extreme, resulting in Libya's being added to the U.S. State Department's list of state sponsors of terrorism. Gaddafi claimed the Gulf of Sidra as Libyan waters, warning foreign navies not to cross a so-called line of death at the 32°30' parallel. The Jimmy Carter administration chose not to challenge the Gaddafi regime over its Gulf claims, but the Ronald Reagan administration did.[224] In August 1981, during a Sixth Fleet exercise pointedly held in the Gulf, two Libyan Su-22s threatened a patrolling Navy E-2 AEW/command-and-control plane and attacked two F-14s vectored to protect it; the F-14s promptly shot both down.[225]

But this lesson did not suffice. In 1985 Gaddafi's anti-"Zionist," anti-American rhetoric became more extreme, as did his regional interventionism, particularly in neighboring Chad.[226] More ominously, the Libyan regime publicly endorsed attacks by the Abu Nidal terrorist group, infamous for massacres at airports in Rome and Vienna on December 27, 1985.[227] At the end of January 1986, at the instigation of the Joint Chiefs, U.S commander in chief Europe (CINCEUR) launched a Sixth Fleet freedom of navigation exercise in the Gulf of Sidra. Called Operation Attain Document, the exercise was undertaken by TF 60, then comprising two carrier battle groups. For six weeks TF 60 exercised above the "line of death," triggering hundreds of Libyan air sorties turned away by Navy fighters but no actual shooting. Then, in March 1986, after President Reagan gave his approval, TF 60, now consisting of three battlegroups built around the carriers *America*, *Saratoga*, and *Coral Sea*, crossed the "line of death" and carried out further exercises in the Gulf. Attain Document included a preapproved contingency plan, Prairie Fire, allowing measured reprisals if Libyan forces attacked TF 60. Thus, when SAM sites at Sirte launched two long-range SA-5s at two F/A-18s (which adroitly evaded them), the Navy went to war. When three Libyan missile boats approached the task force, carrier aircraft sank one and damaged two others, then destroyed Sirte's SAM site.[228]

Outraged, Gaddafi now called for a holy war against Americans, including their "goods, ship, plane or person."[229] On April 2 four Americans perished when a terrorist bomb exploded on board a TWA jetliner, which fortunately managed to land despite grievous damage. Afterward, Gaddafi praised the attack. On April 5 a bomb exploded in the LaBelle discotheque in Berlin, killing two Americans and wounding two hundred people, including seventy-five Americans. Electronic intelligence linked the Gaddafi regime to the bombing, and President Reagan, contemplating a retaliatory air strike on Libya, sought help from America's NATO allies.[230]

Surprisingly, even though the LaBelle disco attack had occurred within a NATO nation, alliance members were cool toward supporting any military action. Spain and France denied overflight permission, and only Britain's prime minister, Margaret Thatcher, agreed but initially most reluctantly. On the afternoon of April 9 she sent Reagan a message promising Britain's "unqualified support," and Reagan then authorized the strike to go ahead.[231]

Various strike assets were evaluated, but two stood out: the Navy A-6E and the Air Force F-111F. Both were precision-attack, all-weather, night-strike aircraft equipped with sophisticated targeting sensors and capable of dropping laser-guided bombs and more advanced than the earlier models of each design that had preceded them. Both had electronic warfare spinoffs that could accompany them into combat: the EF-111A and the EA-6B. These two—supported by screening fighters to protect against air threats, attackers to suppress SAMs and antiaircraft sites, and air refueling tankers—comprised the primary punch of the proposed retaliatory strike.

A larger question was whether a single service, either Air Force or Navy, could undertake the strikes on its own, simplifying command, control, and planning. On the face of it, the logical choice was the Sixth Fleet. Its carriers were in close proximity to the targets and could strike suddenly and unexpectedly from over the horizon. In contrast, the Air Force, because of the reluctance of America's allies to support military action against Libya, would have to operate from Great Britain at a direct-line distance of 1,500 miles. But in reality it was nearly double this: Spain and France's refusal to permit overflights forced a long detour down the Atlantic and through the Straits of Gibraltar, then eastward across the Mediterranean, requiring no less than four separate aerial refuelings off France, Portugal, Algeria, and Tunisia and increasing the danger of detection.

However, there were compelling reasons for employing the Air Force's F-111s. The Navy lacked a sufficient number of A-6Es to attack all targets because the Sixth Fleet, after Attain Document, had reduced its deployed carriers (and, thus, air wings) from three to two, the *America* and *Coral Sea*. Furthermore, the faster F-111F offered a more survivable option going against the Tripoli target set, which was heavily defended by overlaid SA-2, SA-3, SA-5, SA-6, SA-8, and French Crotale SAMs, overseen by three thousand Soviet air defense technicians (plus AAA and fighters). These two factors, rather than a simple desire for "jointness," dominated other concerns and were reflected in the final planning, with the Air Force assigned responsibility to hit the high-threat targets around Tripoli and the Navy assigned to targets around Benghazi.[232]

Planning for what became Operation El Dorado Canyon had begun in late December 1985, after the two airport massacres, when Chief of Naval Operations Adm. James Watkins had proposed a combined Navy–Air Force strike. President Reagan ordered U.S. European Command (USEUCOM) to prepare contingency plans. Sixth Fleet and USAFE collaborated on a lengthy target list sent to Gen. Bernard Rogers, the CINCEUR, for review. After reviewing it, Rogers passed the list to the JCS and Secretary of Defense Caspar Weinberger, who reviewed them, forwarding them to the NSC. The NSC selected a total of five targets: three training complexes implicated in terrorism; Tripoli airport, home to Il-76 transports used to support terrorism; and the Benina air base, home to Libya's MiG-23 fighter force.[233] After securing President Reagan's concurrence, this final listing was sent to USEUCOM for execution. Given the geographic distance between the targets, any such attack would actually have to be two simultaneous strikes, one on Tripoli and the other on Benghazi, separated by over four hundred miles. Rogers then tasked Vice Adm. Frank B. Kelso, the commander of the Sixth Fleet, to command the joint strike (though, as noted later, Kelso "hardly exercised" his authority, given the thorough preplanning of Navy–Air Force operations).[234] No single planning authority existed; rather, USAFE and Sixth Fleet worked closely together with inputs and oversight from CINCEUR, who assigned the Tripoli targets to the Air Force and the Benghazi targets to the Navy. At the execution level, the commander of TF 60 oversaw the planning staffs within the air wings on board *America* and *Coral Sea*. They teamed with Air Force strike planners in USAFE and the wing planning staff of the 48th Tactical Fighter Wing at RAF Lakenheath, exchanging liaison officers between services.[235]

Coral Sea's A-6s would strike Benina airfield outside Benghazi, while *America*'s would hit several terrorist training and military facilities east of the city, the largest of which was the so-called Jamahiriya military complex. The F-111s would attack the Bab al-Aziziyah barracks in Tripoli (a terrorist command center, home to Gaddafi's guard force and sometimes used by Gaddafi both as a residence and as a command post); the Murat Sidi Bilal training camp; and the military flight line at Tripoli airport and its Il-76 transports. The Navy's anti-SAM A-7s, F/A-18s, and F-14s would furnish SEAD and CAP for both Navy and Air Force strikers while the EA-6Bs and EF-111s would blind Libyan radars and jam communications. Altogether the joint-service strike consisted of eighteen F-111s screened by four EF-111s, and fourteen A-6, six A-7, and six F/A-18 strike fighters screened by EA-6B electronic warfare aircraft.[236] The F-111s came from the 48th Tactical Fighter Wing (TFW) at Lakenheath. The EF-111s and Air Force KC-135 and KC-10 tankers from RAF Mildenhall and RAF Fairford would accompany the F-111 strike package from Lakenheath to Libya, together with a KC-10 carrying the Air Force's airborne mission commander, Maj. Gen. David W. Forgan, USAFE's deputy chief of staff for operations. On the long "drag" to Libya and back, each F-111 and EF-111 had its own tanker. The ROE for the operation stressed that "bombs would not be dropped unless weapons systems were fully operational and navigation data was certain, and pilots were forbidden to revisit any targets."[237] Time over target was set at 2:00 a.m. Libyan time on April 15, requiring the Air Force to launch on the evening of April 14.

At midday on April 14, Margaret Thatcher briefed her cabinet. "I said that it was clear that the US was justified in acting in self-defence under Article 51 of the UN Treaty," she recalled. "Finally, I stressed that we had to stand by the Americans as they had stood by us over the Falklands."[238] That evening, at 5:13 p.m. local time, the first tankers took off from their bases, followed, at 5:36 p.m. local time, by the first F-111Fs from Lakenheath. At sea, the *Coral Sea* executed a high-speed run through the Strait of Messina, managing to evade a Soviet intelligence collection destroyer as it steamed to its launching position.[239] The two carrier battle groups launched their strike, SEAD, and CAP aircraft at 12:45 a.m. local on April 15, and at 1:50 a.m. local the EF-111 and EA-6B jammers electronically attacked Libyan air defenses.

Both the Navy and Air Force strike packages arrived over their respective targets on time. The degree to which Libya was prepared for the attack is debatable; radar operators in France, Spain, and Portugal apparently detected the F-111s on their long run to Tripoli but kept silent, while Italian operators informed their counterparts on Malta, who passed on the information to their government, which then (being friendly toward the Gaddafi regime) gave Libya a half-hour warning.[240] The F-111s and A-6s attacked through heavy though largely unaimed antiaircraft fire, and post-strike imagery showed all five of their targets severely damaged or destroyed. Six Navy A-6s destroyed at least a dozen Libyan aircraft at Benghazi and cratered its runway; another six heavily damaged the Jamahiriya complex and an associated MiG-23 assembly facility while Navy SAM-killers disabled SAM sites with radar-homing missiles. The Libyan air force wisely chose not to challenge the F-14s. Five F-111s destroyed five Il-76s at Tripoli airport and damaged several buildings. Three F-111s apiece damaged the Bab al-Aziziyah and Sidi Bilal complexes, blast effects destroying "a number of small training vessels" at Sidi Bilal.[241] Twelve minutes after it started, the last aircraft left Libyan airspace. Navy aircraft had barely "trapped" on board their carriers (the F-111s were still airborne) when the White House had announced the strike, the returning airmen listening to the press conference as they cruised back to their base.

The strike, however, had its losses and disappointments. Of the nine F-111s tasked with striking the Bab al-Aziziyah complex, four aborted from equipment failures, one flew off-course, and one disappeared, likely falling to a SAM because it was last in a stream of attackers. Two of the remaining three hit the complex hard, but the third dropped its bombs over a mile distant, damaging the French embassy. One of the F-111s tasked with striking Tripoli's airport had to abort after losing its terrain-following radar. The large volume of antiaircraft fire and even unaimed SAMs that were fired complicated the determination of collateral damage. The old adage "what goes up must come down" argues that surely some of the urban damage attributed to "air attack" was, in fact, inadvertently caused by the Libyans themselves.[242]

El Dorado Canyon demonstrated how good joint planning and streamlined operational control could lead to smooth tactical execution, though the broader policy implications were less clear. Reagan and Thatcher both came in for great criticism from many of the world's governments (while, quietly, many of these applauded their action) and from their own (at times substantial) political opposition. Critics damned both for assuming that one strike would bring Gaddafi to heel when in fact Reagan (and Thatcher too) had been careful to point out that they were under no illusion that it would do so. Undoubtedly, as both agreed, Gaddafi (as Thatcher termed it) "had been humbled." The strike bound the United States and Britain more closely together and raised Britain's stature in the eyes of the American administration and American people, as Thatcher discovered to her pleasure. It had benefits for both Reagan and Thatcher in that it solidified their image as strong leaders, unafraid to take military action and able to employ forces reaching quickly across thousands of miles.[243] A superpower may be able to achieve a great deal on its own, but even in a relatively trivial example of expressing military power it is important to have allies.

Strategically, while terror attacks continued, some of whose perpetrators cited the raid as a justification for outrages against Americans and Britons, the widely anticipated "wave" attacks forecast in the wake of El Dorado Canyon (and urged previously by Gaddafi himself) did not materialize. Rather than finding solace in common cause with other nations, Libya found itself increasingly isolated, and Gaddafi's image as a strong and dynamic leader willing to stand up to the West was badly tarnished. The "what if?" factor of whether the

El Dorado Canyon operation should have been undertaken at all must remain forever unanswerable. It was certainly both legal and ethical under international law, and any reluctance to take action likely would have been perceived as weakness, encouraging further massacres. El Dorado Canyon certainly seems to have influenced Libyan behavior because afterward its known sponsorship of terror attacks dropped from nineteen in 1986 to six in 1987, and six in 1988.[244]

Operation El Dorado Canyon: Observations, Lessons, and Reflections

Operation El Dorado Canyon demonstrated the importance of joint forces working together harmoniously to achieve a desired outcome. What is remarkable about El Dorado Canyon is the absence of interservice rancor, even though all the elements found in previous conflicts were there: diffuse command, a "route pack" approach (Navy in the west, Air Force in the east), complexity, rival professional communities, and top-down political interest (and political stakes) in the outcome. Winnefeld and Johnson were correct when they noted that El Dorado Canyon succeeded because "all joint command echelons were determined to work together in harmony and to make simplicity and flexibility cardinal joint planning virtues. . . . It demonstrated that a simple plan, full and forthcoming coordination among the services, and flexibility in execution can overcome difficulties presented by friends and foes alike."[245]

Targeting strategies rooted in theater-level recommendations carried forth to national command authorities are useful in "one-off" strikes to achieve some military purpose but are very different from the kind of targeting and outcomes strategy that must be pursued for a broader, lengthier, or more complex air campaign. El Dorado Canyon was a raid, not a campaign, a reflexive punch at a bully. Had it been a more sustained campaign to achieve a different effect, whether regime change or simply destruction of military capabilities, it is likely the two-nation approach would not have worked.

Political, technological, force-structure, and operational factors dramatically influence military options and outcomes. The refusal of Spain and France to permit overflights caused the Reagan administration to turn uncertainly to Britain; fortunately, because of a similar-thinking and forceful personality—Thatcher—Reagan was able to secure support for the Libyan strike. To this degree, El Dorado cemented further the long-standing "special relationship" existing between the two great English-speaking powers straddling the Atlantic divide. But the intransigence of the other European powers (seen earlier in their reaction to the 1973 Arab-Israeli war) forced greater reliance upon long-range tanking, a complication that had many risks of its own.

The limits of the GBU-10 Paveway II laser-guided bomb, optimized for dropping at medium altitudes, made it more susceptible to wider variation in circular error probable when lofted in low-altitude attacks than the GBU-24 Paveway III, developed specifically for low-altitude release. Arguably, the F-111 force would have achieved greater accuracy and destructive effect using Paveway III than Paveway II, but the low-altitude Paveway III had completed its developmental testing only a month previously. The strike illustrated yet again the degree to which mission success can be compromised by the limiting capabilities of weapons.

To succeed, El Dorado Canyon required not only a joint force approach but also the very joint forces that were actually employed. While the Navy had a force-structure advantage in the Air Wing construct (essentially like a shipboard expeditionary air force in that it contains its own attack, SEAD, air superiority, rescue, and reconnaissance force and can plan and train together in a highly effective manner), having so many different types on one ship simply meant that fewer aircraft of any one type were available to guarantee achieving the level of destruction sought in the attack plan. This again forced use of the F-111. Ironically, had the two-place F-14s been qualified (as they later were) to fly as "Bombcat" strike aircraft, it is possible that both air wings would have sufficed to fulfill the mission requirements.[246]

The decision to "stream" low-altitude ingress into a high-threat area greatly increased the risk of aircraft loss. Low-altitude high-speed attack has been (and still is) seriously overrated as a military technique. The proliferation of antiaircraft threats, from missiles down to hand-held weapons, mitigates against it, as does the simple fact that the attacker is coming ever closer to a fixed target, thereby entering an easily predicted zone (actually a cone) of vulnerability. While a single aircraft may possibly survive, a stream of aircraft most likely cannot. Significantly, concern over low-altitude loss drove subsequent Air Force operations in Desert Storm to higher altitudes, and without the loss rates experienced by the RAF when it prosecuted a low-level attack strategy with its Tornado aircraft at war's outset.

JUST CAUSE: AIRPOWER IN HEMISPHERIC CRISIS INTERVENTION

In December 1989 the United States invaded Panama to remove Gen. Manuel Noriega, a corrupt leader who was running a criminal dictatorship and, both through his own actions and his developing ties to the Cuban communist regime, threatened both American and regional interests. Although the operation unfolded rapidly, its planning had the benefit of several key factors. The crisis built slowly, giving planners the opportunity—which they had not enjoyed in previous contingencies such as 1983's Operation Urgent Fury, the Reagan administration's scrambling and somewhat shambolic liberation of Grenada—to study and plan the best way to target the regime. Then, thanks to the nearly century-long American presence in Panama, the American military was largely familiar with the country, its people, its infrastructure—much of which had been American built—its military and security services, and their vulnerabilities.

Noriega combined the classic power-seeking characteristics of a dictator with the corruption of a narcotics trafficker, and the U.S. government issued indictments for drug trafficking against him in 1988. A band of thuggish enforcers, the so-called Dignity Battalions, intimidated regime opponents, many of whom were cast into prison, tortured, and killed, while Noriega formed a special guard, called Battalion 2000, as an elite defense force. As tension grew between the Noriega regime and the United States, the Panamanian Defense Force (PDF) began a program of harassment against American military units on exercises and against individual American military personnel, their families, and dependents. In April 1988 this led to an exchange of fire between Marine security forces and a PDF (and suspected Cuban force) infiltration team attempting to enter a POL tank farm outside Howard AFB.

In May 1989 Noriega overturned the results of a national election that had gone against his hand-picked slate of candidates, and the regime grew more despotic still, his thugs beating and robbing a U.S. sailor. Previously, like the Reagan administration preceding it, the George H. W. Bush administration hoped that building up a large American presence in-country would intimidate Noriega and possibly encourage his own forces to revolt. Now it turned away from a policy of coercion toward direct intervention, using Howard AFB in the Canal Zone as a convenient means to ferry nearly 2,700 Army soldiers and Marines (and nearly 3,000 tons of equipment) under the cover of an operation called Nimrod Dancer. The operation also furnished an excuse to deliver a range of aircraft systems, including attack helicopters and special operations helicopters such as the MH-6, MH-53J, and MH-60. From mid-May through June, the Air Force oversaw an evacuation airlift, Operation Blade Jewel, which brought nearly 6,000 American dependents (and nearly 400 pets!) back to the United States; still, large numbers of other Americans remained.[247] Over this same period, the U.S. Air Force undertook airborne surveillance with OA-37 aircraft from a tactical air support squadron based at Howard, further adding to the intelligence picture.[248]

On December 15, 1989, the Panamanian National Assembly proclaimed Noriega "Maximum Leader for Life" and declared that his regime was "at war" with the United States. The next night, at a roadblock, PDF guards shot three American officers, killing a Marine first lieutenant, Robert Paz. Two witnesses, a naval officer and his wife, were then taken into PDF custody and physically assaulted.[249]

At the outset of this crisis, 13,000 American military personnel were already in Panama confronting 15,000 members of the PDF, of whom only 3,500 were actually soldiers.[250] Despite this force imbalance, the United States faced significant risks. Panama fell within the responsibility of U.S. Southern Command led by Gen. Maxwell Thurman, USA, who had assumed command in September 1989. Thurman had not been happy with a previous campaign plan, Blue Spoon, which envisioned a three-week buildup followed by a relatively linear, sequential, and necessarily lengthy operation to remove Noriega. He feared, with good reason, that the Noriega regime might take numerous American hostages, that the invasion forces might get caught up in a brutal block-by-block urban war, and that other Noriega loyalists might launch a guerrilla war in the thick jungle countryside, with very high casualties on both sides and many collateral deaths.

Therefore, Thurman directed instead that Blue Spoon's buildup be accelerated to three days, and he formed—using his powers as a theater CINC, as authorized under the recently passed Goldwater-Nichols Defense Reorganization Act of 1986—a Joint Task Force headed by Lt. Gen. Carl W. Stiner, USA, the commander of the U.S. Army's XVIII Airborne Corps. Altogether, Stiner's Joint Task Force included 22,000 soldiers, 3,400 airmen, 900 Marines, and 700 sailors.

The relatively straightforward command relationships belied some of the very real complexities facing planners. This operation would not be a conventional invasion from the sea or from the sky; targets and real or potential foes were intermixed with innocents and as many as 35,000 Americans. The situation held great potential for hostage taking and reprisals. Potential attacks would have to be conducted with the greatest of precision and thought to avoid friendly fire and collateral deaths. Although slight, the possibility that Cuba or Nicaragua might seek to intervene, perhaps even imperiling the airlift bridge from CONUS to Panama, could not be dismissed, complicating operations further. Not for nothing had the original planning framework for intervention in Panama been called Elaborate Maze.[251]

On December 17 Thurman met with key staff and informed CJCS Gen. Colin Powell that the forces and plan were ready for execution. The commanders of Military Airlift Command and the Joint Special Operations Task Force assured Powell that the airlift and SOF would be ready in two days. Further high-level meetings involved Powell, Secretary of Defense Richard Cheney, the NSC, and senior defense officials, all of whom favored implementing the plan. President Bush concurred, but only after Powell assured him that a massive and swift intervention was the only way to ensure success, that the intervention was unlikely to end as had Operation Eagle Claw (the Iranian hostage rescue attempt) in the Carter era, and that it would not repeat the interservice disconnects of Reagan's Operation Urgent Fury, where coordination and communication between multiple air-sea-land players was sporadic at best. The next day, December 18, the JCS renamed Blue Spoon Operation Just Cause.[252]

In the early afternoon of Tuesday, December 19, Powell met one last time with President Bush, who reiterated his decision to intervene, and approved the deployment of two F-117 stealth fighters to assist Task Force Red, a Ranger assault on Rio Hato. At 2:30 p.m. Washington time, Powell telephoned Thurman that the operation was on. At 5:56 p.m., the first of over a hundred C-130, C-141, and C-5 airlifters took off. The air armada included refueling tankers, escorting fighters to prevent Cuban or Nicaraguan intervention, and Navy search and rescue aircraft, all overseen by E-3 airborne warning and control system (AWACS) AEW/command-and-control aircraft.[253]

The Noriega regime had watched the airlift into Howard with growing concern, placing the PDF on alert. Then, as with El Dorado Canyon, it received a tip-off about the operation, this one from CBS newsman Dan Rather, who announced at 10:00 p.m. (Eastern time) on the evening news that military transports had left Fort Bragg, North Carolina, adding "The Pentagon declines to say whether or not they are going to Panama"; just before midnight local time, Noriega's Comandancia issued a series of alerts, warning "the ballgame is at 1 a.m." Alarmed by reports that the PDF was rapidly mobilizing and with sporadic gunfire already breaking out across Panama, Stiner ordered an advance in H-hour from 1:00 a.m. to 12:45 a.m., December 20.[254]

The ground operation that followed was short, sharp, occasionally vicious and bitter, and, in the end, decisive. The PDF collapsed, and Noriega went on the run, eventually taking refuge in the residence of the Papal Nuncio in Panama City, from whence he surrendered on January 3, 1990, to be led off in shackles, walked onto a 1st Special Operations Wing (SOW) MC-130, and flown back to Miami to face long-overdue justice.

Operation Just Cause: Observations, Lessons, and Reflections

The airlift was an extraordinary success. In less than thirty-six hours, the Air Force delivered 9,500 combat troops into Panama. Airborne forces from Fort Bragg flew directly to Panama and executed the largest night drop since Normandy—and with much better results. The tanker bridge that is such a necessary part of air mobility operations worked smoothly and efficiently, tankers from 23 squadrons transferring 12 million pounds of fuel from December 20 through January 3—an average of nearly 860,000 gallons per day, over 37,000 gallons per day for each squadron.[255] Over the 56-day contingency, airlifters carried almost 40,000 passengers, delivering 20,650 tons of cargo in 775 missions, an average of approximately 370 tons per day (nearly 27 tons per mission). This proved the wisdom of acquiring a balanced flight of airlifters, from the C-130 to the C-141 and C-5, and of establishing a logistical support system across the services that could take advantage of the potential of these aircraft and turn it to military benefit.[256] All this—the tanking and airlift—presaged what would happen in less than two years' time in Operation Desert Shield, the buildup to Desert Storm.

The F-117 strike at Rio Hato, while not executed precisely as planned, succeeded in stunning the PDF defenders, to the benefit of the assaulting Rangers. Put another way, the two F-117 pilots hit open space, as intended, but the aiming points themselves were off. The bombs were thus technically a "shack," but the strike was misplaced, one bomb hitting just sixty yards from the barracks, thus causing major (if unintended) damage to it.[257] Critics used the bombing to belittle stealth, but again, in two years' time, it would be the F-117's maintainers and pilots who would have the last laugh.

Aside from the airlifters, the 1st SOW was the most important air element supporting Just Cause. The 1st SOW contained the CAS, mobility, and rescue assets and personnel that the ground forces—particularly the joint-service SOF—needed. Commanded by Col. George Gray, it included nine AC-130 gunships, MC-130 SOF transports, two HC-130 refuelers, four MH-60 Pave Hawk light assault/CSAR SOF helicopters, and five MH-53 Pave Low heavy assault/CSAR SOF helicopters.[258] At several key points in the battle to defeat the PDF and collapse the Noriega regime, these SOF air elements proved crucial. For example, the PDF, having been alerted to a possible air assault, quickly rushed antiaircraft guns to Rio Hato. Just prior to the arrival of the Ranger drop force, an AC-130 engaged the PDF, destroying multiple guns and vehicles and furnishing precise fires on pockets of resistance as the Rangers drifted earthward in their parachutes and then formed up to fight.[259] In another case, orbiting AC-130s proved crucial to the rescue of Kurt Muse, an American held under threat of death in the Cárcil Modelo prison. Teamed with Army attack helicopters, the AC-130s supported a Special Forces team entering the prison to rescue Muse (which they did successfully). When PDF forces in the Comandancia threatened the rescue force, the AC-130s tore the building apart with 40 mm and 105 mm cannon fire, one eyewitness declaring, "Night became day when they opened up."[260] Finally, special mention must be made of the Air Force special tactics personnel, who, with exemplary courage, went in ahead of the airborne forces to place navigational marker beacons for the drop zones and then stayed to furnish air traffic control, communications, mission support for other invasion elements, medical treatment, and emergency medical evacuation.[261]

The proximity of friendlies to hostiles raised grave dangers of friendly fire incidents, and only the personal discipline of aircrews prevented what could have been multiple tragedies. In one case an AC-130 aircraft commander was repeatedly ordered by a ground commander to fire on what he believed to be PDF forces. But the gunship's own sensor operators could not confirm that the targets were hostile. His forbearance proved prescient as the supposed "hostiles" proved to be friendlies.[262] This tendency of ground commanders to order immediate fires (from air or ground) without fully identifying an enemy would, alas, crop up with tragic results at the Battle of Khafji two years later. On the positive side, individual discipline and adherence to preestablished ROE were remarkably high, a sign of good training.[263]

Finally, Just Cause showed few of the planning and coordination problems found in earlier joint-service interventions, validating, in the eyes of some, the wisdom of Goldwater-Nichols. General Stiner certainly credited Goldwater-Nichols for producing a clean chain of command, telling the Senate Armed Services Committee that it ensured there were no "ambiguous relationships or units receiving guidance from multiple sources."[264] In truth, this might have reflected more the strong personal relationships and previous associations of many of the key players who knew and trusted each other. Whatever the reason, the degree of mutual support and cooperation/coordination was remarkable by the standards of other conflicts. It left a positive sense of interservice cooperation and joint force planning that benefited America's next crisis intervention, Operations Desert Shield and Desert Storm.

DESERT SHIELD AND DESERT STORM: AIRPOWER IN AMERICA'S FIRST GULF WAR

America's first Gulf War was arguably the last Cold War- and Vietnam-rooted air war in that the force structure, systems, and leadership were all dramatically shaped and influenced by the previous forty-plus year U.S.-USSR standoff and the war in Southeast Asia. It marked the routine use of precision air attack, reflecting technological developments in weapons and sensors that blended the classic elements of the aerospace revolution (aerodynamics structures, propulsion, and flight controls) with the rapidly proliferating computer revolution. The latter produced sensors of extraordinary fidelity and the analytical tools and understanding that led to the so-called low-observable or stealth revolution. Whether or not it constituted a "revolution in military affairs," it constituted a "revolution in aerospace affairs."[265]

From Crisis to Crisis

In June 1990, just weeks before Saddam Hussein invaded Kuwait, Air Force Secretary Donald B. Rice released *The Air Force and U.S. National Security: Global Reach—Global Power*, the most influential white paper issued by the service since its creation.[266] Authored primarily by Lt. Col. David Deptula and

RAND's Christopher Bowie, *Global Reach—Global Power* related how the "inherent characteristics" of the Air Force—speed, range, flexibility, precision, and lethality—could synergistically work to enhance America's national defense strategy. The Air Force could do so by sustaining deterrence (through nuclear forces), providing versatile combat force (for theater operations and long-range power projection), supplying rapid global mobility (via airlift—the tanker "air bridge"), controlling the high ground (via command, control, communications, and intelligence systems in orbit or in the atmosphere), and building American global influence (via strengthening security partners and relationships).[267] *Global Reach—Global Power* triggered controversy because of its almost unprecedented advocacy of air-centric warfare. Critics challenged that, for all its claims, it did not address the realities of war. Then, in August, Hussein's tanks rolled into and over Kuwait.

Confronting Saddam was U.S. Central Command (CENTCOM), established on January 1, 1983. Headquartered at MacDill AFB, Florida, it had various service and joint-service components: Army (ARCENT), Navy (NAVCENT), Marine (MARCENT), Air Force (CENTAF), and joint special operations (SOCCENT).[268] Chief of CENTAF was Lt. Gen. Charles "Chuck" Horner, a career fighter pilot and organizational troubleshooter who had flown in Vietnam during Rolling Thunder and had no wish to repeat the experience, and whose career had been mentored by General Momyer and the legendary Gen. Wilbur Creech. If not "an airpower über alles kind of guy," Horner nevertheless believed airpower could have decisive effect, under the right conditions—something he had learned from history, reading studies and books recommended to him by Momyer.[269] More crucially important to him than debating what air could and could not do was understanding how to manage airpower application in war.[270]

Horner had been appointed CENTAF commander in 1987, working first for Gen. George Crist, USMC (who had enthusiastically endorsed the Joint Force Air Component Commander [JFACC] concept), and then for Gen. Norman Schwarzkopf, USA. As such, Horner was also CENTCOM's JFACC, in essence a single air boss or (as a colleague called him) "the quarterback for all the air players in the Gulf" (though, once Crist had left the area of responsibility, MARCENT representatives had contested Horner's role at various CENTCOM exercises).[271] Although Horner got along well with both Crist and Schwarzkopf, it was the latter who most impressed him. "He really was a profound individual," Horner recalled, "very smart, one who appreciated what air could do for everyone."[272] For his part, Schwarzkopf reciprocated the feeling, praising Horner as "the kind of warrior we need leading our Air Forces."[273]

Signs of trouble in the Gulf had been building ever since the fall of the Shah. It was a bad neighborhood: there had been the punishing war between Iran and

Iraq, culminating in a "tanker war" during which an Iraqi Mirage fighter had hit the frigate USS *Stark* with two Exocet missiles, killing or wounding a number of sailors and severely damaging the ship.[274] Not quite a year later the frigate *Samuel B. Roberts* struck an Iranian mine. American naval forces repeatedly clashed with the Iranian navy. But of the two nations, Schwarzkopf worried more about Iraq, as did Rear Adm. Grant Sharp, CENTCOM's director of plans.[275] In November 1989 Schwarzkopf met with Horner, telling the airman that Hussein was likely poised to move against Kuwait and Saudi Arabia as he needed money and the two nations constituted "the world's largest bank."[276] Schwarzkopf then announced that in any future conflict he would be both theater CINC and commander of land forces. Horner replied that he would speak frankly to him as air commander to land commander, but when Schwarzkopf "put on [his] Unified Commander hat," he would do whatever Schwarzkopf desired; Schwarzkopf agreed.[277]

Thus, even before Saddam's forces rolled off to war, CENTCOM was bracing for an Iraqi strike and thinking about air options. By April 1990 CENTCOM air, sea, and land planners were deep in the preparation of an updated defense plan reflecting the new focus on Iraq, OPLAN (operations plan) 1002-90. From an air standpoint, Horner sought to build an air defense and power-projection deterrent based upon Saudi air defense architecture and its E-3 AWACS aircraft; delay and attrite Iraq's mechanized forces if they attacked; and launch joint-service counterstrikes from land and sea, including attacks on airfields, chemical weapons storage facilities, Scud launch sites, POL targets, power plants, and transportation choke points.[278] Most critical was stopping Iraq at the outset because desert warfare is traditionally warfare on the move, and Horner realized that a rapidly unfolding Iraqi armored advance would require immediate air intervention, for none of the other western Gulf States could withstand so powerful an armored force. Accordingly, he conceived a scheme he called "Push CAS," whereby strike aircraft could be diverted in flight from their preassigned targets if an urgent need arose, depending upon the ground situation. Schwarzkopf, he recalled, "bought that 100 percent."[279] In this can be seen the first glimmerings of the phased Desert Storm air campaign plan, with provisions both for its strategic and operational targeting and its provisions for an emergency "halt phase" if needed.[280]

Iraq was the most powerful nation in the Gulf region, possessing the world's fourth-largest army; over 5,000 main battle tanks; 5,000 infantry fighting vehicles; 3,000 artillery pieces; 700 combat aircraft; a layered, integrated air defense network (with at least 11,000 SAMs of various types, nearly a thousand antiaircraft sites, and over 8,000 antiaircraft cannon); over 800 ballistic missiles; and an annual weapons budget of nearly $13 billion (equivalent to $24 billion in 2016). Baghdad's air defenses alone were denser than any Warsaw Pact target during the Cold War, and seven times as dense as those of Hanoi at the time of Linebacker II.[281] But of all Iraq's capabilities, the most worrisome for Horner and Schwarzkopf were ballistic missiles, derivatives of the 1950s-era Soviet Scud. Iraq had already fired hundreds of missiles against Iran, almost two hundred in 1988 alone. Saddam had attacked both the Iranians and his own Kurds with chemical weapons, and the two men feared he might employ chemical, even "chem-bio" (and, more distantly, atomic) missile warheads. This concern caused them to conceive of ways to use the Army's Patriot SAM, a very sophisticated air defense missile, as a terminal-area antiballistic missile defense. In addition, Horner sought to derive a list of strategic targets that might be used to craft a deterrent strategy to use against the Iraqi regime.[282]

In July 1990 CENTCOM ran Internal Look 90, a command post exercise evaluating how well OPLAN 1002-90 addressed a projected Iraqi invasion of Kuwait and then Saudi Arabia. The analytical tool used to assess results, called TACWAR, predicted that Iraqi armor forces would inflict heavy casualties on defenders. Unknown at that time but appreciated after the Gulf War was that TACWAR was a badly flawed model that overestimated the resilience of ground forces under air attack and underestimated weapons effects by air attackers. As a consequence, TACWAR caused Schwarzkopf to establish a 50 percent attrition goal for Iraqi units, an unnecessarily high requirement.[283] OPLAN 1002-90 was still very much a work in progress when, in the early morning of August 2, 1990, Saddam invaded Kuwait.

Key Bush administration figures reacted to the invasion in different ways, with Secretary of Defense Dick Cheney immediately contemplating military options, CJCS General Powell discussing policy implications, and National Security Advisor Brent Scowcroft recommending immediate and massive aid to Saudi Arabia.[284] On the day of the invasion, at the administration's behest, the Navy ordered the *Independence* battle group to reposition from the Arabian Sea into the Gulf of Oman, and on August 4, after securing permission from Egyptian president Hosni Mubarak, ordered the carrier *Eisenhower* and its battle group to leave the Mediterranean via the Suez Canal and take up station in the Red Sea, which it did on August 7.[285] That same day Schwarzkopf and his component commanders briefed Bush at Camp David on the incomplete OPLAN 1002-90, stressing that airpower constituted "the option most immediately available"; Horner reinforced the message, adding he would have four hundred aircraft in eleven days, and that his airmen were "ready to go."[286] Cheney left for Saudi Arabia the next day, accompanied by Schwarzkopf, Horner, and other senior officials, to secure King Fahd's permission for American forces to enter Saudi Arabia, leaving Powell back in the States as Cheney feared the CJCS' hesitancy would reinforce that of Fahd, thus blocking any action.[287] On August 6

Fahd agreed to accept American forces, and Schwarzkopf said, "Chuck, start them moving," the beginning of Desert Shield.[288] With that, the air deployment from CONUS to Saudi Arabia began; for his part, Horner recalled thinking, "Please God, keep me from screwing things up."[289]

Desert Shield: Protecting Saudi Arabia, Building Forces, and Campaign Planning

On August 7 the 1st TFW at Langley AFB launched 24 F-15Cs, which flew nonstop to Dhahran; 2 DC-10s left Pope AFB with 520 paratroopers from the 82nd Airborne. Within 38 hours of receiving Saudi entry permission, the 24 Langley F-15s were flying combat air patrols in the Gulf. Within 2 days Margaret Thatcher dispatched 24 RAF Tornadoes and Jaguars.[290] By the end of the first week the USAF had deployed 10 fighter squadrons.[291] Within 2 weeks, sufficient force was in theater to ensure the safety of Saudi Arabia. Within a month over 1,200 aircraft had arrived, capable of executing both strategic and tactical missions. Over the first 18 weeks, airlift moved almost 3 times the payload carried in the Berlin Airlift of 1948–49.[292] Critically enabling its functioning was the tanker bridge; over the length of Desert Shield, KC-135 and KC-10 tankers flew 17,285 sorties, off-loading 441 million pounds of fuel. (In the shorter 43-day Desert Storm, they would complete 16,865 sorties, off-loading 800 million pounds of fuel.) During Desert Shield, airlifters delivered 1.7 million ton-miles of cargo to CENTCOM per day, 10 times what their predecessors had flown each day into Berlin.[293] The bed-down of arriving personnel and their equipment posed enormous logistical challenges, but all were successfully met.[294]

As the commander of CENTAF, Horner oversaw preparation of an air campaign plan, working closely with his fellow component commanders, recalling, "The four of us—Walt Boomer, Stan Arthur, John Yeosock, and myself, were like brothers. We would never try to do anything to one another."[295] But he did have disagreements with two other principals, Vice Adm. Henry H. Mauz Jr. (predecessor of Vice Adm. Stanley Arthur as NAVCENT) and Maj. Gen. Royal N. Moore Jr., commander of Marine aviation in the Gulf. Both advocated a "roll-back" campaign, operating against targets on the Iraqi periphery before risking going "down-town" to Baghdad, and Mauz advocated dividing Kuwait and Iraq into Vietnam-style route packages. Appreciating how stealth changed the air defense issue, Horner wanted to go for decisive effect at the outset, shattering Iraq's integrated air defense system to permit simultaneous, parallel air attacks across the entire theater of operations and certainly not tying the coalition's airmen to the rate of advance of surface forces.[296] Mauz left, succeeded by Arthur, a richly decorated "brown shoe" light-attack pilot. Horner regarded Arthur highly, recalling that he "fully appreciated the need for a single commander for air, no matter what service uniform he wore."[297]

Against Horner's advice, Schwarzkopf had turned to the Joint Staff for a "strategic" target list, calling upon Powell and Gen. John "Mike" Loh, the Air Force vice chief of staff, and requesting a plan as well.[298] Loh contacted Maj. Gen. Minter Alexander, the director of plans, who turned to his deputy director for war-fighting concepts, Col. John A. Warden III, a highly regarded air strategist and airpower thinker who ran Checkmate, an Air Staff planning and analysis cell.[299] Warden and his team were already working on a plan, called Instant Thunder (pointedly contrasting with Rolling Thunder), employing effects-based strategic air attacks. Loh and Air Force chief of staff Gen. Michael Dugan authorized its presentation to Schwarzkopf, even though Gen. Robert Russ, commander of TAC, feared a repetition of Rolling Thunder. "What starts as a little bit of help from the Pentagon soon leads to more and more 'help' and pretty soon you get the President in on it," Russ said; "Then you have people in the White House sitting on the floor trying to figure out what targets they are going to hit."[300]

On August 10 Schwarzkopf received Warden's Instant Thunder briefing, exclaiming, "I love it!" The next day the airman briefed Powell, who prudently requested more emphasis on attriting the Iraqi army. Warden briefed the revised plan to Schwarzkopf at MacDill on August 17, and the CINC ordered Warden to brief Horner in Riyadh. The briefing took place on August 20 and went very badly.[301] Horner was still worried about defeating a rolling, unfolding Iraqi mechanized assault, and to his mind Warden's plan was too theoretical, though he considered him "a genius" and "a superb targeteer." When he did not receive any substantive answers to his questions, he ended the briefing. Warden returned to the states (subsequently doing very fine work using Checkmate as a quick-turn intelligence fusion cell to support the war fighters in theater), leaving several of his staff behind, most notably Lieutenant Colonel Deptula, who subsequently headed Horner's strategic attack planning cell, working for Brig. Gen. Buster Glosson, an old Horner associate who became Horner's chief air campaign planner. Washington was very firmly out of the air campaign planning picture, undoubtedly to the relief of those who, like Russ, feared the onset of another Vietnam.[302]

With the deployment and Desert Shield airlift moving at a high pace, Horner assigned units to four air divisions: fighters, electronic combat, strategic (bombers and tankers), and airlift. The division commanders—each a brigadier general—reported to Horner. Coalition air operations had to be integrated into a master attack plan and the daily air tasking order (ATO). While this made sense to airmen, the complexities of air operations confounded those with a traditional surface-centric mindset, Horner stating bluntly, "Air operations are conducted at a speed and range that is difficult for our land forces brethren to capture mentally."[303]

Relations with coalition air forces generally went well, except for a clash between Horner and Air Chief Marshal Sir Andrew "Sandy" Wilson, the air commander of British forces in the Middle East. The two disagreed so strongly over ROE that Horner threatened to pull the RAF out of the campaign. "The RAF saw the Americans as adopting a cowboy approach," Alan Munro (Britain's ambassador to Saudi Arabia) recalled, "while General Horner and his staff regarded the RAF's attitude as wimpish."[304] In mid-November Air Chief Marshal Sir William "Bill" Wratten succeeded Wilson. A supremely capable officer who impressed all who came in contact with him, Wratten quickly smoothed relations.[305]

In early October General Powell ordered Schwarzkopf to send a team to Washington to brief the state of air and ground planning to the defense leadership and President Bush. It constituted a decisive inflection point in campaign planning. Glosson briefed Powell on the plan on October 10. Airmen would strike strategic targets, secure air supremacy, disrupt command and control, sever communications and transport links, and destroy Iraq's fielded forces. (In the final plan each became a sequential phase, with some overlap: phase 1—strategic air campaign; phase 2—air superiority in the Kuwaiti Theater of Operations [KTO]; phase 3—preparation of the battlefield; and phase 4—ground attack.) While CJCS Powell found it "bold, imaginative, and solid," he was also unsettled, fearing that "air power was being portrayed as the 'answer to the problem.'"[306] Ignoring calls to tone down his presentation, and with the fullest support of Schwarzkopf, Glosson ventured to the White House, briefing President Bush the next day, and noting that the old naval aviator asked "many insightful questions."[307]

Next came Schwarzkopf's ground planners, who presented a concept to warm the heart of an eighteenth-century general: straight up the middle into the teeth of Iraqi defenses, at an anticipated cost of two thousand American dead. So bad was the plan that Horner went direct to Cheney "to say I thought we had to do better."[308] Nor was National Security Advisor Brent Scowcroft impressed. "It sounded unenthusiastic, delivered by people who didn't want to do the job," he recalled; "The option they presented us, an attack straight up through the center of the Iraqi army, seemed to me to be so counterintuitive that I could not stay silent. I asked why not an envelopment to the west and north around and behind the forces in Kuwait to cut them off."[309] To Secretary of Defense Cheney, the plan "didn't make any sense: Why would we send our forces—some of which were only lightly armored—up against the heavily armored core of Saddam's defenses?"[310] Bolstered by the VII Corps from Europe, Schwarzkopf completed a revised plan with the "Hail Mary" left hook, briefing it to CENTCOM on November 14.

On November 29 the United Nations passed Resolution 678, authorizing forcible expulsion of Iraqi forces from Kuwait if they did not withdraw by January 15, 1991. By then the airpower forces in theater numbered 2,614 aircraft, 1,990 of which were American. Of these aircraft, 70 percent—1,838—were fighters and attack aircraft. Schwarzkopf had insisted that Horner and his airmen hammer Iraq's Republican Guard and many other divisions, and Glosson emphasized to the tankers of VII Corps that they would pound them thoroughly before Schwarzkopf launched the ground war, using a grid of thirty-mile by thirty-mile "kill-boxes" in which strike aircraft would prowl by day and night. B-52s would carpetbomb deployed Iraqi divisions as well. (His skeptical listeners were not convinced, though they soon would be.[311]) His airmen were more receptive: "Got 'The Plan,' and my heart soared," an F-16 pilot wrote; "The guys that wrote this plan have put together an incredible air campaign." It was far from Rolling Thunder.[312]

In early January the U.S. Congress approved the use of force against Iraq. On January 14 President Bush, Scowcroft, and Cheney reviewed plans with Air Force chief of staff Gen. Merrill McPeak, who "radiated confidence."[313] The next day Bush signed a National Security Presidential Directive authorizing going to war, and Cheney and Powell cosigned its execution order.

Desert Storm: "The Apotheosis of Twentieth-Century Airpower"

At 6:00 a.m. local time on January 16, 1991, Horner issued an alert followed by an execute order shortly after noon: H-Hour was set for 3:00 a.m. January 17. At 12:22 that morning, stealth fighters left Khamis Mushait, deep in Saudi Arabia. At sea, the Navy launched Tomahawk land attack cruise missiles and carrier aircraft, while B-52s from Barksdale launched their own cruise missiles as cells of other B-52s approached with conventional dumb bombs.

At 2:20 a.m., Army AH-64 gunships, led by Air Force Pave Low MH-53 pathfinders, entered Iraq. So too did F-117s and the first cruise missiles. At 2:38, the joint Army–Air Force team destroyed a western radar site, and eighteen F-15Es promptly streaked through the gap to destroy a suspected fixed Scud launch site. Cruising over Baghdad at 3:02 a.m., an F-117 delivered the campaign's first bomb on Iraq's capital, obliterating a telecommunications center and taking CNN off the air, thus providing watchers in Riyadh and Washington with real-time battle damage assessment.[314] Waves of coalition fighters cleared the skies of intervening Iraqi aircraft, for the loss of just one of their own.[315]

By morning the first wave of stealth attacks had shattered Iraq's integrated air defense network and the air force headquarters (among other targets), opening the country to a so-called gorilla package that destroyed much of its remaining air defenses and left such a shambles that by mid-morning coalition aircraft were effectively roaming at will across the Iraqi heartland. "Horner and his planners," Schwarzkopf noted, "clearly succeeded brilliantly at undoing Iraq's high-tech defense network. By jamming and bombing its radars, they'd blinded it; by striking at its command centers, they'd paralyzed it."[316]

The success of the opening night attacks set the stage for the destruction of Iraq's military forces, though not in the way that those who saw airpower's role as one of "shaping" or "preparing" the battlefield might have expected. Precision munitions, which had first appeared in rudimentary (if still telling) form during World War II and then in more influential form during the decade-long war in Southeast Asia, now possessed an accuracy and a power that rendered previous modes of sequential, linear warfare obsolete. Planners could speak with confidence of the likely number of targets destroyed per sortie rather than the number of sorties required to destroy a particular target. Attackers could take advantage of precision capabilities to pursue simultaneous, parallel operations ranging across the entire theater rather than having to plan a repetitive campaign to return and revisit targets as in World War II, Korea, and SEA. Thus, while the campaign followed Horner's broad four-phase outline, the transition between phases was blurred and had considerable overlap. Indeed, from the outset, attackers struck at Iraq's fielded military forces in the KTO while, conversely, at war's end they were still striking at key command, control, communications, and intelligence nodes in Baghdad as the Iraqis worked to rebuild and reorganize them.

Over the length of the forty-three-day conflict, the Iraqi regime attempted to "derail" the coalition's air campaign. Attacking al-Khafji across the Saudi border in late January constituted a brilliant if desperate stroke to trigger a premature launch of the ground war on terms favorable to Iraqi firepower. Though it did not succeed, it did gain for Iraq some alarmist media coverage from journalists (who should have known better) until coalition defenders turned it into a costly defeat, largely through air attack by fixed- and rotary-wing gunships. Over the length of the war, Iraq repeatedly fired Scuds against Israel, hoping to provoke Israeli intervention. But Israel did not rise to the bait and the war went on. Throughout the conflict Iraqi technicians worked vigorously to reassert its ability to effectively command, control, and communicate with its fielded forces, rebuilding destroyed or crippled capabilities, such as its shattered air defense network. Thus, from an air campaign standpoint, this meant that phases were never completely "done," as unexpected enemy action, pop-up threats, and taskings continued to war's end. Though low, coalition losses during low-altitude attacks illustrated yet again the vulnerability of low-level attackers, no matter how fast, when in an environment dominated by shoulder-fired air defense missiles and abundant light flak. Quite frankly, "low is no place to go." In an era where the number of fixed- and rotary-wing CAS aircraft constantly decreases because of their rapidly rising unit cost, this raises questions regarding how willing future commanders will—and should—be to risk using them in such an environment, which might more profitably be left to remotely piloted aircraft and other battlefield support systems such as rocket artillery.

For example, the unexpected Iraqi "flush" of its aircraft to Iran meant that the air superiority war now extended to the Iranian frontier, with the engagement time and geometries challenging the ability of coalition airmen to catch Iranian "fast movers" before they reached the safety of Iranian airspace. In one case, Air Force F-15s inadvertently entered Iranian airspace to shoot down two Iraqi aircraft, something Horner immediately reported to Washington, even though he feared it might lead to imposition of a campaign-constraining buffer zone, as had existed along the Chinese border with North Vietnam a generation previously. The so-called Great Scud Hunt to counter the Saddam regime's use of these weapons forced a serious diversion of strike and intelligence, surveillance, and reconnaissance assets away from confronting the Iraqi fielded forces in the KTO, highlighting for subsequent potential aggressors the great value of these systems as strategic assets whose psychological and political impact was far more significant than the actual physical damage and human loss that they inflicted. Persistent Iraqi efforts to reestablish effective control and shift from compromised or inadequate centers to newer, deeper, and more extensively hardened ones drove the coalition to devote greater efforts to fielding precision strike aircraft with laser-designated bombs (such as the A-6E, F-15E, F-111F, F-117, and British Tornado). They even prompted the coalition to rapidly develop entirely new weapons, the most notable example being the 4,700-pound GBU-28 deep penetration munition designed, developed, tested, fielded, and employed all in the space of seventeen days.

Over forty-three days, airmen flew 109,876 sorties, expending 88,500 tons of ordnance. Approximately half of all sorties attacking Iraq were affected by weather—cloud, rain, and wind—which also resulted in canceled strikes because preestablished ROE dictated that strike aircraft have a clearly identified target before going weapons-free. Even before war's end, Saddam's army had gone from being the fourth-largest army in the world to being the fourth-largest army in Iraq.[317] Obedient to Schwarzkopf's special concern, Horner's airmen made a particular point of battering the Republican Guard. The pace and fury of the attacks on the Guard are seen in the example of two Iraqi divisions that endured "88 B-52 attacks and 579 F-16 strikes" within a single week.[318] On February 24 Schwarzkopf launched the ground offensive, which was in large measure a prisoner collection effort. By that time an estimated 50 percent of Iraqi frontline forces had already deserted or attempted desertion.[319] Abandoned vehicles littered Kuwait and Iraq, and 87,000 Iraqis advanced toward coalition troops with their hands in the air.

The approaching end of the war generated its own frictional pressures threatening the air campaign, particularly the positioning of a too-forward-located fire-support coordination line and fears of inflicting excessive damage and casualties to Iraq and its largely fleeing military. The Army's fire-support coordination line, intended to create an "Army only" free-fire zone (at a time when Army ground maneuver forces were still at a distance) effectively created a sanctuary for Iraqi mechanized forces still on the move. It allowed two Republican Guard divisions to escape, ultimately exposed friendly forces to greater risk of enemy fire, and arguably led to unnecessary ground casualties (from both ground "blue-on-blue" friendly fire and enemy action) in the closing days of Desert Storm.[320] At 8:00 a.m. on February 28, 1991, phase 4 of the Gulf campaign ended. Unlike previous wars, there was no Waterloo, Sedan, Gettysburg, El Alamein, or Stalingrad where one would build a monument signifying the war's culmination or turning point. Instead, Iraq's defeat had come out of the desert sky. "The paralysis and disorganization of the Iraqi Army came as a result of air power," analysts of the Gulf War Air Power Survey concluded; "Air power dominated the military outcome of Operation Desert Storm."[321]

The First Gulf War in Retrospect: Observations, Lessons, and Reflections

The Gulf crisis and subsequent air campaign highlighted and in some cases validated many important developments that had taken place since the war in SEA.

The military-to-military and government-to-government contacts established in the prewar period, intended to confront the Soviet Union, greatly smoothed interactions as coalition members confronted the first aggressor of the post–Cold War period. All coalitions experience difficulty in working together, driven by differing national intentions and the personalities of commanders, and the experiences of multinational commanders in the Gulf certainly reflected this. Nevertheless, with rare exceptions, the commanders who took their national components to war in the Gulf proved an unusually congenial group, reflecting in most cases years of prewar exposure to each other's services and service ethos. This extended to the heads of service in Washington, London, Paris, Riyadh, and other capitals.

Desert Storm transformed the way both political leaders and citizens envisioned air attack, setting a marker (and raising expectations) for future conflicts. On the war's eve, airpower critics pointed to the rubble and destroyed cities of Europe and Japan in World War II, or the futility of Rolling Thunder, arguing that airpower was imprecise, oversold, and ultimately of little consequence except to cause massive collateral damage and much suffering. But Desert Storm turned that view around, reversing decades of skepticism.[322] Central to this was the extraordinary impact of precision attack and a consequent lack of wanton destruction, even when air attacks—whether by aircraft or cruise missiles—took place in densely populated urban areas. When peace activist Erika Monk visited Iraq and witnessed the evidence of precision attack, she concluded that such evidence "doesn't produce the kinds of images that mobilize peace movements."[323] A journalist visiting Iraq marveled at "how little damage allied air raids had actually caused to civilian areas," adding, "Especially in Baghdad, the bombing was eerily precise."[324] Indeed, having seen such results, critics of airpower now have possibly unrealistic expectations of how "clean" air attack can be.

The war confirmed the maturation of American airpower. As Air Vice Marshal Richard A. "Tony" Mason, RAF, stated afterward, "The Gulf war marked the apotheosis of twentieth-century airpower."[325] It also demonstrated the maturation of airpower in that the power of precision enabled a reduction in brute force, allowing smaller and less destructive weapons to produce greater strategic and operational effects. In Desert Storm, the mass of the Iraqi army was less significant than Iraq's nodal vulnerabilities, which strike aircraft could hit precisely. In World War II it had taken dozens, even hundreds of bombs to achieve a reasonable expectation of destroying a target; in the Gulf this took one bomb or one missile. In short, Desert Storm signaled a new stage in the evolution of military operations and capabilities. But above all, as President George H. W. Bush told graduates at the 1991 commencement of the Air Force Academy "Gulf Lesson One is the value of air power."[326]

American mastery of aerospace technology drove coalition success and Iraqi defeat. The war reflected the continued intertwined relationship of air and space power with advanced technology, signaling yet once more the necessity for maintaining technological dominance over potential opponents. It reflected the synergistic confluence of the classic aerospace revolution in aerodynamics, propulsion, structures, and controls with the computer-driven systems revolution and advanced Moore's Law–driven electronic systems. From this came such capabilities as stealth aircraft, "bullet hitting a bullet" antimissile systems, precision sensors and weapons, digital electronic flying controls, and integrated sensor fusion. In particular, coalition operations demonstrated the progress in electronic warfare and low-observables that the United States had made since 1973—the result of investment in technology, testing ranges, and development infrastructure. These advances effectively rendered the air defense architectures and networks of the late Cold War Soviet Union and Warsaw Pact both obsolescent and ineffective. Advances in precision navigation, communications, and weapons technology led to game-changing combat capabilities. These included global positioning system satellites, secure communication systems, smart weapons, and sensors. The combination of low-observable and conventional strike aircraft guided by space-based satellite systems and equipped with precision-attack sensors and weapons proved crucial to the coalition's success in the air, on land, and at sea. It cannot be stressed too strongly that technological mastery, like air supremacy or democracy, is not something that can be assumed as a "given." Rather, every generation has to work to ensure it.

Desert Storm proved the benefits of a single air commander orchestrating the air war via a master attack plan and air tasking-order process. Any likely alternative could easily have resulted in a SEA-style free-for-all with control split among CONUS, CENTCOM, and its constituents, including imposition of a self-limiting "Route Pack"-type system that could have degenerated into little more than a large-scale program of armed reconnaissance. As well, the conflict validated the concept of the ATO. Before and during the war, controversy over the ATO and allegations that it slowed, rather than smoothed, the progress of the air campaign by introducing an overly bureaucratic process threatened to disrupt what was actually a foundational process. The ATO was, as Horner termed it, the "single sheet of music from which everybody played."[327] Schwarzkopf, as CINCCENT, determined what had to be done, tasking the JFACC's planners in Riyadh's "Black Hole," the center of the air campaign direction, planning, and execution. They in turn created a master attack plan, and a planning team then prepared the ATO. ATO criticism largely reflected the larger debate over whether airpower should be centrally or independently controlled via a JFACC. But although critics alleged that the ATO imposed too rigid control, they had—then and afterward—no suitable alternative.[328]

Combat operations validated post-Vietnam emphasis on realistic training and testing. Both air and land combatants afterward remarked on the fidelity of prewar training they had received. Their introduction into combat was vastly different than what their predecessors had experienced a quarter century previously, going to war over North Vietnam in the dolorous days of Rolling Thunder. There were also none of the uncomfortable surprises that occurred in Vietnam when overly touted weapons failed to work as promised. Thanks to more realistic operationally focused testing (to include the dynamics of weapons release in a hard-maneuvering and countermeasures-intensive environment), such advances as stealth aircraft, air-to-air and air-to-surface missiles, laser-guided bombs, and battlefield-scanning radars worked "as advertised."

The deceptive ease of day-to-day logistical and combat operations reflected investment in the Air Force's "tanker bridge"; modern high-capacity, high-bypass-ratio turbofan-powered jet transports and wide-body airliners; and the creation of the Civil Reserve Air Fleet. The "tanker bridge" air refueling infrastructure supported both the combat forces and transports deployed during Desert Shield and then performed routine tanking for coalition aircraft throughout Desert Storm. The airlift illustrated the extraordinary ability of modern transports and mobilized civil jetliners to move personnel and vital equipment into a crisis region within hours of a national command authority go-ahead, and it confirmed the wisdom of establishing processes and a framework to mobilize civil airliners to meet emergency national needs.

Control systems such as AWACS and the joint surveillance target-attack radar system (JSTARS) significantly reduced the traditional "fog of war," aiding situational and battlefield awareness and targeting. In previous conflicts, surprise leading to unanticipated enemy success and confusion leading to the tragedy of "friendly fire" were virtually an accepted part of military life. The highly sophisticated E-3 AWACS to deconflict the air war and prevent "blue-on-blue" fire and the E-8 JSTARS to locate and then track and target enemy ground forces proved themselves in the Gulf. Their inputs made Gulf airmen both more situationally aware and more confident than airmen in previous wars. For example, the JSTARS information picture proved crucial to orchestrating the final collapse of Iraqi forces in the field, even though at the time it was still in the operational test and evaluation stage and thus technically an experimental system.

The Gulf War was the first space war with air, land, and sea forces exploiting—and critically dependent upon—space-based assets for command, control, communications, intelligence, surveillance, antimissile defensive cuing, targeting, weather, and navigation. This, by any reasonable definition, constitutes "space war." Thus, although pundits continue to debate whether the United States and other nations should "militarize space," in truth it has already occurred. Indeed, since then it has expanded to include cuing weapons such as the joint direct attack munition. Space now influences virtually every aspect of modern war. As a subset of this, antiballistic missile (ABM) defense proved its practicality in Desert Storm, confounding long-standing criticism and critics. Iraq launched a total of 93 Scuds against the coalition. Air defenders fired 158 Army PAC-2 Patriot SAMs against 47 Scuds it determined threatened populated areas, hitting 45 of them. While a postwar debate broke out over the effectiveness of the Patriot (given that the warheads of many damaged or destroyed Scuds still came to earth and, in some cases, over populated areas), it is instructive to note that the only unengaged Scud threatening a populated area killed or injured 125 U.S. Army soldiers—the single greatest loss from enemy action American forces suffered in the war. It occurred when a Patriot battery that could have defended the target was down for maintenance. ABM technology since Desert Storm has grown more sophisticated still, with even small rockets and missiles being vulnerable to more recent anti-rocket and -missile systems such as the Israeli Iron Dome.

If these were some of the "successes," the war certainly possessed its share of "fog and friction" as well, much of it well covered in numerous postwar analytical studies and histories.

Intelligence analysis, particularly generating timely "actionable" information and reliable baseline data sets proved problematical, endangering prosecution and fulfillment of the air campaign. Problems occurred in multiple areas, but three primary ones include how to assess nodal, effects-based air war; timely intelligence processing and bomb-damage assessment in general; and overcoming preexisting biases about what air attack "could" do. The first of these was spotlighted by an intelligence debate inside the Beltway over how significantly the air campaign was reducing Iraq's military capabilities, if at all. The debate pitted "traditionalists" looking at a list of targets and measuring remaining capabilities by what percentage of the list had been destroyed against "nodalists" who took a systemic approach, looking at what was actually happening system-wide following attacks on key nodes. In one notable case, after attackers dropped a single bridge that effectively eliminated all rail traffic between Baghdad and Basra, traditionalists held that the rail line was still functional since another bridge further along was left standing. Processing delays impacted daily planning of the unfolding air campaign as it moved through its various phases, causing planners and targeteers in the Black Hole to employ work-arounds such as Warden's Checkmate and Rear Adm. Mike McConnell's J-2 shop to review raw intelligence data sources rapidly enough to keep it "actionable" rather than relegating it to "historical." Bomb-damage assessment proved problematic to analysts unfamiliar with or unused to the deceptive effects of precision munitions. For example, precision bombs often made small entry holes in hardened aircraft shelters and bunkers but then exploded with devastating effect within them. While strike video often showed the tell-tale ejection plume back through the entry hole (reminiscent of the fury of a rocket exhaust) indicative of an energetic explosion within, "after the fact" overhead imagery did not, which led to many cases (when coalition members actually "walked the ground" of Iraqi military facilities) where targets graded as untouched or only slightly damaged were found to have been totally destroyed. Finally, long-standing service-rooted skepticism over the claims of airmen created "fog and friction" issues (and ill will as well) that threatened the air and land campaign. ARCENT analysts initially routinely rejected any claim for destroyed armored vehicles made by a pilot of an aircraft other than an A-10, the only aircraft they were inclined to credit with armor kills since this was its intended purpose. But the war's most successful antitank aircraft were actually the two-place sophisticated night attackers such as the A-6, F-111, and F-15E using advanced sensors (e.g., TRAM, Pave Tack, and LANTIRN) and laser-guided bombs (which the A-10 then lacked). Discounting their kills led to wild overestimates of Iraqi strength, risking unnecessary "return" sorties to no purpose and threatening a delayed launch of the ground occupation phase of the war. ARCENT stopped the practice when confronted with clear evidence of its intellectual bankruptcy.[329] Overall, these problems corrupted analysis and targeting, confounding rather than assisting the war effort.

Iraq's Scuds had great strategic value thanks to their political dimension. Although they could not win the war, the Scud attacks threatened to provoke Israel into a response that might shatter the anti-Iraq Arab-Western coalition; no other weapon possessed such political power. It was hardly by chance that the war's first strikes targeted fixed Scud sites in western Iraq. But the great difficulty in locating "shoot and scoot" Scuds and Scud derivatives and in distinguishing them from decoys posed a challenge that airmen never overcame. Although intense air activity forced caution on Iraqi missileers—the firing rate of Scuds dropped from five per day on average over the first ten days of the war to just one per day on average over the war's remaining month—the Scuds were never temporarily or fully suppressed, a significant "lesson learned" for both would-be aggressors and potential victims. The mobile theater-ranging ballistic missile, capable of being launched within a few minutes, remains a challenging target to engage and defeat by any means other than a "catcher's mitt" strategy of employing defensive ABMs such as PAC-3 Patriot, SM-3 Standard, and THAAD.

Media reaction to destruction and journalists' susceptibility to Iraqi propaganda fueled questionable out-of-theater decision making that constrained coalition air operations. Over the war the Iraq regime sought through mostly ham-fisted efforts to direct the media story of the war, including orchestrating visits by Western antiwar partisans, exploiting damage caused by air strikes such as the so-called Baby Milk Factory strike, and bridge cuts within Baghdad to sever fiber-optic cables to regime command-and-control sites. Surprisingly, such efforts gained a great deal of sympathetic foreign press coverage from journalists who rejected or at least reacted skeptically to coalition spokesmen explaining what the real targets were or why strikes had been prosecuted, preferring to accept the Iraqi narrative of widespread misery and suffering. In at least two cases, Washington's panicked reaction to media accounts influenced campaign execution. An F-117 strike on an al-Firdos bunker (an Iraqi command center that, unknown to coalition planners, doubled as an air-raid shelter), resulted in numerous civilian casualties of senior-level personnel and their dependents. The Cheney-Powell defense team temporarily declared Baghdad off limits, derailing the air campaign against leadership targets in Baghdad until almost war's end. As a result, the Saddam regime was able to restore some key command-and-control functions, secure—at least for a while—in the knowledge that they would not be targeted. Washington's panicked reaction over the alleged "Highway of Death" at war's end when the Iraqi army was in full retreat triggered an early shutdown of the war. With few exceptions, journalists missed that, while the physical destruction was great, the actual loss of life was small because the Iraqis exposed to it immediately fled their vehicles. In short, it was no Wadi al-Far'a, Falaise Gap, or Mitla Pass. Nevertheless, Washington canceled further attacks at precisely the point when they could have been most influential. Both incidents demonstrate that information war is as potentially dislocating as kinetic or cyber war.

The first Gulf War began an operations-cycle tempo for America's military that has lasted for a quarter century. Although not recognized at the time, Desert Shield and Desert Storm marked the beginning of a period of constant air alert and air warfare that has lasted twenty-five years—and with no end in sight. Every day since the arrival of American airpower forces in the Gulf region to confront Hussein's invasion of Kuwait, the U.S. military has maintained a combat footing and operational tempo that has sometimes come close to "breaking" the force by rapidly making its equipment obsolete and wearing down its personnel.

CONCLUSIONS

The half-century from December 1941 to December 1991 witnessed a sea change in American global responsibilities, presence, and power projection. Much as America itself underwent profound changes reflecting its new role in global affairs, so too did joint-service (and civil) airpower transform dramatically.

Although the United States in the last half of the twentieth century was truly an "aerospace nation" defined by its legacy of aerospace accomplishment, robust aerospace industry and infrastructure, use of full-spectrum aerospace power for both civil and military purposes, and clarity of its aerospace vision, it was at successive key points more fortunate than skillful. Well-publicized accomplishments such as achieving the first supersonic flight, developing and practicing routine global air refueling, dominating international air transport for better than a half-century, landing on the Moon, developing the first electronic flight-control systems, and producing the first stealth airplane obscured recognition that the American aerospace community relied more often upon emulation and innovation than upon invention. Given the international stakes—confronting Nazism, fascism, and Japanese militarism, or, after 1945, the Sino-Soviet bloc—it is alarming what the United States missed or came close to missing both before and in the aftermath of World War II. From 1935 through 1961 (the formative years in aerospace technology for building the technical base that undergirded its wartime performance in World War II, Korean War, and Vietnam) the United States dismissed the significance of, minimized, or missed altogether the invention of radar (Britain); the high-speed sweptwing airplane (Germany); the turbojet engine (Britain and Germany); the ramjet (France and Soviet Union); jet fighters (Germany and Britain), jet bombers (Germany), jet airliners (Britain and Canada); battlefield artillery rockets

(Soviet Union and Germany); ballistic missiles (Germany); air-to-surface, air-to-air, and surface-to-air guided missiles (all German); the angled flight deck, mirror landing system, and steam catapult (all Britain); the first earth satellite (Soviet Union), and the first human-carrying spacecraft (Soviet Union). Only in the latter stages of Vietnam did American aerospace inventiveness in materials, flight-control technology, propulsion, applied aerodynamics, sensor technologies, and radar-scattering prediction and reduction come together to enable the development of systems and weapons that constituted at least a generational advance over those of potential opponents. That level of singular, unchallenged advancement no longer characterizes the U.S. aerospace enterprise in the first two decades of the twenty-first century.

In the post-1945 environment, pervasive airpower—more properly aerospace power, after the advent of satellites and ballistic missiles—arguably became the most distinctive feature of American presence and power projection. When critics protested and railed against what they viewed as unwarranted American influence and/or presence, very often they chose symbols emblematic of American aerospace power: airplanes (particularly the B-52), missiles, and helicopters. Protesting the port calls of aircraft carriers and ballistic missile submarines, both of them aerospace systems, became a particular feature of Asian-Pacific unrest, often linked to perceived environmental concerns and campaigns against nuclear energy and nuclear weapons as well. Over much of the 1960s to 1990s, ports, airfields, and cruise missile launch sites became focal points for domestic and foreign protest, as in the well-publicized 1980s demonstrations against NATO deployment of the Pershing II and the ground-launched cruise missile.

The ability of the United States to project airpower into crisis regions rapidly and decisively was crucial to its success in winning the Cold War and then confronting the challenges of the post–Cold War world. Until the Bay of Pigs and then Vietnam, the United States had an unblemished record of success in using airpower to intervene in unfolding crises. American airpower in World War II was considered by the Axis to be the most distinctive aspect of American warfare. The availability of an entire air transport construct, combat proven in World War II, enabled the air supply of Berlin, frustrating Soviet objectives. The presence of on-scene naval forces and the ability to control the sky and furnish long-range airpower as well saved Korea in the summer and fall of 1950, the most critical months of the conflict. Crisis intervention in Quemoy/Matsu and in Lebanon demonstrated America's ability to project protective or retaliatory power rapidly via air-refueled expeditionary forces, as did El Dorado Canyon and the opening stages of Desert Shield subsequently.

Airpower in Vietnam frustrated communist efforts to overwhelm hamlets, defensive forces, and deployed American troops, but its record over the North in Rolling Thunder and over the Ho Chi Minh Trail in Laos was more problematic given both the political dimension of the war, key decision making at the higher levels of government, the convoluted command-and-control process, the uncertain goals and unclear end state of American action, and the limiting factors of technology (particularly shortfalls in precision attack) then extant. Its performance at the time of Linebacker I and II was decisive in the former and sufficient in the latter to achieve the objectives of preventing the collapse of South Vietnam and coercing the North to accept the terms of the Paris peace talks. The failure to adequately support South Vietnam after 1973, particularly with air weapons and logistical support and, in 1975, with direct American air intervention was a tragedy, all the more so because, as in 1972, it is likely such air intervention would have deterred the North from invading in the first place or, if it had, from succeeding.

The rebuilding of American air strength after 1970, reflecting a more realistic appreciation of likely war-fighting circumstances and including the tremendous investment in doctrinal thought, training, and simulation, anticipated the military success of Urgent Fury, El Dorado Canyon, Just Cause, and Desert Storm. That success set the stage for the use of airpower over the next decade, up to September 11, 2001, and the "drone" era that followed.

The story of American airpower—more properly now aerospace power—is, of course, hardly finished. New initiatives in such areas as autonomous systems; microaerovehicles; "smart" structures and skin-embedded sensors; "netted" and sensor-fused aircraft systems; hypersonic precision munitions extending the value and service life of now "legacy" platforms such as the venerable B-52, the near-venerable B-1, and the mature B-2; and pervasive command, control, communications, computers, intelligence, surveillance, and reconnaissance architectures linking air, space, and land forces promise to once again transform the nation's aerospace capabilities. But if American military aerospace is to function as well in future conflicts as it has in the past, its practitioners must recognize the primacy of technological investment, avoiding the too many close-call, "fast second" episodes of the past, keeping in mind as well not merely those institutional structures, doctrines, and approaches that worked but also those that did not.

NOTES

1. U.S. War Department, *Final Report of Gen. John J. Pershing* (Washington, D.C.: Government Printing Office, 1919).
2. Ross E. Rowell, "Aircraft in Bush Warfare," *Marine Corps Gazette* 14, no. 3 (September 1929); and United States Marine Corps, *Small Wars Manual* (Washington, D.C.: Government Printing Office, 1940), sec. 9-23.

3. Roger E. Bilstein, *Flight Patterns: Trends of Aeronautical Development in the United States, 1918-1929* (Athens: University of Georgia Press, 1984), 99-144; and Ronald Miller and David Sawers, *The Technical Development of Modern Aviation* (New York: Praeger, 1968), 47-97.
4. Monte D. Wright, *Most Probable Position: A History of Aerial Navigation to 1941* (Lawrence: University Press of Kansas, 1972), 169-201.
5. Thomas H. Greer, *The Development of Air Doctrine in the Army Air Arm, 1917-1941* (Washington, D.C.: Office of Air Force History, 1985), 40-41; and James A. Mowbray, "Air Force Doctrine Problems: 1926-Present," *Airpower Journal* 9, no. 4 (Winter 1995).
6. Roger G. Miller, "The USAAF and Air Transport on the Eve of Pearl Harbor," in *Air Mobility Symposium: 1947 to the 21st Century* (Washington, D.C.: Government Printing Office, 1998), 10; and Daniel L. Haulman, "Air Mobility Lessons of World War II," in *Air Mobility Symposium: 1947 to the 21st Century* (Washington, D.C.: Government Printing Office, 1998), 26.
7. Robert T. Finney, *History of the Air Corps Tactical School, 1920-1940* (Washington, D.C.: Center for Air Force History, 1992), 64, 67-69; and Stephen L. McFarland, *America's Pursuit of Precision Bombing, 1910-1945* (Tuscaloosa: University of Alabama Press, 1995), 40-44, 68-104.
8. Rudolf Modley and Thomas J. Cawley, eds., *Aviation Facts and Figures, 1953* (Washington, D.C.: Lincoln Press, 1953), tables 2-3 and 2-6, pp. 22, 24.
9. I. B. Holley Jr., *Buying Aircraft: Materiel Procurement for the Army Air Forces, Special Studies, United States Army in World War II* (Washington, D.C.: Office of the Chief of Military History, Department of the Army, 1964).
10. Haywood S. Hansell Jr., *The Air Plan That Defeated Hitler* (Atlanta: Higgins-McArthur/Longino & Porter, Inc., 1972), 55.
11. "Preliminary Plans for the Air Defense of the Hawaiian Islands" (Mitchel Field, NY: Army Air Defense School, April 5, 1941), reprinted as appendix M in William R. Burt, *Adventures with Warlords* (New York: Vantage, 1994), 250-53.
12. Richard Davis, *Carl A. Spaatz and the Air War in Europe* (Washington, D.C.: Center for Air Force History, 1993), 373, 376.
13. Samuel Eliot Morison, *Coral Sea, Midway and Submarine Actions, May 1942-August 1942* (Boston: Little, Brown, 1955).
14. Wesley Frank Craven and James Lea Cate, eds., *Europe: Torch to Pointblank, August 1942 to December 1943* (Chicago: University of Chicago Press, 1949).
15. James A. Winnefeld and Dana J. Johnson, *Joint Air Operations: Pursuit of Unity in Command and Control, 1942-1991* (Annapolis, Md.: Naval Institute Press and RAND, 1993), 13-38.
16. U.S. War Department, *FM 100-20: Command and Employment of Air Power* (Washington, D.C.: Government Printing Office, 1943).

17. Gary Null, *Weapon of Denial: Air Power and the Battle for New Guinea* (Washington, D.C.: Air Force History and Museums Program, 1995).
18. Nathan Miller, *The Naval Air War 1939-1945* (Annapolis, Md.: Naval Institute Press, 1991).
19. Stephen L. McFarland and Wesley Phillips Newton, *To Command the Sky: The Battle for Air Superiority over Germany, 1942-1944* (Washington, D.C.: Smithsonian Institution Press, 1991), 117-60.
20. Arthur B. Ferguson, "Big Week," in *Europe: Argument to V-E Day, January 1944 to May 1945*, ed. Wesley Frank Craven and James Lea Cate, 30-66 (Chicago: University of Chicago Press, 1951); and John S. D. Eisenhower, *Strictly Personal* (Garden City, N.Y.: Doubleday, 1974), 72.
21. Williamson Murray, *Strategy for Defeat: The Luftwaffe 1933-1945* (Maxwell Air Force Base, Ala.: Air University Press, 1983).
22. Richard B. Frank, *Downfall: The End of the Imperial Japanese Empire* (New York: Random House, 1999); Barrett Tillman, *Whirlwind: The Air War against Japan, 1942-1945* (New York: Simon & Schuster, 2010); Herman S. Wolk, *Cataclysm: General Hap Arnold and the Defeat of Japan* (Denton: University of North Texas Press 2010); and Samuel Eliot Morison, *Victory in the Pacific, 1945* (Boston, Mass.: Little, Brown and Co., 1960).
23. Friedrich Ruge, *Rommel in Normandy* (San Rafael, Calif.: Presidio, 1979), 187.
24. Alan Vick, *Proclaiming Airpower: Air Force Narratives and American Public Opinion from 1917 to 2014* (Santa Monica, Calif.: RAND, 2015), 26-27, figs. 2.1 and 2.2.
25. Memorandum, Forrestal to service secretaries, "re Functions of the Armed Forces and the Joint Chiefs of Staff," April 21, 1948; and Truman to Forrestal, "re Functions of the Armed Forces and the Joint Chiefs of Staff," April 21, 1948, in Richard I. Wolfe, ed., *The United States Air Force Basic Documents on Roles and Missions* (Washington, D.C.: Office of Air Force History, 1987), 151-66.
26. Roger E. Bilstein, *Airlift and Airborne Operations in World War II* (Washington, D.C.: Air Force History and Museums Program, 1998), 46.
27. William H. Tunner and Booton Herndon, *Over the Hump: The Story of General William H. Tunner—The Man Who Moved Anything Anywhere, Anytime* (New York: Duell, Sloan and Pearce, 1964), 158-59.
28. Roger D. Launius, "Post World War II Priorities and the Berlin Airlift," in *Air Mobility Symposium: 1947 to the 21st Century* (Washington, D.C.: Government Printing Office, 1998), 34-35.
29. Ibid., 36-42.
30. Readers may note that I have, in previous writings, combined the fourth and fifth phases into a single phase. On reflection, and given the vastly different nature of the early and later periods of fighting, I now consider these as two distinct phases.

31. William T. Y'Blood, *Down in the Weeds: Close Air Support in Korea* (Washington, D.C.: Air Force History and Museums Program, 2002), 7; Air Force History and Museums Program, *Steadfast and Courageous: FEAF (Far East Air Forces) Bomber Command and the Air War in Korea, 1950–1953—Bombing Operations with B-29 Superfortress, Strategic Air Command (SAC), Okinawa Base* (Washington, D.C.: Air Force History and Museums Program, 2000), 12; and Michael Lewis, *Lt. Gen. Ned Almond, USA: A Ground Commander's Conflicting View with Airmen over CAS Doctrine and Employment* (Maxwell Air Force Base, Ala.: Air University Press, June 1996).
32. Warren Thompson, "Shooting Stars over Korea," *Airpower* 15, no. 2 (March 1985), 33.
33. Robert F. Futrell, *The USAF in Korea, 1950–1953* (New York: Duell, Sloan & Pearce, 1961), 94.
34. Office of the Chief of Staff, General Headquarters, United Nations Command, "A General Review of United States Tactical Air Support in Korea, 28 June 1950-8 September 1950," (1950), 1, copy in Air Force History Support Office archives, Bolling Air Force Base, Washington, D.C. The F-47 was World War II's P-47, redesignated from P to F like the P-51/F-51. In April 1951 an F-51 was lost on an average of one per day.
35. Jesse Jacobs, "Air Pressure: Air-to-Ground Operations in Korea," in Richard P. Hallion, ed., *Silver Wings, Golden Valor: The USAF Remembers Korea* (Washington, D.C.: Air Force History and Museums Program, 2006), 81; and Wayne Thompson and Bernard C. Nalty, *Within Limits: The U.S. Air Force and the Korean War* (Washington, D.C.: Air Force History and Museums Program, 1996). The B-26 in Korea was the redesignated Douglas A-26, not the Martin B-26 medium bomber of World War II renown. By the Korean War, the B-29—a very heavy bomber in World War II—was officially a medium bomber.
36. U.S. Navy, Deputy Chief of Naval Operations (Air), Aviation Statistics Section, *Aviation Statistics Special Report* 1-50 (September 20, 1950), 6, Naval History and Heritage Command Archives; and U.S. Air Force Historical Division (USAF HD), *United States Air Force Operations in the Korean Conflict, 25 June–1 November 1950* (Washington, D.C.: U.S. Air Force Historical Division, July 1, 1952), 46.
37. War Department, *FM 100-20*.
38. Air Force History and Museums Program, *Steadfast and Courageous*, 19.
39. USAF HD, HS 71, *USAF Operations in the Korean Conflict*, 46.
40. U.S. War Department, *FM 31-35: Air-Ground Operations* (Washington, D.C.: Government Printing Office, 1946); Joint Logistics Plans Committee, Office of the Joint Chiefs of Staff, *Dictionary of United States Military Terms for Joint Usage (First Revision)* (Washington, D.C.: Government Printing Office, June 1950), 22; Office of the Chief of Staff, General Headquarters, United

Nation's Command, "A General Review of United States Tactical Air Support in Korea, 28 June 1950-8 September 1950" (1950), 1, Air Force History Support Office Archives, Bolling Air Force Base, Washington, D.C.; Allan Millet, "Korea, 1950-1953," in *Case Studies in the Development of Close Air Support*, ed. B. F. Cooling, 345-410 (Washington, D.C.: Office of Air Force History, 1990); Y'Blood, *Down in the Weeds*; and Thompson and Nalty, *Within Limits*.

41. USAF HD, *USAF Operations in the Korean Conflict*, 46; Malcolm W. Cagle and Frank A. Manson, *The Sea War in Korea* (Annapolis, Md.: Naval Institute Press, 1957), 65; and Y'Blood, *Down in the Weeds*, 11-12.
42. Jack Broughton, *Rupert Red Two: A Fighter Pilot's Life from Thunderbolts to Thunderchiefs* (St. Paul, Minn.: Zenith Press, 2007), 146.
43. Tim Cline, "Forward Air Control in the Korean War," *Journal of the American Aviation Historical Society* 21, no. 4 (Winter 1976): 257-62.
44. Donald D. Engen, *Wings and Warriors* (Washington, D.C.: Smithsonian Institute Press, 1997), 116; see also U.S. Navy, *Korean War U.S. Pacific Fleet Operations: Commander-in-Chief U.S. Pacific Fleet Interim Evaluation Report No. 1—Period 25 June to 15 November 1950*, v. 3 (Pearl Harbor: Naval Air Combat Operations Section, COMPACFLT, February 26, 1951), Naval History and Heritage Command Archives.
45. Pat Meid and James M. Yingling, *Operations in West Korea*, vol. 5 of *U.S. Marine Operations in Korea, 1950-1953* (Washington, D.C.: Historical Branch, G-3, Headquarters, U.S. Marine Corps, 1972), 493.
46. Alexandre Y. Mansourov, "Stalin, Mao, Kim, and China's Decision to Enter the Korean War, September 16-October 15, 1950: New Evidence from the Russian Archives," *Cold War International History Project Bulletin*, no. 6-7 (March 1999), Ciphered Telegram #600308/sh, Kim Il-Sung and Pak Hón-Yóng to Stalin, September 29, 1950, 111-12.
47. G. J. Higgins, *Air Support in Korean Campaign*, ATASC-D 373.21 (Ft. Bragg, N.C.: Army Air Support Center, December 1, 1950), 6, Military History Institute Archives, Carlisle Barracks, Pa.
48. U.S. Navy, OCNO, *Combat Activity of Naval Aviation* (November 1950), 3, Naval History and Heritage Command Archives; and Hanson W. Baldwin, "Korea Has Shown Role of Air Power," *New York Times*, November 1, 1950.
49. Xiaoming Zhang, *Red Wings over the Yalu: China, the Soviet Union, and the Air War in Korea* (College Station: Texas A&M University Press, 2002), 73, 82, 116.
50. Lynn Montross and Nicholas A. Canzona, *The Chosin Reservoir Campaign*, vol. 3 of *U.S. Marine Operations in Korea, 1950-1953* (Washington, D.C.: Historical Branch, G-3, Headquarters, U.S. Marine Corps, 1957); William M. Leary, *Anything, Anywhere, Anytime: Combat Cargo in the Korean War*, 50th ann. comm. ed. (Washington, D.C.: Defense Department, Air Force Department, 2000), 17-23; Kenneth W. Condit and Ernest H. Giusti,

"Marine Air at the Chosin Reservoir," *Marine Corps Gazette* 36, no. 7 (July 1952), 18-25; Ernest H. Giusti and Kenneth W. Condit, "Marine Air Covers the Breakout," *Marine Corps Gazette* 36, no. 8 (August 1952): 20-27; and Alexander L. George, *The Chinese Communist Army in Action: The Korean War and Its Aftermath* (New York: Columbia University Press, 1967), 172.
51. Zhang, *Red Wings over the Yalu*, 73, 82, 116.
52. Rept., Chinese Special Aviation Group, in USAF, *Far East Air Forces Intelligence Round-Up*, 69 (December 22-28, 1951), Air Force Historical Research Agency Archives, Maxwell Air Force Base [hereafter AFHRA].
53. Quoted in Zhang, *Red Wings over the Yalu*, 117.
54. Brig. Gen. R. A. Grussendorf, Exec to CSAF, "Memorandum for Colonel Murphy," n.d., in Hoyt Vandenberg Papers, Box 88, "Nam Il" file, Manuscript Division, Library of Congress, Washington, D.C.
55. George, *Chinese Communist Army in Action*, 169.
56. Ibid., 170.
57. Kenneth P. Werrell, *Sabres over MiG Alley: The F-86 and the Battle for Air Superiority in Korea* (Annapolis, Md.: Naval Institute Press, 2005); and Zhang, *Red Wings over the Yalu*.
58. *Oriskany* action report, October 28-November 22, 1952, 4, Naval History and Heritage Command Archives.
59. Richard P. Hallion, *The Naval Air War in Korea* (Baltimore: Nautical & Aviation Publishing, 1986), 92.
60. Quoted in Futrell, *USAF in Korea*, 461.
61. Joseph W. Angell Jr., Charles H. Hildreth, Littleton B. Atkinson, George F. Lemmer, and Lee Bowen, *USAF Tactical Operations: World War II and Korean War with Statistical Tables* (Fort Belvoir, Va.: Defense Technical Information Center, May 1962), table 111.
62. Richard H. Kohn and Joseph P. Harahan, eds., *Air Interdiction in World War II, Korea, and Vietnam* (Washington, D.C.: Office of Air Force History, 1985), 57; see also J. J. Clark, *Carrier Admiral*, with Clark G. Reynolds (New York: David McKay, 1967); and Conrad Crane, *American Airpower Strategy in Korea, 1950-1953* (Lawrence: University Press of Kansas, 2000).
63. Futrell, *USAF in Korea*, 482-89; Cagle and Manson, *Sea War in Korea*, 441-58; and Zhang, *Red Wings over the Yalu*, 188.
64. Futrell, *USAF in Korea*, 515-29; and Cagle and Manson, *Sea War in Korea*, 450-60.
65. Zhang, *Red Wings over the Yalu*, 189.
66. Cagle and Manson, *Sea War in Korea*, 469.
67. Quoted in Futrell, *USAF in Korea*, 669.
68. Zhang, *Red Wings over the Yalu*, 197.
69. A sortie is a single flight by a single aircraft.

70. Statistics from USN, *Combat Activity of Naval Aviation* (April-July 1953), table 15; Angell et al., *USAF Tactical Operations*, table 106; Futrell, *USAF in Korea*, 690; and J. R. P. Lansdown, *With the Carriers in Korea* (Upton, U.K.: Severnside, 1992), 425.
71. Alan Stephens, *Going Solo: The Royal Australian Air Force, 1946-1971* (Canberra: Australian Government Publishing Service, 1995), 241.
72. Air Force History and Museums Program, *Steadfast and Courageous*, 18; and David R. Mets, *The Quest for a Surgical Strike* (Eglin Air Force Base, Fla.: Armament Division, 1987), 23-28. Crews became more proficient over time: 96 percent of the last 150 Razons dropped hit their aim points.
73. *Boxer* action report, August 23-September 6, 1952, 3, 6-7, Naval History and Heritage Command Archives; D. S. Fahrney, "Guided Missiles—U.S. Navy the Pioneer," *Journal of the American Aviation Historical Society* 27, no. 1 (Spring 1982): 21-26; and Mets, *Quest for a Surgical Strike*, 30-32.
74. Matthew B. Ridgeway, *The Korean War* (Garden City, N.Y.: Doubleday, 1967), 244.
75. Ralph D. Bald, *Air Force Participation in Joint Army-Air Force Training Exercises, 1951-1954* (Maxwell Air Force Base, Ala.: Research Studies Institute, 1957), 132.
76. Jacob van Staaveren, *Air Operations in the Taiwan Crisis of 1958* (Washington, D.C.: U.S. Air Force Historical Division Liaison Office, 1962), 19-23; and Bernard C. Nalty, *The Air Force Role in Five Crises, 1958-1965: Lebanon, Taiwan, Congo, Cuba, Dominican Republic* (Washington, D.C.: U.S. Air Force Historical Division Liaison Office, 1968), 1-27.
77. Douglas V. Smith, ed., *One Hundred Years of U.S. Navy Air Power* (Annapolis, Md.: Naval Institute Press, 2010), 240-68, 322-49; and James L. Holloway III, *Aircraft Carriers at War: A Personal Retrospective of Korea, Vietnam, and the Soviet Confrontation* (Annapolis, Md.: Naval Institute Press, 2007), 110-30.
78. For example, James T. Stewart, ed., *Airpower: The Decisive Force in Korea* (Princeton, N.J.: Van Nostrand, 1957).
79. Department of the Air Force, *Strategic Air Operations: Air Doctrine*, AFM 1-8 (Washington, D.C.: Department of the Air Force, May 1, 1954); and James S. Lay, "Basic National Security Policy: A Report to the National Security Council," NSC 162/2 (Washington, D.C.: National Security Council, October 30, 1953), in *National Security Policy*, vol. 19 of *Foreign Relations of the United States, 1955-1957*, ed. John P. Glennon et al. (Washington, D.C.: Government Printing Office, 1990), 32.
80. Lay, "Basic National Security Policy." See also Kenneth W. Condit, *The Joint Chiefs of Staff and National Policy, 1955-56* (Washington, D.C.: Office of the Secretary of Defense, 1992), 9.
81. Century series: the F-100, F-101, F-102, F-104, F-105, and F-106; see Richard P. Hallion, "A Troubling Past: Air Force Fighter Acquisition since 1945," *Airpower Journal* 9, no. 4 (Winter 1990): 4-23.

82. Bruce K. Holloway, "Air Superiority in Tactical Air Warfare," *Air University Review* 19, no. 3 (March–April 1968), 9.
83. Jack B. Pfeiffer, *The Taylor Committee Investigation of the Bay of Pigs* (McLean, Va.: Center Intelligence Agency, 1984), 229, 264–90; and Jack B. Pfeiffer, *Official History of the Bay of Pigs Operation*, vol. 1: *Air Operations, March 1960–April 1961* (McLean, Va.: Central Intelligence Agency, 1979), 205–7, 227–32, 268–93, 303–405. Both approved for release July 2011.
84. Quoted in Steven L. Rearden, *Council of War* (Washington, D.C.: National Defense University Press, 2012), 211.
85. Walter S. Poole, *Adapting to Flexible Response, 1960–1968* (Washington, D.C.: Office of the Secretary of Defense, 2013), 5; and McGeorge Bundy, "National Security Action Memorandum No. 56: Evaluation of Paramilitary Requirements" (Washington, D.C.: National Security Council, June 28, 1961), in the National Security Files, Meetings and Memoranda Series, National Security Action Memoranda, John F. Kennedy Presidential Papers, Kennedy Presidential Library, Boston, Mass., http://www.jfklibrary.org/Asset-Viewer/ex2GImrvWU-Z9Zqyga7ryQ.aspx.
86. John J. Tolson, *Airmobility, 1961–1971* (Washington, D.C.: U.S. Army, 1973), 20–24; and Hamilton H. Howze, *A Cavalryman's Story* (Washington, D.C.: Smithsonian Institution Press, 1996), 233–57.
87. Quoted in David J. Dean, *The Air Force Role in Low-Intensity Conflict* (Maxwell Air Force Base, Fla.: Air University Press, 1986), 88.
88. See Xiaoming Zhang, *Deng Xiaoping's Long War: The Military Conflict between China and Vietnam, 1979–1991* (Chapel Hill: University of North Carolina Press, 2015).
89. Alan L. Gropman, "The Air War in Vietnam, 1961–1973," in *War in the Third Dimension*, ed. Richard A. Mason, 33–58 (London: Brassey's Defence Publishers, 1986); and Thomas C. Thayer, ed., *The Air War* (Washington, D.C.: SEA Intelligence Division, OASD(SA)RP, February 18, 1975), document ADA051611, Defense Technical Information Center, Defense Logistics Agency.
90. Walter J. Boyne, "The Plain of Jars," *Air Force Magazine*, June 1999, 78–83; and John T. Correll, "The Ho Chi Minh Trail," *Air Force Magazine* (November 2005), 62–68.
91. Leslie H. Gelb et al., eds., *Evolution of the War: Origins of the Insurgency, 1954–1960*, v. IV.A.5 of *United States–Vietnam Relations 1945–1967* (Washington, D.C.: Vietnam Task Force of the Office of the Secretary of Defense, January 15, 1969), table 4, 61 (hereafter, abbreviated as VTF, volume title and number, *US-VN*, and pagination). Gelb was director of the Study Task Force. The DoD declassified the series in 2011, which is available from the National Archives and Record Administration at http://www.archives.gov/research/pentagon-papers/.

92. Transcript of interview of Ambassador Leonard Unger by Charles Stuart Kennedy, May 10, 1999, 22, Association for Diplomatic Studies and Training Foreign Affairs Oral History Project, Library of Congress, Washington, D.C. [hereafter ADS-OHP LC]. See also Jacob van Staaveren, *Interdiction in Southern Laos, 1960-1968: The United States Air Force in Southeast Asia* (Washington, D.C.: Center for Air Force History, 1993), 1-4; and Timothy N. Castle, *At War in the Shadow of Vietnam* (New York: Columbia University Press, 1993).
93. John T. Correll, "The Opening Bell in Laos," *Air Force Magazine* 95, no. 12 (December 2012), 63.
94. Unger transcript, 23, ADS-OHP LC. Roger Hilsman, then assistant secretary of state for Far Eastern Affairs, believed the Bay of Pigs turned JFK away from Eisenhower's more aggressive stance to one more accepting of neutralization; see Transcript of interview of Roger Hilsman, JFK no. 1, by Dennis J. O'Brien, August 14, 1970, 20, JFK Library.
95. The sole survivor was Maj. Lawrence R. Bailey, USA, held for nearly two years by the Pathet Lao before his release. See Mark E. Smith, *USAF Reconnaissance in Southeast Asia (1961-66)*, K717.0414-14 (Hickam Air Force Base, Hawaii: HQ PACAF Directorate, Tactical Evaluation, CHECO [Contemporary Historical Evaluation of Combat Operations] Division, October 25, 1966), 1-2, copy in AFHRA.
96. Karl L. Polifka, privately printed memoir, *Meeting Steve Canyon . . . and Flying with the CIA in Laos* (CreateSpace, 2013), 172-73.
97. W. W. Momyer, *Air Power in Three Wars: World War II, Korea, Vietnam* (Maxwell Air Force Base, Ala.: Air University Press, 1978), 85.
98. Unger transcript, 31, ADS-OHP LC.
99. William H. Sullivan, *Obbligato, 1939-79: Notes on a Foreign Service Career* (New York: Norton, 1984), 210; see also van Staaveren, *Interdiction in Southern Laos*, 38; and Victor B. Anthony and Richard R. Sexton, *The War in Northern Laos* (Washington, D.C.: Center for Air Force History, 1993), 112-14.
100. Sullivan, *Obbligato, 1939-79*, 213.
101. Richard Secord, *Honored and Betrayed: Irangate, Covert Affairs, and the Secret War in Laos*, with Jay Wurts (New York: Wiley, 1992), 74-89; Anthony and Sexton, *War in Northern Laos*, 253-56; and Timothy N. Castle, *One Day Too Long: Top Secret Site 85 and the Bombing of North Vietnam* (New York: Columbia University Press, 1999), 251-52.
102. See Jack Ballard, *Development and Employment of Fixed-Wing Gunships* (Washington, D.C.: Office of Air Force History, January 1974).
103. Correll, "Ho Chi Minh Trail," 65; Correll, "Opening Bell in Laos," 65; and HCMT ordnance total from Ramon E. de Arrigunaga, "Laos: The Secret War—Part 4: Combat Operations," *Air Commando Journal* 4, no. 1 (Winter-Spring 2015), 34.

104. Castle, *At War in the Shadow of Vietnam*, 133.
105. Arrigunaga, "Laos," 34; Castle, *At War in the Shadow of Vietnam*, 108-9; and Keith William Nolan, *Into Laos: The Story of Dewey Canyon II/Lam Son 719, Vietnam 1971* (New York: Dell, 1986), 368-71.
106. Arrigunaga, "Laos," 34.
107. Castle, *At War in the Shadow of Vietnam*, 133-37.
108. Michael E. Haas, "Jungle Jim: At the Tip of the Spear," *Air Commando Journal* 4, no. 1 (Winter-Spring 2015), 12.
109. Author's conversation with Richard Secord, January 10, 2016.
110. Darrel Whitcomb, "Farm Gate," *Air Force Magazine* 88, no. 12 (December 2005): 85.
111. Ibid.; and Earl H. Tilford Jr., *Setup: What the Air Force Did in Vietnam and Why?* (Maxwell Air Force Base, Ala.: Air University Press, June 1991), 67.
112. Walter J. Boyne, "Mule Train," *Air Force Magazine*, February 2001, 70-74.
113. See William A. Buckingham Jr., *Operation Ranch Hand: The United States Air Force and Herbicides in Southeast Asia, 1961-1971* (Washington, D.C.: Office of Air Force History, 1982), 31-33.
114. Tolson, *Airmobility*, 26; see also VTF, *The Kennedy Program and Commitments: 1961*, IV.B.1, *US-VN*, 22.
115. Tilford, *Setup*, 67.
116. Author's conversation with Richard Secord, January 10, 2016.
117. For example, see Bernard B. Fall, *Street without Joy: The French Debacle in Indochina* (Mechanicsburg, Pa.: Stackpole, 2005), 184-203.
118. Haas, "Jungle Jim," 13.
119. VTF, *The Advisory Built-Up, 1961-67*, IV.B.3, *US-VN*, vi; and Dennis M. Drew, *Rolling Thunder 1965* (Maxwell Air Force Base, Ala.: Air University Press, 1986), 29.
120. Quotations from U.S. Embassy, Saigon, Memo of a Meeting, Subject: "Conference with COMUSMACV and Staff Prior to Arrival of SecDef," May 11, 1964, in *Foreign Relations of the United States, 1964-1968*, vol. 1: *Vietnam, 1964*, ed. Edward C. Keefer, Charles S. Sampson, and John P. Glennon (Washington, D.C.: Government Printing Office, 1992), Doc. 149.
121. U. S. Grant Sharp, *Strategy for Defeat: Vietnam in Retrospect* (San Rafael, Calif.: Presidio, 1978), 43-44.
122. VTF, *Military Pressures against North Vietnam, July-October 1964*, 14-15.
123. Alan Vick, *Snakes in the Eagle's Nest: A History of Ground Attacks on Air Bases* (Santa Monica, Calif.: RAND, 1995), 76-77; Jacob van Staaveren, *Gradual Failure: The Air War Over North Vietnam* (Washington, D.C.: Air Force History and Museums Program, 2002), 59; and VTF, *The Rolling Thunder Program Begins*, IV.C.3, *US-VN*, 4.
124. Quotation from John Schlight, "The War in Southeast Asia, 1961-1968," in *Winged Shield, Winged Sword: A History of the United States Air Force*, vol. 2:

1950-1997, ed. Bernard C. Nalty (Washington, D.C.: Air Force History and Museums Program, 1997), 256; see also VTF, *Military Pressures Against North Vietnam, November–December 1964*, IV.C.2(c), *US-VN*, viii–ix.

125. Mark Moyar, *Triumph Forsaken: The Vietnam War, 1954–1965* (Cambridge: Cambridge University Press, 2006), 485.

126. George W. Ball, "How Valid Are the Assumptions Underlying Our VietNam Policies?" *Atlantic Monthly* 230, October 5, 1964, 38.

127. VTF, *The Rolling Thunder Program Begins*, IV.C.3, *US-VN*, 4, 141n3. See also van Staaveren, *Gradual Failure*, 59; and R. T. Boiwer, *Rolling Thunder*, K717.423-28 (Hickam Air Force Base, Hawaii: SEA Team, Project CHECO, March 28, 1966), 15, AFHRA.

128. VTF, *The Rolling Thunder Program Begins*, IV.C.3, *US-VN*, 4; see also 23–25.

129. Ibid., 20.

130. This was February 6, Washington, D.C., time.

131. Boiwer, *Rolling Thunder*, 4–10; VTF, *The Rolling Thunder Program Begins*, IV.C.3, *US-VN*, xi–xii, 27; Peter B. Mersky and Norman Polmar, *The Naval Air War in Vietnam* (Annapolis, Md.: Nautical & Aviation Publishing, 1981), 18–26; van Staaveren, *Gradual Failure*, 14–25; and Robert C. Mikesh, *Flying Dragons: The South Vietnamese Air Force* (Atglen, Pa.: Schiffer, 2005), 67.

132. Momyer, *Air Power in Three Wars*, 270.

133. VTF, *Rolling Thunder Program Begins*, IV.C.3, *US-VN*, xi–xii, 28–29.

134. Even including the 8th Air Force's offensive in 1943.

135. VTF, *Rolling Thunder Program Begins*, IV.C.3, *US-VN*, xiii.

136. Van Staaveren, *Gradual Failure*, 84. Losses were 12 percent of the F-105s and a quarter of the F-100s.

137. Norman Polmar and Edward J. Marolda, *Naval Air War: The Rolling Thunder Campaign* (Washington, D.C.: Naval History and Heritage Command, 2015), 5–7; and Mersky and Polmar, *Naval Air War in Vietnam*, 29–30.

138. William Bundy, "A Policy of Sustained Reprisal," reprinted in VTF, *Rolling Thunder Program Begins*, IV.C.3, *US-VN*, 36.

139. John McNaughton, assistant secretary of defense, in Drew, *Rolling Thunder 1965*, 34.

140. Harold Brown, "Airpower in Vietnam," *Air University Review* 20, no. 3 (May–June 1969).

141. Transcript, George Ball Oral History Interview by Paige E. Mulholland, I (July 8, 1971), 17, Johnson Presidential Library, Austin, Texas.

142. See John T. Correll, "Disunity of Command," *Air Force Magazine* 88, no. 1 (January 2005), 34.

143. The researchers were Rear Adm. James A. Winnefeld, USN (ret.) and Dana Johnson; see Winnefeld and Johnson, *Joint Air Operations*, 63.

144. From southeast to northwest, Route Packs I (MACV), II (PACFLT), III (PACFLT), IV (PACFLT), and VI-B (PACFLT). The Air Force had Pack V (Laos eastward) and Pack VI-A (the central heartland north to China).
145. Winnefeld and Johnson, *Joint Air Operations*, 71-76.
146. Doris Kearns Goodwin, *Lyndon Johnson and the American Dream* (New York: Harper & Row, 1976), 264-65.
147. John T. Correll, "Rolling Thunder," *Air Force Magazine* 88, no. 3 (March 2005), 63.
148. For a telling example of how the Johnson White House micromanaged individual targeting in the air war, see Notes of a Meeting, August 18, 1967, in *Foreign Relations of the United States, 1964-1968*, vol. 5: *Vietnam 1967*, ed. Kent Sieg and David S. Patterson (Washington, D.C.: Government Printing Office, 2002), Document 287.
149. Mark Clodfelter, *The Limits of Air Power: The American Bombing of North Vietnam* (New York: Free Press, 1989), 121.
150. BDM, *A Study of Strategic Lessons Learned in Vietnam*, vol. 6: *Conduct of the War*: Book 1: *Operational Analysis* BDM/W-78-128-TR-Vol-6-1 (McLean, Va.: BDM, May 9, 1980), 6-50, 6-53.
151. Transcript, Robert S. McNamara Oral History Interview by Walt W. Rostow, I (January 8, 1975), 31-32, Johnson Presidential Library, Austin, Texas; emphasis added. Rostow had succeeded McGeorge Bundy as National Security Advisor.
152. Sharp, *Strategy for Defeat*, 99.
153. Edward J. Drea, *McNamara, Clifford, and the Burdens of Vietnam, 1965-1969* (Washington, D.C.: Office of the Secretary of Defense, 2011), 82; and VTF, *The Rolling Thunder Program Begins*, IV.C.3 US-VN, 100, 135, 139.
154. A welcome corrective to much misinformed previous scholarship that condemned it as redolent of World War II bombing theory is Charles Tustin Kamps, "The JCS 94-Target List: A Vietnam Myth That Still Distorts Military Thought," *Aerospace Power Journal* 15, no. 1 (Spring 2001). In fact, having actually seen the list, Kamps holds that it "reveals professionalism and shows how airpower was intended to be applied in an effective way" (67).
155. Sharp, *Strategy for Defeat*, 99. See also Malcolm W. Cagle, "TF 77 in Action off Vietnam," U.S. Naval Institute *Proceedings* 98, no. 831 (May 1972): 79.
156. VTF, *The Air War in North Vietnam I*, IV.C.7(a), US-VN, 2, citing a July 30, 1965, McNamara memo to Johnson, JCS recommendation JCSM-670-65, and McNamara memo to CJCS [Wheeler], September 15, 1965.
157. So, too, did his staff of "whiz kids" and advisors, none of whom had credentials as military planners, thinkers, or strategists; see, for example, Paul Nitze's recollection of a March 1967 meeting with McNamara on how to end the war in Paul Nitze, Steven L. Rearden, and Ann M. Smith, *From Hiroshima to Glasnost: At the Center of Decision* (New York: Grove, 1989), 266.

158. Wayne Thompson, *To Hanoi and Back: The USAF and North Vietnam, 1966–1973* (Washington, D.C.: Smithsonian Institution Press, 2000), 35; and Bernard C. Nalty, *Tactics and Techniques of Electronic Warfare* (Washington, D.C.: Office of Air Force History, 1977), 1.
159. CIA Directorate of Intelligence, *Intelligence Memorandum: The Effectiveness of the Rolling Thunder Program in North Vietnam 1 January–30 September 1966*, SC No. 09646/66 (McLean, Va.: CIA, November 1966), 2-3 [Approved for release July 2000]. Hereafter, CIA DOI, *Effectiveness of Rolling Thunder*.
160. Quoted in Stephen Young, "How North Vietnam Won the War," *Wall Street Journal*, August 3, 1995.
161. CIA DOI, *Effectiveness of Rolling Thunder*, 4-9, 51-62. For the record, $1.00 in 1966 equals $7.32 in 2015; $8.70 in 1966 is approximately $64.00 in 2015.
162. John M. Granville, *Summary of USAF Aircraft Losses in SEA*, Report 7409 (Langley Air Force Base, Va.: Directorate of Force Development and Analysis, HQ Tactical Air Command, June 1974), table 5, 24. I thank Dr. Wayne Thompson, formerly of the USAF, for having alerted me to this report.
163. Ibid., table 2, p. 18; table 4, p. 22; table 6, p. 25; table 15, pp. 62-63. There is a two-aircraft discrepancy on the number of F-105s lost to ground fire and SAMs in table 6 compared to table 4; I have chosen to accept the table 4 figure as it agrees with other sources.
164. Correll, "Rolling Thunder," 61.
165. Evident from tabulations and text in the various CHECO reports.
166. Michael B. Oren, *Six Days of War: June 1967 and the Making of the Modern Middle East* (Oxford: Oxford University Press, 2002), 170-78.
167. Nitze et al., *From Hiroshima to Glasnost*, 268-69.
168. U.S. Congress, Senate, Committee on Armed Services, Senate Preparedness Investigating Subcommittee, *Air War against North Vietnam*, 90th Cong., 1st sess. (August 9-29, 1967).
169. Drea, *McNamara, Clifford, and the Burdens of Vietnam*, 215-27.
170. VTF, *Air War in North Vietnam II*, IV.C.7(b), US-VN, 98-99.
171. Rolling Thunder cost 171 aircraft in 1965 and 318 in 1966. In the last week of April 1967 alone the United States lost 16. See VTF, *Air War in North Vietnam I*, IV.C.7(a), US-VN, 178; Granville, *Summary of USAF Aircraft Losses in SEA*, tables 2, 4, 6, 15; and Marcelle Size Knaack, *Post-World War II Fighters, 1945–1973*, vol. 1 of *Encyclopedia of U.S. Air Force Aircraft and Missile Systems* (Washington, D.C.: Office of Air Force History, 1978), 204.
172. CIA DOI, *Effectiveness of Rolling Thunder*, 4-9, 51-62.
173. Eventually 591 POWs returned to the United States after the signing of the Paris Peace Accords in January 1973; see Stuart I. Rochester and Frederick T. Kiley, *Honor Bound* (Washington, D.C.: Office of the Secretary of Defense, 1998).
174. Holloway, *Aircraft Carriers at War*, 242.

175. Ralph A. Rowley, *USAF FAC Operations in Southeast Asia, 1961–1965* (Washington, D.C.: U.S. Air Force, January 1972), 79.
176. Ibid., 80.
177. Ibid., 75–84; see also Ralph A. Rowley, *The Air Force in Southeast Asia: FAC Operations, 1965–1970* (Washington, D.C.: Office of Air Force History, May 1975), 7–8.
178. Rowley, *USAF FAC Operations*, 88–89. Farm Gate officially ended on July 28, 1963.
179. Rowley, *Air Force in Southeast Asia*, 6.
180. Harold M. Moore, quoted in Melvin F. Porter, *The Siege at Plei Me*, K717.0413-1 (Hickam Air Force Base, Hawaii: SEA Team, Project CHECO, February 24, 1966), 7.
181. Tolson, *Airmobility*, 74–83; Melvin F. Porter, *Silver Bayonet*, K717.0413-2 (Hickam Air Force Base, Hawaii: SEA Team, Project CHECO, February 28, 1966), 2–12; and Kenneth R. Pierce, "The Battle of the Ia Drang Valley," *Military Review* 69, no. 1 (January 1989): 88–97.
182. Body counts, questionable on many grounds, soon reached soaring levels as units and services competed with one another to assert their battlefield primacy. Cmdr. Anthony R. DeMarco noted that after one unsuccessful VC ambush on the Rach Gia canal, "The Army guys counted eight bodies in the field; the Navy RivRon [River Squadron] sailors believed that they killed five VC; and the Sea Wolves [USN gunships from VAL-3] rocketed and strafed the area and visually counted six or seven bodies immobile on the ground. The body count-counters at NAVFORV [Naval Forces Vietnam] headquarters counted nineteen dead VC, after totaling them up." See the transcript of his oral history on the Naval History and Heritage Command website at http://www.history.navy.mil/research/library/oral-histories/post-1946/navy-combat-field-historian-in-vietnam.html.
183. Quoted in John J. Sbrega, "Southeast Asia," in *Case Studies in the Development of Close Air Support*, ed. B. F. Cooling (Washington, D.C.: Office of Air Force History, 1990), 469.
184. John T. Correll, "The In-Country War," *Air Force Magazine* 90, no. 4 (April 2007), 68.
185. Tolson, *Airmobility*, 144–46.
186. See Gregory C. Kane, *Air Power and Its Role in the Battles of Khe Sanh and Dien Bien Phu* (Maxwell Air Force Base, Ala.: Air University, 1997).
187. Warren A. Trest, *Khe Sanh*, K717.0413-35 (Hickam Air Force Base, Hawaii: Directorate, Tactical Evaluation, CHECO Division, September 13, 1968), 70, 90; Bernard C. Nalty, *Air Power and the Fight for Khe Sanh* (Washington, D.C.: Office of Air Force History, 1986), 82–88; Tolson, *Airmobility*, 167; and Ralph A. Rowley, *Tactics and Techniques of Close Air Support Operations, 1961–1973* (Washington, D.C.: U.S. Air Force, 1976), 57.

188. Trest, *Khe Sanh*, 82-86; and Peter B. Mersky, *U.S. Marine Corps Aviation* (Annapolis, Md.: Nautical & Aviation Publishing, 1983), 236-38.
189. Lawrence J. Hickey and James G. Bruce Jr., *Operation Attleboro*, K717.0413-13 (Hickam Air Force Base, Hawaii: SEA Team, Project CHECO, 1967), 4. DePuy was frequently fulsome in his praise of the quality of air support the "Big Red One" received, crediting it, in one memorable memo to 7th Air Force Headquarters, with having saved a brigade from being overrun; conversation with Col. Robert Rasmussen, USAF, who was DePuy's chief FAC, at Eglin AFB, FL, March 17, 2016.
190. Hickey and Bruce, *Operation Attleboro*, 470.
191. Douglas Kinnard, *The War Managers* (Hanover, N.H.: University Press of New England, 1977), 63.
192. Westmoreland quote from Nalty, *Air Power and the Fight for Khe Sanh*, 88; David Chanoff and Doan van Toai, *Portrait of the Enemy* (New York: Random House, 1986), 109, 154, 171, 185; and Jeffrey J. Clarke, *Advice and Support: The Final Years, 1965-1973* (Washington, D.C.: US Army, 1988), 486.
193. Elizabeth H. Hartsook, *Air Power Helps Stop the Invasion and End the War, 1972* (Washington, D.C.: U.S. Air Force, 1978), 40-41. See also Walter J. Boyne, "The Easter Halt," *Air Force Magazine*, September 1998, 60-65; and Rebecca Grant, "Linebacker I," *Air Force Magazine*, June 2012, 71-74.
194. Hartsook, *Air Power Helps Stop the Invasion and End the War*, 42-85.
195. Statement of Brig. Gen. John R. McGiffert, USA, in *Airpower and the 1972 Spring Invasion*, ed. John A. Doglione et al. (Washington, D.C.: Government Printing Office, 1976), 103; see also Hartsook, *Air Power Helps Stop the Invasion and End the War*, 107-10.
196. Bùi Tín, *Following Ho Chi Minh*, trans. by Judy Stowe and Do Van (Honolulu: University of Hawaii Press, 1995), 71.
197. "Mild protest" from Thomas C. Hone, "Strategic Bombardment Constrained," in R. Cargill Hall, ed., *Case Studies in Strategic Bombardment* (Washington, D.C.: Air Force History and Museums Program, 1999), 508; see also Holloway, *Aircraft Carriers at War*, 289, 300-301; and Hartsook, *Air Power Helps Stop the Invasion and End the War*, 85 and following.
198. Quoted in Lewis Sorley, "Courage and Blood: South Vietnam's Repulse of the 1972 Easter Invasion," *Parameters* 29, no. 2 (Summer 1999): 56n26.
199. John A. Doglione et al., *Airpower and the 1972 Spring Invasion* (Washington, D.C.: Government Printing Office, 1976), 106, table VI-1, "Fixed Wing Strike Sorties in South Vietnam, March-June 1972."
200. Giap quote in Grant, "Linebacker I," 74.
201. Kenneth P. Werrell, *Archie, Flak, AAA, and SAM* (Maxwell Air Force Base, Ala.: Air University Press, 1988), 116.
202. Quoted in Hone, "Strategic Bombardment Constrained," 513.

203. W. Hays Parks, "Linebacker and the Law of War," *Air University Review* 34, no. 2 (January–February 1983): 2–30.
204. Momyer, *Air Power in Three Wars*, 236.
205. Fired SA-2 numbers vary according to source; I accepted Hone's 844 from his "Strategic Bombardment Constrained," 516; see also James R. McCarthy and George B. Anderson, eds., *Linebacker II: A View from the Rock*, with Col. Robert E. Rayfield (Washington, D.C.: Government Printing Office, 1976), 171; Walter J. Boyne, "Linebacker II," *Air Force Magazine*, November 1997, 50-57; and Karl J. Eschmann, *Linebacker: The Untold Story of the Air Raids over North Vietnam* (New York: Ballantine, 1989).
206. Kenneth P. Werrell, "Linebacker II: The Decisive Use of Air Power?" *Air University Review* 38, no. 2 (January–March 1987): 58–61.
207. Parks, "Linebacker and the Law of War," 27-30; see also U.S. Department of State, *The Department of State Bulletin* 68, no. 750 (January 8, 1973): 33-41.
208. Parks, "Linebacker and the Law of War," 27–30.
209. In an interview with Stephen Young, Staff Col. Bùi Tín told Young, "When Nixon stepped down because of Watergate we knew we would win. . . . We tested [Gerald] Ford's resolve by attacking Phuoc Long in January 1975. When Ford kept American B-52's in their hangars, our leadership decided on a big offensive against South Vietnam." Young, "How North Vietnam Won the War."
210. See Leslie H. Gelb and Richard K. Betts, *The Irony of Vietnam: The System Worked* (Washington, D.C.: Brookings Institution, 1979); James Clay Thompson, *Rolling Thunder: Understanding Policy and Program Failure* (Chapel Hill: University of North Carolina Press, 1980); Norman Podhoretz, *Why We Were in Vietnam* (New York: Simon and Schuster, 1983); Loren Baritz, *Backfire* (New York: Ballantine, 1986); Clodfelter, *Limits of Air Power*; Tilford, *Setup*; Robert Buzzanco, *Masters of War* (Cambridge: Cambridge University Press, 1996); Lewis Sorley, *A Better War: The Unexamined Victories and Final Tragedy of America's Last Years in Vietnam* (San Diego: Harcourt, 1999); Thompson, *To Hanoi and Back*; van Staaveren, *Gradual Failure*; and Ronald B. Frankum Jr., *Like Rolling Thunder: The Air War in Vietnam, 1964-1975* (Lanham, Md.: Rowman & Littlefield, 2005).
211. Jack Broughton, *Thud Ridge: F-105 Thunderchief Missions over Vietnam* (New York: J. B. Lippincott, 1969).
212. In addition to Broughton's *Thud Ridge* and his later *Going Downtown: The War against Hanoi and Washington* (New York: Orion, 1988), see Richard S. Drury, *My Secret War* (Fallbrook, Calif.: Aero, 1979); John Trotti, *Phantom over Vietnam* (Novato, Calif.: Presidio, 1984); John B. Nichols and Barrett Tillman, *On Yankee Station: The Naval Air War over Vietnam* (Annapolis, Md.: Naval Institute Press, 1987); Ken Bell, *100 Missions North: A Fighter Pilot's Story of the Vietnam War* (Washington, D.C.: Potomac Books, 1993); Tom Clancy and

Charles Horner, *Every Man a Tiger: The Gulf War Air Campaign* (New York: Putnam's, 1999); George J. Marrett, *Cheating Death: Combat Rescues in Vietnam and Laos* (Washington, D.C.: Smithsonian Books, 2003); Rick Newman and Don Shepperd, *Bury Us Upside Down: The Misty Pilots and the Secret Battle for the Ho Chi Minh Trail* (Novato, Calif.: Presidio, 2006); Moyar, *Triumph Forsaken*; and Robin Olds, *Fighter Pilot: The Memoirs of Legendary Ace Robin Olds*, with Christina Olds and Ed Rasimus (New York: St. Martin's, 2010).

213. Charles A. Horner personal communication with the author, June 1, 2011.
214. Goodwin, *Lyndon Johnson*, 264.
215. The best-known and most influential being Harry G. Summers Jr.'s *On Strategy: A Critical Analysis of the Vietnam War* (Novato, Calif.: Presidio, 1982).
216. Quoted in Drew Middleton, *Can America Win the Next War?* (New York: Scribner's, 1975), 7.
217. See, for example, C. R. Anderegg, *Sierra Hotel: Flying Air Force Fighters in the Decade after Vietnam* (Washington, D.C.: Air Force History and Museums Program, 2001).
218. NATO, *Offensive Air Support*, ATP-27A (Brussels: NATO, 1975); and NATO, *Tactical Air Doctrine*, ATP-33 (Brussels: NATO, 1976). See also David J. Stein, *The Development of NATO Tactical Air Doctrine*, R-3385-AF (Santa Monica, Calif.: RAND, 1987).
219. Department of the Army, *FM 100-5: Operations* (Washington, D.C.: Government Printing Office, 1976); see also John L. Romjue, *From Active Defense to AirLand Battle: The Development of Army Doctrine, 1973–1982* (Fort Monroe, Va.: Historical Office, U.S. Army Training and Doctrine Command, 1984); Richard G. Davis, *The 31 Initiatives: A Study in Air Force–Army Cooperation* (Washington, D.C.: Office of Air Force History, 1987); Romie L. Brownlee and William J. Mullen III, eds., *Changing An Army: An Oral History of General William E. DePuy* (Carlisle, Pa.: U.S. Army Military History Institute / Center of Military History, 1988); and Donn A. Starry, "A Perspective on American Military Thought," *Military Review* 69, no. 7 (July 1989): 2–11 (Starry was DePuy's successor as TRADOC's commander).
220. John A. Warden III, *The Air Campaign: Planning for Combat* (Washington, D.C.: National Defense University Press, 1988); and Office of the Secretary of the Air Force, *The Air Force and U.S. National Security: Global Reach—Global Power* (Washington, D.C.: U.S. Department of the Air Force, 1991); see also Dennis M. Drew, "Two Decades in the Air Power Wilderness: Do We Know Where We Are?," *Air University Review* 37, no. 6 (September–October 1986): 2–13; and Richard P. Hallion, "Doctrine, Technology, and Air Warfare: A Late Twentieth-Century Perspective," *Airpower Journal* 1, no. 2 (Fall 1987): 4–27.

221. See Richard P. Hallion, "Girding for War: Perspectives on Research, Development, Acquisition, and the Decision-Making Environment of the 1980s," *Air University Review* 37, no. 6 (September-October 1986): 46-62.
222. Nichols and Tillman, *On Yankee Station*, app. C, 168.
223. Numbers vary slightly according to source, some differences reflecting methods of accounting for loss and time periods; USMC numbers are combat only, not including operational. This does not include "black" losses such as those of Air America in Laos.
224. For background, see Brian L. Davis, *Qaddafi, Terrorism, and the Origins of the U.S. Attack on Libya* (New York: Praeger, 1990).
225. John F. Lehman Jr., *Command of the Seas* (New York: Scribner, 1988), 361-62; and Caspar W. Weinberger, *Fighting for Peace: 7 Critical Years in the Pentagon* (New York: Warner, 1990), 176-77.
226. In February 1986 the United States used Air Force C-141 jet airlifters to support French forces fighting in Chad.
227. Judy G. Endicott, "Raid on Libya: Operation El Dorado Canyon," in *Short of War: Major USAF Contingency Operations, 1947-1997*, ed. A. Timothy Warnock (Maxwell Air Force Base, Ala.: Air University Press / AFHRA, 2000), 146-48.
228. David R. Arnold, *Conflict with Libya: Operational Art in the War on Terrorism* (Newport, R.I.: Naval War College, November 1993), 10-13; Robert E. Stumpf, "Air War with Libya," U.S. Naval Institute *Proceedings* 112, no. 8 (August 1986): 42-48; Lehman, *Command of the Seas*, 364-76; and Weinberger, *Fighting for Peace*, 182-201.
229. Todd R. Phinney, *Airpower versus Terrorism* (Maxwell Air Force, Ala.: Air University Press, March 2007), 11.
230. Endicott, "Raid on Libya," 148.
231. Margaret Thatcher, *The Downing Street Years* (London: HarperCollins, 1995), 445; see also Arnold, *Conflict with Libya*, 13; and Endicott, "Raid on Libya," 148.
232. William T. Y'Blood, "Peace Is Not Always Peaceful," in *Winged Shield, Winged Sword: A History of the United States Air Force*, vol. 2: *1950-1997*, ed. Bernard C. Nalty (Washington, D.C.: Air Force History and Museums Program, 1997), 419. The decision-making issue is detailed in Winnefeld and Johnson, *Joint Air Operations*, 88-93.
233. Endicott, "Raid on Libya," 150.
234. Winnefeld and Johnson, *Joint Air Operations*, 88.
235. Ibid., 84-86.
236. A total of twenty-four F-111Fs and six EF-111s launched; six of the Fs and two of the EFs that took off as spares returned to base once it was clear that the strike force had eighteen "good" F-111Fs and four "good" EF-111s. On standby but not used were less technically capable F-111Es of the 20th TFW at Upper Heyford.

237. Arnold, *Conflict with Libya*, 14; see also Endicott, "Raid on Libya," 151.
238. Thatcher, *Downing Street Years*, 446.
239. Robert E. Venkus, *Raid on Qaddafi: The Story of History's Longest Fighter Mission* (New York: St. Martin's, 1992), ix; and Arnold, *Conflict with Libya*, 15.
240. Endicott, "Raid on Libya," 153.
241. Ibid. The Tripoli airport attackers dropped sixty Vietnam-legacy Mk 82 500-pound high-drag "Snakeyes"; Bab al-Aziziyah and Sidi Bilal attackers dropped four GBU-10 Paveway II laser-guided bombs apiece.
242. Endicott, "Raid on Libya," 153–54.
243. Thatcher, *Downing Street Years*, 447–49.
244. Bruce H. Curry, *Conflict with Libya: Use of Military Force against Terrorism* (Newport, R.I.: Naval War College, 1994), 19.
245. Winnefeld and Johnson, *Joint Air Operations*, 95.
246. In theory, the strike could have employed the F-117 stealth fighter, which had attained its "initial operational capability" in late 1983. However, it was still an immature system, and deploying it from CONUS would have risked revealing its existence and perhaps even some of its capabilities to Soviet/Warsaw Pact intelligence.
247. William J. Allen, "Intervention in Panama: Operation Just Cause," in *Short of War: Major USAF Contingency Operations, 1947–1997*, ed. A. Timothy Warnock, 167–78 (Maxwell Air Force Base, Ala.: Air University Press / Air Force Historical Research Agency, 2000), 171.
248. Forrest L. Marion, "First Fight: Special Tactics in Panama," *Air Commando Journal* 3, no. 3 (Fall 2014): 15-16.
249. Ronald H. Cole, *Operation Just Cause: The Planning and Execution of Joint Operations in Panama, Feb. 1988–Jan. 1990* (Washington, D.C.: Joint Chiefs of Staff, 1995), 2, 15-16, 27.
250. Jennifer Morrison Taw, *Operation Just Cause: Lessons for Operations Other Than War* (Santa Monica, Calif.: RAND, 1996), vii.
251. Elaborate Maze covered a series of contingency plans. Begun in February 1988, it spawned a series of operations orders collectively called Prayer Book. One of these was Blue Spoon. See Cole, *Operation Just Cause*, 8.
252. Ibid., 30, 32. For Eagle Claw and Urgent Fury, see Edward T. Russell, "Crisis in Iran: Operation Eagle Claw," in *Short of War: Major USAF Contingency Operations, 1947–1997*, ed. A. Timothy Warnock, 125–34 (Maxwell Air Force Base, Ala.: Air University Press / Air Force Historical Research Agency, 2000); and Daniel L. Haulman, "Crisis in Grenada: Operation Urgent Fury," in *Short of War: Major USAF Contingency Operations, 1947–1997*, ed. A. Timothy Warnock, 135–44 (Maxwell Air Force Base, Ala.: Air University Press / Air Force Historical Research Agency, 2000).
253. Cole, *Operation Just Cause*, 33.
254. Ibid., 38.

255. Allen, "Intervention in Panama," 174.
256. Ibid., 177; and Taw, *Operation Just Cause*, 19.
257. As witnessed by the author over a decade later; it was still unrepaired.
258. Darrel D. Whitcomb, *On a Steel Horse I Ride* (Maxwell Air Force Base, Ala.: Air University Press and the Air Force Research Institute, 2012), 264.
259. Marion, "First Fight," 18-19.
260. William Walter, "Operation Acid Gambit: The Rescue of Kurt Muse from Modelo Prison," *Air Commando Journal* 3, no. 3 (Fall 2014): 44.
261. Summarized in Allen, "Intervention in Panama," 175; and examined more fully in Marion, "First Fight," 15-20.
262. The pilot was Maj. (later Maj. Gen.) Clay McCutchan, USAFR.
263. Taw, *Operation Just Case*, 24-26.
264. Quoted in ibid., 14.
265. Thomas A. Keaney and Eliot A. Cohen summarized the uncertainty, noting, "The ingredients for a transformation of war may well have become visible in the Gulf War, but if a revolution is to occur someone will have to make it." Keaney and Cohen, *Gulf War Air Power Survey Summary Report* (Washington, D.C.: Government Printing Office, 1993), 251.
266. Office of the Secretary of the Air Force, *Air Force and U.S. National Security*. A useful review is found in Barbara J. Faulkenberry, *Global Reach—Global Power: Air Force Strategic Vision, Past and Future* (Maxwell Air Force Base, Ala.: Air University Press, 1995).
267. Faulkenberry, *Global Reach—Global Power*, 15. Personal recollections of the author, who was one of *Global Reach—Global Power*'s reviewers.
268. Diane T. Putney, *Airpower Advantage: Planning the Gulf War Air Campaign, 1989-1991* (Washington, D.C.: Air Force History and Museums Program, 1994), 1-3.
269. Author's conversation with Horner, December 13, 2011.
270. Horner to Hallion, June 1, 2011.
271. Clash remark from Horner to Hallion, June 1, 2011. Quarterback remark from Michael A. Nelson, "Aerospace Forces and Power Projection," in *The Future of Air Power in the Aftermath of the Gulf War*, ed. Richard H. Shultz Jr. and Robert L. Pfaltzgraff Jr., 115-26 (Maxwell Air Force Base, Ala.: Air University Press, July 1992), 120.
272. Ibid.
273. Gen. H. Norman Schwarzkopf, Memorandum thru Chief of Staff, U.S. Air Force [Gen. Merrill A. McPeak] for Secretary of the Air Force [Hon. Dr. Donald Rice], Subject: Commander Evaluation—Lt Gen Charles A. Horner (August 9, 1991), 1, copy in files of the Secretary of the Air Force's Staff Group, SAF/OSX, Headquarters Air Force, Pentagon.
274. Harold Lee Wise, *Inside the Danger Zone: The U.S. Military in the Persian Gulf, 1987-1988* (Annapolis, Md.: Naval Institute Press, 2007), xi-41.

275. Rear Adm. Grant Sharp was the son of Adm. U. S. Grant Sharp of Vietnam War fame.
276. Horner to Hallion, June 1, 2011; see also H. Norman Schwarzkopf, *It Doesn't Take a Hero*, with Peter Petrie (New York: Bantam, 1992), 282–83.
277. Horner to Hallion, June 1, 2011; for Sharp's influence on Schwarzkopf's thinking, see Edward J. Marolda and Robert J. Schneller Jr., *Shield and Sword: The United States Navy and the Persian Gulf War* (Washington, D.C.: Navy Historical Center, Department of the Navy, 1998), 42.
278. Transcript of interview of Horner by Suzanne Gehri and Rich Reynolds, December 2, 1991, 5, Cat. No. K239.0472-93, AFHRA (hereafter, Horner Interview 1).
279. Horner Interview 1, 2–3. For additional detail, see transcript of interview of Horner by Barry Jamison, Richard Davis, and Barry Barlow (March 4, 1992), 13, Cat. No. K239.0472-94, AFHRA, 11–12 (hereafter, Horner Interview 2).
280. William T. Y'Blood put it in his "From the Deserts to the Mountains," in *Winged Shield, Winged Sword: A History of the United States Air Force*, vol. 2: *1950-1997*, ed. Bernard C. Nalty (Washington, D.C.: Air Force History and Museums Program, 1997), 446.
281. Ibid., 444.
282. Horner Interview 2.
283. Putney, *Airpower Advantage*, 18; and Steve McNamara, "Assessing Airpower's Importance," *Armed Forces Journal International* (March 1997): 36–37. I thank Lt. Gen. David A. Deptula (ret.) for further insights.
284. Dick Cheney, *In My Time: A Personal and Political Memoir*, with Liz Cheney (New York: Threshold Editions, 2011), 425; Colin L. Powell, *My American Journey*, with Joseph E. Persico (New York: Random House, 1995), 132–33; George H. W. Bush and Brent Scowcroft, *A World Transformed* (New York: Alfred A. Knopf, 1998), 334; Bob Woodward, *The Commanders* (New York: Simon and Schuster, 1991), 233–34; and Putney, *Airpower Advantage*, 24.
285. Marolda and Schneller, *Shield and Sword*, 61.
286. Schwarzkopf, *It Doesn't Take a Hero*, 300; Bush and Scowcroft, *A World Transformed*, 327; and Clancy and Horner, *Every Man a Tiger*, 165.
287. Cheney, *In My Time*, 187; and Powell, *An American Life*, 465.
288. Schwarzkopf, *It Doesn't Take a Hero*, 305.
289. Quoted in Clancy and Horner, *Every Man a Tiger*, 185; see also Cheney, *In My Time*, 190–91.
290. Thatcher, *Downing Street Years*, 820–23.
291. Schwarzkopf, *It Doesn't Take a Hero*, 312.
292. Keith A. Hutcheson and Charles T. Robertson, *Air Mobility: The Evolution of Global Reach* (Vienna, Va.: Point One, 1999), 71.
293. Y'Blood, "From the Deserts to the Mountains," 451, 454.

294. Horner to Hallion, June 1, 2011. See also Schwarzkopf, *It Doesn't Take a Hero*, 351; and Rob A. Scofidio, "Transportation and Maintenance at King Fahd," in *From the Line in the Sand*, ed. Michael P. Vriesenga, (Maxwell Air Force Base, Ala.: Air University Press, March 1994), 62.
295. Horner Interview 2, 26, 73.
296. As noted by Marolda and Schneller, *Shield and Sword*, 114; and Horner to Hallion, June 1, 2011.
297. Horner to Hallion, June 1, 2011. Arthur, an A-4 pilot, had completed over five hundred combat missions over SEA.
298. Horner Interview 2, 13; Schwarzkopf, *It Doesn't Take a Hero*, 313, 320; Clancy and Horner, *Every Man a Tiger*, 186-87; and Putney, *Airpower Advantage*, 32-43. The chief, Gen. Michael Dugan, was out of town.
299. For Warden, see David R. Mets, *The Air Campaign* (Maxwell Air Force Base, Ala.: Air University Press, 1999); and John Andreas Olsen, *John Warden and the Renaissance of American Air Power* (Washington, D.C.: Potomac Books, 2007).
300. Quoted in Putney, *Airpower Advantage*, 55.
301. Horner Interview 1 discusses this; see also Clancy and Horner, *Every Man a Tiger*; Olsen, *John Warden and the Renaissance of American Air Power*; Putney, *Airpower Advantage*; Richard T. Reynolds, *Heart of the Storm: The Genesis of the Air Campaign against Iraq* (Maxwell Air Force Base, Ala.: Air University Press, 1995); and Frederick W. Kagan, *Finding the Target: The Transformation of American Military Policy* (New York: Encounter Books, 2006), 132-35.
302. Horner Interview 2, 14; and Gary Waters, "Master of Air Power—General Buster Glosson," in *Masters of Air Power*, ed. Keith Brent, 133-52 (Canberra: RAAF Air Power Development Centre, 2005), 147.
303. Horner to Hallion, June 1, 2011.
304. Alan Munro, *Arab Storm: Politics and Diplomacy Behind the Gulf War* (London: Tauris, 2006), 83.
305. Peter de la Billière, *Storm Command: A Personal Account of the Gulf War* (New York: HarperCollins, 1992), 84-87, 114; and author's personal recollection.
306. Powell, *My American Journey*, 484; see also Buster Glosson, *War with Iraq: Critical Lessons* (Charlotte, N.C.: Glosson Family Foundation, 2003), 45.
307. Glosson, *War with Iraq*, 58-59.
308. Horner Interview 2, 19.
309. Bush and Scowcroft, *A World Transformed*, 381.
310. Cheney, *In My Time*, 198, 200.
311. Glosson, *War with Iraq*, 105-6. The "kill box" was devised by Lt. Col. (later Maj. Gen.) Richard B. H. "Rick" Lewis. See also Barry D. Watts and Williamson

Murray, *Operations,* part 1, vol. 2, *Gulf War Air Power Survey* [hereafter GWAPS] (Washington, D.C.: Government Printing Office, 1993), 266.
312. William Andrews, "Gulf War Journal (I)," *Code One* 6, no. 4 (January 1992), 10.
313. Bush and Scowcroft, *A World Transformed,* 447–48.
314. Clancy and Horner, *Every Man a Tiger,* 341.
315. The casualty was Lt. Cmdr. Michael Speicher, USN, an F/A-18 pilot.
316. Schwarzkopf, *It Doesn't Take a Hero,* 415.
317. Statistics from Merrill A. McPeak, "Desert Storm: The Air Campaign," DoD News Briefing, Pentagon, Washington, D.C., March 15, 1991, reprinted in Merrill A. McPeak, *Selected Works: 1990-1994* (Maxwell Air Force Base, Ala.: Air University Press, 1995), fig. 14, p. 31.
318. Watts and Murray, GWAPS, 271.
319. Fred Frostic, *Air Campaign against the Iraqi Army in the Kuwaiti Theater of Operations,* Report MR-357-AF (Santa Monica, Calif.: RAND, 1994), 63–64. The psychological effects of Gulf War attacks are detailed in Andrew P. N. Lambert, *The Psychology of Air Power* (London: Royal United Services Institute for Defence Studies, 1994), 64–69. For the KTO air campaign, see Perry D. Jamieson, *Lucrative Targets: The U.S. Air Force in the Kuwaiti Theater of Operations* (Washington, D.C.: Air Force History and Museums Program, 2001).
320. Richard B. H. Lewis, "JFACC Problems Associated with Battlefield Preparation in Desert Storm," *Airpower Journal* 8, no. 1 (Spring 1994): 4–21.
321. Watts and Murray, GWAPS, 264, 381. This does not mean, of course, that there were not individual cases where Iraqi armored forces did fight—for example, at the famed "73 Easting" encounter, or as Marine armored forces advanced on Kuwait City—but these were the isolated exception, not the hourly norm.
322. Joel Achenbach, "The Experts in Retreat," *Washington Post,* February 28, 1991.
323. Monk, quoted on the NPR morning show "Morning Edition," WAMU-FM, Washington D.C., May 27, 1991.
324. Joost R. Hiltermann, "Bomb Now, Die Later," *Mother Jones* 16, no. 4 (July–August 1991), 46.
325. Richard A. Mason, "The Air War in the Gulf," *Survival* 33, no. 3 (May–June 1991): 211–29.
326. Remarks of President George H. W. Bush, Air Force Academy, Colorado Springs, Colorado, May 29, 1991, in *Weekly Compilation of Presidential Documents* (Washington, D.C.: Executive Office of the President, June 3, 1991), 683–86.
327. Quoted in Keith E. Kennedy, "Geeks Go to War: Programming Under Fire," in *From the Line in the Sand,* ed. Michael P. Vriesenga (Maxwell Air Force Base, Ala.: Air University Press, March 1994), 80.

328. "The Navy had no system for planning and directing sustained air campaigns, and even lacked a mechanism to plan integrated strikes from more than one carrier," Naval History and Heritage Command historians Marolda and Schneller conclude, adding, "With no viable alternative, NAVCENT had to adapt to the ATO system"; see their *Shield and Storm*, 184–85. After the war, the Navy markedly strengthened its airpower command, control, and projection capabilities, as evidenced over the Balkans and in varied continuing operations since the September 11, 2001, terrorist attacks.

329. Watts and Murray, GWAPS, 262–64; Jamieson, *Lucrative Targets*, 81–85; and Glosson, *War with Iraq*, 187–89.

Chapter 2

AMERICAN AND NATO AIRPOWER APPLIED
From Deny Flight to Inherent Resolve

—*Benjamin S. Lambeth*

After the stunningly successful first days of Operation Desert Storm in 1991, airpower underwent a quantum leap in its worldwide reputation for combat effectiveness. The harmonious blend of the latest in air weaponry with unmatched aircrew skill and the bold strategy that guided the coalition's move to evict Iraq's occupying forces from Kuwait revealed a breakthrough in airpower's leverage after a promising start in World War II and more than three years of misuse in the American bombing of North Vietnam from 1965 to 1968. The prompt attainment of air supremacy and what that allowed allied air assets to do thereafter, by way of enabling the earliest possible achievement of the coalition's goals on the ground with so few losses, marked—in the view of many—the final coming of age of airpower.[1]

In the early wake of that remarkable performance, some who had long doubted airpower's ability to shape the course and outcome of a major conflict so singlehandedly tended for a time to dismiss it as a one-off anomaly. It was, they suggested, the clear and open desert environment, or the unusual vulnerability of Iraq's exposed armored forces to precision attack from above, or any number of other unique geographic and operational circumstances that made the 1991 Persian Gulf War an exception to the general rule that it takes a clash between opposed troops in high-intensity *land* combat to achieve a final and decisive win against a well-endowed enemy.[2]

In the twelve years that followed that epic experience, however, the world saw American-dominated airpower likewise prevail in four widely dissimilar subsequent instances, starting with the two successive showdowns against Serbia in the Balkans by the North Atlantic Treaty Organization (NATO) in Operations Deliberate Force in 1995 and Allied Force in 1999 and followed in turn by the opening round of Operation Enduring Freedom in 2001 against al-Qaeda's terrorist stronghold in Afghanistan and the ruling Taliban in that country, who provided it safe haven. A year after that signal success came the three-week major combat phase of Operation Iraqi Freedom that finally toppled Saddam Hussein and his regime in early 2003. Those twelve years truly represented a triumphal time for modern airpower. By their end, the air weapon could fairly be said to have finally matured in its ability to deliver the sorts of decisive enabling results that its pioneer advocates had foreseen and predicted generations before.

The years since those path-breaking achievements, however, have largely been dominated by a less dramatic form of warfare and a resultant diminished role for kinetic air employment. Throughout those more recent years, the United States and its allies have been consumed by lower intensity counterinsurgency (COIN) and counterterrorist operations in which decisive aerial strikes like those typified by Desert Storm and its early successors have been overshadowed by slower-motion wars of attrition on the ground—to a point, indeed, where it had become fashionable among some for a time to proclaim that the sorts of cutting-edge airpower applications that proved to be so pivotal between 1991 and 2003 had since been superseded by a new era of fourth-generation asymmetric warfare in which high-technology weapons had become largely irrelevant.[3] In both Iraq and Afghanistan after the initial successes, overly ambitious American goal-setting aimed at unattainable democratic nation building, coupled with inappropriate land-centric warfighting strategies, led the United States into seemingly unending combat entanglements on the ground that cost the nation dearly. U.S. and allied airpower played only a supporting role in the penumbra of costly and protracted terrestrial slugfests in both arenas, with friendly troop fatalities in the two countries eventually rising to exorbitant levels, reaching more than four thousand U.S. and allied combatants killed in action in Iraq by 2011 and more than two thousand killed in Afghanistan thus far with still no end in sight.

Even the banner first twelve years of U.S. and NATO air employment after Desert Storm began with a badly flawed performance by a now uniquely able air weapon under the aegis of a newly elected American president who was unwilling at first to deal forcefully with the Serbian atrocities in the Balkan civil war that had erupted in the early aftermath of the collapse of the former Yugoslavia. No sooner had the resounding success of Desert Storm faded in popular memory when, just two years later, the United States and its NATO allies forgot altogether the exemplary teachings of the Gulf War and reverted instead to long-discredited Vietnam-think in the desultory and half-hearted character of their ineffectual Operation Deny Flight to enforce a no-fly zone against Serbia in the gathering Balkan civil war. The United States and NATO only got truly serious about addressing Serbian atrocities in the former Yugoslavia in 1995 with their more determined and ultimately successful two-week coercive air offensive against the Bosnian Serbs in response to the latter's shelling of innocents in Sarajevo.

Four years later, not long after a four-day American and British punitive bombing campaign in response to Saddam Hussein's repeated failure to comply with UN resolutions regarding the inspection of Iraq's suspected effort to develop weapons of mass destruction (WMD), the United States and NATO committed essentially the same mistakes of Deny Flight all over again in the similarly hesitant and gradualist character of their air-only war against Serbian strongman Slobodan Milošević aimed at halting his ethnic cleansing of Kosovar Albanians. After that slow and feckless start, the campaign only began to show real progress when the United States and NATO finally ramped up the intensity of their bombing toward the end of their needlessly prolonged seventy-eight-day effort once their leaders realized that their hitherto irresolute campaign was failing. In the end, the United States and NATO pulled a decisive victory from the jaws of near defeat at the last minute and, to nearly everyone's surprise, achieved the first-ever campaign win by airpower alone.

Similarly, after the substantial American troop surge that was finally set in motion in Iraq in 2007, President George W. Bush essentially handed his successor, President-elect Barack Obama, a costly and hard-earned military win there in 2009. However, Obama proceeded not long thereafter to squander all the hard-won gains of the preceding six years by summarily withdrawing the stabilizing residual U.S. military presence from Iraq in toto at the end of 2011. That purely politically driven move to satisfy an earlier campaign pledge, a move undertaken against the emphatic counsel of his top military and diplomatic subordinates not to do it, created an ensuing power vacuum in the region that allowed the former al-Qaeda in Iraq to metastasize into the even more noxious Islamic State in Iraq and Syria (ISIS) that, in turn, has occasioned today's still-festering and uncontrolled violence in both countries.

For its part, Operation Inherent Resolve, the still only half-serious U.S.-led air response that was belatedly launched by the Obama administration against ISIS in August 2014, has thus far failed completely to stem the continued vitality and growth of that emergent radical Islamist movement. Despite more than two years of desultory bombing with no coherent strategy or any involvement even of American forward air controllers on the ground to help the able Kurdish rebels in resisting the depredations of ISIS, allied airpower has yet to apply its fullest potential in that continuing failure of the United States to produce any significant outcome-determining gains on the ground.

Along the way to this latest disappointment involving U.S. and NATO airpower, the American-led Operation Odyssey Dawn, expanded soon thereafter into the NATO-led Operation Unified Protector against Libyan dictator Muammar Gaddafi, appeared in its initial aftermath in late 2011 to have been another airpower success story, with the United States this time having consciously led from behind in that air-only effort. However, although it succeeded (without so intending) in ending Gaddafi's rule in the short run, that campaign, with no

American and NATO diplomatic effort made thereafter to see to the needs of a stable endgame in the country, likewise opened up a regional Pandora's box that has since rendered Libya not just a failed state but another breeding ground for radical Islamist terrorism, just as Afghanistan was until the initial success of Operation Enduring Freedom in late 2001.

This chapter revisits the highlights of those eight U.S. and NATO air warfare experiences since Desert Storm, with a view toward reconstructing the operations that largely distinguished them and summarizing the successes registered and problems encountered in each case. It further explains the various factors that accounted for the wide variance in airpower's effectiveness throughout the past quarter century. It concludes by offering seven overarching generalizations extracted from this uneven record of aerial performance. In all, the discussion that follows shows that since its initial success in the first Persian Gulf War of 1991, U.S. and NATO airpower has steadily matured into a uniquely capable instrument of modern warfare. It also shows, however, that that same eventful quarter century has been marred by an unfortunate recurrence of hard-earned lessons forgotten and only sometimes relearned, varying degrees of success achieved, and some needless failures in American and NATO air employment thanks to flawed and wanting senior leadership and strategy.

OPERATION DENY FLIGHT

NATO's first-ever offensive air operation, launched in half-hearted support of beleaguered Bosnia, began on April 12, 1993, in what eventually proved to be a hapless enterprise called Operation Deny Flight. That endeavor entailed around-the-clock fighter patrols to enforce a declared no-fly zone, maintain a NATO air "presence" in the region, and provide on-call air support as needed in response to the unconscionable killing of innocents that the Yugoslav civil war had come to represent since it resumed in 1991, after more than three generations of quiescence under communism. Quite apart from the degradation in overall aircrew mission readiness these patrols occasioned, thanks to the many long hours spent merely boring holes in the sky, those diffident and ineffectual sorties were, to all intents and purposes, pointless with respect to any tangible gain produced on the ground. Over the two years during which they occurred, they saw only limited contact with Bosnian Serb forces. For example, out of more than a hundred close-air support (CAS) "presence" requests, only four authorized CAS attacks were ever conducted. There was a grand total of only five precision air strikes, one of which resulted in a temporary shutdown of a runway at Udbina by an attacking force of thirty NATO aircraft on November 21, 1994, in response to a launching of Serb fighters from that airfield against Croatian targets inside a designated UN safe area.

Apart from that, Operation Deny Flight had little practical effect on Serbian behavior and was little more than a costly exercise in converting jet fuel into noise. Lt. Gen. Michael Ryan, the U.S. Air Force commander of Allied Air Forces in NATO Southern Command, later remarked with studied tact that it entailed "a use of airpower in a way we don't normally use airpower"—namely, under oppressive UN-imposed restrictions that were "very frustrating for us."[4] The many UN constraints that hampered the effective use of allied airpower included a firm ban against NATO attacks on Serbian aircraft or air defenses at Udbina and strictly limited authorization for NATO to engage only those Bosnian Serb air defense positions that had actually fired on NATO aircraft. In all, said General Ryan, the UN-mandated limitation of NATO airpower to little more than "making noise" quickly accustomed Bosnian Serb leaders to the fact that NATO would not follow through on its repeated threats to unleash air strikes.

The Wages of Predictability

As a testament to the strategic amnesia that the UN's initial rules of engagement (ROE) seemed to indicate, a British Royal Navy Sea Harrier was shot down near Goražde during the first week of Deny Flight on April 16 by a handheld, infrared-guided SA-7 missile on the aircraft's third pass in a vain attempt to identify and destroy the single offending Serb tank that UN authorities had approved for attack. Because of a fatally flawed concept of operations, the aircraft's mission was strategically purposeless, its tactics were entirely predictable, and its mode of use was in violation of every rule of rational force commitment that had consistently been honored in Desert Storm.

The next year, in roughly similar circumstances, a U.S. Air Force F-16 was shot down by a radar-guided Serbian SA-6 surface-to-air missile (SAM) on June 2 while orbiting in a totally predictable high racetrack pattern southwest of Banja Luka. Subsequent indications suggest that the aircraft may have been lured into a trap. Even worse, it was said not to have been equipped with the latest radar warning equipment. Worse yet, there were conflicting reports from the U.S. military about the extent of prior awareness of a SAM threat in the area, with the chairman of the Joint Chiefs of Staff (JCS), Gen. John Shalikashvili, stating that "we had absolutely no intelligence [of an active SAM threat]," and the Supreme Allied Commander in Europe, Gen. George Joulwan, countering that the area had been a known "high threat environment" with an integrated air defense system (IADS).[5]

Whatever the case, airborne U.S. electronic surveillance assets operating in the area reportedly acquired real-time indications of an active SA-6 tracking radar within range of the targeted aircraft but were unable to communicate that awareness in sufficient time to prevent the shootdown. U.S. Secretary of Defense William Perry later conceded that he was "not satisfied . . . that we did the best job in transmitting and relaying the information to the person who most needed the information."[6] Immediately after the shootdown, NATO planners moved with alacrity to develop a credible option against the Serbian IADS, and all subsequent Deny Flight missions were accompanied by strike assets dedicated expressly to the suppression of enemy air defenses (SEAD). However, that scarcely counterbalanced the fact that the downing of the F-16 was an embarrassment to the United States and a setback for airpower's hard-earned reputation for effectiveness won in Desert Storm.

Past Teachings Forgotten

During the ensuing weeks, recurrent allied threats to carry out air strikes in response to Serbian acts of aggression, followed by increasingly predictable backpedaling and inaction by the principal UN authorities, suggested that all involved at the highest levels both at the UN and in the administration of President Bill Clinton had forgotten not only the United States' cardinal mistakes in Vietnam but also the teachings of its remarkably successful use of airpower in Desert Storm. In a reflection of the frustration felt by most American air commanders, both on scene and elsewhere, the commander of NATO's airborne warning and control system (AWACS) wing observed that during the more than two years of Operation Deny Flight, there had been no fewer than 5,300 recorded violations of the no-fly zone (albeit by helicopters), and U.S. Air Force F-16s had downed only four Serbian Galeb light attack jets, one with an AIM-120 advanced medium-range air-to-air missile, in a single episode on February 28, 1994.[7]

When Deny Flight was finally concluded on December 20, 1994, after more than two years of effort by the United Nations to maintain an air "presence" over Bosnia, allied aircraft had flown 100,400 sorties, rivaling Operation Desert Storm in total number. Of those sorties, however, a full third were passive combat air patrol missions, with reconnaissance, in-flight refueling, command and control, and other support sorties accounting for most of the remainder.[8] In all, this near-disastrous flirtation with failure for more than two years of UN ineffectuality was reminiscent of every bad strategy choice the U.S. government made throughout its long and costly misadventure in Vietnam. It offered a powerful reminder that, however capable a tool modern airpower may have become in principle since Desert Storm, there is nothing foreordained about its ability to produce winning results.

OPERATION DELIBERATE FORCE

The first serious test of airpower in the post–Cold War era was the successful conduct of U.S.-led NATO air strikes against Bosnian Serb forces in 1995 in support of continued UN peacemaking efforts in the ongoing Yugoslav civil war. The action that ultimately triggered NATO's response in this case was a shelling attack against Sarajevo on August 28, 1995, which resulted in thirty-eight civilians being killed. Confirmation of Bosnian Serb complicity in that attack led two days later to the unleashing of Operation Deliberate Force, an eleven-day campaign of coordinated NATO air strikes against preapproved Serbian targets in Bosnia-Herzegovina. The operation's purpose was to deter further Serbian attacks against declared UN safe areas and to respond as necessary to any such attacks until they ceased.[9]

The operation's essential elements had been preplanned over the preceding two months and fully coordinated among all scheduled participants. It took the Serbian shelling of Sarajevo, however, to give UN authorities the final impetus to action. UN peacekeeping forces were moved out of threatened areas to give NATO airpower the latitude it needed to engage all targets selected by allied strategists. The guiding assumption underlying the now-imminent campaign was that fear of being dominated by outside forces was the Bosnian Serbs' main center of gravity. That belief in turn dictated an attack against their advantages, most notably their freedom to maneuver and their ability to supply their combatants, with the ultimate goal of transforming those into disadvantages.[10]

Combat Highlights

The air campaign commenced at 2:00 a.m. local time on August 30, with forty-three NATO strike aircraft attacking command-and-control sites, SAM and antiaircraft artillery (AAA) sites, and supporting radar and communications facilities. The strike force was made up mostly of U.S. Air Force aircraft operating out of Aviano Air Base, Italy, with additional U.S. Navy and Marine Corps aircraft from the carrier USS *Theodore Roosevelt* operating on station in the Adriatic Sea. The declared intent of these initial attacks was to destroy all fixed and truck-mounted air defense positions in eastern Bosnia and to take down the Bosnian Serb IADS completely.[11] The target array was not, as the popular image of the fighting in Bosnia might have suggested, a ragtag threat wielded by untutored rebels in a nasty civil war. It was a sophisticated Soviet-style IADS consisting of SA-2 and SA-6 radar-guided SAMs and AAA. It was operated, moreover, by former Yugoslav air defense professionals who had been trained to counter massed air attacks in the context of a major Warsaw Pact offensive and who knew from both radar and other sources where NATO's aircraft were at all times.

More than three hundred strike and support sorties were flown during the first twenty-four hours, with attacks against twenty-three targets resulting in ninety weapon impacts. Among the most important early targets engaged were hardened Serbian underground command bunkers that had been designed for use during the Cold War. These were taken out by F-15Es using GBU-10 2,000-pound laser-guided bombs (LGBs). Later targets consisted of ammunition dumps, artillery positions, communications links, and supply storage areas, with a view toward reducing the Bosnian Serb army's ability to conduct further offensive operations. Additional targets included a number of key bridges used to support Bosnian Serb military activity, although without any underlying goal of destroying the entire Serbian infrastructure. AC-130 gunships and A-10 CAS aircraft worked selected aim points along with the faster-moving fighters, with the AC-130 operating mainly at night against IADS and command-and-control targets. Serbian troop concentrations were kept strictly off limits, and there were highly restrictive ROE beyond that.

NATO suspended its bombing for two days starting September 2 in an attempt to test Serbian compliance with the alliance's demands. When none was forthcoming, the attacks resumed on September 5. In a tactic highly reminiscent of what Israeli air and land forces did during the opening moments of their 1982 Bekaa Valley operation in southern Lebanon, air strikes against selected SAM and AAA emplacements were coordinated with artillery attacks by the UN Rapid Reaction Force, with NATO ground-based tactical air-control parties providing that force with precise targeting data.[12] As before in Desert Storm, weather was a complicating factor in the air delivery of precision munitions, with thunderstorms topping out as high as 38,000 feet, forcing an overall abort rate of 25–30 percent of all scheduled U.S. ground-attack sorties and 30–35 percent of those by other NATO participants. Nevertheless, the overall assessed average success rate of allied precision weapon attacks was around 60 percent, with the GBU-12 yielding the highest success rate at 76 percent.[13]

Portions of the Bosnian Serb IADS were sufficiently sophisticated that NATO's air commanders initially wanted to use the F-117 stealth attack aircraft, with its very low observability to enemy acquisition and tracking radars, against the most heavily defended targets. Indeed, planning for the use of F-117s had progressed to the point where a detachment of the aircraft had begun taxiing to the runway at their home base at Holloman Air Force Base, New Mexico, for deployment to the theater. At that moment, the Italian government denied permission for that high-profile U.S. aircraft to operate out of Aviano, in an understandable expression of pique over having been excluded from the so-called Contact Group despite all Italy had done to make its facilities available to UN and NATO forces.[14] NATO planners elected instead to use Tomahawk land-attack missiles (TLAMs) against the most heavily defended IADS targets and standoff GBU-15 precision-guided munitions (PGMs) against the rest.

A New Emphasis on Precision

Roughly 70 percent of the weapons employed in Operation Deliberate Force were LGBs and electro-optical-guided bombs. Unguided munitions as well as Maverick and high-speed antiradiation missiles were also used, along with thirteen TLAMs, which were targeted against several particularly well-protected Serbian IADS sites. The latter weapons were fitted with global positioning system (GPS) receivers and other upgrades that rendered them more accurate than those employed during the 1991 Persian Gulf war. In addition, U.S. Navy F/A-18s employed the standoff land-attack missile to good effect.[15] After the campaign ended, 338 Serbian aim points spread over 56 discrete targets had been struck by more than 600 precision weapons.[16] As in Desert Storm, the SEAD portion of the operation succeeded by intimidation in shutting down the Serbian IADS around Sarajevo and in much of the remainder of Bosnia. No radar-guided SAMs were fired after the operation began, although NATO aircraft continued to draw fire from AAA and shoulder-fired infrared-guided SAMs.[17]

Concern over collateral damage was extremely high, since even a single stray bomb that resulted in unintended civilian casualties would end instantly any UN confidence in NATO's ability to be precise. Accordingly, each weapon's desired mean point of impact (DMPI) was personally vetted by General Ryan, the combined force air component commander (CFACC) at Vicenza, Italy, with special attention given to such considerations as attack axis, time of day or night, aircraft system limitations, munitions capabilities, and possible secondary effects. Efforts were made as well to use the smallest weapon possible, such as a 500-pounder rather than a 2,000-pound bomb, to minimize the undesired side effects of shrapnel and blast. Careful battle damage assessment (BDA) was conducted after each strike using a combination of pilot mission reports, ground reporting, cockpit weapon-system video, postattack aerial reconnaissance by U-2s and other air vehicles, and national imagery and signals intelligence.

In the end, NATO's efforts to minimize any unintended destruction paid off well. There were no Serbian complaints about noncombatant fatalities or other harm to innocents since no collateral damage to speak of was inflicted.[18] No civilians were reported to have died from the allied air attacks, and only a small number of Bosnian Serb military personnel were killed. In some cases, weapon placement accuracy criteria were so exacting that if a bomb did not hit within seven feet of its intended target, it was not counted as mission effective. Overall reported force effectiveness was 1.5 attack sorties flown and 2.8 PGMs expended per DMPI engaged, with 6.6 general-purpose bombs released per DMPI in the case of nonprecision attacks.[19]

Operation Deliberate Force featured 3,515 sorties flown by 293 aircraft of 8 NATO countries operating from 18 locations across Europe, along with the carriers USS *Theodore Roosevelt* and, later, USS *America*. Of that total, 750 were strike sorties. The majority of sorties flown (65 percent) were American. The remainder were flown mainly by the United Kingdom and France, with token participation by the Netherlands, Spain, Germany, Turkey, and Italy. Air tasking was conducted out of NATO's Combined Air Operations Center (CAOC) at Vicenza, with orchestration of the attacks by NATO AWACS aircraft and an EC-130 airborne command-and-control aircraft.[20] Target detection, acquisition, and destruction proved to be more challenging than they had been during the 1991 Gulf War. Nevertheless, the sensors and information systems that had worked so well in Desert Storm were more than adequate for enabling NATO airpower to produce the results it did. The only aircraft lost during the 11-day operation was a French Mirage 2000D, which was downed by a shoulder-fired SA-7 infrared SAM while the fighter was operating at low altitude on the first day.[21]

The Campaign's Achievements

This was NATO's first serious and determined air offensive as well as the largest military action to have taken place in Europe since World War II. Although limited in scope, it finally produced, after four years of unspeakable killing of innocents, a shaky truce in Bosnia that has persisted to this day. Operation Deliberate Force successfully achieved its designed objectives, including the restoration of safe areas from any threat of attack, the removal of offending heavy weapons, and the reopening of the Sarajevo airport and road access to Sarajevo for relief supplies. In so doing, it demonstrated that U.S. and allied airpower possessed credible leverage for show-of-force roles short of major war.

Assessed against some of the earlier cases of air employment addressed in this book, Operation Deliberate Force did not constitute an especially historic event in the evolution of airpower even though it was no less effective than Desert Storm in helping to enable a sought-after strategic outcome on the ground. There were no surprises in its performance, and it did what it was expected to do once approved by the UN authorities. That said, as in the case of Israel's surprise attack on Iraq's nuclear reactor in 1981, it provided a textbook illustration of airpower in action not to "win a war" but rather to achieve a discrete and important campaign goal short of full-fledged war.[22] The result was a successful exercise in coercion. In underscoring the limited intent of the operation, U.S. Air Force chief of staff Gen. Ronald Fogleman stressed afterward that the aim of the NATO bombing was "not to defeat the Serbs, but simply to relieve the siege of UN safe areas and gain compliance with UN mandates and thus facilitate ongoing negotiations to end the fighting."[23]

In the end, the Bosnian Serb leaders acceded to NATO's demands by withdrawing specified heavy weapons from the Sarajevo exclusion zone. More important, the air attacks paved the way for the Dayton Peace Accords, which were initialed not long afterward on November 21 and signed in Paris on December 14, 1995. To be sure, it was not just allied airpower but a confluence of other factors as well that ultimately drove the Bosnian Serb leadership to the negotiating table. The latter included increased allied artillery fire, the credible threat of a Croatian ground attack, and mounting diplomatic pressure and other sanctions. Nevertheless, Richard Holbrooke, then the assistant secretary of state, who had successfully negotiated the Dayton Accords, later observed that although it had taken a Bosnian Serb outrage to trigger the launching of Deliberate Force in the first place, the air campaign had made a "huge difference" in helping to bring about an acceptable outcome.[24] Viewed in hindsight, only the 3,515 sorties of Operation Deliberate Force, of which fully 70 percent were penetrating and directly combat related, counted as far as any practical payoff from allied operations over the Balkans up to that point since 1992 was concerned.

OPERATION DESERT FOX

American attention to Iraq never really abated after Desert Storm ended, thanks to the subsequent imposition and enforcement of the northern and southern no-fly zones over the country by U.S. Central Command (CENTCOM) to help secure that war's gains, and became further heightened in the summer of 1998 in response to repeated Iraqi "cheat and retreat" experiences. Saddam Hussein would thwart previously agreed-upon efforts by UN inspectors to monitor Iraq's suspected development of WMD, only to back away from such obstructionism at the last minute whenever it seemed that CENTCOM might resort to combat action in punitive reprisal. On August 5 of that year, in yet another episode in what had long since become a familiar pattern, Iraq again ejected the UN's inspectors from the country and demanded that the UN certify Iraq as being free of WMD. That affront prompted the United States the next month to begin preparing for a serious bombing effort in response. The ensuing force buildup, along with the concurrent passage of UN Security Council Resolution (UNSCR) 1134 excoriating Iraq's interference with the inspections, was enough to induce Hussein to back down yet again. On November 1, however, Iraq declared anew that it would cease cooperating with the UN Special Commission (UNSCOM) tasked with conducting the weapons inspections, prompting CENTCOM this time to begin refining two retaliatory strike options code-named Desert Viper and Desert Viper Plus, the latter to be implemented if additional attacks were deemed necessary once the impending campaign was under way.

The Final Countdown

By November 11 CENTCOM had reinforced its forces already deployed forward for Operation Southern Watch with fifty-four additional U.S. and British strike aircraft stationed in the Gulf region outside Saudi Arabia, which had refused to make its bases available to CENTCOM for the gathering operation. These reinforcements included twelve B-52s, six B-1s, and twelve F-117 stealth attack aircraft. The Desert Viper plan was scheduled to commence with a barrage of nearly a hundred conventional air-launched cruise missiles (CALCMs) launched by a dozen B-52s. Those aircraft were actually airborne and just eight minutes from releasing their CALCMs when Foreign Minister Tariq Aziz suddenly announced on Iraqi television that Baghdad had chosen once again to accept resumed UN inspections unconditionally. That eleventh-hour move, which plainly indicated that Iraq had been alerted to the impending attack in adequate time, occasioned an immediate order from CENTCOM to recall the bombers, thus negating in the blink of an eye all the hard work that had gone into preparing for the attack. As British defense analyst Michael Knights well put it, "Iraq had once again tricked the trillion-dollar-a-year [U.S.] military with a simple ruse."[25]

After experiencing that rude awakening, the U.S. government swore never again to allow itself to be caught short by such last-minute Iraqi connivance. It accordingly began planning another air offensive, this time code-named Operation Desert Fox, to be unleashed immediately after the upcoming release of UNSCOM's next report, which was expected to announce new egregious violations of Iraq's commitments to the inspection regime. This time CENTCOM was determined not to allow Iraqi diplomatic gamesmanship once again to rob it of the tactical surprise that it failed to achieve through the false start of Desert Viper.

Since the twelve F-117s had all returned to their home base in the United States in the early aftermath of the aborted Operation Desert Viper, CENTCOM's air component decided this time to exclude them from the now-incipient Operation Desert Fox, since any return of those highly symbolic aircraft to the theater would send a clear message to Iraq that another allied air offensive was in the offing. Accordingly, amid numerous additional deception measures implemented by the Clinton administration and by CENTCOM, planning for a short but intense four-day aerial assault against key Iraqi targets now aimed at a December 16 start date, the day after the slated release of UNSCOM's next report.

Strike Operations in a Nutshell

As planned, the first night's attacks began with a barrage of 250 TLAMs fired from U.S. and British surface naval ships and submarines operating in the Persian Gulf, along with appropriately time- and space-deconflicted CALCMs launched concurrently from airborne B-52s. This opening round of cruise missiles hit its assigned targets throughout Iraq shortly before 1:00 a.m. local time. It was followed thirty-nine minutes later by several successive waves of U.S. Navy F-14 and F/A-18 strike fighters launched from the aircraft carrier USS *Enterprise*. To minimize the likelihood of any leaks that might give Iraq advance notice of the impending attack, CENTCOM chose for its first night of operations to employ no land-based fighters operating from forward bases in its geographic area of responsibility (AOR) and to exercise command and control of the opening-night attacks from *Enterprise* rather than from its air component's CAOC at Prince Sultan Air Base, Saudi Arabia, which would have been the normal practice.

In its planning for Desert Fox, CENTCOM's air component considered more than 2,600 candidate targets before settling on the 102 that it eventually chose for inclusion in its final master air-attack plan. In support of this daunting effort, the prior on-site work of UNSCOM's weapons inspectors before the campaign's initiation had given American targeteers unprecedented insights into the interstices of Iraq's Ba'athist regime, far more than had been available to them on the eve of Desert Storm eight years before. Accordingly, the first targets struck during the offensive's opening night were the barracks and associated facilities of Iraq's Special Security Organization and Special Republican Guard, the two most pivotal instruments of Hussein's social and political control machinery. The barracks of these organizations were assigned top priority in the campaign's opening-night flow plan so as to exploit to the fullest the element of surprise and kill as many of their occupants as possible. Initial BDA that first night reported that as many as 1,400 members of Hussein's Special Republican Guard and security forces lost their lives during the initial attacks.

Other target sets for the first night included known WMD production facilities, most notably missile final-stage fabrication plants; leadership command-and-control centers, including Hussein's last known personal sleeping quarters on the outskirts of Baghdad; four airfields that harbored attack helicopters used after Desert Storm to suppress the Kurdish rebellion in the north and the Shi'ite rebellion in the south; and critical nodes of Iraq's IADS, including the ring of twenty-four SA-2 SAM sites and associated acquisition and tracking radars that composed the heart of the so-called Super MEZ (missile engagement zone) that surrounded Baghdad. These IADS targets were only struck selectively, however, and with just enough concentration of force on their most critical nodes to achieve the desired temporary defense suppression throughout the four-night campaign.

In announcing the campaign's start, the Clinton administration went out of its way to stress that its mission was simply to "degrade" Iraq's WMD equities and war-waging capability rather than to destroy both entirely. As Secretary of State Madeleine Albright remarked candidly the next day, "we are being very honest [here].... What it means is that we know we can't get everything."[26] Only years later in a future U.S. air operation over post-Ba'athist Iraq (see below, on Operation Inherent Resolve) would an American administration once again invoke "degrading" as a strategy goal, only this time not to indicate a clearly understood limitation on what precision air attacks could practically accomplish but instead to telegraph an underlying lack of leadership determination to go the full length of effort needed to vanquish a detested enemy.

The second night of Desert Fox began much as the night before, with ninety CALCMs fired from B-52s and targeted principally against Iraq's missile-related industries. The initial cruise-missile volley was followed this time by 213 fixed-wing strike sorties in two successive waves of land-based F-15Es, F-16s, A-10s, and British Royal Air Force (RAF) Tornado GR1s operating out of Kuwait and joining the U.S. Navy's carrier-based F-14s and F/A-18s. Now that ensuring operational security was no longer a pressing concern with the offensive well under way, command and control of air operations for the remainder of the campaign reverted to CENTCOM's CAOC in Saudi Arabia. The second night's attacks also included four B-1s operating out of Oman and targeted mainly against the barracks of Hussein's Special Republican Guard. This second night of operations featured more cruise missiles and strike aircraft than were used during the first night. It also was more comprehensive in the breadth of its target coverage. Indeed, after the initial BDA results began filtering in, CENTCOM's air component commander, Lt. Gen. Hal Hornburg, was persuaded that four nights of such bombing would probably be enough to meet the operation's declared goals.[27]

In all, Operation Desert Fox was the most extensive combat action taken by the United States against Iraq since Operation Desert Storm in 1991. The fact that CENTCOM could sustain its operations throughout the campaign with no enemy SAMs fired and no loss of aircraft or aircrews showed that the United States could now strike at key targets throughout the country with essential impunity. Although the operation serviced only ninety-seven targets in the end and used just a tenth the number of aircraft that had taken part in the first Gulf War, it represented the epitome of precision bombing, with no reported civilian fatalities or collateral damage. All combat sorties were conducted at night, with fully half the total number of assigned targets struck during the first night. Except for the unguided general-purpose bombs dropped by the four B-1s, every air-delivered munition was precision guided, as was the case in NATO's earlier two-week war against the Bosnian Serbs in 1995. Those two combat operations taken together established a new standard for force employment that would not only persist but also show ever more refined and discriminating potential into the first decade and a half of the twenty-first century and beyond.

As for operational "firsts" achieved, Desert Fox saw the B-1 finally make its combat debut, and in a conventional role rather than in the nuclear delivery mode for which it had originally been designed and fielded. The campaign also saw the first-ever combat use of the U.S. Navy's F-14D in a night and all-weather strike role, with that once purely air-dominance fighter now configured with the low-altitude navigation and targeting infrared for night targeting pod and armed with as many as four 2,000-pound GBU-24 laser-guided bombs. This first combat employment of the B-1 and F-14D heralded the later workhorse roles that both aircraft would fulfill with distinction in subsequent air wars over Afghanistan and Iraq starting in 2001 and 2003, respectively. Finally, in a notable precedent, Desert Fox represented the first time that American female fighter pilots participated in air warfare, with U.S. Navy lieutenants Lyndsi Bates, Carol Watts, and Kendra Williams, all in F/A-18s from USS *Enterprise*, flying night bombing missions in the operation.

Mission Results

Regarding what the four-night effort accomplished, most observers saw Desert Fox as a resounding success from a purely military viewpoint. However, as one early assessment rightly noted, the main concern in judging the campaign's success was not "how many targets of what character were struck with what level of damage" but rather "what was the political and strategic impact on the enemy."[28] In the view of this latter assessment, the Clinton administration "did not [adequately] explain what Britain and the U.S. really hoped to achieve by launching Desert Fox."[29] Although the campaign's stated goal was to "degrade" Iraq's suspected WMD effort, it became clear during the operation's conduct that the administration's real underlying intent was "to destabilize Iraq and support the policy of 'containment plus replacement' that the president had openly endorsed after calling off the [previously planned] strikes in mid-November."[30]

To expand further on this important point, in announcing the campaign's onset, President Clinton said the effort's aim was to "degrade" Iraq's WMD program by destroying the facilities that Baghdad had declared off limits to UNSCOM's weapons inspectors.[31] Before the bombing ended, he reiterated in a statement from the White House that "our mission is clear—to degrade Saddam's capacity to develop and deliver weapons of mass destruction and threaten the region."[32] Yet while the campaign's openly avowed rationale was to "degrade"

Iraq's ability to produce WMD and to "diminish" the Ba'athist regime's ability to threaten its neighbors, the list of targets actually struck during the four nights of bombing told a very different story. Out of the ninety-seven targets included on the list in all, forty-nine represented the central nervous system of the regime. Another thirty-five were associated with Iraq's IADS. Only eleven of the targets struck were known WMD facilities, and those few centered mainly on Iraq's short-range missile program since CENTCOM did not know for sure where the regime had hidden the majority of its WMD development facilities. Instead CENTCOM mainly attacked targets more directly identified with Hussein's close control over the country, including command-and-control centers, Special Republican Guard barracks, and internal security facilities.

In this regard, as defense analyst William Arkin observed a month after the campaign ended, the essence of Desert Fox's targeting scheme "was more than [simply] a reflexive reaction to Saddam Hussein's refusal to cooperate with UNSCOM's inspectors." In his assessment, national security insiders in the Clinton administration had "convinced themselves that bombing Saddam Hussein's internal apparatus would drive the Iraqi leader around the bend" by showing him that "we've penetrated your security, we're inside your brain."[33] A later assessment likewise noted that although Desert Fox remains "routinely misremembered" to this day as a campaign aimed at targeting Iraq's WMD program, in fact "it was designed and executed to punish [Hussein's] regime by degrading Iraq's air defenses [and] killing Hussein's security forces." At bottom, this more recent assessment concluded, "the 1998 military operation had little to do with Iraq's WMD program and everything to do with punishing Saddam Hussein."[34] Indeed, the single most significant departure of Desert Fox from the principal weight of targeting effort in Desert Storm nearly eight years before was in the latter's more concentrated attention paid to leadership-related centers of gravity such as the Ba'ath Party and Hussein's internal security apparatus that were most essential to his continued survival in power.

To be sure, Operation Desert Fox did indeed "degrade" significant aspects of Iraq's military posture, just as was claimed in the Clinton administration's overt rationale for it. The four nights of bombing showed convincingly that the United States and its British ally were prepared to use force majeure against Hussein's regime as deemed necessary to enforce UN sanctions and to limit Iraq's capacity to harm its neighbors. Relatedly, the campaign showed during its first night that the United States could sustain air strikes solely from the decks of aircraft carriers operating in the Arabian Sea and by long-range bombers based on the British island base of Diego Garcia in the Indian Ocean, thereby tacitly affirming that, if need be, it could get by without basing support from any of the adjacent Gulf states. Interestingly, this experience was an almost exact precursor to the initial retaliatory bombing of Taliban and al-Qaeda targets in Afghanistan that occurred three years later in the wake of the terrorist attacks against the United States on September 11, 2001.

As for the campaign's strategic effects achieved, Secretary of Defense William Cohen remarked toward the end of Desert Fox that as a result of CENTCOM's successful target coverage, "we are advancing our goal of containing Saddam Hussein."[35] Both Cohen and the chairman of the JCS, Gen. Hugh Shelton, denied that the strikes were aimed at destabilizing the Ba'athist regime. Yet that was surely the campaign's undeclared intent, as was best attested by the distribution of effort reflected in CENTCOM's actual target list. In the view of Kenneth Pollack, a long-time observer of Gulf security affairs, "Desert Fox actually exceeded expectations" in that regard. "Saddam," he wrote several years later, "panicked during the strikes. Fearing that his control was threatened, he ordered large-scale arrests and executions, which backfired and destabilized his regime for months afterwards."[36]

That observation was consistent with earlier reports that when CENTCOM was visibly readying itself to unleash Desert Viper the previous November, the Iraqi leadership similarly reacted in "a state of near panic" that induced it to back away instantly from refusing to cooperate with UNSCOM.[37] It also was affirmed less than a month after Desert Fox ended when CENTCOM's commander in chief, Gen. Anthony Zinni, raised the assessed number of Special Republican Guard troops thought to have been killed in the first night's bombing to as many as two thousand, adding that the resultant indications of resentment and disloyalty among Hussein's most elite palace guards had prompted a brutal crackdown by the dictator, indicating that the Iraqi leader had indeed been rattled by the bombing. Said Zinni on this point: "I do believe, personally, that he is shaken." Added General Shelton: "I think that Saddam is feeling the pressure, is becoming more desperate."[38]

It bears noting at least in passing that Desert Fox is regarded in some circles even to this day as "Monica's War" since the commencement of bombing coincided almost to the minute with the start of U.S. Senate impeachment hearings of President Clinton on charges of perjury and obstruction of justice emanating from his testimony regarding earlier involvement with White House intern Monica S. Lewinsky. In light of this all-too-suspicious-looking overlay of events, some administration critics quickly concluded that the operation was nothing but a Clinton ruse aimed at drawing attention away from the impeachment proceedings and undermining them. (Indeed, the Senate's impeachment debate was postponed for at least twenty-four hours to avoid appearing to undermine CENTCOM's just-begun campaign.) Others went even further and insinuated that the suspiciously timed bombing represented a real-world replay of the scenario in the popular recent movie *Wag the Dog*, which featured presidential assistants conjuring up an international crisis requiring force employment to divert public attention away from a sex scandal involving the president.

As convenient as the onset of Desert Fox may have been for President Clinton's personal fortunes, however, it remains an overarching fact that his administration faced an all-too-real need for prompt retaliatory action once UNSCOM's report on Iraqi inspection violations was issued on December 15. The administration wanted to avoid having to take the unpalatable step of continuing combat into the month-long Ramadan season of Muslim prayer and fasting, or else postponing the start of Desert Fox for another month or more, after which the original rationale for the operation might well have faded in popular memory. That meant that the administration had no alternative but to exploit the narrow time window of just four days between December 15 and the imminent start of Ramadan by striking while the iron was hot. On this important count, former secretary of state James Baker III, a staunch Republican and no Clinton admirer, freely conceded that "there probably was some imperative with respect to speed here, [because] the last couple of times that Saddam has stuck his finger in our eye, we've diddled around."[39] This time Baker agreed that immediate action was needed to capitalize on the element of surprise and end the bombing before the onset of Ramadan.[40]

Desert Fox in Strategic Context

Viewed in hindsight, Operation Desert Fox turned out to have been considerably more consequential in its practical impact on Iraq than the Clinton administration's principals had surmised in its initial aftermath. In a telling testament to this, David Kay, the former head of the Iraq Survey Group that had been tasked by the Department of Defense and Central Intelligence Agency (CIA) with finding Hussein's presumed stocks of WMD after the major combat phase of Operation Iraqi Freedom ended in early 2003 (described further below), was initially a skeptic regarding the strategic worth of the four-day offensive. After having interrogated more than two hundred Iraqi officials involved with Hussein's WMD program once the Ba'athist regime was finally toppled, however, he concluded that the 1998 bombing had in fact left Iraq's weapons specialists both demoralized and convinced that their efforts had all been for naught. In a post-2003 reflection, Kay said that his interviews with Hussein's WMD specialists were "a bit of an eye-opener, because I had always denigrated Desert Fox. What I failed to understand was that [the campaign's effectiveness] was cumulative, coming on top of eight years of sanctions."[41] This belated appreciation totally escaped the Clinton administration's defense leaders in the immediate aftermath of Desert Fox. It also bears strong witness to the continued limits of conducting accurate BDA solely through the medium of remote imagery and sensing.

As for the campaign's downsides, Saddam Hussein survived Desert Fox and remained firmly ensconced in power until finally driven out by U.S.-led combat action more than four years later in early April 2003. Yet another negative result of the four-day campaign was that it ensured that Hussein would never again allow UNSCOM's weapons inspectors into Iraq. As attested by those two unhelpful returns from Desert Fox, Kenneth Pollack was on target when he later characterized the campaign as "a limited punitive operation uncoupled from any coercive demands on Saddam."[42] In that regard, Anthony Cordesman similarly noted in the operation's early aftermath that Desert Fox was "likely to prove to be just one more engagement in a nearly decade-long process of containing Saddam Hussein." Cordesman further remarked instructively that "the issue is not whether Desert Fox was a failure; rather, [it is] whether its successes at the tactical level were matched by equal success in the battle for perceptions and by proper planning to use military force to achieve policy-level objectives."[43]

To their credit, both the Department of Defense's and CENTCOM's lead spokesmen bent every effort throughout the campaign to remain true to the facts by avoiding any unseemly spin in exaggerating what the bombing was producing. However, in Cordesman's bottom-line assessment, even though the campaign's execution was all but flawless from a tactical perspective, the U.S. government "did little to describe other specific goals for Desert Fox [besides "degrading" its WMD posture] or to create the climate for a successful political and strategic endgame."[44]

For his part, in the immediate aftermath of Desert Fox, President Clinton's national security advisor, Samuel "Sandy" Berger, rejected all ensuing calls for the administration to strive more forcefully to topple Hussein and his regime as soon as possible, insisting that the only sure way to do that would be for the United States "to commit hundreds of thousands of American troops to fight on the ground inside Iraq." Berger added, with what now resonates in hindsight as ominous foreboding: "I do not believe the cost of such a campaign would be sustainable at home or abroad. And the reward of success would be an American military occupation of Iraq that could last for years."[45] Berger did, however, call for a review of options aimed at *eventually* bringing down Hussein and at enforcing a continued containment of Iraq until any such regime change occurred. In doing that, he and the Clinton administration, albeit unwittingly at the time, helped lay the initial groundwork for President George W. Bush's fateful Operation Iraqi Freedom that would commence its long and costly slog more than four years later.

OPERATION ALLIED FORCE

Between March 24 and June 7, 1999, the near debacle of Operation Deny Flight conducted haplessly between mid-1993 and the end of 1994 came close—at least for a time—to replaying itself out on a far grander scale. During that period, NATO, led by the United States, conducted an air campaign against Serbia in an effort to halt the continuing human rights abuses being committed against the citizens of its Kosovo province by Slobodan Milošević. As it turned out, the seventy-eight-day campaign called Operation Allied Force represented the third time in a row after Operations Desert Storm and Deliberate Force in which airpower proved pivotal in determining a regional combat outcome. Yet, notwithstanding its ultimate success, what began as a hopeful gambit for producing quick compliance on Milošević's part soon devolved into a situation suggesting to many that those most responsible for the campaign had forgotten all they had learned—or should have learned—not only from Desert Storm and Deliberate Force but also from Vietnam. That and more made NATO's air war for Kosovo a step backward in terms of efficiency in the use of airpower when compared to Desert Storm.

The air offensive had its origins in the steadily mounting Serbian atrocities against those ethnic Albanians who made up the majority of Kosovo's population. After two unsuccessful diplomatic attempts by the United States and NATO in February 1999 to induce Milošević to desist, in mid-March U.S. officials presented NATO's ambassadors with a bombing plan, the stated aim of which was to "reduce" Serbia's ability to continue abusing the Kosovars. The plan's declared goals were to achieve a halt to Serbian ethnic cleansing in Kosovo; a withdrawal of all Serbian military, police, and paramilitary forces; the deployment of a NATO-led international peacekeeping presence; the return of all ethnic Albanian refugees and assurance of their unhindered access to aid; and the laying of groundwork for a future settlement that would allow for Kosovar autonomy under continued Serbian sovereignty.[46]

A Halting Start

The operational setting of the former Yugoslavia contrasted sharply with that presented to coalition planners by Iraq in 1991. Defined by a series of interwoven valleys partly surrounded by mountains and protected by low cloud cover and fog, Serbia and Kosovo made for an arena smaller than the state of Kentucky (39,000 square miles), with Kosovo itself no larger than the Los Angeles metropolitan area. Its topography and weather promised to present a unique challenge for NATO airpower, compounded further by an able enemy IADS that was guaranteed to make allied offensive operations both difficult and dangerous.

The campaign plan was conceived from the start as a coercive operation only, with the implied goal of merely inflicting enough pain to persuade Milošević to capitulate. It was expected by U.S. and NATO leaders that he would settle very quickly.[47] Indeed, so confident were those leaders that merely a symbolic bombing effort would suffice to persuade Milošević to yield to NATO's demands that the initial attack was openly announced in advance.[48]

Operation Allied Force began on the night of March 24. Targets included SAM batteries and radar and military communications sites in Kosovo and southern Serbia, plus a radar site at Podgorica, the capital city of Montenegro. Allied pilots were instructed to remain above an altitude floor of 15,000 feet at all times so as to take no chances with the enemy IADS.

No Serbian SAMs were fired in self-defense the first night. However, numerous enemy fighters, including at least a dozen MiG-29s, were launched to intercept the attacking NATO aircraft. Two MiG-29s were downed by U.S. Air Force F-15Cs and one by a Royal Netherlands Air Force F-16. In all, some 400 sorties were flown by NATO the first night. Of these, however, only 120 were actual strike sorties, which attacked a mere 40 Serbian targets in all.

Once it became clear that the air offensive was not having its desired effect, NATO's military commander in chief, Gen. Wesley Clark, received authorization from the North Atlantic Council, the political arm of NATO, to proceed to phase 2 of the campaign, which entailed ramped-up attacks against a broader spectrum of fixed targets in Serbia and against fielded Serbian ground forces in Kosovo. Despite the seeming escalation suggested by the campaign's shift to phase 2, the intensity of effort continued to average no more than around fifty strike sorties a night throughout the first week, in sharp contrast to the first week of Operation Desert Storm, in which the allied combat sortie rate had been as high as a thousand or more a day.

After the second week, the campaign's focus shifted from SEAD to interdiction, with predominant emphasis on Serbian lines of communication, choke points, storage and marshaling areas, and any tank concentrations that might be found. These air attacks continued to be hampered by bad weather, Serbian dispersal tactics, and air defenses that were proving to be considerably more resilient than initially anticipated. In the absence of a credible NATO ground threat, which the United States and its NATO allies had ruled out from the start because of an assumed lack of popular willingness to accept casualties, Serbia's ground forces were able to survive the air attacks simply by dispersing and concealing their tanks, armored personnel carriers, and other battlefield vehicles.

By the end of the third week, Clark requested that three hundred more aircraft be committed to Allied Force. That request, which would increase the total number of U.S. and allied aircraft assigned to the campaign to nearly a thousand, entailed more than twice the number of aircraft (430) that had been on hand when the campaign started on March 24—and almost half of what the allied coalition had had available to conduct the far more ambitious Operation Desert Storm eight years before. For the United States, it represented a 60 percent increase over the 500 U.S. aircraft already committed to the campaign.[49]

As a part of his requested force increment, Clark also asked for a deployment of twenty-four Army AH-64 Apache attack helicopters. Although the other aircraft were eventually approved by Secretary of Defense William Cohen and the JCS, this particular request was initially turned down on the avowed premise that, since attack helicopters are typically associated with land combat, the introduction of any Apaches might be misperceived by the shakier NATO allies as a precursor to a ground operation. A more serious, if unstated, concern was that the Apaches would not be survivable if they were to be committed to combat in the still-lethal Serbian SAM and AAA environment. In the end, despite Army and JCS reluctance, Clark prevailed in his request for the Apaches and announced that they would be deployed to Albania. Pentagon officials went out of their way, however, to stress that the Apaches were intended solely as an extension of the air campaign and not as any implied prelude to future ground operations.[50]

In the meantime, in one of the first tentative strikes against enemy infrastructure, the main telecommunications building in Pristina, the capital city of Kosovo, was taken out by a cruise missile on April 8. Yet the campaign as a whole still remained but a faint shadow of Operation Desert Storm, with only 28 targets throughout all of Serbia attacked out of 439 sorties in a 24-hour period during the campaign's third week. As for the hoped-for "strategic" portion of the campaign against the Serbian heartland, Clark was still being refused permission by NATO's political leaders to attack the state-controlled television network throughout Yugoslavia. Before the campaign was even a week old, indications began to mount that American officials were starting to have second thoughts about the advisability of having peremptorily ruled out a ground option before launching into Allied Force. By the end of the second week, Secretary of State Madeleine Albright openly acknowledged Washington's growing appreciation of the attractiveness of a credible ground threat when she allowed that NATO might change its position and put in ground troops should the bombing succeed in creating a "permissive environment."[51]

Before long, however, a pronounced rift began to emerge between Clark and senior Pentagon authorities over Clark's insistence on stepping out aggressively toward undertaking concrete preparations for a NATO ground invasion. Despite their hedged comments, top Clinton administration decision makers continued to nurture hopes that the air campaign would eventually produce the desired response on Milošević's part. Deep doubts that it would do so, however, prompted a steady rise in military support for developing at least a ground option, notably including from many U.S. Air Force leaders involved in the campaign. By the start of the third week, a consensus had begun to form in Washington that ground forces might be needed, if only to salvage the increasingly shaky credibility of NATO.[52]

As the campaign entered its fourth week, NATO's targeting efforts began to focus not only on fielded Serbian forces in Kosovo but also on what NATO officials had come to characterize as the four main pillars of Milošević's power—the political machine, the media, the security forces, and the economic system. New targets added to the approved list included national oil refineries, petroleum depots, road and rail bridges over the Danube River, railway lines, military communications sites, and factories capable of producing weapons and spare parts.[53]

The first attacks against enemy radio and television stations in Belgrade took place on April 21, with three cruise missiles temporarily shutting down three channels after NATO had issued a warning to employees to vacate the buildings. With that escalation NATO finally brought the campaign to Yugoslavia's political and media elite after weeks of hesitation, indicating that it was now emboldened enough to go directly after the business interests of Milošević's family and friends.

Less than two weeks later, during the predawn hours of May 3 and in possibly the single most consequential attack of the campaign up to that point, U.S. Air Force F-117s dropped CBU-94 munitions on five transformer yards of Belgrade's electrical power grid, temporarily cutting off electricity to 70 percent of Serbia. The sought-after effects were achieved by means of scattered reels of treated wire that unwound in the air after being released as BLU-114/B submunitions, draping enemy high-voltage power lines like tinsel and causing them to short out. The declared intent of the attack was to shut down the installations that provided electrical power to the Serbian 3rd Army so as to disrupt military communications and to confuse Serbian air defenses.[54] Very likely an unspoken additional intent was to tighten the air campaign's squeeze on the Serbian political leadership and rank and file.

By the end of the seventh week there began to be reports of Serbian officials openly admitting that the country was on the verge of widespread hardship due to the mounting damage that the campaign was causing to the nation's economy, which had already been weakened by almost four years of international sanctions imposed for Serbia's earlier role in the war in Bosnia.[55] By the time the campaign had reached its halfway point, the bombing of infrastructure targets had halved Serbia's economic output and deprived more than 100,000 civilians of jobs. Local economists reported that the effect was more damaging than that of the successive Nazi and allied bombing of Yugoslavia during World War II, when the country was far more rural in its economic makeup.[56]

The Bombing Intensifies

Only during the last two weeks of Operation Allied Force did NATO finally strike with real determination against Serbia's electrical power-generating capability, a target set that had been attacked in Baghdad from the very first days of Desert Storm. The earlier "soft" attacks at the beginning of May with graphite filament bombs against the transformer yards of the Serbian power grid had caused a temporary disruption of the power supply by shorting out generators and disabling them rather than destroying them. This time, on May 24, Belgrade's electrical power grid was severely damaged by high-explosive PGMs. That attack affected the heart of the Serbian air defense network as well as the computers that ran Serbia's banking system.

In what was initially thought to have been a pivotal turn of events in the war's effort against enemy ground troops, the Kosovo Liberation Army (KLA), a paramilitary group of Kosovar Albanian nationalists whose members had earlier begun a partisan war against the Serbian army and police forces that controlled the increasingly conflicted province, launched a counteroffensive on May 26 against Serbian troops in Kosovo. That thrust, called Operation Arrow, involved upward of four thousand guerrillas, with the aim of driving into Kosovo from two points along the province's southwestern border and securing a safe route so that the KLA could resupply its beleaguered fighters. The attack was thwarted at first by Serbian artillery and infantry counterattacks, indicating that the Serbian army still had plenty of fight left in it after seventy days of intermittent bombing by NATO.

However, as the KLA's counteroffensive forced Serbian ground units to come out from hiding and to marshal their forces to defend themselves, their movements were often detected by the E-8 joint surveillance target-attack radar system (JSTARS) aircraft and other overhead sensor platforms, even though enemy troops sought to maneuver in small enough numbers to avoid such detection. The JSTARS crews then transmitted the coordinates of suspected enemy ground-force concentrations to airborne forward air controllers who, in turn, directed both RQ-1 remotely piloted aircraft (RPA) and strike fighters in for closer looks and ultimately for attacks on the Serbian units.[57]

As the campaign's endgame neared, Russia's envoy to the Balkans, former prime minister Viktor Chernomyrdin and Finnish president Martti Ahtisaari, representing the European Union, flew to Belgrade on June 2 and offered Milošević a plan to bring the conflict to a close. Ahtisaari was brought into the process because allied leaders had been concerned that Chernomyrdin, operating alone, had not faithfully conveyed NATO's demands to Milošević during his four previous visits to the Yugoslav capital. Two days later the Serbian leadership accepted an international peace plan by which it would accede to NATO's demands for a withdrawal of all Serbian forces from Kosovo, an unmolested return of the refugees to their homes, and the creation of self-rule for the ethnic Albanian majority that acknowledged Serbia's continued sovereignty over Kosovo.

No sooner had this accord been reached in principle, however, when NATO and Serbian representatives failed to agree on the terms for Serbian withdrawal. The talks then degenerated into haggling over when NATO would terminate its air attacks and whether Belgrade would have more than a week to get its troops out of Kosovo. That breakdown suggested that the Serbs were looking for more time to continue their battle against the KLA. In response to this willful foot-dragging, NATO's air attacks, which had been scaled back after Milošević initially accepted the proposed plan, resumed their previous level of intensity.

At the same time, on June 7, Serbian forces launched a redoubled attack against the KLA in an area south of Mount Pastrik, where they had been locked in an artillery duel since May 26. This time, thanks to improved weather, a significant degradation of Serbian air defenses, and the effective role that had been played by the KLA in forcing Serbian forces to come out of hiding, two B-52s and two B-1s dropped a total of 86 Mk 82 500-pound bombs and cluster munitions on an open field in a daytime raid near the Kosovo-Albanian border where those enemy troops were thought to have been massed. The estimated number of Serbian troops was 800 to 1,200, with initial assessments suggesting that fewer than half of those had survived the attack.[58] The Serbian counteroffensive against the KLA came to a halt after that raid, which the Pentagon later called the single heaviest air attack against fielded enemy forces in the entire campaign.[59]

In the end, Serbia acceded to an agreement authorizing a presence of 50,000 international peacekeepers commanded by a NATO general and with sweeping occupation powers over Kosovo. After 78 days of bombing, the agreement was signed on June 9, after which NATO ceased its air attacks upon confirming that the Serbian withdrawal had begun. The UN Security Council then approved, by a 14–0 vote with China abstaining, a resolution putting Kosovo under international civilian control and the peacekeeping force under UN authority. With that, President Clinton declared that NATO had "achieved a victory."[60]

Airpower's Accomplishments

Operation Allied Force was the first air campaign in which all three U.S. heavy bomber types saw combat employment. Of some 700 combat aircraft committed to the campaign altogether, a mere 21 U.S. Air Force heavy bombers (10 B-52s, 5 B-1s, and 6 B-2s) dropped 11,000 out of the 23,000 bombs and missiles that were expended during the campaign's 78-day course.[61] Also of major note, the first night saw the long-awaited combat debut of the B-2 stealth bomber, which flew nonstop to its targets directly from its home base in Missouri, on 30-hour round-trip missions. Each B-2 delivered up to 16 GPS-aided GBU-31 joint direct attack munitions (JDAMs) from 40,000 feet, usually through cloud cover, against hardened enemy targets, including command bunkers and air defense facilities.

To the surprise of many, the B-2 turned out to have been the most consistently effective performer of the entire air campaign. Protected by U.S. Navy and Marine Corps EA-6B electronic jamming, as were all other NATO combat aircraft that flew into hostile airspace, it was the first manned platform to penetrate Serbian air defenses the first night.[62] In addition to its normal load of JDAMs, the B-2 also carried the GPS-aided GBU-37 for special missions against deeply buried or super-hardened targets.[63] Having contributed only fifty combat missions all told, the B-2 flew fewer than 1 percent of the total number of strike sorties in Allied Force, yet it dropped a full third of all the precision munitions expended during the campaign. It also proved itself capable of operating effectively above weather that grounded all other allied combat aircraft.[64]

Once Serbia's air defenses became less of an ever-present threat, the campaign saw a heightened use of B-52s, B-1s, and other combat aircraft carrying unguided bombs. By the end of May, some four thousand free-fall bombs, around 30 percent of the total number of munitions expended altogether, had been dropped. They included the Mk 82 general-purpose bomb and the CBU-87 cluster bomb. In sharp contrast to the indiscriminate carpet bombing that was all the B-52 could accomplish from high altitude with unguided munitions both over Vietnam and during Operation Desert Storm, the B-1 repeatedly demonstrated a capability to drop cluster munitions within a footprint only a thousand feet long against enemy barracks and other military area targets.

More than in any previous air warfare experience, Predator RPAs equipped with synthetic-aperture radar, electro-optical, and infrared-imaging sensors were used in Allied Force for intelligence, surveillance, and reconnaissance (ISR) support, most notably in locating mobile SAMs, Serbian troop concentrations, and enemy aircraft parked in the open. Some were flown as low as a thousand feet above Serbian troop positions to gather real-time imagery, which enabled prompt attacks by A-10s and F-16s against often fleeting targets. Several were lost when controlling commanders requested closer looks at such positions, forcing the drones to descend into the lethal envelopes of Serbian AAA and man-portable SAM systems. These losses did not evoke much concern, however, since the RPAs had been intentionally sent out on missions known beforehand to be especially dangerous. Despite the losses, RPAs offered NATO air commanders and planners the advantage of close battlespace awareness without any accompanying danger of incurring aircrew casualties.[65]

In the final tally, allied aircrews flew 37,465 sorties, of which 14,006 were strike sorties.[66] One-third of the 23,000 munitions expended were general-purpose Mk 82 unguided bombs dropped by B-52s and B-1s during the campaign's last two weeks. Between 3,000 and 5,000 of these munitions were delivered against some 500 fixed targets in Serbia and Montenegro. The remainder were dropped on fielded enemy forces in Kosovo. In a telling reflection of the extent of allied determination not to lose a single aircrew member, some 35 percent of the overall air effort was directed against enemy air defenses. Thanks largely to that, only 2 allied aircraft were downed and not a single friendly fatality was incurred.[67]

Assessing the Experience

Because of the campaign's ultimate success in forcing Milošević to yield to NATO's demands, many hastened to characterize it afterward as a watershed achievement for airpower. On closer examination, however, it is hard to accept that characterization as the right way to remember Operation Allied Force. After the campaign ended, the former commander of NATO forces during the earlier successful Operation Deliberate Force, Adm. Leighton W. Smith Jr., remarked more properly that the Kosovo experience should go down as "possibly the worst way we employed our military forces in history."[68] The air component commander for the campaign, Lt. Gen. Michael Short, likewise declared later that "as an airman, I'd have done this a whole lot differently than I was allowed to do. We could have done this differently. We should have done this differently."[69]

To be sure, there is much to be said of a positive nature about Operation Allied Force. To begin with, it did represent the first instance in which the application of airpower coerced an enemy leader to yield with no friendly land combat action whatsoever. Moreover, although there were some unfortunate and highly publicized cases in which innocent civilians were killed, Secretary of Defense Cohen was on point when he characterized the campaign after the cease-fire went into effect as "the most precise application of airpower in history."[70]

Nevertheless, despite the campaign's successful outcome in the end, Operation Allied Force fell considerably short of being a stellar performance by airpower. To begin with, it could have failed miserably. The incremental campaign plan chosen by NATO's leaders at the outset risked squandering much of the capital that had been built up in airpower's account since its ringing success in Desert Storm nearly a decade before. By metering their initial air strikes with such hesitancy, NATO's leaders remained blind to the fact that airpower's very strengths can become weaknesses if the air weapon is used in a way that undermines its credibility. The opportunity costs incurred by NATO's anemic start of the campaign without any accompanying ground threat included, most notably, a failure to exploit airpower's inherent shock potential and the encouragement it gave Serbian ground forces to disperse and hide while they had time.

As for what airmen and other observers should take away from Allied Force by way of points worth pondering for the future, the commander of the U.S. military contribution, Adm. James Ellis, a career U.S. Navy fighter pilot, offered a good start when he later charged that NATO's leaders "called this one absolutely wrong" and that their failure to anticipate what might occur once their initial strategy of hope failed occasioned most of the untoward consequences that ensued thereafter. These included the overly hasty activation of a joint task force, a race to find suitable targets, an absence of coherent campaign planning, and lost opportunities caused by the failure to think through unpleasant excursions from what had been expected.[71]

On the plus side, the campaign's successful outcome, despite its many frustrations, suggested that American and NATO airpower might by then have become capable enough to underwrite a strategy of incremental escalation irrespective of the latter's inherent inefficiencies. What made the gradualism of Allied Force more bearable than that of the earlier war in Vietnam was that in the more recent case, the allied advantages in stealth, precision standoff attack, and electronic warfare meant that NATO could fight a one-sided war against Milošević with near-impunity and achieve the desired result, even if not in the most ideal way.[72] That was not an option when U.S. airpower was a less developed tool than it was by 1999.

OPERATION ENDURING FREEDOM

Two years later, on September 11, 2001—a clear and fateful morning that will be forever remembered in American history—four commercial jetliners on routine transcontinental flights were taken over by radical Islamist terrorists not long after their near-concurrent departures for the West Coast from Boston, Newark, and Washington, D.C. Upon being commandeered, the fuel-laden aircraft were promptly converted into what would soon become de facto WMDs against the United States. The first two jetliners were flown within eighteen minutes of each other into the Twin Towers of the World Trade Center in New York City, causing nearly three thousand fatalities among innocent civilians. The third was flown forty minutes later into the southwest side of the Pentagon in Arlington, Virginia. The fourth, its target believed to have been the White House or the U.S. Capitol building, fortunately had its mission thwarted by some brave passengers on board who had turned on their captors once they learned from cell phone conversations what the other three airliners had just done. After a fierce struggle between the terrorists and their resisters, that fourth and last aircraft was brought to earth in a ball of fire in an empty field in western Pennsylvania.

These horrific attacks caught the American government completely off guard. It did not take long, however, for it to conclude that Osama bin Laden and his al-Qaeda terrorist network had been behind them. The U.S. military response to the attacks, code-named Operation Enduring Freedom, did not begin until nearly a month later. Yet it became clear from the very first days after the historically unprecedented provocation that the still-new administration of President George W. Bush would take forceful and determined action in reprisal by means of an air-dominated campaign to extirpate bin Laden's network in Afghanistan and that country's ruling Taliban theocracy, which had provided it safe haven.

Shaping a Plan

As the administration's response began to unfold, its first challenge was to build a worldwide coalition to lend the forthcoming effort the greatest possible legitimacy and material support. A second challenge entailed developing a concrete course of action that specified the impending campaign's priorities and goals. A third was to craft a detailed concept of operations for meeting those priorities and achieving the administration's immediate goals. Last, there was the associated need to begin fielding and prepositioning the required assets of all U.S. services for any such action. All of that occurred within the scant twenty-six days that separated the attacks of September 11 and the campaign's onset the following October 7.

As for the needed instruments for implementing the emerging campaign plan, CENTCOM would rely heavily on U.S. Navy and Marine Corps carrier-based strike fighters, supported by U.S. Air Force and RAF tankers for providing in-flight refueling, owing to the limited immediate availability of forward shore bases in the region within easy reach of Afghanistan by land-based fighters. Two aircraft carriers, USS *Carl Vinson* and USS *Enterprise*, were already operating on station in CENTCOM's AOR with their embarked air wings ready for action, with a third carrier battle group led by USS *Theodore Roosevelt* ordered to deploy to the AOR from its home port of Norfolk, Virginia, on September 18. At the same time, USS *Kitty Hawk* departed for the AOR from her home port at Yokosuka, Japan, without her full air-wing complement so as to provide what later came to be called a sea-based "lily pad" from which teams of U.S. special operations forces (SOF) would be staged into Afghanistan.

Less than a week before the campaign commenced, the number of U.S. aircraft in the region had grown to between four hundred and five hundred, including seventy-five on each of the Navy's three aircraft carriers on station.

Many dozens of Air Force combat aircraft were deployed to the Persian Gulf states of Kuwait, Saudi Arabia, and Oman; to Diego Garcia in the Indian Ocean; and—in an unprecedented post–Cold War move—to the two former Soviet republics of Uzbekistan and Tajikistan. These included B-52s, B-1s, F-15Es, and F-16s as well as E-3s and tanker and other support aircraft.[73]

A New Kind of Air War

The campaign began under clear skies on the night of October 7, 2001, against preplanned targets in and around Herat, Shindand, Mazar-i-Sharif, and the southern Taliban stronghold area of Kandahar. The attacks were carried out by five U.S. Air Force B-1 and ten B-52 heavy bombers operating out of Diego Garcia and by twenty-five Navy F-14 and F/A-18 fighters launched from USS *Enterprise* and USS *Carl Vinson* in the North Arabian Sea. Two B-2 stealth bombers flying nonstop all the way from their home base in Missouri also took part in the opening-night attacks, each carrying sixteen 2,000-pound satellite-aided JDAMs directed against Taliban early warning radars and military headquarters buildings.[74]

The heaviest bombing that first night was conducted by U.S. Air Force B-52s, which rained both JDAMs and hundreds of Mk 82 unguided bombs on al-Qaeda terrorist training camps in the valleys of eastern Afghanistan. For their part, strikes from the Navy's carriers involved distances to target of more than six hundred nautical miles, with an average sortie length of more than four and a half hours and a minimum of two in-flight refuelings each way to complete the mission. The United Kingdom's RAF provided Tristar and VC-10 tankers to help supplement Air Force KC-135s and KC-10s in providing in-flight refueling for the Navy fighters.[75]

The second day of air operations saw only about half the number of aircraft that had been committed the first night. Attacks again began at night but this time continued on into daylight hours, indicating CENTCOM's heightened confidence that the Taliban's minimal air defenses had been largely neutralized. By the time the fifth consecutive day of strike operations began, mountain cave complexes harboring al-Qaeda combatants and equipment were attacked for the first time, using GBU-28 5,000-pound laser-guided hard-structure munitions.[76]

After the campaign's tenth day, the effort shifted from mainly attacking fixed targets to seeking out targets of opportunity, notably enemy troop concentrations and vehicles. Attention turned to what were called "emerging targets," including Taliban vehicles that had been moved after the initial attacks, as well as other enemy troops and weapons as they were detected and identified. As a key part of this shift in emphasis, the successful insertion of a small number of SOF combatants into southern Afghanistan after eleven days of bombing signaled the beginning of a new use of airpower in modern warfare. In this new phase of operations, airborne forward air controllers flying in carrier-based strike fighters would visually confirm and validate targets that had been designated by allied SOF teams and then clear other aircraft to attack them.[77]

On November 9 friendly indigenous Afghan Northern Alliance ground forces finally took Mazar-i-Sharif. That success made for the first tangible breakthrough in Operation Enduring Freedom as well as a notable morale booster at a time when concerns about the campaign's initial halting progress had begun to mount. The subsequent capture of Kabul by Northern Alliance forces, aided decisively by American airpower working in close harmony with allied SOF teams, made for another timely breakthrough. At the same time, Taliban forces continued to fight hard to retain control of Kunduz and Kandahar, the latter of which was the movement's primary and last remaining stronghold.

Accordingly, CENTCOM's center of focus shifted to those two areas where the majority of U.S. air strikes were now concentrated. Allied SOF teams engaged systematically in enabling the aerial plinking of enemy targets by sealing off roads, selectively blowing up bridges, and calling in air attacks on moving vehicles. All of this was aided by a multispectral ISR umbrella that stared relentlessly down from a multiplicity of air and space assets operating constantly overhead.

As the siege of Kunduz got under way, allied air strikes increased in number and intensity. In yet another sign of progress, reports indicated that the bombing in the Kandahar area had finally succeeded in eliminating some senior al-Qaeda leaders.[78] Principal among them was bin Laden's military chief, Mohammed Atef. He was inside a targeted house and was killed by an LGB dropped by an Air Force F-15E, which, by happenstance, was in the midst of conducting what turned out to have been the longest-duration combat sortie by a fighter ever recorded in history (15.8 hours).

With the Taliban's remaining days in power now numbered, the Pentagon indicated that the campaign had entered a new phase, with less well-defined front lines and with the emphasis now placed on "Taliban-plinking" and on rooting out al-Qaeda combatants wherever they might be found. Around 10,000 air-delivered munitions had been expended during the first 45 days of combat. That expenditure rate was roughly comparable to the daily weapons delivery rate of NATO's air war for Kosovo in 1999. A major difference between the two campaigns was the overall proportion of precision weapons employed (around 60 percent in Operation Enduring Freedom, as compared to only 35 percent in Allied Force).[79]

Air attacks on Kandahar intensified on December 1 as opposition forces moved to within ten miles of that last remaining Taliban holdout and a loose encirclement of the city progressively became a siege. The battle for Kandahar was fought mainly from the air and entailed more than two months of strikes against the city's outskirts. With the city's fall sixty-three days after the start of the campaign, the war effort entered a new phase, with the main focus now on finding bin Laden and his top lieutenants and on stabilizing post-Taliban Afghanistan. Hard-core al-Qaeda combatants continued to hold out in the Tora Bora mountains, having found shelter there in as many as two hundred separate caves.[80]

After the bombing of the Tora Bora mountains had continued nonstop for three weeks, it was suspended for a brief interlude to allow friendly Afghan forces to advance on the caves in search of al-Qaeda fugitives. Earlier, U.S. and British SOF teams had begun checking some caves after receiving a confirmed report that bin Laden had recently been spotted in the White Mountains.[81] In light of the unusual fierceness of the al-Qaeda resistance, it was presumed at first that bin Laden had been surrounded and cornered in Tora Bora. Later, however, administration officials conceded that there was only a fifty-fifty chance that he was still there.

With the Tora Bora cave complex now all but obliterated, some of the al-Qaeda survivors sought to regroup in caves in eastern Afghanistan at Zhawar Kili and nearby in the vicinity of Khost. That development prompted 118 consecutive attack sorties in the area over a 4-day period beginning on January 3, 2002, by B-52s, B-1s, F/A-18s, and an AC-130. It took nearly 2 weeks of continuous bombing to complete the destruction of the al-Qaeda complex there, with U.S. Air Force combat controllers attached to American SOF teams identifying and designating most of the aim points.[82]

As in Operation Desert Storm a decade before, many weapon effects achieved in Enduring Freedom were primarily psychological in nature. Bombs dropped by aircraft that were too high to be seen or heard by the enemy exploded as though they had come out of nowhere. Friendly Afghan Northern Alliance fighters often overheard Taliban soldiers on the radio speaking frantically of running for cover any time jet noise was heard. In one instance at night, early during the campaign, Taliban forces were preparing to cross a bridge in foggy weather conditions. The bridge was taken out by three concurrent JDAM hits right before their eyes.[83]

On December 18 the aerial bombardment was finally brought to a halt. By mid-January 2002 Operation Enduring Freedom had evolved from a high-technology air war into what essentially became a domestic policing function as the United States now found itself striving to manage and pacify feuding warlords, protect the embryonic interim Afghan government that had supplanted the Taliban, and ensure adequate force protection from sniper fire and other hostile action for the 4,000 U.S. ground troops who were now in the country. In the end, the Taliban regime was brought down only 102 days after the terrorist attacks of September 11. Although indigenous Afghan ground forces and allied SOF teams were essential to the success of this achievement, American air and space power were the principal enabling elements.

The Anaconda Imbroglio

After two months of relative quiet following the fall of the Taliban and the installation of an interim successor government under Hamid Karzai, U.S. ground forces met their fiercest test of the war in a bold attempt to encircle and capture or kill those al-Qaeda fugitives who had escaped into the high mountains overlooking the Shah-i-Kot valley of eastern Afghanistan. The lead role for the planning and execution of this effort, code-named Operation Anaconda, fell to Maj. Gen. Franklin Hagenbeck, the commander of the U.S. Army's 10th Mountain Division, who, for the upcoming operation, was formally designated commander of Combined Joint Task Force (CJTF) Mountain.

Despite its nominal designation as a "joint" entity, however, CJTF Mountain had no representation from any services other than the Army in its organizational makeup. More important, at no time throughout the elaborate planning for Anaconda almost up to the day of its scheduled start had Hagenbeck made any effort whatever to enlist the air component's involvement, notwithstanding the fact that the undertaking had grown under his direction into the largest pending commitment of U.S. ground troops (more than a thousand) to combat since Operation Desert Storm more than a decade before.

Anaconda's declared mission was to capture or kill any al-Qaeda and Taliban fighters who might be encountered by allied forces in the Shah-i-Kot area of Afghanistan's eastern hinterland. Toward that end, more than 1,400 conventional U.S. Army infantrymen and an additional 200 SOF troops were assigned to participate, along with around 1,000 friendly Afghan Northern Alliance fighters who were also involved in the planned blocking and track-down effort. It would prove to be an experience in which fixed-wing airpower, left out of the initial planning entirely and summoned in full force only at the eleventh hour when events seemed headed toward a major calamity for the Army, would be pivotal in producing what ultimately was a successful, if costly, outcome.

In one of the first harbingers of more trouble yet to come, a flight of Army AH-64 Apache attack helicopters preceded CJTF Mountain's move into the valley by reconnoitering the air assault's planned landing zones. Immediately after being inserted, however, CJTF Mountain's troops found themselves beset by withering enemy fire from both the valley floor and the adjacent high ground. All seven of the Apaches that had initially been committed to the fight were hit by al-Qaeda heavy-weapons fire. After they were withdrawn from the fight, the complexion of Anaconda changed almost instantly—in the words of one informed account, "from an operation focused primarily on land power to an operation increasingly dependent on Air Force, Navy, and later Marine air assets."[84]

However, because CJTF Mountain had not enlisted the involvement of CENTCOM's air component or laid any of the needed groundwork for an optimally effective joint air-ground operation until the last minute, this sudden dependence on fixed-wing airpower was bound to encounter trouble once calls for emergency CAS arose. No CAS cell was manned in the air component's CAOC at the time Anaconda began. The two Air Force air liaison officers attached directly to CJTF Mountain quickly learned that their undermanned and poorly equipped air support cell was at the brink of being overwhelmed by the need to prioritize multiple CAS requests simultaneously and to deconflict the limited airspace over the valley as a profusion of calls for immediate fire support came pouring into CJTF Mountain's command post from the thirty-seven U.S. Air Force enlisted terminal attack controllers who were dispersed throughout the area.[85]

Once the air contribution to Anaconda improved in effectiveness, Air Force forward air controllers and enlisted terminal attack controllers controlled hundreds of munitions deliveries from every platform in every U.S. service contributing kinetically to Enduring Freedom, with no fratricide and no friendly losses to enemy fire. In a situation in which five times the expected enemy strength was taken on by CJTF Mountain, air support to Anaconda saw the greatest number of precision munitions dropped into the smallest geographic space in the history of air warfare.

Yet because the CAOC had not been brought into Hagenbeck's planning for Anaconda from its first day onward, CENTCOM's air component did not figure in his evolving concept of operations except by happenstance and at the last minute, once the CAOC's leaders finally got wind of it. After that, thanks entirely to rushed eleventh-hour improvisation on the CAOC's part, American fixed-wing air assets provided the overwhelming preponderance of force for CJTF Mountain and did most of the work that was originally envisaged for organic Army fires. To this day, there is no smoking-gun evidence that might prove beyond question that CJTF Mountain deliberately excluded the CAOC from its planning for Anaconda so the Army could finally have its chance to look good again after having for so long languished in the shadow of airpower's superior performance both during and since Desert Storm. For sure, however, numerous faulty assumptions on Hagenbeck's part resulted in CJTF Mountain's having been left only barely covered by needed air support once its eventual insertion encountered unexpected resistance. In reflecting on all of this, the CAOC director for the first month of Enduring Freedom later concluded: "The message that needs to come out of this issue is that to optimize air-ground synergy, the air component must be included in all phases of planning surface operations and vice versa. That is what went awry in Anaconda, not CAS."[86]

Distinctive Aspects

Operation Enduring Freedom was a SOF-centric application of joint and combined airpower that, in the end, added up to a new way of war for the United States.[87] Among other things, even more than in the case of Desert Storm over a decade before, the campaign's results showed the ability of the United States to conduct successful force projection from land bases thousands of miles away from the target area as well as from carrier operating stations farther away from a land-locked combat zone than ever before in the history of naval air warfare.[88]

The three ingredients that made this unprecedented achievement possible were long-range precision airpower managed by a uniquely sophisticated and capable CAOC, consistently good real-time tactical intelligence, and mobile SOF teams on the ground working in close concert with indigenous Afghan resistance forces and equipped with enough organic firepower and electronic support to maintain adequate situation awareness, operate independently, and avoid ambushes. Beyond that, Operation Enduring Freedom saw a continuation of some important trends that were set in motion during the first Persian Gulf War of 1991. For example, precision weapons accounted for only 9 percent of the munitions expended during Desert Storm, yet they totaled 29 percent in Operation Allied Force and nearly 60 percent in Enduring Freedom. That dramatic improvement in overall force leverage reaffirmed that one could now speak routinely not of the number of sorties required to engage a given target but rather of the number of desired weapon aim points that could be successfully attacked during a single sortie.

Moreover, for the first time ever, Operation Enduring Freedom was conducted under an overarching ISR umbrella that stared down relentlessly in search of enemy activity. That umbrella was formed by a constellation of overlapping sensor platforms, starting with various satellites on both low and higher orbits in space. It also included a multiplicity of manned and unmanned aircraft sporting a broad spectrum of electro-optical, radar, and other sensor suites and packages. These interlinked and mutually supporting platforms enabled a greatly increased refinement of ISR input over that which had been available during earlier conflicts. It also permitted a degree of ISR fusion that distinguished Enduring Freedom from all previous air campaigns.

The integration of Air Force terminal attack controllers with U.S. and allied SOF teams was arguably the single greatest tactical innovation of the war. These controllers would rack and stack a dozen or more fighters and bombers like layers of a wedding cake over a segment of the battlefield and then direct pilots toward specific targets to be struck. As the campaign shifted from attacking fixed targets to engaging emerging time-sensitive targets, aircrews would routinely get airborne without any preassigned targets. By the time the air war was over, some 80 percent of all targets attacked by U.S. aircrews had not been preplanned but rather were assigned while their aircraft were en route to their assigned holding points over Afghanistan.

Problems in Execution

At the same time, Operation Enduring Freedom was not without its share of friction and inefficiencies. To begin with, much as in the previous case of Operation Allied Force against Serbia in 1999, some severe shortcomings in securing target approvals under tight time constraints were revealed. Thanks to the recent revolution in global communications and ISR fusion, the sensor-to-shooter information cycle time was reduced from hours—or even days—to single-digit minutes. Yet an overly cumbersome target-approval process with multiple layers of involved participants often nullified the potential effects of that breakthrough by extending decision timelines, making the human factor rather than the command-and-control and ISR systems the principal rate limiter.

Some operator complaints about the inhibiting ROE and time-consuming target-approval provisions were entirely appropriate. Yet those constraints emanated from the highest echelon of the U.S. government and were anything but arbitrary. President Bush was personally determined to avoid any untoward occurrence resulting from errant bombing that might even remotely suggest that the campaign was an indiscriminate war against the Afghan people. That determination led to a requirement for a minimally destructive air campaign using tactics that would not risk alienating the Afghan rank and file and inflaming Arab passions elsewhere around the world. For that reason, infrastructure targets were expressly excluded from attack.

In actual practice, however, the approach followed by CENTCOM in honoring these onerous restrictions sometimes occasioned a tendency on the part of CAOC staffers to be gun-shy in proposing targets out of anticipatory fear of CENTCOM disapproval on grounds of collateral-damage sensitivities. At times, things got to a point where mission accomplishment took a back seat to collateral-damage avoidance. There was a tendency at all levels to forget that information on time-sensitive targets is highly perishable and often must be acted on within minutes to produce desired results. More than in any previous campaign, Operation Enduring Freedom saw not just centralized planning but also a pronounced expansion of centralized execution that reached from the highest echelons of government all the way down to engaged combatants at the tactical level. The result was a complex target-approval process involving many tiers of the chain of command that sometimes had the adverse effect of lengthening rather than shortening the kill chain.

One overarching lesson that emerged from the Enduring Freedom experience, given the heightened communications connectivity and battlespace awareness that predominated throughout the campaign, is that senior leaders need to stay focused on their proper level of war and to know when their hands-on involvement is appropriate and when it is not. CENTCOM's former air component commander during Operation Desert Storm, Gen. Charles Horner, bluntly observed in this regard, "the most dangerous thing we face [as a result of increased ISR and communications connectivity worldwide] is the 8,000-mile screwdriver simply because it is possible."[89] Doctrine and practice, he added, must accordingly own up to this new reality squarely and find effective ways of addressing it preemptively lest that reality be allowed, by operator default, to undermine and destroy one of America's most precious military advantages.

On Balance

Beyond its historic role as the first military move in the gathering American global war on terror, Operation Enduring Freedom was a battle laboratory for testing, in a live combat setting, some of the most significant airpower developments to have appeared in more than two decades. Among other things, the war saw the first use of an unmanned ISR platform, the MQ-1 Predator RPA armed with Hellfire air-to-surface missiles, as a precision-attack weapon. The campaign's dominant features were persistence of pressure on the enemy and rapidity of execution, thanks to the improved data fusion enabled by new technologies, a better managed CAOC, more help from space, and smarter concepts of operations. Much of the persistent pressure that CENTCOM applied stemmed also from the widespread availability of precision munitions. During NATO's air war for Kosovo in 1999, only the B-2 was configured to drop JDAMs. In Enduring Freedom two years later, nearly every U.S. strike platform was equipped with that capability.

Furthermore, a new concept of offensive air employment against enemy ground forces was successfully tested in Enduring Freedom. Although often mistakenly equated with CAS, it was, in fact, something fundamentally new by way of airpower application that entailed air attacks against fielded enemy forces that were *not* in direct contact with friendly troops.

In all, Operation Enduring Freedom represented a unique blend of airpower, allied SOF teams, and indigenous Afghan opposition-group combatants on the ground. It was further marked by a complete absence of heavy-maneuver

U.S. ground forces. Notwithstanding the later involvement of a large number of conventional allied ground troops in Operation Anaconda, the campaign was not a land war but rather a SOF-centric air war that largely accounted for the ultimate successes of the indigenous Afghan resistance forces. SOF teams and airpower produced a unique synergy in which each enabled the other. The SOF units rendered airpower more effective than it would have been otherwise, and airpower allowed the SOF teams to succeed with opposition groups in land operations against Taliban and al-Qaeda forces in a fashion that otherwise would not have been possible. In this, the SOF presence was critical to Enduring Freedom's initial outcome. Neither airpower alone nor airpower in support of conventional ground troops could have produced the same results.

If there was anything "transformational" about the way Operation Enduring Freedom was conducted, it was the dominance of fused information over platforms and munitions as the principal enabler of the campaign's success in the end. That new dynamic made possible all other major aspects of the war, including the integration of SOF teams as human ISR sensors with precision-strike airpower, the minimization of target location error, and collateral-damage avoidance. Thanks to real-time imagery and increased communications connectivity, the kill chain on occasion was shorter than ever before, and target-attack accuracy was truly phenomenal. Such network-enabled operations were the cutting edge of a continuing paradigm shift in combat style that may eventually have greater influence on future warfighting than did the introduction of the tank at the start of the twentieth century.[90]

OPERATION IRAQI FREEDOM

America's second war against Iraq differed notably from its first. Operation Desert Storm in 1991 was a purely coercive effort by U.S. and coalition forces to drive out those Iraqi troops who had brutally invaded and occupied neighboring Kuwait nearly six months before. In contrast, the major combat phase of Operation Iraqi Freedom, conducted in the spring of 2003, was a more ambitious effort by U.S., British, and Australian air, land, and maritime forces to bring about a decisive end to Saddam Hussein's regime. Unlike the first Persian Gulf War, it featured a concurrent and synergistic rather than sequential application of air and ground power. During the course of this three-week campaign, U.S. and British troops pressed from Kuwait to the outskirts of Baghdad within just days. As the main enabler of this rapid ground push, allied airpower quickly neutralized an already heavily degraded Iraqi air defense system and established uncontested control of the air while at the same time paving the way for the allied ground thrust by shredding in detail Iraq's Republican Guard divisions, even as a three-day sandstorm reduced visibility on the ground to just meters.

Unlike most previous major combat experiences throughout American history, this war was clearly one of choice rather than necessity. Even the darkest assessment by senior members of the Bush administration did not regard Hussein's regime as presenting an imminent threat to U.S. security. Nevertheless, given the president's understanding at the time of Iraq's involvement in the development of WMD and his responsibility for the nation's security in light of the terrorist attacks on September 11, 2001, and the even worse possible future horrors they portended, he judged that timely and decisive U.S. action against Hussein was warranted. Some argued at the time that the nation should withhold any such action until a firmer casus belli was in hand. To such arguments President Bush replied that he could not afford to wait and have the eventual proof of any such involvement end up being a nuclear mushroom cloud over an American city as a result of Hussein's having provided the needed wherewithal to Osama bin Laden and his al-Qaeda movement. As he later recalled in his memoirs, "if we waited for a danger to fully materialize, we would have waited too long."[91]

In the years that followed the successful three-week major combat phase of Operation Iraqi Freedom, the progressive revelations that Hussein and his regime neither possessed WMD stocks nor had any direct complicity with al-Qaeda thrust the nation into an acrimonious debate over the wisdom of the administration's decision to go to war in the first place. That debate grew all the more heated with the steadily mounting incidence of American and allied combat fatalities that were incurred by mid-2011 as a result of the festering insurgency and sectarian violence that ensued in Iraq for more than five years after the war's initial phase ended in early April 2003. These and other untoward developments that have occurred in the region since Hussein's fall have led a growing number of informed and responsible Americans, with the benefit of more than a decade's hindsight, to doubt now whether going to war against Iraq in 2003 was the wisest choice at the time for the nation on President Bush's part. Yet whatever position one may take with respect to that still-unsettled larger question, the now nearly forgotten three weeks of major combat that ended Hussein's rule remain a casebook example of successful joint and combined warfare at the operational and tactical levels.

An Unseen War

A novel feature of Iraqi Freedom's major combat phase in 2003 was the early decision by CENTCOM's commander, Gen. Tommy Franks, to embed civilian reporters within many of the combat units that would conduct the war in the interest of fostering journalistic accounts that were informed by firsthand observation. Unlike CENTCOM's eventual ground offensive, however, allied air operations over Iraq did not benefit from such firsthand reportage, partly because there was no easy way in which journalists could routinely fly in combat aircraft on strike missions, but even more so because various host-nation sensitivities precluded the presence of foreign journalists in CENTCOM's CAOC in Saudi Arabia and at most other forward locations throughout the region from which they could have observed the air war's conduct from the most senior level on down. As a result, of the roughly five hundred embedded reporters who accompanied U.S. combat forces altogether, fewer than thirty were assigned to U.S. Air Force units that operated from four locations in the war zone.

Because most of the media representatives were embedded within CENTCOM's ground units, the overwhelming majority of the subsequent journalistic accounts of the war were naturally ground-focused. For their part, allied air operations and their effects were all but unseen by outside observers. Furthermore, there was a greater public awareness that airpower was playing a pivotal role during Operation Desert Storm in 1991 because, for all but the last four days of that war, there was nothing else of major note by way of coalition operations to report. As a result, weapon-system video clips of precision munition attacks from the cockpit displays of coalition fighters appearing on the nightly television news did not have to compete with reporters in Kevlar helmets riding in armored fighting vehicles as the latter raced northward across the Iraqi desert toward Baghdad.

Even after CENTCOM's campaign reached peak intensity after the first few days as allied air attacks moved from fixed targets to Hussein's fielded forces, the popular image of unfolding events remained distorted because the majority of reportage was provided through the eyes of journalists who were embedded with advancing allied ground units. In light of that, it was hardly surprising in hindsight that anyone who watched the three-week offensive unfold solely through the lenses of CNN or Fox News would have been left with the impression that the war had been fought and won almost entirely by allied soldiers and marines equipped with tanks, rifles, and other appurtenances of land warfare.

To be sure, televised video clips also showed recurrent images of U.S. Navy and Marine Corps strike fighters being launched from aircraft carrier flight decks and, less frequently, of U.S. Air Force combat aircraft operating from selected forward land bases. Those images, however, conveyed no impression whatever of the full extent and accuracy of CENTCOM's bombing effort and its profound physical and psychological effects on Iraqi ground forces. Yet those effects were overwhelming in their contribution to the three-week campaign's ultimate course and outcome. As Anthony Cordesman later remarked in this regard, "the fact that so many reporters were embedded with ground forces led to a near-reversal [from Desert Storm and other past experiences] and [to] a focus on ground power. [Yet] the fact remains that it was [CENTCOM's] ability to tailor new *joint* mixes of ground-air-sea power to the needs of a particular campaign that proved decisive."[92]

Effects of the Air Offensive

In a telling characterization of the air war's cumulative impact on the three-week campaign, an Australian analyst writing as the major combat phase of Iraqi Freedom was nearing its end noted that "the coalition air fleet has, to date, accounted for most of the heavy damage to the Iraqi land force. Often the ground force only mops up remnants left after sustained battlefield air strikes." This writer went on to portray the plains of the Tigris and Euphrates Rivers south of Baghdad as "an enormous kill zone for an ongoing aerial turkey shoot unseen since 1991."[93]

After Hussein's regime fell, a team sent in by U.S. Joint Forces Command (JFCOM) to interrogate captured Iraqi army leaders got a firsthand confirmation of these statements. One Iraqi general told JFCOM's interrogators that the main result of the air attacks had been to make every soldier feel as if he was in "a sniper's sight."[94] As this division commander later said to JFCOM's interviewers,

> the air attacks were the most effective message.... Overall, [the air attacks] had a terrible effect on us. I started the war with 13,000 soldiers. By the time we had orders to pull back to Baghdad, I had less than 2,000; by the time we were in position in Baghdad, I had less than 1,000.... When my division pulled back across the Diyala bridge, of the more than 500 armored vehicles assigned to me before the war, I was able to get fifty or so across the bridge. Most were destroyed or abandoned on the east side of the Diyala River.[95]

JFCOM's analysts later concluded from their interviews with Iraqi officers that "in effect, precision airpower and the fear it engendered [had] made an entire division of the Republican Guard combat-ineffective."[96] One could fairly render the same observation across the board with regard to the counter-land portion of CENTCOM's air operations throughout the campaign.

A True Joint Campaign

Unlike the first Persian Gulf War of 1991, Operation Iraqi Freedom's major combat phase was not principally an air war, even though allied airpower—

including the critically important air- and space-based ISR aspects of it—contributed significantly toward setting the conditions for its outcome. Neither, however, was it predominantly a ground combat affair, despite the fact that nearly all writings about it thus far, even this many years later, have focused almost exclusively on the land portion of the three-week campaign.

In fact, leaving aside its grossly inadequate resourcing at the strategic level by the Bush administration when it came to hedging against the likely needs of postcampaign stabilization, the offensive that brought down Saddam Hussein and his regime was, at the more operational and tactical levels, an all-but-flawless undertaking that included not just CENTCOM's land component but also the indispensable involvement of virtually the entire spectrum of allied air, maritime, and space capabilities. Just as the regime's undoing could not have occurred without a substantial allied ground presence, the land offensive could not have succeeded with such speed and such a relatively small loss of friendly life to direct enemy action (only 108 American and 27 British military personnel) without the contribution of allied airpower toward establishing prompt air supremacy over Iraq and then beating down enemy ground forces to a point where they lost both their will and their capacity to continue fighting.

By the same token, the rapid allied ground advance could not have progressed from Kuwait to the heart of Baghdad in less than three weeks without the essential contribution of the ISR portion of the air- and space-power equation in providing the coalition's land commanders the needed confidence that their exposed flanks were free of threats on either side, thanks to allied air attacks keeping the enemy pinned down and unable to fight as a coherent entity. That relentlessly unblinking ISR eye over the war zone gave commanders at the brigade level and above not just the proverbial ability to "see over the next hill" but also a high-fidelity picture of the entire Iraqi battlespace along their line of northward movement.

The major combat phase of Operation Iraqi Freedom was a true team effort in which all force elements played influential roles and in which, in the apt words of two historians writing an early synopsis of the campaign, there was "little of the petty parochialism that too often marks interservice relations within the [Washington] Beltway."[97] Speaking as CENTCOM's maritime component commander, Vice Adm. Timothy Keating characterized the operational payoff of this unusual interservice amity as "joint warfighting at the highest form of the art I'd ever seen. . . . There was understanding, friendship, familiarity, and trust among all the services and special forces working for General Franks. He did, in my view, a remarkable job of engendering that friendship, camaraderie, and trust. In fact, he insisted on it. . . . There was no service equity infighting—zero."[98]

Breakthrough Achievements

Viewed in hindsight, the major combat phase of Operation Iraqi Freedom was more than just a preventive joint and combined exercise in regime takedown. It also turned out to have been yet another live battle laboratory for refining some novel approaches to air warfare that had first been conceptualized and applied during Operation Enduring Freedom in Afghanistan two years before.

To begin with, a major improvement during the preceding year in the trust relationship between President Bush and CENTCOM's commander, General Franks, as well as between General Franks and the air component's commander, Lt. Gen. T. Michael "Buzz" Moseley, now allowed General Moseley essentially full autonomy in approving target nominations. It also enabled an automatic delegation arrangement from CENTCOM to the CAOC for nearly all target categories, if only because there were too many targets and aim points to be struck on short notice each day to lend themselves to detailed micromanagement from above.

On the trust issue, General Moseley himself later recalled that the good working relations between himself and General Franks (and between CENTCOM and its air component more generally) had become so solidified after the last weeks of major combat in Afghanistan that once the first night of full-scale air operations was under way, CENTCOM's director of operations back at MacDill Air Force Base in Florida, Maj. Gen. Gene Renuart, pressed him almost plaintively for an update by asking, "Will you tell us what you're bombing when you get a chance?" With regard to this significant improvement in the CAOC's freedom of action in setting the pace and focus of strike operations compared to the first halting weeks of Operation Enduring Freedom, General Moseley frankly characterized the earlier air war over Afghanistan as "the JV [junior varsity] scrimmage" for the more complex and consequential major combat phase of Iraqi Freedom that followed a year later. Of the substantial improvement in joint-force performance that the latter experience reflected, he further stressed, as perhaps the single most basic operational-level teaching of the three-week campaign, that "you learn to fight by fighting."[99]

In its execution of the campaign plan, CENTCOM enjoyed complete control of the air over Iraq essentially from the opening moments of formal combat onward. The earlier Desert Storm experience started out with thirty-eight days of air-only operations that focused mainly on suppressing the Iraqi air force and Iraq's ground-based IADS until the campaign could finally proceed to attack Hussein's forces in and near Kuwait. By contrast, Iraqi Freedom began with allied air superiority and moved swiftly to air dominance, thanks to more than a decade of prior Northern and Southern Watch operations to enforce the UN-imposed no-fly zones over northern and southern Iraq, plus seven months of escalated attacks in connection with those operations under the rubric of the precursor Operation Southern Focus before the start of formal combat to further degrade Iraq's IADS and prepare the battlespace for the impending second Gulf war.

During his postcampaign wrap-up briefing at a conference attended by working-level air-war participants at all echelons who had gathered at Nellis Air Force Base, Nevada, in July 2003 to assess and document the air war's main events, General Moseley put forward a long list of accomplishments that he personally deemed to have been CENTCOM initiatives that had worked especially well. At the top of his list, he put General Franks' campaign plan that, in his view, was distinguished by an unprecedented level of jointness and coalition cooperation. He further noted the close integration of air and SOFs, the air component's ability to operate deep inside defended Iraqi airspace from the campaign's opening moments, and the land component's air-enabled march to Baghdad in what became, in the end, the fastest mechanized ground advance ever. Finally, he singled out the air component's total crushing of the Iraqi air force, navy, Republican Guard, Special Republican Guard, and Special Security Organization as functioning entities and its all but complete dismantling of Iraq's command-and-control network.[100]

Nevertheless, although the campaign set new records for air warfare achievement, its execution was not without shortfalls in performance that were judged by General Moseley to have been disappointments. In this regard, he spotlighted a number of activities that, in his view, "worked less well," including insufficiently timely delivery of accurate battle damage assessment, inadequate transfer of information between the CAOC and airborne aircraft, inefficient management of CAS in the battlespace controlled by the Army's V Corps, and a totally unsatisfactory performance by the firing logic and deconfliction procedures of the Army's Patriot surface-to-air missile system that had occasioned two (and nearly three) allied fighters having been inadvertently downed with a loss of three crew members. In the end, however, a comprehensive assessment conducted by the U.S. Air Force's Air Combat Command concluded that new levels of achievement shown by allied air forces while pursuing CENTCOM's goals had included the early establishment of complete and uncontested control of the air; a dominance of mass precision; and the unprecedented rapidity of combat action, connectivity and integration of ISR and command and control, efficacy of joint warfare, and service flexibility in rapid adaptation throughout the campaign.[101]

As for the tangible results made possible by this uniquely effective performance, Air Combat Command's review concluded that "the coordinated use of coalition airpower quickly created the conditions that allowed land forces to achieve high rates of maneuver and tempo in response to enemy activity."

It further observed: "Captured senior Iraqi General Staff officers reported that the fighting effectiveness of the Republican Guard divisions had been largely destroyed by air strikes."[102] Essentially confirming this observation, Col. William Grimsley, commander of the 1st Brigade of the U.S. Army's 3rd Infantry Division, later recalled: "We never really found any cohesive unit of any brigade, of any Republican Guard division."[103]

A Failure of Prior Resourcing

Unfortunately, this remarkable story about the substantial advances registered in American and allied air warfare capability since the first Gulf War of 1991 was almost completely overshadowed for nearly five years after the coalition's takedown of Hussein's regime by the seemingly unending postcampaign insurgency and sectarian violence in Iraq that dominated the world's headlines every day from months into years thereafter. Only in 2007 did Gen. David Petraeus, with President Bush's approval, finally develop and implement a new approach aimed at providing genuine security to the Iraqi people to supplant the more heavy-handed approach that a succession of previous U.S. Army joint-force commanders had sought to apply, to no avail, throughout the preceding four years of the allied occupation of Iraq. The steadily mounting political, economic, and human costs of that deadly turmoil tended, for a disturbingly long time, to render the initial three-week campaign in March and April 2003 that drove out Hussein's regime an all-but-forgotten achievement.

Whether or not one believes today that Washington's going to war against Iraq was in the best interest of American and international security to begin with, the latest consensus among most informed commentators is that CENTCOM's campaign plan, abetted and approved by the Bush administration, completely failed to address the needs of postcampaign stabilization. That manifest failure, along with subsequent sins of commission on the administration's part such as the ill-advised wholesale dismantling of the Iraqi army and police force and its forced displacement of all Iraqi civil servants with any senior Ba'ath Party connections into the ranks of the unemployed after Hussein's regime was toppled, aggressively ignored the most fundamental tenet of democratic nation-building theory—namely, that an indispensable precondition of successful political modernization must be the establishment and lasting entrenchment of effective institutions of state governance.[104]

To be sure, CENTCOM's toppling of Hussein's regime had the salutary effect of bringing to an end not only the iron rule of an odious dictator who had brutalized his people for more than thirty years but also the continuing regional security challenge from Ba'athist Iraq that had occasioned a costly American and British military presence in Southwest Asia ever since the end of

Operation Desert Storm. The flawed and incomplete way in which that laudable objective was pursued, however, points up most uncompromisingly the crucial importance of never forgetting the abiding rule that no plan, however elegant, survives initial contact with the enemy. It further provides a sobering reminder that any truly exhaustive plan for a complete regime takedown must anticipate and duly invest against the most likely political hereafter in addition to merely planning the campaign's course and outcome through the major phase of combat operations. As the journalist Thomas Ricks rightly noted in his thoughtful postmortem on the American-led invasion, "speed didn't kill the enemy—it bypassed him. It won the campaign, but it didn't win the war, because the war plan was built on the mistaken strategic goal of capturing Baghdad, and it confused removing Iraq's regime with the far more difficult task of changing the entire country."[105]

The Takeaway that Matters Most

Whatever errors the Bush administration's most senior leaders may have made in planning for the campaign by having failed to insure adequately against the most likely needs of the endgame, there can be no denying that the allied combatants in all services who prosecuted the campaign at the operational and tactical levels, thanks in substantial part to the enabling contributions of CENTCOM's air component, performed in an exemplary manner when it came to the execution of Iraqi Freedom's major combat phase. As a former U.S. Marine Corps F/A-18 pilot later wrote of that experience, none of what ensued by way of the bedeviled postcampaign occupation and stabilization effort "should detract from what was done and learned during [the three weeks of major combat in] Operation Iraqi Freedom. The successes were spectacular in a way that was unlike anything seen before."[106]

In achieving unprecedented levels of combat performance, allied airpower was crucial in setting the conditions for the campaign's rapid conclusion. In contributing to that outcome, moreover, it did not merely "support" friendly land operations by "softening up" the enemy's ground forces. Quite to the contrary, it conducted wholesale destruction of Iraqi ground units both prior to and independently of allied land action. On other occasions, it both supported allied land actions and in turn was supported by them in shaping enemy force dispositions for more effective attack from the air. The intended effect of allied air operations, which the air component ultimately achieved, was to facilitate the quickest possible capture of Baghdad without the occurrence of any major head-to-head battles between allied and Iraqi ground forces.

With respect to the air component's contribution toward that outcome, it bears stressing that its performance bore powerful witness not only to the many investments that the U.S. Air Force, Navy, and Marine Corps, along with their British and Australian counterparts, had made in the hardware ingredients of their combat repertoires since Desert Storm but also to such crucial intangibles as the cutting-edge aircrew training at the postgraduate level that had been provided by the Air Force Weapons School, the Naval Strike and Air Warfare Center, and Marine Aviation Weapons and Tactics Squadron One. The air component's banner performance further resulted from the repetitive case-hardening of allied aircrews and their commanders that had been inculcated at all levels over the course of the preceding decade through recurrent realistic large-force training exercises conducted both day and night, exacting operational readiness inspections and tactical evaluations at regular intervals in between, unrelenting frankness in training mission debriefings, and continuous joint and combined real-world enforcement of the northern and southern no-fly zones over Iraq for nearly a decade. All of that finally culminated in an opportunity for CENTCOM's air component to exercise those many investments in high-intensity combat under the leadership of an able and aggressive commander and with the help of the most experienced CAOC staff in the history of air warfare.[107]

OPERATIONS ODYSSEY DAWN AND UNIFIED PROTECTOR

Nearly a decade later, beginning in Tunisia in mid-December 2010, a spontaneous popular uprising called the Arab Spring spread across North Africa like wildfire, driving out the existing autocratic regimes in Tunisia and Egypt within weeks. Inspired by those examples, a similar regional quest for democracy showed its first stirrings two months thereafter in Libya's second-largest city of Benghazi. In that instance, however, Libya's long-time dictator, Col. Muammar Gaddafi, swore to crush the rebellion, threatening to pursue the rebels "house by house" in a crackdown that would "show no mercy" if they failed to back down.[108] At the start of this nascent movement, the poorly organized Libyan resistance was no match for Gaddafi's forces, with their far superior firepower both on the ground and in the air. The mounting showdown, which soon escalated into wanton bombing of helpless civilians by Gaddafi's air force, quickly became a humanitarian crisis in the making that begged for outside intervention.

Having previously reversed a long-standing Gaullist stance under the pro-American leadership of French president Nicolas Sarkozy four years before by rejoining NATO's military command structure in 2007, France took the lead, along with the United Kingdom, in pressing for the establishment of a no-fly zone over Libya to prevent Gaddafi from any further use of his air force against the mounting resistance. On March 12, 2011, the Arab League, in a major first for the organization, endorsed France's proposal for such a zone to be maintained by a coalition of the willing in support of the Libyan National Transitional Council that had recently emerged and coalesced in response to Gaddafi's repression.

At first the United States was disinclined to intervene, with Secretary of Defense Robert Gates insisting that "what was happening in Libya was not a vital interest of the United States." As Gates later put that conviction in his memoirs, he was "running out of patience ... with people blithely talking about the use of military force as though it were some kind of video game."[109] On March 19, however, at a summit meeting hastily convened in Paris, a quorum of concerned nations agreed to undertake prompt action against Gaddafi's forces that were advancing rapidly on the resistance. The same day, President Obama reversed his administration's earlier unwillingness to engage in the Libyan situation and joined the coalition to enforce UNSCR 1973, which had been passed two days before and which aimed at preventing Gaddafi from conducting air strikes against antiregime forces in Benghazi and Tripoli. In addition to allowing for the imposition of a no-fly zone over northern Libya, UNSCR 1973 authorized UN member states to impose and enforce an arms embargo against Libya and to employ any and all other measures deemed necessary short of actual foreign occupation to protect Libyan civilians from Gaddafi's depredations.[110]

Genesis of the Campaign

The U.S.-led coalition's first move was its activation of Joint Task Force (JTF) Odyssey Dawn as a contingency measure on March 3, two weeks before UNSCR 1973 was issued. The coalition's use of force against Gaddafi soon to follow was to be air-only by express decree, with the enabling Security Council resolution having ruled out any allied ground combat involvement. President Obama echoed that UN ruling a day later by declaring categorically that "the United States is not going to deploy ground troops into Libya."[111] Still embroiled in operations in Iraq and Afghanistan, he and his administration were indisposed to enter a new fight against yet another Islamic state and sought from the very start to hand control of it over to NATO as soon as possible.

In the campaign's first kinetic move, French Air Force Rafale and Mirage 2000 fighters struck and destroyed several government armored vehicles in the early afternoon of March 19 to head off an imminent threat of beleaguered rebel forces being slaughtered by Gaddafi's army. The avowed aim of that opening move, as one assessment later put it, was "to produce an immediate impact on the ground."[112] The next installment in Operation Odyssey Dawn, as the campaign's initial phase was dubbed, was a concerted aerial offensive beginning later that night and conducted largely by U.S. forces against Libya's Soviet-style

IADS as a precursor to establishing a no-fly zone over the entire northern stretch of Libya from its western to eastern borders.

Because the U.S. intelligence community had paid so little attention to Libya throughout the preceding decade due to its preoccupation with supporting ongoing operations in Iraq and Afghanistan as well as to the easing of tensions with Libya that had followed in the wake of Gaddafi's abandonment of his pursuit of WMD after Saddam Hussein's toppling in 2003, the provision of up-to-date information on Libya's IADS capabilities to U.S. attack planners and aircrews on such short notice proved to be all but impossible. As a result, both were forced to hedge on the worst-case side in their tactics development and weaponeering. Further complicating this challenge was the fact that the formidable Soviet long-range SA-5 SAM that dominated Libya's IADS had never before been engaged by U.S. forces in actual combat. For both of these reasons, and because the attack would be the first time that American aircrews would go up against a full-scale enemy IADS since the opening night of Operation Iraqi Freedom in 2003, attack planners overinsured in the number and types of platforms and weapons they allocated against Libya's acquisition and tracking radars, SAM sites, and fighter aircraft dispersed in hardened shelters.

The first round of the IADS takedown featured a coordinated attack against Gaddafi's SAM sites and radars by 112 TLAMs launched by U.S. and British destroyers and submarines that were positioned offshore in the Mediterranean, followed by three U.S. Air Force B-2 stealth bombers, each loaded with sixteen 2,000-pound JDAMs, that flew nonstop from Whiteman Air Force Base, Missouri, for precision attacks against forty-five shelters that harbored Gaddafi's MiG-23, Su-22, and Su-24 fighters. By the end of their third day, the JTF commander for Odyssey Dawn, Adm. Samuel Locklear, reported that these attacks had "rendered Gaddafi's long-range air defenses and his air force largely ineffective."[113]

U.S. Air Force F-15Es and F-16CJs operating out of the United Kingdom and Germany then struck Libyan army troops that were marshaling along the approach to Benghazi. Sea-based U.S. Marine Corps AV-8B Harriers from the amphibious assault ship USS *Kearsarge* conducted similar strikes against regime forces, with supporting electronic jamming of Libyan communications provided by U.S. Navy E/A-18Gs operating out of Aviano Air Base, Italy. The main goal of these follow-on attacks was to prevent Gaddafi's forces from savaging innocent Libyan civilians, with the overarching mission imperative being the strict avoidance of any harm done to noncombatants and civilian infrastructure. None of Gaddafi's fighter aircraft ever rose to challenge these operations, although the Libyan air force did launch a single Galeb jet trainer over Misrata on March 24, with French Rafales destroying it on the ground soon after it landed. Because of the considerable distances to prospective targets in northern Libya, U.S. and allied aircrews operating out of land bases in the region flew combat missions averaging eight hours in duration and requiring as many as five in-flight refuelings to support just one hour on station.[114]

In all, Operation Odyssey Dawn lasted less than two weeks. The administration's intent from the start was to front-load the American contribution into that initial U.S.-led effort and then, after NATO assumed the lead role, to provide only unique U.S. air assets that the other allies largely lacked, such as AWACS, JSTARS, the U-2, and tankers. A particularly notable achievement on the diplomatic side of its planning for Odyssey Dawn was the administration's successful organization of a coalition of the willing of fifteen participating nations within just a few scant weeks.[115]

From American to NATO Leadership

On March 31 combat operations against Gaddafi shifted from Odyssey Dawn into a NATO-led effort code-named Operation Unified Protector. That expanded undertaking—which now included the United States in a subordinate role, at least nominally—entailed the first significant NATO air endeavor to have taken place since Operation Allied Force a dozen years before. One of its many distinguishing features was its enlistment of a uniquely diverse multinational spectrum of air arms that included not only the U.S. Air Force, Navy, and Marine Corps and, under NATO's auspices, the Royal Air Force, Royal Canadian Air Force, Royal Danish Air Force, Royal Norwegian Air Force, Italian Air Force, Royal Netherlands Air Force, Turkish Air Force, Spanish Air Force, and Belgian Air Force, but also the Qatar Emiri Air Force, United Arab Emirates Air Force, Royal Jordanian Air Force, and Swedish Air Force. Participating combat and combat-support aircraft operated from land bases in Crete, Cyprus, Greece, Italy, France, Spain, and the United Kingdom. In addition, sea-based strike operations were conducted by French Navy Rafales and Super Étendards from the carrier *Charles de Gaulle*, with Marine Corps AV-8Bs continuing for a limited time to fly ground-attack sorties from *Kearsarge*.

Once it was up and running by early April, Unified Protector became the first air offensive since the Cold War's end in which NATO European and other participating air forces carried most of the operational load. It also represented the first time since World War II when a combat operation involving U.S. participation saw non-American airpower making up as large a percentage of the total as it did in the campaign against Gaddafi. In that regard, the Libyan air war will most likely be remembered by at least some as the first-ever instance of the United States' having consciously chosen in such a situation to "lead from behind," as one unnamed administration official, no doubt with subsequent remorse and regret, publicly characterized Obama's unenthusiastic and indifferent approach to the campaign as it was nearing full swing.[116]

At about the time NATO assumed the lead role in the campaign, Gaddafi's forces had regained their earlier combat footing and were configuring to resume their offensive against the resistance. That meant that the operation's end was nowhere in sight for some time yet to come. Regime forces had also learned the hard way from the two weeks of pounding they had already sustained during Odyssey Dawn that their best chance of minimizing the effectiveness of future air strikes was to alter their tactics from advancing in easily targetable formations to adopting unconventional measures to blend in with civilian vehicular traffic and to use Libyan civilians as human shields. That naturally required allied aircrews to rely more heavily than before on more fine-grained ISR for better target discrimination so as to avoid causing any noncombatant casualties. That strict requirement in turn added considerably to the time required for coalition planners and aircrews to identify, target, and engage Gaddafi's troops, who were often closely commingled with resistance fighters on the ground. It also made for an unavoidable prolongation of the campaign.

In the end, opposition forces finally ran Gaddafi down and summarily killed him in his home town of Sirte on October 20, at which point the town fell into the hands of the resistance, and what was left of Gaddafi's regime promptly collapsed. With that milestone successfully passed, NATO declared Operation Unified Protector over on October 31 after seven months of sustained air operations. As in previous allied combat involvement in the Balkans in the 1990s and during the initial round of the Afghan war in 2001, airpower proved pivotal in achieving the campaign's immediate objectives, even though in this particular case, regime collapse was never an avowed goal of U.S. and NATO strategy.

Successes and Problems

This was not by any means an air-only war, and allied airpower did not determine its outcome singlehandedly. On the contrary, it was the Libyan resistance forces on the ground who took the fight to Gaddafi and brought about his eventual demise through their own increasingly effective direct action. Allied airpower, as a pronounced asymmetrical edge offered to the resistance by NATO, simply leveled the playing field by forcing the Libyan army into dismounted formations that were incapable of massing, thereby making them more exposed and susceptible to attack by rebel forces. In that regard, events were comparable to the earlier case of Operation Enduring Freedom in Afghanistan during its major combat phase in late 2001, when American airpower enabled the forces of the indigenous Northern Alliance to take on the Taliban with the help of a small contingent of allied paramilitary units and terminal air controllers working with them to identify and target enemy fighters for precision attacks from above.

Similarly, during Odyssey Dawn early on, there were reports that small teams of British Special Air Service SOF troops offered covert assistance to allied air attacks by conducting on-the-ground target location, identification, and designation, much as U.S. and allied SOF teams had done before in Afghanistan.[117] To that extent as well, friendly ground involvement was an indispensable contributor to the campaign's ultimately successful course and outcome. Yet any such SOF involvement would have entailed an extremely modest allied ground presence at best, rendering the Libyan campaign, like NATO's air war for Kosovo a dozen years before, yet another joint and combined offensive in which allied airpower achieved desired campaign goals without the need to commit any NATO conventional ground troops to the fighting.

The campaign also was conducted without any of the participating countries incurring a single casualty or losing a single aircraft to enemy fire, although one F-15E experienced an in-flight mechanical emergency during Odyssey Dawn's first week that required its two crew members to eject from the aircraft. Both did so safely and were recovered soon thereafter. The campaign as well was one of unprecedented bombing accuracy, with every munition expended having been precision guided.

As for air warfare "firsts," the campaign featured the first combat employment of the RAF's Eurofighter Typhoon, which flew both air policing and strike sorties as well as the first combat exposure for the U.S. Navy's E/A-18G in its advanced electronic warfare role. It also saw the first combat use of B-1s flying directly from the United States, striking dynamic targets in faraway Libya that were assigned as the bombers were en route and then recovering at allied forward bases in Europe. Qatar, for its part, sent six Mirage 2000 fighters to Crete and flew air policing missions over Libya from the military airfield at Souda Bay beginning on March 25, making for the first-ever combat missions flown by an Arab League country.

This is not to say, however, that NATO's air war against Gaddafi was flawlessly conducted, by any means. Most early after-action assessments portrayed the successive efforts as having been resoundingly successful. On closer examination, however, one informed appraisal rightly warned that the campaign experience "should in many ways serve as a wake-up call for everyone involved."[118] To begin with, as in the earlier case of Operation Allied Force in 1999, the extent of NATO's involvement was highly uneven. Although half of its member states contributed materially to Operation Unified Protector in one way or another, only six actually took part in kinetic strike operations. Furthermore, the performance of allied air assets and the overall efficiency of the effort were bedeviled by manifold shortcomings in such areas as force and communications interoperability, intelligence sharing, and reported shortages of PGMs in the inventories of some of the smaller allied air forces, all of which had suffered reduced annual funding throughout the preceding two decades of a "peace dividend" that had been presumed possible because of the Soviet Union's collapse. These deficiencies will need attention and rectifying, at least to some degree, if NATO is ever again to undertake a similar air operation for higher stakes. (Of course, one mitigating factor here with respect to assessed shortfalls in capability in some NATO air arms is the fact that NATO was never envisaged as going into combat, either in whole or in part, without the indispensable top cover of American involvement in a major way.)

Beyond these alliance-related concerns, because of Libya's geographic location, responsibility for the planning and conduct of Odyssey Dawn naturally fell to U.S. Africa Command (AFRICOM), which had only been established four years before and was intended mainly to serve in a humanitarian assistance role. Although its air component commander, Maj. Gen. Margaret Woodward, quickly rose to the many challenges she inherited, it became clear from the first moment the campaign was assigned to it that AFRICOM lacked the needed expertise and command-and-control wherewithal to plan and oversee a highly kinetic air war, especially on such short notice. Owing to its lack of enough properly trained and experienced personnel to conceive and conduct such a war on its own, AFRICOM's air component, called AFAFRICA, which was General Woodward's 17th Air Force headquartered at Ramstein Air Base in Germany, was obliged to call on help from the far more robust air component of U.S. European Command, which fortunately was collocated with General Woodward at Ramstein. In responding to this urgent need on AFRICOM's part, the nearby 603rd Air Operations Center supporting U.S. Air Forces in Europe found itself suddenly enlisted, in the words of one informed account, into performing "as a sort of airpower Gulliver supporting AFAFRICA's Lilliputian joust with an ogre at the edge of its own operational back yard."[119]

Furthermore, as NATO assumed responsibility for the campaign under the new rubric of Operation Unified Protector, the transfer of command-and-control oversight from AFRICOM was anything but seamless. To begin with, ongoing combat operations placed a high premium on real-time ISR in a dynamic setting dominated by a need for frequent time-sensitive targeting. In this crucial mission application, most of the non-U.S. staff officers assigned to NATO's combined force air component (CFAC) were at a distinct disadvantage when it came to being familiar with the practices and procedures of the CFAC's air operations center from previous hands-on experience.

Compounding this source of frustration, the distances from the available bed-down airfields in the region to the coastal span of Libya covered by the no-fly zone was such that nearly all of the campaign's strike sorties depended on in-flight refueling, and most of the available tankers arrived in theater only after the heaviest combat operations in Odyssey Dawn had been completed. The lack of enough tanker and ISR aircraft on the part of many of the participating NATO countries made for what one observer called a "disequilibrium between the spear and the shaft" in their respective air arms that promised to hinder any future operations on their part that did not feature strong American involvement.[120] Even during the NATO-led Operation Unified Protector, the United States provided 75 percent of the ISR and tanker sorties and most of the experienced targeteers and weapons experts who populated the CFAC.

In addition, as was the case before in Operations Allied Force, Enduring Freedom, and Iraqi Freedom, information sharing between and among the allies was hampered by multiple national restrictions regarding allowable access, with few workarounds to resolve this problem having been established and sustained by the United States and its NATO partners since those campaigns. There also was a lack of familiarity on the part of the American airmen who occupied most of the CFAC's billets with various allied aircraft systems, communications capabilities, and data-link arrangements.

Finally, to note but one more of the many force-integration and compatibility issues encountered by the various participants in Unified Protector, there were reports of increasingly severe shortages of precision munitions among some of the involved air forces as the campaign continued on from weeks to months.[121] Fortunately on this count, the air component commander for the NATO-led campaign, Lt. Gen. Ralph Jodice, assured all that any such shortages never impinged adversely on his day-to-day combat operations. "I never once," he said, "had to cancel or postpone a sortie because I didn't have the right munitions that I needed."[122]

On the positive side, the ingrained professionalism of the many allied liaison officers assigned to the CFAC's air operations center and their strong mutual respect and trust relationships with the American principals there helped immensely toward offsetting at least some of the material and procedural shortcomings noted earlier. Their various countries' political leaders were also uncommonly accommodating when it came to securing approvals for target nominations that might have been of less than self-evident acceptability within their respective national ROE. For example, unlike in the case of Operation Allied Force in 1999, in which pervasive top-down political oversight by the North Atlantic Council often delayed decision making with respect to target selection and approvals, most of such decisions were made by uniformed national representatives at the working level within the CFAC in Operation Unified Protector, which made for far greater target-servicing efficiency.

The War in Retrospect

In the campaign's early aftermath, most observers tended to portray it as a singularly successful allied achievement. Its two principal overseers, Ivo Daalder and Adm. James Stavridis, the U.S. permanent representative to NATO and the Supreme Allied Commander for Europe, respectively, set the tone for many subsequent assessments when they described it as a "model intervention."[123] Without question, Operations Odyssey Dawn and Unified Protector did indeed make the crucial difference in helping indigenous rebel forces successfully fend off atrocities that otherwise almost surely would have been visited upon helpless civilians by Gaddafi's forces. Furthermore, the willingness of the United States and its NATO allies and others to lend a collective hand to Libya's beleaguered civilians in the face of Gaddafi's threatened abuses, along with the measured and limited level of effort they envisaged, almost certainly ensured that the campaign would entail an effective and relatively low-cost undertaking when viewed retrospectively in the short run.

However, as a more inquiring and critical assessment concluded four years later, "this hands-off strategy [also] ensured that the subsequent political transition was chaotic" and that "instead of shielding Libya's civilians from atrocities, a nominally humanitarian intervention deepened societal cleavages that continue to feed civil strife to this day."[124] In a sad affirmation of this harsh conclusion, four years after Gaddafi was toppled by the resistance with the help of NATO and other coalition air arms, the UN support mission in Libya was reluctantly forced to conclude from events that had transpired there since the end of Unified Protector that it had little to show for its effort to rebuild the failed state that Libya had become in the campaign's early aftermath.

The failure of the campaign's political planners to establish the needed preconditions for ensuring the growth of effective institutions of state governance after the collapse of Gaddafi's regime created numerous adverse consequences for Libya. Preeminent among them, the civil disorder that ensued in the campaign's wake soon became a virtual magnet for the influx of al-Qaeda and other Islamist terrorists into the country, just as Afghanistan had been for al-Qaeda until Operation Enduring Freedom finally crushed its protectorate there in 2001. In particular, the mass migration of ISIS and like-minded jihadists into Libya that soon began, thanks to the shortsightedness of American and allied political planning for the campaign's hereafter, ultimately led to the well-planned and effective terrorist rocket and mortar assault on the American diplomatic compound in Benghazi on the symbolically important date of September 11, 2012, that resulted in the murders of Ambassador J. Christopher Stevens and three members of his security contingent.

Regarding this infamous and still-inflammatory issue in American domestic politics, former U.S. secretary of state Hillary Clinton, who had aggressively backed the campaign against Gaddafi going into it, had the temerity to characterize it in retrospect more than three years *after* the subsequent fatal assault on the U.S. consulate that took place under her watch as an American exercise in "smart power at its best."[125] Yet, however flawless the campaign's planning and conduct may have been from a short-term operational and tactical perspective, it fell so far short of its hoped-for promise in terms of ultimate *strategic* achievement that once its final history is written, it will more likely be fairly judged an "abject failure," as another critical assessment described it four years later.[126]

Looking back on the campaign as a testament to "the limits of liberal intervention," one postmortem review of the experience noted that the effort's overarching promise was to provide "an opening toward a richer and more meaningful kind of freedom that might allow Libya's new citizens to go about their lives with less fear and greater dignity."[127] Such a hoped-for outcome, however, was not to be realized in the end—nor could it possibly have been, given the absence of any effective top-down strategic guidance given to the campaign's planners beyond its immediate stated goal of stopping Gaddafi's forces from committing here-and-now atrocities against innocent Libyan civilians. On this important count, barely a week into Odyssey Dawn, the editor of the respected journal *Foreign Affairs* presciently warned that the Obama administration had "launched the United States into battle with no clear vision of what a successful and stable outcome looks like."[128] True enough, any follow-through effort that might have helped more fully to meet the needs of postcampaign stabilization in Libya would almost certainly have required an American or NATO ground involvement of some sort. There was no way, however, that the Obama administration or any of its NATO allies would have committed to such an open-ended and risky gamble.

Assessing Operations Odyssey Dawn and Unified Protector more narrowly as case studies in airpower employment, those two campaigns in close succession did not depart in any fundamental way from the six previous American and NATO air combat experiences since 1991 explored earlier. Nor did they pioneer any significant new tactical applications with respect to the diverse roles played by the various fighters, bombers, ISR platforms, mobility aircraft, and myriad space assets on orbit that took part in the fighting. In the latter regard, as the most thorough assessment of the two campaigns to date rightly observed, "the more one knew about airpower, [and] particularly about recent developments in airpower, the less surprising the course and outcome of the Libyan air campaign and broader war. The Gulf War [of 1991], Bosnia, Kosovo, and the opening phase of Operation Enduring Freedom all provided signposts on the road to Libya."[129] That said, the campaign *did* represent one major milestone with respect to the continuing evolution of air warfare. And that was the indisputable reminder it offered to airpower's most vocal detractors—that after a decade of low-intensity counterinsurgency operations in Iraq and Afghanistan in which kinetic air employment had seemingly been overtaken once and for all by more prosaic irregular combat on the ground, those who for a time had concluded so self-assuredly that modern high-technology airpower had finally outlived its relevance were completely misguided in propounding that false and baseless claim.

OPERATION INHERENT RESOLVE

The most recent case of U.S. and NATO air warfare since Operation Desert Storm entails the still-ongoing American-led effort against the self-proclaimed Islamic State in Iraq and Syria (ISIS), a uniquely abhorrent jihadist movement that first erupted in the ungoverned spaces that were opened up in 2012 by the steadily intensifying Syrian civil war. The movement soon thereafter metastasized into the power vacuum that had previously been created by the Obama administration's withdrawal of all remaining U.S. troops from Iraq at the end of 2011. The administration's response to the manifold abuses against innocent civilians subsequently perpetrated by ISIS throughout the portions of Iraq that it controlled was slow to gain headway at first. It finally began with limited U.S. air strikes against ISIS positions in Iraq on August 8, 2014, that President Obama, in announcing them the day before, characterized *not* as the start of a major move to defeat the Islamist movement but simply as an event-driven and specifically targeted reaction intended to "protect . . . American [diplomatic] personnel" in the area and as "a humanitarian effort to save thousands of civilians . . . trapped on a mountain without food and water."[130]

The strikes that took place the next day were conducted by U.S. Navy F/A-18s operating from the aircraft carrier USS *George H. W. Bush* and delivering 500-pound LGBs, along with U.S. Air Force MQ-1 Predator RPAs firing Hellfire missiles, against ISIS positions along the approach to the Kurdish capital of Erbil in northern Iraq. Those attacks were solely intended to turn back an imminent ISIS advance on the city and to break the siege that the jihadist militia had imposed on tens of thousands of Yazidi refugees who had been stranded on nearby Sinjar Mountain in the wake of the assault.[131] A week later continued air strikes against selected ISIS targets, with the largely uncoordinated support of able Kurdish *peshmerga* combatants on the ground, finally allowed 35,000 to 45,000 of the stranded refugees to be evacuated from the mountain and returned to their homes.[132] The strikes constituted the first American use of kinetic airpower in Iraq since the departure of the last U.S. troops there nearly three years before.[133]

Fast-forwarding more than two years to this writing, that latest U.S.-led air war has continued to play itself out in its now-familiar, overly measured, and halting way. More to the point, it is still being conducted with a conspicuous lack of evident seriousness and senior leadership determination when judged against the standards of earlier air wars going back to Desert Storm, albeit with an encouraging and fortunately sustained recent uptick in its initially lethargic pace, thanks to an accumulation of egregious outrages that the Obama administration could no longer ignore, committed in close succession both in the immediate region and beyond and by ISIS directly or by terrorists acting in its name beginning in late 2015. Yet, despite this long-overdue ramping up of the intensity of daily air strikes and an associated belated concentration on more significant enemy targets more than a year after its start, the effort still shows little progress from an overall campaign perspective and still lacks a coherent strategy aimed at seeking realistic and achievable goals any time soon. Since it remains an ongoing endeavor with no end yet in sight, it can only be addressed here insofar as it has taken place to date.

How the ISIS Challenge Arose

As the then-controversial troop surge that eventually brought a modicum of internal order and stability to Iraq was showing its first signs of promise in July 2007, President Bush offered during a meeting with White House reporters what, in retrospect, turned out to have been a remarkably prophetic warning:

> I know some in Washington would like us to start leaving Iraq now. To begin withdrawing before our commanders tell us we're ready would be dangerous for Iraq, for the region and for the United States. It would mean surrendering the future of Iraq to Al-Qaeda. It would mean that we'd be risking mass killings on a horrific scale. It would mean we'd allow the terrorists to establish a safe haven in Iraq to replace the one they lost in Afghanistan. It would mean increasing the probability that American troops would have to return at some later date to confront an enemy that is even more dangerous.[134]

Today, with the passage of nearly nine troubled years in the region, that well-advised warning has proven prescient in every respect.

By way of essential background to the continuing chaos in Iraq and Syria that enabled the rise of ISIS in the first place, President Obama announced a month after his inauguration in January 2009 that he would end the American combat role in Iraq on August 31, 2010. He further swore to make good on his earlier campaign pledge to end the Iraq war once and for all by withdrawing all remaining U.S. troops from the country by the end of 2011 unless an acceptable status-of-forces agreement could be reached with the government of Prime Minister Nouri al-Maliki. Such an agreement would allow for a continued American military stabilizing presence in Iraq for as long as might be needed to offset persistent Iraqi shortcomings in the needed wherewithal for preventing a resumption of the insurgency that had nearly destroyed the country after the war's major combat phase ended in 2003.

On this important count, a well-informed assessment remarked in late 2014, after the initial gains of ISIS had become undeniable to all, that "everything that [had] happened [in Iraq] since 2011 was foreseeable—and, in fact, was foreseen by U.S. military planners and commanders, who years earlier [had] cautioned against the complete withdrawal of the nearly 50,000 U.S. troops that still remained in Iraq in 2011." Yet despite that good counsel, this observer went on to say, "Obama and senior members of his national security team [failed] to reach an agreement with the government of Iraq that would have allowed a residual U.S. force to remain there temporarily, and also [failed] to establish a strategy for how to leave Iraq in a manner that would secure the gains made" during the ensuing years since the successful 2007 U.S. troop surge. All of that, he concluded, "set the stage for the rapid advance of ISIS and the potential disintegration of the country."[135]

With respect to the ensuing wreckage in the region that followed President Obama's withdrawal of all remaining U.S. troops from Iraq, some of his supporters have lately offered the all-too-facile rationalization after the fact that Obama "had no choice in the matter," since the agreement that President Bush had signed with al-Maliki's government in 2008 had demanded that all U.S. forces leave Iraq no later than December 31, 2011. Any amendments to that agreement would have required Iraqi acceptance of a U.S. demand that American troops be granted immunity from Iraqi law, something to which no factions in Iraq's parliament allegedly would have agreed.[136] Nevertheless, President Obama did not pursue a determined effort toward that end, despite the fact that many Iraqi government officials and military leaders had privately voiced their support for a continued post-2011 American military presence in the country. Moreover, the commander of U.S. forces in Iraq at the time, Lt. Gen. Lloyd Austin, had recommended a residual force of more than 20,000 U.S. troops remaining in Iraq to help the Iraqi Security Forces maintain domestic order and keep what was left of the by-then largely vanquished al-Qaeda in Iraq on the run.[137]

Owing in large part to that failure, not long after the last U.S. soldier had left Iraq, a knowledgeable reporter wrote from firsthand experience how "the country [had] become something close to a failed state." This commentator went on to note that even as early as 2009, the Obama administration had abandoned any further interest in inculcating democratic values in the still-embryonic post-Hussein Iraqi government and had instead directed all of its energies toward the country's mercurial Prime Minister al-Maliki "so that it could more easily withdraw U.S. forces." The net result was that the administration failed to preserve the significant gains finally achieved after exorbitant sunk cost by President Bush's 2007 troop surge, a result that ultimately "would mark a total defeat for the United States in terms of its aims for the country."[138] With respect to this unfortunate and avoidable denouement, former Secretary of Defense Gates, who had served under both Bush and Obama, later remarked in his memoirs that the final withdrawal of all U.S. forces from Iraq "was a regrettable turn of events for our future influence in Iraq and our strategic position in the region." However, he added revealingly, "President Obama simply wanted the ... war in Iraq to be ended."[139] Gates' successor, Leon Panetta, who had just taken office when the last American troops left Iraq at the end of 2011, likewise later wrote of what he regarded as "the essential mistake of the transition in Iraq—an abrupt departure that left the United States without any presence to continue exercising influence."[140] Nearly five years after that precipitous final U.S. troop withdrawal insisted on by Obama, a universally respected British news weekly frankly characterized the president's peremptory move in informed hindsight as "reckless."[141]

The ensuing turmoil in Syria that has since provided such fertile ground for the rise of ISIS began with the onset of the Arab Spring in Tunisia at the end of 2010, which in turn prompted similar antiregime demonstrations in southern Syria that rapidly spread throughout the country. It was further aided by the vast lawless terrain created along Iraq's now unenforced and all but meaningless border with Syria when the last American combat units left on December 18, 2011. Significantly in this respect, al-Qaeda in Iraq had been all but neutralized by the time President Bush left office in 2009. Yet that jihadist organization still retained enough life to seek a new foothold in Syria, where it took full advantage of the opportunity presented to it there between 2012 and 2014 to rebrand itself as ISIS. In the process, it gained renewed strength in the now-raging Syrian civil war that Obama had refused to engage in after having first declared, and then reneged on, his avowed conviction that any use of chemical weapons by Syria's President Bashir al-Assad against innocent Syrian civilians, which actually occurred in August 2013, would constitute a "red line" for him warranting a forceful American response.

Yet even as ISIS gained in strength and capability to a point where it seized and took over the highly symbolic Iraqi city of Fallujah in early January 2014, President Obama could still say of it dismissively a week later: "The analogy we use around here [in the White House] sometimes, and I think it is accurate, is if a jayvee team puts on Lakers uniforms, that doesn't make them Kobe Bryant."[142]

The following June, however, it became ever harder for the administration to sustain that blithe and indifferent attitude when ISIS forces, now equipped with expropriated U.S.-made Iraqi M1 Abrams tanks, up-armored Humvees, and heavy weapons suddenly and unexpectedly drove into the heart of Mosul, capturing and occupying Iraq's second-largest city and causing an estimated half a million residents there to flee for their lives. In rapid succession thereafter, ISIS took over additional towns throughout Anbar Province and finally declared itself a caliphate now in control of large swaths of Syria and Iraq. Only when faced with a humanitarian crisis the following August to which he could no longer turn a blind eye did Obama finally feel compelled to make a first tentative resort to U.S. airpower on behalf of Erbil's Yazidi refugees in an eleventh-hour move to forestall an imminent catastrophe that would have been intolerable for any U.S. government. As one of the most well-informed scholarly treatments of the rise of ISIS aptly remarked of this rapid devolution of events, had this been Iraq in 2008, "the Islamic State would have been defeated. . . . But in 2014, . . . the Americans were gone, and [Iraqi] government troops could no longer pacify the Arab Sunni hinterland in western Iraq."[143]

The Air War Thus Far

In the early aftermath of the administration's initial and studiously limited air strikes in northern Iraq, its bombing of ISIS targets continued at first in just handfuls from one day to the next, with a White House feeling no evident urgency to ramp up the effort's tempo and intensity. On the contrary, President Obama stressed even before the bombing's first week had ended that "this is going to be a long-term project."[144] Later on, three weeks into his continued desultory effort against the jihadist movement, the president conceded that "we [still] don't have a strategy yet" when pressed by reporters as to his long-term intentions regarding the challenge posed by ISIS.[145]

As the administration's air strikes continued through August at a snail's pace compared to the intensity of previous air campaigns going back to Desert Storm, the United States expanded the effort by enlisting and leading an Arab coalition in attacking targets not only in Iraq but also now in Syria, with attacks carried out by supporting combat aircraft from Bahrain, Jordan, Saudi Arabia, Qatar, and the United Arab Emirates. Still, however, by the end of the effort's first month, although coalition pilots had flown 1,871 CAS, escort, and interdiction sorties against ISIS, only 280 of the strike sorties had accomplished at least 1 weapon release, making for an average of fewer than 10 aim points struck each day.

Finally, on September 10 Obama announced what he billed as his "comprehensive strategy" for dealing with ISIS, with an overarching intent to "degrade and ultimately destroy" the jihadist movement.[146] As the Clinton administration's earlier four-day Operation Desert Fox in 1998 was just getting under way, Secretary of State Albright had spoken likewise of an intent to "degrade" Iraq's presumed WMD production capabilities on the valid ground that the U.S. government lacked the needed intelligence to do anything more than that with any confidence. Yet in marked contrast to that earlier instance, Obama's resort to "degrade" as the immediate goal of his response (with "ultimately destroying" it presumably to be left to his successor at some indeterminate future date) gave every impression of being a carefully contrived rhetorical ploy intended to telegraph his unwillingness to pursue anything more than a minimalist response to the spread of ISIS throughout Iraq and Syria and eventually beyond.

Of this still-limited and uncommitted performance, Anthony Cordesman remarked in early October 2014 that it "seems to be doing too little, too slowly, failing to have the impact needed in Iraq, and drifting toward mission creep in Syria." He added that the administration's effort to date was "so small by the standard of recent [past] conflicts that it amounts to little more than military tokenism." Indeed, when compared to the Desert Storm experience, Cordesman noted that the effort against ISIS as it had progressed to date "looks like a statistical hiccup," suggesting that, if continued, it could "well be a warning that the [United States] is now embarked in leading and conducting a high-risk air campaign that will do too little and do it too slowly."[147]

Yet another telling sign of the administration's irritation at having been saddled with an inconvenient new threat to address and of its deep and abiding reluctance to come to terms with it effectively was the fact that its halting effort against ISIS went unnamed for more than two months. Only on October 15, 2014, did CENTCOM, which had been tasked with organizing and conducting the effort, finally announce that it would be known henceforth and retroactively as Operation Inherent Resolve, with that code name said to be "intended to reflect the . . . deep commitment of the U.S. and partner nations . . . to degrade and ultimately destroy ISIL [Islamic State of Iraq and the Levant, the administration's preferred alternative name for the movement]."[148]

Yet, despite that grandiose characterization, the ground truth five weeks into the effort was that CENTCOM had conducted a total of just 412 strike sorties against an expanding ISIS that now controlled some 50,000 square miles of Iraq and Syria, making for an average of just 7 strike sorties a day. In contrast, during the same length of time, the allied coalition in Operation Desert Storm flew 48,224 strike sorties in all for a daily average of around a thousand a day. That contrast prompted two former U.S. Air Force airmen and later Washington-based defense analysts to suggest that the main underlying motivation behind the administration's approach to countering ISIS seemed to be "to apply the least amount of force possible while still claiming credit for doing something about the Islamic State."[149]

Eight months later, commenting on a map released by the Pentagon in early April 2015 that purportedly showed that ISIS was no longer able to operate in 25 to 30 percent of the populated areas of Iraq and Syria it formerly held, observant critics dismissed the claim as misleading in that it failed to show other parts of the two countries in which ISIS had made substantial gains since the bombing began the year before. As for the Defense Department's failure also to show the continued ability of ISIS to conduct offensive operations in those parts of Iraq and Syria that it still controlled, a visiting fellow at the Brookings Institution's Doha Center in Qatar, Charles Lister, concluded that "in this respect, I'd say ISIS has been very minimally challenged since August 2014."[150]

As that year was drawing to a close, U.S. government officials were reportedly projecting that the ongoing strikes against ISIS might have to continue for at least 3 more years.[151] The following August, more than a year into the still-lethargic bombing, the chairman of the JCS, Gen. Martin Dempsey, went further yet and suggested that vanquishing ISIS once and for all could eventually take up to 20 years.[152] Given the administration's minuscule level of effort up to that point, it was not hard to see why. As of mid-November 2015, U.S. and coalition aircrews had flown more than 57,000 combat and combat-support sorties into Iraq and Syria in all in their endeavor against ISIS up to that point, including nearly 8,300 strike sorties that had reportedly attacked some 16,000 individual ISIS target aim points. However, that made for an average of fewer than 20 strike sorties a day over a course of 450 days, yet at an assessed overall cost of $5 billion, or $11 million a day, for the little gain they had achieved.[153] Nearly the same level of kinetic output was reached within the first week of Operation Desert Storm.

Moreover, the roster of participants in the air war against ISIS thus far has made for a coalition far more in name than in fact. In all, since the effort began in August 2014, fourteen foreign air arms have taken part at one time or another in strike operations against ISIS targets in Iraq and Syria, including those from Australia, Britain, Bahrain, Belgium, Canada, Denmark, France, Jordan, Morocco, the Netherlands, Qatar, Saudi Arabia, Turkey, and the United Arab Emirates. By far the majority of those operations, however, have been conducted by the United States, which by the end of 2015 had flown 94 percent of all strike sorties into Syria and 78 percent of those into Iraq.[154] This should hardly have come as any surprise, since the Obama administration to this day has yet to provide its would-be coalition partners with any incentives to run risks and incur costs that the United States itself has been unwilling to assume.

On the positive side of this otherwise undistinguished latest chapter in the history of air warfare, after seventeen months of mostly low-impact and ineffectual bombing, reenergized units of the Iraqi Security Forces finally succeeded at the end of 2015 in recapturing Ramadi, the capital city of Anbar Province that had been held by ISIS since the preceding May. Of this encouraging breakthrough, the U.S. Army colonel serving as the spokesman for Operation Inherent Resolve declared that "we're hitting them with combination punches now. They're getting hit in multiple places simultaneously."[155] He added that coalition air strikes had been responsible for 80 percent of that success and that it had been the air effort that had "really . . . enabled the Iraqi forces to move in."[156] Notably, this push for Ramadi also saw an effective use for the first time of Iraqi F-16s, whose pilots had recently been trained in the United States. The overall gain, however, as welcome as it was as a first clear sign of tangible progress at long last, raised the obvious first question as to why such a more serious and determined approach to combating ISIS had not been pursued by the Obama administration from the very start.

The Effort Assessed to Date

Operation Inherent Resolve has not been notable for having represented any major new advances in the evolution of modern airpower. It has, however, as in all earlier instances of U.S. and NATO air warfare since Desert Storm, seen the coalition's aircrews flying their day-to-day missions, along with their fellow airmen in the CAOC serving as weaponeers and planners, all working at the top of their game. This exemplary professionalism shown by all at the execution level has consistently reflected the refined skills that were first developed and assimilated by all three U.S. air services during the first decade after Vietnam and then further ingrained as their standard operating repertoire ever since.

By the same token, the still-ongoing coalition air effort against ISIS has also seen the involvement of just about every platform and weapon that might conceivably play a useful role in such an endeavor. Throughout the operation's course since its onset in early August 2014, the various combat aircraft contributing to the fight have included a total of more than two hundred F-15E, F-16, F/A-18, Mirage 2000, Rafale, Super Étendard, Tornado, Typhoon, and B-1 strikers, along with MQ-1 Predator and MQ-9 Reaper armed RPAs, supporting ISR aircraft like the U-2, JSTARS and AWACS, and an additional raft of tankers and transports that have been essential for their sustainment. Whatever else one might say about the many flaws in the way the effort has been conducted thus far with respect to its leadership and intensity, its effectiveness when it comes to putting bombs on target with consistent accuracy has in no way been compromised by any shortfalls in the available hardware or aircrew skill and proficiency.

To note one case in point here, the coalition's extensive use of the 250-pound GPS-aided GBU-39 small-diameter bomb against such ISIS targets as vehicles and tactical positions in built-up areas with innocent civilians nearby has contributed significantly to the CAOC's entirely apropos claim that the strikes conducted under its aegis to date have been "the most precise and disciplined in the history of aerial warfare."[157] As a telling measure of this laudable performance, as of the end of September 2015, U.S. and coalition forces had expended more than 20,000 precision-guided weapons against ISIS aim points in all, with that number comprising a full 99 percent of all munitions employed throughout the effort.[158]

In yet another notable milestone event, the war against ISIS has also finally seen the combat debut of the U.S. Air Force's fifth-generation F-22 stealth fighter that first entered service more than a decade ago in 2005, albeit not in the air-dominance role for which it was initially acquired but rather as a highly survivable ground-attack platform and one also mounting an unsurpassed suite of sensors for providing enhanced battlespace awareness for all players in the execution chain. These first-ever combat sorties flown by the Raptor took place during the initial night of coalition air strikes against ISIS targets in Syria on September 23, 2014, when a four-ship flight was tasked first with attacking an ISIS command post with 1,000-pound GBU-32 JDAMs and then serving as strike escorts for a B-1 attacking its own assigned targets inside Syria's well-defended airspace.[159]

Despite these and other praiseworthy aspects of the air war at the tactical level, however, the main distinguishing feature of the oxymoronic Operation Inherent Resolve from an overall campaign perspective has continued to be its manifest *absence* of any such resolve. This ironic fact has stemmed in substantial part from the imposition of stultifying constraints on the most effective use of airpower by an administration led by a president who has shown every sign of refusing to allow the sorts of measures that will be essential to defeating ISIS decisively and who instead has asked the American people for their "strategic patience" with his dilatory handling of such challenges.[160] To begin with, the administration's determination at first not to return any U.S. ground troops to Iraq instantly precluded the availability of a winning approach previously proven in Afghanistan of partnering small teams of American SOF combatants and joint terminal attack controllers with indigenous friendly ground forces—in this case, the able Kurdish *peshmerga* fighters in northern Iraq—to locate, identify, validate, and designate enemy targets in enough numbers for daily air attacks to make a real difference.

Second, in contrast to most of the previous U.S. and NATO air wars since Desert Storm, the predominant characteristic of CENTCOM's effort against ISIS to date seems to have been principally a reflexive day-to-day exercise in mindless target servicing in support of no overarching strategic course of action or clearly defined goal. Instead it has largely entailed reactive attacks against pop-up targets of opportunity in ones and twos, such as ISIS sniper positions and vehicles, as they get detected by overhead ISR platforms in the absence of friendly SOF teams and joint terminal attack controllers on the ground who can scout out and designate targets of greater significance and value. In effect, as Anthony Cordesman has wryly noted, such largely responsive strike operations with no apparent broader rhyme or reason have turned "the classic description of pointless tactical activity in counterinsurgency from 'whack a mole' to 'whack a sand castle.'"[161]

A third and most inhibiting constraint on the effort's effectiveness to date has been the uniquely stringent ROE regime imposed by a micromanaging White House that has limited the number of ISIS targets available for aerial attack each day through its absolute insistence on no civilian casualties being occasioned by any coalition weapon detonation. As a result, CENTCOM has had far fewer targets that have been eligible for attack each day than it has platforms and munitions available to engage them. This largely explains why only one out of four strike sorties flown throughout the effort's first five months actually dropped bombs on ISIS targets.[162]

These ROE, it should be added, far exceed the requirements embodied in the Laws of Armed Conflict, which insist that all reasonable measures be undertaken to avoid causing noncombatant casualties in warfare, but which also stipulate that ensuring the lives of innocent civilians instantly becomes the responsibility of any enemy who would willfully use them as human shields. International law also expressly allows for the occurrence of civilian fatalities, even if knowingly caused, should an attack meet the law's reasonable standards of proportionality that require a target's military importance to be deemed high enough to justify the possibility, or even certainty, of civilian byproduct fatalities.

With respect to Operation Inherent Resolve, however, as one analyst well put it, the highly capable ISR and strike platforms available to CENTCOM in principle have remained "tied up in obsessive platinum-standard target vetting" dictated by politically driven ROE that are "without a doubt the most obsessively restrictive of any air campaign ever fought by a U.S. coalition."[163] Most target-attack approvals are reportedly granted not in the air component's CAOC but rather by the general officer on duty in CENTCOM's U.S. Army-dominated Joint Operations Center in Baghdad. In cases involving an especially high likelihood of significant civilian casualties, a request for approval to drop may be forwarded by the Joint Operations Center up the chain of command to a more senior general at CENTCOM headquarters in Tampa, Florida, or even to senior civilian authorities in Washington in the most sensitive cases.[164]

In this needlessly exacting political and legal environment, pilots flying missions into Iraq and Syria are routinely required to have their attack requests wend their way through a maddening gauntlet of bureaucratic wickets before they can receive approval to bomb or strafe a lucrative but possibly also fleeting target. One U.S. Air Force A-10 pilot complained frankly of this onerous constraint early on in a private e-mail to a friend:

> I've never been more frustrated in my career. After thirteen years of the mind-numbing low-intensity conflict in Afghanistan, I've never seen the knife more dull. All the hard lessons learned in Vietnam and fixed during the first Gulf war have been unlearned again. The level of centralized execution, bureaucracy, and politics is staggering. . . . In most cases, unless a general officer can look at a video picture from a UAV [unmanned aerial vehicle] over a satellite link, I cannot get authority to engage. I've spent many hours staring through a targeting pod screen in my cockpit, watching ISIS sh - - heads perpetrate their acts until my eyes bleed, without being able to do anything about it. The institutional fear of making a mistake that has crept into the central mindset of the military leadership is endemic. We have not taken the fight to these guys. We haven't targeted their centers of gravity in Raqqa. All the roads between Syria and Iraq are still intact with trucks flowing freely. The other night I watched a couple hundred small tanker trucks lined up at an oilfield in ISIS-held northeast Syria. . . . It's not uncommon to wait several hours overhead a suspected target for someone to make a decision to engage or not. It feels like we are simply using the constructs built up in Afghanistan, which was a very limited fight, in the same way here against ISIS, which is a much more sophisticated and numerically greater foe. It's embarrassing.[165]

In the face of the rising groundswell of well-founded criticisms from credible witnesses like those quoted above ever since the administration's bombing of ISIS began, CENTCOM's leaders, remarkably even including those heading up its air component, have lately taken to explaining away the overly draconian ROE that have largely occasioned the low number of daily strikes compared to earlier air campaigns with the condescending we-know-better reply that such critics "frankly haven't been in a fight like the one we're in now."[166] What those leaders fail to understand and appreciate in adhering to that long-habituated but now inappropriate stance is that they have, from the very start, been wrongly applying a U.S. Army-developed planning template designed for winning indigenous hearts and minds in a COIN war to a totally different sort of enemy in ISIS that needs to be viewed and dealt with by airpower instead as a self-avowed nation-state possessing territory, an infrastructure, an economy, a central nervous system, targetable leadership, and the beginnings of a capable conventional army. As for CENTCOM's still-meager level of effort as reflected in its overly parsimonious air strikes into Iraq and Syria now more than two years into it, even Obama's own respected former undersecretary of defense for policy, Michèle Flournoy, complained two months after that lame and unconvincing reply from the CAOC was proffered that the administration's efforts to combat ISIS to date "convey a sense of creeping incrementalism . . . that simply will not turn the tide given ISIS's size, spread, and momentum."[167]

The still-gradualist and indecisive pace of operations reflected in Operation Inherent Resolve to date has been all too reminiscent of the worst U.S. practices of the Vietnam War now being repeated by a successor generation of American leaders who seem to have forgotten all the hard-earned lessons of air warfare and strategy first borne out in Desert Storm and later validated by subsequent air campaigns, culminating in allied airpower's casebook performance in enabling the takedown of Saddam Hussein's regime in just three weeks in 2003. One example of this reversion to Vietnam-era practices can be seen in CENTCOM's most recent resort, in the absence of any more telling measures of merit, to such long-discredited metrics of combat performance as the numbers of sorties flown, targets struck, and enemy combatants killed (the daily "body count") when such figures merely reflect level of effort rather than any extent of actual progress. Another has been reflected in the increasingly outspoken complaints from CENTCOM's rank-and-file intelligence analysts after more than a year into the effort that their superiors have repeatedly rewritten their unflattering fact-based assessments so as to spin a more positive portrayal of the bombing's effectiveness up the chain of command.[168]

Fortunately for the future prospects for Operation Inherent Resolve, repeated terrorist outrages planned or inspired by ISIS both in the region and abroad in late 2015 finally forced the Obama administration to expand its roster of approved targets to a point where ISIS command centers in the heart of Raqqa in Syria and oil-bearing ISIS trucks on the move in quest of revenue for the would-be caliphate have since become fair game for U.S. and coalition aircrews. Indeed, in the weeks after the ISIS-planned terrorist attacks in Paris on November 13, 2015, that killed 130 innocent civilians and wounded hundreds more, the administration ramped up the intensity of its air attacks to the highest level since the effort began in early August the year before.[169]

Still, more than two years now into the Obama administration's would-be effort against ISIS, Operation Inherent Resolve has yet to attain to the level of a full-fledged military campaign, as that notion is typically understood and used by military professionals. The official dictionary of military terms published by the U.S. Department of Defense defines a campaign as "a series of major operations aimed at attaining strategic and operational objectives within a given time and space."[170] Nothing to date in CENTCOM's continuing flail against ISIS can be convincingly shown to have entailed "a series of major operations" driven by a well-defined strategy and course of action aimed at seeking achievable combat goals on a realistic timetable. On the contrary, its vague assigned charter simply to "degrade and ultimately destroy" ISIS remains about as nonspecific and indeterminate a mission statement as one could possibly imagine.

By early 2016 CENTCOM's performance in its still-hesitant effort against ISIS had finally begun to show further signs of improvement at least at the margins. To begin with, the intensity of aerial weapon releases against individual ISIS targets had steadily grown from fewer than two hundred a month in August 2014 to more than three thousand a month by mid-July 2016.[171] Better yet, as 2016 continued to unfold, CENTCOM relaxed some of its previously oppressive ROE aimed at preserving the lives of would-be noncombatant civilians and expanded its list of approved ISIS targets to include weapons manufacturing facilities, secret cash coffers, and major infrastructure assets like oil refineries used to raise millions of dollars of illicit revenue each day. As further aids to more effective targeting, it deployed small numbers of American SOF teams to work with indigenous friendly ground forces, and it also granted at least a partial delegation of target-approval authority from CENTCOM's headquarters in Florida to more closely involved senior generals in the forward area.[172] All of this succeeded by mid-2016 in allowing an eventual hard-won Iraqi recapture of Fallujah and a decisive reversion of ISIS to the tactical defensive for the first time since its emergence as a thriving would-be caliphate more than two years before.

Despite this notable growth in apparent U.S. effort since Inherent Resolve began in August 2014, CENTCOM's increased bombing and target coverage more than 2 years thereafter had still registered no significant strategic gains toward achieving the Obama administration's ultimate avowed goal of defeating ISIS decisively. By the end of July 2016, the effort's overall total cost had risen to $8.7 billion, accrued over time at an average rate of $12.1 million per day throughout the operation's 724 days to date. Furthermore, by the end of the next month, American and partner-nation aircraft had flown some 111,410 sorties in all in support of allied operations over Iraq and Syria since early August 2014, with 11,442 actual target attacks performed in both countries by U.S. combat aircraft and nearly 3,400 additional strikes by coalition aircraft, producing an overall total of more than 26,000 ISIS target types struck in all to date, nearly half of which consisted of individual enemy buildings and fighting positions.[173] Yet for all this seemingly herculean level of expanded effort by CENTCOM in sheer numerical terms, Iraqi troops remained no closer than ever before toward achieving their most important near-term goal of recapturing Mosul, the center of gravity of ISIS's dominating presence in Iraq. To make matters even worse, a new complicating factor arose as a result of Russia's having opportunistically inserted itself into the war zone by conducting aerial strikes on behalf of Syria's embattled President Assad, thanks to its ability to exploit the regional power vacuum created by President Obama's earlier refusal to honor his declared "red line" against Assad by engaging in the ongoing Syrian civil war in support of rebel forces. Furthermore, although CENTCOM's combat effort by mid-May 2016 had reportedly driven ISIS out of some 45 percent of the territory it formerly held in Iraq and out of 20 percent of the areas it once controlled in Syria, the terrorist movement effectively reconstituted and reinvigorated itself by extending its toxic reach and presence into ungoverned post-Gaddafi Libya and by either conducting or inspiring additional terrorist atrocities in major cities worldwide, including in the U.S. homeland.

The continued vitality and successes shown by ISIS since its initial rise in early 2014 prompted the director of the National Security Agency and commander of U.S. Cyber Command, Adm. Michael Rogers, to declare by late 2016 that the terrorist organization represented by far "the most adaptive target [he'd] ever worked [in 25 years] as an intelligence professional."[174] As for CENTCOM's most recently heightened effort to counter ISIS with a more effective application of kinetic force, the U.S. Air Force's newly installed chief of staff, Gen. David Goldfein, was doubtless on firm ground when he declared at the end of August 2016 that Operation Inherent Resolve in principle was "absolutely going in the right direction."[175] That said, however, the former commander of CENTCOM from 2010 to 2013, Gen. James Mattis, was no less on target when he offered the more overarching observation at roughly the same time that the Obama administration's would-be campaign against ISIS remained "unguided by a sustained policy or sound strategy [and continued to be] replete with half-measures."[176]

In these still-troubled circumstances, a more promising way ahead for the U.S. and allied effort against ISIS was suggested by the former chief air campaign planner for the 1991 Persian Gulf War, Lt. Gen. David Deptula, who finally proposed toward the end of 2015 that any truly effective and productive approach "will require moving beyond the current anemic, pinprick air strikes to a robust, comprehensive use of airpower—not simply in support of indigenous allied ground forces but as the key force in taking down the Islamic State. It will [also] require focusing on the Islamic State as a government, not as an insurgency, and for Central Command and [its] subordinate task force [against ISIS] to stop fighting the last war and start the serious use of airpower."[177] Otherwise, as an informed British assessment concluded not long before, "the campaign risks becoming another expensive lesson that despite their best efforts and intentions, expert personnel and superb equipment in the air cannot by themselves deliver strategic victory."[178] Anthony Cordesman added in a similar vein that if a more determined restart of the effort against ISIS is not initiated by CENTCOM soon, then the legacy of this latest U.S. and NATO air war "may well be that the [Obama administration] could talk a fight but not execute one" by having repeatedly pursued ineffective half-measures that "have proved so reactive that events have consistently outpaced every new increment in U.S. military activity."[179]

SEVEN LESSONS

Each of the eight U.S. and NATO air operations discussed here, including the still-ongoing evolution against ISIS, is unique with respect to its initial intended goals, number of participants involved, level of effort expended, and degree of success achieved. Yet all were prosecuted by variations on the same transformed instruments of air warfare that were first showcased with such dramatic effectiveness in Operation Desert Storm in 1991. Among the many operational constants that distinguished the conduct of these diverse experiences, the most prominent were consistently high levels of aircrew professionalism and performance, uniformly skilled and adaptive planning and execution at all levels of the kill chain, a sought-after and generally attained avoidance of inadvertent civilian casualties, and precise delivery of right-sized munitions to designated targets around the clock and in any weather.

Beyond these and other unifying similarities at the operational and tactical levels, some broader strategic generalizations can also be drawn regarding airpower and its varied applications from the contrasting cases explored earlier.[180] To be sure, when it comes to the many pitfalls that abound in pursuing such overarching insights, one must take care to honor an important cautionary reminder offered by the British military historian Sir Michael Howard, who wrote in 1991 that "history, whatever its value in educating the judgment, teaches no 'lessons,' and professional historians will be as skeptical of those who claim that it does as professional doctors are of their colleagues who peddle patent medicines guaranteeing instant cures. Historians may claim to teach lessons, and often they teach very wisely. But 'history' as such does not."[181] With that crucial caveat duly noted, the rest of this chapter offers seven broad-based conclusions from the overall record of U.S. and NATO air employment since 1993 that have important implications for future leaders regarding core questions of force planning and strategy.

Airpower Will Inevitably Be a Player in Tomorrow's Wars

The eight cases summarized earlier all point to a safe conclusion that air operations will henceforth figure prominently in future conflicts around the world, albeit in different ways and with varying degrees of criticality depending on the particular circumstances of tomorrow's armed conflicts. At one end of the spectrum, in both Operations Deliberate Force and Allied Force in 1995 and 1999, U.S. and NATO airpower was the *only* force element that played any active part in the fighting. Likewise, during the major combat phase of Operation Enduring Freedom in Afghanistan in late 2001, U.S. airpower, facilitated by merely some three hundred embedded CIA paramilitary operatives and allied special operations combatants, allowed the indigenous Afghan Northern Alliance to drive out the ruling Taliban in less than three months of precision bombing with no conventional U.S. ground combat involvement whatever.

Slightly more than a year later, in the very different major combat phase of Operation Iraqi Freedom in early 2003, the American and allied air and ground offensives began roughly concurrently. However, thanks to its constantly staring overhead ISR sensors both in the air and on orbit in space, CENTCOM's air component in that campaign was able to give allied ground commanders unquestioned confidence that their unprotected flanks were secure as they pressed northward. That contribution, along with the simultaneous precision air attacks against Iraq's ground forces independent of allied land action, was indispensable in making possible the land component's unimpeded race from Kuwait to the outskirts of Baghdad within days and to eventual enemy regime collapse in just three weeks. In marked contrast, during the more protracted COIN phases of Operations Enduring Freedom and Iraqi Freedom that went on for years thereafter, CENTCOM's air component took a back seat to allied ground troops as the main force element employed. Even in those cases, however, airpower remained both central and indispensable to the war effort through its mostly nonkinetic but still essential enabling contributions by way of armed overwatch, on-call CAS, inter- and intra-theater mobility, medical evacuation, and ISR support.

The future naturally remains uncertain as to what the next global tests of strength might entail for the United States and NATO. At one extreme, should a successor U.S. administration ever feel compelled to defend Taiwan against threatened Chinese military action, American airpower will be not just preeminent but pivotal because of the broad open-ocean arena in which any such conflict would take place. The associated tyranny of distance will place a unique premium on survivable and effective U.S. long-range strike capabilities to counter China's increasingly sophisticated offensive and defensive force posture in the region. Yet at the opposite end of the conflict spectrum as well, even in the most low-intensity and land-centric future threat scenarios around the world, the ISR, mobility, and strike offerings of American and perhaps also NATO airpower will remain key to the successful pursuit of joint- and combined-force success.

Airpower Can Sometimes Achieve Campaign Goals All by Itself

The eight cases explored in this chapter all suggest that, in at least some situations, well-conducted air operations can bring about desired wartime objectives singlehandedly, without any need for committing large numbers of conventional ground troops to early combat. To be sure, no responsible American or NATO airman has ever suggested that such a welcome opportunity will present itself in *every* future confrontation or that it should be something that airpower's continuing development should strive for as its ultimate performance standard. Yet based on the undeniable facts of the historical record since 1993, one can say unequivocally that allied airpower alone enabled the achievement of NATO's goals both in Operation Allied Force over Serbia in 1999 and in the subsequent Operations Odyssey Dawn and Unified Protector over Libya in 2011, without any need to commit allied ground forces to combat.

In the first case, for all its many shortcomings by way of excessive gradualism and irresolution, NATO's air war for Kosovo represented the first time ever that airpower coerced an enemy leader to yield with no supporting friendly land-force involvement. True enough, heated arguments later ensued between some airmen and land combatants over the extent to which Milošević feared a possible NATO ground invasion and whether that imputed factor was the main consideration behind his decision to accede to NATO's demands in the end. Most outspokenly in this regard, the overall commander of Allied Force, General Clark, later claimed in his memoirs that by mid-May of 1999, "NATO had gone about as far as possible with the air strikes" and that, in the end, it had been the prospect of a NATO ground intervention that "*in particular*, pushed Milošević to concede" (emphasis added).[182]

That would-be NATO ground threat imputed by Clark, however, had no basis in fact by way of any actual allied preparations for a land invasion. Milošević knew that. He also knew that NATO's precision standoff air attacks against key infrastructure targets in Belgrade could go on indefinitely. After the campaign ended, allied airpower turned out to have been the only force element that actually figured in delivering combat effects from start to finish. To that extent, one can honestly say that for the first time in its still relatively brief lifetime, airpower alone forced the wholesale withdrawal of an enemy force from disputed terrain. The British military historian John Keegan, hitherto an avowed doubter of airpower's oft-vaunted capabilities, freely conceded as the campaign's endgame drew near that the looming settlement represented "a victory for airpower and airpower alone."[183] In reluctantly acknowledging that emerging fact, he added that he felt "rather as a creationist Christian being shown his first dinosaur bone."[184] NATO's air-only achievement against Serbia in 1999 roundly repudiated a parochial pronouncement made just the year before by former U.S. Army chief of staff Gen. Gordon Sullivan, who said, "We are now out of the era—if we were ever in it—of airpower being able to cause someone to do something."[185]

Of course, campaign planners in no way can routinely *count* on airpower alone being the decisive force element in tomorrow's combat operations. Yet in future showdowns featuring such permissive circumstances as those that prevailed in the Balkans in 1995 and 1999—and also later in Libya in 2011—the air weapon has now become so precise and so effective that it offers every promise of yielding a welcome situation in which allied ground troops will no longer need to go head to head in large numbers at the outset against well-armed opposing forces and suffer needless casualties as a result.

Land-Force Availability Will Usually Make Airpower More Effective

Several of the armed conflicts involving the United States and NATO since 1993 have shown convincingly that a credible ground-force component to any campaign plan can almost always enhance airpower's potential. For example, in perhaps the most revealing case of NATO's air war for Kosovo in which allied airpower turned out to have been the sole force element actually committed to the fight, former U.S. Air Force chief of staff Gen. Merrill McPeak nonetheless remarked afterward that the Clinton administration's and NATO's having ruled out any ground combat involvement from the start was "a major blunder." He wrote, "I know of no airman, not a single one, who welcomed that development. Nobody said, 'Hey, finally, our own private war. Just what we've always wanted!' It certainly would have been smarter to retain all the options. . . . Signaling to Belgrade our extreme reluctance to fight on the ground made it less likely that the bombing would succeed, exploring the limits of airpower as a military and diplomatic instrument."[186] In a similar vein, the RAF's chief of staff later faulted NATO's decision to rule out a ground option as "a strategic mistake" that relieved Serbian forces of any need to prepare anticipatory defensive positions. It also allowed them to hide their tanks and artillery to make the fullest possible use of concealment against air attacks. It further freed them to conduct their ethnic cleansing of Kosovo with impunity.[187]

As for the concern voiced by some at the time over the possibility that NATO could have sustained intolerable friendly losses had it opted to back up its air offensive with a serious ground threat, there would most likely have been no need for the alliance actually to commit troops to combat in the end. By simply being there poised and ready—and highly visible to the enemy—a substantial forward presence of NATO troops along the Albanian and Macedonian borders would have made the Serbs more easily targetable by allied airpower by forcing them to bunch up in anticipatory defensive formations. Because of the absence of such a NATO ground threat, the air war had almost no effect on the Serbian Third Army's campaign of ethnic cleansing.

All the same, a combat-ready NATO ground presence might still have aided the air war and helped to deter, or at least lessen, Milošević's ethnic cleansing by giving his Third Army a more serious threat to worry about. It might also have allowed a swifter end to the campaign. This suggests an important corrective to the seemingly unending argument between airmen and land warriors over the relative merits of airpower versus "boots on the ground." Although NATO's air war for Kosovo confirmed that the alliance's principal members no longer need to commit their ground troops to early combat in every case, it also confirmed that, in most cases, airpower cannot perform to its fullest effectiveness without the presence of a credible ground constituent to the campaign strategy—even if only as a passive shaper of desired enemy behavior.

By the same token, the major combat phase of Operation Enduring Freedom in late 2001 was also almost entirely an air war in terms of American combat involvement. Yet in that instance as well, it took the supporting participation of small teams of CIA operators and coalition SOF troops working in close harmony with indigenous Afghan Northern Alliance forces, both empowered by U.S. aerial strike operations, to destroy al-Qaeda's sanctuary in Afghanistan and eventually rout the Taliban. The decisive role played by U.S. airpower in that initial phase of CENTCOM's Afghan war could not have achieved its immediate goal without the indispensable enabling contribution of friendly indigenous ground troops in enough numbers and with enough combat prowess to leverage the air input to the fullest in consummating its assigned mission. Much the same can be said of NATO airpower's essential role in enabling the toppling of Gaddafi by indigenous Libyan resistance forces in 2011.

Airpower Will Not Always Be Preeminent in Joint Warfare

The lower intensity, land-centric COIN operations that ensued in Iraq and Afghanistan for years after the relatively brief period of successful major combat in each country ended had the effect of putting air warfare professionals on notice that airpower will not invariably be the principal force element in future joint and combined combat. As noted earlier, the most recent U.S. and NATO COIN involvements since 2003 had the effect for a time of casting air operations—or at least kinetic air operations—into a seemingly permanent subordinate role in the eyes of some. Yet if one takes a longer view and thinks of airpower not just in terms of how it has been used most recently but in the broader sweep of history in which its future payoff will be delivered, one will quickly see how its operational and strategic relevance is neither universal nor unchanging but rather is contingent entirely on the particular circumstances of a situation. More directly put, kinetic airpower can range from being single-handedly decisive to being largely irrelevant to a combat challenge depending on the operational exigencies of the moment. Because its relative import, like that of all other force elements, is directly related to a joint-force commander's most immediate needs at any given moment, airpower need not disappoint its proponents and others when it is not always the main producer of desired results.

Although kinetic air employment on a large and sustained scale such as that seen from Desert Storm through the major combat phase of Iraqi Freedom has been largely overshadowed in more recent engagements by the greater cost in casualties and effort typically associated with more ground-centric COIN warfare, there will surely be future challenges that will again test American and NATO air assets to the fullest extent of their deterrent and combat potential. Notwithstanding the natural tendency of most to fixate on the here and now to the exclusion of all else, there remains an infinite span of future still lying before us to present new and more challenging threats of a different order. Accordingly, whether airpower should be regarded as "supported by" or "supporting of" other force elements is not a question that can ever have an unchanging answer. Instead, context will rule in every case, with the answer invariably hinging on the predominant circumstances of combat at any given moment.

Airpower and Ground Forces Have Reversed Roles in Major Air-Land Warfare

The major precedents set first in Operation Desert Storm in 1991 and again in the subsequent three-week major combat phase of Operation Iraqi Freedom in March and April 2003 attested that, at least when it comes to major conventional war against modern mechanized opponents, the classic roles of air and land power have switched places. In this recent role reversal, ground forces have now come to do most of the shaping and fixing of enemy forces, with airpower carrying out most of the actual killing of those forces. This major change has stemmed, first and foremost, from airpower's around-the-clock, all-weather, precision standoff attack capability. It has been further facilitated by the availability of accurate munitions in large numbers, electro-optical and infrared sensors on board strike aircraft, and airborne synthetic-aperture radars and ground-moving-target indicators to geolocate and target enemy tanks and troop concentrations.[188]

This changed phenomenon of joint and combined warfare in the past two decades has not been simply a matter of the notional "hammer" of friendly airpower now smashing enemy forces against the "anvil" of friendly ground power. Rather, as a former U.S. Army colonel and now practicing military historian has explained, it more entails "a case of ground power flushing the enemy, allowing airpower to maul his forces, with ground power [then] finishing the fight against the remnants and controlling the ground dimension in the aftermath of combat."[189] Such performance was at the root of the allied air-land engagement of Iraq's fielded armored and infantry forces during the three-week major combat phase of Operation Iraqi Freedom.

In a telling expression of this, CENTCOM's air component commander during the campaign, Lt. Gen. Buzz Moseley, remarked in his first meeting with media representatives toward the campaign's end: "Our sensors show that the preponderance of the Republican Guard divisions that were outside of Baghdad are now dead. We've laid on these people. I find it interesting when folks say we're 'softening them up.' We're not softening them up. We're killing them."[190] In a later ground affirmation of this testament, a platoon commander at the leading edge of the final push to Baghdad by the 1st Marine Expeditionary Force, Lt. Nathaniel Fick, wrote: "For the next hundred miles, all the way to the gates of Baghdad, every palm grove hid Iraqi armor, every field an artillery battery, and every alley an antiaircraft gun or surface-to-air missile launcher. But we never fired a shot. We saw the full effect of American airpower. Every one of those fearsome weapons was a blackened hulk."[191]

What has largely accounted for this role reversal between land and air forces in major conventional combat is that fixed-wing airpower has by now proven itself to be far more effective than ground-force capabilities in creating the necessary conditions for rapid offensive success. In the most instructive illustration of that change, throughout the three weeks of major combat in Iraq in 2003, the U.S. Army's V Corps launched only 2 deep-attack attempts with a force consisting of fewer than 80 Apache attack helicopters. The first came close to ending in disaster, and the second achieved only modest success. Similarly, U.S. Army artillery units expended only 414 of their longest range battlefield tactical missiles, primarily because of the wide-area destructive effects of that weapon's submunitions and their certain prospects of causing unacceptable collateral damage. In marked contrast, CENTCOM's air component during the same 3 weeks generated more than 20,000 strike sorties, enabled by a force of 735 fighters and 51 heavy bombers. In all, those aircraft struck more than 15,000 target aim points in direct and effective support of the allied land campaign.[192]

In light of that experience, it is fair to conclude that evolved airpower in its broadest sense, to include its indispensable ISR adjuncts, has fundamentally altered the way the United States and NATO might best fight any future large-scale engagements through its ability to perform battlespace functions long fulfilled at greater cost and risk, and with less efficiency, by more traditional ground-force elements. Most notable in this regard is modern airpower's repeatedly demonstrated ability to neutralize an enemy's army while incurring a minimum of friendly casualties along the way and to establish the conditions for achieving strategic goals almost from the very outset of fighting. Reduced to basics, modern airpower now allows JTF commanders and their subordinate units both freedom *from* attack and freedom *to* attack—something fundamentally new in the last two decades.

Evolved Airpower Has Yet to Have Been Fully Tested in High-Technology Combat

By way of a cautionary note against drawing excessive confidence from this recently evolved attribute of airpower, American and NATO air assets were in no way tested to the limit of their combat potential in any of the eight instances of armed conflict in which they have taken part since 1991. Without question with respect to its precision-strike capability, along with the indispensable ISR and command-and-control wherewithal that has enabled that heightened effectiveness, the air warfare equities fielded by the United States and its main NATO allies have become unsurpassed when it comes to taking out high-value targets around the clock and in any weather. Yet in each campaign experience reviewed in this chapter, American and NATO airpower was pitted against second-tier opponents who offered little or no combat pushback of the sort that a peer or near-peer enemy would present at the higher end of the conflict spectrum in the realms of air-to-air, surface-to-air, counterspace, and cyberspace operations.

To offer just one example of how relatively easy the combat going was for American and NATO airpower throughout the past quarter century, Iraq had thirty-three of its fighter aircraft shot down by allied fighters during the first days of Operation Desert Storm for the loss of just one U.S. aircraft in the air-to-air arena. That was a U.S. Navy F/A-18 downed during the campaign's first night, almost certainly by an unobserved and lucky AA-6 radar-guided missile from an Iraqi MiG-25 that had eluded detection by AWACS and fired on the U.S. jet from beyond visual range. After that early exposure otherwise to vastly superior American air combat prowess, Saddam Hussein mounted no further aerial resistance and flushed much of his remaining fighter force to what he wrongly hoped would be a safe haven in Iran. Some of those fighters as well were shot down by U.S. Air Force F-15s during their high-speed dash eastward to escape at low level, with most of their pilots unaware that they were even being engaged and making no attempt to countermaneuver in self-defense.

Fast-forwarding to NATO's air war for Kosovo in 1999, as noted earlier, the Serbian air force launched many of its fighters, including a dozen or more MiG-29s, during the first night of allied air operations in an attempt to disrupt NATO's bombing attacks. Two MiG-29s were downed by U.S. Air Force F-15s and a third by a Dutch F-16 that night. Two days, later, two additional MiG-29s attempting to engage allied fighters were shot down by American F-15s. Only rarely after those one-sided losses did Serbia's fighters rise again to challenge NATO's bombing operations. For its part, the country's Soviet-style IADS with its well-trained professional operators, while sufficiently threatening to keep NATO's pilots constantly on guard against any sudden SAM launches, mostly withheld radar-guided SAM fire throughout the seventy-eight-day campaign as a result of the near-certainty that its launch crews would receive prompt and lethal counterfire from allied F-16s armed with antiradiation missiles if they left their tracking radars locked on long enough to allow their missiles to home on targeted NATO fighters.

The air-to-air and SAM threats in all subsequent U.S. and NATO air wars became of even less concern after those initial air combat successes. The Taliban's rudimentary air force, with just a few flyable MiG-21s and with poorly trained and barely competent pilots to man them, never once got airborne and was soon decimated on the ground by precision bombing attacks during the first few nights of Operation Enduring Freedom. Less than two years thereafter, what remained of Iraq's fighter force, still chastened by the drubbing it had received from allied air-to-air fire during the first week of Desert Storm, was ordered by Hussein to stand down entirely from the first night onward in Operation Iraqi Freedom and never once attempted to offer any resistance. Later, as the continuing wars in Iraq and Afghanistan evolved from their initial major combat phases into more protracted COIN fighting, the absence of any residual functioning air defenses in either country meant that CENTCOM's air component could operate its vulnerable propeller-driven MC-12 ISR aircraft and unmanned Predator RPAs at will and in a way that would have been completely nonsurvivable in more well-defended enemy airspace.

In short, as well-equipped and proficient in aerial combat as U.S. and NATO fighter pilots continue to be, they would face a far more daunting and stressful operational challenge if they were exposed to the growing array of fourth- and fifth-generation fighters, advanced air-to-air missiles, long-range SAMs, and supporting counterspace and cyberspace capabilities that are now being fielded by China and Russia. To sum up this important caveat regarding the eight combat experiences discussed above, *all* of the kinetic and supporting ISR and mobility assets that accounted so impressively for the effective performance of U.S. and NATO airpower in those conflicts since 1991 would find themselves at far greater risk in any future showdown against a more able opponent armed with such high-technology threat systems.[193]

No Air Posture, However Capable, Can Make Up for a Deficient Strategy

Last and by far the most important teaching to be drawn from the collective record of U.S. and NATO air warfare since 1991, the wide variations in relative success among the eight cases reviewed in this chapter clearly reveal that even the most advanced air weapon imaginable can never offset the failed results that can emanate from the application of a flawed or bankrupt strategy. This abiding fact of life, hardly unique to the post–Cold War era but convincingly reaffirmed throughout it, was well attested to in the early aftermath of NATO's air war for Kosovo when the commander of Allied Forces South, Admiral Ellis, declared in an after-action briefing to U.S. military leaders that *luck* played the main role in ensuring that campaign's success. Ellis concluded that the need for consensus within a widely divergent assemblage of NATO allies had resulted in an incremental war rather than more decisive operations. He further remarked that excessive concern over avoiding collateral damage had created both sanctuaries and opportunities that the enemy successfully exploited and that the absence of a credible NATO ground threat made the air war last longer than necessary to achieve its goals.[194] The importance of having a well-founded and sufficiently resourced strategy from a campaign's start was again highlighted by the rude awakening that the second Bush administration experienced in early 2003 when the masterfully conducted major combat phase of Operation Iraqi Freedom devolved within just days into an ugly domestic sectarian struggle and eventual insurgency. The resulting chaos consumed U.S. troops and resources for four prohibitively costly years until an appropriate COIN strategy was finally approved and funded in a way that allowed for an eventual stabilization of daily life in that long-embattled country.

To repeat, as was amply attested to by those instructive past examples, no air arm—or, for that matter, *any* combination of force elements—can ever be more effective than the overarching strategy it seeks to underwrite. As Colin Gray has rightly admonished in this regard, for airpower's inherent advantage "to secure strategic results of value, it must serve a national and . . . overall military strategy that is feasible, coherent, and politically sensible. If these basic requirements are not met, [then] airpower, no matter how impeccably applied tactically and operationally, will be employed as a waste of life, taxes, and, frankly, trust between the sharp end of [a nation's] spear and its shaft." More to the point, Gray reminds us, a nation's strategy can be so dysfunctional that it "cannot be rescued from defeat by a dominant airpower, no matter how that airpower is employed."[195]

One could hardly ask for a more compelling indictment than that as it relates to the most recent effort that the United States has conducted in a half-hearted way for more than two years and continues to pursue in its still open-ended and ineffectual would-be campaign against ISIS. After a reluctant start in August 2014 with mere pinprick air attacks and with no clear direction or seriousness of purpose ever since, subsequent terrorist outrages committed by ISIS in late 2015 and thereafter finally forced the Obama administration to approve more forceful strikes against more lucrative targets, albeit still in a piecemeal and seemingly purposeless manner whose ultimate payoff remains yet to be seen. As that administration's and CENTCOM's continuing refusal to honor and apply in this latest flawed effort the many teachings offered by previous U.S. and NATO air war successes and failures since Desert Storm so well attests, lessons *indicated* by such past experiences can never become truly lessons *learned* until they are first understood and accepted implicitly by a nation's most senior leaders and then assimilated as enduring features of their warfighting repertoire.

NOTES

1. The United Kingdom's most respected commentator on air warfare, Air Vice-Marshal Richard A. Mason, RAF (ret.), best summarized this take on the experience when he wrote after the campaign ended that "the Gulf war marked the apotheosis of twentieth-century air power." Richard A. Mason, "The Air War in the Gulf," *Survival* (May–June 1991): 225. The only remaining question at the time, in the words of another able observer, was whether Desert Storm symbolized not just a sea change in modern airpower's capability but also an emergent "domination of air power and a new paradigm of warfare" presaging "a fundamental shift in the way many wars will be conducted and the need for a new way of thinking about military operations." Dennis Drew, "Desert Storm as a Symbol: Implications of the Air War in the Desert," *Airpower Journal* 6, no. 3 (Fall 1992): 6, 13.
2. Indeed, a claim to the continued validity of that would-be general rule was implied in the chosen title for the official account of the U.S. Army's contribution to Desert Storm; Robert H. Scales, *Certain Victory: The U.S. Army in the Gulf War* (McLean, Va.: Brassey's, Inc., 1994).
3. At least one purveyor of this outlook went so far as to argue that, as a result of the onset of predominantly COIN fighting in Iraq and Afghanistan after the relatively brief major combat phases of those two wars, "air power clearly is in real trouble" now and that, given the likelihood that the wars of the twenty-first century will continue to be "mainly of the low-intensity kind, . . . there probably is no compelling case [any longer] for independent air power at all." Martin van Creveld, "The Rise and Fall of Air Power," in *A History of Air Warfare*, ed. John Andreas Olsen (Washington, D.C.: Potomac Books, 2010), 369–70. For a further development of this eccentric and studiously provocative viewpoint, see also Martin van Creveld, *The Age of Airpower* (New York: Public Affairs, 2011). A compelling refutation of it is offered in Karl P. Mueller, "Airpower: Two Centennial Appraisals," *Strategic Studies Quarterly* 5, no. 4 (Winter 2011): 123–132; and Karl P. Mueller, "Sky King," *American Interest* 7, no. 3 (January–February 2012): 104–8.

4. Michael E. Ryan, "Deliberate Force: The Bosnian Air Campaign—Lessons for the Future," briefing at a conference on "Canada's Air Power in the New Millennium" sponsored by the Canadian Forces Air Command, Winnipeg, Manitoba, Canada, July 30, 1997.
5. See "Washington Outlook," *Aviation Week and Space Technology*, June 12, 1995, 37. The F-16 pilot, Capt. Scott O'Grady, was rescued a week later by a team of forty U.S. Marines and a force of forty mission and support aircraft.
6. Barbara Starr, "Deny Flight Shootdown May Put USAF on the Offensive," *Jane's Defense Weekly*, June 24, 1995, 24.
7. Brig. Gen. R. T. Newell III, USAF, personal letter to the author, September 2, 1995.
8. Ryan, "Deliberate Force."
9. The most thorough treatment of that operation is the final report of Air University's Balkans Air Campaign Study edited by Robert C. Owen, *Deliberate Force: A Case Study in Effective Air Campaigning* (Maxwell AFB, Ala.: Air University Press, 1999).
10. Ryan, "Deliberate Force."
11. Craig Covault, "Air Power Alters Bosnia Equation," *Aviation Week and Space Technology*, September 4, 1995, 22–24.
12. For more on Israel's air operations in the 1982 Bekaa Valley offensive, see Benjamin S. Lambeth, *The Transformation of American Air Power* (Ithaca, N.Y.: Cornell University Press, 2000), 92–96.
13. "NATO Air Operations over the Balkans," SHAPE briefing charts, no date given.
14. See Celestine Bohlen, "Italy Demands a Little Respect," *New York Times*, September 17, 1995; and Arturo Zampaglione, "Italy Blocks Stealth Fighters," *La Repubblica*, September 12, 1995.
15. Craig Covault, "Precision Missiles Bolster NATO Strikes," *Aviation Week and Space Technology*, September 18, 1995, 22–23.
16. Rick Atkinson, "Deliberate Force," *Washington Post*, November 15, 1999.
17. Barbara Starr, "NATO Strikes Strive to Stop Serb Shelling," *Jane's Defense Weekly*, September 9, 1995, 3.
18. "NATO Air Forces Inflicted No Collateral Damage in Bosnian Air Campaign," *Inside the Air Force*, July 19, 1996, 1–2.
19. Ryan, "Deliberate Force."
20. Craig Covault, "NATO Air Strikes Target Serbian Infrastructure," *Aviation Week and Space Technology*, September 11, 1995, 28.
21. See "French Mirage Loss Highlights Threat," *Aviation Week and Space Technology*, September 4, 1995, 22–23.
22. For the essential details of the Israeli Air Force's successful strike against Iran's nuclear reactor, see Rodger W. Claire, *Raid on the Sun: Inside Israel's Secret Campaign That Denied Saddam the Bomb* (New York: Broadway Books,

1984). See also Shelomoh Nakdimon, *First Strike: The Exclusive Story of How Israel Foiled Iraq's Attempt to Get the Bomb* (New York: Summit Books, 1987).
23. Gen. Ronald R. Fogleman, "What Air Power Can Do in Bosnia," letter to the editor, *Wall Street Journal*, October 11, 1995.
24. Richard Holbrooke, *To End a War* (New York: Random House, 1998), 104.
25. Michael Knights, *Cradle of Conflict: Iraq and the Birth of the Modern U.S. Military* (Annapolis, Md.: Naval Institute Press, 2005), 199.
26. Secretary of State Madeleine Albright, "Interview with Jim Lehrer," *PBS Newshour*, December 17, 1998.
27. Lt. Gen. Hal Hornburg interview with Michael Knights, cited in Knights, *Cradle of Conflict*, 204.
28. Anthony H. Cordesman, *The Lessons of Desert Fox: A Preliminary Analysis* (Washington, D.C.: Center for Strategic and International Studies, February 16, 1999), 11.
29. Ibid., 18.
30. Ibid.
31. Norman Kempster, "U.S. and Britain Strike Iraq; Impeachment Debate on Hold," *Los Angeles Times*, December 17, 1998.
32. Quoted in Robin Wright and John Daniszewski, "Air Assault on Iraq Called off after 4 Nights," *Los Angeles Times*, December 20, 1998.
33. William M. Arkin, "The Difference Was in the Details," *Washington Post*, January 17, 1999.
34. Micah Zenko, "Is Operation Desert Fox a Useful Comparison for Bombing Iran?" *Council on Foreign Relations* (blog), April 15, 2015, http://blogs.cfr.org/zenko/2015/04/15/is-operation-desert-fox-a-useful-comparison-for-bombing-iran/.
35. Quoted in Tyler Marshall, "U.S., British Pound Military Sites," *Los Angeles Times*, December 18, 1998.
36. Kenneth M. Pollack, *The Threatening Storm: The United States and Iraq: The Crisis, the Strategy, and the Prospects after Saddam* (New York: Random House, 2002), 93.
37. Robin Wright, "Endgame in Iraq Still Elusive Despite Strikes," *Los Angeles Times*, December 21, 1998.
38. Quoted in Paul Richter, "U.S. Says Strikes Badly Disrupted Iraqi Regime," *Los Angeles Times*, January 9, 1999.
39. Quoted in Kempster, "U.S. and Britain Strike Iraq."
40. In the end, fewer than one in three Americans polled said that they thought the action was timed to delay the impeachment hearings. "Most in U.S. Back Strikes, Polls Say," *Los Angeles Times*, December 18, 1998.
41. Quoted in Thomas E. Ricks, *Fiasco: The American Military Adventure in Iraq* (New York: Penguin Press, 2006), 21.
42. Pollack, *Threatening Storm*, 92.

43. Cordesman, *Lessons of Desert Fox*, 1–2.
44. Ibid., 18–19.
45. Tyler Marshall, "U.S. Rejects Calls for Efforts to Oust Hussein," *Los Angeles Times*, December 24, 1998.
46. Jane Perlez, "Holbrooke to Meet Milosevic in Final Peace Effort," *New York Times*, March 22, 1999.
47. Secretary of State Madeleine Albright declared in a television interview on the evening of March 24, "I don't see this as a long-term operation." Quoted in John T. Correll, "Assumptions Fall in Kosovo," *Air Force Magazine* (June 1999): 4.
48. Jane Perlez, "U.S. Option: Air Attacks May Prove Unpalatable," *New York Times*, March 23, 1999.
49. Steven Lee Meyers, "Pentagon Said to Be Adding 300 Planes to Fight Serbs," *New York Times*, April 13, 1999.
50. Bradley Graham and Dana Priest, "Allies to Begin Flying Refugees Abroad," *Washington Post*, April 5, 1999.
51. Rowan Scarborough, "Momentum for Troops Growing," *Washington Times*, April 5, 1999.
52. Dan Balz, "U.S. Consensus Grows to Send in Ground Troops," *Washington Post*, April 6, 1999.
53. Eric Schmitt and Steven Lee Meyers, "NATO Said to Focus Raids on Serb Elite's Property," *New York Times*, April 19, 1999.
54. David A. Fulghum, "Electronic Bombs Darken Belgrade," *Aviation Week and Space Technology*, May 10, 1999, 34.
55. Robert Block, "In Belgrade, Hardship Grows under Sustained Air Assault," *Wall Street Journal*, May 12, 1999.
56. Steven Erlanger, "Economists Find Bombing Cuts Yugoslavia's Production in Half," *New York Times*, April 30, 1999.
57. Tony Capaccio, "JSTARS Led Most Lethal Attacks on Serbs," *Defense Week*, July 6, 1999, 13.
58. William Drozdiak, "Yugoslav Troops Devastated by Attack," *Washington Post*, June 9, 1999.
59. R. Jeffrey Smith and Molly Moore, "Plan for Kosovo Pullout Signed," *Washington Post*, June 10, 1999.
60. Quoted in Tim Weiner, "From President, Victory Speech and a Warning," *New York Times*, June 11, 1999.
61. David Atkinson, "B-2s Demonstrated Combat Efficiency over Kosovo," *Defense Daily*, July 1, 1999, 1.
62. Dale Eisman, "Over Balkans, It's Beauty vs. the Beast," *Norfolk Virginian-Pilot*, April 26, 1999.
63. Adam Hebert, "Air Force Follows Roadmap in Employment of Bombers against Serbia," *Inside the Air Force*, April 2, 1999, 2.

64. Paul Richter, "B-2 Drops Its Bad PR in Air War," *Los Angeles Times*, July 8, 1999.
65. "Despite Losses, Backers Say Unmanned Systems Excelling over Kosovo," *Inside the Pentagon*, June 10, 1999, 1.
66. Wesley K. Clark, "When Force Is Necessary: NATO's Military Response to the Kosovo Crisis," *NATO Review* (Summer 1999): 16, 18.
67. That said, Operation Allied Force was by no means without manifold problems in execution, including a highly challenged SEAD effort, shortcomings in intelligence cycle time, occasional inadvertent civilian casualties as a result of stray munitions, and an accidental bombing of the Chinese embassy in Belgrade, among numerous other sources of headaches for U.S. and allied commanders and planners. For a comprehensive discussion of these and other aspects of the campaign, see Benjamin S. Lambeth, *NATO's Air War for Kosovo: A Strategic and Operational Assessment* (Santa Monica, Calif.: RAND, 2001), 101–77.
68. "Reporters' Notebook," *Defense Week*, July 19, 1999, 4.
69. Quoted in William Drozdiak, "Allies Need Upgrade, General Says," *Washington Post*, June 20, 1999.
70. Quoted in Bradley Graham, "Air Power 'Effective, Successful,' Cohen Says," *Washington Post*, June 11, 1999.
71. Elaine M. Grossman, "For U.S. Commander in Kosovo, Luck Played Role in Wartime Success," *Inside the Pentagon* 15, no. 36 (September 9, 1999): 1.
72. See Phillip S. Meilinger, "Gradual Escalation: NATO's Kosovo Air Campaign, though Decried as a Strategy, May Be the Future of War," *Armed Forces Journal International* (October 1999): 18.
73. Thomas E. Ricks, "Warplanes Begin Deploying to Gulf, Central Asia," *Washington Post*, September 20, 2001.
74. Thomas E. Ricks and Vernon Loeb, "Initial Aim Is Hitting Taliban Defenses," *Washington Post*, October 8, 2001.
75. Michael Evans, "U.S. Troops and Helicopters Set for Ground War," *London Times*, October 11, 2001.
76. Bradley Graham and Vernon Loeb, "Cave Complexes Smashed by Bombs," *Washington Post*, October 12, 2001.
77. For more on this new mode of air warfare involving allied SOF teams on the ground working closely with friendly indigenous ground forces in directing precision air attacks against enemy ground troops, see Richard B. Andres, Craig Wills, and Thomas E. Griffith Jr., "Winning with Allies: The Strategic Value of the Afghan Model," *International Security* 30, no. 3 (Winter 2005–2006): 124–60.
78. James Dao, "More U.S. Troops in bin Laden Hunt; Hideouts Bombed," *New York Times*, November 19, 2001.

79. Tony Capaccio, "Sixty Percent of Bombs Dropped on Afghanistan Precision-Guided," *Bloomberg.com*, November 20, 2001.
80. Anthony Cordesman, *The Lessons of Afghanistan: Warfighting, Intelligence, Force Transformation, Counter-Proliferation, and Arms Control* (Washington, D.C.: Center for Strategic and International Studies, June 28, 2002), 20.
81. Stephen Farrell and Michael Evans, "SAS Searches bin Laden Cave System," *London Times*, December 4, 2001.
82. Steve Vogel and Walter Pincus, "Al-Qaeda Complex Destroyed; Search Widens," *Washington Post*, January 15, 2002.
83. Keith Richburg and William Branigan, "Attacks Out of the Blue: U.S. Air Strikes on Taliban Hit Military Targets and Morale," *Washington Post*, November 18, 2001.
84. Mark G. Davis, "Operation Anaconda: Command and Confusion in Joint Warfare," unpublished thesis presented to the faculty of the School of Advanced Air and Space Studies, Maxwell Air Force Base, Alabama, June 2004, 113.
85. Interview with Lt. Gen. John D. W. Corley, USAF, Headquarters United States Air Force, Washington, D.C., May 13, 2003. The year before, General Corley had been the air component's CAOC director throughout the course of Operation Anaconda.
86. Comments on an earlier portion of this chapter by Maj. Gen. David A. Deptula, USAF, Director of Operations, Pacific Air Forces, Hickam AFB, Hawaii, October 4, 2002.
87. The term "joint," in standard military usage, refers to the cooperative involvement of two or more of a nation's armed services in a combat, peacekeeping, or humanitarian operation. "Joint and combined" refers to both multiservice and allied participation in such operations.
88. For a fuller treatment of the U.S. Navy's important contributions to Operation Enduring Freedom, see Benjamin S. Lambeth, *American Carrier Air Power at the Dawn of a New Century* (Santa Monica, Calif.: RAND, 2005), 9–38.
89. Comments on an earlier version of this chapter, personal e-mail to the author, January 8, 2004.
90. For a full account of the planning and execution of this campaign, see Benjamin S. Lambeth, *Air Power against Terror: America's Conduct of Operation Enduring Freedom* (Santa Monica, Calif.: RAND, 2005).
91. George W. Bush, *Decision Points* (New York: Crown, 2010), 229.
92. Anthony H. Cordesman, "The 'Instant Lessons' of the Iraq War: Main Report," third working draft (Washington, D.C.: Center for Strategic and International Studies, April 14, 2003), 8.
93. Carlo Kopp, "Iraqi Freedom—The Hammer and Anvil," *Australian Aviation* (May 2003), 29.

94. Kevin M. Woods, with Michael R. Pease, Mark E. Stout, Williamson Murray, and James G. Lacey, *Iraqi Perspectives Project: A View of Operation Iraqi Freedom from Saddam's Senior Leadership* (Norfolk, Va.: Joint Center for Operational Analysis, U.S. Joint Forces Command, March 2006), 125.
95. Quoted in ibid.
96. Ibid., 126.
97. Williamson Murray and Robert H. Scales, *The Iraq War: A Military History* (Cambridge, Mass.: Harvard University Press, 2003), 114.
98. Timothy J. Keating, "Interview with Vice Adm. Timothy J. Keating, USN—'This Was a Different War,'" U.S. Naval Institute *Proceedings* 129, no. 6/1,204 (June 2003): 30.
99. Interview with Gen. T. Michael Moseley, USAF, Chief of Staff, Headquarters U.S. Air Force, Washington, D.C., August 2, 2006.
100. Lt. Gen. T. Michael Moseley, USAF, "Operation Iraqi Freedom: Initial CFACC Roll-up," briefing given at a symposium to assess and document allied air operations during the three weeks of major combat in Operation Iraqi Freedom, Nellis Air Force Base, Nevada, July 18, 2003.
101. Mark Simpson, "Air Power Lessons from Operation Iraqi Freedom" (Langley Air Force Base, Va.: Headquarters Air Combat Command, ACC/XPSX, November 25, 2003).
102. Ibid.
103. Quoted in ibid.
104. This theme was first developed in depth more than four decades ago in the widely acclaimed study by Samuel P. Huntington, *Political Order in Changing Societies* (New Haven, Conn.: Yale University Press, 1968).
105. Ricks, *Fiasco*, 127–28.
106. Jay A. Stout, *Hammer from Above: Marine Air Combat over Iraq* (New York: Presidio Press, 2005), 378.
107. The most thorough assessment of the air contribution to the major combat phase of Operation Iraqi Freedom may be found in Benjamin S. Lambeth, *The Unseen War: Allied Air Power and the Takedown of Saddam Hussein* (Annapolis, Md.: Naval Institute Press, 2013).
108. William Branigin, Liz Sly, and Sudarsan Raghavan, "Obama Demands Pullback of Libyan Troops, Tripoli Declares Cease-Fire," *Washington Post*, March 18, 2011.
109. Robert M. Gates, *Duty: Memoirs of a Secretary at War* (New York: Knopf, 2014), 511–12.
110. The precise language of UNSCR 1973 authorized "all necessary measures" for protecting Libyan civilians under threat of attack, "while excluding a foreign occupation force of any form on any part of Libyan territory." UN Security Council, "Security Council Approves 'No-Fly Zone' over Libya, Authorizing All Necessary Measures to Protect Civilians, by a Vote of 10 in

Favour with 5 Abstentions," SC/10200, 6498th Meeting [night], New York: UN Department of Public Information, March 17, 2011.
111. "Remarks by the President on the Situation in Libya," White House, Office of the Press Secretary, March 18, 2011.
112. Christian F. Anrig, "Allied Air Power over Libya: A Preliminary Assessment," *Air and Space Power Journal* 25, no. 4 (Winter 2011): 89–90.
113. Adm. Samuel Locklear, USN, press briefing, March 22, 2011.
114. Margaret Woodward, "Operation Odyssey Dawn—United States," in *Air Power and Coercive Diplomacy*, Proceedings of the 2012 RAAF Air Power Conference, Canberra, Australia: National Convention Centre, May 10-11, 2012, 174.
115. A concise synopsis of the essential facts of this brief first phase of the campaign may be found in Jeremiah Gertler, "Operation Odyssey Dawn [Libya]: Background and Issues for Congress," *Congressional Research Service*, March 28, 2011, 7.
116. Quoted in Ryan Lizza, "The Consequentialist: How the Arab Spring Remade Obama's Foreign Policy," *New Yorker*, May 2, 2011.
117. See, for example, Nicholas Cecil and Nick Pisa, "SAS Using Lasers to Guide Missiles on to Key Targets," *Evening Standard*, March 21, 2011.
118. Jason R. Greenleaf, "The Air War in Libya," *Air and Space Power Journal* 27, no. 2 (March–April 2013), 29.
119. Robert C. Owen, "The U.S. Experience: National Strategy and Campaign Support," in *Precision and Purpose: Airpower in the Libyan Civil War*, ed. Karl P. Mueller (Santa Monica, Calif.: RAND, 2015), 94.
120. Anrig, "Allied Air Power over Libya," 95.
121. See, for example, Karen De Young and Greg Jaffe, "NATO Runs Short on Some Munitions in Libya," *Washington Post*, April 15, 2011.
122. Quoted in John Tirpak, "Lessons from Libya," *Air Force Magazine*, December 2011, 34–38.
123. Ivo H. Daalder and Adm. James G. Stavridis, "NATO's Victory in Libya: The Right Way to Run an Intervention," *Foreign Affairs*, March–April 2012, 2.
124. Colin Hunt, "NATO Has Little to Show from Its Libya Intervention," *Cicero Magazine*, August 12, 2015.
125. "Full Transcript: Democratic Presidential Debate," *New York Times*, October 14, 2015.
126. Alan J. Kuperman, "Obama's Libya Debacle: How a Well-Meaning Intervention Ended in Failure," *Foreign Affairs*, March–April 2015, 67.
127. Christopher S. Chivvis, *Toppling Qaddafi: Libya and the Limits of Liberal Intervention* (New York: Cambridge University Press, 2014), 169.
128. Gideon Rose, "Tell Me How This One Ends," *Washington Post*, March 27, 2011.

129. Karl P. Mueller, "Victory Through (Not by) Airpower," in Mueller, ed., *Precision and Purpose: Airpower in the Libyan Civil War* (Santa Monica, Calif.: RAND, 2015), 373–74.
130. "Statement by the President," White House, Office of the Press Secretary, August 7, 2014.
131. Alissa J. Rubin, Tim Arango, and Helene Cooper, "U.S. Jets and Drones Attack Militants in Iraq, Hoping to Stop Advance," *New York Times*, August 9, 2014.
132. Helene Cooper and Michael D. Shear, "Militants' Siege on Mountain in Iraq Is over, Pentagon Says," *New York Times*, August 13, 2014.
133. It bears mention in passing here that CENTCOM began aerial reconnaissance operations over northern Iraq as early as June 2014 to monitor and assess the progress of ISIS's forces. Adam Entous and Julian E. Barnes, "U.S. Secretly Flying Drones over Iraq," *Wall Street Journal*, June 12, 2014.
134. Quoted in Marc Thiessen, "George W. Bush Was Right about Iraq Pullout," *Washington Post*, September 8, 2014.
135. Rick Brennan, "Withdrawal Symptoms: The Bungling of the Iraq Exit," *Foreign Affairs*, November/December 2014, 26, 28.
136. Fred Kaplan, "Obama's Way: The President in Practice," *Foreign Affairs*, January–February 2016, 58–59.
137. Frederick W. Kagan, "The President and the Generals," *Weekly Standard*, December 12, 2011.
138. Ned Parker, "The Iraq We Left Behind: Welcome to the World's Next Failed State," *Foreign Affairs*, March–April 2012, 94, 96, 99.
139. Gates, *Duty*, 555, 569.
140. Leon Panetta, *Worthy Fights: A Memoir of Leadership in War and Peace*, with Jim Newton (New York: Penguin, 2014), 415.
141. "From Beirut to Baghdad," *Economist* (London), May 14, 2016, 13.
142. David Remnick, "Going the Distance: On and Off the Road with Barack Obama," *New Yorker*, January 27, 2014.
143. William McCants, *The ISIS Apocalypse: The History, Strategy, and Doomsday Vision of the Islamic State* (New York: St. Martin's Press, 2015), 125.
144. Michael D. Shear, "U.S. Airstrikes on Militants in Iraq," *New York Times*, August 10, 2014.
145. Aaron Blake, "Why Obama's 'We Don't Have a Strategy' Gaffe Stings," *Washington Post*, August 29, 2014.
146. David Hudson, "President Obama: We Will Degrade and Ultimately Destroy ISIL," White House blog, September 10, 2014.
147. Anthony H. Cordesman, *The Air War against the Islamic State: The Need for an "Adequacy of Resources"* (Washington, D.C.: Center for Strategic and International Studies, October 13, 2014), 1–2, 5, 23.

148. Dan Lamothe, "Operation against Islamic State to be Called Inherent Resolve," *Washington Post*, October 15, 2014.
149. Mark Gunzinger and John Stillion, "The Unserious Air War against ISIS," *Wall Street Journal*, October 14, 2014.
150. Quoted in Tim Mak, "Exclusive: Pentagon Map Hides ISIS Gains," *Daily Beast*, April 22, 2015.
151. Robin Wright, "The War against ISIS, by the Numbers," *Wall Street Journal*, December 30, 2014.
152. Jim Garamone, "Dempsey Makes Case for Long-Term Effort to Defeat ISIL," Washington, D.C.: U.S. Department of Defense news release, August 17, 2015.
153. Department of Defense, "Operation Inherent Resolve: Targeted Operations against ISIL Terrorists," Department of Defense special report, November 23, 2015.
154. Tom Vanden Brook, "Anti-ISIL Strikes Now Aimed at Moving Targets," *USA Today*, December 14, 2015.
155. Amar al-Shamary and Tom Vanden Brook, "Iraqi Military Claims Key Victory in Ramadi, Says ISIL Is in Retreat," *USA Today*, December 27, 2015.
156. Department of Defense, "Department of Defense Press Briefing by Col. Warren via Teleconference from Baghdad, Iraq," Washington, D.C.: U.S. Department of Defense news transcript, December 29, 2015.
157. Department of Defense, "Lieutenant General John W. Hesterman III, USAF, Combined Force Air Component Commander, Holds a Defense Department News Briefing via Teleconference," Washington, D.C.: U.S. Department of Defense press release, June 5, 2015.
158. Nolan Peterson, "Inside the U.S. Air War against ISIS," *The Daily Signal*, September 28, 2015.
159. These top-of-the-line fighters were sent to the war zone in the first place not with the intent to be used in routine strike operations but rather as an added source of deterrence, given Syria's possession of an unusually sophisticated and capable Soviet-style IADS that American and NATO aircrews had never before encountered in a combat setting. In the end, that hedge proved to have been well advised but superfluous, once Syria's air defenders wisely chose to stand down rather than react, when their air sovereignty was breached for the first time by coalition combat aircraft. Amy McCullogh, "With the Raptors over Syria," *Air Force Magazine*, February 2016, 26–33.
160. Gregory Korte, "Obama Embraces Doctrine of 'Strategic Patience,'" *USA Today*, February 6, 2015.
161. Anthony H. Cordesman, "Looking Beyond the Tragedy in Paris: Still No Clear Strategy and No Public Measures of Effectiveness for Dealing with ISIS," draft manuscript (Washington, D.C.: Center for Strategic and International Studies, December 1, 2015), 10.

162. John C. K. Daly, "Operation Inherent Resolve: The War against Islamic State's Oil Network," *Terrorism Monitor* 13, no. 1, Jamestown Foundation, January 9, 2015.

163. Michael Knights, "Campaign Acceleration: How to Build on Progress and Avoid Stalemate against ISIL," *War on the Rocks* (blog), November 2015, http://warontherocks.com/2015/11/campaign-acceleration-how-to-build-on-progress-and-avoid-stalemate-against-isil/.

164. Karen De Young and Missy Ryan, "As Bombing in Syria Intensifies, a Debate about the Rules of Engagement," *Washington Post*, December 22, 2015.

165. Quoted in Andrew Cockburn, "War by Remote: How Armchair Generals Pretend They're on the Front Lines," *Harper's Magazine*, March 18, 2015.

166. Lt. Gen. John Hesterman press briefing in the Pentagon via video teleconference, June 5, 2015. General Hesterman's successor as CFACC, Lt. Gen. Charles Q. Brown, USAF, later countered in a similar vein regarding the recent rise in reasoned calls for more permissive ROE in the interest of greater mission effectiveness as to how much harder it would be for the United States to earn and retain the support of the Iraqi and Syrian rank and file "if we just start wiping out civilians," something that no responsible critic of the administration's current ROE regime has ever come close to espousing. Quoted in Aaron Mehta, "Carter 'Prepared' to Change Rules of Engagement against ISIS," *Defense News*, November 19, 2015.

167. Michele Flournoy and Richard Fontaine, *An Intensified Approach to Combatting the Islamic State*, Policy Brief (Washington, D.C.: Center for a New American Security, August 2015), 3–6.

168. Matt Apuzzo, Mark Mazetti, and Michael S. Schmidt, "Inquiry Grows into Intelligence on ISIS Surge," *New York Times*, November 22, 2015.

169. Jeff Schogol, "U.S. Dropping More Bombs on Islamic State than Ever Before," *Air Force Times*, November 25, 2015.

170. Department of Defense, *Department of Defense Dictionary of Military and Associated Terms*, Joint Publication 1-02 (Washington, D.C.: Joint Staff, November 8, 2010 as amended through November 15, 2015), 27.

171. Oriana Pawlyk, "Anti-ISIS Airstrikes in Iraq, Syria Hit 2016 High," *Air Force Times*, July 19, 2016.

172. Kimberly Dozier, "How Special Ops Is Taking ISIS Out," *Daily Beast*, May 28, 2016; and Eric Schmitt, "U.S. Says Its Strikes Are Hitting More Significant ISIS Targets," *New York Times*, May 26, 2016.

173. Department of Defense, "Operation Inherent Resolve: Targeted Operations against ISIL Terrorists," Washington, D.C.: U.S. Department of Defense news release, September 14, 2016.

174. Mark Pommerleau, "Cyber Command Leader: ISIS Is 'Most Adaptive Target' Seen in 35 Years of Intel," C4ISRNet.com, September 13, 2016.

175. Quoted in "Air Force Chief of Staff Describes Major Role in Fight against ISIS," NPR, August 30, 2016.
176. Quoted in Mark Thomas, "Former U.S. Commanders Take Increasingly Dim View of War on ISIS," *Time*, August 31, 2016.
177. David A. Deptula, "We Can't Stop the Islamic State with a 'Desert Drizzle,'" *USA Today*, November 15, 2015.
178. Elizabeth Quintana and Jonathan Eyal, eds., *Inherently Unresolved: The Military Operation against ISIS*, RUSI Occasional Paper (London: Royal United Services Institute for Defence and Security Studies, October 2015).
179. Cordesman, "Looking Beyond the Tragedy in Paris," 11.
180. A fuller development of these and other teachings offered by the world's major conflicts of the past quarter-century may be found in Benjamin S. Lambeth, "Lessons from Modern Warfare: What the Conflicts of the Post–Cold War Years Should Have Taught Us," *Strategic Studies Quarterly* 7, no. 3 (Fall 2013): 28–72.
181. Michael Howard, *The Lessons of History* (New Haven, Conn.: Yale University Press, 1991), 11.
182. Wesley K. Clark, *Waging Modern War: Bosnia, Kosovo, and the Future of Combat* (New York: Public Affairs, 2001), 425.
183. Quoted in Elliott Abrams, "Just War, Just Means?" *National Review*, June 28, 1999, 16.
184. John Keegan, "Modern Weapons Hit War Wisdom," *Sydney Morning Herald*, June 5, 1999.
185. Quoted in Sean D. Naylor, "Army Panels Warn of Technology Dependence," *Defense News*, August 31–September 1, 1998.
186. Merrill A. McPeak, "The Kosovo Result: The Facts Speak for Themselves," *Armed Forces Journal International*, September 1999, 64.
187. Michael Evans, "Ground War 'Error,'" *London Times*, March 24, 2000.
188. For further discussion, see Benjamin S. Lambeth, "AirLand Reversal," *Air Force Magazine* (February 2014): 60–64.
189. David E. Johnson, *Learning Large Lessons: The Evolving Roles of Ground Power and Air Power in the Post–Cold War Era* (Santa Monica, Calif.: RAND, 2006), 115, 140.
190. T. Michael Moseley, "Coalition Forces Air Component Commander Briefing, April 5, 2003," Department of Defense news transcript, April 5, 2003.
191. Nathaniel Fick, *One Bullet Away: The Making of a Marine Officer* (New York: Houghton Mifflin, 2005), 289.
192. Jody Jacobs, David E. Johnson, Katherine Comanor, Lewis Jamison, Leland Joe, and David Vaughn, *Enhancing Fires and Maneuver through Greater Air-Ground Joint Interdependence* (Santa Monica, Calif.: RAND, 2009), 6.
193. For a well-informed fictional portrayal of how such advanced threat systems might figure in future warfare, see P. W. Singer and August Cole, *Ghost*

Fleet: A Novel of the Next World War (New York: Houghton Mifflin Harcourt, 2015).
194. Grossman, "For U.S. Commander in Kosovo," 1.
195. Colin S. Gray, *The Airpower Advantage in Future Warfare: The Need for Strategy* (Maxwell Air Force Base, Ala.: Air Force Research Institute, 2007), 15, 18, 20.

Chapter 3

MODELING AIRPOWER
The Arab-Israeli Wars of the Twentieth Century

—Alan Stephens

War can only make sense when viewed within its political context, and for the Arab-Israeli wars of the twentieth century that context was absolute. Nothing reveals the extreme nature of this struggle more starkly than the contrasting names given by the protagonists to their first conflict in 1948. To the Israelis, it was "the War of Independence"; to the Palestinians and their Arab allies it was "the Catastrophe."

Israel was established in May 1948 as a Jewish state within the territory of the former British Mandate of Palestine, with a population comprising pre-independence residents, refugees, and immigrants (many of the latter two groups being survivors of the Holocaust). From the first day its very existence was challenged by its predominantly Muslim neighbors. Defeat in war could have meant annihilation. The situation was no less acute for the Palestinians, confronted as they were with the loss of both their homeland and their national identity. Between 1948 and 1949 around 750,000 Palestinians were driven from their homes by Israeli armed forces under a systematic program of land seizure and ethnic cleansing.[1] The number of Palestinians displaced by that process has since grown to 5 million, living in some 60 UN-recognized refugee camps in Jordan, Lebanon, Syria, the West Bank, and Gaza.

In other words, the Arab-Israeli wars of the twentieth century concerned nothing less than national survival. Thus, while the objectives of a particular military operation might have been expressed in limited terms—for example, the Israeli Air Force's (IAF) strike against the Iraqi nuclear reactor at al-Tuwaitha in 1981 was intended to disrupt Iraq's nuclear program for about ten years—the consequences of unconditional defeat for both the Israelis and the Palestinians (represented on the field of battle by their Arab allies) were unthinkable and provided an implicit subtext for every decision and action.

Airpower became central to this continuing struggle and is examined here through seven conflicts: the First Arab-Israeli War, 1948–49; the Suez War, 1956; the Six-Day War, 1967; the War of Attrition, 1969–70; the October War, 1973; the al-Tuwaitha Raid, 1981; and the First Lebanon War, 1982. Throughout this period Israel's exploitation of airpower was exceptional and played a vital role in the nation's survival, while that of the Arab states and organizations more often than not was inept—a failing that contributed to a succession of military defeats and, therefore, to the Palestinians' inability to achieve statehood. The fundamental question arising from this is: why were the Israelis so good and their Arab opponents so bad? This chapter seeks to answer that question by analyzing the protagonists' evolving models of airpower.

THE FIRST ARAB-ISRAELI WAR, 1948-49

The Ottoman (Turkish) Empire dominated the Middle East from the early sixteenth century until the late nineteenth century, at which point the United Kingdom and France intervened. When World War I started in July 1914, the power struggle had not been resolved. In May 1916, anticipating victory, the British and French governments concluded a secret treaty to divide the Arab provinces of the Ottoman Empire to suit their strategic and commercial interests. Known as the Sykes-Picot Agreement after the two principal negotiators, the treaty took no account of traditional tribal and ethnic borders.[2] At the same time, British officials were conferring privately with Arab leaders and seemed to offer them independence, should they join the war against Turkey. The prospect of independence was a key factor in the Arab Revolt of June 1916, a broadly based uprising against the Ottomans that contributed significantly to the allies' victory in the Middle East.

In November 1917 British foreign secretary Arthur Balfour informed the Zionist Federation of Great Britain and Ireland that his government was prepared to "facilitate . . . the establishment in Palestine of a national home for the Jewish people." Britain's position in part reflected sympathy for the plight of the Jewish people, who for centuries had been the victims of dislocation, social exclusion, and pogroms. However, it was also cynical, as the timing indicates. The outcome of World War I remained in the balance, and the British government was hoping to mobilize support among influential Jewish populations in the United States, Russia, and Germany. British and French politicians also thought the establishment of a pro-Western Jewish state within the chaotic politics of the Middle East might help to secure their access to the region's oil fields and the Suez Canal.

Once the war ended, the spirit of cooperation that had informed the Arab Revolt was unable to overcome the region's tradition of suspicion and hostility. With the Arabs again divided and politically powerless, the allies reneged on the suggestion of independence and redrew the Middle East's boundaries in accordance with the Sykes-Picot Agreement. Regional geopolitics relapsed into an inchoate arrangement of protectorates, kingdoms, and tribal fiefdoms dominated by self-serving elites and foreign powers. Egypt provided the classic case study. The region's most important territory because of its strategic location and size, Egypt had been a puppet state for centuries, first as part of the Ottoman Empire and then as a British protectorate. Even when in 1922 it was granted independence, it remained under the rule of a sultan appointed by the British government and under the thumb of the Western banks that owned the Suez Canal. An unfortunate consequence of this exercise in geopolitical cynicism was that when the questions of Palestine and a Jewish homeland were debated in international forums in the years between the world wars, the opinions of Arabs in general and Palestinians in particular counted for little.

Israel and the Trenchard Model

In the hundred years of organized aerial warfare, only a handful of countries have succeeded in developing effective, balanced, and sustainable airpower. Most have lacked the essential combination of technical, financial, and human resources. That combination was first translated into organizational form in the 1920s by Hugh Trenchard, chief of staff of the world's first air force, the (British) Royal Air Force (RAF). Trenchard identified the building blocks of professional airpower as follows: a central flying school to set and maintain standards; research and development units for the technological edge; a staff college to train leaders; an apprentice scheme to train mechanics; and an indigenous industrial base to build and maintain the infrastructure and the machines.[3] Implicit in Trenchard's model were two external components: a strong national economy and a progressive, broadly based education system because high-quality airpower is expensive and requires a skilled workforce. Nothing has changed since.

From the outset, the Israelis understood the Trenchard model (even if they did not identify their approach as such) and were capable of implementing it, whereas the Arabs neither comprehended what was needed nor had the wherewithal to apply it even if they had. Creating the system of people, standards, infrastructure, and resources was the key, and in this social and organizational contest the Israelis were vastly superior.

Encouraged by the Balfour Declaration, Jewish immigration to Palestine (much of it illegal under international law) increased rapidly after World War I, amounting to 483,000 people between 1919 and 1948.[4] This provoked a succession of violent anti-Jewish riots from Palestine's majority Muslim population. In order to protect themselves, local Jewish leaders formed a number of unofficial defense organizations known collectively as the Haganah.

Initially limited to land forces, the Haganah expanded its capabilities in 1937 by establishing the Palestine Flying Service, followed ten years later by an air service. The notion of a distinctive air arm was opposed by the Haganah's dominant army faction, who had a "mystifying aversion to air power," but a handful of World War II veteran pilots argued their case forcefully and were supported by the preeminent figure in the Jewish independence movement, subsequently Israel's first prime minister, David Ben-Gurion.[5]

That this precursor to the IAF was tiny, organizationally ad hoc, sometimes ill disciplined, and had only obsolescent aircraft and equipment was not the point. What mattered was that the importance of independent airpower to any future Jewish state had been recognized. This intellectually and strategically bold initiative constituted the first step toward forming an instrument of policy that would become one of the world's best air forces.

The pivotal event in Arab-Israeli history occurred on November 29, 1947, when the United Nations adopted a resolution to partition the Mandate of Palestine into separate Jewish and Arab states. Under the proposal, 56 percent of the territory was to be allocated to the 600,000 Jews currently living in Palestine and 43 percent to the 1.2 million Palestinians.[6] (The other 1 percent was Jerusalem, which, because of its significance to the three major monotheistic religions, was to be administered by a special regime.) The Jewish allocation included two-thirds of the Mediterranean coast and exclusive access to the Red Sea via the Gulf of Aqaba. The resolution was generally well received within Jewish circles and rejected by Arabs.

The State of Israel came into being on May 14, 1948; one day later it was invaded by armies from Egypt, Syria, Iraq, Lebanon, and Jordan and attacked by aircraft from the Royal Egyptian Air Force. Shortly afterward the Haganah's air service became Israel's air force.[7] The new service's leaders had to organize recruiting, training, planning, equipment acquisition, intelligence, and logistics while fighting a war of national survival.

Thanks to the legacy of the Palestine Flying Service, planning had at least begun and some of the pieces were already in place. Noteworthy initiatives in the early days included conducting a census to determine the numbers of trained air and ground crews in the country (many Jews had served with allied air forces during World War II) and contacting friendly nations to try to obtain any hardware a new air force might be able to use.[8] Important financial backing came from sympathizers in the United States, where another future Israeli prime minister, Golda Meir, was prominent in marshaling resources.

The IAF started combat operations with a collection of secondhand light aircraft. Early missions included handheld photography and manual "bomb chucking" onto advancing Arab armies. Better equipment was soon acquired, notably Bf-109, Spitfire, and P-51 fighters and a few B-17 bombers, C-47 transports, and antiaircraft guns. Simultaneously, skilled pilots were recruited from local and international volunteers: of the 607 men who served in the IAF and its associated transport command in 1948-49, 70 percent had combat experience from World War II.[9]

In sum, the IAF took constructive steps toward building an effective organizational structure and conducting an air force's primary roles of control of the air; intelligence, surveillance, and reconnaissance (ISR); strike; and maneuver.

Egypt, Syria, Iraq, and the Oriental Despotism Model

While Israel moved purposefully toward building a professional air force, its Arab neighbors were trapped within a socioeconomic model that in many ways was resistant to intellectual and technological progress. That model might be likened to oriental despotism, a condition identified by historians as disparate as Herodotus and Karl Marx, which was characterized by the domination of the many by the few (kings, dictators, tribal lords, etc.), an agrarian economy based on feudal relationships, the absence of a broad-based meritocracy, and an archaic education system. The term may seem unusual, but understanding the extent to which modernity had bypassed the Middle East is essential to understanding the Arab world's approach to airpower.

According to Marx, the constraints on progress inherent in oriental despotism might be broken by the "civilizing influence" of an occupying power whose wealth, advanced technologies, and relative freedoms would not go unnoticed by repressed populations.[10] The Ottomans were not modernizers, but the British and French diplomats, financiers, businessmen, and soldiers who increasingly controlled Middle Eastern affairs from the late nineteenth century onward were. However, there were strict limits to the reforms those self-interested groups permitted; consequently, Arab societies in 1948 were still dominated by elites and remained undeveloped, poor, and badly educated.

Taking Egypt as an example, despite several half-hearted attempts at industrialization in the early decades of the twentieth century, by the start of World War II the economy was still based on growing and exporting cotton and on a few related industries such as transport and warehousing. Even when change was introduced following the nationalist revolution led by army colonel Gamal Abdel Nasser in 1952, the effects took years to flow through the broader society. Almost a quarter of a century after the revolution, Egypt's literacy rate was a dismal 38.2 percent compared to Israel's 95 percent, and its gross domestic product (GDP) per capita was $324 compared to Israel's $3,500.[11] It was within that unfavorable setting that Egypt took its first steps toward building airpower.

The Egyptian Army Air Service was formed in 1930, invariably stifled by the dead hand of either its British masters or its army generals. Training, logistics, and aircraft were supplied by the RAF, and tasking was controlled by the Army.[12] Nominal independence in 1937 brought a name change to the Royal

Egyptian Air Force (REAF), and measures were taken to form an air academy. New bases were built adjacent to the strategically vital Suez Canal, and squadrons received obsolescent army support aircraft such as the Gloster Gladiator and Westland Lysander from the United Kingdom.

World War II served as an agent of change in the Middle East. Among other things, the RAF expanded its infrastructure in the region, an initiative that benefited the REAF. Egyptian pilots gained operational experience when they occasionally and unofficially flew with the RAF against the Italian and German air forces (Egypt was formally neutral until the final weeks of the war). Small numbers of Hurricane and Tomahawk fighters were added to the REAF's inventory, later supplemented by Spitfires and C-47s.

Nevertheless, Egyptian airpower remained marginalized. On the eve of the first Arab-Israeli war, the REAF consisted of only two hundred officers and two thousand airmen. Operational standards were low; the REAF had little planning capacity, few training services, insufficient technicians, no national technological support, no repair depot, and an inadequate recruitment pool.[13]

With due alteration for detail, similar circumstances inhibited progress in Iraq, Syria, and Jordan. The Royal Iraqi Air Force (RIrAF) claimed April 1931 as its foundation date, when newly graduated pilots who had trained in England arrived back home. Also heavily dependent on the RAF, the RIrAF may have achieved better standards than the Egyptians because of regular participation in operations against rebel indigenous tribes. But in 1941 the RAF destroyed the RIrAF when the United Kingdom struck back harshly against an attempt by Iraqis to assert independence. The modern state of Syria was established as a French mandate after World War I. Independence came after World War II, and the Syrian Arab Air Force (SyAAF) was formed in 1948. It entered the first Arab-Israeli war with a small number of RAF-trained pilots and limited capabilities. Jordan also gained independence after World War II, but while its army was to play a role in the war against Israel, its air capability was irrelevant.

Modern versus Archaic

As noted, on the day after declaring independence, Israel was invaded by a combined Arab League force from Egypt, Syria, Iraq, and Jordan; Lebanon joined in later. The war lasted fourteen months and was fought mainly between land forces. Israel started with about 30,000 personnel under arms and finished with 118,000, while for the Arabs the numbers were 13,000 and 64,000. Some 6,400 Israeli soldiers and civilians and about 6,000 Arab League soldiers were killed. The Palestinians fared worst, with anywhere up to 13,000 fighters and civilians killed and hundreds of thousands of civilians displaced or ethnically cleansed. By the time a cease-fire was accepted, Israel not only held all of the territory allocated to it under the UN Partition plan but had also had seized 50 percent of Palestine's territory.

Air operations were peripheral to the outcome, but some noteworthy combat and doctrinal events occurred. As mentioned earlier, the IAF's first wartime sorties included intelligence gathering with a handheld camera from a light aircraft. While the means may have been primitive, the mission was modern in its objective. So too was the REAF's combat debut on May 15, 1948, when four Spitfires attacked a power station in Tel Aviv and parked aircraft at an IAF base. These were classic airpower targets, hinting at a strategic outcome in the first instance and control of the air in the second. But Egypt's airmen were unable to sustain that intellectual model. Within days the REAF shifted its attention to attacks against civilians in towns and rural settlements, indicating that their campaign had degenerated into the discredited concept of terror bombing. And a strike against a British air base that the Egyptians wrongly believed was occupied by the IAF attracted a severe lesson in professionalism when the RAF retaliated by shooting down five REAF Spitfires.

The Arab air forces' association with the RAF had given them a veneer of competence, but it was no more than that. Following the UN's partition resolution, the British government wanted to get out of its mandate responsibilities for Palestine as quickly as possible, which meant distancing itself from the now-warring parties. This included withdrawing the RAF's support, a move that exposed the REAF's structural weakness. There was no indigenous training system to augment the small number of skilled pilots and technicians, and abysmal maintenance practices meant that aircraft were unserviceable more often than not. When missions were flown, planning was haphazard and cooperation between the Arab air forces nonexistent.

The contrast with the IAF could not have been more pronounced. The Israelis had to scramble to obtain aircraft, ancillary equipment, and expert assistance, and often had to make do with what they could get rather than what they wanted. In order to circumvent American restrictions on the export of aircraft, spare parts, and weapons, Israeli agents established fake companies through which transactions could be processed. Countries sympathetic to the Jewish cause were approached for material and political help, which in some instances involved unofficial approval to use airfields to ferry equipment to Israel. By the end of 1948 the IAF had assembled a useful force of World War II–vintage fighter aircraft complemented by an assortment of airlifters, ground attack, and army liaison aircraft.

Simultaneously, air bases and logistics chains were set up, which meant that, unlike the Arab air forces, the IAF could keep its aircraft flying. The recruitment of experienced air and ground crews continued, with training conducted in Italy, Czechoslovakia, and South Africa as well as Israel. Planning services were established, including a department of operations, an intelligence branch, and an aerial photography unit.

By the end of the year the numerically outnumbered but qualitatively superior IAF had established control of the air and was conducting battlefield resupply, command-and-control, intelligence, and close-attack missions. This cleverly assembled bits-and-pieces air force provided the Israeli Army with a significant warfighting advantage.

Commentary

By early 1949 both sides had had enough and eventually agreed to an armistice brokered by the United Nations. The Arabs, while strategically and organizationally inept, were sufficiently astute to accept that they should call a halt before things got worse and they lost even more territory, while the Israelis, although militarily dominant, decided they should take their winnings while they could, lest world opinion turned against them because of their illegal annexation of large amounts of Palestinian land.

Although airpower's role in the war was marginal, some useful observations can be drawn. Laboring under the combined weight of colonial oppression, a near-feudal socioeconomic system, and inadequate public schooling and lacking united leadership, the Arab states were incapable of constructing effective airpower. It should not have been surprising that the façade of competence applied by their European mentors crumbled within weeks or that the longer the fighting went, the worse the Egyptian, Iraqi, and Syrian air forces became. The critical issues for the Arabs at the end of the war were whether they could grasp what had happened and whether they were capable of implementing the necessary socioeconomic reforms.

Israel's experience, by comparison, could scarcely have been more impressive. Applying the Trenchard model either deliberately or intuitively, Israel's political and military leaders marshaled their financial, industrial, technological, and, most importantly, human resources within a clear strategic framework. Consequently, the IAF was able to play an increasingly useful role in the fighting.

Israel emerged from the war as the political winner. Military success against an ostensibly more powerful enemy attracted international respect, consolidated the new nation's territory, and added legitimacy to its status. By contrast, the Arab states that supported Palestine not only lost the war but also lost face. The Palestinians themselves were by far the biggest losers, with the conflict signaling the beginning of an unmitigated catastrophe.[14]

THE SUEZ WAR, 1956
Egyptian Nationalism

Following its completion in 1869, the Suez Canal became one of the world's most important transport links. By greatly shortening the maritime route between Europe and the Indian Ocean, the canal enhanced the passage of trade, warships, and armies; later, from the 1950s until the 1990s, it became the "oil highway" between the Middle East and Europe, providing transit for two-thirds of all shipments. Although the canal's utility diminished with the evolution of supertankers that could carry enough oil to make longer routes profitable (and that were too big to use the canal anyway), for more than a century it was one of the central components of the international political and financial power structure.

The canal was built with French and Egyptian money and was nominally under the management of an Egyptian company. In 1882 the United Kingdom invaded Egypt and, in association with France, seized control of the canal. When German and Ottoman forces tried to capture the canal during World War I, Britain established a garrison of 80,000 troops at Suez. From then on the canal was treated as a British territorial possession, with the UK government infringing "almost every article" of the relevant international conventions.[15]

Anticolonial movements around the world were invigorated by the shock of World War II, which undermined the authority and wealth of the imperial powers. British statesmen managed to disengage the United Kingdom from most of its overseas possessions with a degree of civility, but the Suez Canal was an exception: because of its importance to trade, military deployments, and the flow of oil, guaranteed access was regarded as a strategic imperative.

In July 1952 a revolution in Egypt led by army officers saw the overthrow of the king, the establishment of a republic, the replacement of constitutional monarchy with parliamentary government, and a reduction in British garrison forces. In mid-1956 the leader of the revolution, Nasser, now the president, nationalized the Suez Canal, a move that precipitated military intervention by the United Kingdom, France, and Israel.[16]

Before addressing that intervention, the modernization program initiated by Egypt's new government in 1952 must be outlined because of its implications for airpower. Reform was introduced across most sectors of society—political, legal, educational, financial, agricultural, military, and industrial. Included in the latter was the establishment of the Egyptian Aircraft Construction Factory at Helwan, near Cairo. The factory drew on expert (if unsavory) assistance from foreign sources such as the renowned designer of the Bf-109 and convicted Nazi collaborator Willy Messerschmitt and the air force of fascist Spain. A primary trainer based on the German Bucker Bu 181D went into production, as did aero engines also derived from imported technology. Cairo's Kader Factory for Developed Industries was another center of aircraft engineering.[17]

As reform gathered pace, Egypt experienced something of a socioeconomic renaissance. But the country was starting from a very low base and, after "centuries of infantilizing colonial rule," transformation of the necessary magnitude represented an enormous challenge.[18] Social and educational progress continued to be constrained by religious conservatism, which favored the rote learning of scriptures over critical thinking. By the time of the Suez crisis, four years of effort had managed to inch Egypt's literacy rate up to only 25 percent and its GDP per capita to $275. Israel's rates stood at 95 percent and $2,000.[19]

The Egyptian Air Force

President Nasser had served in the Egyptian Army in the 1948-49 war against Israel and was aware of the military's deficiencies; consequently, postrevolution modernization was extended to the armed services.

After the war the United Kingdom had reequipped the REAF with small numbers of jet fighters and trainers, including the frontline Gloster Meteor. But the British attitude was disrespectful. Twelve Meteor F8s were promised, but five were diverted to Brazil and three to Israel, while the four that arrived in Egypt had had their guns removed. Several years later fourteen more Meteors were delivered, but half were dual-seat trainers, and drop-tanks that increased the aircraft's range and, therefore, its combat capability were withheld. Requests to the United States for F-86 Sabres were rejected.

RAF instructors who trained Egyptian pilots on the Meteor found their students to be enthusiastic but below average.[20] Poor standards extended to maintenance and logistics procedures, which were under-resourced and disorganized. At least leadership and flying training were placed on a potentially more professional basis with the formal establishment in 1951 of the Egyptian Air Academy.

As Egypt sought to exercise greater independence, the United Kingdom sought to maintain its grip on the Suez Canal. Additional strain was placed on the relationship by a series of terrorist raids by the Israeli secret service against British and U.S. interests in Egypt, intended to be perceived as the work of local anti-imperialists. In what became known as the "Lavon Affair" after the defense minister who approved it, Israeli agents placed bombs in British- and U.S.-sponsored libraries, movie theaters, and cultural centers around Egypt. Israel simultaneously pursued a policy of "active defense" against its prospective enemies, including "preemptive" strikes against Palestinian communities in the Egyptian-ruled Gaza Strip.

In an atmosphere of deteriorating relations with the West, the Egyptian government turned to the Union of Soviet Socialist Republics (USSR) for military aid. For the Soviets, this was an opportunity to strengthen their hand in the Cold War. Toward the end of 1955 air warfare matériel started pouring in to Egypt. Eighty-six MiG-15 interceptor/fighters headed the list, together with thirty-nine Il-28 twin-engine bombers, twenty Il-14 airlifters, training and support equipment, and ground-based defense systems.[21] Egyptian Air Force (EAF) pilots were given hurried conversions, and on January 15, 1956, a flight of MiG-15s overflew Cairo to show the Egyptian people their new air force.

MiG-15s and Il-28s were good aircraft. The question was: did the EAF have the full suite of competencies—all of the elements of the Trenchard model—to use its equipment effectively? The challenge of changing from Western-bloc aircraft, systems, and practices was enormous. The language shift alone was demanding, affecting flight manuals, cockpit instrumentation, and maintenance publications. Furthermore, Russian air force training was notoriously rigid and controlled (like Soviet society itself), so while basic flying instruction was reasonable, pilots received little exposure to advanced combat maneuvers and tactics.[22]

A report submitted to London early in 1956 by the British air attaché in Cairo noted that while the EAF's handful of experienced pilots were good, the majority were ill disciplined, had poor flying techniques, were below standard in instrument and night flying, and had little comprehension of air warfare operations and tactics. And the shortage of qualified mechanics was a greater problem. In the attaché's opinion, the EAF was in "no position to take on the Israelis."[23] In truth, the EAF's ability to attack Israel was more image than substance, and the assertion made by some commentators that the influx of Soviet aircraft had altered the balance of power in the Middle East was disingenuous.[24]

The Israeli Air Force

Although the IAF was nominally independent, its leaders had been excluded from higher Israel Defense Forces (IDF) planning during the 1948–49 war.[25] Given the IAF's limited capabilities and the land-centric nature of the conflict, that was perhaps understandable. But it was also short sighted.

Israel has very little strategic depth. In places it can take a jet aircraft only minutes to overfly the border and reach major population centers, and it can take only hours for an invading army to do the same. The corollary, of course, is that IAF aircraft can threaten potential targets with little warning. In other words, only airpower has the necessary speed of response and range to defend the nation against sudden attack, regardless of whether that attack comes from land, sea, or air, and to take the initiative, perhaps preemptively. Moreover, much of the region is open, flat, and featureless—an ideal setting for the classic combination of airpower and fast-moving armor and infantry. Those factors indicated that, rather than being relegated to a subordinate role, airpower should have been regarded as Israel's strategic force of first choice. Many countries have large armies that fight capably close up, but very few have high-quality air forces. For Israel, the point was to deny its enemies the first prospect and derive maximum advantage from the second.

Arguments to that end fell on deaf ears, in the case of the IDF's higher command because the army generals simply did not understand them and in the case of Prime Minister Ben-Gurion because he was trying to balance competing priorities. Israel's position was parlous. It was a new state surrounded by enemies and had minimal strategic depth. Almost every community service had to be developed from the ground up, not least the economy and social cohesion. Ben-Gurion consequently wanted to base national defense on a mass reserve force that would be called up only during crises, thus leaving the population free to build the nation. While the policy seemed reasonable, it failed to grasp the significance of airpower to Israel's geostrategic position and the centrality to airpower of highly trained, full-time practitioners.

Frustration within the IAF provoked a number of senior commanders to resign. In the end, this proved fortuitous. Under the new leadership of the administratively expert Maj. Gen. Haim Laskov and the respected World War II pilot Col. Dan Tolkowsky, the IAF prospered.[26] Laskov inherited an organization weakened by its previous commander's struggle with the army. He wisely adopted a path of least resistance by ostensibly acceding to the IDF's insistence that the IAF was a supporting service and got on with the business of building an elite force that would establish its worth not by internecine doctrinal disputes but by combat success.

Laskov established three warfighting priorities for the IAF: controlling the air, "disabling" Arab air forces, and supporting surface forces. Plans were developed, training programs revised, maintenance and other technical facilities strengthened, and equipment procured. Consistent with that approach, standards at the recently established Israeli Air Force Flight Academy were exacting. Underpinning everything was Tolkowsky's insistence that the air force had to maximize its unique combat capabilities—that control of the air and strike had to take priority. The right course had been set.

Also on the right course were Israel's aerospace industries. In 1953 the Bedek Aviation Company, subsequently renamed Israel Aerospace Industries (IAI), was founded at the initiative of Defense Ministry official Shimon Peres (later prime minister and president of Israel and Nobel laureate).[27] Bedek's task was to support the IAF, which it did not merely by completing routine maintenance but also by developing modifications specific to a particular conflict, by adapting aircraft to use new or different weapons, or by reverse engineering covertly obtained technologies, and so on. Within six years Bedek was manufacturing its first aircraft, a derivative of the French Fouga Magister light attack/trainer. Additional defense research and development capacity came from the government-sponsored Science Corps, later re-formed as the Division of Research and Planning and then as Rafael Advanced Defense Systems Ltd.[28]

Overcoming financial constraints, the IAF managed to upgrade its fleet through a combination of hard work and ingenuity involving conventional international arms sales and backroom deals. By mid-1956 the existing fleet of second-line but still useful Meteors and Vampires had been supplemented by a frontline force of sixty supersonic Mystère IVAs and twenty-two Ouragan strike/fighters. Supplied by France, these aircraft tipped the never-ending technological battle Israel's way. A fleet of C-47 airlifters and a variety of communications/liaison aircraft rounded out the IAF's evolving force structure.

In the months leading up to the Suez War Israeli strike/fighters regularly infringed Egyptian airspace. When on one occasion the EAF retaliated by sending four Vampire fighter/trainers across the border into Israel, IAF Meteor pilots provided a cameo of what was to come by shooting down two of them.

War as Policy

Friction over control of the Suez Canal had existed from the time the canal opened. Britain quelled dissent by establishing a powerful garrison in the canal zone during World War I, but tensions resurfaced following Egypt's revolution in 1952. President Nasser nationalized the canal in July 1956, and on October 29 Egypt was invaded by the United Kingdom, France, and Israel. The protagonists' objectives differed fundamentally. For Egypt, the Suez Canal represented nationalism, independence, and economic opportunity; for Britain and France, it was central to their desire for cheap oil and strategic influence; while for Israel, the dispute opened a back door to territorial opportunism.

Passage to and from Asia and East Africa from the Israeli port of Eilat was possible only through the Gulf of Aqaba, which was dominated by the Straits of Tiran. Egypt had blockaded the straits by placing a battery of guns on the adjacent Sinai Peninsula and had denied access to all Israel-bound and Israeli shipping. As the likelihood of an Anglo-French military intervention against Egypt over the Suez Canal grew, the Israeli government saw an opportunity to join in and pursue their own ambitions. Israel's goals were to gain access to the Gulf of Aqaba via the Straits of Tiran and to deal with the perceived military threat from Egypt sooner rather than later. Sensitive to the United Kingdom's commercial interests with Arab nations, the British government initially opposed Israel's participation. But British sensibilities were of little concern to France and Israel, which began joint planning, and eventually the United Kingdom acquiesced. Two separate but complementary campaign plans to invade Egypt were developed, one reflecting Anglo-French interests and the other Israel's.

The Anglo-French plan centered on a large-scale amphibious and airborne invasion to seize control of the canal, but the British Army commander in chief of British and French forces, Gen. Charles Keightley, thought that a "strategic" bombing campaign might by itself be sufficient to achieve victory. An advocate of advanced technology, Keightley believed that the RAF's new fleet of Valiant and Canberra jet bombers would be able to achieve a politically inexpensive victory by destroying the Egyptian economy and national will and precipitating a popular uprising against Nasser.[29]

General Keightley's analysis suffered from considerable technical, doctrinal, and political shortcomings. Technically, the Valiants and Canberras had only recently entered service, and concepts for their use were immature. Bombing accuracy was an issue. Because several daytime reconnaissance flights over Egypt by RAF Canberra PR7s had been attacked by EAF MiG-15s, British planners decided that the offensive would be conducted at night and from high altitude. Those parameters enhanced safety but at the cost of bombing accuracy. Doctrinally, while Egypt was making economic and industrial progress, it was still an undeveloped, agrarian-based society, and as the failed U.S. Air Force (USAF) campaign against North Korea several years previously had revealed, a scarcity of high-value targets can negate the concept of strategic bombing.[30] Finally, in the postcolonial world, there was already international unease at the prospect of two advanced, wealthy states attacking a backward, poor state for entirely selfish reasons. Even before the fighting began, the United Kingdom and France had very little political capital to expend.

A three-phase plan for the invasion was endorsed on September 8, 1956. Phases 1 and 2 were to be solely air campaigns in which winning air supremacy over Egypt would be followed by a ten-day "aero-psychological" offensive directed against "transportation, communication, and economic centers [and] Egyptian morale" that would, if General Keightley were correct, bring about the country's collapse and Nasser's overthrow. Air- and sea-borne forces would then land unopposed in phase 3 and seize the canal.[31]

The Israelis' primary objective was to reopen the Straits of Tiran; thus, their plan emphasized air-land operations in the Sinai Peninsula. Clearing out Palestinian fedayeen guerrilla forces from the densely populated Egyptian-held Gaza Strip was another goal. Any damage the Anglo-French campaign might inflict on Egypt's broader capacity to threaten Israel would be a bonus.

IAF staff worked closely with IDF commander Lt. Gen. Moshe Dayan, who planned a rapid-maneuver assault in the Sinai. Dayan's concept required IAF strike/fighter units to win air superiority, immediately after which fast-moving infantry, artillery, armor, and close-air attack forces would "encircle" and then capture Egyptian strong points. Other IAF units would provide maneuver through paradrop and airlift missions and perform intelligence, liaison, and communications services.

Egypt's air strategy was shaped as much by its air force's limitations and the defensive doctrine of its Soviet mentors as it was by the prevailing circumstances. Controlling Egyptian airspace and protecting the army were the EAF's primary tasks, followed by close attack (noting that the EAF's best aircraft, the MiG-15 air superiority fighter, was unsuited to that role).[32] Given the EAF's low standards—including a reluctance to fly at night—and the qualitative and numerical superiority of the Anglo-French land- and naval-based air forces, neither of those objectives was credible.

The war started on October 29, 1956, when, before the Anglo-French offensive in the Suez zone had begun, Israel invaded the Sinai Peninsula. As part of Dayan's maneuver and encirclement plan, C-47 airlifter crews flew at low level under enemy radar to drop paratroopers, and P-51 Mustang pilots disrupted the Egyptian command-and-control system by cutting telephone lines with specially designed chain devices attached to their aircrafts' wings or, if that failed, with their propellers. Air defense was provided by patrols of Mystère fighters. Once Israeli soldiers were on the ground, the IAF turned its attention to close attack and interdiction.

For a period the EAF fought back. MiG-15, Meteor, and Vampire units attacked the Israeli Army, and MiG-15s clashed with Mystères. However, the IAF quickly asserted its dominance. The Israelis also dominated another vital component of airpower: the contest for management and maintenance superiority. IAF engineers were able to generate four sorties a day from their strike/fighters—a rate twice that of their enemies, which effectively doubled the size of the IAF's fleet.[33] Fighting between the opposing armies was sometimes intense, but within days the Sinai was under Israeli control.

On October 30 the British and French governments formally warned President Nasser that unless all Egyptian forces were withdrawn from the canal zone within two days, air attacks would be launched against military and industrial targets. The ultimatum generated a degree of panic among Egyptian civilians but was rejected by Nasser. Part success, part failure, and part farce, the ensuing offensive was to become a classic illustration of the truism that a bombing campaign can only be conducted in accordance with the prevailing political ethos.

The campaign began on the night of October 31, when RAF Canberra and Valiant bombers attacked targets around Cairo. The Anglo-French ultimatum and reconnaissance flights over Egypt in the preceding days should have been more than enough warning for the Egyptians to place their air defenses—blackouts, camouflage, radio silence, early-warning radars, fighter squadrons, antiaircraft batteries—on full readiness. Yet as the first RAF bombers approached Egypt, their crews were astonished to find almost no opposition and every city in the Nile Delta "ablaze with light."[34] Targets were clearly illuminated by red markers dropped by a pathfinder Canberra. Unworried by desultory low-altitude flak, the British crews dropped their bombs from 30,000 feet. Accuracy was poor and the material damage slight, but the political ramifications in the United Kingdom were severe.

British prime minister Anthony Eden was "horrified" to learn that one of the targets was a civilian airfield near Cairo from which, by chance, American citizens were being evacuated. Already sensitive to the opprobrium of the international community and worried by the possibility of civilian casualties, Eden personally intervened to divert a follow-up force of Valiants to alternative targets.[35] From then on, all bombing operations were subject to strict political oversight. The strategic campaign continued, focusing on airfields, military bases, supply depots, oil facilities, road and rail systems, and radio and communications links. British planners also still clung to the dubious objective of terrorizing the Egyptian people.

Shorter-range strike/fighters operating off aircraft carriers and from airfields in Cyprus, which attacked with greater accuracy from lower altitudes, were more successful. The EAF's unpreparedness extended to leaving aircraft parked on tarmacs in neat lines, making them ideal targets for strafing, fragmentation bombs, and rockets. The morning after the first strategic strike, scores of Anglo-French Venoms, Sea Venoms, Corsairs, Thunderstreaks, and Seahawks, with top cover from Hunters, swept in for what amounted to little more than an air-to-ground weapons exercise against the carelessly arrayed EAF. As many as two hundred aircraft were destroyed, leaving the EAF in ruins. According to two former RAF instructor pilots who were working for the Egyptians and who observed the raid, the EAF was "stunned . . . into inactivity."[36] Problems were compounded by disorganized communications, which made it difficult for commanders to collate information and exercise authority.

President Nasser responded with two profound decisions. First, he ordered the forty or so ships transiting the Suez Canal to be sunk, an action that at one stroke closed the canal, stopped the flow of oil to Britain and France, boosted his popularity at home, and increased political pressure on the aggressor states. Second, he instructed the EAF to withdraw most of its remaining assets, including MiG-15s and Il-28s, to safety in southern Egypt, Saudi Arabia, and Syria. Clearly the EAF was out of its depth, and by fleeing the field its pilots and aircraft were saved for another time and place when they might be more effective. On the other hand, their retreat so early in the war was ignominious and left the Egyptian Army exposed. But Nasser's rationale was sound: as he explained after the war, "At some stage the British and French are going to withdraw. But we are going to be in a state of war with Israel for years, and we shall need all the pilots we can get. Planes can be replaced overnight, but it takes years to train a pilot."[37]

With the EAF removed from the equation, Anglo-French strike/fighter pilots were free to soften up the Egyptian Army in preparation for the next phase of the campaign. The invasion of the canal zone started on November 5 and was briefly resisted by elements of the Egyptian Army. Many units could not, however, cope with the ferocious assault and the "no prisoners" code of merciless French paratroopers, while others were "annihilated" by close-attack aircraft as the battle along the canal degenerated into a rout.[38]

Nasser again demonstrated his political acuity. He had weapons issued to civilians, instructed his soldiers to wear civilian clothing, and declared the conflict to be a "people's war." Anthony Eden and his French counterpart, Guy Mollet, were confronted with a major problem. It was already clear that civilian casualties had become a central concern for France and the United Kingdom, and that "excessive" Egyptian deaths—whatever that meant—would precipitate demands from the United Nations and the United States for French and British forces to get out of the country. And now they were fighting a vicious, one-sided war against "civilians."

The Politics of War

Eight days after the conflict began France and the United Kingdom had won the battle. Their armies and navies had fought professionally and fiercely, their air forces had been dominant, and they had achieved their military objectives. They had, however, lost the war. Prime ministers Eden and Mollet had misjudged the international mood, and for them this particular armed conflict was no longer an acceptable form of the continuation of policy by other means.

Pressure to quit came from numerous sources. In the United Kingdom the First Sea Lord and member of the royal family, Adm. Louis Mountbatten, opposed the invasion because of the political costs and his fear British servicemen would kill "thousands of innocent women and children."[39] Antiwar protests were led by prominent left-wing politicians and intellectuals, who made frequent references to war crimes. Anger was also widespread in the Muslim world, where anti-Western rallies were held, Western-owned businesses sabotaged, and an embargo placed on oil exports to the United Kingdom and France by Saudi Arabia.

The most compelling opposition came from the United States, for whom international politics was dominated by the Cold War. President Dwight Eisenhower was concerned that anti-Western sentiments arising from the invasion would drive the Middle East into the Soviet camp, with potentially disastrous consequences for oil supplies and the world balance of power. Eisenhower had taken the lead in the international condemnation of the USSR's recent invasion of Hungary and could be accused of hypocrisy if he supported a no less reprehensible incursion by the West into Egypt. The United States therefore placed intense political and economic pressure on its two allies.

On November 2 the United Nations overwhelmingly endorsed a U.S. proposal for a cease-fire, the withdrawal of all invading forces, and the reopening of the canal. Several days later the resolution came into effect. This represented a stunning success for Nasser and Egypt, who, in contrast to their Anglo-French enemies, had lost the battle but won the war.

Israel's political outlook was different. For Prime Minister Ben-Gurion and his cabinet, the war had not been about oil or economics or prestige but national survival. Thus, Israel initially rejected the UN resolution by refusing to withdraw from the Gaza Strip and the Sinai Peninsula and not allowing peacekeepers into areas its forces controlled. Ben-Gurion eventually relented under the threat of U.S. sanctions, and the IDF pulled out from the Sinai in March 1957, but not before systematically destroying roads, railways, telephone lines, and villages.[40] Shortly afterward the Suez Canal was reopened to all shipping and the Straits of Tiran to Israeli and Israel-bound vessels.

Commentary

For the United Kingdom and France, the Suez crisis was a military success but a humiliating political failure; for Egypt, it was a military defeat but a resounding political victory; and for Israel, it was both a military and political success. Britain in particular suffered a severe loss of prestige, leading to Prime Minister Eden's resignation. The confirmation by the United States and the United Nations of Egypt's sovereignty over the Suez Canal saw President Nasser's reputation soar within the Arab world. Nasser's admirable leadership deserved praise, but perhaps in the afterglow of the political triumph he and other Arab leaders chose to forget the dismal performance of Egypt's armed forces; if so, it was an indulgence they would come to regret. No such self-satisfaction distracted Israel's leadership from the job still at hand. Immediate objectives might have been achieved, but the threat to their state had not diminished.

As far as airpower was concerned, the RAF's strategic campaign bordered on the eccentric. Aircraft intended for nuclear war against the USSR—a setting that implied the existence of numerous high-value targets and the need for only modest bombing accuracy—were deployed against a third-world nation in which hitting the few worthwhile targets from high altitude with unguided bombs demanded a degree of precision that could never be achieved.

That aside, the Anglo-French air operations were predictably professional, routing the EAF in days and paving the way for the land invasion. The EAF by contrast was predictably abysmal. President Nasser's decision to order the remnants of his air force to flee after only two days was courageous and strategic: trained pilots are airpower's most hard-won and perishable commodity, and it made sense to save them for another day. The question, though, was whether the EAF's leaders understood what was needed to reach an acceptable standard and, if they did, how long it might it take.

Israel provided the main airpower story. During the 1948-49 war the IAF had been a useful but marginal contributor, but by 1956 it was an essential component of a highly effective joint force. Operations in the Sinai confirmed that the IAF had all the components of the Trenchard model in place and that the institutional commitment to excellence was working. Furthermore, Air Force leaders had accepted the importance of cooperating with their Army colleagues and had integrated their service's capabilities into the overall IDF concept of operations. In turn, the Army better understood air's war-winning potential, especially given Israel's distinctive geostrategic setting. No one questioned the place of airpower in the IDF's future; rather, it was a matter of making the IAF bigger and better—and as quickly as possible.

The Suez War left two profound legacies for Arab-Israeli relations. First, Israeli scientists had been secretly gathering the knowledge and technology for building nuclear weapons since 1949. As part of the pre-Suez invasion negotiations France agreed to sell Israel a research reactor and uranium fuel. Construction began at Dimona in the Negev Desert in 1958, concealed from the inspection regime of the International Atomic Energy Agency. The second legacy was the formation in 1964 of the Palestine Liberation Organization (PLO), whose prime objective was to wage armed struggle against Israel.

The Suez cease-fire did not lead to an effective peace agreement. Constant cross-border incursions and acts of terrorism by both sides continued to increase tensions, which for the Israelis reached a breaking point in June 1967.

THE SIX-DAY WAR, 1967
Preemption as Strategy

Airpower is purpose built for preemption, a strategy that can be both devastating and controversial. Two of the better-known examples are the attacks by the Japanese Naval Air Force against Pearl Harbor on 7 December 1941, and by the IAF against Egypt on 5 June 1967. The Japanese Naval Air Force came close to dealing a terminal blow to the U.S. Pacific fleet, while the IAF effectively destroyed the EAF in a morning. As for controversy, U.S. president Franklin D. Roosevelt described Japan's attack as a "day of infamy," while a quarter of a century later official American sources praised the IAF's strike as a "brilliant opening" to a "war of daring."

Any hope of resolving the hostility between Israel and the Arab states following the Suez crisis quickly evaporated. Led by Egypt, most Arab nations refused to acknowledge Israel's right to exist, while Israel refused to comply with near-unanimous UN resolutions regarding peacekeeping measures and illegal territorial annexations. Both protagonists supported terrorist incursions against each other's populations, and border clashes between their armies occurred regularly. The rise of the PLO was a reflection not only of that mutual hostility but also of the growing frustration of a displaced people. Given the often profoundly moving history of the Jewish diaspora, this was a dark irony. By 1967 it was a case of when, not if, another war would be fought.

Swift Intuition

Writing in 1928, the great Italian airpower theorist Giulio Douhet argued that the war in the air is the "true war of movement," in which "swift intuition, swifter decision, and still swifter execution" are needed.[41] Douhet might have been describing the IAF of 1967. In the eleven years between the end of the Suez crisis and the start of the Six-Day War, the IAF largely completed its transformation into an airpower of the highest caliber—into a force that moved with swift assurance and could win wars.

Notwithstanding the IAF's strong performance in 1956, there was still considerable scope for improvement. People had to be the starting point, followed by planning and equipment. Skilled strike/fighter pilots were the most pressing need. Control of the air and close attack had been central to Lieutenant General Dayan's rapid-maneuver strategy in the Sinai and would be again in the next war. Pilot numbers had to be increased and standards raised. Flying in the Air Force was not the military profession of choice for talented young Israelis for whom service with the commandos held most appeal. Major General Tolkowsky, who had become the IAF's commander in May 1953, challenged that mindset. He wrote to all suitable high school graduates and encouraged them to become pilots; insisted on all new flying instructors having a fighter background; and reorganized the training syllabus so that students progressed sooner onto jet aircraft.[42] Within a year annual recruitment numbers increased from seventeen to eighty, and graduation standards were as rigorous as any in the world.

The Israelis continued to get the personnel side of the equation right when in mid-1958 Tolkowsky was succeeded by the "swashbuckling" Maj. Gen. Ezer Weizman.[43] Weizman's combat feats had made him a hero to his fellow pilots, and few doubted his intellect and leadership qualities, but there were fears his advocacy of airpower would alienate the army. But Weizman turned out to be an outstanding commander who hastened the IAF's drive toward modernization and excellence. He also shrewdly promoted the notion that "Israel's best defense is in the skies of Cairo," a catchphrase that both gave the men and women of the IAF a clear sense of purpose and the IDF's senior commanders a concept of operations for the next war.

The same progressive mindset was apparent in the recruitment and management of technical staff. Emphasis was placed on high-quality training, personnel retention, and the use of reservists as a surge capability. Individuals at all levels were encouraged to think independently and to suggest methods for getting the most out of the IAF's fleet, such as reducing aircraft turnaround times between sorties, streamlining maintenance and rearming practices, rationalizing the physical disposition of aircraft and their auxiliary systems (weapons stocks, spare parts, servicing tools, refueling points), and so on. Some squadrons started to generate six sorties a day compared to the usual two.[44]

Planning came next. Defense planners tend to acquire their force structure—platforms, weapons, installations, and so on—and then develop a strategy to fit that structure, whereas logic dictates the reverse; namely, first identify the way (the strategy) and then obtain the means (the structure). Geostrategic imperatives drew the IAF's leaders inexorably toward one solution to their national defense challenge. Israel's lack of strategic depth meant that the country had no capacity to absorb the first wave of an assault by making a controlled withdrawal into a hinterland as, for example, Russia had done when invaded by Napoleon in 1812 and the Nazis in 1941. Geographical reality was accentuated by the geometry of war in the Middle East, in which Israel would always be surrounded and outnumbered. And the open, flat expanses of much of the region favored rapid movement and made targets hard to conceal, factors with obvious warfighting implications.

Israeli planners were familiar with the work of the British strategist Basil Liddell Hart, whose theory of "expanding torrent" warfare had been one of the foundations of the German blitzkrieg tactic of World War II, and which had been reflected in Moshe Dayan's campaign in the Sinai in 1956. They also believed that the lack of strategic depth that constituted a weakness might be used as a strength: if Israel were to take the initiative, its air force could strike against Egypt, Syria, Jordan, Lebanon, and Iraq with little warning. The logical conclusion was that a campaign based on preemptive attack and rapid maneuver would best exploit Israel's geostrategic circumstances and the superior quality of the IDF.

For the IAF, this translated above all else into offensive counterair operations. Control of the air was a prerequisite for almost any strategy the IDF might adopt, but the endorsement of preemption refined that conclusion. Winning control defensively as, say, the RAF had done in the Battle of Britain would have been inconsistent with the need to seize the initiative and to win quickly—only offensive action could satisfy the broader strategic logic. And as Douhet had reasoned decades previously, "the surest and most effective way of achieving... [control of the air is to] ... destroy the enemy air force at its bases, which are found on the surface."[45]

From the early 1960s onward the IAF turned the aphorism "Air Power is targeting, [and] targeting is intelligence" into an institutional article of faith.[46] A comprehensive program to translate theory into practice was introduced across the IAF. Because the EAF had been identified as the enemy's center of gravity, a vast amount of intelligence was collected on its component parts such as air-defense radars, command-and-control systems, leadership, air bases, runways and movement areas, hangars, aircraft types, fuel stocks, maintenance facilities, and weapons dumps. That intelligence was then synthesized into a detailed campaign plan by Major General Weizman's chief of operations, the scholarly fighter pilot Yak Nevo. Code-named "Moked" (Focus), Nevo's plan called for the IAF first to close the EAF's runways so that its aircraft would be trapped on the ground and then to destroy those stranded targets. Nevo and his team calculated hundreds of times-on-target, allocated aircraft types and weapon loads, assessed enemy defenses, selected ingress and egress routes, determined fuel loads, allowed for contingencies such as repeat attacks and losses, and scores of similar details. During the four years it took to construct the plan, IAF pilots assiduously practiced their skills.[47]

Turning to the final component of the Israeli airpower model—advanced technology—by the mid-1960s, the IAF and the country's aerospace industries had made remarkable progress. Weizman envisaged a force structure in which capability and cost were balanced. He wanted a minimum but sufficient number of leading-edge (expensive) strike/fighters to achieve control of the air and a large number of workhorse (cheaper) aircraft for air-to-ground attack.

Requests to modernize the IAF's fleet with U.S. jets were rejected by the Americans, so with the assistance of prime ministers Ben-Gurion (to June 1963) and then Levi Eshkol, Weizman turned to France. The French obliged by supplying the Dassault Mirage III, a Mach-2 air superiority fighter the equal of any then flying, and the Sud Aviation Vautour twin-engine bomber, which, while not state-of-the-art aircraft, offered a radius of action and payload that would allow the IAF to attack distant targets. Support would come from the existing fleet of Super Mystères, Mystères, Ouragans, and Magisters.

Hawk surface-to-air missiles (SAMs) were another noteworthy acquisition. While circumstances were to marginalize the role of SAMs in the Six-Day War, they were an essential component of a modern air-defense network. The Hawks complemented the IAF's fighters, and their mere presence created a deterrent effect.[48]

Israel's aerospace industry was fundamental to the IAF's modernization. The Mirage and Vautour might not have been built locally, but indigenous companies were capable of modifying aircraft and weapons systems to meet the IAF's specific needs. For example, because Weizman was planning to destroy his enemies' air forces on the ground, the Mirages' avionics were customized for air-to-ground operations and their fuel load increased.[49] Israeli industry was also skilled in battle-damage repair, an under-valued expertise that, by keeping aircraft in the fight, effectively increases the size of a force.

Local expertise extended to purpose-designed weapons, two of which were especially significant. In 1959 the Rafael Armament Development Authority began work on an infrared-guided air-to-air missile, initially called Shafrir and later renamed Python. While the original missile was disappointing, subsequent models contributed to the IAF's superiority.

The second weapon was a runway penetration bomb built by Israel Military Industries (IMI) in collaboration with French companies, which was developed with the preemption strategy in mind.[50] Runways are difficult to hit and can be quickly repaired. If the IAF's plan were to succeed, the EAF's runways had to be closed for hours. IMI's solution was a high-drag, rocket-boosted bomb. High-drag bombs fall slowly, allowing the attacking aircraft to fly at low altitude, thus ensuring accuracy, but still escape from the blast area before detonation; the rocket-booster propelled IMI's bomb through the surface into the runway substructure before the bomb exploded, causing greater damage.

Two other research and development activities warrant mention. First, trials between the IAF's Mirage III and a MiG-21 flown to Israel by an Iraqi Air Force (IQAF) defector yielded valuable air-to-air combat performance data. And second, in 1966, a computing and electronic product design division was established within the Elron Electronic Industries.[51] Later to become the Elbit Systems, the new division specialized in developing systems for aerospace weapons delivery, navigation, and avionics. Israel and the IAF were making technology serve strategy.

Platforms without Policies

In February 1958 Egypt and Syria merged as the United Arab Republic, a union that reflected Nasser's popularity in the Arab world because of his political victory at Suez and which also, it was hoped, signaled the beginning of a wider pan-Arab movement. Three years later constant disagreements saw Syria withdraw, an action more representative of Arab interstate relations.

Suez may have been a political triumph for President Nasser, but he could not hide from the fact that his defense forces had been trounced. Egypt's most pressing tasks were to learn from that experience and to rebuild the military. Considerable emphasis was placed on the EAF because of the now-obvious importance of control of the air and strike. Soviet premiers Nikita Khrushchev and Leonid Brezhnev took the opportunity to strengthen the USSR's position in the Middle East by providing Egypt with generous amounts of equipment, training, and technical support.

By 1967 the EAF had been reequipped with more than 400 combat aircraft, including large numbers of MiG-21s, the USSR's best fighter and a match for the IAF's Mirage IIIs. There were also replacement Il-28 medium bombers and new Tu-16 heavy bombers, the latter perceived by Israeli leaders as a serious threat because of their 3,000-mile range and 20,000-pound payload. Future Egyptian president Hosni Mubarak at one stage commanded a Tu-16 squadron and was typical of EAF senior officers who believed that as long as their bombers were protected by MiG-21s, they could attack any Israeli target.[52]

There were also significant developments in ground-based air defense (GBAD), with the USSR providing batteries of ZSU-57-2 self-propelled antiaircraft guns and SA-2 SAMs. The guns were effective up to an altitude of about 15,000 feet and out to a distance of 3 miles, while the missiles had a kill envelope from 10,000 to 60,000 feet out to a range of 25 miles. If properly coordinated with early-warning systems and command-and-control centers, the two weapons could constitute a formidable barrier.

The Egyptian aerospace industry continued on its challenging path. The Helwan factory built jet trainers based on the Spanish Hispano Ha-200 and initiated an ambitious scheme to develop an indigenous supersonic fighter known as the Ha-300. Both projects eventually foundered, the trainer because of technical and sustainment problems, the fighter because of financial pressures. Helwan's reliance on imported technologies compared unfavorably with Israel, where local design and innovation were well established.

Similar technology/workforce weaknesses were exposed by attempts to build long-range surface-to-surface missiles. In the early 1950s Egypt assembled a project team led by former Nazi scientists and army officers, but the program disintegrated, not least because key staff members were assassinated by the Israeli secret service. The Egyptian government persisted, and local engineers eventually managed to build several prototypes based on the Nazi V-2 rocket. None, however, became operational, and the project petered out.[53] By contrast, Israel's equivalent venture typically drew on better leadership, planning, and resources and, with help from the French Dassault company, test-fired the three-hundred-mile-range Jericho I ballistic missile in 1965.

Egypt's failed indigenous fighter and missile projects were indicative of the nation's struggle to build airpower, a process that continued to be suffocated by poor leadership, a low economic base, and underdeveloped social and educational institutions.

The EAF was plagued by maintenance shortcomings. A fleet of 450 warplanes sounded impressive, but on the eve of the Six-Day War less than 50 percent were serviceable.[54] Passive defense was another concern. The Suez campaign had made it clear that offensive airpower would be a factor in any future conflict, which made it equally clear that high-value assets should be protected. An integrated air-defense system—fighters, radars, SAMs, antiaircraft artillery (AAA), command-and-control centers—is the best solution, but an integrated air-defense system is complex, very expensive, and difficult to operate. By contrast, passive defense measures such as hardened shelters, revetments, dispersal, and camouflage are relatively cheap, easy to implement, and can be effective. A few of the EAF's aircraft were protected by revetments, but overall the passive defense measures were woefully inadequate. The omission is difficult to explain other than in terms of incompetent leadership.

Leadership in fact remained a problem across the EAF. President Nasser's modernization program had tried to raise standards, but long-standing cultural and social practices constituted formidable barriers. The notion of merit-based promotion remained elusive, and cronyism and corruption continued to undermine the ethos of the profession of arms.[55]

Similar models evolved in the other Arab states that fought in the Six-Day War: Syria, Iraq, and Jordan. (Lebanon also participated but had so little capability as to be irrelevant.) Syria had become an independent republic in 1946 following a protracted struggle to overthrow French rule and had initially looked to the United Kingdom for assistance. The SyAAF was equipped with British aircraft, and its pilots and technicians were trained by the RAF; one early graduate was the future president and dictator, Hafez al-Assad, who in the 1950s was a prominent fighter pilot. Like Egypt, Syria then turned to the USSR and, following the Suez War, sent large numbers of personnel to Warsaw Pact countries for training and bolstered its fleet with MiG-17s and -21s and Il-28s. But also like the EAF, the SyAAF struggled with leadership, planning, training, maintenance, and logistics.

Iraq experienced a number of political shocks in the 1950s and 1960s that affected its defense alliances. Following a military-led revolution in 1958 in which the monarchy was replaced by a republic, Iraq's new leaders cut their ties with the United Kingdom and the RAF and turned to the USSR, reequipping their air force with MiG-17s, -19s, and -21s; Il-28s; and Tu-16s. After another coup in 1963 Iraq sought to restore relations with the West, which led to renewed but cautious links with the RAF.

The Royal Jordanian Air Force was established in 1955 using facilities built in the 1930s by the RAF. At the start of the Six-Day War the Royal Jordanian Air Force was operating a moderately competent, daylight-only fleet of about twenty Hawker Hunter transonic fighters. Lebanon also had a handful of Hunters.

The Arab air forces were not helped by the doctrinal influence of their Soviet advisors. Soviet airpower thinking was shaped by a combination of the

Red Air Force's analysis of the Korean War, the Kremlin's fear of being attacked by nuclear-armed bombers, and Marxist-Leninist ideology. Consequently, there was an emphasis on obedience to orders, centralized control, and ground-controlled intercepts.[56] Unfortunately for the Arabs, that model was unsuited to the Middle East in 1967, and it was the antithesis of the IAF's flexibility and resourcefulness.

Still, there was nothing wrong with the Arab commanders' strategic thinking. They were fully aware of the threat the IAF posed and, like their enemies, believed that preemption was the best option. Several days before the war began, EAF commander Air Marshal Mohamed Sedky Mahmoud urged President Nasser to authorize preemptive strikes against the IAF's runways, movement areas, aircraft, radars, and fuel dumps.[57] Nasser refused, wanting Israel to deliver the first blow and thus attract international opprobrium, and he believed that Egypt was capable of absorbing any losses before hitting back.

An Airpower Master Class

Tensions in the Middle East peaked in May 1967 when the Soviets erroneously informed their Arab allies that Israel was massing forces along its border with Syria.[58] The Arabs' reliance on the USSR for intelligence represented a serious failure of airpower. Most strike/fighters can be used as ISR platforms, even if their only sensor is the pilot's eyes. And in this instance there was plenty to see. In the weeks leading up to the war the IDF covertly redeployed aircraft and troops for the forthcoming attack; indeed, some of those movements were detected by EAF reconnaissance flights.[59] But the uncoordinated nature of the EAF's ISR activities and the inability of its commanders to use any information they did collect meant that although the Arabs knew war was imminent, they did not know where or how it might start.

There can be no excuse for the Arab commanders' failure to mount a comprehensive ISR campaign, especially during a period of heightened tension. Once again the contrast with the IAF was extreme: Israel's airmen had spent years gathering and analyzing an enormous amount of information in a systematic and intellectually disciplined ISR program that constituted the foundation of their war plan.

In response to the incorrect Soviet intelligence, President Nasser ordered Egyptian forces to deploy along the border with Israel in the Sinai and, in a provocative move, again closed the Straits of Tiran to Israeli shipping. Simultaneously, Iraq and Egypt moved troops and armored units into Jordan, closer to Israel. With both protagonists primed for preemption, it was a matter of who would strike first. Believing that to wait any longer could risk catastrophe, the

Israeli cabinet resolved on June 4 to attack the next morning. Nasser's decision to wait and absorb the first blow was the single biggest mistake of the war.

Once preemption had been chosen as the strategy, everything depended on whether the IAF's first wave of aircraft could penetrate Egyptian airspace undetected and implement Douhet's theory by defeating the EAF on the ground. Only if the initial strike were successful would the broader Israeli campaign plan, including land operations, be viable.

In the months leading up to the war the IAF had implemented a ploy that, it was hoped, would engender a sense of complacency within Egypt's high command. Each morning at dawn IAF jets were launched westwards toward Egypt, to which the EAF responded by sending patrols over the northern Sinai.[60] For the Egyptians, this daily routine became little more than posturing—exactly the mindset the Israelis were hoping to induce.

On the morning of June 5 the IAF's first attack wave took off in accordance with Yak Nevo's schedule. The pilots observed radio silence and flew low to stay under enemy radar, assisted by C-47s dispensing radar-spoofing chaff. As it happens, those tactics might not have been necessary. In one of the war's more bizarre episodes, Egypt's GBAD system had been temporarily deactivated. Apparently the Egyptian chief of staff was scheduled to fly to the Sinai on an inspection visit, and in order to prevent his aircraft being accidentally shot down by friendly fire, antiaircraft radars and guns had been placed on standby.

Also ineffectual when most needed was the Arabs' command-and-control system. The Israeli strike force was detected by Jordanian radar, but communications failures prevented the message from reaching the EAF bases that were about to be bombed. Some 180 jets—85 percent of the IAF's frontline inventory—arrived over their targets at 7:45 a.m., minutes after the EAF's routine patrols had landed and so could not be scrambled.[61] That was also the time at which many senior officers were commuting to their offices and could not be contacted. Given the feeble state of Egypt's communications and the reluctance of junior officers in an intellectually inflexible organization to make decisions, the EAF's ability to respond was immobilized at the precise moment when decisive action was needed.

Nevo's plan incorporated a bold but calculated risk. The concept of defeating the EAF on the ground meant that priority had to be given to closing down airfields and destroying aircraft; consequently, the first attack wave could not prosecute other dangerous targets such as GBAD.[62] Furthermore, because so many aircraft were committed, there was a brief period when only twelve were available for the air defense of all of Israel. If the Arab air forces had been able to construct a system of information sharing and operational coordination, they might have been able to counterattack; as it was, they were incapable of even recognizing the opportunity.

The IAF struck eleven airfields concurrently. At some bases EAF aircraft were lined up in the open, so once runways had been closed, the Israeli pilots were able to bomb and strafe to great effect. Where high-value aircraft such as the Tu-16s were in revetments, gun-only attacks were made. Within an hour some two hundred Egyptian aircraft had been destroyed on the ground. Rapid turnaround by skilled ground staff enabled the IAF to launch a second wave and repeat the process while the EAF was still in chaos. Air-defense radars and batteries were added to the target list.

Just after midday the Jordanian, Iraqi, and Syrian air forces joined the war by attacking Israel. Their action invited retribution, which the IAF exacted in full. Emulating the EAF during the Suez War, the remnants of the Jordanian and Iraqi air forces fled to bases beyond the IAF's reach.[63]

By the end of the day the IAF had destroyed more than 400 aircraft and had established air supremacy; by the end of the war only five days later, 451 of the 600 Arab jets had been demolished. Remarkably, 391—86 percent—were destroyed on the ground.[64]

Nevertheless, the air war was not entirely one-sided. Pockets of professionalism existed within all of the Arab air forces and many of their pilots fought courageously. Egypt's SA-2 missile batteries were relatively new to Western air forces and compelled the Israelis to develop new tactics. The IAF found the going particularly hard on the Golan Heights, on the border with Syria, where dug-in gun positions were difficult to hit. During the six days of fighting the Israelis lost twenty-one pilots and 13 percent of their aircraft.[65]

The annihilation of the Arab air forces allowed the IAF pilots to join the land war. By the evening of the first day Israeli tanks and troops were breaking through Egyptian defensive positions; within six days the Israelis had occupied the Sinai, Jordan's West Bank (including East Jerusalem), the Golan Heights, and the Gaza Strip.

The nature of the IAF's victory created an intriguing consequence. Because the Arab air forces were defeated primarily on the ground, their most perishable and valuable asset—combat pilots—largely escaped: in the EAF, for example, while 34 pilots were killed, about 120 survived. Defense Minister Dayan later acknowledged that one of the IDF's "greatest mistakes was that [we] did not destroy the Egyptian pilots ... [we] destroyed the material but not the people."[66]

Commentary

It would be dismissive of the professionalism and courage of the IAF to suggest that the Six-Day War was effectively won before it started, just as it would be disrespectful to those Arab airmen who fought bravely. Regardless of the IAF's superiority, its people still had to execute their tasks in opposition to deadly force, and in the knowledge that the stakes were nothing less than national survival; moreover, during the first hours their margin for error was dangerously slight.

At the same time, the contrast between the Israeli and Arab air forces could scarcely have been more pronounced. Whereas the IAF's model was an exemplary combination of people, plans, and technology, the Arabs' was deficient in every respect. Platforms alone did not equate to power.

The conflict did not end when the fighting stopped. So extreme was the Arabs' military failure that the Palestinians no longer believed their allies could win back their homeland for them, and when Israel refused to return the Sinai and the West Bank, they also stopped believing negotiation was viable. Consequently, many Palestinians became radicalized. And because the PLO could not directly challenge the Israeli Army or Air Force, it turned to the kinds of asymmetric tactics almost invariably favored by the weak against the strong.

THE WAR OF ATTRITION, 1969-70
The Politics of Victory and Defeat

The Six-Day War changed the geopolitical landscape of the Middle East. By annexing the Sinai, the West Bank, the Gaza Strip, and the Golan Heights, Israel more than tripled its territorial holdings. Thanks in large part to the IAF, Israel's strategic depth and, therefore, its security had been substantially extended. Moreover, the stunning nature of the victory by an apparent David over an apparent Goliath greatly enhanced Israel's international prestige. The opposite was the case for the Arab nations, who were humiliated by their failure. President Nasser lowered his ambition from the lofty aim of becoming a pan-Arab leader to the more pragmatic goal of regaining respect and the Sinai.

For the Palestinians, the outcome was more misery. Around 300,000 fled or were forced from their newly occupied homelands, mostly into Jordan's East Bank, and many of their villages were demolished "not in battle," as Moshe Dayan said, "but as punishment."[67] Most Palestinians now lived outside the boundaries of the land that until 1948 had been their home.

Military victory brought Israel security for the immediate future but had no effect on the toxic political situation. Several months after the war Arab leaders announced a "three nos" policy toward Israel: "no" to peace; "no" to recognition; and "no" to negotiations. Only military action, Nasser declared, would compel Israel to withdraw from the territories it had illegally seized. Skirmishing between the Egyptian and Israeli armies began on the east bank of the Suez Canal (having occupied the Sinai, Israel now controlled that side of the canal), and the radicalized PLO stepped up its asymmetric warfare by attacking Israeli civilians with rockets, mortars, and antipersonnel bombs.

As far as modeling airpower was concerned, it was clear that the Israelis had the correct formula and should maintain their existing flight path, whereas if the Arabs were serious about competing, drastic change was needed.

Learning from Failure

If the aphorism that we learn more from failure than from success is true, then the Arabs had plenty to work with. The starting point for reform had to be leadership. Following the Six-Day War, Israeli Army major general Ariel Sharon praised Egypt's rank-and-file soldiers, commending their bravery and discipline under fire, but with typical candor dismissed their officers as "shit," criticizing their lack of flexibility, initiative, and imagination.[68]

President Nasser had attempted to improve the quality of military leadership after the 1952 revolution, but promotion still depended on cronyism and patronage. Now the magnitude of the disaster and the need to find scapegoats demanded genuine reform. A failed coup immediately after the Six-Day War led by the commander in chief of the Joint Military Command of Egypt and Syria, Field Marshal Abdel Hakim Amer, added more urgency to the situation. Nasser appointed a committee of inquiry that absolved him and attributed all blame to the military high command. Courts-martial were convened and around eight hundred officers were imprisoned or discharged, including all full generals and most lieutenant generals and major generals. Air Marshal Sedky Mahmoud was jailed for fifty years for dereliction of duty, and Field Marshal Amer allegedly committed suicide. Nasser then promoted "the best officers he could find" to fill the vacancies.[69] Merit was said to replace influential connections as the main criterion for advancement, and Nasser reportedly reinstated officers who were known to be competent but had previously been dismissed for disloyalty.

Egypt's recast defense hierarchy demonstrated a keener understanding of airpower than its predecessors by introducing three important reforms. First, military intelligence was overhauled and ordered to direct its full attention against Israel instead of its own officer corps, as had previously been the case (as a means of uncovering disloyalty to the regime). Second, the EAF commenced a systematic program of reconnaissance flights intended to guard against another surprise attack and to assemble a data base for future operations. Finally, an independent Air Defense Command (ADC) was established with the express purpose of avoiding a repeat of 1956 and 1967. Emulating the Soviet model, the ADC would be required to maintain continuous radar coverage over all Egyptian territory, which it would protect from the IAF with a network of GBAD weapons backed-up by the EAF's fighter force.[70]

The attitudinal shift implicit in those reforms was complemented by practical initiatives. Pilot training was rationalized, resulting in more and better pilots graduating in less time. Operational training began to incorporate aggression, low-altitude maneuvering, navigation, and weapons application. New airfields were constructed, dispersal areas added to existing bases, hundreds of hardened aircraft shelters built, and sections of highways upgraded as emergency runways.[71] The Soviets contributed engineering and instructional knowledge, but much of the work was done by the EAF in what proved a valuable learning experience. Rationalization was also applied to the Egyptian aerospace industry, whose objectives the government accepted were unrealistic. Indigenous projects such as the Ha-300 supersonic fighter and guided missiles were cancelled and priority shifted to assembling, repairing, and modifying imported aircraft and weapons systems.

The least of the EAF's problems was replacing the aircraft the IAF had destroyed. Soviet self-interest saw the delivery of hundreds of strike/fighters, including MiG-17s, -19s, -21s, and -23s, and Su-7s. But they were neither the most advanced variants nor fitted with the latest weapons.

Strategy was the final task, and here too Egypt's leaders showed that they finally understood the reality of airpower in the Middle East. The initiative that best revealed their new outlook was the establishment of the ADC and the decision to assign it, rather than the EAF, prime responsibility for control of the air. Without understating the effort involved, constructing and operating a GBAD system is less demanding than developing an air combat force. The reforms introduced into the EAF were a step in the right direction, but realistically it would be years before the service might be capable of competing with the IAF. In the meantime, it made sense to prioritize GBAD.

Strategy and technology thus came together as the USSR supplied Egypt with GBAD radars, command-and-control links, and weapons, the latter including the formidable low- to medium-altitude mobile SA-3 and SA-6 missiles and the self-propelled ZSU-23-4 antiaircraft gun.

Intellectual substance was added to this new approach with a strategy that sought to exploit Egypt's strengths and Israel's weaknesses. Israel's small population of 2 million and its increasingly skill-based economy forced the IDF to rely on reservists who were called up in times of national emergency. Egyptian strategists realized that if a conflict were prolonged rather than concluding within days, as had happened in 1956 and 1967, there was a good chance Israel would feel the strain and become more amenable to negotiations to return occupied territory. Egypt's population of 30 million largely insulated it from workforce issues.

The Egyptian high command consequently endorsed a strategy of attrition, under which major confrontations would be avoided in favor of continual, low-level harassment that, it was hoped, would force the IDF to remain mobilized, damage Israel's economy, steadily inflict casualties, and drain morale.[72] For the first time since 1948 the Arabs had combined people, technology, and ideas into a coherent whole.

Consolidating Success

The IAF's model had proven so successful that the service's main challenges were to avoid complacency and to continue on its trajectory of excellence. Constant skirmishes with the Egyptians and Palestinians meant that complacency was not a problem. Nor was the management of people and strategy. In combination with the prestige now attached to serving in the IAF, Israel's modern school system sustained a well-educated workforce. And strategy remained a constant. The realities of geography, population, regional hostility, and the superiority of the IAF made it plain that preemption was Israel's best option. The fact that the strategy was common knowledge did not make it any less valid: knowing your opponent's likely course of action and doing something about it can be entirely different things.

Maintaining the technological edge presented obstacles, but excellent leadership found answers. IAF commanders knew that they could not stand still, that they had to keep pushing the boundaries. Their preference was to upgrade their fleet with the latest Mirage strike/fighter, but French president Charles de Gaulle imposed an arms embargo, supposedly in response to a provocative raid by Israeli commandos in Beirut, more likely to safeguard the flow of oil from the Middle East. This was a crucial moment in the continual struggle for technological supremacy. The Israeli government decided to pursue two separate solutions: local production and international diplomacy.

The aircraft de Gaulle had embargoed (even though Israel had paid for the first thirty) was the Dassault Mirage V. Reportedly using blueprints stolen from Dassault, Israel Aircraft Industries started production of an Israeli variant in 1969. Renamed the Nesher, the multirole fighter was fitted with Israeli avionics and could apply a wide range of weapons, including the indigenous Shafrir air-to-air missile. Deliveries to the IAF began in May 1971.

Israel's leaders simultaneously turned to the United States. Previously the Americans had been reluctant to send arms to the Middle East, but the French embargo and the influx of Soviet weapons into Egypt and Syria convinced President Lyndon Johnson to restore the balance. A delegation to the United States in late 1965, led by Major General Weizman, had secured approval to acquire 48 A-4 Skyhawks. All were in service by the end of 1968; eventually the IAF operated 300. Armed with a 30 mm cannon and able to carry around 6,000 pounds of ordnance, the Skyhawk was an outstanding air-to-ground platform. And perhaps just as important as the aircraft was the access it provided to the United States' unsurpassed training and logistics services.

A meeting in January 1968 between Johnson and Israeli president Levi Eshkol produced an even better outcome when the Americans agreed to provide fifty F-4E Phantoms. Arguably the best combat aircraft of its era, the Phantom represented a quantum leap over the Mirage III in terms of performance, avionics, the variety and weight of ordnance it could employ, and its electronic warfare systems.

Another technological development during this period was, however, the most momentous. Disappointed by the failure of the Six-Day War to bring lasting peace and disturbed by the intransigence of the Arabs' "three nos" policy, the Israeli government approved the production of atomic weapons at its Dimona reactor. It seems probable that by 1970 a "handful" of bombs had been built.[73]

Fighting Smart—Attrition Warfare

President Nasser publicly announced the beginning of a "War of Attrition" in March 1969. Both protagonists had been conducting small-scale incursions, air strikes, artillery attacks, and terrorist raids since the end of the Six-Day War, but now the intensity increased. Much of the early fighting took place along the Suez Canal, which since 1967 had been heavily fortified by the Egyptians along the west side and the Israelis along the east.

Fixed fortifications are by their nature defensive, so while in Egypt's case the approach was consistent with their emphasis on GBAD, attrition, and trying to minimize their exposure to the IDF's strengths, in Israel's case a static posture was inconsistent with the dynamic air/land operations of 1956 and 1967. Despite opposition from senior IDF commanders, including Major General Sharon, Israel constructed a massive ninety-three-mile defensive barrier incorporating sand and concrete walls, forts, strongpoints, trenches, minefields, barbed wire, bunkers, artillery, machine gun posts, mortars, and tank positions. Named the Bar Lev Line after the IDF chief of staff, the fortification had to be continuously manned by hundreds of soldiers to ensure the integrity of the whole, which could only be as strong as any one link at any one moment. In that sense alone, the line was playing into the hands of the Egyptian plan to exhaust Israel's limited manpower.

Because the Egyptians' intention was to contest the IAF's dominance with the ground-based weapons of their newly formed ADC, the centerpiece of their fortifications in the Suez zone was a concentrated system of SAM batteries and antiaircraft artillery supported by radars and command-and-control links. GBAD was also deployed around high-value centers such as military bases, essential infrastructure, and cities.

There was, of course, much more to the fighting than the war in the air. Heavy artillery exchanges took place, especially along the Suez Canal, and both sides mounted commando-style raids against civilian and infrastructure targets deep inside enemy territory. But those kinds of activities offered little that was new to the student of military affairs. By contrast, the air war incorporated two relatively novel dimensions; namely, aircraft versus SAMs, and electronic warfare systems as weapons in their own right.

A subtext to the air war in the Middle East was provided by the concurrent American bombing campaign against North Vietnam. U.S. politicians and military commanders were understandably preoccupied with their own problems and were not always able to respond to requests for assistance as quickly as the Israelis might have liked. This situation did, however, confirm once again the importance of Israel's indigenous aerospace industry, which often was able to satisfy urgent operational requirements. And because the air war over North Vietnam was the first in which aircraft were opposed by a comprehensive SAM-based defensive system, the IAF benefited from the Americans' learning experience as deficiencies in U.S. capabilities—inadequate electronic countermeasures (ECM), unsuitable weapons, flawed tactics, and so on—were exposed.

Operations during the War of Attrition were shaped by the imperative to establish control of the air over the Suez Canal zone. Unfortunately for President Nasser, Egypt's new GBAD weapons and MiG fighters turned out to be insufficient compensation for the shortcomings of his air-defense operators and fighter pilots, who were overpowered by an aggressive IAF air superiority campaign.

Then, having neutralized the enemy's air defenses, the IAF used its long-range Phantoms to mount a punishing bombing campaign against targets deep inside Egypt.[74] This was a clever move: by changing the tempo and nature of the fighting the Israelis had countered the Egyptians' strategy of attrition.

With his GBAD barrier breached and his strategy faltering, President Nasser called on the Soviets for help. The response was rapid. Dozens of SAM batteries, antiaircraft guns and MiG-21s were rushed to Egypt, together with radars and command-and-control systems. And this time the hardware came with a serious sting in its tail. Experience had shown that the Egyptians were not ready to fight a war based on broadly based institutional skill and advanced technology, so the USSR also sent around 15,000 men to command, operate, and maintain the equipment.[75]

The Soviets brought tactical sophistication to the fight. Initially they focused on regaining control of the air around Cairo, and when that had been achieved they gradually pushed their defensive barrier eastward toward the Suez Canal. They also formed SAM and AAA batteries into concentrated clusters rather than dispersed lines. Simultaneously, EAF fighter squadrons, which had been reinforced with Soviet pilots, were ordered to remain on their own side of the canal and within range of their GBAD, which gave them more say over how they engaged the IAF.[76]

By reasserting control over the nature and location of the air war, the Soviets resuscitated the Egyptians' strategy of attrition. Forced into a situation antithetical to its preferred way of fighting, the IAF began to feel the strain. More strain was felt when Israeli pilots discovered that the ECM in their aircraft was ineffective against some of the newer Soviet SAMs. Urgent requests for American assistance brought a response but mixed results as the United States itself was scrambling to develop countermeasures for its own fight against the same weapons in North Vietnam.[77] Eventually the Americans were able to provide improved ECM pods, which the IAF complemented with locally developed systems.

Because much of the fighting took place along the Suez Canal and in the Sinai, the participation of other Arab states was limited. Syria and Jordan made a few incursions, but both were wary of exposing their air forces. The PLO was more active, notably with fedayeen raids into Israel from Jordan, Lebanon, and the Gaza Strip and with indiscriminate rocket and mortar attacks against border settlements. Those latter operations, incidentally, were in part a reaction to the regional airpower imbalance. If Israel wished to strike against its enemies' homes it could do so almost when and where it liked. Arab states with traditional air forces knew they were outclassed and so were cautious about engaging the IAF, while entities without air forces, such as the PLO, turned to asymmetric alternatives.

The Soviet Union's participation in the War of Attrition raised the temperature of the Cold War to the extent that in mid-1970, concerned by the possibility of escalation, U.S. president Richard Nixon began to push for a cease-fire. As it happened, the timing suited both protagonists. The Egyptians had made their point, and after more than a year of fighting the Israelis were fatigued. Nixon's proposal took effect on August 8–9, and despite immediate violations from both sides, the truce more or less held.

Commentary

By most military measures Israel won the War of Attrition. It held all the territory it had taken in the Six-Day War, and once the IDF adjusted to Egypt's new tactics and weapons, the fighting followed a familiar pattern. Between 700 to 1,400 Israeli soldiers and civilians were killed and 14 to 30 IAF aircraft were lost, while for the Egyptians and the PLO the figures were 4,700 to 12,000 soldiers and civilians killed and around 110 aircraft destroyed.[78] Significant losses were also inflicted on the Egyptian Army's artillery and armor.

The IAF again performed splendidly. Its defeat of the first iteration of Egypt's air-defense force was critical, as was its ability to change the nature of the war by conducting deep strikes. In air-to-air combat the IAF's kill ratio over the EAF was 18:1 (compared to 3:1 in 1967), an achievement made even more meritorious by the presence in the enemy ranks of Soviet pilots.[79] Once more the IAF benefited from the support of the local and U.S. aerospace industries.

But the prognosis was not all positive. Fighting a war that lasted more than a year proved far more draining on Israel's (and the IAF's) small population than the preceding ten- and six-day campaigns; indeed, toward the end of the conflict one IAF squadron commander had to decline a directive to scramble because "we [had] no strength left."[80] Aircraft could always be replaced, but pilots could not. Furthermore, the IAF was exposed to some extent by the Soviet-Egyptian change of tactics and the unexpected effectiveness of some of the newer Soviet GBAD.

While the Egyptians may have been defeated on the battlefield, genuine improvement was evident in their people, technology, and plans. Aspects of their planning were impressive, notably the decision to accept the reality of the IAF's supremacy and to find an alternative way of dealing with it. Scaling back the ambition of the indigenous aerospace industry to focus on repair and maintenance rather than design and construction also seemed indicative of a newfound common sense. Overall, the war helped to restore Egypt's confidence and status, to the extent that there was now a belief in the Arab world that in the near future a broadly based military campaign against Israel might succeed.

The War of Attrition concluded with a wretched endnote arising from the civil war that broke out in Jordan in September 1970. The Emirate of Transjordan, later renamed the Hashemite Kingdom of Jordan, was another of those Arab "nations" whose borders were drawn up so carelessly by European statesmen after World War I. By 1970 about two-thirds of Jordan's inhabitants were Palestinian, many of whom were refugees from the wars with Israel. Jordan's King Hussein was a moderate who favored peace with Israel but who at the same time had to accommodate a substantial proportion of his population that had become radicalized. But accommodation could only extend so far, and when shortly after the War of Attrition extremist elements of the PLO and some of its offshoots tried to overthrow the Jordanian monarchy, Hussein ordered his army to crush them, which it did. The PLO was driven out of Jordan and largely resettled in Lebanon, a relocation that was to set the scene for the First Lebanon War twelve years later.

Jordan's civil war and the continuing failure of the Arab world to regain the Palestinians' homeland also precipitated the creation of the Black September terrorist movement, later responsible for aircraft hijackings, a series of assassinations (including that of Jordan's prime minister), and the murder of eleven Israeli athletes at the 1972 Olympic Games.

THE OCTOBER WAR, 1973
A Strategy for "Winning"

President Nasser died in September 1970 and was succeeded by his vice president, former army officer and fervent nationalist Anwar Sadat. Sadat was eager to resolve the conflict with Israel peacefully, preferring to direct Egypt's resources toward nation building. However, his overtures were rebuffed by Israel, where the one-sided nature of the Six-Day War and the strategic depth gained from the occupation of the Sinai had created a heightened sense of confidence.[81] Sadat therefore decided to revert to military means to achieve his objectives. It was the way he defined those objectives that determined the next chapter of the Arab-Israeli war.

Before contemplating any action, Egyptian planners analyzed the strengths and weaknesses of the protagonists' respective means (for example, air forces, armies, economies, industrial bases) and possible ways (such as preemption, air campaign, invasion, blockade). Only when that process was finished did Sadat settle on an acceptable end (objective). His decision was conspicuous for the absence of any notion of either "destroying" Israel or "restoring the legitimate rights" of the Palestinian people. Regarded by Henry Kissinger as a statesman of the first order, Sadat instead concluded that, given the means and ways available to each side, his immediate objectives should be to strengthen Egypt's bargaining power by fighting credibly and to regain a foothold in the Sinai.[82] Anything beyond that would be a bonus. This was a refreshingly realistic attitude. By defining what, in the prevailing circumstances, he meant by "winning," President Sadat had established a rational basis for the Arabs' campaign.

Sadat started his war preparations by appointing the loyal and capable Gen. Ahmed Ismail Ali as his war minister and commander in chief, and the well-regarded air marshal Hosni Mubarak as head of the EAF. Simultaneously, he attended to the political side of the equation by strengthening ties with the Soviets, on whom he depended for armaments, and with Syria's president, Hafez al-Assad, who was as eager to regain the Golan Heights as Sadat was the Sinai.

Egyptian planners identified four main Israeli strengths: air superiority, technological expertise, highly skilled personnel, and rapid logistics support from the United States. Weaknesses included extended lines of communications, multiple fronts that needed defending, and a small population. General Ismail also believed the Israelis suffered from "the evils of wanton conceit"—a condition he believed the Arabs could exploit.[83]

It would be "disastrous," Ismail noted, if in the next campaign Egypt and its allies tried to replicate the protracted nature of the War of Attrition. He knew the Israelis had learned from that experience and were likely to respond to any aggression with an immediate and "violent" air campaign the Arabs would not be able to withstand. His conclusion was that his own forces would have to strike first—quickly and hard.

Ismail decided that Egypt and Syria should attack preemptively and simultaneously, the former along the length of the Suez Canal on Israel's western flank, the latter at the Golan Heights on the east. Preemption offered the best chance of catching the IDF off guard, and attacking at a number of places would stretch the IAF.

The Egyptian plan was qualified by two tactical considerations. First, Arab land forces had to be protected from Israeli airpower; and second, the fight to control the air should not be allowed to take place on the IAF's terms. This meant avoiding air-to-air combat, from which it followed that Egypt and Syria would have to rely on GBAD. In turn, this would limit how far their armies should advance since they would have to remain under the protective umbrella of their SAMs and AAA.

General Ismail's concept was not wholly defensive. Egypt's and Syria's GBAD systems were in the process of being upgraded with advanced Soviet radars, fire-control units, and ECM, and it was feasible that if the IAF were caught off guard, Israel's "Shield of David" might sustain serious losses. Ismail also hoped that if his army were able to breach the Bar Lev Line and advance rapidly (but not too far) into the Sinai, it might be able to inflict similar damage on unwary Israeli armored units.

President Assad initially rejected Sadat's limited strategic objectives, insisting that the only acceptable aim was the destruction of Israel. He eventually acknowledged that this was unrealistic and in mid-1973 endorsed the Egyptian concept and began making preparations to recapture the Golan Heights and the adjacent area west to the Jordan River. Syria's plan centered on a massed assault by five armored and infantry divisions against Israeli positions on the heights operating under the protection of GBAD.[84]

It is axiomatic that the timing of any attack is critical, and here too the Arab planning revealed a degree of sophistication previously absent. Scores of factors were taken into account, including weather forecasts, hours of daylight/moonlight, national holidays or religious observances (which might increase the chance of catching the enemy off guard and increase the difficulty of mobilizing), stocks of war supplies, the operational readiness of one's own forces, and so on. In mid-June General Ismail selected October 6. As well as offering favorable meteorological conditions, the date encompassed two important religious events that might work in the Arabs' favor. For the Muslims it would be the tenth day of Ramadan, and the general staff in Cairo thought the Israelis would not expect them to attack during their holy month; for the Jews it would be Yom Kippur, the Day of Atonement, their holiest day of the year, when almost every Israeli reservist would be off duty.

"The Evils of Wanton Conceit"

A successful preemptive strike depends entirely on surprise. Israel's intelligence services were aware of the Arabs' preparations for war; indeed, some agencies predicted the timing of the forthcoming attack almost to the minute.[85] The issue, though, was whether Israel's leaders had their priorities right and were paying their enemies sufficient respect. As it happens, they were preoccupied with the wrong threat and dangerously overconfident.

Prime Minister Meir and her advisors had become distracted by frequent PLO attacks against civilians. But regardless of how distressing those experiences may have been, arbitrary small-scale violence was never going to constitute an existential threat. On the other hand, the War of Attrition had demonstrated the Arabs' growing military potential.

Reacting more to populist clamor than to reasoned priorities, Israel's leaders removed intelligence analysts from agencies charged with reporting on Egypt and placed them in a new office whose sole task was to monitor Palestinian guerrillas.[86] This was a serious mistake. Focused on the PLO and inclined to ignore reports from military and foreign affairs specialists, Meir and her colleagues failed to take adequate measures in response to clear signs of Arab mobilization. Fuel was added to this smoldering fire by the IDF's contemptuous opinion of the Arabs. Defense Minister Dayan and his commanders were dismissive of their enemies' air forces and armies, contending that their opponents had turned to guerrilla tactics because of their fear of facing the Israelis in conventional warfare.

The dangers inherent in this mindset were compounded by the surprising narrowness of the IAF's strategic thinking. Almost everything the IAF did was based on the assumption that in any major conflict they would have the initiative—that they would be the aggressors. The question no one seemed to ask was what would happen if the Arabs appropriated the strategy of preemption? In the event, the IAF's "lack of a coherent operational doctrine" to deal with precisely that situation represented a major intellectual failure.[87]

Social Change

The unflattering assessment of Arab leadership and fighting qualities made by generals Sharon and Dayan was a harsh truth President Sadat and General Ismail had to confront. If the Arabs were ever going to challenge Israel's military dominance, then social mores that were inimical to modernization had to change. Sadat and Ismail acknowledged the problem by revisiting the educational and behavioral reforms President Nasser had tried to introduce.

By the mid-1970s Egypt's literacy rate still lagged behind Israel's by almost 60 percent.[88] However, that bare number disguised the progress that had been made in sectors of Egyptian society since 1952. At the time of the Six-Day War in 1967 only 25 percent of the Egyptian defense force's enlisted ranks had completed secondary school, but just six years later, immediately before the October War, the ratio had doubled to 51 percent.[89]

The humiliation of 1967 had also prompted Nasser to revoke the military draft exemption previously available to college students and graduates. This had an even more positive effect on the quality of Egypt's armed forces. Between 1967 and 1973 the proportion of officers with university degrees rose from less than 2 percent (little wonder the EAF had struggled intellectually and technologically) to 60 percent. Simultaneously, emphasis was placed on recruiting engineering graduates to the extent that by 1973 half of all Egyptian engineers were serving in the military, most with the Air Force and the Air Defense Command.[90]

Reform was extended to military culture. The rise in the educational standard of enlisted personnel fostered better relations between the ranks, a helpful development in a technology-oriented, skills-based service. And the creative egalitarianism of air forces was further enhanced by the withdrawal of unwarranted privileges for officers. Across all services, commanders were urged to embrace adaptability, independence, and innovation, and officers were directed to make honest reports of operational readiness, regardless of how painful their content might be.

The implications of those changes were profound. Nasser and Sadat had put in place the single most important component of the Trenchard model, which their air forces previously had lacked—namely, a systematic and merit-based approach to recruiting, training, and supporting high-quality people. As long as they continued to promote the other components, the air superiority on which Israel's national defense rested might be at risk.

In that context, the failure of Israel's national leadership to comprehend the implications of Egypt's change of personnel management practices was as damning as their failure to respond adequately to the signs of their enemy's preparations for war.

Technology and Training

In contrast to the shortcomings of their planning and intelligence processes, the Israelis remained at the leading edge of technology. About a dozen U.S.-made Hawk mobile SAM batteries were acquired in the mid-1960s; some missiles may have been fired unsuccessfully during the Six-Day War. The systems' radar and optical tracking and guidance systems were upgraded by local industry, and in 1969 a Hawk recorded its first kill in the Middle East by shooting down an EAF MiG-21.[91] Local industry was also building an improved version of the Nesher strike/fighter, an initiative that in June 1973 saw the first flight of the Kfir, perhaps the best variant of the Mirage V made anywhere.

The Egyptians may have adopted a different approach to air strategy by favoring the GBAD of the ADC over the fighters of the EAF, but that did not mean they were ignoring the more traditional form of airpower. The IAF was Israel's greatest military advantage, and if the Arabs were ever going to succeed, the EAF had to at least become competitive. An obvious starting point was to avoid the disasters of 1956 and 1967 by surviving any initial onslaught; consequently, hardened bunkers were built for every combat aircraft, and operational redundancies such as emergency runways, dispersed facilities, and concealed fuel and weapons supplies were established. SAM batteries were deployed around airfields and passive defense measures enhanced.

Improvements to infrastructure were complemented by changes to pilot training. Recruitment standards were raised, flying hours increased, and operational training made more realistic through practice attacks with live weapons on mockups of Israeli targets. Pilots flew exercises with other Arab air forces to enhance cooperation.[92] But the EAF was a still an immature institution, and its commanders continued to face many challenges—a situation not helped by the inflexible doctrine and boorish attitude of their Soviet mentors. As it happens, Soviet prestige was periodically punctured when USSR pilots flying missions in EAF aircraft were routinely outclassed by the IAF, an embarrassment some commentators believe the Egyptians quietly enjoyed.[93]

Syria's development of airpower followed much the same pattern. President Assad entered an alliance of convenience with the Soviets primarily because he needed their weapons. A former commander of the SyAAF, Assad understood his old service's limitations. Like Sadat, he decided to rely on GBAD as his first line of air defense, in 1969 authorizing the establishment of an independent Syrian ADC and relegating the SyAAF to a secondary role.

By mid-1973 massive assistance from the Soviet Union had seen the Egyptians and the Syrians construct powerful air-defense barriers along the Cairo–Suez Canal axis and in the Golan Heights, incorporating some 180 SAM batteries and scores of AAA. Quantity was complemented by quality with the inclusion of missiles such as the SA-3, -6, and -7.

During and immediately after the War of Attrition the IAF had made a considerable effort to analyze the Egyptians' GBAD. However, the Soviet air-defense specialists who were supervising the Egyptian ADC had gained valuable experience operating similar systems during the U.S. bombing offensive against North Vietnam and were adept at adjusting their tactics. The Soviets demonstrated their skill when the IAF attacked the GBAD in the Suez Canal zone in April 1971. This was one of the first times the IAF had used its Shrike antiradiation missiles, designed to home in on radar emissions. Drawing on their Vietnam experience, the Soviets either turned on all radars, which confused the Shrikes' attempts to lock on to an individual emission, or they turned them all off, thus removing the homing source. Seventy-two Shrikes were fired but only one radar was destroyed.[94] The upshot was that on the eve of the October War the IAF's comprehension of the enemy's air-defense doctrine and operational specifications was "fundamentally wrong."[95]

A War in Two Parts

By mid-1973 the contest of ideas that is the essence of strategy was a dead heat. Both protagonists had decided on preemption, so the question was: who would act first?

Presidents Sadat and Assad had chosen their time and place, but the Israeli government prevaricated. Indeed, Prime Minister Meir and her cabinet repeatedly considered striking first right up until the morning of October 6 but, under American pressure to hold their fire for the sake of appearances, chose to wait.

The war began just after midday on October 6 when Egyptian and Syrian forces launched massive coordinated attacks against Israeli positions along the Suez Canal and in the Golan Heights, catching their enemy off guard. Two of the Arabs' initial actions warrant special mention. On the northern end of the Golan Heights, in an operation that demonstrated the importance of electronic warfare, Syrian commandos knocked out an IDF electronic monitoring station known as "The Eyes of Israel."[96] Against all expectations, the Syrians had seized an early advantage in the information war. Meanwhile, on the Suez Canal, inventive Egyptian soldiers stunned complacent Israeli defenders by unexpectedly using high-pressure water cannons to blast large gaps in the Bar Lev Line.

Within minutes, Egyptian tanks, artillery, and infantry were crossing the canal, breaching not only the Bar Lev Line's defenses but also its flawed strategic logic. At the same time, about two hundred EAF aircraft, including missile-armed Tu-16s, attacked Israeli air bases, SAM sites, and command centers. On the Golan Heights, Israeli positions were bombarded by a hundred SyAAF aircraft and massed artillery, after which the Syrian Army advanced in strength.

Endangered on two fronts, outnumbered by about three to one, and with most of its reservists not mobilized, Israel was confronting its most serious threat since 1948. Predictably, its leaders turned to the IAF. This time, however, the IAF was facing different circumstances and a well-prepared enemy. In previous wars the IAF had been able to establish control of the air before conducting close-attack, interdiction, and strategic strike missions. The strength of the Arab GBAD on both fronts indicated that this sequence would again be necessary, and that a concerted suppression of enemy air defenses (SEAD) campaign should precede all other air operations. But with its army in danger of being overrun, especially on the Golan Heights, the IDF high command had little choice other than to use the IAF for close attack before air superiority had been established.

IAF pilots found themselves flying ground attack missions without the favorable air environment they had enjoyed in the past and ill equipped to counter powerful defensive barriers. Furthermore, the need to fight on two fronts diminished the IAF's capacity to concentrate force. An already fraught situation was made worse by flawed decision making within IAF headquarters, where analysts identified AAA as the most dangerous component of the Arabs' air-defense system, when in fact SAMs were the more potent threat. Planners also gave priority to attacking air bases, a curious choice given the EAF's history of failure.

Egyptian ADC commanders "could scarcely believe it" when the IAF's SEAD campaign left their SAMs untouched. Insult was added to injury for the Israeli pilots when their strikes against AAA were largely unsuccessful. And when an attempt was made to retrieve the situation by redirecting the SEAD effort against SAMs in the Golan Heights, the mission was badly planned and "failed in every respect."[97] Things became worse still for the Israelis as losses mounted on both fronts. The combination of the mobile, rapid-firing ZSU-23-4 AAA and the SA-6 missile proved especially dangerous, more so because the SA-6 was impervious to the IAF's electronic countermeasures. The IAF started the war with about 290 F-4s and A-4s and within days had lost about 50, many during close-attack missions on the Golan Heights. That loss rate was unsustainable.

Replicating their tactic from the War of Attrition, the Israeli high command tried to change the tempo and nature of the fighting by directing some of the IAF's effort against interdiction and strategic targets deeper inside Syria. The idea was to buy time while electronic countermeasures were developed and aircraft replaced, and to ease pressure on their army on the Golan front by interrupting Syrian supply lines. The shift in targeting also reduced the likelihood of aircraft losses.

Relief arrived on October 8, when the IAF received self-protection antiradar chaff and antimissile flares for its strike/fighters, followed by replacement F-4s and A-4s that were flown in as part of a massive American aerial resupply operation. Also added to the IAF's inventory were new electronic countermeasures, more Shrike antiradiation missiles, and AGM-62 Walleye television-guided glide bombs. Now adequately prepared, the IAF was ready to resume its battle with the Arabs' GBAD.

It was ironic, therefore, that the vital breakthrough in the fight to control the air overhead the Suez zone came not from fighter pilots but from tank crews and infantrymen. After only five days the Egyptian Army had achieved

President Sadat's prewar aim of crossing the Suez Canal and recapturing a reasonable portion of the Sinai. Then, however, Sadat ordered his army to press on into the Sinai. This was the worst strategic decision of the war. By continuing the offensive, Sadat violated the Arabs' carefully determined logic of a limited end state; furthermore, by pushing his army out from under its GBAD umbrella, he undermined his own military strategy. His ground forces were now overextended, and exposed to Israeli forces that were fully mobilized, reequipped, and ready to advance. The Egyptian Army rapidly lost the initiative and began to retreat.

On October 15, charging Israeli armored formations and paratroopers crossed the Suez Canal into Egypt. In the process they destroyed scores of SAM and AAA sites, opening up a gap in the Arab GBAD barrier through which the IAF could fly. The Israeli Army, not the Air Force, had established control of the air.

The prospect of land forces winning control of the air should not be surprising. In World War II, for example, Allied armies did precisely that when they overran Luftwaffe air bases and air-defense systems during their march into Germany from France and the USSR, while during the American war in Vietnam, Viet Cong soldiers (who never even had an air force) frequently asserted local control of the air by dominating landing zones and runways with machine guns and light AAA.

With the Israelis advancing and the Arabs retreating, the war entered its second part, in which the action resembled June 1967 rather than the first week of October 1973. If the Israeli counterattack was to be stopped, the IAF's dominance had to be curtailed, and with his GBAD neutralized Sadat's only option was the EAF. For the first ten days of the war the EAF had been confined to tasks in which it could not get into too much trouble, such as hit-and-run strikes against lightly defended targets. Fighter sweep and close-attack missions had been kept to a minimum. Now the EAF was thrust into the front line.

Despite six years of reform, the EAF was not up to the job. In some 50 air-to-air clashes EAF pilots managed to shoot down about 8 IAF aircraft while losing over 170 themselves.[98] The IAF's kill ratio of 20:1 was far greater than their rate of 7:1 from 1967. Because the Israelis were using their most advanced fighter, the F-4E, primarily for strike missions, the majority of dogfights were between technologically equivalent IAF Mirage IIIs and EAF MiG-21s. In other words, highly skilled, tactically flexible IAF pilots were outclassing pedestrian, doctrinaire EAF pilots. The SyAAF (which included elements of the IQAF) fared no better.

As the war progressed and the Israelis continued to upgrade their ECM and weapons, the IAF became much more effective against GBAD, destroying 43 SAM sites in one 4-day period alone.[99] The Israelis also enjoyed some success with their own comparatively modest GBAD array, downing between 12 and 24 aircraft with the 75 Hawk SAMs they fired. That kill rate of 1 enemy aircraft per 3 to 6 missiles fired was vastly superior to the ratio achieved by the Egyptian ADC, whose operators fired around 1,000 SA-2s, -3s and -6s and as many as 8,000 shoulder-launched SA-7s to bring down some 25 IAF aircraft; that is, about 360 missiles were launched for every aircraft shot down.[100] (Egyptian AAA claimed an additional 20 IAF aircraft.)

Aircraft maintenance was another contest in which the IAF established an overwhelming advantage. At the start of the conflict the IAF had about 400 strike/fighters and the EAF and SyAAF about 850. However, the Israelis consistently achieved an on-line rate of 85 percent compared to the Arabs' 60 percent, in effect changing those numbers to 340 and 510. The real change came, though, when the daily sortie rate per platform was applied. By getting four sorties per day out of each platform, the IAF "increased" the size of its combat force to 1,360 strike/fighters, whereas by averaging only 0.6 of a sortie per aircraft per day the Arab air forces "reduced" theirs to 306.[101]

The final air warfare event of note occurred on October 22, when the Egyptians fired three Scud missiles (derived from the German World War II V-2 rocket) into Israel. Inaccurate but with a 200-mile range and a 2,000-pound warhead, the Scud was to become something of a strategic strike weapon of choice in the Middle East for countries with second-rate air forces. Following the Scud attack the IAF made very few deep strikes into Egypt, whereas it maintained a punishing campaign against dual-use (civilian and military) targets in Syria, including power stations, electrical grids, and transportation systems. Perhaps the Scuds generated a deterrent effect.

By late October Israeli forces on the Suez front were only a hundred kilometers from Cairo with open ground ahead of them, and their artillery on the Golan front was shelling the Syrian capital of Damascus. Nevertheless, the Israeli leadership was uncomfortable. Their resources were stretched, casualties were mounting, and they were sensitive to international criticism of territorial expansionism. And in any case, after a disastrous start their military forces had again prevailed, and all of the land the Arabs had retaken in the first week had been regained, plus some.

If Israel's leaders were uncomfortable, the Arabs' leaders were in crisis. Both capital cities seemed vulnerable to Israeli attack—an event sufficient to trigger coups against Sadat and Assad—while near the Suez Canal an Egyptian army was surrounded. Moreover, although the Arab forces were on the verge of being routed yet again, their impressive performance in the first week had won respect and had demonstrated that in the right circumstances they could compete with the Israelis. Sadat could reasonably claim to have satisfied his prewar objective. More pressure to call a halt came from the United States and

USSR, who wanted to defuse the tension created by their roles as sponsors. A cease-fire brokered by the United Nations was accepted on October 25 after an earlier attempt had collapsed.

Logistics as Strategy

It is a truism that wars are won by people, but it is also true that, all else being equal, the side with the best weapons is likely to prevail. In that context, Israel's indigenous military/industrial base represented a major advantage. However, there is a limit to how much nations can spend on otherwise nonproductive war supplies—an economic imperative that is especially pronounced in the war in the air. In 1970 a single F-4E cost $3 million and a Shrike $7,000. High unit costs are compounded by the extreme usage and loss rates typical of air warfare. During the three weeks of the October War the IAF lost 102 jets and the Arabs 433, and the Arabs fired about 9,000 SAMs.[102]

Governments consequently have to make fine judgments regarding how many weapons—which represent stranded expenditure until they are used—they can afford to have parked on ramps and stored in warehouses for a contingency that may never arise. What that meant in 1973 was that neither the Israelis nor the Arabs were capable of fighting an air war for more than about a week without material assistance from their American and Russian sponsors. Thus, on October 9 the Soviets started a massive airlift to resupply the Egyptians and Syrians with missiles, ammunition, radars, and much more; shortly afterward the United States did the same for the Israelis.[103] The United States also made good the IAF's aircraft losses by flying in about a hundred F-4s, A-4s, and C-130s, some of which arrived still bearing USAF markings.

Strategic airlift was not new, as the sustained resupply over "The Hump" in World War II and the Berlin Airlift of 1948–49 illustrate. However, the October War introduced a new dimension. Airlifters such as the Soviets' An-22 and the Americans' C-5 and C-141 were fast, big, and long range, and could move very large loads between continents in hours. It was this capability alone that made it possible for the Israelis and Arabs to continue to fight in the air.

The point bears emphasis. Israel was militarily far superior to the two Arab states, but it is not unreasonable to suggest that, had Egypt and Syria been resupplied and Israel had not, the war would have ended differently.

The concept of logistics as strategy was given broader expression immediately afterward when Arab states reacted to U.S. support for Israel by using oil as a weapon. On October 17 the Organization of the Petroleum Exporting Countries, led by Saudi Arabia, decided to cut oil production by 5 percent, a move intended to punish the West by forcing a price rise. When just two days later U.S. president Richard Nixon announced a massive increase in military aid to Israel, OPEC responded by placing an embargo on oil shipments to America, later extended to other Western states. Perhaps even the Arabs were surprised by the effectiveness of this new form of coercion. By the time the embargo was lifted in March 1974 the price of oil had quadrupled from $3 to $12 per barrel and had created chaos in global financial markets. This so-called first oil shock had a lasting effect on international politics and was yet another unforeseen cost of the Arab-Israeli wars.

Commentary

The October War was widely regarded as a comprehensive military victory for Israel. Nevertheless, Egypt and Syria earned respect for their greatly improved performance in both planning and on the battlefield. That respect translated into enhanced international status, as a consequence of which Israel's leaders became more amenable to returning territory seized in 1967. In 1979 Israel and Egypt signed a peace treaty that included the withdrawal of all Israeli military forces and civilian settlers from the Sinai, a process that was completed by 1982. During the same period Egypt gradually distanced itself from Soviet influence and, under the authoritarian rule of former EAF commander Hosni Mubarak, became a comparatively moderate voice in Middle Eastern politics for the next three decades.

As far as airpower was concerned, three intriguing points could be drawn from the war. Control of the air in the Suez Canal zone was won first by a GBAD system and then by an army; as the fighting evolved, Israel's dynamic strike/fighter-based model of airpower proved vastly more effective than the Arabs' inflexible GBAD-based model; and strategic airlift assumed a decisive dimension.

THE al-TUWAITHA RAID, 1981

The Begin Doctrine

The policy of preemption may be contentious, but in the Arab-Israeli setting it made sense: for the Israelis, because of the vulnerabilities arising from their small population and minimal strategic depth; for the Arabs, because striking first was one way of mitigating their military inferiority. The Israelis also believed that the perception they might at any time make a punishing strike generated a powerful deterrent effect.

Although the Egyptian government had softened its approach toward Israel's right to exist, most other Arab states and the PLO remained implacably hostile. That attitude seemed especially pronounced in Iraq following the formal accession to power in July 1979 of the ruthless and belligerent Saddam Hussein.

Iraq's purchase of a nuclear reactor from France in 1976 (a deal completed with the complicity of several other Western states) had already caused concern in Israel; now the prospect of a nuclear-armed Saddam raised yet again the specter of an existential threat. Located at al-Tuwaitha about ten miles southeast of Baghdad, the reactor was known as "Tammuz" by the Iraqis and "Osirak" by the West.

On June 7, 1981, in a brilliant and daring operation, the IAF seriously damaged the Iraqi reactor. Israeli prime minister Menachem Begin subsequently justified the raid in terms of "preventive strike" and "counterproliferation."[104] The Begin Doctrine, as it became known, combined an explicit threat to act preemptively with an implicit intention to deter.

Because Israel had been "stealing nuclear secrets and covertly making bombs since the 1950s," some commentators believed the Begin Doctrine represented a double standard.[105] More moral ambiguity was introduced by Iraq's status as a signatory to the Treaty for Nuclear Non-Proliferation, under which it accepted a requirement for independent inspections of its facilities, whereas Israel was not, and in any case denied the existence of its program.

Israel's objectives for the raid were to eliminate any nuclear threat for ten or so years and to reinforce its policy of deterrence. (The concept of deterrence is intrinsically subjective, so any organization wishing to generate a deterrent effect may need to apply force from time to time to demonstrate that its muscle is complemented by the will to use it.) A successful strike against Saddam's reactor would satisfy both goals.

The operational aspects of the al-Tuwaitha raid that stand out are the IAF's professionalism and Iraq's incomprehensible carelessness. But before discussing those points, the context must be set. For once that context was not defined by the Arab-Israeli conflict but by the war between Iraq and Iran that began in September 1980 and continued until August 1988.

Tension over disputed borders had existed between Iran and Iraq for years. When in early 1979 Iran's pro-Western monarch, Shah Mohammad Reza Pahlavi, was overthrown and replaced by a "revolutionary" Islamic Republic, Saddam Hussein became concerned that Shi'ite-dominated Iran might encourage Iraq's repressed Shi'ite majority to rebel. Saddam decided to take advantage of Iran's political turmoil and ordered his armed forces to invade the disputed areas. The ensuing war was by any measure depraved: in many respects it was a reprise of World War I, involving trench warfare, human-wave attacks, bayonet charges, poison gas, and no apparent concern for casualties.

Paradoxically, amid the intellectually bankrupt land operations, the protagonists occasionally displayed some imagination in their attempts to create a strategic effect with airpower, even if the operations themselves were crude. Between 1980 and 1988, Iraq fired more than 300 Scud-B ballistic missiles at

30 Iranian cities, contributing to 60,000 civilian casualties. In 1988 alone, 160 Scuds were launched at the Tehran area. Iran returned fire with numerous rocket attacks against Baghdad and other Iraqi cities.[106]

A more reasoned outlook was evident in September 1980 when the Islamic Republic of Iran Air Force (IRIAF) attacked the Iraqi reactor at al-Tuwaitha. During the shah's rule, Iran's military had been the beneficiary of U.S. largesse. Although American support was withdrawn following the revolution, Iran had enough indigenous expertise to keep advanced weapons systems operational, including F-4 Phantom and F-14 Tomcat jets. The attack on al-Tuwaitha was made by two F-4s and caused some damage. Simultaneously, another pair of Phantoms hit Baghdad's main power plant and reportedly shut down the city's electricity supply for a few days.

Israeli officials had publicly urged Iran to attack al-Tuwaitha. In fact, the Israelis had been considering doing so themselves for about five years, during which time their agents clandestinely destroyed reactor components under construction in France, threatened senior French and Iraqi officials, and assassinated a key project scientist in a hotel in Paris.[107] When the Iranian air strike failed to cause sufficient damage, the Israelis decided to finish the job.

Opinions differ regarding the threat the Iraqi program represented. According to Prime Minister Begin the reactor was almost ready to become operational—that is, it could be used to make nuclear weapons—and constituted a serious threat. On the other hand, French and Iraqi officials insisted the that reactor was designed only for scientific research, a claim endorsed by Harvard physics professor Richard Wilson, who inspected the reactor after the Israeli raid and stated that it was "unsuited" for making bombs.[108] Whatever the truth may be, once the IAF had received its orders, its leaders proceeded with characteristic professionalism.

Operation Opera

The broad concept for the strike against the al-Tuwaitha facility, code-named Operation Opera, was agreed to as early as November 1979, but the sensitive nature of the target and its distance from Israel demanded a great deal of preparation. When the idea was initially conceived the round-trip distance of 1,500 miles meant that the aircraft then available—Skyhawks and Phantoms—would have required in-flight refueling over hostile territory, a major complicating factor. The delivery to the IAF in 1980 of F-16s resolved that problem. Although the distance would test the F-16s and their top cover F-15s, meticulous planning would allow the mission to be flown unrefueled. A key factor in that calculation was retaining access to the airfield at Etzion, near the Gulf of Aqaba on the Sinai Peninsula. As part of the 1979 peace treaty with Egypt, Israel was in the process of evacuating the Sinai, but because Etzion was the most suitable location for launching a strike deep into Iraq, its handover was delayed.

Another notable event was the cooperation between Israel and Iran, a country whose postrevolution leaders regularly called for the "annihilation" of the Jewish state. Prior to the start of the Iran-Iraq War, Israel provided Tehran with intelligence on Iraq's military readiness, including details of the Tammuz reactor. The IRIAF returned the favor with a well-planned strike against three Iraqi air bases on April 4, 1981, destroying some thirty to forty IQAF aircraft and a substantial amount of infrastructure.[109] In addition to weakening the IQAF, the Iranian raid diverted Iraq's attention from Israel and exposed shortcomings in their air defenses that the IAF later exploited. Iran also gave Israel technical details of the Iraqi reactor. Additional intelligence came from the United States, whose KH-11 satellites routinely monitored al-Tuwaitha.

Even without the setback caused by the IRIAF strikes, the IQAF was struggling. Following the 1973 October War a faction of the IQAF attempted to replace Soviet doctrine and equipment with Western ideas and matériel, a push that led to the acquisition in 1976 of Mirage F-1 strike/fighters from France. However, Western aircraft were expensive and their operational concepts difficult to master; consequently, progress stalled and the IQAF became embroiled in an internecine three-way quarrel in which some favored organizational modernization, others wanted to retain the discredited but comparatively undemanding Soviet approach to air warfare, and others still wanted to revive the doctrines taught by the RAF in the 1950s.[110] If there was a model of Iraqi airpower, it could only be described as "confused."

While Iraq's airmen procrastinated, Israel's got on with the job. Gaps in the air-defense networks in Jordan, Saudi Arabia, and Iraq were identified, and a route and flight profile was chosen to minimize the risk of detection and maximize fuel efficiency. Deception techniques were prepared, under which the IAF pilots would make radio transmissions in Arabic and, if challenged, pretend to be a Jordanian or Saudi air force formation that had wandered off course.[111] Pilots practiced navigation, tactics, and weapons-delivery techniques, attacking a replica of the reactor.

While the IAF's preparations were impeccable, they involved little that was new: the IAF simply did what first-class air forces do. One aspect that did offer professional interest, however, was the choice of weapon. Weapon selection centered on two issues: how much damage was needed to achieve the objective, and was there a risk of releasing nuclear-contaminated material into the atmosphere? In order to minimize the possibility of radioactive fallout, the reactor would have to be bombed before it became operational ("hot"), a condition Israeli intelligence reportedly believed would be reached in late 1981.

Exhaustive investigations by specialist engineers satisfied the Israeli government that the risk of causing atmospheric contamination was slight.

That left the size, type, fuzing, and number of weapons to be determined. After analyzing the reactor's construction, Israeli planners concluded that unguided, 2,000-pound high-explosive bombs should be used. Eight should be sufficient; twelve would provide a margin of error. Since the F-16s would be carrying full fuel, they were limited to two bombs each, indicating a formation of six aircraft, to which IAF commander Maj. Gen. David Ivry added two backups, making a strike force of eight. Some bombs would be fuzed to explode instantaneously to crack the casing, while others would have delayed fuzing to allow them to reach the reactor's core before exploding, maximizing damage.[112]

The use of unguided ("dumb") bombs was noteworthy. U.S. pilots had used precision-guided munitions extensively ten years previously in North Vietnam, and there was no technical reason why the IAF could not have done the same; indeed, given the sensitivity of the target, it might seem odd that they chose otherwise. Perhaps because the mission was already pushing the boundaries of range, payload, and planning the IAF wanted to control as many other variables as possible—in this instance, the risk of malfunctioning or unusable (because of weather) bomb guidance systems. The F-16s were fitted with an excellent continuously computed impact point sight, which, together with the pilots' skill, gave the IAF's commanders every confidence the target would be hit. During practice for the raid, the IDF chief of staff, Lt. Gen. Rafael Eitan, flew in a two-seat F-16B to observe progress.

The execution of the plan was near flawless. Eight F-16s with six F-15s as top cover took off from Etzion in the early afternoon of June 7 and flew unchallenged at low level over Jordan and Saudi Arabia. Remarkably, as the formation crossed the Gulf of Aqaba, it was seen by King Hussein of Jordan, who was holidaying there. Hussein deduced that the aircraft were heading for al-Tuwaitha and ordered his military headquarters to advise the Iraqis.[113] The message either never reached Baghdad or was not heeded.

Crossing the Euphrates River well inside Iraq, the Israeli pilots were astonished that their antimissile warning systems remained silent, indicating that the enemy's air-defense radars either had not detected them or were inactive. No Iraqi SAMs were launched, and no IQAF fighters were scrambled.

Situated in a drab suburban area and surrounded by a prominent wall, the al-Tuwaitha reactor was easily identified. The Israeli pilots pulled up to about 8,000 feet for a dive attack. Rolling-in at 5-second intervals, they dropped their bombs from 3,500 feet before breaking away hard and releasing missile-avoidance flares. Of the 16 bombs, 12 hit the main reactor.[114] Leaving the site smoking and on fire, the formation climbed to 42,000 feet for the 90-minute flight home, again untroubled by the enemy.

A final small but thoughtful contribution was made by Major General Ivry as the strike force crossed the Israeli border. It can be easy in the excitement of completing an operational mission—let alone one of this significance—for a pilot to lose concentration and make a careless mistake during approach and landing. Ivry took the microphone, congratulated his pilots, and asked them to remain focused until they were safely on the ground.[115] It was a nice touch, and a reminder that for all its seeming invincibility, the IAF was a small and personal organization. Saddam Hussein, by contrast, reportedly ordered the executions of the head of Iraq's Western Air Defense Zone and all of the command's officers above the rank of major.[116]

International reaction to the raid was overwhelmingly critical, even from Israel's staunchest supporter, with the American ambassador to the United Nations likening it to the USSR's 1979 invasion of Afghanistan.[117] But much of the outrage was token: not many governments, including those of Iraq's nominal Arab allies, were upset to see Saddam's nuclear ambitions disrupted. And in Israel there was only satisfaction, with postmission intelligence revealing it was likely to be ten years before the reactor could be repaired.

Commentary

As a military operation and statement of intent, the al-Tuwaitha raid was an unqualified success. The planning and execution were exceptional and the results decisive. If Saddam Hussein's nuclear program did indeed constitute an existential threat to Israel, then it had been eliminated for about a decade; furthermore, the sheer brilliance and audacity of the operation burnished the IAF's already imposing reputation. The raid thus served three of the Begin Doctrine's objectives of counterproliferation, preventive strike, and deterrence.

It might seem contrary, therefore, to suggest that, as an exercise in airpower, the raid should be viewed with some caution. The issue is not the IAF but their Arab opponents. The fact that 14 hostile aircraft could spend 3 hours flying 1,500 miles over three enemy countries without being challenged beggars belief. That Iraq was already in a state of war, that the al-Tuwaitha reactor was a high-value target and had already been attacked, and that Israel's policy of preemption was public knowledge merely compounded the offense. Given Egypt's and Syria's early success with GBAD in the 1973 October War, it does not seem unreasonable to suggest that the Baghdad area, including al-Tuwaitha, should have been defended by a 24/7 system.

As the sporting truism has it, we can only beat the opposition that takes the field. But when that opposition performs as badly as the Iraqis, it is necessary to ask: how would we have performed against someone else, against someone even moderately competent? Regardless of that, Operation Opera was an exemplary demonstration of playing to one's strengths. In the Middle East, the Israeli model of airpower was supreme, and it made perfect military sense to use it preemptively and forcefully.

Once again, in the short term, Israel had thwarted a perceived threat to its existence, but also once again, the deeper strategic/political implications were less certain. According to the prominent American political commentators Bob Woodward and Richard Betts, the raid may have had the opposite effect to that intended. Looking back a quarter of a century after the event, Woodward reported that "Israeli intelligence were convinced that their strike in 1981 on the Osirak nuclear reactor . . . had ended Saddam's program. Instead [it initiated] covert funding for a nuclear program . . . involving 5,000 people testing and building ingredients for a nuclear bomb."[118] Betts went even further, concluding that the additional resources Saddam allocated to Iraq's nuclear program after the IAF's raid "may actually have accelerated [Iraq's nuclear program]."[119] But probably neither of those opinions would have worried the IAF, whose masterful application of the Begin Doctrine had bolstered its standing as Israel's weapon of first choice.

THE FIRST LEBANON WAR, 1982
"Dislodging" the Problem

Political stability in Lebanon depended on cooperation between the Muslim and Christian communities. Never entirely comfortable, relations between the two groups were destabilized by the influx of tens of thousands of Palestinians who in 1948-49 had been ethnically cleansed from their homeland (now Israel) and then in 1970-71 driven out of Jordan. Replicating events in Jordan, the PLO in Lebanon operated as a state within a state, a development that kindled the tension between Christians and Muslims. Simultaneously, frustrated by their marginalization, many Palestinians became more radicalized. Refugees throughout Lebanon armed themselves and factions of the PLO clashed with Lebanese Christian militias. In April 1975 a full-scale civil war broke out following the massacre of twenty-six Palestinians in a Christian area of Beirut.

Although essentially Christian against Muslim, the civil war was much more complicated than that, with each group comprising numerous factions. Perceiving Syria's interests to be at risk, in 1976 President Hafez al-Assad ordered his armed forces to invade Lebanon, marking the start of a twenty-nine-year occupation.

In the south of the country militant elements of the PLO increased their rocket attacks against Israeli settlements in the Galilee, just over the border. Israel responded with IAF bombing raids and, in 1978, a relatively low-scale army incursion into southern Lebanon. However, when the rockets continued and the

PLO carried out several high-profile attacks against Jewish targets in other parts of the world, the Israeli government decided to mount a major invasion.

Disingenuously titled "Operation Peace for Galilee" by the Israelis—in Lebanon it was known more prosaically as "The Invasion"—the IDF's ostensible objective was to penetrate no more than twenty-five miles into Lebanon and, working in cooperation with Christian militias, "dislodge" the PLO. However, a vastly more ambitious aim was shared by Israeli Defense Minister Ariel Sharon and IDF chief of staff Rafael Eitan, who wanted to advance all the way to Beirut, crush the Lebanese Muslims and, if necessary, the Syrian army, and establish a Christian "pro-Israeli satrapy over all of Lebanon."[120] In the end, the Israeli Army did occupy Beirut, at which stage the Sharon-Eitan scheme unraveled disastrously.

In the meantime the IDF's commanders had not forgotten their chastening experience from the first week of the October 1973 war. If the IAF were to be effective in the reconnaissance, strike, maneuver, and close-attack roles during the invasion, it would first have to win control of the air. Consequently, the IAF was tasked with clearing out an ostensibly powerful air-defense system the Syrians had constructed in Lebanon's Bekaa Valley, the site of the Beirut-Damascus highway. The scene had been set for another remarkable air campaign.

The Arnold Doctrine

Writing just after World War II, the commander of the U.S. Army Air Forces, Gen. H. H. Arnold, contended that air forces must remain open to new ideas and advanced technologies and keep their vision "far into the future." An air force whose doctrine was tied "solely to the equipment and processes of the moment," he continued, would endanger national safety.[121] The air war between Syria and Israel overhead the Bekaa Valley in June 1982 confirmed the wisdom of Arnold's analysis.

Syria had enjoyed early success in the October 1973 war with its GBAD in the Golan Heights before being crushed by the IAF. Apparently satisfied that a model that partially succeeded almost ten years previously was still good enough, the Syrian Air Defense Command packed the seventy-five-mile-long Bekaa Valley with nineteen SA-2, SA-3, and SA-6 batteries, large numbers of short-range antiaircraft missiles, and about four hundred antiaircraft guns.[122] But while the defensive barrier was intense and the short-range missiles modern, the larger SAMs had been upgraded only incrementally, their electronic warfare systems were obsolescent, and the Syrians' operational practices were careless.[123] The notion that a dated GBAD system might prove superior to a high-quality, constantly modernizing force indicated the limitations of Syrian airpower thinking.

Doctrinal problems of a different kind were apparent in the SyAAF, which continued to rely on the MiG-21, an excellent fighter in its time but now twenty years old. President Assad had a better knowledge of airpower than most national rulers and was committed to the concept of technological "strategic parity" with Israel.[124] This was the kind of forward thinking SyAAF airpower doctrine needed, but it had to be managed carefully lest it conflict with the service's modest abilities. Unfortunately for Assad that was precisely what happened with the two main additions to the SyAAF's inventory between 1973 and 1982.

The first, the MiG-23, featured a variable-geometry wing, a technical innovation whose complexity taxed even advanced air forces and that survived only one design generation; the second, the MiG-25 Foxbat, was a high-altitude interceptor intended to combat the American developmental B-70 Valkyrie nuclear-armed bomber, which in the end never entered production. Although the MiG-25 achieved something of a cult status because of its exotic purpose and Mach-3 speed, it was of questionable use to a substandard air force, which needed to concentrate on mastering the basics of control of the air, close attack, interdiction, and reconnaissance.

The Syrians' reliance on the past (the October War) and delusion over the future (the Foxbat) contained a dangerous assumption—namely, that the IAF would not have improved during the previous decade. But, unlike the SyAAF and Syrian ADC, the IAF had spent a great deal of time analyzing its failings in the October War, paying special attention to technologies and techniques that might defeat GBAD systems. New strike/fighters were the starting point. The design and systems of the F-15s and F-16s that had been so successful at al-Tuwaitha incorporated lessons learned from the Americans' air war over North Vietnam. Both jets had outstanding maneuverability, excellent cockpit visibility, look-down shootdown radar, advanced ECM, and the capacity to launch a wide range of weapons, including antiradiation missiles. Regular upgrades to the Phantoms, Skyhawks, and Kfirs since 1973 meant that they too were still highly effective.

Complementing the strike/fighters was the Middle East's first airborne early-warning and control capability, four E-2 Hawkeyes. The Hawkeyes raised battlespace awareness and coordination to new levels by providing command and control, real-time intelligence, fighter vectoring, and strike direction. It was typical of the IAF's innate understanding of the Arnold Doctrine that the IAF was the first E-2 operator to modify the aircraft for air-to-air refueling.

Two locally developed weapon systems were also to prove critical in the Bekaa Valley: remotely piloted vehicles (RPVs, later known as unmanned aerial vehicles) and antiradiation ordnance. RPVs were acquired from the United States following the War of Attrition as both a promising technology and a means of easing the stress of prolonged conflict on pilots. At around the same time, Israel Aerospace Industries began designing and building its own RPVs. Some officials questioned the initiative, believing RPVs to be nothing more than toys. But encouraged by Major General Ivry, IAI persisted and became a world leader in one of the most important developments in aviation for decades.[125] Whereas the U.S. RPVs carried only photographic cameras, it seems IAI's were fitted with a television camera to relay information in real time, and perhaps also weapons.

Antiradiation ordnance developed by the Israeli Armament Development Authority during the 1970s was later acclaimed by the former IAF fighter pilot and squadron commander Shmuel L. Gordon as the IAF's "most important advantage" in the campaign against SAMs in the Bekaa Valley. Writing some thirty-five years after the event, Gordon described the weapons as "revolutionary . . . standoff air-to-ground precision-guided munitions" that have "completely changed the aircraft-SAM balance ever since."[126]

Dynamic versus Inflexible

The First Lebanon War started on June 6, 1982, when the IDF invaded southern Lebanon. While the ground war was to end badly, the air battle in the Bekaa Valley, which began three days later, was a triumph for the IAF. In a reversal of the first days of the October 1973 war, Israel's dynamic air force crushed Syria's inflexible GBAD. And when the destruction of his missiles and guns compelled Hafez al-Assad to send the SyAAF into combat, the contest was one of the most one-sided in the history of air warfare.

This time the IAF had done its homework. In addition to information collected by reconnaissance aircraft and satellite imagery, the IAF had made skillful use of RPVs. In the months preceding the battle, RPV flights into the Bekaa Valley were used to trigger the Syrians' air-defense radars, enabling the Israelis to plot the position of SAM batteries and compile emission data from which ECM could be constructed.

Meticulous coordination characterized the IAF's campaign, titled Operation Arzav. A pleasing feature for any military strategist was the use of deception. At around 2:00 p.m. on October 9 Syrian radar operators reported the apparent presence of large formations of unidentified aircraft at numerous locations around Lebanon; shortly afterward, their communications, early-warning sensors, and command-and-control networks were disrupted by electronic countermeasures. More confusion was added by RPV decoys, which flew into the Bekaa Valley and deceived air-defense operators into firing SAMs.

With the Syrian ADC in disarray, about forty IAF aircraft attacked SAMs, AAA, radars, and headquarters buildings. Perhaps referring to Israel's "revolutionary standoff air-to-ground precision-guided munitions," Syria's Defense

Minister Mustafa Tlass later noted that IAF F-4s used "television" bombs.[127] IAF Hawkeyes coordinated activities, and an electronic intelligence B-707 jammed Syrian command-and-control services. As soon as the attack finished, battle-damage assessment was carried out to redefine targeting priorities for the next tranche of strikes.

The Syrians' reaction was instructive. Prior to the IAF strike SyAAF fighters were on combat air patrol near the Bekaa Valley and in most circumstances would have been vectored to engage the Israelis. Instead they were ordered to withdraw, apparently to create a free-fire zone into which SAMs and AAA could be fired without having to identify targets.[128] Either Syria's commanders doubted their fighter pilots or were very confident in their GBAD. If it were the latter, their confidence was misplaced. Within two hours all nineteen SAM batteries had been either destroyed or damaged, and Syria's strategy for protecting the Damascus-Beirut highway had been shattered.

The question now was whether or not the SyAAF would be called up to try to regain control of the air over the Bekaa Valley. Numerous factors indicated that Syria's pilots were likely to struggle. Israel's fighter pilots were the equal of any in the world and were flying leading-edge F-15s and F-16s and very good Kfirs armed with advanced air-to-air missiles. They were operating as one component of an integrated system featuring centralized command and control, real-time battlespace management, ECM superiority, and information dominance. By contrast, the Syrians' standards were modest, their MiG-21s and -23s were obsolescent, and they were fighting blind because of the destruction of their early-warning radars and communications and the inadequacies of their command-and-control arrangements.

Major General Ivry personally managed the air-to-air battle from his command post in Tel Aviv. Although the IAF committed about ninety aircraft to the fight, Ivry preferred to vector waves of four-ship formations into the combat zone, where engagements with courageous but confused Syrian pilots generally lasted only a minute or two. By the end of the first day almost thirty SyAAF jets had been shot down for no IAF losses; six days later the ratio had increased to more than eighty to nil.

The IAF's remarkable kill rate did not mean the victory was easily achieved. On the contrary, it represented thirty-four years of constant striving for excellence across the full spectrum of airpower skills. In this instance, Ivry and his staff managed an extremely complex situation with a degree of real-time control never previously achieved. Ivry later provided a neat musical analogy: rather than "playing" a set of individual instruments that more or less supported each other, he was "conducting" a full orchestra.[129]

In Moscow the extent of the failure by association of Soviet training, tactics, and technology caused shockwaves and prompted a root-and-branch review of warfighting concepts.[130] The USAF also learned from the experience, and nine years later during the first Gulf War the IAF model from the Bekaa Valley served as a prototype for the most successful air campaign in history.

The Economics of Airpower

In the one hundred years since airpower was first applied systematically, only a small number of countries have been able to construct high-quality air forces. Not the least of the reasons is that airpower is very expensive. It is no coincidence that advanced airpower has been the province of either first-world nations such as the United States, the United Kingdom, Germany, and France, or the large command economies of the USSR and China. Nor is it a coincidence that when third-world nations or entities have managed to apply airpower successfully, their chosen models have been cheap, asymmetric, and event specific. During the French and American wars in Vietnam, for example, Viet Minh and Viet Cong forces regularly gained temporary local control of the air through the shrewd deployment of machine guns and AAA, or by ambushing landing strips and helipads, or by attacking air bases. And on September 11, 2001, a handful of al-Qaeda operatives asserted control of the air over the continental United States by subterfuge, having been trained in simulators to fly airliners to minimal standards and at minimal cost.

That minimalist, asymmetric model is not, incidentally, broadly applicable. The al-Qaeda example is unsustainable, and Vietnam's was purpose designed to counter an invading force that was not supported by the majority of the occupied nation. Both would have been useless in the kinds of crises Israel faced between 1948 and 1982.

By the time of the Lebanon war, Israel was a first-world country. Unlike its Arab enemies, it was a successful democracy with a strong economy, including impressive research and development and industrial sectors (albeit skewed toward military technology) and a high-quality public education system. GDP per capita was $6,095, compared to $545 in Egypt and $1,695 in Syria; while the respective literacy rates were around 92 percent, 44 percent, and 56 percent.[131] But having been in a continual state of war since its inception and with a population of only 4 million, Israel faced intense budgetary pressure.

Precisely how much of Israel's GDP has been spent on defense is difficult to establish. Estimates can vary wildly depending on the parameters applied; furthermore, defense spending is notoriously secretive. Thus, numbers cited for Israel can range from around 5 percent of GDP to more than 30 percent.[132] But even though that is a big discrepancy, in this context it does not matter. Regardless of which end of the spectrum is used, both sums are immense and both imply an unsustainable airpower model—unless external economic assistance is available.

Most of that assistance has come from the United States. Since World War II, Israel has been the largest recipient of American military aid. In the nine years leading up to the 1982 Lebanon invasion, the United States gave Israel $6.1 billion in military grants and $7.83 billion in military loans.[133] Over the same period Israel's average annual GDP was $16.87 billion, meaning that each year the United States added 9 percent to Israel's economy, all of which was spent on defense. In short, notwithstanding the quality of its people, planning, and technology, the IAF could not have built its model of airpower without external aid.

Plainly, the same logic applies to Israel's enemies, who over the time covered by this study received massive amounts of Soviet assistance. Immediately after the Lebanon war, for instance, the USSR gave Syria military hardware worth $2 billion, including 160 new strike/fighters.[134]

Whether or not donor states receive value for money in terms of geopolitical influence is a matter of opinion. The point here does not concern geopolitics or great power rivalries or Israelis or Arabs. It is simply about the cost of advanced airpower. Economics is almost always a factor in war; in the case of advanced airpower, it is an imperative.

Creating Hezbollah

The six-day Bekaa Valley air war marked the high point for the Israelis, as their army sank into the quagmire of a three-year occupation of Lebanon. Directed by Defense Minister Sharon and supported by IAF fixed- and rotary-wing aircraft, the Israeli Army pushed the PLO out of the twenty-five-mile zone inside Lebanon's southern border. The IDF then continued northward as IAF jets bombed Beirut. Lebanon's fragile political equilibrium collapsed, as did unity within the PLO. Revenge as much as the pursuit of rational political objectives seemed to become the motivation for many combatants as interstate war branched into civil and factional war, involving, among others, Lebanese Christian and Muslim sects, the Syrian Army, Kurdish separatists, leftists, PLO factions, and Israelis. Beirut was reduced to rubble and eventually split into separate Christian and Muslim zones.

The low point for Israel came in September 1982, when the IDF stood by and allowed their Christian Phalangist allies to murder about 2,000 captured Muslims, mostly Palestinians, in Beirut's Sabra and Shatila refugee camps.[135] International condemnation forced Sharon to briefly stand aside from his position.

By the end of 1982 Israel had achieved one objective by forcing the PLO to relocate yet again, this time to Libya. However, Lebanon was unmanageable and the IDF's occupation became increasingly untenable. When the Israeli Army finally withdrew in June 1985, none of the other outcomes could be regarded as successful. Syria was taking over Lebanon; Israel's international standing and the reputation of its armed forces had been sullied; and a new and dangerous movement had emerged to fill the vacuum left by the PLO.

Known as Hezbollah, that movement was conceived by Muslim clerics and funded by Iran in direct response to Israel's occupation of Lebanon. Hezbollah's ideology of Islamic nationalism, anti-Westernism, anti-Zionism, and anti-Semitism as well as its commitment to armed struggle left no doubt as to its purpose. In the three decades since then, Israel has annihilated scores of terrorist cells, but Hezbollah has survived every attempt to destroy it. Instead, it has become a state within a state and today is arguably Israel's most serious threat. The PLO was not so much "dislodged" from Lebanon as "replaced," and by a more dangerous enemy at that.

Commentary

The IAF's extraordinary campaign in the Bekaa Valley formalized the status of electronic warfare as an airpower capability in its own right and set new standards for planning and command and control. It also seems the experience convinced some of Israel's enemies that they could not compete with the IAF and should develop alternative models of airpower. According to Major General Ivry, it was immediately after the Bekaa Valley that Syria's defense minister concluded his country should rely on ballistic missiles for strategic strike, at which time Syria started acquiring Scuds.[136]

When analyzed strictly in terms of the mechanics of airpower, Operation Arzav was a brilliant success and a model for the future. But when analyzed in terms of Israel's broader campaign in Lebanon, which was an unmitigated disaster, it was of little consequence. Chief of the IDF Eitan once told his troops that they "had to do everything to make [the Palestinians] so miserable they will leave."[137] The problem was that while Eitan and Defense Minister Sharon were very good at applying force, they were less so at understanding its limits.

CONCLUSION

Israeli airpower in the twentieth century was built on the foundations of an educated workforce, rigorous standards, advanced technology, and, for the most part, exemplary planning. The addition of strong leadership and a clear strategic vision created an exceptional combat force. The Arab nations, meanwhile, labored under the legacies of colonialism and a socioeconomic system that was in many ways resistant to intellectual and technological progress. An unsurprising consequence was that too often their air forces were inept. Their only noteworthy successes came in the War of Attrition, when a smart strategy played to their strengths; and the 1973 October War, when their pilots were relegated to a secondary role and the skillful use of GBAD won them temporary control of the air. Other significant points to emerge from this study include electronic warfare as a capability in its own right, the strategic application of logistics, the evolution of RPVs as a transformative technology, the Israelis' development of maintenance practices and local aerospace industries as force multipliers, and real-time battlespace management.

None of those points, however, is as important as the demonstrated need for a great and powerful friend. Air warfare is characterized by skilled practitioners, advanced technology, and high usage rates, which in combination can be prohibitively expensive. By 1973 the IAF was one of the best air forces in the world, but it is not unreasonable to suggest that without the matériel and financial support of the United States, the IAF would have failed in the October War, thus placing Israel's existence at risk. Nor could the Arab air forces have developed to any extent without the sponsorship of the USSR. The point is broadly applicable.

Caution is needed when seeking to translate the IAF's experiences from the specific to the general. During the period under review, the IAF's performance was brilliant, and even when problems did arise the organization was intellectually strong enough to acknowledge failings and take remedial action. Nevertheless, the Arabs often were so bad that analysts must consider how the IAF might have fared against a more capable foe.

It might seem to follow that the Arabs should not have bothered with airpower, that they perhaps should have directed their resources elsewhere. But that would be to ignore the very low base from which they started and the magnitude of their task. Change can take a long time, and everything is relative. Only six years after the IQAF was ineffectual during Israel's strike against al-Tuwaitha, it was able to generate a strategic effect of sorts through its politically astute campaign against oil tankers in the Persian Gulf during Iraq's war with Iran.

There is a final, superseding conclusion. The Arabs' inability to construct an effective airpower model was the main reason for their persistent failure on the battlefield. The IAF's model, by contrast, enabled airpower to play a vital role in Israel's survival. From an (entirely reasonable) Israeli perspective, other conclusions presumably are beside the point.

NOTES

My thanks to associate professor Rodger Shanahan from the Lowy Institute for International Policy for his insights into politics and society in the Middle East.

1. Ilan Pappé, *The Ethnic Cleansing of Palestine* (Oxford: Oneworld, 2011); and Benny Morris, *1948: A History of the First Arab-Israeli War* (New Haven, Conn.: Yale University Press, 2008).
2. In an interview with the *New Statesman* in 2002, British foreign secretary Jack Straw observed, "A lot of the problems we are having to deal with now ... are a consequence of our colonial past.... The Balfour Declaration and the contrary assurances which were being given to the Palestinians in private at the same time as they were being given to the Israelis ... are interesting history for us, but not an entirely honorable one." Quoted in Sykes-Picot Agreement, http://www.saylor.org/site/wp-content/uploads/2011/08/HIST351-9.2.1-Sykes-Picot-Agreement.pdf.
3. H. N. Wrigley, "Some Notes on Air Strategy," in *The Decisive Factor*, ed. Alan Stephens and Brendan O'Loghlin, 29–86 (Canberra: Australian Government Publishing Service, 1990).
4. Eli Barnavi, ed., *A Historical Atlas of the Jewish People* (New York: Schocken, 2003); and Pappé, *Ethnic Cleansing of Palestine*, 571–91.
5. Lon O. Nordeen, *Fighters over Israel* (New York: Orion Books, 1990), 4; and Ehud Yonay, *No Margin for Error* (New York: Pantheon, 1993), 13, 45–46.
6. UN General Assembly Resolution 181 (Partition Plan for Palestine), Medea Institute, http://www.medea.be/en/themes/international-organizations-and-diplomacy/un-ga-resolution-181-partition-plan-of-palestine/.
7. Israeli Air Force, http://www.iaf.org.il/3199-7566-en/IAF.aspx.
8. Eliezer Cohen, *Israel's Best Defense* (New York: Orion, 1993), 4–6.
9. Smoky Simon, "The Israeli Air Force (IAF) in the War of Independence," World Machal, http://www.machal.org.il/index.php?option=com_content&view=article&id=413&Itemid=708&lang=en.
10. Karl Marx and Frederick Engels, "Austria's Weakness," *New York Daily Tribune*, May 7, 1855, in *Collected Works*, vol. 14 (London: Lawrence and Wishart, 1975–1983), 689–93.
11. TheGlobalEconomy.com, Egypt Economic Indicators, http://www.theglobaleconomy.com/Egypt/Literacy_rate/; and Google Search, Egypt and Israel Literacy and GDP Rates, https://www.google.com.au/?gfe_rd=cr&ei=xiY_Vbm-CcaN8QelkYA4&gws_rd=ssl#q=israel+gdp+per+capita, both accessed October 1, 2015.
12. Lon Nordeen and David Nicolle, *Phoenix over the Nile* (Washington D.C.: Smithsonian Institution Press, 1996), 15–19.
13. Ibid., 67–68.
14. Benny Morris, *The Birth of the Palestinian Refugee Problem* (Cambridge: Cambridge University Press, 1988).
15. Anthony Gorst and Lewis Johnman, *The Suez Crisis* (London: Routledge, 1997), 6; and Keith Kyle, *Suez* (London: I. B. Tauris, 2011).

16. Motti Golani, "Chief of Staff in Quest of a War: Moshe Dayan Leads Israel into War," *Journal of Strategic Studies* 24, no. 1 (March 2001): 49-70.
17. Joe Stork, "Arms Industries of the Middle East," Middle East Research and Information Project, www.merip.org/mer/mer144/arms-industries-middle-east; and Kader Factory for Developed Industries, Arab Federation for Engineering Industries, www.arabengineeringindustries.org.
18. "Entangled: Why America Must Stay Engaged in the Middle East," *Economist*, June 6-12, 2015.
19. UNESCO, *World Illiteracy at Mid-Century* (Switzerland: UNESCO, 1957), 32-39, 52-53, http://unesdoc.unesco.org/images/0000/000029/002930eo.pdf. Syria's literacy rate was about 30 percent and Iraq's 20 percent. Although Egypt's literacy rate had improved, population growth meant that the number of illiterate people had increased since the beginning of the century.
20. Nordeen and Nicolle, *Phoenix over the Nile*, 138-42.
21. Ibid., 145, 157.
22. Sanu Kainikara, *Red Air: Politics in Russian Air Power* (Boca Raton, Fla.: Universal Publishers, 2007), 173-233; Nordeen and Nicolle, *Phoenix over the Nile*, 174; and Benjamin S. Lambeth, *Russia's Air Power in Crisis* (Washington D.C.: Smithsonian Institution Press, 1999), 72-73.
23. Nordeen and Nicolle, *Phoenix over the Nile*, 147.
24. Shmuel L. Gordon, "Air Superiority in the Israel-Arab Wars, 1967-1982," in *A History of Air Warfare*, ed. John Andreas Olsen, 127-56 (Washington D.C.: Potomac Books, 2010), 130; and Robert Jackson, *Suez 1956: Operation Musketeer* (London: Ian Allen, 1980), 25.
25. R. A. Mason, "Air Power as a National Instrument: The Arab-Israeli Wars," in *The War in the Air, 1914-1994*, ed. Alan Stephens (Fairbairn, Canberra: Air Power Studies Centre, 1994), 182-83.
26. "General Haim Laskov of Israel; Former Chief of Staff, 1958-61," Obituary, *New York Times*, December 9, 1982; Cohen, *Israel's Best Defense*, 68-69; and Yonay, *No Margin for Error*, 110-16.
27. Israel Aerospace Industries Ltd., www.iai.co.il/.
28. Rafael Advanced Defense Systems Ltd., www.rafael.co.il/.
29. Derek Varble, *The Suez Crisis 1956* (Oxford: Osprey Publishing, 2003), 188-96.
30. Alan Stephens, "The Air War in Korea, 1950-1953," in *A History of Air Warfare*, ed. John Andreas Olsen, 86-106 (Washington D.C.: Potomac Books, 2010), 101-2.
31. Varble, *Suez Crisis*, 364.
32. Nordeen and Nicolle, *Phoenix over the Nile*, 156.
33. Nordeen, *Fighters over Israel*, 52.
34. Jackson, *Suez 1956*, 59.
35. Varble, *Suez Crisis*, 933.

36. Jackson, *Suez 1956*, 61; and Varble, *Suez Crisis*, 948.
37. Quoted in Nordeen and Nicolle, *Phoenix over the Nile*, 164.
38. Varble, *Suez Crisis*, 1060–68.
39. Kyle, *Suez*, 201–2.
40. Donald Neff, "Ike Forces Israel to End Occupation after Sinai Crisis," *Washington Report on Middle Eastern Affairs*, February–March 1996, 89–91.
41. Giulio Douhet, *The Command of the Air* (Washington D.C.: Office of Air Force History, 1983), 206.
42. Mason, "Air Power as a National Instrument," 186–87.
43. William A. Orme and Greg Myre, "Ezer Weizman, Former President of Israel and Hero of 1967 War, Dies at 80," *New York Times*, April 25, 2005; and Nordeen, *Fighters over Israel*, 56.
44. Martin van Creveld, *The Sword and the Olive* (New York: Public Affairs, 2002), 162.
45. Douhet, *Command of the Air*, 53–54.
46. Phillip S. Meilinger, *10 Propositions Regarding Air Power* (Washington D.C.: Air Force History and Museums Program, 1995), 20.
47. Mason, "Air Power as a National Instrument," 186–87.
48. David Tal, "Symbol Not Substance? Israel's Campaign to Acquire Hawk Missiles, 1960-1962," *International History Review* 22, no. 2 (June 2000): 304–17.
49. Creveld, *Sword and the Olive*, 162.
50. Israel Military Industries, http://www.imi-israel.com/.
51. Elbit Systems Ltd, https://www.elbitsystems.com/.
52. Nordeen and Nicolle, *Phoenix over the Nile*, 186.
53. Ibid., 179–80.
54. Mason, "Air Power as a National Instrument," 187.
55. Kenneth M. Pollack, *Arabs at War: Military Effectiveness, 1948–1991* (Lincoln: University of Nebraska Press, Kindle eBook, 2002), loc. 433–35.
56. Ibid., loc. 1076–87; and Nordeen and Nicolle, *Phoenix over the Nile*, 174, 183.
57. Mason, "Air Power as a National Instrument," 187.
58. Henry Kissinger, *Years of Upheaval* (London: Weidenfeld and Nicolson, 1982), 196–97.
59. Gordon, "Air Superiority," 132.
60. Nordeen, *Fighters over Israel*, 71–72.
61. Itai Brun, "Israeli Air Power," in *Global Air Power*, ed. John Andreas Olsen (Washington D.C.: Potomac Books, 2011), 146–48; and Nordeen, *Fighters over Israel*, 71.
62. Gordon, "Air Superiority," 132–33.
63. Tom Cooper, "Iraqi Air Force Since 1948, Part 1," ACIG.org, August 26, 2007, http://www.acig.info/CMS/index.php?option=com_content&task=view&id=66&Itemid=62.

64. Brun, "Israeli Air Power," 147–48; and Gordon, "Air Superiority," 133.
65. Gordon, "Air Superiority," 133–35.
66. Nordeen and Nicolle, *Phoenix over the Nile*, 221.
67. Quoted in Benny Morris, *Righteous Victims: A History of the Zionist-Arab Conflict, 1881–1999* (New York: Knopf, 1999), 328–29; see also Avraham Shapira, *The Seventh Day: Soldiers' Talk about the Six-Day War* (New York: Simon and Schuster, 1971).
68. Quoted in Pollack, *Arabs at War*, loc. 1140.
69. Nordeen and Nicolle, *Phoenix over the Nile*, 220; and Pollack, *Arabs at War*, loc. 1295.
70. The Tactical Operations Center, "Egyptian Air Defense During the Yom Kippur War," http://www.tacticaloperationscenter.com/Air%20Defense.htm; Global Security.org, "Air Defense Force: Egypt," http://www.globalsecurity.org/military/world/egypt/adf.htm; Nordeen and Nicolle, *Phoenix over the Nile*, 230–1; and Pollack, *Arabs at War*, loc. 1313.
71. Nordeen and Nicolle, *Phoenix over the Nile*, 225–27.
72. Pollack, *Arabs at War*, loc. 1318–30.
73. Martin van Creveld, *Nuclear Proliferation and the Future of Conflict* (New York: Free Press, 1993), 100.
74. Gordon, "Air Superiority," 137.
75. Ibid., 138.
76. "The F-4 Phantom in Israeli Service," http://www.oocities.org/capecanaveral/hangar/2848/phantom.htm.
77. Gordon, "Air Superiority," 138.
78. Murray Rubenstein and Richard Goldman, *The Israeli Air Force Story* (London: Arms and Armour Press, 1979), 108.
79. Gordon, "Air Superiority," 140–41.
80. Mason, "Air Power as a National Instrument," 191.
81. Pollack, *Arabs at War*, loc. 1439.
82. Kissinger, *Years of Upheaval*, 482.
83. The Insight Team of the Sunday Times, *The Yom Kippur War* (New York: ibooks, 2002), 66.
84. Simon Dunstan, *The Yom Kippur War*, vol. 1 (Oxford: Osprey Publishing, 2003), 11–14.
85. Gordon, "Air Superiority," 142–43.
86. Insight Team, *Yom Kippur War*, 64–65.
87. Central Intelligence Agency, *Intelligence Report: The 1973 Arab-Israeli War: Overview and Analysis of the Conflict*, September 1975, http://www.foia.cia.gov/sites/default/files/document_conversions/1699355/1975-09-01A.pdf, 26, 30; and Brun, "Israeli Air Power," 155.
88. TheGlobalEconomy.com, Egypt Economic Indicators, http://www.theglobaleconomy.com/Egypt/Literacy_rate/.

89. Pollack, *Arabs at War*, loc. 1523–28.
90. Ibid., loc. 1528.
91. Chaim Herzog, *The Arab-Israeli Wars* (London: Arms and Armour, 1982), 209–10.
92. Nordeen and Nicolle, *Phoenix over the Nile*, 259–60; and Pollack, *Arabs at War*, loc. 1528–34.
93. Dani Asher and Moshe Tlamim, *The Egyptian Strategy for the Yom Kippur War: An Analysis* (Jefferson, N.C.: McFarland, 2009), 69.
94. Lester W. Grau and Jacob W. Kipp, "Maintaining Friendly Skies: Rediscovering Theater Aerospace Defense," *Aerospace Power Journal* 16, no. 2 (Summer 2002), 41. Turning off radars removed the GBAD's primary tracking source and forced operators to fire visually.
95. Brun, "Israeli Air Power," 152.
96. Dunstan, *Yom Kippur War*, 14.
97. CIA, *Intelligence Report:1973 Arab-Israeli War*, 59–60; Gordon, "Air Superiority," 144–45; see also Brun, "Israeli Air Power," 154.
98. Pollack, *Arabs at War*, loc. 1781–1806.
99. H. P. Willmott and Michael B. Barrett, *Clausewitz Reconsidered* (Santa Barbara, Calif.: Greenwood Publishing, 2010), 104.
100. CIA, *Intelligence Report: The 1973 Arab-Israeli War*, 49; and Pollack, *Arabs at War*, loc. 1806.
101. Pollack, *Arabs at War*, loc. 1800.
102. Brun, "Israeli Air Power," 155–56; and Pollack, *Arabs at War*, loc. 1806.
103. M. J. Armitage and R. A. Mason, *Air Power in the Nuclear Age* (Urbana: University of Illinois Press, 1985), 129–31.
104. Assaf Sharon, "The Jewish Terrorists," *New York Review of Books* (September 24, 2015); and Dmitry Adamsky, "Why Israel Should Learn to Stop Worrying and Love the Bomb," *Foreign Affairs* (March 31, 2012), https://www.foreignaffairs.com/articles/israel/2012-03-31/why-israel-should-learn-stop-worrying-and-love-bomb.
105. Julian Borger, "The Truth about Israel's Secret Nuclear Arsenal," *Guardian*, January 16, 2014; and Seymour M. Hersh, *The Samson Option: Israel's Nuclear Arsenal and American Foreign Policy* (New York: Random House, 1991).
106. Alan Stephens and Stuart McKenzie, "Bolt from the Blue: The Ballistic and Cruise Missile Problem," Air Power Studies Centre Paper No. 20 (Canberra: Air Power Studies Centre, 1994).
107. Ronen Bergman, "Killing the Killers," *Newsweek*, December 13, 2010, http://www.newsweek.com/killing-killers-69081.
108. Donald Neff, "Israel Bombs Iraq's Osirak Nuclear Research Facility," *Washington Report on Middle Eastern Affairs*, June 1995, 81–82, http://www.wrmea.org/1995-june/israel-bombs-iraq-s-osirak-nuclear-research-facility

.html; and Mehdi Hassan, "Bomb Iran and It Will Surely Decide to Build Nuclear Arms," *Guardian*, March 26, 2012, http://www.theguardian.com/commentisfree/2012/mar/25/bomb-iran-nuclear-arms-iraq-israel.
109. Tom Cooper and Farzad Bishop, "Target: Saddam's Reactor," *Air Enthusiast*, no. 110, http://www.angelfire.com/art2/narod/opera/.
110. Pollack, *Arabs at War*, loc. 2520–26.
111. Trevor Dupuy and Paul Martell, *Flawed Victory: Arab-Israeli Conflict and the 1982 War in Lebanon* (Fairfax, Va.: Hero Books, 1986), 69.
112. Cohen, *Israel's Best Defense*, 450–58.
113. Ze-ev Raz (who led the mission), cited in Avraham Shmuel Lewin, "Osirak Revisited," *Jewish Press*, Frontpagemag.com, December 18, 2007, http://archive.frontpagemag.com/readArticle.aspx?ARTID=29258.
114. My thanks to Dr. Benjamin S. Lambeth for authoritative information on the types of bombs used and the results achieved. Some thirty-five years after the event numerous sources still present contradictory details. There were two reactors, the large "Tammuz 1" and the small "Tammuz 2." Tammuz 1 was the target. See also Cooper and Bishop, "Target."
115. Cohen, *Israel's Best Defense*, 459.
116. Cooper and Bishop, "Target."
117. Duncan M. Currie, "Remember Operation Babylon," *Harvard Crimson*, September 18, 2002, http://www.thecrimson.com/article/2002/9/18/remember-operation-babylon-as-the-debate/.
118. Bob Woodward, *State of Denial* (New York: Simon & Schuster, Kindle eBook, 2006), loc. 3926–33.
119. Richard K. Betts, "The Osirak Fallacy," *National Interest* (Spring 2006).
120. Lawrence Joffe, "Obituary, Lieut-Gen Rafael Eitan," *Guardian*, November 25, 2004; and Pollack, *Arabs at War*, loc. 7377–82.
121. "Future of Air Power—Report by General Arnold, Commanding General of the United States Army Air Forces," *U.S. News*, November 30, 1945, Box 1634, CRS 5954, National Archives of Australia.
122. Nordeen, *Fighters over Israel*, 170; Brun, "Israeli Air Power," 160–61; and Gordon, "Air Superiority," 149.
123. Matthew M. Hurley, "The BEKAA Valley Air Battle, June 1982: Lessons Mislearned?" *Airpower Journal* 3, no. 4 (Winter 1989).
124. Neil MacFarquar, "Hafez al-Assad, Who Turned Syria into a Power in the Middle East, Dies at 69," *New York Times*, June 11, 2000.
125. Israel Aerospace Industries, "Unmanned Air Systems," http://www.iai.co.il/2013/18892-en/BusinessAreas_UnmannedAirSystems.aspx; Cohen, *Israel's Best Defense*, 430; and Brun, "Israeli Air Power," 161–62.
126. Gordon, "Air Superiority," 149; see also "Rafael—Armament Development Authority," Israel Association of Electronics and Software Industries, http://www.iaesi.org.il/Eng/?CategoryID=163&ArticleID=556.

127. Quoted in Gordon, "Air Superiority," 150; see also GlobalSecurity.org, Air Defense Command, http://www.globalsecurity.org/military/world/syria/air-defense.htm.
128. Quoted in Rebecca Grant, "SEAD/DEAD: Bekaa Valley 1982. Israel Sets New Standard," Defence Pakistan, July 23, 2013, http://defence.pk/threads/sead-dead-bekaa-valley-1982-israel-sets-new-standard.266363/.
129. Quoted in ibid.
130. Benjamin S. Lambeth, "Moscow's Lessons from the 1982 Lebanon War," RAND Project Air Force Paper R-3000-AF (Santa Monica: RAND, September 1984).
131. Public Data, World Development Indicators (derived from The World Bank), http://www.google.com.au/publicdata/explore?ds=d5bncppjof8f9_&met_y=ny_gdp_mktp_cd&idim=country:ISR:IRN:EGY&hl=en&dl=en; The World Bank, Literacy Rate, adult total (% of people ages fifteen and above), http://data.worldbank.org/indicator/SE.ADT.LITR.ZS. The literacy percentage for Israel is from 1983, Egypt 1986, and Syria 1981.
132. Alex Minz, "The Military-Industrial Complex: The Israeli Case," *Journal of Strategic Studies* 6, no. 3 (September 1983): 103–27, reported indicative defense expenditures as a percentage of gross national product as follows: in 1966, 10.4; in 1967, 17.7; in 1973, 32.7; and in 1980, 25.2. See also Simon Rogers, "Military Spending: How Much Does the Military Cost Each Country?" (sourced from SIPRI), *Guardian World News*, April 17, 2012; Niall McCarthy, "The Biggest Military Budgets as a Percentage of GDP," *Forbes Business*, June 25, 2015, http://www.forbes.com/sites/niallmccarthy/2015/06/25/the-biggest-military-budgets-as-a-percentage-of-gdp-infographic-2/; and Moti Bassok, "Israel Shells out Almost a Fifth of National Budget on Defense," *Haaretz*, February 14, 2013.
133. Jeremy M. Sharp, *U.S. Foreign Aid to Israel* (Washington, D.C.: Congressional Research Service, June 10, 2015); United States Arms Control and Disarmament Agency, "World Military Expenditures and Arms Transfers 1972-1982," Washington D.C.: April 1984, http://www.state.gov/documents/organization/185658.pdf.
134. MacFarquar, "Hafez al-Assad."
135. Seth Anziska, "A Preventable Massacre," *New York Times*, September 16, 2012.
136. Grant, "SEAD/DEAD."
137. Quoted in Joffe, "Obituary, Lieut-Gen Rafael Eitan."

Chapter 4

THE ISRAELI AIR FORCE AND ASYMMETRIC CONFLICTS, 1982–2014

—*Raphael Rudnik and Ephraim Segoli*

Operation Peace for Galilee, also known as the First Lebanon War (1982), may mark the turning point of the armed conflicts in which the Israel Defense Forces (IDF) have participated.[1] The IDF entered a war that resembled the American experience in Vietnam: in Lebanon it fought simultaneously against the Syrian state and Palestinian guerrilla forces. In fact, this was the last war the IDF waged against a state military, at least up to the time of writing.

From its inception, the IDF has fought against nonstate, asymmetric enemies but shaped its forces primarily in preparation for "big wars" against state armies that threatened Israel. The IDF viewed the guerrilla warfare and terrorist activities of nonstate organizations as secondary problems and little more than a nuisance. The Israeli Air Force (IAF), too, was preparing mainly for a struggle against the seemingly more challenging enemy: the Syrian military.

In the summer of 1982 the IDF's definition of conflicts comprised two concepts: "war," which signified a conflict with state militaries, and "day-to-day security," which mainly consisted of continuous struggle with nonstate entities and sometimes included a large military operation. Responsibility for day-to-day security fell mostly to the army; the IAF played a relatively marginal role in this mission. Gradually the IDF and the IAF in particular perceived that asymmetric conflicts were replacing conventional wars between states. It took even longer for the IDF to begin grasping the complexity of asymmetric conflicts and to recognize the necessity of investing many different types of resources in the struggle. Throughout, the debate centered on what would constitute "victory" and on the IAF contribution to achieving such a victory.

POINT OF DEPARTURE: FROM THE FIRST LEBANON WAR TO A NEW CONCEPT OF WARFARE

The IAF benefited from an impressive learning process after the blow it had sustained in the 1973 war, and it developed a fitting response to the challenge posed by Soviet air-defense systems. That response included a profound conceptual change that defined both technological and organizational modifications. The air force understood that only optimal linkage among concept, organizational structure, and technology could produce the required systemic change.

The First Lebanon War again demonstrated the importance of the air superiority that allows aircraft to operate freely and ground forces to maneuver with no fear of enemy air attack. Operation Peace for Galilee was awe inspiring in operational terms: the IAF neutralized the Syrian air force and its air-defense system. Maj. Gen. David Ivry, the commander of the air force during that time, summed up the results in a paraphrase of Ezer Weizman's statement following the 1973 war: "After this war one can state without any doubt that the plane bent the missile's wing."[2] Unmanned aerial vehicles (UAVs) proved especially successful in combat by providing intelligence in real time and directing fighter aircraft to attack points. The IAF understood the potential of these platforms and initiated development and expansion that generated internal tensions owing to the need to transfer resources and missions from manned platforms to unmanned ones. Still, air superiority did not suffice to achieve a decisive victory, and it seems that in this operation the IAF missed an opportunity to produce lasting results.

By contrast, it seems that Syria rested on the laurels of its 1973 success and did not properly appreciate the IAF's ability to recover and learn. For this Syria paid a stiff price, but Operation Peace for Galilee motivated it to undertake its own significant process of drawing lessons that pushed it—among other things—to adopt a strategy of indirect conflict against Israel.

It executed this strategy first through a proxy in the form of Hezbollah and, second, by abandoning air-to-air confrontation in favor of massively enlarging its arsenal of missiles and surface-to-surface rockets for various ranges. Moreover, by understanding the IAF capabilities of gathering intelligence and attacking, Syria improved its air-defense system, reorganized its command-and-control structure, and devoted considerable effort to all activities connected with camouflage and decoys.

Despite the brilliance displayed in the air war and the benign operational conditions, the IDF's achievements on the ground were less impressive. Senior IDF ground commanders claimed that various difficulties encountered by ground troops resulted from poor air support. One of the commanders even commented that "first and foremost it should be remembered that in spite of having worked extensively together and in spite of the important achievements of that cooperation, at the conclusion of the war both sides were dissatisfied and even somewhat frustrated. This feeling stems from the assessment that in those conditions much more could have been achieved."[3] By contrast, the Syrian military believed at the end of the war that its ground troops had executed their missions well, notwithstanding the defeat in the air.

Conceptual gaps and the different characteristics of fighting in the surface dimension and that of the air dimension have historically created an almost regular source of tensions in the management of military campaigns, with both operational and tactical implications. Some commanders in both ground and air forces have considered the tensions as inherent and insoluble; therefore, they concluded that the best solution would consist of creating a separation—or deconfliction—in which each force receives whatever resources it needs to perform its missions. According to this concept, the allocation of attack helicopters to the army in Operation Peace for Galilee should have given soldiers the responsibility for close-air support (CAS) and allowed the fighter-bombers to concentrate on other missions, such as strategic strikes and interdiction. The controversy about this issue continued throughout the years following the operation.

From Operation Peace for Galilee Israel learned that the strategic objective of creating a new political reality in Lebanon was too ambitious. Still, Israel achieved other strategic objectives relative to the Syrian and Palestine Liberation Organization (PLO) presence in Lebanon: Syrian military units evacuated Beirut and were pushed to northern Bekaa, whereas the PLO was badly beaten and most of its armed activists as well as its headquarters were banished and absorbed in Tunis. A United Nations Interim Force in Lebanon (UNIFIL) force supervised the implementation of the agreement to end the fighting.

Operation Peace for Galilee represented the IDF's last attempt to wage a decisive war. Since then Israel has deterred aggression mainly by operations designed to preserve the status quo and consolidate the security situation.[4] This state of affairs, together with technological advances and Western culture in the contemporary era, has given the IAF an opportunity to dominate military operations.[5] The concept of deterrence gave rise to dilemmas crucially concerned with the best methods of operation: launching instant and massive strikes or escalating gradually; relying on indirect approaches in the form of damaging the power structure or executing direct assaults to erode military capabilities; maximizing force and the number of targets or limiting force and focusing on the quality of targets. Concurrently, the IDF debated the best allocation of resources—structuring forces to execute asymmetric conflicts or continuing to preserve competence and advantage for the "real" interstate war to come.

This chapter explores these dilemmas and issues by describing and analyzing seven military operations conducted in the two main theaters where the IAF has fought during the last two decades: Lebanon and the Gaza Strip. It examines the learning process in which each side engaged—or failed to engage—in the intervals between operations. Fundamental changes took place in the IAF and its missions throughout these years. Advances in technology drove most of the changes in the IAF force structure and concept of operations. Changes in the characteristics of the adversary's system and challenges in the battlespace also had a major influence. The chapter shows how the IAF adapted its strategic and operational thinking and planning as it came to accept the inevitability of asymmetric conflicts. In the IDF this process was described as the IAF's transition from the role of "bombing contractor" to that of "operational architect."

OPERATION ACCOUNTABILITY, 1993
Strategic Context

The First Lebanon War did create a strategic change, but not in the manner Israel had planned or expected. Israel's aspirations at the end of 1982 to find allies—or at least entities with which it could come to a political agreement and who could lead Lebanon—quickly faded. The Iranian Revolutionary Guard exploited the war by setting up Hezbollah to implement Ayatollah Khomeini's revolutionary values and extremist ideology in Lebanon and function as one of Iran's strategic forces. Hezbollah would grow steadily and turn into the main threat to the IDF throughout the following years. Initially it functioned as an Islamic terror organization, directing its attacks at foreign elements that had invaded Lebanon. It carried out the first suicide attacks in Lebanon—against the U.S. embassy, the U.S. Marine Corps headquarters, and the headquarters of the French forces in Beirut.

In 1985 Israel wished to scale down its political involvement in Lebanon and resolved to remove its forces south of the Litani River, hoping that the "security buffer zone" would serve as a barrier between Israel and the terrorist organizations in Lebanon. Following Israel's retreat, Hezbollah improved and strengthened its guerrilla activities against IDF units and the Christian militia they supported in southern Lebanon. Hezbollah attacked its adversaries with rocket and mortar shelling, explosive devices, and antitank missiles.[6]

Not long after the evacuation of Syrian forces from Beirut and the removal of the PLO from Lebanon, Syria took advantage of the political vacuum created by the Israeli retreat and the turmoil in Lebanon and returned to center stage. By the end of the 1980s Lebanon had practically turned into a Syrian protectorate. The Syrians enabled Hezbollah to strengthen its influence among the Shi'ites and before long Hezbollah became the dominant organization in south Lebanon, serving Syria as a proxy for deterrence and indirect action against Israel as well as for preserving Syrian interests in Lebanon.[7]

The retreat to the security buffer zone also enabled the Palestinians to broaden their renewed consolidation in Lebanon and their aggressive operations against Israel. In October 1985, when the Palestinians again started to launch Katyushas at Israel from south Lebanon, Israel responded with an air attack on PLO headquarters in Tunisia. Throughout the 1990s, with Iranian and Syrian support, Hezbollah established itself ever more firmly as a Lebanese military and political entity. It adopted a well-organized structure, set up a widespread social service network, joined in Lebanon's political life, developed semi-military operational patterns, and acquired numerous advanced weapons. Assistance from Iran and Syria enabled Hezbollah to establish an advanced military infrastructure, but at no point did the organization abandon its terrorist characteristics. In fact, Hezbollah represented a perfect example of a "terrorilla" (terror and guerrilla) organization, possessing military capabilities whose quality and quantity resembled those of a state and adjusting its tactics to the given context. Its direct operations against the state of Israel consisted mainly of launching rockets and assisting different Palestinian terror organizations. Hezbollah's operational logic emphasized that victory consisted of survival and continued rocket attacks on Israel, making the Israeli hinterland and IDF troops pay the highest price.

The IDF and the South Lebanese Army deployed in the security buffer zone, mainly in the permanent outposts near major townships and traffic axes. Over time they carried out primarily defensive missions while the number of assaults and offensive actions dwindled. They gradually turned over assault missions within populated regions to the IAF, which executed them mainly with attack helicopters. In 1992 the IAF used recently acquired AH-64 helicopters in an attack that killed the Hezbollah leader, Sheikh Abbas al-Musawi. Sheikh Hassan Nasrallah, who replaced Musawi, retaliated for his predecessor's death by ordering a terror attack on the Israeli embassy in Buenos Aires.

In 1993 Hezbollah increased its attacks on IDF forces in the security buffer zone and its Katyusha launches against the Galilee settlements. The Israeli leadership concluded that the IDF concept of operations in Lebanon was not achieving its goal; a different, more active strategy was needed. Prime Minister Yitzhak Rabin therefore ordered a large-scale operation in Lebanon, with the strategic aim of preventing Hezbollah from continuing its terror attacks on Israel. The undeclared objectives of the operation were to return to the status quo ante—those oral understandings that excluded the northern settlements from the fighting—and to weaken Hezbollah by eroding its popular support.

Concerns about again having the ground forces sink into the "Lebanese quagmire," and the Israeli public's unwillingness to "sacrifice" soldiers in what they viewed as elective wars led the IDF to decide that the IAF would lead the main effort. This decision was also influenced by the recognition of technological advances in airpower and by the U.S. performance during Operation Desert Storm in Iraq in 1991. The IDF defined the objective of the operation as "strike Hezbollah targets and Palestinian terrorists in Lebanon, key infrastructures and their civilian operators, to create pressure on the Lebanese government and other power brokers in Lebanon to restrain Hezbollah and Palestinian operations against the security sector and change their patterns of operation against targets in Israeli territory."[8] The IAF was to focus its strikes on Hezbollah in spite of its decentralized command-and-control system and the integration of Hezbollah forces into the local population. The difficulty was even greater because the Hezbollah terrorists anticipated it and sought to blend even more deeply into the civilian population. Moreover, the Israeli government directed the IAF to operate under strict constraints: minimize collateral damage, avoid any harm to UN forces, and prevent any loss of Israeli aircraft. Hezbollah had some three thousand to five thousand armed activists and only a few hundred combatants armed with light weapons and antitank missiles as well as rocket and artillery. Hezbollah was limited in mobilizing forces; therefore, it based its fighting on the prior deployment of forces and local activists who fought in spaces and from positions previously prepared for it.

Hezbollah had no military bases in south Lebanon. The military, logistic, and command infrastructure of the organization was based in the Bekaa region and in Beirut. Fighting equipment and the fighters' staging bases were spread all around Lebanon and were absorbed mainly in the environment of the Shi'ite population. The houses of many Shi'ite activists in south Lebanon served as firing positions for mortars or rockets stored in their cellars.

Concept and Execution

The concept of operations rested on an indirect approach. The IAF's original idea was to attack the outskirts of villages in order to persuade the villagers to vacate their houses and move northward, thus creating free space for direct attack. This idea evolved into a broader concept of creating a chain of pressures starting with the inhabitants of south Lebanon and reaching to the Lebanese administration and the Syrian leader, ideally convincing them to restrain Hezbollah.[9] At the same time, the IAF was to place south Lebanon under an air blockade that would prevent any reinforcements and provisions from passing southward and would facilitate attacks on combatants. According to this concept, the IAF would attack terrorist targets as well as military and civilian infrastructures in south Lebanon, bomb the outskirts of villages, and destroy identified antiaircraft artillery emplacements.

The IDF opened the campaign on July 25 with artillery fire and air assaults on the outskirts of southern villages, accompanied by radio broadcasts and leaflets encouraging the population to leave their houses. As a result, nearly 300,000 Shi'ite inhabitants fled north. The IAF then attacked Hezbollah targets from the air, with some of the attacks led by Special Forces and UAVs. Hezbollah reacted by directing massive fire against the Galilee settlements. The IDF debated whether to expand the operation to Beirut and the Bekaa or to stay with the original plan. The Israeli government chose the latter course; meanwhile, the United States sought to mediate between the parties. Israel stopped the air strikes after seven days, when a cease-fire reached with American mediation went into effect on July 31.

This operation featured a compressed command-and-control structure that significantly shortened the distance between the political leadership and the cockpit. The IDF's Northern Command was excluded from the chain of command. Strict political supervision of the form and scale of all missions led to precise planning and close analysis of each sortie, giving IAF pilots very limited autonomy. The requirement to obtain preapproval of every target led to a long and cumbersome delay between target identification and strike. Missions such as bombing the outskirts of villages or attacking very small targets (such as a team of two terrorists, which was defined as a legitimate target) with precision munitions sometimes caused tensions between the field operators and IAF headquarters, which was repeatedly called upon to explain the goal and character of each operation to the pilots.

Among other targets, the IAF attacked infrastructures in south Lebanon and several power stations, which drew broad condemnation in Israel and around the world. The air strikes exhausted their potential at an early stage of the operation because the IAF quickly exhausted all known targets and identified no new ones. The pilots faced no serious challenges, as Hezbollah lacked an efficient air-defense system and Israel's mode of operation was very restrained. The IAF succeeded in striking several launch teams and launchers, which reduced the number of missile launches but did not stop them altogether. The entire operation killed 54 terrorists and destroyed 300 houses but also killed 184 Lebanese citizens. Israel lost 2 civilians and 1 soldier.

The cease-fire included an oral agreement by both sides to refrain from attacking civilian targets: Hezbollah undertook not to launch missiles into northern Israel, and Israel undertook not to attack Lebanese villages. The agreement allowed Hezbollah and Israel to continue fighting inside the security buffer zone as long as they did not target civilians. In essence, the sides returned to the status quo ante.

In total, the IAF conducted 1,588 sorties in Operation Accountability: 646 by fighters, 259 by attack helicopters, 183 by transport and utility helicopters, and 500 from UAVs. Of the 1,503 strikes, 200 used precision-guided munitions, 984 used general-purpose bombs, and 319 used missiles from attack helicopters.

Observations

The IAF's technical capabilities enabled the political leadership to control the conduct of Operation Accountability in detail. This micromanagement raised many questions as to the relative responsibilities of the political and the military leadership for planning and conducting military operations. This shortening of the command chain also complicated the process of confirming, planning, and executing attacks.

At the IAF debriefing a dispute arose about the fundamental character of the conflict and the difficulty of operating in a state of ambiguity. Some thought the air force should not invest resources in developing concepts and structuring its forces to combat terror organizations that posed only a marginal, fleeting threat. In their opinion, such fervor might divert the focus from the real threat: regular state military forces. Others predicted that these asymmetric confrontations would represent the very type of conflict that the IAF would have to cope with from that point on. As Dan Halutz said, "I am sometimes worried by those statements that 'it's not like war' and eventually we have about 15 years between one 'real' war and another; meanwhile we experience 'other wars.' I am saying these things here are exactly like war."[10] Halutz was to become the IAF commander and later the chief of General Staff.

Since the operation did not try to achieve a decisive outcome, it was very difficult for any of the IDF services to determine the level of success they had achieved. The Northern Command concluded that the cease-fire agreement had "legitimized" Hezbollah operations and reinforced its motivation to act against both the IDF and Israeli settlements in the north. In the leadership's opinion, the agreement tied the IDF's hands.[11] Conversely, senior IAF staff officers believed that Hezbollah's morale had sustained a severe blow that would undermine its motivation to carry on.[12] Yet even within the IAF, and especially among the pilots who took part in the operation, there was a sense that success had eluded them because of the ineffectiveness of the attacks.[13]

The concept of operations received harsh criticism for targeting civilians, and there was lingering doubt as to the effectiveness of operations and the implementation of escalation. Still, the IDF in general and the IAF in particular would have to resolve the dilemmas involved in planning deterrence operations. At the operational level, the IAF again stressed the importance of creating tighter linkages between sensors and shooters through the use of Special Forces or UAVs.

For its part, Hezbollah became aware of its technological inferiority and the need to conceal its activities and the structure of its command-and-control system. The organization also perceived the fine granularity at which the IDF examines collateral damage; therefore, it continued intensifying efforts to blend within the population.

Although carried out mainly by the IAF, Operation Accountability did not enable the IAF to understand its systemic responsibility for planning such operations. The IAF did not fully recognize that conflicts of this kind presented complex, enduring challenges, and that the air force itself would have to adapt conceptually, organizationally, and technologically in order to develop a relevant, effective response.

OPERATION GRAPES OF WRATH, 1996
Strategic Context

In the short term Operation Accountability had indeed created tensions between Hezbollah and the Lebanese population and administration. However, Hezbollah's intensive activities to rehabilitate the Shi'ite villages in the south, conducted with Iranian assistance, and the establishment of aid mechanisms in southern Lebanon eventually restored and even considerably improved Hezbollah's standing in the country. As Hezbollah embedded itself further in Lebanon's political structure, it made a large investment in setting up its own system of government as an alternative to the official political establishment in Lebanon. In many ways Lebanon became a state ruled by an organization; Hezbollah did not take formal responsibility for the government but in fact determined its agenda.

The agreements concluded at the end of Operation Accountability benefited Hezbollah: because they prohibited Israel from attacking inhabited regions, they enabled—even encouraged—Hezbollah's military consolidation within the civilian population. Hezbollah understood that to neutralize IAF capabilities, it had to minimize its own operational signature and that of its combatants as much as possible. Hezbollah therefore deployed its expanding rocket arsenal at the perimeter of villages, towns, and various other locations that were difficult for the IDF to attack. In Hezbollah's view, this fit the image it was establishing for itself as the "defender of Lebanon." Meanwhile, Hezbollah's fighting force grew to more than five thousand combatants, prepared for long-time independent and local operation.

After Operation Accountability, the IDF troops in the security buffer zone in Lebanon stayed primarily in their fortified outposts as concern about possible casualties limited any initiative. This encouraged Hezbollah to renew firing rockets and continue its attempts to exact a price from Israel for keeping IDF soldiers in Lebanon. These actions prompted Israel to increase air strikes on Lebanon. The intensity of the fighting varied, with attacks sometimes initiated by Hezbollah and sometimes by Israel. Concurrently, the IAF's ability to conduct assaults at night and in bad weather conditions improved considerably, and great advances occurred in both the quantity and quality of the collection and direction capabilities of Special Forces and UAVs.

The IAF devoted considerable effort to studying the Hezbollah troop dispositions and modus operandi, especially to analyzing the characteristics of its rocket operations. In June 1994 attack helicopters assaulted a Hezbollah training camp near Ein Dardara in the Lebanese Bekaa. Six weeks later Hezbollah retaliated with a massive terrorist attack on the Jewish community center in Buenos Aires. The two sides continued exchanging blows well into 1995, and operations intensified when Hezbollah resumed launching Katyushas at Israel's northern settlements. Fairly successful operations by Israeli special ground forces did not undermine Hezbollah's resolve. Israel again tried to use diplomatic channels, but when this did not yield the desired results, the government decided to undertake another military operation.

The large gap between its improved assault capabilities and its ability to identify viable targets presented a great challenge for the IAF. Hezbollah's compartmentation, decentralization, and integration into the civilian environment made it very difficult to collect intelligence. As the IAF chief of operations aptly stated in a briefing before an operation, "We should at some point wise up—we won't have better intelligence on Hezbollah than we have today.... The Katyushas... are based on independent work in terrain cells without depending too much on central control from above."[14] In addition, the IAF had to cope with challenges similar to those it had experienced in Operation Accountability: the need to conduct attacks while minimizing collateral damage and without losing any aircraft.

Concept and Execution

Israel did not assume it could fully subdue Hezbollah and instead sought a significant truce. The goal of Operation Grapes of Wrath was to deter Hezbollah from continuing to shoot missiles at the northern settlements. Israel also had another aim: to create optimal conditions for the political leadership to obtain a clear agreement that would constrain Hezbollah even more severely. In the back of their minds the decision makers again hoped that putting pressure on the population would bring about a degradation of Hezbollah's status in Lebanon.[15]

Since Operation Grapes of Wrath began as a reaction to Hezbollah activity, its detailed objectives were defined only after the assaults started. The operational plan stated: "The IDF will hit Hezbollah targets in Lebanon and, if needed, in environment infrastructure and the civilian presence enabling their operation in reaction to the damage done to the settlements of the north, aiming to create pressure on Lebanese powers that be to take action to restrain Hezbollah operations against the settlements in north Israel and the security buffer zone and change the pattern of their activity against targets in Israeli territory."[16]

The IAF commander, Maj. Gen. Herzl Bodinger, had also commanded Operation Accountability and was among those who believed that the operation had met its objectives. Therefore, he directed the IAF to follow the same concept of operations, which combined direct and indirect action against Hezbollah. Direct actions would consist of simultaneous, multidimensional attacks on Hezbollah fighters and infrastructures throughout Lebanon and on identified sources of antiaircraft fire, accompanied by an aerial blockade and naval interdiction to increase the effectiveness of the air strikes. The concept also included the possible early insertion of Special Forces to identify targets and direct the assaults. The indirect operations would include assaults on Lebanese national infrastructure and on the outskirts of villages, again intended to force the inhabitants to move north and create pressure on the Lebanese government in the hope that it would in turn pressure Syria to restrain Hezbollah. To maximize the effect, the IAF planned a large-scale opening move that would produce considerable economic loss.

As in the previous operation, Israel had no intention of involving significant ground forces. To shorten the process of approving strikes in the blockaded areas and make them more efficient, the IAF delegated authority to confirm targets to the commander of the Northern Command—a task that he executed through the forward headquarters of the IAF in his command. Should the conflict escalate, the air force was also required to be ready for action against the Lebanese military. Due to constraints and the high sensitivity of the attack plans, the IAF main headquarters exercised precise, rigorous control over all changes and cancellations of missions.

The first sortie was aimed at a Hezbollah logistics base deep in Lebanon, near the border with Syria and the territory it controlled. Later on the IAF attacked the Hezbollah headquarters in Beirut, which it had not done since the summer of 1982, carrying out a pinpoint assault with AH-64s. Then, in accordance with prior plans, the operation continued with IAF raids on infrastructures and assaults on the outskirts of villages by the air force and artillery. Concurrently, the IAF began to enforce the air blockade in areas well known for launching Katyushas while the navy laid siege to Lebanese ports.

With the air blockade in place, the IAF began hunting for launch teams. Fighter-bombers and helicopters continuously flew over launch sites that had been analyzed in advance and identified for attack by Special Forces and UAVs. Bad weather conditions sometimes disrupted the assaults but did not stop them altogether.

At the start of the operation the UN Security Council showed understanding of Israel's motives, and the UN attempted to mediate between the sides to stop the conflict. The Lebanese government demanded a cease-fire and a return to the previous agreements that favored Hezbollah but refused to renegotiate the terms. Israel made it clear that its attacks would cease only if Hezbollah ceased its shelling of Israel, but instead Hezbollah actually increased the number of targets at which it aimed its rockets. Most of the launches took place in daytime because Hezbollah had determined that at night most citizens were in shelters, and they estimated that the IAF had a higher likelihood of identifying launch sources at night. In accordance with its early deployment, Hezbollah operated from within civilian areas and in the proximity of protected areas such as UN camps and mosques. In keeping with its standard practices, Hezbollah executed some launches from stationary launchers with delay mechanisms.

Contrary to IDF expectations, relatively few inhabitants of southern Lebanon vacated their houses and fled northward as they had done three years previously. This undermined a major component of the IDF campaign concept. The IAF leadership recognized this weakness and warned of potential harm to civilians and its impact on the operation as a whole.[17]

On April 18 a dramatic turnaround occurred: an IDF artillery battery fired mortars to assist a force in distress near a UN outpost. Four stray shells hit a stronghold in which several hundred civilians had taken refuge, killing about a hundred refugees and several UN soldiers. The Israeli prime minister apologized and ordered an immediate halt to all attacks. Nevertheless, the incident triggered worldwide indignation and international pressure to stop hostilities. On April 25 the UN Security Council approved a resolution condemning Israel and demanding that it cease its assaults in south Lebanon. Two days later Israel ceased fire and signed a new memorandum of understanding with Syria and Lebanon.

In total, the IAF executed 2,000 assault sorties with jets and helicopters. In these assaults 22 Hezbollah terrorists, 173 civilians, and 3 Lebanese soldiers were killed. Hezbollah launched 840 Katyushas, of which 600 landed in Israeli territory. On the Israeli side, 24 civilians and 31 soldiers were wounded; no one was killed. The IAF flew 2,950 sorties in Operation Grapes of Wrath: 1,785 by fighter aircraft, 938 by attack helicopters, and 227 by UAVs. Ordnance dropped numbered 2,278, of which 466 were precision-guided munitions, 1,516 general-purpose bombs, and 296 missiles from helicopters.

Observations

The memorandum of understanding signed at the end of the conflict—largely imposed on Israel—made both sides content to exit the conflict. Hezbollah, however, gained recognition of the legitimacy of its struggle against the Israeli "conquest." The IDF Northern Command therefore argued at the conclusion of this operation that Hezbollah had again emerged as the overall winner.

Contrary to Israel's continued expectation that pressure on the population would weaken Hezbollah, the attacks actually enhanced the group's status. Hezbollah again rushed to aid in the restoration of houses that had been damaged, thus underscoring its image as the defender of the Shi'ites in Lebanon. The IAF chief of staff at that time, Brig. Gen. Amos Yadlin, who would later become the chief of the IDF intelligence branch, referred to Operation Grapes of Wrath when he wrote that in fact the operation had not implemented the original plan of attacking infrastructures and instead the IDF had "sent signals" that were not understood and only "contributed to the enemy's strength."[18]

The IAF had failed to conduct a thorough, in-depth examination of the fundamental nature of the conflict and its implications for the use of airpower, even though that issue had already arisen in Operation Accountability. Again leaders argued for the necessity of a rigorous definition of "other wars," stating, "It takes us a very long time to tell ourselves, well, this isn't war, this is something else, but we don't exactly define that other thing, because we don't have any such term."[19] This issue was later addressed again by Dan Halutz, this time when he was the IAF chief of staff. He stated that because the IDF lacked the option of conducting a direct, decisive ground operation against Hezbollah, and going to war against Syria to force it to restrain Hezbollah was not feasible, the only choice had been to execute a short, focused operation against Lebanon that would prompt outside intervention and force an agreement.[20]

Once again the IAF had executed a campaign that concluded without a real decision and left considerable leeway for defining "victory." The IAF commander sought to present the operation as a success because it achieved the political leadership's objective: obtaining a written peace agreement. He argued that "the great achievement is the confidence the political echelon places in the air force."[21] Despite poor weather conditions, the IAF successfully carried out all of its missions except for locating and destroying launch crews. Yet staff of the Northern Command and IAF pilots held a different view because the operation had not met another of the principal goals: reducing the number of rocket launches against Israel.

Debate surrounding the IAF's assumption of full responsibility for suppressing the launches against Israel naturally arose. Some maintained that the IAF had no choice but to perform this task given the absence of any other force capable of executing the entire mission. Others argued that the IAF would make a mistake by accepting this mission because this type of operation would distract it from its primary purpose of attacking strategic targets. This controversy would persist in later years as well.

Throughout the operation the political and military leadership engaged in intense strategic discussions. Given the central role of the air force in the fighting, the IAF commander took part in these talks. Senior air force officers later commented that these meetings had not produced useful results because the political leadership, which did not understand how to manage airpower, demanded frequent changes while conducting the campaign: "We didn't know exactly what they wanted of us. There was no discourse with the political echelon; the performance of the air force as it was operated was very deficient. It should be put loud and clear: we didn't fulfill the mission. We didn't reinstate deterrence."[22]

Reviving the concept of operations of Operation Accountability also came under sharp criticism: "In the absence of discourse, one does not manage to implement lessons. We didn't learn from Accountability that one should not go for civilians but for infrastructures that hurt, right in the first act. All this theory of levers, that we pressure the Lebanese, the Lebanese will pressure the Syrians and the Syrians the Hezbollah—it has to be checked as well. By my assessment it didn't actually work out."[23]

The halt in the campaign as the result of an artillery targeting error clearly demonstrated the significance of legitimacy in such operations. In addition, it emphasized the need to conduct short operations in order to minimize the possibility that an error could change the character of the operation as a whole.

The IAF leadership also examined the implications of centrally commanded and controlled activity on one of the main pillars of the air force concept of operations: the leader's actual decision-making authority: "Every action and every decision were examined through a magnifying glass so in practice the leader was left with very small area of decision. For the air force pilots that was a deep culture change."[24] This concern derived from the possibility that cultural change would influence the pilots' mode of operation even in conflicts without such centralized control, when individual leaders should exercise their own judgment in the air. The requirement that pilots operate overcautiously to minimize both collateral damage and opportunities for Hezbollah to shoot down an aircraft affected the IAF's ability to maintain focus on its goals. "Most of the attention in each sortie focused on the fear of making a mistake that could prompt Katyusha launches. Hezbollah understood that; they behaved as if they controlled the intensity of the situation even though we were much stronger."[25]

DEVELOPMENTS BETWEEN 2000 AND 2004

The end of one century and the beginning of another provided a good opportunity for analyzing prevailing concepts and theories. Military discourse and theoretical debates in Israel both expanded and intensified in view of the different characteristics and lessons of the large military campaigns that took place at the end of the twentieth century in Kosovo and at the beginning of the twenty-first in Afghanistan and Iraq.

In December 1999 the IAF commander, Maj. Gen. Eitan Ben Eliyahu, wrote an article describing air force challenges in the twenty-first century. Ben Eliyahu's central scenario focused on threats posed by nation-state adversaries with distinct strategic assets that could be efficiently hit from the air, mainly by fighter aircraft. He stated that "operating fire in an efficient manner from the air is in many cases more economical and effective than a ground maneuver against those very same targets. Moreover, it is less problematic from the political aspect—therefore we have to build up airpower capable of hitting the enemy strategic targets."[26] Ben Eliyahu concluded that the centrality of airpower had dramatically increased to the point where it had become the deciding factor in military campaigns.

Major General Halutz, who replaced Ben Eliyahu as the commander of the IAF in 2000, also referred to the issue of military decision and the role of the air force in achieving it. He maintained that "the concept of 'physical decision' should be removed from the lexicon and replaced by 'perceptual decision.'" As he saw it, "victory means achieving the strategic purpose, not necessarily obtaining territory."[27] Halutz maintained that the character of wars had changed, necessitating a reexamination of the concepts of operations.

Colonel Amir Eshel, then a wing commander and later to become the IAF commander, wrote an article on a similar theme. The title of that article, "Ma'arachtan" ("Operator" in Hebrew), summarized his thesis: the IAF should take a central role in the shaping and planning of campaigns.[28]

A dramatic strategic development occurred in May 2000, when Israel unilaterally withdrew all its forces from Lebanon. The withdrawal enabled Hezbollah to boost its image as the "protector of Lebanon." While UN confirmation that Israel had fully implemented UN Security Council Resolution No. 425 of 1978 somewhat undermined the perception of Hezbollah's legitimacy in continuing to fight against Israel, it definitely did not convince Hezbollah to change its course. Instead, Hezbollah immediately began to consolidate its military presence in south Lebanon and to intensify its integration into the Lebanese government. With assistance from Iran and Syria, the organization grew swiftly and significantly. Hezbollah followed several lines of operation: increasing its ground defensive and offensive fire arsenals for wartime, expanding its support and guidance to various terrorist organizations in their fight against Israel, and maintaining controlled tension vis-à-vis Israel through sporadic attacks. Hezbollah maintained a strict deterrence-reprisal balance with Israel. The antiaircraft fire aimed at Israel represented an unmistakable response to what Hezbollah described as violation of Lebanese sovereignty by Israeli aircraft and UAVs.[29]

After its withdrawal from Lebanon, Israel restrained its actions toward Hezbollah, trying to avoid any escalation. Israel's decision makers sought to suppress the Hezbollah threat while devoting their attention to the Palestinian theater. Some hoped that over time Hezbollah's rockets would simply rust away. The political leadership instructed the IDF not to open a second front in the north. This gave Hezbollah freedom of action near the border, creating a situation that was intolerable for the IDF but ideal for Hezbollah.

In October 2000 a Hezbollah platoon disguised as a UNIFIL force attacked an IDF patrol moving along the border and abducted three wounded IDF soldiers to Lebanon. In the same month an Israeli civilian, a reserve colonel, was also abducted in Dubai. In January 2004 Israel and Hezbollah carried out an exchange: Hezbollah returned the bodies of the 3 soldiers as well as the civilian in exchange for Israel's liberation of 435 Palestinian and Lebanese citizens.

The IDF based its strategic planning for the Lebanese theater on an indirect approach, defined as "manipulating levers," with the IAF as the primary actor. Even though the IDF had conducted operational planning for a broad ground maneuver in Lebanon, it believed that exerting pressure on Syria constituted the most effective strategy for influencing Hezbollah. This approach rested on the assumption that Israel had no interest in invading Lebanon again and that Syria was responsible for all activity in Lebanon and had the capacity to sway Hezbollah. The IDF also believed that kinetic attacks directed toward a state entity such as Syria were more efficient than kinetic attacks directed at an organization such as Hezbollah or a failing state such as Lebanon.

In June 2000 Syria's president Hafez al-Assad died and was succeeded by his son Bashir. This considerably weakened Syria's influence on Lebanon in general and on Hezbollah in particular. In September 2004 the UN ratified Resolution 1559, which demanded Syria's withdrawal from Lebanon and the dismantling of all militias in Lebanon. Meanwhile, Iran's influence in the region grew.

Concurrently with Israel's continuous struggle with Hezbollah, the last decade of the twentieth century was characterized by positive trends: the processes designed to settle the conflicts between Israel and its neighbors. In 1993 Israel signed a peace agreement with Jordan, and that same year another agreement—even more dramatic—was signed: the Oslo Accords between Israel and the PLO. It paved the way for the PLO to operate in Judea, Samaria, and the Gaza Strip.

The following years saw remarkable prosperity and cooperation with relative calm, though occasionally broken by terror operations executed by Hamas. Islamic jihad also resumed, encouraging PLO terrorist strikes. Toward 2000 Israeli-Palestinian relations took a turn for the worse, leading to a violent struggle. Israel responded mainly by carrying out ground operations while airpower made only a marginal contribution to this effort.

Palestinian suicide bombings that took the lives of hundreds of civilians in Israeli towns, and the broad escalation of fighting in Judea and Samaria in September 2000 defined as the Second Intifada, prompted a wide-ranging IDF campaign in the territories ceded to the Palestinian Authority. Ground forces led the struggle, with relatively limited air support by UAVs and attack helicopters, which were used for their surgical assault capabilities. When the situation deteriorated, jet aircraft took part in the assaults. The IAF's gradual involvement in the conflict raised critical questions about the air force's suitability or willingness to play a central part in the campaign terrorist threats.

In 2002 the IDF launched Operation Defensive Shield to eliminate terrorist infrastructure in the Palestinian territories in Judea and Samaria. That operation, and the security fence later installed between Israel and the Palestinian territories, in fact defeated the terrorist organization in the West Bank. The armed Palestinian struggle moved to the Gaza Strip.

At that time about eight thousand Israeli Jews lived in the Gaza Strip, concentrated in several blocks of settlements. The security fence around the Gaza Strip and the presence of IDF ground troops made it difficult for the terrorists to "export" attacks to Israeli territory. Therefore, at the beginning of the intifada most of the Palestinian fighters targeted IDF forces and the Jewish settlements within Gaza. In April 2001 a Qassam rocket launched from the Gaza Strip toward a town in southern Israel opened a new phase in the campaign principally characterized by the launch of long-range rockets and missiles at the Israeli hinterland.

The IAF transferred the experience and knowledge it had gained in the Lebanese theater to the Palestinian theater, mainly in all operations related to targeted killing. At first the IDF focused on field commanders and carried out the first assault as early as November 2000. The aircraft of choice was the attack helicopter, which was capable of very precise targeting and created minimal collateral damage, but later on the IDF employed jets as well. Over time the category of permissible targets broadened to include senior military commanders and even members of the civilian leadership. The most prominent of these leaders was Ahmed Yassin, the founder of Hamas, who was both its religious and political leader. He was eliminated in March 2004.

Subsequent air raids did not succeed in reducing terrorist activity in the Gaza Strip or preventing its spillover to Israeli territory. Prime Minister Ariel Sharon understood that the Israeli settlements and military presence in the Gaza Strip constituted an intolerable burden on the state and made a dramatic decision to unilaterally evacuate both the settlers and members of military. This decision, declared by Sharon in December 2003, encouraged the terrorist organizations to increase their missile attacks, most of them launched from the crowded refugee camps in the northern Gaza Strip toward the Israeli settlements bordering it.

In May 2004 the IAF set up a new campaign planning department. This structural change clearly indicated the IAF's intention, under the leadership of Major General Halutz, to assume a more central role in all activities related to shaping and planning campaigns. That month the air force held a conference at the Fisher Institute titled "The IAF and its War on Terror," with participants including both retired and active duty senior officers. They all fully understood the potential that the IAF might become entangled in significant ground force operations and needed to define a new direction that would allow the air force to reach its full potential. The speakers emphasized the IAF's duty to take a leading role in the war on terror and develop relevant capabilities, such as control of the ground from the air and stealth operations against any threat, quickly and with minimal friction with the other services. Major General Halutz summed up the consensus of the conference in a few clear words: "I don't accept the dictum that the air force must participate in the ground forces' battle. The air force should lead the war on terror as much as it can. . . . For three and a half years we have been expecting some classical war in which a MiG 29 faces an F-15 and we shoot a missile at it. . . . Too bad there's no such thing. Meanwhile 931 Israeli citizens were killed in that war."[30]

Fighting against Palestinian terrorism forced the IAF to rethink its mission. Even so, an apparent gap persisted between theories about missions and emergence of concepts that changed the organization's culture and led to development of actual capabilities. The ground forces retained responsibility for planning strategic campaigns and directing the overall campaign against guerrillas and terrorists.

OPERATION DAYS OF RETURN, 2004
Strategic Context

Throughout 2004 Hamas accelerated the rate of its rocket attacks, launched primarily from two crowded refugee camps in the northern part of the Gaza Strip toward neighboring Israeli settlements. The Hamas teams that perpetrated the shelling merged easily into the civilian population, eliminating any option for Israel to take preventive action or retaliate after an attack without causing grave collateral damage. Thus, the IDF had reached an impasse: it hesitated to perform a ground operation in densely populated areas such as the refugee camps because of the significant potential for casualties, but the IAF could propose no relevant alternative in the form of air operations. The Regional Division received CAS from attack helicopters and air observation platforms, but that did not suffice to deter Hamas, especially because the ground commander had no authority to order an attack unless all targets had been thoroughly vetted and IAF headquarters had given permission.

The tension and frustration ground forces felt toward the IAF reached their height in September 2004. The commander of the northern brigade of the Gaza Division identified a terrorist squad preparing to launch rockets into Israel. He ordered the leader of the attack helicopters assigned to him to strike the squad immediately. While the helicopter pilot relayed that demand to IAF headquarters for confirmation, the squad launched several rockets at the town of Sderot and killed two children. The brigade commander threw the attack helicopters out of the area, and the frustration turned into anger and caused a serious crisis of trust.[31] The commanders of the Regional Division and the Northern Brigade helplessly watched a demonstration by the inhabitants of Sderot following the tragedy.[32] This incident caused the Israeli government to authorize an operation against the rocket threat from the northern portion of the Gaza Strip.

Brigadier General Eshel, then deputy commander of the IAF, decided that the IAF had to take an active part in examining the challenge and finding a solution. Eshel understood the need for a systemic change that would require a new concept of operations through the reorganization and coordination of the relevant technology. To better understand the problem, Eshel met with the commander of the Regional Division, Brig. Gen. Shmuel Zakai. The meeting of these two senior commanders, in which personal ego was laid aside and the walls came down, created a cultural shift that set in motion an intensive and highly sophisticated learning process. The best operations and intelligence officers of the Regional Division, the IAF, and the General Security Service (Shabak) participated in this process.

The Regional Division and the IAF had to establish a new capability that would enable a succession of pinpoint strikes on Hamas fighters with minimal injury to innocent bystanders. To end the shelling of Israeli settlements and deter Hamas from renewing it, they defined three military objectives: remove the threat posed by the Qassam rockets to Sderot and its vicinity, execute a serious strike that would exact a heavy price from the terrorist organizations in the Gaza Strip, and reinforce defensive capabilities in the settlements.[33]

Concept and Execution

In this operation the air forces and ground forces exchanged their traditional roles: airpower became the main form of attack and the ground force, three brigades strong, became the supporting element. Air elements, both manned and unmanned, would hover above the theater of operations and produce a primary assessment of the situation. Then various formations of ground troops would execute raids with the objective of alarming the area and forcing enemy fighters to reveal themselves. The IDF expected that the nonstop surveillance would enable rapid identification of enemy fighters, followed by immediate attacks, mainly from the air.

For optimal realization of the concept, the IDF set up an integrated war room for all the partners planning and conducting the operation. Numerous air options—manned and unmanned—were allocated to the operation, including some previously reserved for "big wars." In addition, the IAF assembled an attack "toolkit" that included all the components of a strike mission: identification, verification, and attack.[34]

The operation started on September 30, 2004, exactly as planned. Small infantry formations began penetrating into the refugee camps in the northern Gaza Strip, forcing Hamas fighters to oppose them. The direct contact between IAF headquarters and the integrated headquarters, and the delegation of authority to that headquarters without the mediation of the Southern Command and the General Staff, permitted very rapid decision making and immediate target confirmation. The interval between identifying a target and attacking it was reduced to a few seconds. The commander of the infantry brigade described the fighting thus: "in those places where we have no targets we reinforce the maneuver as an incitement action, producing targets, at which point we operate fire and kill the targets. In those places where we have targets we amplify the fire for destroying the targets."[35]

On October 17 the IDF declared that the operation had achieved its objectives, and its forces withdrew from the refugee camps. During the operation 1 Israeli citizen and 2 IDF soldiers were killed. On the Palestinian side 108 died, 80 of them identified as active terrorists; most of the casualties resulted from air raids.[36]

Israel considered the operation highly successful. The joint mode of operations was seen as a great achievement and an impressive advance in IDF operations. The relatively hard blow suffered by Hamas launch teams and fighters did not prevent the Hamas leadership from declaring victory in the campaign, but Hamas ceased firing rockets at Israel and announced a temporary halt to the launches.

Analysis of data from the campaign indicated an impressive improvement in the IDF's ability to destroy targets while minimizing collateral damage. The IAF commander, Maj. Gen. Eliezer Shkedy, pointed out that throughout Operation Days of Return the IAF struck 55-60 percent of all targets (compared to 10 percent in earlier operations). Moreover, he noted that the ratio of casualties between combatants and noncombatants dramatically improved from 1:1 in the preceding operations to 1:12 (one civilian casualty for every twelve Hamas activists) during Operation Days of Return.[37]

Observations

This operation demonstrated the beginning maturation of the concept of achieving "operational dominance" through airpower. That concept rests on the development of a capability for "holding terrain" that requires continuous observation of the battlespace by a variety of sensors, both to improve the effectiveness of power operation and to minimize harm to noncombatants. In May 2005 Commander Shkedy stated, "We are still far from achieving this capability but we are advancing toward the capability to control terrain or understand very well from the air what is happening on the ground."[38]

Operation Days of Return clearly revealed the parallel cycles of observation and learning between the adversaries. In the years preceding the operation, Hamas had come to understand and successfully exploit the limits of IDF operations in densely populated areas such as refugee camps. Yet the parallel learning process undertaken jointly by the IAF and the Gaza Division created a new concept of operations that surprised Hamas. The head of Shabak at the time, Avi Dichter, described it by stating, "the capability to identify and attack people from the air impressed the Palestinians in a big way and created significant deterrence. The IDF succeeded in fighting the lone terrorist, not just the infrastructure.... The terrorists understood that Big Brother is watching from above.... This fact alone caused Hamas declaration of 'thahadiya'—calm."[39]

Everyone who took part in the operation, directly or indirectly, understood the potential inherent in the concept of asymmetric operations that combined the relative advantages of every dimension of operations and synchronized all efforts. Maj. Gen. Eyal Eizenberg stated: "This operation contributed more than any other thing to the development of the IDF future concept—and to my own insights as the commander of the Gaza division during Operation Cast Lead."[40]

But alongside the enthusiasm for the new approach and its successful application, some questions arose about the feasibility of turning it into a generic IDF concept of operations. Brigadier General Eshel foresaw that IDF personnel would find it difficult to understand and internalize the profound learning process that had taken place and the changes it produced, and to implement that process more broadly. He thought it was "a completely different thinking... the laboratory experiment we did in Gaza with the participation of the division and the air force proved the potential of this combination, but in other areas this joining is still very far from being exploited."[41] On several other occasions Eshel expressed his frustration with the revival of organizational turf wars, with each side trying to claim credit for the success of an operation.

THE SECOND LEBANON WAR, 2006
Strategic Context

Dan Halutz, the man nominated in June 2005 to become the new chief of General Staff, had performed most of his service in the IAF, but choosing an airman for this position did not create any significant change in the air force's thinking and planning processes. Halutz became the chief of General Staff of a military force involved mainly in a limited conflict with the Palestinians that affected the IDF concept of operations as well as its force buildup and organization. At that time many senior officers in the IDF—the new chief among them—discounted the possibility of a traditional military victory on the battlefield and favored the operational idea of changing the enemy's perceptions. In fact, the IDF comprised two militaries: a rather outdated ground force that had received little training and was mainly occupied with policing missions alongside an advanced air force built and trained for high-intensity fighting in both neighboring and distant countries. As a result, air support doctrine and training received very little attention.

Halutz believed that traditional military victory, based on ground forces, is irrelevant in twenty-first century conflicts, yet he maintained that the IAF had the capability to significantly contribute to the required military decision. The IAF was consolidated as the long strategic arm of the IDF; the IAF and the intelligence branch had the largest budgets in the IDF. Indeed, the IAF began to structure its forces to mirror its responsibility for defending Israel by "fighting from the air" against multiplying threats (SS-class missiles, rockets, and UAVs), but it continued to concentrate improvements on its tactical capabilities. The IAF specialized in carrying out "targeted killings," especially in the Gaza Strip, while dramatically reducing collateral damage, and it trained for systematic, broad attacks against enemy targets, guided by information gathered and analyzed by its intelligence organs.

In February 2005, apparently with Syrian support or guidance, members of Hezbollah murdered Lebanon's ex–prime minister, Rafik al-Hariri. The murder drew popular outrage as well as international pressure that eventually caused the Syrians to withdraw all their forces from Lebanon in April 2005. A month later, an anti-Syria, anti-Hezbollah coalition headed by Sa'ad Hariri, son of the late prime minister, took office in Lebanon.

On June 28, 2006, IDF troops executed Operation Summer Rains in the Gaza Strip to put an end to the missile launches from Gaza and create conditions for the return of an abducted soldier. This joint operation lasted for four months but was overshadowed by the campaign in Lebanon.

The changing realities in both Lebanon and Syria brought home to the IDF commanders the need to update their plans for the Lebanese front. At the time the Second Lebanon War broke out the IDF General Staff had three operational plans: Magen Ha'aretz, a full-scale ground maneuver in south Lebanon; the Ice-Breaker, a short, precise, and powerful air attack with limited ground maneuver both to severely damage Hezbollah and to leverage any potential escalation to create conditions for restraining the organization; and Mei Marom, a simultaneous air and ground maneuver to overpower Hezbollah in south Lebanon.[42]

The Second Lebanon War started on July 12, 2006, with a Hezbollah attack on an IDF patrol moving in Israeli territory along the border. The well-planned ambush was accompanied by heavy artillery shelling of Israeli settlements and IDF outposts along the border. Several soldiers were killed and injured and two were abducted to Lebanon. Another five soldiers were killed in a follow-up incident.

The attack did not surprise Israel's leaders because for several months they had seen warnings of Hezbollah's intention to take such action. Northern Command troops were on alert. Between February and May 2006 the new prime minister, Ehud Olmert, Defense Minister Amir Peretz, and Chief of General Staff Dan Halutz had agreed that if Hezbollah carried out its threat of abducting soldiers, this would serve as justification for an aggressive strategy to change the equation vis-à-vis Hezbollah and improve the security situation in the north.[43] Still, the Hezbollah strike caught Israel and the IDF unprepared.

Not only Israel was surprised. About two weeks after the Second Lebanon War ended, Hassan Nasrallah, leader of Hezbollah, gave an interview on NTV, a Lebanese television channel. During that interview, in addition to proclaiming a great Hezbollah victory, Nasrallah added apologetically that "had I thought on July 11 that taking those soldiers captive would bring on such a war, I would certainly not have done it because of moral, human, military and political considerations."[44]

In 2006 Hezbollah's military infrastructure had five main components.[45]

Offensive: Based on rockets with various ranges, this arsenal was dispersed and hidden deep within Lebanon, with the main portion deployed south of the Litani River. According to several assessments, in July 2006 the organization had about 15,000 to 20,000 rockets (Katyusha, Fajar), including some with a range of up to 250 kilometers (Zalzal). Hezbollah also established a limited array of unmanned aircraft (Ababil) for strike missions; according to assessments, this array also encompassed man-portable missiles (SA-7, SA-18) and a few shore-to-sea missiles (C-802).

Defensive: Deployed around the offensive array, mainly near the Shi'ite population in south Lebanon, Hezbollah's defenses included some 10,000 combatants who were prepared to conduct independent, prolonged fighting. This force was armed with a large amount of advanced ordnance that included antiaircraft missiles (SA-7, SA-14) and especially antitank missiles (particularly Cornets and Concourses).

Logistics: Drawing on equipment warehouses spread around Lebanon, in which most of the materiel from Syria and Iran were stored, the logistics train was concentrated mainly in the Bekaa region. From there equipment was distributed to the various units.

Command and control: The command structure was decentralized among various operational units and zones of operation but had an orderly hierarchy. The operations center was located in the Dahiya quarter, an autonomous Hezbollah area in the Shi'ite sector of south Beirut; it housed the main headquarters, offices, and living quarters of Hezbollah's senior leaders. The command-and-control infrastructure was based on various communication systems, including advanced means of communication.

Intelligence and information security: Hezbollah had high-quality means for collecting human, imagery, and signals intelligence and tried to maintain strict information security inside the organization.

Concept and Execution

On July 13 the IDF hurriedly prepared and confirmed its first operations plan for the campaign in Lebanon. It was based on the principles of the Ice Breaker plan and the strategic framework remained similar, but the plan's name was later changed to "change of direction." Numerous documents and testimonies indicate that Israel's objectives in the campaign were to alter the security situation and change the deterrence balance between Israel and Hezbollah. Israel sought to eliminate the Hezbollah terrorist threat by reducing Hezbollah's freedom of action, capabilities, and status; expanding regional deterrence by imposing concrete consequences for aggression against Israel; motivating Lebanon to exert its sovereignty over the whole of Lebanon and restrain Hezbollah; stimulating international involvement in enforcing UN resolutions and the cease-fire; and creating conditions for the return of the abducted Israeli soldiers. The IDF defined several constraints and limiting conditions for the campaign: minimizing casualties among its fighting forces; avoiding widespread war in Lebanon and especially with Syria; leaving no Israeli presence in Lebanon at the end of the conflict; protecting Israel's international legitimacy; and maintaining public support for the operation within Israel.

The concept of operations involved immediately striking Hezbollah directly with more force than it would expect, applying mounting pressure on the Lebanese government to restrain Hezbollah, and mobilizing the international community to ensure a stable settlement in Lebanon while preparing the Israeli public for the possibility of a widespread, protracted campaign.[46] The lines of operation included surprising, rapid, and powerful strikes over the whole of Lebanon, especially against long-range missile sites, the command-and-control apparatus, and as many combatants as possible. By targeting Hezbollah infrastructure, the operation was designed to convince Hezbollah operatives that they were being hunted throughout the whole area. The operation was intended to destroy Hezbollah infrastructure close to the border, disrupt launches of short-range rockets, execute limited ground maneuver in the form of raids, and attempt to minimize casualties, enabling civilians to maintain their daily routines. Concurrently, Israel planned to exert indirect influence, which included imposing maritime and air closure on Lebanon, executing a limited attack on infrastructure, warning the population and prompting the Shi'ites to move from south to north, and concretizing the implications of fighting by damaging Hezbollah status symbols in the heart of Beirut (the Dahiya). The government planned a public relations effort to accompany the campaign with the goals of building legitimation for Israeli operations, delegitimizing Hezbollah as a terror organization, and demonstrating the dangers of regional escalation.

The campaign took place in five main stages.[47]

Stage 1: Air strike (July 12–18). This stage was designed to produce shock and awe, eliminate strategic threats posed by Hezbollah, and demonstrate Israel's change of policy. In thirty-four minutes on July 13 a painstaking multiyear planning and intelligence effort bore fruit: the IAF executed Operation Specific Gravity, which destroyed most of Hezbollah's long- and medium-range rockets.[48] In addition, the IAF attacked Hezbollah's command-and-control structures and transportation infrastructure and imposed a maritime and air blockade on Lebanon.

Stage 2: Raids (July 19–28). The IDF carried out limited ground maneuvers in key areas and towns near the border to annihilate the enemy and augment pressure on Hezbollah. The main missions included ground raids on key areas and towns to destroy the enemy, air raids against all Hezbollah assets, and a hunt for launchers and rockets as well as attacks on ordnance transfers from Syria to Lebanon. In addition, the IDF began to mobilize ground forces.

Stage 3: Control of the security buffer zone (July 29–August 8). The IDF launched a large ground maneuver aimed at destroying the enemy and taking over territory to push Hezbollah back from the border, minimize launches of short-range rockets, and increase pressure on Hezbollah. On July 30 an accidental strike on a building in Kfar Kana caused the deaths of twenty-eight people, including nineteen children. The incident dramatically increased international pressure to end the war, and as a result the IAF halted almost all of its raids on Lebanon for forty-eight hours. On August 2 about two hundred Special Forces fighters, commanded by the IAF commander, carried out a large raid in the Lebanese Bekaa. The ground maneuver penetrated to six kilometers from the border while Special Forces operated deep inland. The IDF extended attacks on the Dahiya and Bekaa and increased the recruitment of reserve forces.

Stage 4: Offensive (August 9–14): Next the IDF executed a deep maneuver in all sectors to achieve an operational decision over Hezbollah in south Lebanon and end the launches of short-range rockets. It included a raid by four divisions and an air assault to destroy the enemy and gain control over territory up to the Litani River. Israel stopped the assault operation on the second night after Hezbollah shot down a CH-53, while the IAF continued supporting the ground maneuver and hunting for the launchers.

Stage 5: Cease-fire (August 15–October 1): The UN Security Council passed Resolution 1701, calling for a cease-fire, the disarmament of Hezbollah in south Lebanon, and deployment of a multinational force with Lebanese troops in south Lebanon. The cease-fire took effect on August 14. The IDF troops withdrew from Lebanon when the multinational UN force and the Lebanese military took over responsibility for south Lebanon.

The air campaign constituted the IDF's main effort throughout most of the fighting, and the scope of IAF operations was unprecedented. IAF missions included attacking long- and medium-range rocket positions, command-and-control structures, and infrastructure; eliminating senior Hezbollah leaders; defending Israel's skies against UAVs; interdicting transfer of equipment and weapons; imposing an air blockade; collecting intelligence; supporting the ground forces; and conducting air assault, air supply, and medevac.[49]

In thirty-four days of fighting, the IAF carried out about 19,000 sorties—an average of 550 sorties per day, more than half of them by jets. During the war Israel lost 121 soldiers and 45 civilians. On the Lebanese side, between 300 and 450 civilians, 36 soldiers of the Lebanese military, and about 600 to 850 Hezbollah fighters were killed.

Hezbollah fired about four thousand rockets and missiles at population centers in Israel. The IAF's opening strike destroyed most of Hezbollah's strategic and operational rocket arsenal; other missile sites were successfully attacked after the first launch using short-turnaround strikes. Hezbollah also attacked Israel twice using three armed UAVs, which Israel successfully intercepted.

Israel's ability to decapitate the senior leadership structure of Hezbollah decreased because the leaders went into hiding when the campaign broke out. The IAF struck Hezbollah headquarters in Beirut as well as command-and-control centers all over Lebanon. However, the synchronization and coordination demonstrated by Hezbollah's use of force—especially during cease-fires—indicated Hezbollah's capability to retain efficient centralized control.

Despite prior planning and IDF recommendations Israel's political leadership did not permit a wide-ranging attack on Lebanon's infrastructures, but Israel did attack a few bridges, roads, fuel depots, and airstrips in various airports. Since most of Hezbollah's infrastructure was concentrated in the Dahiya quarter, this area suffered the most damage.

Israeli forces attacked several hundred border crossings and central traffic axes between Syria and Lebanon as well as trucks and vehicles carrying weapons and munitions. Attacks against several hundred checkpoints on the Litani and Zahrani Rivers proved less effective because Hezbollah had prepared for the conflict by minimizing its dependence on supplies that had to be brought to the front.

Regarding air support missions in general, the clear gaps between the established doctrine (which had not been updated) and the immediate needs of the ground forces compelled the IAF commander to approve many deviations from the doctrine. The IAF operated under a basic assumption that Hezbollah might possess man-portable air-defense systems. Therefore, the jets had to fly above a certain minimum altitude, which decreased the effectiveness of some missions. The deviation from the minimum safety range in many CAS missions did not lead to any friendly fire incidents.[50] The Northern Command was responsible for attacking short-range rockets south of the Litani River, and the IAF served as its main instrument for executing that mission. The IAF succeeded in hitting a few dozen launchers, but this had only a marginal effect on Hezbollah's continuous shelling.

During the Second Lebanon War, Israel attacked the following target sets: bunkers, command posts, and tunnels (3,000); launch area denial (2,400); bridges, roads, and fuel stations (500); launchers and suspected vehicles (700); combatants (200); and radar communications (100). Despite Israel's complete air superiority over Hezbollah, the IAF lost 8 aircraft in the campaign. The crew had to bail out of an F-16 upon takeoff; 2 Apache helicopters collided while hovering above Israeli territory; an Apache-Longbow disintegrated in the air above Israeli territory due to technical failure; a CH-53 helicopter was shot down by a man-portable air-defense system; and 3 UAVs crashed because of technical failure and operator errors.

The achievements of the operation clearly demonstrate that Israel had changed the way in which it "contained" incidents. In fact, the Israeli campaign discredited Hezbollah's strategic logic, which had viewed its rocket artillery capabilities as the factor that deterred Israel.[51] Hezbollah received extraordinarily strong and sharp criticism from the Arab world for recklessly starting the fighting, sacrificing Lebanon and its citizens, being responsible for the destruction of Lebanon, acting as an armed militia that undermined Lebanon's stability and sovereignty, encouraging civil war, and acting as an operational branch of Iran's military. The war apparently aggravated the political conflict and critical debates among several elements in Lebanon that opposed Hezbollah. In addition, the political struggle in Lebanon took on the characteristics of sectarian strife, to the deep dissatisfaction of Nasrallah, leading Hezbollah to invest considerable resources in the internal struggle.

The war badly eroded Hezbollah's military power, although the organization managed to regain most of its strength several years later.[52] Its outposts along the border with Israel were destroyed, and its underground facilities in south Lebanon were exposed and partially hit. Hezbollah's medium- and long-range rocket arsenal was almost wiped out—in some cases before it became operational. About 10 percent of its militants were killed and its logistics pipeline was severely degraded. Hezbollah's symbolic Dahiya quarter was completely destroyed and Shi'ite villages in south Lebanon, Hezbollah's main source of support, suffered severely. Heavy damage to Lebanese infrastructures and the northward flight of nearly a million inhabitants of the south put pressure on the government of Lebanon. Israel had devoted great effort to distinguishing Hezbollah targets from other Lebanese targets, which it left relatively intact. Still, the results of the fighting left their mark on the whole of Lebanon.[53]

The operation led to the adoption of UN Security Council Resolution 1701, which sought to create better conditions in Lebanon. Hezbollah was now defined as an international terror organization supported by Syria and serving as the operational branch of fundamentalist Iran. The war also became a catalyst creating cohesion among Sunni regimes, which in this case sided with Israel either publicly or covertly and combined efforts for long-term operation against the radical Shi'ite axis.

Daily life in northern Israel and along the Lebanese border radically improved after the campaign. Still, many perceived the war as a missed opportunity. The Israeli public was both disappointed and frustrated by the results of the campaign and the way the leadership had prepared the country for war and managed the conflict. Many saw the war as a demonstration, at times disillusioning, of the limits of military power in general and airpower in particular.[54] Public protest in Israel prompted the resignations of most of those involved in conducting the war. The IDF commanders were the first to resign, including the commander of the Northern Command, the commander of the navy, two division commanders, and finally Chief of General Staff Halutz. Eventually Minister of Defense Peretz also resigned.

Observations

Despite the public's dissatisfaction with the outcome, the war had some notable results that perhaps can be appreciated only in retrospect. At the end of the campaign the Israeli public had formed the impression that the IAF was the only military branch that met expectations. The Winograd Commission stated that the air force had attained the most impressive achievements and that it had shown extraordinary capabilities throughout the war. Still, the commission stressed that the IAF particularly excelled at carrying out preplanned missions. The majority of the criticism aimed at the IAF dealt with the strategy and conduct of the campaign, which the commission defined as "weakness in strategic thinking."[55] In 2006 the IAF had not yet adopted a functional concept of operations with a wide strategic outlook and long-range planning and had not managed to free itself from acting simply as the IDF's bombing contractor.

Operation Specific Gravity demonstrated the IAF's flexibility and capacity to rapidly concentrate power for a massive surprise attack based on high-quality intelligence. This opening strike shocked the enemy, but the central problem was that the campaign planning of the IDF and of the IAF in particular did not exploit the effect created by the attack to launch an accompanying ground operation or to use it as political leverage for creating a possible end to hostilities.

The lack of cooperation and jointness represented one of the major failures during this campaign. Before the campaign the IAF did not engage in detailed discussions, deliberation, and planning with the General Staff and Northern Command. The services planned their missions separately and barely explored the possibility of joint operation between supporting and supported elements; as a result, during the campaign in Lebanon each branch executed its missions almost independently.

One mission that the IDF and IAF did not design or implement sufficiently well was the acquisition and prosecution of targets, although at the end of the fighting this aspect of the war was credited with better results than expected. The large-scale use of the IAF's UAVs contributed greatly to the execution of this mission, demonstrating yet again the importance of unmanned platforms in an intensive campaign against nonstate entities.

Throughout the war the IAF functioned like an industrial production line. Intelligence elements collected and ranked as many targets as possible and organized them into a series of air strikes. Control centers in the Northern Command and Tel Aviv directed the attacking aircraft, leaving the pilots with very limited autonomy. The IAF rapidly collected and processed the results of the strikes, evaluating them on the basis of intelligence about targets, efficiency, precision, speed, and especially strike quantity—which, from the Second Lebanon War onward, had apparently become the IAF's central criterion in planning and assessing operations. As a consequence, the IAF allocated collection and execution resources on the basis of the number of targets attacked rather than the quality of those targets. Analysis also noted a decline in the quality of CAS operations. Overcautiousness and a strict limit on minimum altitude seriously hampered the pilots' performance in identifying and striking their targets and their maintenance of the aims.

In general, the Second Lebanon War alerted the IDF and the IAF to various needs and shortcomings. Among the lessons that emerged were the importance—and the difficulty—of executing a large-scale preemptive strike on the enemy leadership. Analysis also revealed the need to develop a response to short-range SS-class rockets and to conduct combat operations in densely populated areas, terrain with heavy undergrowth, and underground.

OPERATION CAST LEAD (DECEMBER 27, 2008-JANUARY 19, 2009)
Strategic Context

Under the leadership of Ariel Sharon, the state of Israel had evacuated all its citizens and soldiers from the Gaza Strip in September 2005. Hamas soon exploited this new situation to accelerate its military buildup and reinforce its power among Palestinians and within the Gaza Strip in particular. Having won a majority in the elections to the Palestinian Legislative Council, Hamas formed a Palestinian government in March 2006. On June 13, 2007, Hamas forcibly took over the Gaza Strip, exiled many members of the Fatah party, and started to conduct an independent interior and foreign policy separate from that of the Palestinian Authority in the West Bank, led by Mahmoud Abbas. Following the coup, Israel and Egypt imposed a blockade on the Gaza Strip to isolate Hamas politically and economically. The closure of the Gaza Strip intensified Hamas's digging of smuggling tunnels under the border between the Gaza Strip and Egyptian territory. The hundreds of tunnels became the main lifeline for the residents of Gaza and an active channel for military buildup. Egypt mostly turned a blind eye to the underground complex formed on its frontier.

After the Second Lebanon War Hamas took Hezbollah as a model. Syria and Hezbollah assisted Hamas with money and ordnance and provided military advice. The Hamas strategy exemplified the idea of brinkmanship. It expressed itself through the controlled use of terror, including rocket launches to send messages, but sought to avoid an all-out conflict with the IDF. All the while, Hamas prepared for an IDF attempt to take over the Gaza Strip.

Hamas had two principal components: the internal security apparatus and the military branch, composed of the Izz ad-Din al-Qassam battalions, which were well trained to carry out terrorist actions against Israel and defend the Gaza Strip from the IDF. In case the IDF entered the Gaza Strip, Hamas expected the internal security forces and other terror organizations in Gaza to participate in the fighting alongside the military branch.

The Hamas military buildup included an increase in the order of battle and organization of Hamas fighters in a semi-military structure (some 20,000 armed men subordinate to Hamas or incorporated in its forces in an emergency); training both within and outside Gaza, mainly in Iran and in Syria; production of arms and smuggling of advanced ordnance with emphasis on improved rockets (ranges up to 40 kilometers); deployment of advanced antitank weaponry (Concourse, Sager, RPG-7/29) and antiaircraft artillery (14.5 mm, 12.7 mm, SAM-7); advanced underground infrastructures for fighting and shelter; development of powerful explosive devices (Shawaz); and emplacement of these devices in high-traffic areas and houses in expected fighting focal points.

From 2000 to 2008 repeated rounds of fighting took place between Israel and Hamas and other terror organizations in the Gaza Strip, with about 12,000 rockets and mortars launched from the Gaza Strip into Israeli territory.[56] The launches continued on and off until December 24, 2008—a day on which more than sixty rockets were launched at Israeli towns and settlements. Israel faced two central challenges in the Gaza Strip: stopping the rocket launches and shelling from Gaza for as long as possible, and halting the military buildup, especially through the smuggling tunnels from the Sinai Peninsula. Israel sought to avoid full occupation of Gaza and a lengthy stay in that area. The government also directed the IDF to fight without causing a humanitarian crisis and thus maintain the legitimacy of Israel's armed operations in one of the most densely populated areas in the world, where the population served as human shields for a semi-military terror organization.

Concept and Execution

There were three approaches in the Israeli government regarding how to address the challenge. The prime minister wanted to expand the campaign until the UN Security Council reached a decision about deployment of an international force; the minister of defense wanted to launch a very powerful operation that would be ended by Egyptian interference and pressure; the minister of foreign affairs thought there was no chance to reach any agreement and therefore sought to hit Hamas hard and then unilaterally end the operation. The IDF was able to define five main objectives for the campaign: (1) cause heavy damage to the Hamas organization; (2) create conditions for improving the security situation; (3) restore Israeli deterrence; (4) end terrorist strikes and rocket launches from the Gaza Strip; and (5) create a settlement mechanism to preserve peace and delay the next confrontation as long as possible. The constraints and limitations on force operation included avoiding escalation in other theaters, maintaining the separation between the Gaza Strip and the West Bank, preserving relations with Egypt, and avoiding the creation of a humanitarian crisis.

The IDF had already begun preparing for a broad campaign in the Gaza Strip at the end of Operation Summer Rains in 2006. While the Southern Command planned the ground maneuvers, the IAF planned the opening blow. Building on lessons from the Second Lebanon War, the IAF and Southern Command collaborated closely in planning and vetting the target list. They also cooperated with Shabak, which had collected valuable intelligence in the Gaza Strip. The General Staff synchronized the entire process.

Another lesson from the Second Lebanon War led the ground forces to re-equip and conduct intensive exercises tailored to the type of conflict expected in the Gaza Strip. The level of cooperation between IAF squadron leaders and brigade and battalion commanders in both training and operational planning represented the most impressive improvement since 2006. Interactions between the political and the military leadership showed another advance: unlike the situation in July 2006, the political leadership fully understood the IDF's operational plans.

In 2008 the IDF had several General Staff plans in place for the Gaza Strip, all predicated on gradual escalation in the level of force used and the required results.[57]

>*Fires*: Extracting a price, preventing escalation, and shortening the campaign as much as possible.
>
>*Limited maneuver*: Operating standoff fires accompanied by a limited surface effort focused on the town of Gaza, exacting a price from Hamas, minimizing rocket launches at Israel, and enforcing first a cease-fire and then the desired settlement.
>
>*Operational takeover*: Partially occupying the Gaza Strip to enforce the desired settlement and change the security situation.
>
>*Occupation*: Full occupation of Gaza to cause the collapse of the Hamas regime and shape a new political-security reality.

Operation Cast Lead began at 11:30 a.m. on December 27, 2008, with a sustained kinetic attack by the IAF, preceded by a deception operation to conceal the timing of the strike. Israel executed the strike according to a plan called "Birds of Prey," designed to hit Hamas hard and induce shock and awe, in the style of the U.S. opening blow against Iraq in 2003.[58] The IAF set the precise starting point as the weather improved and the air force received intelligence about a graduation ceremony for police cadets that would take place next to the police headquarters in the heart of Gaza, in which several prominent Hamas activists from the security organs were to participate.

The surprise air strike with which the IAF opened the campaign was designed to inflict the maximum destruction while demonstrating Hamas's vulnerability and the futility of continuing to fight. The blow was planned to be as powerful and broad as possible, accompanied by a gradual offensive for exerting continuous, growing pressure on Hamas leadership. The purposes were to execute a precise hit with the least possible collateral damage and to minimize the damage to the civilian homeland in Israel. In addition to running the kinetic force, the IDF planned information operations and cease-fires to allow the distribution of humanitarian equipment as well as the evacuation and treatment of casualties in order to avert a humanitarian crisis and enable Hamas leadership to assess the price of continued fighting. The intention was to create a mechanism for ending the fighting and achieving political settlement in cooperation with the Palestinian Authority in the West Bank and Egypt. The IDF also readied itself for a lengthy campaign until the entire Gaza Strip was taken.

Hamas's defensive plan consisted of an asymmetric response to IDF military and technological superiority, refraining from full military engagement during the first stages of the conflict and limiting friction with the IDF in open areas. Instead, Hamas planned to channel the fighting into densely populated urban areas, where it would target and exhaust the IDF (mostly by using explosives and antitank weapons) and undermine the legitimacy of Israeli actions while simultaneously wearing down the Israeli populace with massive rocket launches.[59] Concurrently, Hamas fighters followed patterns of "disappearing" to ensure the survival of its activists and of Hamas military infrastructures. Hamas intended to make great use of Palestinian, Arab, and international communication to gain sympathy and decrease Israel's freedom of action, enabling Hamas to declare "victory" over the IDF while it removed its forces from the Gaza Strip.

Operation Cast Lead had four main components.[60]

Phase 1: Air strikes (December 27, 2008–January 2, 2009). The IAF delivered a devastating blow against Hamas with standoff fire alone. Since it was not clear whether the political leadership would allow the IDF to carry on with the air operation as well as the ground maneuver as planned, the IDF attempted to achieve many results in very short time. The main missions consisted of striking Hamas activists and conducting targeted killing of Hamas leaders and members of other terrorist organizations in the Gaza Strip; destroying tunnels between Gaza and the Sinai Peninsula (Egypt); damaging Hamas assets; eliminating rocket launchers; and paving the way for future delivery of humanitarian aid into Gaza. In the first 4 minutes the IAF struck a hundred targets and fired some hundred tons of munitions;

88 fighter aircraft and attack helicopters participated. On the first day the IAF attacked a total of 170 targets, killing 270 Palestinians and wounding 750, most of them Hamas activists.

Phase 2: Ground offensive (January 3–9). Five brigade combat teams advanced to attack the enemy, take over key areas in order to minimize rocket launches, and bring greater pressure to bear on Hamas leadership while demonstrating IDF capabilities. The advance was accompanied by massive fire and with close support from the IAF. The main missions consisted of separating the Gaza Strip into three parts; removing the civilian population from regions of ground fighting; capturing and clearing territory, with emphasis on the open areas in the northern Gaza Strip; continuing strikes on Hamas activists and leaders; and delivering humanitarian aid.

Phase 3: Intensified ground maneuver (January 10–17). Through action on the ground, the IDF increased pressure on the Hamas political and military leadership in order to create conditions for ending the campaign. The main missions carried out included reinforcing the encirclement and taking the assault deeper into Gaza; obliterating rocket launchers; establishing a humanitarian cease-fire; and calling up and training reserve soldiers (10,000 combatants).

Phase 4: Cease-fire and withdrawal (January 18–21). On January 17 Israel's prime minister announced a unilateral cease-fire and the withdrawal of IDF forces from the Gaza Strip because Israel had attained the campaign objectives. The next day Hamas, too, announced a cease-fire. In the background a multilateral cease-fire agreement was put together, with Egypt leading and mediating. On January 21 all IDF troops withdrew from the Gaza Strip.

The IAF played an especially significant role throughout Operation Cast Lead.[61] The air force meticulously planned the opening strike, executed it perfectly, and then carried out a succession of intelligence collection and strike sorties throughout the campaign. The IAF's main missions were eliminating terrorists, especially their senior leaders; hitting the rocket launchers and hunter-killer mode; obliterating the infrastructures, smuggling tunnels, production capacity, ordnance storage, headquarters, and situation rooms of Hamas and other organizations; collecting intelligence; carrying out electronic warfare; providing CAS to ground forces, including rescue and medevac (thirty-two sorties); warning the civilian population of impending attacks (using the "Eye of Storm" system operated by antiaircraft forces); and dropping 2.5 million propaganda leaflets. Airpower was also the main weapon used against the underground tunnels that the enemy employed for obtaining reinforcements and smuggling ordnance from Iran to Hamas, far from Israel's borders.[62]

Most of the sorties were defined as CAS, demonstrating considerable improvement in cooperation between the branches; in turn, ground activity helped to create assault targets for the IAF. Fighter planes executed some three hundred assaults in the coordination area with the ground forces. The sensor-to-shooter link proved highly efficient: continuously collected intelligence was quickly passed directly to the attack aircraft and ground forces.

The enemy fighting forces were the central targets, and most were hit from the air. During the operation about 700–850 Hamas activists were killed, as were some 250–500 civilians; thousands of Palestinians were injured. On the Israeli side 10 soldiers and 3 civilians were killed, and hundreds of Israelis—both military and civilians—were wounded. Hamas continued shooting missiles at Israel throughout the whole campaign, with about 820 rockets and shells launched at Israel over 23 days, but the number of launches decreased significantly as the campaign progressed.

Hamas openly used the population as human shields to deter Israel from action, at times even taking women and children up to the roofs of buildings in order to prevent attacks. In response, the IAF developed a unique procedure named "knock on the roof" to remove civilians from military sites designated for attack. The IAF carried out this procedure in a fixed order. First the IDF would make telephone calls asking the inhabitants to leave. The IAF would conduct observation sorties to ascertain if civilians had left the area and after that fire a small rocket at the corner of the roof as additional warning. Finally, the IAF would launch a precision-guided missile to destroy the structure. The desire to prevent harm to civilians prompted Israel to use expensive, precision-guided munitions, which constituted 81 percent of all the munitions launched throughout the campaign. Given the difficulties of fighting in densely populated area, the collateral damage ultimately caused was extremely low.

For the first time in Israel's armed conflicts, unmanned vehicles accumulated more flight hours than manned platforms (about a third of the sorties and some 60 percent of the flight hours in total). Attack helicopters also played a highly significant role in the fighting, shooting more munitions than the total expended throughout the Second Lebanon War.

The underground tunnels presented the IAF with a new challenge. Guided by precise intelligence, the IAF bombed tunnels used mainly for smuggling ordnance from the Sinai Peninsula to the Gaza Strip as well as underground structures all around the Gaza Strip that terrorist organizations used for fighting, hiding weaponry, rocket launches, and operational headquarters. Yet the operation also revealed the difficulty of neutralizing underground assets, especially from the air. The IAF had great difficulty in assessing the damage caused, and most of the tunnels were quickly restored after the operation.

Operation Cast Lead did not stop the military buildup of terrorist organizations in the Gaza Strip via the underground tunnels. Nevertheless, it mobilized an international effort to prevent the smuggling of ordnance from Iran to the Gaza Strip and even aided the Egyptian effort to locate and block tunnels between Gaza and the Sinai Peninsula.

Observations

In the IAF debriefing on the operation, Maj. Gen. Ido Nechushtan, then the IAF commander, stated that the operation had exemplified "a new sort of fighting" and that in many ways it set a "record of airpower operation in fighting terror and supporting ground forces fighting in densely populated urban areas." Nechushtan also stated that "a powerful, surprising opening blow has substantial influence on the rest of the campaign." This assertion appears correct, but the effect of the opening strike evidently dissolves when no continuous operational or diplomatic pressure prolongs it. It also seems that in this campaign the IDF and the Israeli government did not know how to leverage the achievements of the opening strike, and that the IAF did not prepare itself sufficiently for the phase following the attack on the preplanned targets.

The IAF planning processes had not included any broad and deep systemic thinking about issues pertaining to fighting in Gaza prior to actual operations. In fact, the first discussion of this kind took place only on December 28, after the operation had begun. Some commanders realized throughout the operation that the IAF must engage in strategic-operational thinking—not just perform concrete operational-tactical planning.[63]

Operation Cast Lead again raised questions about the contribution and the significance of airpower vis-à-vis ground forces. One of the foremost complaints was that airpower had inflicted the main damage done to the enemy throughout the operation, but the Israeli public only recognized the victory and the deterring message produced by ground maneuvers, which—it must be acknowledged—was rather limited. From Israel's perspective, the operation had an important deterrent effect, but given the rapid renewal of fighting cycles, the extent of its influence on the Palestinians in Gaza was unclear.

The operation also led the UN Human Rights Council to establish the Goldstone Commission to investigate Israel's conduct of the war. The commission's report echoed widespread international condemnation of Israel's alleged violations of international law during the operation. Clearly the IDF and various establishments and institutions around the world had a widely divergent understanding of the challenges of asymmetric fighting.

OPERATION PILLAR OF DEFENSE, 2012
Strategic Context

Operation Cast Lead achieved only a temporary lull.[64] Just one week after the operation, terrorist organizations opposed to Hamas rule resumed attacks on Israel along the border and began launching rockets from the Sinai Peninsula. The IDF reacted primarily by executing targeted killings or precision attacks of military infrastructure or smuggling tunnels. At times the sides were drawn into limited exchanges of fire that lasted several days.

Hamas and other organizations in the Gaza Strip exploited the partial lull to conduct a massive military buildup. They smuggled large amounts of ordnance into Gaza through tunnels from the Sinai Peninsula while simultaneously upgrading indigenous production capabilities. The military equipment included long-range rockets, Kornet-type advanced antitank missiles, and UAVs. Israel undertook various types of operations in the Gaza Strip and away from its own borders, trying to prevent the transfer of munitions into Gaza, and achieved partial success.

During 2010 the IDF began deploying the Iron Dome system for active air defense against rockets. This technological development had a substantial bearing on the asymmetric balance between Israel and its enemies, especially those in the Gaza Strip. On April 7, 2011, the system registered its first operational interception. The IAF assumed operational command of this array; consequently, the designation "antiaircraft array" was changed to "air defense command."

Beginning in December 2010 the Middle East underwent upheavals that swept through Egypt, among other countries. The Muslim Brotherhood's rise to power in Egypt in June 2012 gave Hamas great psychological support and self-confidence. Hamas began to solidify its relations with the new regime, which seemed its natural ally.

In October 2012 fighting between Israel and Hamas escalated. Israel attacked launch crews and other terrorist targets while the Palestinians launched scores of mortars and rockets, attacking Israeli patrols along the security fence. On November 12 Hamas launched more than a hundred rockets at Israel. Israel characterized the security situation as intolerable and sought to design a surprise opening blow for a military campaign to minimize the threat from the Gaza Strip.

In late 2012 Israel had five operational Iron Dome systems, but on the eve of the armed conflict with Hamas in November 2012 Israel did not yet have full confidence in the potential effectiveness of the systems in a broad conflict scenario. The large rocket arsenal in Gaza presented a clear and tangible threat to the state of Israel, but destruction of this arsenal posed a special challenge because it was concealed among the dense civilian population.

Israel's central challenges were strategic. In the near term, opinions were divided between wanting to deal Hamas a serious blow and wishing to keep the campaign short while preserving Hamas rule in the Gaza Strip. Likewise, it was not clear if mediation by the new Muslim Brotherhood government in Egypt could provide an exit mechanism from the conflict. Israel also perceived Egypt as an essential factor in limiting Hamas's ability to build up military capability in Gaza over the longer term.

Concept and Execution

The IDF designed an overwhelming kinetic campaign against preplanned targets to minimize the rocket threat and exact a severe penalty from Hamas. According to the plan, after a few days Israel would gradually reduce the intensity of its kinetic effort in tandem with political efforts to end hostilities or would launch a ground effort to further damage Hamas and other terror organizations. It is not clear if the ground effort was planned as a deception and pressure ploy or if the IDF had any serious intention of implementing it. Regardless, when a gap occurred between fully exploiting the fire campaign and creating conditions for realizing an exit mechanism, the IAF had to bridge it by reinforcing missile-hunting missions and carrying out an intensive effort to identify new targets for attack.

The operation commenced at around 4 p.m. on November 14 with the targeted killing of Ahmed Jabari, the head of Hamas's military branch in the Gaza Strip, as he rode in a car with his son. Immediately thereafter Israel attacked Hamas's long-range rocket array (mainly the Fajer-5, whose range exceeded forty kilometers). Various deception messages about cooling off and the Israeli government's intention to stop the escalation of the preceding few days made the surprise attack possible.

The operation took place in three main stages. The first stage included the preparation and execution of the opening strike. In the second stage Israel conducted the kinetic campaign, mainly from the air, with the intention of causing maximum, continuous damage to the military infrastructures in Gaza while deploying troops for a ground offensive. The third stage included attempts to stop the fighting and to shape the "rules of the game" for the aftermath of the operation.

The campaign involved four parallel efforts: (1) airstrikes seriously damaged military infrastructures; (2) threat through escalation mainly involved deploying ground forces around Gaza and mobilizing reserves (about 50,000 troops); (3) defense consisted of preventing terrorist actions on Israeli territory and operating five batteries of Iron Dome, in parallel with disseminating instructions for conduct and civil defense in the hinterland; and (4) political efforts sought a mechanism for establishing a cease-fire and creating conditions for a long-term agreement.

The IAF dominated the fighting, conducting an armed dialogue with Hamas while eroding its military capabilities and making clear the penalty for continuing a policy of terror toward Israel. The IAF's main missions included reducing the rocket and UAV arsenals; destroying military infrastructures such as production layouts, smuggling tunnels, warehouses, and communications; and conducting active defense of the Israeli hinterland against rockets. The targets attacked during Operation Pillar of Defense included senior Hamas and Islamic Jihad terrorists (30), high-level command centers (19), underground rocket launchers (980), smuggling tunnels (140), operational tunnels (66), Hamas operations rooms (42), and weapon manufacturing and storage facilities (26).[65] Of the sorties flown in Operation Pillar of Defense, 1,096 were flown by fighter-bombers, 465 by UAVs, 360 by ISR platforms, and 103 by attack helicopters.

For the first time in Israel's asymmetric conflicts an adversary fired rockets at Tel Aviv and Jerusalem (a distance of over 60 kilometers). In all, Hamas launched 1,506 rockets at a rate of about 200 per day. Hamas also fired about 20 man-portable air-defense systems, among them some advanced models.

On the eighth day of the fighting (November 21) the foreign ministers of Egypt and the United States declared that they had coordinated a cease-fire between the opponents. The close relations between Hamas and the new regime in Egypt enabled this relatively fast resolution.

During the conflict 2 Israeli soldiers and 4 civilians were killed. The IAF executed the air strikes with extreme caution to minimize collateral damage and casualties among civilians. In the Gaza Strip about 170 people were killed, of whom over a hundred were terror organization activists and fewer than 70 innocent citizens.[66]

The campaign apparently exacted a heavy price from Hamas. Its main strategic arrays were badly damaged, including the long-range Iranian rockets and the UAVs, which became inoperable. Hundreds of launch sites were hit and about 50 percent of the Hamas rocket arsenal was destroyed. The IAF also struck the organization's fighters and commanders; as noted, the casualties included the head of Hamas's military branch. Hamas government infrastructures were badly damaged, as were the residences of Hamas senior officials and the smuggling tunnels.

Israel could boast a unique, unprecedented strategic achievement with the Iron Dome. The new system achieved 85 percent success by intercepting 431 rockets. In spite of many Hamas launches, the Iron Dome enabled civilians in the hinterland to carry on their day-to-day activities. It also gave the political leadership a broader scope for decision making. Yet, while successful in minimizing concrete harm to Israel, the serious damage inflicted on Hamas also undermined the campaign's legitimacy.

Observations

Pillar of Defense was primarily an air operation, but when it began the IAF confronted intelligence gaps and lacked the ability to identify targets for attack—the same problems that had plagued the Second Lebanon War and Operation Cast Lead. The IAF performed remarkably well in meticulously planned operations, but when it had destroyed preplanned targets, or when rules of engagement prevented attacks on designated targets, the effectiveness of the air branch declined severely.[67]

The IAF concluded that it should make more comprehensive and longer term plans, and institute more effective processes for identifying targets in real time. Looking ahead, the IAF commander saw the need for greater IAF autonomy in attacking targets. He also concluded that attacking targets to exercise influence and deterrence was more efficient than executing direct hits on enemy military assets. The main lesson that the IAF drew from the operation was that the key to victory lies in extending attack capacity to strike thousands of targets in twenty-four hours.

The operation prompted discussion about the role of defense in victory in a campaign. The defensive Iron Dome system was crowned "Queen of the Campaign." The protective envelope it provided against an enemy such as Hamas turned the rocket attacks from a severe threat into a mere nuisance. Consequently, pressure to shorten the campaign decreased and plans for ground missions changed.

Major General Eshel's taking office as commander of the IAF in May 2012, coupled with the absolute dominance of the air effort throughout the campaign, may have motivated the IAF to take on a more significant role in planning at the strategic and campaign levels. Thus, in the service debriefing of the operation, the IAF commander characterized the air force as a "system architect," not merely an "executive branch." He went on to explain that the IAF "had a great influence on the campaign—acting to change the rules of engagement, the kind of targets attacked, the pace and the capacity of attacks, etc.—issues that affect the whole campaign. Still, we did not manage to persuade the decision-makers to stop the operation at an earlier stage exploiting the fire effort."[68]

In this campaign as in previous ones, both sides could declare victory and claim they had achieved their objectives. Operation Pillar of Defense can be seen as a learning experience in which the combatants went through trial and error and tested each other with a view toward the next campaign.

OPERATION PROTECTIVE EDGE, 2014
Strategic Context

The Muslim Brotherhood regime under Mohamed Morsi did not survive for long.[69] A year after it took power, protestors demanded that President Morsi resign. On July 3, 2013, Egypt's minister of defense, Abdel Fattah al-Sisi, led a military coup that ousted Morsi. The new government outlawed the Muslim Brotherhood movement. This chain of events abruptly changed Hamas's plans; Hamas not only lost its potential strategic ally but also had to deal with a hostile Egyptian regime. The new government started to operate resolutely, closing the smuggling tunnels from the Gaza Strip to the Sinai Peninsula, which had remained very active during Morsi's rule. Egypt's policy of prolonging the closure of the Gaza Strip and stopping the transfer of money from the Palestinian Authority in the West Bank to the Gaza Strip caused Hamas to become isolated within the Arab world. The movement's political status was at a low ebb, and the population of Gaza was reduced to penury.

The agreements reached at the end of Operation Pillar of Defense produced only relative peace; Hamas did not entirely cease its mortar and rocket fire. However, it seemed that in the Iron Dome system Israel had found a satisfactory, albeit expensive, response to the relatively limited threat of medium- and long-range rockets launched from the Gaza Strip. In July 2014 Israel already had nine operational Iron Dome batteries but lacked an adequate technological counter to the threat that mortar shelling and short-range rockets posed to settlements close to the Gaza Strip.

The IAF collaborated exhaustively with various intelligence elements to expand the target list as much as possible, while a separate planning effort sought to increase the IAF's potential attack capacity. In its force structuring the IAF attempted to increase elements of intelligence collection and processing in general and the number and capabilities of UAVs in particular. The IAF also continued its effort to reinforce cooperation with IDF army units and the territorial commands.

Hamas's concept of operations relied on waging a war of attrition against Israel in parallel with shaping an image of the Palestinians as victims and thus undermining the legitimacy of Israeli actions in Gaza. The lessons it had learned from previous operations prompted Hamas to significantly increase its arsenal of rockets, with emphasis on redundancy and obtaining even longer range rockets. The launchers were spread all over the Gaza Strip and were better camouflaged or concealed deep underground in densely populated urban areas. In June 2014 the analysis division of the IDF intelligence branch assessed that the number of rockets possessed by the terror organizations in Gaza had doubled since Operation Pillar of Defense.[70]

Concurrently, Hamas devoted its greatest efforts to building a capability for fighting underground. A huge area in the Gaza Strip was excavated to create a grid of reinforced tunnels for mobilization, logistics, command and control, combat, and the abduction of Israeli soldiers. In addition, Hamas dug more than thirty tunnels that led into Israeli territory for use in attacking civilian settlements and military targets.

The IDF had coped with the underground threat in the Gaza Strip for many years but only began to recognize the enormous scope of this challenge in the aftermath of Operation Pillar of Defense. In 2013 Israel located and destroyed three tunnels designed for carrying out terror operations in Israeli territory; another tunnel that penetrated about seven hundred meters into Israeli territory was discovered and destroyed in March 2014.

Signs of escalation appeared in the beginning of 2014. On March 12 alone Palestinian Jihad launched sixty rockets at Israel and in June launched more than fifty rockets. On June 12 a Hamas team kidnapped three teenagers near the Jewish settlement of Alon Shvut, southwest of Bethlehem (later it emerged that they were murdered immediately). After the abduction the IDF began an operation in the West Bank and arrested some four hundred Hamas members. The number of rocket launches from the Gaza Strip increased, especially those aimed toward nearby Israeli settlements; Israel reacted with pinpoint air strikes on the weapon sites in the Gaza Strip.

On July 2, after the bodies of the three teenagers were found, a team of fundamentalist Jews abducted and murdered a Palestinian boy in East Jerusalem. Following this incident violence escalated in the West Bank, while mortar bombs and rocket launches from the Gaza Strip intensified. Between July 2 and 7 about 230 rockets were launched from the Gaza Strip against Israeli towns, and for the first time since Operation Pillar of Defense Hamas acknowledged responsibility for some of the launches. The Hamas senior leadership subsequently went into hiding.

A warning of a planned terrorist action to be executed in Israel via a tunnel from Gaza led to discovery of an infiltration tunnel in the southern part of the Gaza Strip. On July 7 the IAF attacked the tunnel and killed six Hamas activists. Hamas and other terror organizations intensified their rocket and mortar shelling of Israel, launching about 120 rockets and a large number of mortars at Israel in a 24-hour period. On the evening of July 7 Israel's government decided to execute Operation Protective Edge in order to degrade and destroy terrorist infrastructures.

Israel did not wish to escalate hostilities in the Gaza Strip, and intelligence organs in Israel assessed that Hamas did not wish to do so either. In fact, both sides had a strategic interest in promoting economic stability in the Gaza Strip and even in preserving Hamas authority, but regional political realities and the military capabilities each side had developed led them to become embroiled in a fifty-day-long conflict. Israel had begun the campaign to stop the barrage of rockets aimed at its settlements and towns but extended it because of the opportunity to destroy the tunnels—Hamas's "strategic weapon." Hamas wished to break out of its political isolation, end the blockade of the Gaza Strip, and above all resume transfers of the money needed to pay salaries in Gaza.

The objectives Israel defined did not differ substantially from those of its preceding campaigns: restore the peace, protect Israeli civilians, and damage Hamas and other terror organizations operating in the Gaza Strip. This meant preventing and disrupting attacks from the Gaza Strip, stopping the rocket launches, and restoring relative calm. In parallel, Israel wished to stabilize the situation in the West Bank while separating it from the Gaza Strip.

The challenges that Israel had faced in the preceding campaigns in the Gaza Strip characterized this campaign as well. Israel wanted to hit Hamas hard without causing it to collapse, wanted to avoid being sucked into exercising civilian authority over the Gaza Strip and to overcome the difficulty of fighting in a densely populated area where the enemy used civilians as human shields, and wanted to create an agreement that would remain in force for a long time, limiting the future military buildup of Hamas and other terror organizations.[71] Operation Protective Edge presented unique challenges as well. At the tactical level, the central problem was finding ways to cope with the reinforced underground complexes that Hamas had prepared. Because the tunnels were hidden under private homes in cities, dealing with them—a complex mission in itself—would inevitably cause severe friction with the population.

At the strategic level, Israel faced two main challenges. The first stemmed from its dependence on Egyptian mediation to craft an agreement for ending the operation. Egypt had no urgent reason to stop the fighting and no interest in promoting any rapprochement between Israel and Hamas. The second, longer term challenge was to shape an effective control mechanism to ensure that Hamas would not rebuild its terror infrastructures by diverting the financial contributions and equipment designated for humanitarian assistance and restoration of the Gaza Strip—a restoration that was also in Israel's interest.

Concept and Execution

During the operation Minister of Defense Moshe Ya'alon changed Israel's traditional concept of operations, which dictated that Israel should end all campaigns as soon as possible by achieving superiority through a decisive ground maneuver in enemy territory. Ya'alon believed that the Iron Dome system would give Israel the time needed to wear down the enemy. In fact, time itself constituted attrition against the enemy because Israel felt no pressure to shorten the campaign or to execute a powerful but potentially controversial maneuver whose results might have proven a double-edged sword for Israel. The Iron Dome restored some luster to the idea of "offensive defense."

The campaign can be divided into four major stages.

Stage 1: Exchange of fire (July 8-17). On the night of July 7-8, the IAF attacked about 50 targets, among them 4 houses belonging to activists in Hamas's military branch, rocket launch pads and concealed launchers, the shafts of infiltration tunnels, training camps, and ordnance storage sites.[72] Unlike preceding operations, the IAF did not start the campaign with intensive airstrikes. The Gaza Strip had prepared itself for an Israeli attack, and Israel did not want to set a standard that would make it difficult to end the campaign. During the next 10 days Israel primarily bombed missile sites, headquarters, warehouses, tunnels, and the houses of Hamas activists and of other terror organization members in Gaza. Every day the Palestinians launched about 120 rockets at Israel, with ranges up to 150 kilometers. Israel's air-defense units used Patriot missiles (MIM-104D) to intercept 2 UAVs launched from the Gaza Strip toward Israel. From the beginning of the campaign various international intermediaries attempted to broker a cease-fire, but Hamas rejected all offers.

Stage 2: Ground offensive (July 17-August 3). On the morning of July 17 the IDF discovered and photographed thirteen terrorists attempting to penetrate the border through a tunnel and attack the Sufa kibbutz south of Gaza. As a result, the Israeli government directed the IDF to carry out a plan that Southern Command was assembling to destroy the infiltration tunnels from the Gaza Strip. This led to a new concept of operations that included a reinforced defensive effort to minimize the enemy's chances of success and an intensive kinetic effort to strike hard at military infrastructures and the assets of Hamas and other terror organizations in the Gaza Strip while trying to minimize harm to civilians. It also encompassed a limited ground effort aimed at neutralizing the tunnel complexes and hit the forces fighting in those spaces.

That evening the IDF began a ground offensive with seven armored infantry brigades. The forces advanced with massive support from air and artillery fire. The ground effort sought principally to secure an area in Palestinian territory that would permit the IDF to locate and destroy the infiltration tunnels. The Palestinians were widely deployed in the built-up area and made considerable operational use of the underground complexes. Concurrently the Palestinians continued launching rockets at Israel from sites throughout the Gaza Strip and the IAF continued destroying targets in Gaza.

On July 22 a rocket fired toward Israel's Ben Gurion International Airport landed on the roof of a house about two kilometers from the airport, causing no casualties. Even so, the incident triggered a chain reaction among American and European aviation authorities and many airlines, prompting them stop their flights to Israel for some thirty-three hours.[73] The incident had wider implications in that Hamas leveraged it to raise its profile by claiming it had shut down all air traffic to Israel. It also served as a warning of the indirect implications of the continued fighting, despite the success of the Iron Dome.

Stage 3: Withdrawal and negotiations for cease-fire (August 3–18). After an intensive effort to locate and neutralize all of the Palestinians' offensive tunnels, the Southern Command announced on August 3 that the mission was complete. In an attempt to reach a cease-fire and avoid any friction that might cause escalation, Israel decided to withdraw all its ground forces from the Gaza Strip and deploy them on the border, ready to reenter Gaza if necessary. The combatants also agreed on a temporary cease-fire to enable negotiations on a long-term agreement. At this stage, discussions took place in Cairo in an attempt to sustain the cease-fire and reach a mutual accord. The intense negotiations were periodically interrupted when the Palestinians violated the cease-fire.

Stage 4: Final accord (August 18–26). The failure of the talks in Cairo led Hamas to engage in heavy shelling of Israel from rockets and mortars. The IDF, especially the IAF, intensified the kinetic effort to extend their gains and increase pressure on Hamas to put an end to the conflagration. The strikes focused mainly on Hamas senior leaders and other terror organizations in the Gaza Strip, but the IAF also attacked some key civilian assets that served military purposes, among them the skyscrapers in midtown Gaza City. Third-party negotiations continued in parallel with the exchange of fire, and on August 26 both sides agreed to the Egyptian proposal for a cease-fire.

The net assessment of Operation Protective Edge showed that fighter-bombers flew 10,150 hours; attack helicopters, 2,900; assault helicopters, 931; transport, 622; and UAVs, 21,745. The fighter-bombers flew 6,373 sorties; attack helicopters, 1,285; and assault helicopters, 659. As for ordnance, Israel dropped 970 general-purpose munitions, 9,662 precision-guided munitions, and 1,020 attack helicopter missiles. During Operation Protective Edge 6 Israeli civilians and 67 IDF soldiers were killed. In the Gaza Strip about 2,125 Palestinians were killed. Some 50 percent of the casualties were members of Hamas militias or of other terror organizations.

The IDF neutralized thirty-two infiltration tunnels, of which fourteen penetrated into Israeli territory in the direction of Israeli settlements. Another eighteen tunnels were incomplete at the time the operation began; most of those reached the border area. Ground forces destroyed most of the tunnels, while the IAF struck thousands of Hamas targets and those of other organizations, killing about a thousand militants and combatants. Hamas launched scores of Strella SA-7 man-portable air-defense systems that missed their target.

Israel achieved its primary goals: Hamas remained very much isolated politically, and the approach to the Gaza Strip and the West Bank as two different entities was preserved. In fact, Israel accepted none of Hamas's demands, and at the end of the conflict Hamas accepted almost the same conditions that mediators had offered at the beginning of the campaign (July 15). Israel managed to retain the support of its allies throughout the campaign, but by the end of the campaign the legitimacy of Israel and its policies was broadly questioned and several international judicial commissions of inquiry were set up to investigate Israel's alleged crimes against civilians.

Still, at the end of the campaign Hamas could boast of several achievements. It continued to exist as a functioning organization both politically and militarily. The IDF did not penetrate deep into the Gaza Strip and the built-up areas. Missile launches at Israel from Gaza continued throughout the campaign and constantly harassed the majority of Israel's population (including residents of Jerusalem, Tel Aviv, and even Haifa). Hamas carried out several successful strikes on Israel from the sea and through the tunnels. Thousands of Israelis abandoned their houses in settlements close to the Gaza Strip and moved to more secure areas. The Palestinians also scored a substantial success by forcing the cancellation of numerous commercial flights to Israel for more than a day.

The Iron Dome system again excelled as the "Queen of the Campaign," achieving a remarkable success rate of more than 90 percent in intercepting about 735 rockets. This technology bestowed a level of protection on Israel's civilian hinterland unique in military history. Iron Dome created an almost hermetic defense against rockets launched at the greater part of Israeli territory, which threatened about 70 percent of its population. Although the Israeli public was apprehensive throughout the campaign, the citizens exhibited disciplined behavior and followed the instructions of the Home Front Command. The Iron Dome gave the Israeli government flexibility in decision making, but it also raised complex questions regarding its influence on prolonging the campaign and on Israeli deterrence, the legitimacy of sending forces into the Gaza Strip, and even the economic cost of operating the system.

For most of the campaign the IAF operated under restrictive rules of engagement. Some claimed that the IAF attacked only 10 percent of available targets for fear of hitting civilians and causing large amounts of collateral damage.[74] For this reason most of the ordnance used was precision guided. Still, a relatively high proportion of the casualties on the Palestinian side were civilians (an equal number of civilians and combatants). This occurred largely because the fighting took place in one of the most congested areas in the world, but the change in the IAF's offensive aims may have had some bearing on this as well. Perhaps as a lesson learned from Operation Pillar of Defense or as a result of incomplete intelligence, the guidance for offensive operations in Protective Edge shifted toward minimizing direct attacks on Hamas military capabilities—especially fighting forces—and instead broadened attacks against infrastructures and the residences of Hamas activists, which had been put to dual civil and military use. The change reflected Israel's wish to influence Hamas's decision-making calculus rather than erode the organization's capabilities.

The campaign placed special emphasis on the IAF's support missions, which included providing real-time intelligence, sharing information with ground forces, and providing fire support for strike and rescue missions at extremely close ranges. Updated procedures made it possible for jets to play a vital role very near ground forces fighting in urban areas.[75]

The tunnels presented a special challenge, largely because of the difficulty in obliterating such an extensive underground infrastructure entirely from the air. Furthermore, carrying out a preparatory air strike to support ground forces designed to locate and destroy the tunnels was complicated.

Observations

Despite its relatively long duration, Operation Protective Edge produced only limited achievements. As noted, the Iron Dome system gave Israel a defensive shield from rocket attacks; therefore, Israeli decision makers felt no urgency either to intensify or to end the campaign, especially after commercial flights to Israel resumed. The IDF took a relatively long time to meet the government's declared objective of destroying the tunnels. Meanwhile, Hamas did not perceive the operation as a major threat to its existence and ability to govern and therefore maintained its opposition to a cease-fire under the onerous conditions offered and continued its attrition and harassment warfare. Egypt played a key role in creating an agreement to end the conflict, but the hostility between the new Egyptian regime and Hamas undermined the possibility of conducting efficient and short negotiations.

One of the central lessons the IAF learned from Operation Protective Edge was that an emphasis on increasing its attack capacity was perhaps inappropriate to asymmetric conflicts of the sort Israel actually confronts. It became apparent that the quality of the targets attacked mattered far more than the quantity. The enormous destruction caused by air strikes in the Gaza Strip apparently did not influence the decisions of the Hamas leadership throughout the fighting, even though it probably helped to prevent a new cycle of escalation.

Israel recognized that its asymmetric enemies would not give up underground warfare and would continue to invest large resources in developing this capability. Hamas's tunnels served as an essential strategic resource, especially in view of Israel's absolute air superiority and its antimissile and antirocket defense systems. Since the IDF had not invested sufficient effort in understanding the complexity and implications of this challenge, and no air operation was likely to eliminate the problems posed by the tunnels, the IDF had to deploy considerable ground forces to locate the shafts of the tunnels, determine their extent, and destroy them. In the future, Israel should make a concerted effort to counter this threat and allow greater flexibility for decision makers. Israel may also need to develop more effective air capabilities for this purpose.

Routine joint learning and training—one of the lessons from the Second Lebanon War—enabled cooperation between fighter aircraft and ground forces to achieve unprecedented effectiveness. During the operation the safe altitude limits for air support attacks were reduced by 50 to 75 percent thanks to strenuous staff work and collaboration between branches and commanders that increased mutual trust and professionalism.

It is difficult to assess whether the air or the ground effort had the greatest effect on attaining the campaign's objectives. An earlier ground maneuver that would have penetrated deeper into the enemy territory might have achieved better results in the campaign and shortened it as well. In his summary of the operation, the IAF commander indicated that he had been wrong to recommend against initiating the ground maneuver at the beginning of the operation because he had not correctly assessed its operational significance.

Next to the uniquely important role of Iron Dome, UAVs became the dominant mechanism for executing diverse missions throughout the campaign. UAVs flew above the Gaza Strip almost twice as long as all other aircraft combined. Almost all the missions during the operation involved UAV support, thus demonstrating the tremendous effectiveness of this resource and the growing need for a continuous air presence in such conflicts.

In comparison to Operation Pillar of Defense, the IAF played a less prominent role in planning and conducting activities throughout Protective Edge and had relatively less influence on decision making. It seems that Major General Eshel did not realize his aspiration for the IAF to become a "system architect" and exercise more influence on campaign planning and management—perhaps because only an intensive ground effort could neutralize the tunnels. Still, the IAF may simply not have generated important strategic insights that its commander could have contributed to the overall planning and conduct of the campaign. Eshel's comment at the end of the campaign that the strategic thinking sessions he chaired did not take place often enough during the operation may support this assessment.

Growing international doubts as to the legitimacy of Israeli policy during the operation prompted Israel to draw two related lessons: the importance of minimizing harm to civilians in its asymmetric campaigns and the need to find ways of closing the constantly growing gap between Israel's efforts to minimize collateral damage and the criticism it received for causing disproportionate casualties among noncombatants. The organizations that condemned Israel apparently failed to recognize the challenges posed by asymmetric conflicts and Israel's strategic environment.

CONCLUDING THOUGHTS

Israel has acknowledged the IAF as its primary strategic arm because of the air force's operational reach and power. Advances in technology, together with the imperative to minimize casualties and the application of a policy of deterrence, resulted in the IAF's playing the central role in IDF operations over the last three decades. In the seven major armed conflicts the IDF has waged since 1990, air strikes inflicted the greatest damage on the enemy. In three of those campaigns—Operations Accountability, Grapes of Wrath, and Pillar of Defense—the IAF executed the majority of the effort by itself. The IAF also made extensive contributions to the other four campaigns, both in parallel to and in combination with ground maneuver. All these airpower campaigns gave Israeli decision makers vital flexibility in operating forces.

The IAF had shaped its forces to extend its operational reach and increase its offensive capability, but this direction proved inappropriate to the asymmetric conflicts in which the IDF has actually engaged throughout the last few decades. In its race to increase power and capacity, the IAF did not apply Carl von Clausewitz's principle, which says that "the first, the supreme, the most far-reaching act of judgment that the statesman and commander have to make is to establish the kind of war on which they are embarking, neither mistaking it for, nor trying to turn it into something that is alien to its nature. This is the first of all strategic questions and the most comprehensive."[76] The IAF still finds it difficult to envision conducting a campaign by means and capabilities other than those originally designed for a different type of conflict. It should release itself from the "independent service thinking" that confines it to traditional air force missions and instead increasingly adopt the strategic-systemic thinking that exploits current technology and various air platforms creatively and in an advanced way.

Since the First Lebanon War in 1982 the IAF has undertaken a difficult learning process that has led it to reexamine its concept of operations and its force structure and seek to match them to the battlespace realities that Israel must confront. The process poses challenges because at times it demands that the IAF shift from established paradigms to think creatively within unique new contexts. For example, in Operation Grapes of Wrath (1996) several senior commanders in the IAF maintained that "we know how to play the game for which fighter planes were invented. A fighter plane carries large bombs... but for big strategic targets which affect the war, not for pipes.... Our organization is not made to catch a Katyusha, a few pipes or a terrorist jumping in through the window and doing guerrilla warfare."[77] Some commanders in fact viewed these asymmetric conflicts as so irrelevant to the air force that they believed the IAF should ignore them.

The IAF also found it difficult to free itself from a "one size fits all" mentality. Dan Halutz, IAF chief of staff during Operation Grapes of Wrath and chief of General Staff during the Second Lebanon War, outlined the solution following Grapes of Wrath, recommending that "the same things can be done with greater intensity and at a higher rate.... We should invest less in striking targets of opportunity.... The most adequate method is dealing more painful blows, at shorter fixed times."[78] Since then, the IAF has applied this method with tactical success but limited strategic effect. Only after Operation Protective Edge did IAF commander Eshel conclude that the IAF would do better to concentrate on striking targets of high importance within the specific context of each operation.

The IAF established an almost predictable operational pattern that consisted of opening the campaign with a powerful surprise airstrike. Some senior officers ironically described this as an operational concept of "starting at maximum power and then intensifying it." Unfortunately, under this approach the IAF usually only assumed responsibility and constructed plans for the opening phase of a campaign. Because the IAF rarely constructed in-depth plans for building on the effects of the opening strike, and strikes were not sufficiently synchronized with parallel systemic efforts, the strategic impact of the opening move often eroded and was not leveraged into lasting achievements.[79]

Over the years the IAF has proven its great capability and impressive flexibility, demonstrating ad hoc adaptation to available technology and to the immediate challenges the air force must meet. The IAF must develop innovative, relevant concepts of operations and coordinate technological development with those concepts to better prepare for the challenges of the future. At present the

IAF is advancing with small, hesitant steps, sometimes almost unconsciously, toward a concept of operations of "operational dominance" from the air. This concept is based on a theory of optimal use of the air dimension to produce a consistent presence that aids the IAF to assess and understand the situation and exert military power optimally throughout the battlespace. "The General Staff Concept of Operations for the IDF," published in 2006 and shelved after the Second Lebanon War, identified this trend. It also noted that the revolution in technology enabled the "change in the role of fire from an assisting component to a central component in reaching decisions . . . identifying the air medium and its superiority as a central dimension makes it possible to efficiently realize more maneuver, collection, destruction, command-and-control capabilities while lessening the friction created by asymmetric components developed by the enemy."[80]

The IAF is shifting from an operational theory of "raiding" toward a theory of "presence." Major General Nechushtan, a former IAF commander, referred to this in 2011 when he wrote that "the classic mission of fighter aircraft is that of a kind of a raid while the unmanned air vehicles have added a dimension of presence or lengthy 'stay' above the battlefield." It is an essential change in the way airpower is operated.[81] The IAF recognizes that aircraft speed and missile power are not the most important determinants of effectiveness when using airpower to meet the strategic challenges of the asymmetric battlespace. Instead, after seven asymmetric conflicts with nonstate actors, the IAF has learned that the ability of UAVs to loiter over an area for a long time, the UAV's observation capacity, a short sensor-to-shooter cycle, and precision have become the essential factors in the optimal operation of airpower. Increased loiter time can reduce the intensity of fire required, enable the use of less expensive (nonprecision) munitions, and further decrease collateral damage.

The IAF has made a significant effort to minimize harm to noncombatants. Statistics gathered over the years show that, despite conducting operations over densely populated urban areas and against enemies that use civilians as human shields, the IAF has achieved highly impressive results in this regard. However, the IAF has not yet found the optimal formula to balance direct attacks against the enemy's operational capabilities and indirect approaches designed to influence the enemy's decision making. Such a balance is essential in complex conflicts whose primary objective is to affect the enemy's perceptions and priorities rather than to defeat or annihilate the adversary. The IAF faces a similar dilemma with regard to choosing whether to define offensive achievements quantitatively or qualitatively. To some degree this represents a choice between a scientific or artistic approach to warfare, where decision by destruction represents the former approach whereas decision by influence is linked to the latter.

The IAF achieved most of its tactical successes during the first stages of its campaigns, when it struck targets for which it had planned well in advance. Over the years the IAF acquired impressive capabilities for collecting intelligence about targets and destroying those targets with great accuracy. It is more difficult to assess the IAF's success from the strategic perspective. Many factors influence the long-term deterrent effects of military campaigns, and therefore the IAF's contribution cannot be analyzed in isolation. The IAF's clear asymmetric air advantage undoubtedly deterred and coerced the enemy, but it also substantially lowered the need to execute ground force operations, which the enemy would view as more decisive and dangerous. In general, whenever the IDF applied military power in a combined, synchronized way, the campaigns achieved better results.

To energize the discourse about different dilemmas in the operation of airpower, and to generate and select among various operational alternatives, the IAF must develop and instill an organizational culture of strategic and systemic thinking that will match its current tactical excellence. The centrality and importance of the air dimension in the armed conflicts of the twenty-first century indeed oblige airmen to act as architects of the military system, not just as engineers or builders within it.

NOTES

The authors wish to express their gratitude first and foremost to IAF commander Maj. Gen. Amir Eshel, for enabling us to access data. We are thankful to Lt. Col. Moti Havakuk and Maj. Michal Izraeli Bachar from the History Branch for their help, and to Lt. Col. Ronnie Amir (Res.) of the Operational Planning Department for his advice. We would also like to thank Maj. Gen. Herzl Bodinger (Ret.), Ph.D., Brig. Gen. Aviem Sella (Ret.), Brig. Gen. Itzhak Amitai (Ret.), Brig. Gen. Shmuel Zakai (Ret.), and Col. Avi Levi (Ret.) for having been so generous with their time and knowledge. Special thanks go to the Fisher Institute for Air and Space Strategic Studies and its chief executive officers, Brig. Gen. Abraham Assael (Res.) and Brig. Gen. Asaf Agmon (Res.), for their firm support and active interest. Although indebted to all those who contributed, the authors wish to emphasize that all the opinions in this study are their own.

1. Saul Bronfeld, "Fighting Outnumbered: The Impact of the Yom Kippur War on the U.S. Army," *Journal of Military History* 71 (April 2007): 465-98.
2. David Ivry, "The Destruction of the Syrian Air Defense in Operation Peace for Galilee" (in Hebrew), *Maarachot* 413 (July 2007): 70; see also interview with Brig. Gen. Itzhak Amitai (Ret.) (a senior planner in the IAF Operation Branch in Operation Peace for Galilee), August 20, 2015.
3. A. Rotem, "The Unraveled Stitch, IAF Participation in the Land Warfare" (in Hebrew), *Maarachot* 413 (July 2007): 61.

4. Some describe Operation Defensive Shield against the Palestinians in the West Bank in 2002 as a decisive operation. The air force role was marginal; therefore, we do not take it up at this time.
5. Itai Brun, "Where Has the Maneuver Disappeared?" (in Hebrew), *Maarachot* 420–21 (September 2008): 4.
6. For further reading about Hezbollah, see "Hezbollah," The Meir Amit Intelligence and Terrorism Information Center, http://www.terrorism-info.org.il/en/Hezbollah.
7. Reuven Erlich, "The 'Syrian Order' in Lebanon (1975–2005): Lebanon as a Syrian Satellite during the Hafez Assad Régime and the Weakening of Syria's Hegemony under Bashar Assad," April 2005, http://www.terrorism-info.org.il/Data/pdf/pdf3/APR18_05_30980064.pdf.
8. IAF, Operation Accountability Operations Plan, July 24, 1993. IAF History Branch.
9. Interview with Maj. Gen. Herzl Bodinger (Ret.), September 11, 2015.
10. IAF, Operation Accountability Debriefing, August 25, 1993. IAF History Branch.
11. Moshe (Chiko) Tamir, "War without Decoration" (in Hebrew), *Maarachot* (2005): 65.
12. IAF, Operation Accountability Debriefing, 1993.
13. Ibid.
14. IAF, Operation Grapes of Wrath Briefing, April 10, 1996. IAF History Branch.
15. Interview, Bodinger.
16. IAF, Operation Grapes of Wrath Operations Plan, April 12, 1996. IAF History Branch.
17. IAF, daily order, April 17, 1996. IAF History Branch.
18. A. Yadlin, "Response: Will Airpower Be the Decisive Power in Wars?" (in Hebrew), *Thoughts in the Air*, December 25, 2000.
19. IAF, Operation Grapes of Wrath Briefing, April 10, 1996. IAF History Branch.
20. Ibid.
21. Ibid.
22. Ibid.
23. Ibid.
24. Ibid.
25. Ibid.
26. E. Ben Eliyahu, "Airpower for the 21st Century" (in Hebrew), *Maarachot* 368 (December 1999): 28–30.
27. D. Halutz, "Airpower as a Decisive Power" (in Hebrew), *National Defense Studies* (July 2001): 98.
28. Amir Eshel, "Ma'arachtan" (in Hebrew), *IAF Magazine* (Summer 2000).

29. Daniel Sobelman, "New Rules of the Game: Israel and Hizbollah after the Withdrawal from Lebanon," Memorandum No. 69 (Tel Aviv: Tel Aviv University: Jaffee Center for Strategic Studies, January 2004), http://www.inss.org.il/uploadimages/Import/(FILE)1190276456.pdf.
30. "The IAF and Its War on Terror" (in Hebrew), Fisher Institute Publication 24 (May 2004): 39.
31. Interview with Col. Avi Levi (Ret.), brigade commander in Operation Days of Return, September 3, 2015.
32. Interview with Brig. Gen. Shmuel Zakai (Ret.), Regional Division commander in Operation Days of Return, August 13, 2015.
33. IAF, Operation Days of Return report, November 15, 2004.
34. Ibid.
35. Interview with Maj. Gen. Eyal Eizenberg (then one of the infantry brigade commanders), published in the Ground Forces Site, http://mazi.idf.il/7176-11345-he/IGF.aspx [Hebrew].
36. Ibid.
37. Maj. Gen. Eliezer Shkedy, lecture at the Fisher Institute conference "Airpower Counter Terrorism," May 2005, Herzeliya.
38. Ibid.
39. Avi Dichter (former head of Shabak), lecture at the Fisher Institute conference "Airpower Counter Terrorism," March 11, 2004, Herzeliya.
40. Interview, Eizenberg.
41. Brig. Gen. Amir Eshel, lecture at the Fisher Institute conference "Airpower Counter Terrorism," March 11, 2004, Herzeliya.
42. *The Winograd Commission Report on the Lebanon Campaign*, partial report (April 2007), 54–57, http://www.jewishvirtuallibrary.org/jsource/History/winograd.html.
43. Testimonies of the prime minister, minister of defense, and chief of staff, on the Winograd Report. http://www.jewishvirtuallibrary.org/jsource/History/winograd.html.
44. Yoav Stern, *Haaretz*, August 8, 2006, http://www.haaretz.co.il/misc/1.1132044.
45. *Winograd Commission Report*, 40–41; and *Hezbollah's Operations in 2006*, the National Security Council archive, http://web.archive.org/web/20090124171428/www.nsc.gov.il/NSCWeb/Docs/chapterd.pdf.
46. From the beginning of the campaign the political leadership prohibited the IDF from deliberately damaging Lebanese infrastructure.
47. IDF, Second Lebanon War debriefings, December 14, 2006. IAF History Branch; and *The Winograd Commission Final Report* (January 2008), 591, http://www.jewishvirtuallibrary.org/jsource/History/winograd.html.
48. For further information, see I. Ben Israel, *The First Israel Hezbollah Missile War* (in Hebrew) (Tel Aviv University, 2007), 36–37.

49. For further information, see *Winograd Commission Final Report*, 328; Itai Brun, "The Second Lebanon War, 2006," in *A History of Air Warfare*, ed. John Andreas Olsen, 297–324 (Washington, D.C.: Potomac Books, 2010); and Benjamin S. Lambeth, *Air Operations in Israel's War against Hezbollah: Learning from Lebanon and Getting It Right in Gaza* (Santa Monica, Calif.: RAND, 2011).
50. Israel, *First Israel Hezbollah Missile War*, 35.
51. Ephraim Kam, "The Impact of the War on Arab Security Concepts," in *The Second Lebanon War: Strategic Perspectives*, ed. Shlomo Brom and Meir Elran, 197–208 (Tel Aviv: Institute for National Security Studies, 2007), 202, http://www.inss.org.il/uploadimages/Import/(FILE)1285063319.pdf; and Edward. N. Luttwak, "Misreading the Lebanon War," *Jerusalem Post*, August 20, 2006.
52. See also A. Kulik, "Hezbollah and the Next War," *Strategic Review* 3, no. 10 (November 2007): 33–42.
53. See United Nations Environmental Programme, *Lebanon: Post-Conflict Environmental Assessment* (Nairobi, Kenya: UNEP, 2007), http://unep.org/pdf/lebanon_PCOB_Report.pdf.
54. Brun, "Second Lebanon War."
55. *The Winograd Commission Final Report*, 326–31.
56. For further reading, see State of Israel, *The 2014 Gaza Conflict, 7 July–26 August 2014: Factual and Legal Aspects*, May 2015, http://mfa.gov.il/ProtectiveEdge/Documents/2014GazaConflictFullReport.pdf.
57. Fisher Institute conference, "Operation Cast Lead—Strategic Decision Making Processes," September 7, 2012, Herzeliya.
58. R. Ben Ishai, "Military Doctrine: Barak, Olmert and Cast Lead 2" (in Hebrew), YNET, December 12, 2010, http://www.ynet.co.il/articles/0,7340,L-4004902,00.html; and S. Fogelman, "Two Years after Operation Cast Lead—Back to the Bombing of the Policemen Academy in Gaza," *Haaretz*, December 23, 2010, http://www.haaretz.co.il/misc/1.123685.
59. "Hamas's Military Buildup in the Gaza Strip," Intelligence and Terrorism Information Center at the Israel Intelligence Heritage & Commemoration Center, April 8, 2008, http://www.terrorism-info.org.il/data/pdf/PDF_19009_2.pdf.
60. State of Israel, *The Operation in Gaza (27 December–18 January): Factual and Legal Aspects*, 2009, https://www.jewishvirtuallibrary.org/jsource/Peace/GazaOpReport0709.pdf.
61. For further information, see Lambeth, *Air Operations in Israel's War*, 221–76.
62. See ABC reports about the attacks in Sudan; Michael James, "Exclusive: Three Israeli Airstrikes against Sudan," ABC News, August 6, 2011, http://blogs.abcnews.com/politicalradar/2009/03/exclusive-three.html.

63. IAF, Operation Cast Lead Debriefing, January 20, 2009. IAF History Branch.
64. IDF, "13 IDF Aircraft Oddly Similar to the Animals They're Named After," December 29, 2012, https://www.idfblog.com/blog/2012/.
65. IDF, "2012 Operation Pillar of Defense," https://www.idfblog.com/about-the-idf/history-of-the-idf/2012-operation-pillar-of-defense.
66. "Analysis of the Ratio between the Names of Terrorist Operatives Killed during Operation Pillar of Defense and Civilians Killed in Error," Meir Amit Intelligence and Terrorism Information Center, December 16, 2012, http://www.terrorism-info.org.il/en/article/20444.
67. IAF, Pillar of Defense Debriefing, November 15, 2013. IAF History Branch.
68. Ibid.
69. For further reading, see State of Israel, *The 2014 Gaza Conflict, 7 July –26 August 2014: Factual and Legal Aspects*, May 2015, http://mfa.gov.il/ProtectiveEdge/Documents/2014GazaConflictFullReport.pdf.
70. "The Threat of Rockets from the Gaza Strip—The Situation on the Ground," Meir Amit Intelligence and Terrorism Information Center, July 8, 2014, http://www.terrorism-info.org.il/en/article/20666.
71. Hamas used to force civilians to stay on roofs, which were expected to be attacked by the IAF. See "Hamas Again Uses Gazan Civilians as Human Shields to Prevent the Israeli Air Force from Attacking Operatives' Houses," Meir Amit Intelligence and Terrorism Information Center, July 10, 2014, http://www.terrorism-info.org.il/en/article/20669.
72. "News of Terrorism and the Israeli-Palestinian Conflict (July 2–8, 2014)," Meir Amit Intelligence and Terrorism Information Center, http://www.terrorism-info.org.il/en/article/20665.
73. See Asaf Agmon, "Targeting and Safeguarding Ben Gurion International Airport," *Israel Defense*, October 13, 2014, http://www.israeldefense.co.il/en/content/targeting-and-safeguarding-ben-gurion-international-airport.
74. Amnon Lord, "IDF Attacked only 10% of Identified Targets in Gaza," August 31, 2014, http://mida.org.il/2014/08/3.
75. Elad Halperin, "The Cooperation between the IAF and the Ground Forces Reached a Climax," August 12, 2014, IDF Spokesman site (in Hebrew), http://www.idf.il/1133-21109-he/Dover.aspx.
76. Carl von Clausewitz, *On War*, edited and translated by Michael Howard and Peter Paret (Princeton, N.J.: Princeton University Press, 1976), 88–89.
77. IAF, Operation Grapes of Wrath Debriefing, April 10, 1996. IAF History Branch.
78. Ibid.
79. In conversations the authors held with IAF commanders, they emphasized the importance of the idea of the "opening strike." However, it became evident that they did not understand the logic of the move in the same way,

and it seems that a profound clarification is needed. Major General Shkedy, Major General Eshel, and Major General Sheffer referred to this issue in interviews we held with them for an earlier study conducted by the Fisher Institute, *The Asymmetric Conflict—the Conceptual Revolution in the Operation of Airpower and the Air Dimension* (in Hebrew), Publication 51 (May 2013).
80. IDF, *Force Operation Doctrine*, 1st ed. (April 2006). IDF Archive.
81. Ido Nechushtan, "Israeli Airpower—Future Directions," in *Flying High— the Israeli Air Force Missions and Challenges* (Tel Aviv: Ministry of Defense, 2011), 122.

Chapter 5

THE AIRPOWER PROFESSION

—John A. Warden III

The earliest works on the profession of arms date back to ancient Greece and Rome. For good reason, almost all describe land warfare; even those that address war at sea use the vocabulary and concepts of land warfare. Dominant among these concepts is the centrality of defeating an enemy's military forces, an idea carried to the extreme by Carl von Clausewitz in the early nineteenth century. Almost a hundred years later, however, something unique happened: warfare moved from the surface to the third dimension of air (and later space). Although many see this dimensional change as little different from the advent of new techniques in war—ranging from the fourteen-foot *sarissa* of Alexander the Great to the cannons of Napoleon—in reality it ushered in a change in warfare that made all previous changes pale in comparison. The advent of third-dimension warfare made it possible to conduct war without necessarily attacking the fielded military forces of the opponent. The concept of strategic attack, far different from force-on-force battle, emerged and enabled nations to affect the very essence of an enemy in order to achieve politico-military objectives.

Despite the real revolution that has taken place in a remarkably short period of time, both serving military officers and theorists still discuss the profession of arms in much the same way as did Antoine de Jomini or Helmuth von Moltke the Elder. It has now become more than appropriate to define the profession of airpower ("airpower" used as shorthand for third-dimension power, which includes space) as largely different from the old profession of arms (with its connotations of sabers and charging stallions) and to rethink how the profession of airpower should be conducted and taught. To this end, this chapter delineates the unique aspects of airpower, explores the special roles of the air professional, describes the ideal characteristics of an airpower professional, examines the macro events likely to occur in the next half century that will profoundly affect the air profession, and considers the education appropriate for the new air professional.

AIRPOWER IS DIFFERENT

The most obvious difference between airpower and its predecessors is that airpower operates in the third dimension. In a certain sense, it has even affected the fourth dimension—time—by enabling rates of movement orders of magnitude faster than movement on the surface. Operations in the third dimension are game changing because they make it possible to avoid Clausewitz's essence of war—the battle—and go directly to the strategic heart of an opponent where it becomes feasible to so alter an opponent as to force him into compliance with legitimate war objectives. Although this strategic capability seems obvious, the attachment to ancient ideas of warfare has made it difficult to think clearly about this new capability and to use it appropriately.

The ability of airpower to operate against the essence of an opponent makes it imperative to link airpower plans and employment directly to national objectives. Surface operations in most cases depend on accumulated success in serial battle (tactical actions) to achieve military objectives. By definition, serial operations are time consuming, expensive, and unpredictable. Their long duration gives the opponent ample time to react, making it increasingly difficult to link military operations to national policy. As an example, linking German policy objectives for the Soviet Union with serial military operations became dramatically more difficult as the summer of 1941 ended and fall weather began. The reason is simple. With serial operations (one battle or one country at a time), there is no strategic information that tells you whether you are better off. Under these circumstances, the overwhelming tendency is to make important decisions after each episode, which results in an almost random path. Conversely, with strategic operations, it is relatively easy to link policy with airpower because the policy can be executed in relatively short time frames with objectively measurable results.

The world has thousands of years of experience with serial surface operations and only decades of experience with parallel strategic air operations. The former are considered well understood while the latter are subject to wildly differing views that in turn create great controversy about the development and execution of airpower. The apparently high cost of airpower platforms in comparison to surface implements intensifies the controversy surrounding airpower.

Most states that employ airpower today subscribe to a cult of "jointness" that postulates combined operations as a prerequisite of success. While the concept has no inherent flaws, in many or perhaps even most instances joint operations actually prove counterproductive because all services rarely will or should have an equal role—or perhaps any role at all—in a given conflict. The real issue lies not so much in the conduct of operations, joint or otherwise, but in the planning process that precedes them. Jointness tends to take the form of a committee approach in which all potential players want to vote and participate, often for reasons that have more to do with service interests than with creating efficient war plans. A significant problem arises when committees plan complex operations. The problem stems from the compromises made during the planning and execution process to satisfy the bureaucratic imperatives of all services without regard for their potential contribution. Often it makes far more sense for the service that would play the leading role in operations to perform the planning and indicate where others might assist, but joint dogma makes this kind of solution difficult.

Given airpower's strategic capabilities, in many or even most instances the airpower representative could and should make a case for building plans around an airpower solution. In typical interservice deliberations and in discussions between military officers and political leaders, however, the airpower representatives will be seen as not "joint" and not team players if they assert (even with good rationale) that airpower should play the sole or dominant part and thus form the core of the operation. The underlying suspicion of airpower complicates planning. This perception can easily lead to decisions about operations based on equality rather than effectiveness. The true airpower professional must be able to address and deal with this situation.

Land surface operations do not inherently require technology. At the most basic level, people can walk to an engagement and then fight their opponents with their bare hands. Conversely, both sea and air operations depend entirely on technology for any degree of execution. What can or cannot be accomplished in the air varies rapidly with changes in technology. In conversations with the author prior to the first Gulf War, Gen. Norman Schwarzkopf, the commander in chief of Operation Desert Storm, estimated that he would need a half million men on the ground to overcome the Iraqi army in Kuwait—an estimate that would have been the same had the confrontation taken place a half century earlier. On the other hand, estimates of the air forces needed to realize national objectives were a fraction of what they would have been a half century earlier, in large measure due to the dramatic changes in technology.

The last major airpower differentiator is its disruptiveness. From an external standpoint, war changed more as a result of airpower than of any other technology in its long history because it affected everyone, everywhere. Internally, airpower has created great strains within military establishments as well as within airpower establishments themselves. Dealing with the disruptiveness of airpower presents one of the major challenges for the airpower professional.

SPECIAL ROLES FOR THE AIR PROFESSIONAL

Since airpower itself is different from the other forms of warfare, the profession of airpower must differ from the traditional profession of arms. The airpower professional must fulfill five special roles that all stem to one degree or another from the airpower differences just noted: managing the direct link between national policy and airpower application, planning and executing airpower operations that exist in a space and time dimension outside of normal human experience, developing and managing disruptive technology, securing support and adequate funding for airpower, and demonstrating tactical proficiency with airpower without losing the necessary focus on the strategic aspect.

Linking Policy and Airpower

As a prelude to examining the first role of the airpower professional, it is useful to summarize briefly an activity basic to creation of national strategy. The process involves establishing a comprehensive postwar future picture, complete with strategic measures for both one's own nation and for the opponent. A future picture is a high-resolution view of what one intends to be and what one intends one's opponent to be in the postwar period. It may seem strange that the first step in creating war strategy consists of developing a future picture for one's own state, but failure to do so can easily result in self-destructive actions even while operations against the opponent might succeed militarily. Numerous historical events show that a belligerent may win the war but destroy itself in the process: Pyrrhus's wars against Rome in antiquity and the campaigns of all the major European belligerents in World War I represent well-known examples. With respect to the latter, consider whether any of the European belligerents would have gone to war in 1914 had they known what their circumstances would be in 1919.

World War I may seem an anomaly because of the outcome for so many of the belligerents, but the difference between this and other wars may be less dramatic than it seems. In World War II both Germany and Japan lost everything and presumably would not have gone to war had they suspected the outcome. What about the victors? The United States realized substantial gains compared to the costs and would probably have embraced those costs had they been known in 1941. The Soviet Union would probably have done the same, even given what seems to Western observers like a disproportionate cost. By contrast, although Great Britain was on the winning side, the cost to the economy and to British power around the world was extraordinarily high. Might some of these belligerents have made different strategic decisions had the future picture been clear?

Foresight as good as hindsight would obviously be invaluable, but is impossible. In the absence of true foresight, however, the answer still lies in forming a solid future picture for both friend and foe. Good future pictures make it possible to create strategic measures that in turn suggest exit points. Had Germany and Japan had good future pictures with good strategic measures, both might have taken advantage of many opportunities to end their wars long before enduring the calamities that eventually befell them. But in case after case, rather than create a future picture of their desired postwar situation, countries put all their energies into fighting their opponents regardless of the cost or the emerging outcomes. This aspect of national strategy construction lies somewhat outside the expertise of airpower professionals, but these professionals must ensure that political leaders form such a picture and that they understand the implications for military strategy and operations

Another aspect of constructing a future picture consists of determining the desired condition of the opponent post war. Choices clearly range from total elimination (Rome's punishment of Carthage) to restrictions on armaments such as those imposed on Germany following World War I. Airpower professionals must remember that the future picture for the opponent reflects what their government believes that picture should be to further its broader interests; at this point it in no way concerns the means to make it happen. From a military standpoint, constructing the future picture for the opponent is absolutely essential, as all subsequent operations should be designed to make it a reality. This step is especially the province of airpower professionals rather than surface warfare officers because only the airpower professional has the wherewithal in today's world to craft direct operations to convert the opponent strategically to meet future picture requirements.

This exclusive ability has not always existed. Naval forces have created genuine direct strategic effects at least since the Spartan blockade of Athens 2,500 years ago and more recently with the blockades of Germany during World War I. In concept, naval action can still produce direct strategic effects, but probably not without the simultaneous employment of air vehicles. Likewise, land forces have had direct strategic effect, for example, when a walled city was the strategic objective. In these circumstances, a successful assault led directly to war-winning (or at least campaign-winning) results. Today, however, opportunities for these kinds of operations may no longer exist, so surface officers have far less motivation to concern themselves with direct strategic effects than do air professionals.

The airpower professional needs to work closely with political leadership to ensure the creation of a good future picture that is thoroughly understood and vetted by all parties. In many cases the airpower professional must take on the task of teaching strategy to political leaders, who rarely have any familiarity with strategic concepts. Ideally, this will be a collegial process from the beginning, but the airpower professional must be prepared to develop the future picture with little or no input from political leaders. Needless to say, before it becomes part of the national strategy, any future picture must receive approval in accordance with the laws and customs of the land.

With the future picture established, the airpower professional must next identify the centers of gravity (the leverage points) within the enemy system that operations must address to trigger the system change needed to force the opponent into the future picture envisioned for it. The airpower professional must be highly competent at identifying and selecting the right centers of gravity, for it is through attacks on centers of gravity that airpower can exert its direct strategic effect on the enemy. By contrast, surface operations today can rarely have the ability to produce a direct strategic effect, depending instead on a series of battles to lead in the right direction. Surface officers will generally lack a high degree of facility with identifying strategic centers of gravity simply because they have little opportunity for practice or application.

The most reliable form of warfare is that of attacking centers of gravity directly so as to change the enemy system to match future picture objectives. Anything short of direct attack carries major risks, but centers of gravity also play a major role in less comprehensive operations. For example, if a nation hopes to deter an opponent from a particular action, deterrence is more likely (though not certain) to the extent the opponent realizes the vulnerability of his centers of gravity. Containment falls into the same category. Blockade really consists of an attack on one or two strategic centers of gravity and may achieve its objectives, but it depends on a single point rather than a parallel attack. Graduated response could entail attacks on actual centers of gravity but poses so many risks that decision makers should reject it as a serious option.

The new option that decision makers should consider is strategic conversion, which means affecting opponents through their centers of gravity to reduce their physical capability to a level that matches the future picture for them. As a hypothetical example, imagine that Sparta had strategic conversion capability and was only concerned with Athens's sea power. Had it possessed the airpower equipment of today, Sparta could have eliminated Athens's sea power simply by attacking the centers of gravity associated with sea power. While Athens might have remained a functional city-state, that would have been largely irrelevant to Sparta, and Sparta would not have chosen to fight a long and ultimately self-destructive war of attrition.

The airpower professional has primary responsibility for identifying and nominating strategic centers of gravity, but—as with the future picture—final decisions about these centers require political approval because, unlike battle plans, selection of the centers of gravity forms an integral part of national policy. Here again, the airpower professional must be comfortable working persuasively with the highest levels of political leadership.

After developing a future picture and centers of gravity, decision makers must determine a time frame for war operations. In this case, the right strategic question is always "How long do we have to succeed?" and never "How long will it take?" Once established, this time frame becomes part of the future picture. Organizations of all kinds often fail to ask and answer the right questions, perhaps because historical experience with surface operations put time beyond control and made the combatant its servant rather than its master.

The last special responsibility of the airpower professional in formulating strategy centers on the development of exit points and plans for both success and failure. Airpower professionals are well suited to help craft exit points and plans because airpower operations can shift quickly between cessation to dramatically intensified attack. Decision makers must develop and agree upon both the points and plans before hostilities commence if forces are to have much hope of following the plans.

Ideally, airpower professionals will work closely with political leadership from the beginning to craft a plan that meets military and political requirements simultaneously. When this collaboration does not occur—as has been the standard for the last half century, at least in the West—airpower professionals may find themselves faced with an a priori political decision that is not militarily feasible. Under the best of circumstances, they may be able to convince the political leadership to change course. If this is not possible, they have two choices: salute smartly and do the best job possible (like most of Hitler's generals in World War II and U.S. generals in Korea and Vietnam) or resign. The first choice is easy to rationalize on the basis that perhaps they can ensure the policy creates as little damage as possible; the second requires more certainty and moral courage but has an aura of quitting that is countercultural.

Planning and Executing Airpower Operations: Parallel War

The second special role for the airpower professional is planning and executing airpower operations, which take place in a space and time dimension outside normal human experience. For virtually all of human history, the general speed of movement has barely exceeded a walking pace; as a result, movement in a day was normally less than twenty miles on land and perhaps only five to six times farther on the water. Information moved at about the same pace. Even today, while we regularly make flights at hundreds of miles an hour, cover thousands of miles in a day, and observe events from around the world in near-real time, our walking speed and range and the distance we can see still heavily influence our concepts of time and distance.

In the surface realm, the constraints of time and distance forced military thinking and operations into a serial mode. In serial warfare, a commander assembles a force, directs it against an enemy whose size and capability is only partly known, engages, assesses the situation, and then either mounts another attack or perhaps pulls back. At the same time, the enemy executes an identical process. Despite advances in mobility, the rate of movement of operational-level forces still tends to remain in the range of twenty miles per day. Each engagement takes place in relatively confined space, with duration measured in days or even more. Ultimately, success depends on winning a series of engagements, each of which has a probability of success of less than one. Thus, the overall probability of success falls rapidly as the number of engagements increases, even if each engagement has a good probability of success. All this happens over extended time frames (many days to months or years), during which the cost of operations (in terms of casualties, lost equipment, and money) climbs steadily. Despite the obvious problems associated with serial operations, commanders have been forced to live with them, although in a few cases—notably Alexander's conquest of Persia, the Mongol incursions into Eurasia, and the German conquest of France in 1940—commanders reduced the costs and poor odds somewhat by moving relatively faster than their opponents in both space and time, which tilted the odds in their favor.

The advent of airpower over a century ago laid the foundation for parallel war—the antithesis of serial operations. In parallel war, one side brings so many key elements (strategic and operational centers of gravity) under attack in such a compressed time frame (hours to days) that the attacked side can be shocked into paralysis with little or no ability to react or respond effectively. An entire parallel war may take place in a fraction of the time that would have been required to create equivalent results through land or sea operations—if creation of equivalent results were even possible. Compression of time and operations also significantly raises the odds of overall success and simultaneously lowers the cost of the war as a whole. Glimmers of the effects of parallel war appeared toward the very end of World War II in both Germany and Japan and in the 1967 Arab-Israeli war, but not until the first Gulf War did the effects and methodology become clear.

Parallel war is so different from serial war that it requires special professionals to explain and plan it. Indeed, familiarity with the old ways is actually detrimental to understanding the new. Political leaders often have a limited grasp of war, and their views are heavily influenced by such popular movies as *The Longest Day*, *Apocalypse Now*, and *Band of Brothers*, all of which not only describe serial operations but also focus on surface operations. Thus, explaining parallel war to political leaders becomes especially difficult even though it offers overwhelming political advantages. Failure in this endeavor, however, means that the leaders will adopt a serial war strategy and the country will pay a high price.

Explaining parallel war is as difficult as is waging it effectively. Part of the problem in planning and execution stems from human discomfort with compression of speed and time as well as from the inability to comprehend complex opponents spread over potentially large geographic areas. Airpower professionals clearly have an advantage in these areas, but that does not automatically mean they will be comfortable with and capable of planning and executing parallel operations. Added to the temporal and spatial issues is the apparent risk inherent in parallel war, which requires up-front application of substantial forces. To the untrained and uninitiated, serial operations seem to offer a safer approach that puts fewer forces at immediate risk. In reality, however, the serial approach carries far higher risk because of the multiplicative nature of probability and because it gives the opponent ample opportunity to react in creative and possibly dangerous ways. Given that their tasks can really only be executed in the third dimension, air professionals must be well versed in the parallel methodology.

Developing and Managing Disruptive Technology

The third special role for the air professional consists of developing and managing disruptive technology while adapting to rapid changes in the general technology base. A technology or concept is termed "disruptive" when it makes its predecessor technologies or concepts irrelevant by enabling a vastly better way to accomplish something—or perhaps even to do something unprecedented. In the military sphere, the airplane was and remains enormously disruptive: it allowed man to fly—something never done before; it allowed man to move at speeds orders of magnitude beyond anything possible in the past; and it allowed man to operate in the third dimension. Operations in the third dimension in turn enabled completely new areas of military endeavor: observing the enemy at any depth and from the beginning almost in real time, bypassing surface forces and significantly reducing the importance of battle, and bringing the strategic depths of an opponent under attack from the inception of hostilities.

Disruptions also typically encounter desperate resistance, and this indeed occurred—and continues to occur—with airpower. Overcoming this resistance and introducing new concepts of operations made possible by disruption become key roles for airpower professionals and are among the most challenging and enduring tasks. Even though airpower has now existed for over a century, the refrain of "You can't do that with airpower" has remained constant, with the only changing aspect being the specific identification of "that." Central to the role of the airpower professional is accelerating the "that" cycle so airpower can realize its real potential as quickly as possible because speed of adaptation wins wars and saves lives. Two examples should illustrate this point.

Gen. Billy Mitchell demonstrated convincingly that aircraft could sink capital ships when he successfully sank the former German battleship SMS *Ostfriesland*, ignoring the claims of U.S. Navy officers who said they would be willing to stand on the ship's deck while it was under aerial bombardment, so certain they were that it would be safe. Yet twenty years later HMS *Prince of Wales* and *Repulse* sailed into range of Japanese land-based aircraft and were sunk within hours at a great cost in casualties and prestige. In World War II, tanks proved highly vulnerable to aircraft attack, and American actions in Korea and Israeli operations in two wars produced similar results. Nevertheless, Iraq confidently deployed thousands of tanks into Kuwait in August through November 1990 only to see the majority destroyed by coalition air operations in January and February 1991. Interestingly, before the antitank operations began in January 1991, senior political and military leaders in the United States expressed great skepticism over the feasibility of destroying tanks (and other ground forces) largely from the air. Fortunately for coalition forces, General Schwarzkopf was not one of those skeptics.

As a final illustration of stubborn resistance to disruption, Gen. John K. Herr, the last U.S. Army Chief of Cavalry, closed his 1953 book, *The Story of the U.S. Cavalry*, with a strong observation about the importance of the horse (the oat-eating variety) that is worth quoting in full: "The Achilles heel of our army today is its lack of horse cavalry and it may well prove just as fatal. One basic and immutable truth stands out through all our wars. Sometimes our commanders have had to learn it the hard way: *There is no substitute for cavalry!*"[1]

Failure on the part of airpower professionals to understand the near-limitless and disruptive capabilities of airpower means that an extraordinary capability will be neither developed nor employed. Solutions in many cases will involve radical reorganization of the airpower professional's own service and dramatically diminished importance for his oldest comrades.

Real disruptions, such as the airplane itself or the precision bomb, are in themselves challenging to manage, but the airpower professional must also manage the inexorable change in the general technology base. If we assume that technology advances at roughly the rate of Moore's Law for transistors (capacity doubling every eighteen months to two years) the technology available in ten years will be about a hundred times as capable as current equivalents and in twenty years will be ten thousand times as capable. Although this increase will affect all forms of military operations, it will have the largest impact on those services most dependent on technology, of which airpower offers the best example (with undersea a close second). Airpower professionals must internalize the exponential growth of technological power from two perspectives: designing and fielding new weapon systems and preparing for technology-based surprises by an opponent. As in many cases, recognition of the problem is key. To help with recognition, it is worth expanding on both of these situations.

In the United States today, with a few exceptions, it takes twenty years to field a new aircraft, with the B-2, the C-17, the F-22, and the F-35 offering good examples. During that time, the general capability of technology will increase by four orders of magnitude, which means that an aircraft twenty years in the making will be technologically obsolescent compared to the state of the art when it becomes operationally ready. The airpower professional should devote enormous energy to solving this problem—which may be as simple as using the F-80, the U-2, the SR-71, and the F-117 as the development models.[2]

The second aspect of the issue—preparing for technology-based surprises—actually presents a far more difficult problem because humans cannot predict the future. For this reason, the airpower professional should focus on developing such an array of offensive capabilities that the odds will be so good that one of them will trump the enemy surprise.

Securing Support and Funding

The fourth special role for the airpower professional is related to the previous three and consists of securing support and adequate funding for airpower even though it is neither well understood nor well liked. In simple terms, this amounts to selling airpower. To succeed in this, airpower professionals must possess skill in both strategic analysis and proper framing of the debate. Although officers from other services also need to secure support and funding, the airpower professional has the special challenge of explaining the rationale for esoteric systems whose use and application are not well understood. Conversely, political leaders and the public alike think they understand the function of tanks, ships, and artillery, so the "selling" process is generally much easier.

Airpower systems and equipment are expensive, especially on a unit-cost basis. Because all national defense budgets are limited, any expenditure on airpower reduces the money available to spend on non-airpower forces—thus generating automatic and strong opposition to airpower. The opposition may be mostly a function of the budget, but as competitors search for ways to reduce airpower allocations, they expand their attacks to include nonbudgetary issues. These often target the overall value of airpower and the air arm's lack of jointness, and sometimes even accuse airpower proponents of dishonesty. That opposition will not disappear, so the problem for the airpower professional becomes one of securing adequate funding and support in spite of it.

Opposition to airpower has subjective and objective elements. The objective elements are easier to counter. It is customary in military as well as commercial enterprises to measure the cost of a piece of equipment on a unit-cost basis—generally a very accurate measurement but not always a relevant one. A good measure would address a key aspect of accomplishing a task acknowledged as important to realize a future picture: a strategic objective. In the case of war operations, a key aspect of the future picture consists of forcing the opponent into a new configuration. The important measures are those that show the desired configuration exists or is materializing at the required pace. If they follow this paradigm, decision makers must then measure the cost of military equipment not by its unit cost but by the effect it has on an opponent. Viewed in this way, even a costly airpower weapon or weapon system can be remarkably inexpensive.

The measurement issue offers a good illustration of the importance of asking and answering the right questions and then educating the target audience. This approach becomes even more compelling when considering the cost of an operation in human lives (on both sides). Casualty forecasts for the first Gulf War made between the Iraqi invasion of Kuwait in August 1990 and initiation of hostilities in January 1991 typically ranged into the tens of thousands and included predicted shortages of body bags. Actual U.S. killed in action came to less than 150. These remarkably low numbers resulted largely from airpower and its associated precision weapons—which were very expensive from a procurement standpoint. When measured from an output side—rapid realization of strategic objectives and very low casualties—the input cost proved trivial.

Developing and Maintaining Tactical and Strategic Proficiency

The last special role of the airpower professional is that of simultaneously developing and maintaining tactical and strategic proficiency. In airpower operations, a single mission in which a single platform deploys a single weapon may or may not have a very large strategic effect, but in all cases it should be planned and executed as part of a broader strategy. This contrasts significantly with almost all non-airpower operations, where strategic effect comes about indirectly as a result of multiple tactical actions. Thus, the non-airpower officer can focus almost exclusively on developing tactical prowess, whereas the airpower professional should from the very beginning learn to combine tactical execution with strategic effect.

Airpower professionals must become proficient in all the roles just discussed in order to make the greatest possible contribution to national defense, of which airpower is the most critical military part. Becoming proficient and executing these roles effectively are not easy tasks and will depend on the airpower professional's having appropriate characteristics and talents—the subject of the next section.

CHARACTERISTICS OF AIRPOWER PROFESSIONALS

Beyond the responsibilities common to all military officers, airpower professionals have special roles that other military professionals either do not share at all or share only at reduced levels. In addition to these special roles, however, the airpower professional has most of the same responsibilities as other professionals. It is important to focus on the special characteristics of the airpower professional.

The Boy Scouts of America promulgate the "Scout Law," which states: "A Scout is trustworthy, loyal, helpful, friendly, courteous, kind, obedient, cheerful, thrifty, brave, clean, and reverent." Although the Scout Law does not specifically address leadership, most would agree that its components would be important (although historically not absolutely necessary) for a good leader to possess. Clearly, other components could be added and the literature abounds in lists of this sort. What should be added to apply either uniquely or in special measure to the airpower professional? Three required characteristics stand out: knowledge, leadership, and creativity.

Knowledge

All professionals in every field need to know a great deal about their profession, but the airpower professional's knowledge must extend far beyond the bounds of airpower itself. It should include a deep understanding of military and geopolitical history, a solid grasp of economic theory and practice, conversance with technology and science, and facility in marketing (in its broad sense).

Humans have interacted with, and warred with, other tribes or states since time immemorial. Over this lengthy period, tactics and weapons have changed dramatically, but the basic concepts of strategy have changed little, as they are based on human nature and on the physical realities of existence. Knowledge of these aspects of history is important for all military professionals but especially for airpower professionals—who, as described earlier, are directly and inherently involved with strategy from the beginning of their careers. Knowing what led to strategic successes and failures in the past means that the airpower professional can apply airpower to repeat the successes and avoid the failures.

An example of each should illustrate the point. When Alexander the Great marched out of Greece in 334 BC, his objective was to conquer and assimilate the Persian Empire—not merely to defeat the Persian army or plunder the countryside. He recognized that to realize these goals he would have to depend on local rulers to maintain order in territories stripped from Persian control as he advanced to the east. That meant honoring the local gods and recognizing that the local rulers had probably demonstrated capability and were reasonably tolerated. By pursuing this approach, he found that he could maintain practical control over the conquered lands with only tiny garrisons of Macedonians. The Germans pursued a diametrically opposite approach in the eastern territories they occupied in World War II, which led to the necessity of maintaining very large forces to ensure a modicum of control in their rear areas. Although the intentions and means were much different, the United States encountered great difficulties following the second Iraq War when it displaced the people and tribes who had ruled the territory for centuries.

In the geopolitical arena, it is more than instructive to recall how Otto von Bismarck ordered Moltke the Elder not to destroy the retreating Austrian army in 1866—which would have been the normal military course under the circumstances—because of the deleterious effect it would have on enlisting Austrian support in the future. Presumably any intelligent military professional would have made the same decision in similar circumstances but would be far more likely to do so with knowledge that such a policy was successfully followed in the past.

Economic theory and practice are arcane and challenging even for economists, so it might seem strange that they should be important for the airpower professional. Their importance stems from the imperative for the airpower professional to secure funding for airpower that may amount to a noticeable part of the state budget. Part of the opposition will flow from questions about affordability, and the airpower professional must be able to counter the arguments—or, even better, to preempt objections by developing innovative ways to finance airpower or to complete the acquisition at a fraction of the "normal" cost. The airpower professional's grasp of economic theory and practice should extend well beyond the theory in vogue at any given time to cover the gamut from Austrian to Keynesian to Marxist.

Technology is the essential underpinning of airpower, so it goes without saying that the airpower professional must be thoroughly comfortable with both technology and with scientific principles in general. This does not mean that all airpower professionals need sufficient expertise to design and build airpower systems, but they should understand the underlying concepts and be able to visualize systems based on new technologies.

The fourth field of knowledge important for the airpower professional is marketing. The term has both a technical meaning in business, where it focuses on developing brand awareness and a demand for a product, and a less precise general meaning of "selling." Professional military education rarely includes marketing, and the military culture of hierarchy tends to suppress the natural exuberance and persistence of the good commercial marketer and salesman. If, however, the airpower professional must secure funding and support for a product that is not well understood or appreciated, then expertise in the mechanisms for developing support and funding is critical.

In airpower history, a handful of officers have demonstrated real skill in marketing, with Gen. Billy Mitchell being the best known. Mitchell was undoubtedly successful in capturing the imagination of his country and subsequently in building sufficient political support to continue airpower development. For this he paid a heavy personal price and is often denigrated by current airpower representatives and historians, but this is not important compared to his achievements. Especially useful to the real airpower professional is a sufficiently deep understanding of the marketing techniques Mitchell employed to be able to analyze and improve them for future application.

Invention is necessary but verges on the futile without good marketing. The nineteenth-century exhortation "Build a better mousetrap and the world will beat a path to your door" would seem like a truism but is in fact rarely, if ever, accurate. The world will beat no path to any door if it is ignorant of what lies behind the door or does not understand or believe that the new "mousetrap" fills some important unmet need at an attractive price.

As recent examples, consider the U.S. Air Force's experience with acquiring the B-2 bomber and the F-22 fighter—both superior mousetraps by any standard. However, the B-2 and F-22 lacked a compelling case to justify their cost. Neither the public nor political leaders understood the necessity of follow-ons in large numbers to replace the successful B-52 and F-15, as few believed a general nuclear war or air battles requiring hundreds of fighters were likely—especially when the power of the enemy against which these systems had been postulated had shrunk dramatically by the time production decisions had to be made to pursue large buys.

Another part of the problem lay in the "marketing" realm, as Air Force leaders based much of their case on technical superiority and the need to replace older systems. Both of these arguments made some sense, but they were esoteric and did not provide any easily explainable, compelling rationale for the huge sums of money requested. A far better argument would have built a credible case for new concepts of operations for both systems that would have led to faster victories at far less cost. That approach, however, would have meant escaping the cultural issues associated with dedicated nuclear bombers and dedicated air superiority fighters. The other interesting question that arises is really a strategic one. In retrospect, should the Air Force have requested (or agreed to) a much smaller and less expensive program for both platforms rather than spending enormous political capital even as the opposition became overwhelming?

Leadership

The next broad requirement for the airpower professional is leadership ability. Leadership is essential in every kind of organization and seems to function in about the same way whether the organization is military or commercial. Until fairly recent times, military leadership, even at senior officer levels, involved extreme personal danger, to include physical contact with an opponent. Although physical danger from enemy actions still exists, especially in land operations and in some air operations, senior officers rarely face it directly and even junior officers are becoming more separated from it. Physical bravery as a key part of leadership may no longer be as important as it previously was, but moral and intellectual bravery remain essential for the airpower professional to provide the leadership needed to advance and use airpower successfully. Whether planning or executing a novel operation or proposing adoption of a new approach to operations, the airpower professional must lead believers and doubters alike to venture into the unknown and untried.

The kind of leadership needed is not without historical precedent. Adm. Horatio Nelson is best remembered as the fighting admiral who won the crucial battle of Trafalgar during which he was fatally wounded while standing in the open on the quarterdeck of his flagship, HMS *Victory*. Without a doubt, he was a great battle leader with immense personal bravery. Less well known, and especially apropos to this subject, is his intellectual leadership. Rather than simply issue imperious orders to his captains, he went to great pains to educate them in higher tactics so that they did not merely follow orders but understood the reason for those orders. In part because of this intellectual leadership, Nelson's captains continued the battle after he fell and brought it to a successful conclusion, almost as if he were still in command.

In the early airpower era, Maj. Haywood S. Hansell, along with a handful of other brilliant officers who had served together at the Air Corps Tactical School, led the effort to create Air War Plans Division 1, the blueprint for unprecedented American strategic attacks on Germany and Japan. He and his fellow planners risked their careers in creating a plan to be presented to the president that called for aircraft to receive disproportionate funding—an idea not popular with Hansell's Army superiors.

At a less senior level, Col. Al Whitley was a key officer in bringing the F-117A stealth fighter into the Air Force inventory and served as commander of the stealth wing that played such an overwhelming role in the success of the first Gulf War. He demonstrated his leadership by shepherding his fellows through the trying experience of developing the tactics for the untested stealth aircraft and then personally leading the first wave against Baghdad—at that time probably the most heavily defended city in the world. Nobody knew whether stealth would really work under combat conditions, so leading the attack required immense physical bravery, but the more important aspect of his leadership consisted of giving his fellow flyers confidence that they would succeed in this daring attempt with an untried technology.

All this by no means implies that officers in other services have not led with enormous bravery and skill. What it does suggest, however, is that airpower professionals are more likely to lead efforts, in peace or war, to acquire or employ an untested new technology or concept. Without this kind of leadership, airpower is unlikely to prosper or prevail.

Creativity

The last special characteristic to address is creativity—the ability to find innovative solutions to tough problems. This ranges from invention to creation of new concepts of operations for existing systems. Of the two, the latter applies to far more airpower professionals simply because relatively few airpower professionals have either the opportunity or the inclination to carry out the in-depth academic study behind most modern airpower inventions. On the other hand, developing new concepts of operation depends far more on an open and inquisitive mind than on academic study. Of great importance is the willingness to ask a series of questions: "Why are you doing it that way?" "Who says that is the only way to do it?" "What difference does it make if we have always done it this way?" "Why don't we give it a try?" The majority of people can probably be creative to some degree if they simply force themselves to ask these kinds of questions. Of course, it helps if they find themselves in an organization whose leaders possess intellectual bravery. If many (ideally most) airpower professionals have the ability to be creative, the effectiveness of air operations will increase dramatically while costs plummet.

THE NEXT FIFTY YEARS

It has always been essential that airpower professionals have the characteristics just discussed, but this will become even more important over the next half century, which promises a plethora of challenging changes. Accurate prediction is impossible, as evidenced by the litany of spectacularly failed forecasts about the telephone, automobile, airplane, radio, television, and personal computers—to name but a few. Given this terrible record, a section on the "next fifty years" may cause readers to raise their eyebrows by more than a little. On reflection, however, the famously failed predictions concerned micro-events, which is what products are, no matter what consequences they eventually have. A more fruitful approach to thinking about the profession of airpower in the next half century lies in taking a macro look. It is useful to start by examining what happened in the last several fifty-year periods around the world: 1865 to 1915, 1915 to 1965, and 1965 to 2015. This look focuses on three major categories of events important to the airpower professional: geopolitics, technology (to include weapons), and medicine. Fifty years seems an appropriate time period, as this is about the longest time that an officer might serve on active duty. More important, actions taken or not taken in the first three or four decades of the period will probably have an impact at least through its remainder.

A long-serving officer in 1915 looking back on his commissioning in 1865 would have seen the rise of the United States to become a significant major power, the dominance of Prussia over the German states, the collapse of the Spanish Empire, the meteoric modernization of Japan culminating in Japan's defeat of Russia, the outbreak of the first general European war in a century, the completion of the first transcontinental railroad, the replacement of the sailing ship by the steamship with the attendant advances in speed and reliability, the advent of instant intercontinental communication via undersea cables, the explosion in automobile ownership, the first manned flight, and the widespread adoption of asepsis and anesthesia in medicine.

An officer who began his service in the next period, from 1915 to 1965, such as Gen. Dwight Eisenhower, would have witnessed even more dramatic changes, to include the collapse of the German and Austro-Hungarian Empires, the fall of the Russian czars followed by communist rule, the resurgence of Germany, the imperial expansion of Japan, World War II and the accompanying destruction of Germany and Japan, American and Soviet ascendancy to superpower status, the birth and heavy employment of strategic bombing, the start of the Cold War, and the conquest of China by Mao Zedong and the communists. In the technology and weapons area, this officer would have seen the maturation of airpower, the transition from propeller to jet aircraft, and the development of radar, nuclear weapons, and satellites. Events in the medical world ranged from the terrible Spanish influenza epidemic that killed tens of millions to the invention of penicillin and the polio vaccine. Needless to say, this observer lived in interesting times!

The last period of observation begins in 1965 and concludes in 2015. In this period, the long-serving officer would see the defeat of the United States by North Vietnam, constant turmoil in the Middle East to include several Arab-Israeli wars, the overthrow of the shah of Iran by the mullahs, the collapse of the Soviet Union, the first war planned and executed as an air campaign with subsequent defeat of Iraq in forty-two days, and the rise of the Islamic State (ISIS). In the technical and weapons areas, highlights include the advent of stealth and precision, the personal computer, the Internet, the cell phone, and the first-ever manned flight to the moon. In medicine, organ transplants became common and the human genome was decoded.

The point of reciting the world-changing events of the last 150 years is to illustrate that the only constant is change itself. For example, although we cannot with any certainty predict the rise and fall of another major power in the next fifty years, we would probably be quite surprised if it did not happen. In addition to the great changes likely to continue in geopolitics, technology, and medicine, the demographic aging of the developed countries will likely have a marked effect on their economic capability and on both their will and capacity for war.

At the risk of wandering into the deadly seas of micro-prediction, it is well within the realm of probability that the airpower professional beginning a career in 2015 might see robotics (with drones as a subset) and beam weapons assume a dominant place in operations, and that mining and other exploitation of heavenly bodies will lead to true space-based military operations. It is even possible that mankind will harness the power of gravity and antigravity, will leap into hypersonic transport speeds, and will learn how to create all-spectrum invisibility.

The conclusion, then, about the next fifty years is that they are certain to be momentous, that much will change by 2065, and that any assumptions about linear development in geopolitics, technology, or medicine will almost certainly be ill founded. All this means that airpower professionals will face significant and—if the trends of the last 150 years continue, perhaps unprecedented—challenges. How can nations prepare airpower professionals to succeed in this tumultuous world?

THE EDUCATION OF THE AIRPOWER PROFESSIONAL

Given the uniqueness of the airpower profession, it would seem obvious that airpower professionals would require a special and carefully crafted education. This section deals with education, not training, on the assumption that anyone engaged in airpower as a career will go through programs to become tactically proficient with the weapon system or support function central to their particular specialty. It is also important to note that everyone (at least all officers) in an airpower role should be an airpower professional and should be expected to perform all the special roles previously identified. In other words, this is not just about those who operate manned or unmanned weapon systems.

As this chapter has shown, the ability to apply airpower strategically is of paramount importance, and airpower education should ensure that airpower professionals can think and act strategically throughout their various responsibilities. This in turn depends on a good understanding of strategy and on the ability to avoid becoming mired in tactics.

The education of the strategist should include significant exposure to military and geopolitical history, to accounts of great strategists beginning with Alexander the Great, to foundational literature that in the West necessarily starts with the *Iliad*, to secular and religious philosophy, and to a thorough exposure to the professional's national history. Of particular importance are studies on the rise and especially the fall of empires. The test of success in this aspect of education is the air professional's demonstrated ability to discuss and extract strategic lessons from each area studied.

The curriculum should encompass not only history but also high-quality fiction, particularly science fiction that blends technology and human behavior in ways that spur thought and innovation. Likewise, historical fiction may provide valuable insights that professional historians may either fail to recognize or be uncomfortable presenting.

Airpower, as previously mentioned, depends completely on technology, and a decided advantage today can swing to inferiority very quickly. Some airpower professionals should have the ability to create new systems, but all must have a broad enough exposure to technical concepts to comprehend technical proposals and to employ the results of technology. As a minimum, this requires an exposure to basic engineering disciplines such as astrodynamics and mechanics. Comfort with technology also means comfort, or at least familiarity, with mathematics. Of special importance in this area are statistics because so much in the commercial and political world depends on statistical analysis.

Clearly, airpower education must also include in-depth study of airpower itself as an instrument of war. This should be a relatively straightforward part of the curriculum because it is a focused subject that covers little more than a century and has been concentrated in a handful of nations.

Because of the special importance of marketing for air professionals, airpower education should include both this skill and the art of persuasion. To this end, educational institutions should revive the study of logic and rhetoric, with the former designed to assist in finding and verifying truth and the latter to provide the tools of persuasion. For marketing itself, a good exposure to business publications on the diffusion of innovation and on how disruption works and is sold can be invaluable.[3] Advertising in itself is fascinating and relevant. Airpower professionals may not place advertisements on television or erect billboards outside government buildings, but they might employ certain analogues in a variety of circumstances. As with history, people who have no awareness of how something was accomplished in another field or time or place are much less likely to conceive or execute equivalent processes in a contemporary setting. Lastly, the education of air professionals should instill comfort with change.

The education just proposed is of great importance but can fail to deliver results if those educated lack the capacity for disciplined thinking. Airpower professionals should take Richard Feynman's two celebrated statements to heart: "It doesn't matter how beautiful your theory is, it doesn't matter how smart you are. If it doesn't agree with experiment, it's wrong." And "The first principle is that you must not fool yourself and you are the easiest person to fool."[4]

CONCLUSION

The old-style officer of the profession of arms faced daunting challenges driven by slow rates of movement, the need to get very close to the enemy in order to fight, the lack of sound information about the opponent, difficult and slow communications, variable reliability of men and equipment, and the imprecision of weapons. These problems manifested themselves as tactical issues to overcome with practice and with marginal changes in capability. Military leaders had some appreciation of the importance of strategy but in the profession of arms strategy took a distant back seat to tactics. Indeed, the promotion of officers was almost exclusively a function of demonstrated tactical expertise or success such as being the first to scale the ramparts of a besieged city. Strategy languished, and only a few great commanders are remembered for their strategic brilliance as opposed to their battle-winning tactical brilliance.

Airpower professionals live in a different world in which their real task consists of conceiving and executing strategy that is not a function of winning battles. In the world of the third dimension, strategy is the only legitimate starting point because third-dimension operations can and should have a direct strategic effect on the opponent. Failure to understand and use the principles of strategy means that airpower will either fail when employed or will achieve far less than it otherwise should.

The salient importance of strategy is one of the most important and most distinguishing difference between the old world and the new. In the world of today and tomorrow, the airpower professional must be able to develop and execute airpower strategy that is highly unlike traditional war strategy, must recognize air wars as fundamentally different from Napoleonic wars, and must be able to explain and defend the difference. Developing the concept of strategic conversion may be the next step.

Weapons technology tended to change slowly in the world of surface warfare, where even major steps such as the introduction of gunpowder actually had little immediate impact, and firearms took many years to displace the bow and the catapult. Conversely, the introduction of stealth aircraft in the late 1980s had a near-instantaneous impact around the world—not just where such aircraft were employed in operations. Airpower professionals must understand, perhaps invent, and incorporate disruptive technology into both platforms and plans and must know how to market and sell concepts and products little understood and much disliked by many—and be comfortable doing so. They must understand and promote radical change, even though this is difficult and may mean that familiar weapon systems such as fighter aircraft rapidly lose their relevance. Parting with the horse was traumatic for the cavalry officer, but the trauma was spread over at least a half century, as opposed to the few years (and perhaps even months) of today. As in virtually all fields, resistance to change will be intense and will often manifest itself in aggressive ways. Airpower professionals must know how to convince decision makers of the value of their product so that airpower can make the appropriate contribution to their country and can garner the monetary and political support needed to keep third-dimension warfare on an accelerating development path.

In the same manner, the airpower professional must break away decisively from the old concepts most succinctly stated by Clausewitz and his modern acolytes. This again demands the intellectual and emotional strength needed to confront and counter the "consensus" view of proper military behavior.

The broad education described here is a necessary but insufficient prerequisite for airpower professionals on active service. The other prerequisite is that their service organization provide an atmosphere where asking "why?" and proposing novel ideas are celebrated, not castigated. Achieving both presents a formidable challenge.

If nations that wield airpower can succeed in defining the airpower profession and adequately educating its professionals, airpower will have the equipment and concepts necessary to deal effectively with the broadest range of opponents while causing the least possible loss of human life. To the extent that airpower develops the right capabilities, it will reduce both the probability of war and the negative effects of wars that take place—the ultimate objective of the profession of airpower.

NOTES

1. John K. Herr and Edward S. Wallace, *The Story of the U.S. Cavalry, 1775-1942* (Boston: Little, Brown, 1953), 261.
2. For a good description of how this was accomplished, see Ben R. Rich and Leo Janos, *Skunkworks: A Personal Memoir of My Years at Lockheed* (New York: Little, Brown, 1994).
3. See, for example, Everett M. Rogers, *Diffusion of Innovation*, 5th ed. (New York: Free Press, 2003); Clayton Christensen, *Innovator's Dilemmas: When New Technologies Cause Great Firms to Fail* (Cambridge, Mass.: Harvard Business School Press, 1997); and Adam Morgan, *Eating the Big Fish: How Challenger Brands Can Compete against Brand Leaders*, 2nd ed. (Hoboken, N.J.: Wiley, 2009).
4. Richard Feynman as quoted in "Richard P. Feynman Quotes," Brainy Quotes, http://www.brainyquote.com/quotes/authors/r/richard_p_feynman.html#pqYI37MekX5c5UQP.99.

Afterword

The United States and Israel, the two liberal-democratic states at the center of this study, have had extraordinary military success for the last seventy years. They have rarely encountered battlefield defeat (the initial Chinese intervention in Korea and the successful Syrian-Egyptian onslaught during the first few days of the Yom Kippur War are exceptions), but even when they have, their airpower helped blunt and eventually reverse those defeats. Some of the American and Israeli successes have been dramatically lopsided. And for the most part, these successes have been, by historical standards, relatively low in total numbers of victors' lives lost. There are many reasons for this, but one of the most important among them has been their ability to maintain air superiority, and in some cases, air supremacy.

There has always been a danger that this would be taken for granted. Air superiority can cover many sins in modern warfare, including logistical recklessness and lack of tactical skills by ground forces. More deeply, it can make, and to some extent has made, war seem easier than it is and can vitiate strategic thinking about how to achieve objectives—a dose of bombing is a kind of universal prescription that can be applied to any strategic ailment.

Air superiority, moreover, prevented real debacles and certainly defeats, but it could not deliver victory. Mostly that was because victory had to be decided, as it so often is, by troops seizing terrain and holding territory. Sometimes it is because, particularly under modern political conditions, tactical success does not necessarily translate into strategic accomplishment.

The high-end airpower that the United States has had since World War II, and that Israel had developed by 1967, was always contested but—a few scary moments aside—never challenged in depth and over a long period of time. Air defense systems from the early surface-to-air missiles to Russian quad-mounted 23 mm cannon netted together in integrated air defense systems were overcome eventually. The Vietnamese, Syrians, and Iraqis could inflict damage, but they could not, in the end, prevent American and Israeli planes from dominating the skies over battle zones and even capital cities.

This era may be changing. Israel now encounters Hezbollah UAVs, and the air raid shelters in Beersheba are used when war erupts with Hamas-ruled Gaza. American planners realize that their air bases are within the threat rings of Iranian and Chinese surface-to-surface missiles, some of which will almost surely get through. In the unmanned revolution and the proliferation of cruise and ballistic missiles—and who knows, in the future perhaps even hypersonic vehicles or conventional projectiles from space—the other side will increasingly find ways to even up the score. Air superiority will still be there and in the hands of the West (we think), but air supremacy probably will not. Rear areas, to include bases and population centers, will probably come under attack. It will be a new reality encountered first virtually, in the experience of war gamers and planners, and then in a very different way viscerally. Indeed, in Israel's conflicts with both Hezbollah and Hamas, it has already happened.

Air superiority will nonetheless continue to be an enormous advantage. It will be one thing to occasionally land a punch at an airbase or a city but another thing entirely to be exposed to continuous surveillance and consequent fires that prevent movement. But war will become more costly for the advanced liberal democracies: a historical moment is therefore ending.

Why is it that dominant airpower has been so much the domain of the West? There is a deeper connection here well worth exploring. The liberal democracies are technologically advanced—but then, in many areas, so too was the Soviet Union. Indeed, so too in a limited way are the jihadi movements that can use both social media and modern gadgets like webcams, small drones, and advanced weaponry. Similarly, although Western air forces are largely meritocratic in their recruitment and promotion patterns, other militaries are not as far behind as one might wish. The key Western strengths go deeper.

One advantage has certainly been the discretionary authority that states like the United States and Israel are willing to give to lower-level operators—that is, pilots. Another has to do with the willingness of such societies to freely share information, which is essential to modern air warfare. A third attribute—a strength but not a monopoly—has to do with creativity, innovation, and learning.

These strengths remain, but they too may come under challenge. The highly skilled lower-level operator may be replaced, to some degree, by the semiautonomous or autonomous robotic aircraft; information sharing may also become somewhat less a human function than a cybernetic one. And the truth is that some of the West's opponents are actually learning machines too, if not quite as effectively as the West is. These intangible elements of the West's airpower edge must be protected vigilantly, but they will to some extent be weakened.

The scrupulousness of Western militaries in the application of airpower is both weakness and strength. Reduced-size bombs (even inert bombs), scrupulous target selection and bomb damage assessment, tactics like "knocking" on the roofs of buildings before attacking them are all commendable from a purely humanitarian point of view. But we have to recognize that our opponents share no such scruples. To the extent that war retains an element of terror and large-scale destruction works—and both are true, unfortunately—they will have an advantage.

For a time at the end of the twentieth century there was a period of what one might call airpower triumphalism. It was misplaced. The evolution of technology, the shrewd countermeasures of serious opponents, and the development of our own restrictions have limited, and will limit, what robust Western airpower has been able to do. But it is inconceivable that we would conduct war without it. To the extent that air dominance is rooted in the civilization of the advanced liberal democracies, it will persist in the ways that they build not only technology but also organizations. And persisting will be not merely relevant but vital.

—Professor Eliot A. Cohen
John Hopkins University's School of Advanced International Studies

Selected Bibliography

Abrams, Elliott. "Just War, Just Means?" *National Review*, June 28, 1999.

Achenbach, Joel. "The Experts in Retreat." *Washington Post*, February 28, 1991.

Adamsky, Dmitry. "Why Israel Should Learn to Stop Worrying and Love the Bomb." *Foreign Affairs*, March 31, 2012.

Agmon, Asaf. "Targeting and Safeguarding Ben Gurion International Airport." *Israel Defense*, October 13, 2014. http://www.israeldefense.co.il/en/content/targeting-and-safeguarding-ben-gurion-international-airport.

Air Force History and Museums Program. *Steadfast and Courageous: FEAF (Far East Air Forces) Bomber Command and the Air War in Korea, 1950–1953—Bombing Operations with B-29 Superfortress, Strategic Air Command (SAC), Okinawa Base*. Washington, D.C.: Air Force History and Museums Program, 2000.

Air Mobility Symposium: 1947 to the 21st Century. Washington, D.C.: Government Printing Office, 1998.

Albright, Madeleine. "Interview with Jim Lehrer." *PBS NewsHour*, December 17, 1998.

al-Shamary, Amar, and Tom Vanden Brook. "Iraqi Military Claims Key Victory in Ramadi, Says ISIL Is in Retreat." *USA Today*, December 27, 2015.

Anderegg, C. R. *Sierra Hotel: Flying Air Force Fighters in the Decade after Vietnam*. Washington, D.C.: Air Force History and Museums Program, 2001.

Andres, Richard B., Craig Wills, and Thomas E. Griffith Jr. "Winning with Allies: The Strategic Value of the Afghan Model." *International Security* 30, no. 3 (Winter 2005–2006): 124–60.

Angell, Joseph W., Jr., Charles H. Hildreth, Littleton B. Atkinson, George F. Lemmer, and Lee Bowen. *USAF Tactical Operations: World War II and Korean War with Statistical Tables*. Fort Belvoir, Va.: Defense Technical Information Center, May 1962.

Anrig, Christian F. "Allied Air Power over Libya: A Preliminary Assessment." *Air and Space Power Journal* 25, no. 4 (Winter 2011).

Anthony, Victor B., and Richard R. Sexton. *The War in Northern Laos*. Washington, D.C.: Center for Air Force History, 1993.

Anziska, Seth. "A Preventable Massacre." *New York Times*, September 16, 2012.

Apuzzo, Matt, Mark Mazetti, and Michael S. Schmidt, "Inquiry Grows into Intelligence on ISIS Surge." *New York Times*, November 22, 2015.

Arkin, William M. "The Difference Was in the Details." *Washington Post*, January 17, 1999.

Armitage, M. J., and R. A. Mason. *Air Power in the Nuclear Age*. Urbana: University of Illinois Press, 1985.

Selected Bibliography

Arnold, David R. *Conflict with Libya: Operational Art in the War on Terrorism.* Newport, R.I.: Naval War College, November 1993.

Arrigunaga, Ramon E. de. "Laos: The Secret War—Part 4: Combat Operations." *Air Commando Journal* 4, no. 1 (Winter–Spring 2015).

Asher, Dani, and Moshe Tlamim. *The Egyptian Strategy for the Yom Kippur War: An Analysis.* Jefferson, N.C.: McFarland, 2009.

Atkinson, David. "B-2s Demonstrated Combat Efficiency over Kosovo." *Defense Daily*, July 1, 1999.

Atkinson, Rick. "Deliberate Force." *Washington Post*, November 15, 1999.

Bald, Ralph D. *Air Force Participation in Joint Army–Air Force Training Exercises, 1951–1954.* Maxwell Air Force Base, Ala.: Research Studies Institute, 1957.

Baldwin, Hanson W. "Korea Has Shown Role of Air Power." *New York Times*, November 1, 1950.

Ball, George W. "How Valid Are the Assumptions Underlying Our Viet-Nam Policies?" *Atlantic Monthly* 230, October 5, 1964.

Ballard, Jack. *Development and Employment of Fixed-Wing Gunships.* Washington, D.C.: Office of Air Force History, 1974.

Balz, Dan. "U.S. Consensus Grows to Send in Ground Troops." *Washington Post*, April 6, 1999.

Baritz, Loren. *Backfire.* New York: Ballantine, 1986.

Barnavi, Eli, ed. *A Historical Atlas of the Jewish People.* New York: Schocken, 2003.

Bassok, Moti. "Israel Shells Out Almost a Fifth of National Budget on Defense." *Haaretz*, February 14, 2013.

BDM. *A Study of Strategic Lessons Learned in Vietnam*, vol. 6: *Conduct of the War*: Book 1: *Operational Analysis.* BDM/W-78-128-TR-Vol-6-1. McLean, Va.: BDM, May 9, 1980.

Bell, Ken. *100 Missions North: A Fighter Pilot's Story of the Vietnam War.* Washington, D.C.: Potomac Books, 1993.

Bergman, Ronen. "Killing the Killers." *Newsweek*, December 13, 2010. http://www.newsweek.com/killing-killers-69081.

Betts, Richard K. "The Osirak Fallacy." *National Interest*, Spring 2006.

Bilstein, Roger E. *Airlift and Airborne Operations in World War II.* Washington, D.C.: Air Force History and Museums Program, 1998.

———. *Flight Patterns: Trends of Aeronautical Development in the United States, 1918–1929.* Athens: University of Georgia Press, 1984.

Blake, Aaron. "Why Obama's 'We Don't Have a Strategy' Gaffe Stings." *Washington Post*, August 29, 2014.

Block, Robert. "In Belgrade, Hardship Grows under Sustained Air Assault." *Wall Street Journal*, May 12, 1999.

Bohlen, Celestine. "Italy Demands a Little Respect." *New York Times*, September 17, 1995.

Boiwer, R. T. *Rolling Thunder.* K717.423-28. Hickam Air Force Base, Hawaii: SEA Team, Project CHECO, March 28, 1966.

Borger, Julian. "The Truth about Israel's Secret Nuclear Arsenal." *Guardian*, January 16, 2014.

Boyne, Walter J. "The Easter Halt." *Air Force Magazine*, September 1998, 60-65.

———. "Linebacker II." *Air Force Magazine*, November 1997, 50-57.

———. "Mule Train." *Air Force Magazine*, February 2001, 70-74.

———. "The Plain of Jars." *Air Force Magazine*, June 1999, 78-83.

Branigin, William, Liz Sly, and Sudarsan Raghavan. "Obama Demands Pullback of Libyan Troops, Tripoli Declares Cease-Fire." *Washington Post*, March 18, 2011.

Brennan, Rick. "Withdrawal Symptoms: The Bungling of the Iraq Exit." *Foreign Affairs*, November–December 2014.

Brent, Keith, ed. *Masters of Air Power.* Canberra: RAAF Air Power Development Centre, 2005.

Brom, Shlomo, and Meir Elran, eds. *The Second Lebanon War: Strategic Perspectives.* Tel Aviv: Institute for National Security Studies, 2007.

Bronfeld, Saul. "Fighting Outnumbered: The Impact of the Yom Kippur War on the U.S. Army." *Journal of Military History* 71 (April 2007): 465-98.

Brook, Tom Vanden. "Anti-ISIL Strikes Now Aimed at Moving Targets." *USA Today*, December 14, 2015.

Broughton, Jack. *Going Downtown: The War against Hanoi and Washington.* New York: Orion, 1988.

———. *Rupert Red Two: A Fighter Pilot's Life from Thunderbolts to Thunderchiefs.* St. Paul, Minn.: Zenith Press, 2007.

———. *Thud Ridge: F-105 Thunderchief Missions over Vietnam.* New York: J. B. Lippincott, 1969.

Brown, Harold. "Airpower in Vietnam." *Air University Review* 20, no. 3 (May–June 1969).

Brownlee, Romie L., and William J. Mullen III, eds. *Changing an Army: An Oral History of General William E. DePuy.* Carlisle, Pa.: U.S. Army Military History Institute / Center of Military History, 1988.

Buckingham, William A., Jr. *Operation Ranch Hand: The United States Air Force and Herbicides in Southeast Asia, 1961–1971.* Washington, D.C.: Office of Air Force History, 1982.

Burt, William R. *Adventures with Warlords.* New York: Vantage, 1994.

Bush, George H. W., and Brent Scowcroft. *A World Transformed.* New York: Knopf, 1998.

Bush, George W. *Decision Points.* New York: Crown, 2010.

Buzzanco, Robert. *Masters of War.* Cambridge: Cambridge University Press, 1996.

Cagle, Malcolm W. "TF-77 in Action off Vietnam." *U.S. Naval Institute Proceedings* 98, no. 831 (May 1972).

Cagle, Malcolm W., and Frank A. Manson. *The Sea War in Korea*. Annapolis, Md.: Naval Institute Press, 1957.

Capaccio, Tony. "JSTARS Led Most Lethal Attacks on Serbs." *Defense Week*, July 6, 1999.

———. "Sixty Percent of Bombs Dropped on Afghanistan Precision-Guided." *Bloomberg.com*, November 20, 2001.

Castle, Timothy N. *At War in the Shadow of Vietnam*. New York: Columbia University Press, 1993.

———. *One Day Too Long: Top Secret Site 85 and the Bombing of North Vietnam*. New York: Columbia University Press, 1999.

Cecil, Nicholas, and Nick Pisa. "SAS Using Lasers to Guide Missiles on to Key Targets." *Evening Standard*, March 21, 2011.

Central Intelligence Agency. *Intelligence Report: The 1973 Arab-Israeli War: Overview and Analysis of the Conflict*. September 1975. http://www.foia.cia.gov/sites/default/files/document_conversions/1699355/1975-09-01A.pdf.

Chanoff, David, and Doan van Toai. *Portrait of the Enemy*. New York: Random House, 1986.

Cheney, Dick. *In My Time: A Personal and Political Memoir*. With Liz Cheney. New York: Threshold Editions, 2011.

Chivvis, Christopher S. *Toppling Qaddafi: Libya and the Limits of Liberal Intervention*. New York: Cambridge University Press, 2014.

Christensen, Clayton. *Innovator's Dilemmas: When New Technologies Cause Great Firms to Fail*. Cambridge, Mass.: Harvard Business School Press, 1997.

CIA Directorate of Intelligence. *Intelligence Memorandum: The Effectiveness of the Rolling Thunder Program in North Vietnam 1 January–30 September 1966*. SC No. 09646/66. McLean, Va.: CIA, November 1966.

Claire, Rodger W. *Raid on the Sun: Inside Israel's Secret Campaign That Denied Saddam the Bomb*. New York: Broadway Books, 1984.

Clancy, Tom, and Charles Horner. *Every Man a Tiger: The Gulf War Air Campaign*. New York: Putnam's, 1999.

Clark, J. J. *Carrier Admiral*. With Clark G. Reynolds. New York: David McKay, 1967.

Clark, Wesley K. "When Force Is Necessary: NATO's Military Response to the Kosovo Crisis." *NATO Review* (Summer 1999): 14–18.

———. *Waging Modern War: Bosnia, Kosovo, and the Future of Combat*. New York: Public Affairs, 2001.

Clarke, Jeffrey J., *Advice and Support: The Final Years, 1965–1973*. Washington, D.C.: US Army, 1988.

Clausewitz, Carl von. *On War*. Translated and edited by Michael Howard and Peter Paret. Princeton, N.J.: Princeton University Press, 1976.

Cline, Tim. "Forward Air Control in the Korean War." *Journal of the American Aviation Historical Society* 21, no. 4 (Winter 1976): 257–62.

Selected Bibliography

Clodfelter, Mark. *The Limits of Air Power: The American Bombing of North Vietnam.* New York: Free Press, 1989.

Cockburn, Andrew. "War by Remote: How Armchair GeneralsPretend They're on the Front Lines." *Harper's Magazine,* March 18, 2015.

Cohen, Eliezer. *Israel's Best Defense.* New York: Orion, 1993.

Cohen, Eliot A. "The Historical Mind and Military Strategy." *Orbis* 49, no. 4 (Fall 2005): 575–88.

Cole, Ronald H. *Operation Just Cause: The Planning and Execution of Joint Operations in Panama, Feb. 1988–Jan. 1990.* Washington, D.C.: Joint Chiefs of Staff, 1995.

Condit, Kenneth W. *The Joint Chiefs of Staff and National Policy, 1955–56.* Washington, D.C.: Office of the Secretary of Defense, 1992.

Condit, Kenneth W., and Ernest H. Giusti. "Marine Air at the Chosin Reservoir." *Marine Corps Gazette* 36, no. 7 (July 1952): 18–25.

Cooling, B. F., ed. *Case Studies in the Development of Close Air Support.* Washington, D.C.: Office of Air Force History, 1990.

Cooper, Helene. "As U.S. Hails Iraqi Success in Ramadi, Focus Turns to Next Move in ISIS Fight." *New York Times,* December 30, 2015.

Cooper, Helene, and Michael D. Shear. "Militants' Siege on Mountain in Iraq Is over, Pentagon Says." *New York Times,* August 13, 2014.

Cordesman, Anthony H. *The Air War against the Islamic State: The Need for an "Adequacy of Resources."* Washington, D.C.: Center for Strategic and International Studies, October 13, 2014.

———. "The 'Instant Lessons' of the Iraq War: Main Report." Third working draft, Washington, D.C.: Center for Strategic and International Studies, April 14, 2003.

———. *The Lessons of Afghanistan: Warfighting, Intelligence, Force Transformation, Counter-Proliferation, and Arms Control.* Washington, D.C.: Center for Strategic and International Studies, June 28, 2002.

———. *The Lessons of Desert Fox: A Preliminary Analysis.* Washington, D.C.: Center for Strategic and International Studies, February 16, 1999.

———. "Looking Beyond the Tragedy in Paris: Still No Clear Strategy and No Public Measures of Effectiveness for Dealing with ISIS." Draft manuscript. Washington, D.C.: Center for Strategic and International Studies, December 1, 2015.

Correll, John T. "Assumptions Fall in Kosovo." *Air Force Magazine* 82, no. 6 (June 1999): 4.

———. "Disunity of Command." *Air Force Magazine* 88, no. 1 (January 2005): 34–39.

———. "The Ho Chi Minh Trail." *Air Force Magazine* 88, no. 11 (November 2005): 62–68.

———. "The In-Country War." *Air Force Magazine* 90, no. 4 (April 2007): 64–69.

———. "The Opening Bell in Laos." *Air Force Magazine* 95, no. 12 (December 2012).

———. "Rolling Thunder." *Air Force Magazine* 88, no. 3 (March 2005): 58–65.

Covault, Craig. "Air Power Alters Bosnia Equation." *Aviation Week and Space Technology*, September 4, 1995.

———. "NATO Air Strikes Target Serbian Infrastructure." *Aviation Week and Space Technology*, September 11, 1995.

———. "Precision Missiles Bolster NATO Strikes." *Aviation Week and Space Technology*, September 18, 1995.

Crane, Conrad. *American Airpower Strategy in Korea, 1950–1953*. Lawrence: University Press of Kansas, 2000.

Craven, Wesley Frank, and James Lea Cate, eds. *Europe: Argument to V-E Day, January 1944 to May 1945*. Chicago: University of Chicago Press, 1951.

———, eds. *Europe: Torch to Pointblank, August 1942 to December 1943*. Chicago: University of Chicago Press, 1949.

Creveld, Martin van. *The Age of Airpower*. New York: Public Affairs, 2011.

———. *Nuclear Proliferation and the Future of Conflict*. New York: Free Press, 1993.

———. *The Sword and the Olive: A Critical History of the Israeli Defense Force*. New York: Public Affairs, 2002.

Currie, Duncan M. "Remember Operation Babylon." *Harvard Crimson*, September 18, 2002. http://www.thecrimson.com/article/2002/9/18/remember-operation-babylon-as-the-debate/.

Curry, Bruce H. *Conflict with Libya: Use of Military Force against Terrorism*. Newport, R.I.: Naval War College, 1994.

Daalder, Ivo H., and Admiral James G. Stavridis. "NATO's Victory in Libya: The Right Way to Run an Intervention." *Foreign Affairs*, March–April 2012.

Daly, John C. K. "Operation Inherent Resolve: The War against Islamic State's Oil Network." *Terrorism Monitor* 13, no. 1, Jamestown Foundation, January 9, 2015.

Dao, James. "More U.S. Troops in bin Laden Hunt; Hideouts Bombed." *New York Times*, November 19, 2001.

Davis, Brian L. *Qaddafi, Terrorism, and the Origins of the U.S. Attack on Libya*. New York: Praeger, 1990.

Davis, Mark G. "Operation Anaconda: Command and Confusion in Joint Warfare." Unpublished thesis presented to the faculty of the School of Advanced Air and Space Studies, Maxwell Air Force Base, Alabama, June 2004.

Davis, Richard G. *Carl A. Spaatz and the Air War in Europe*. Washington, D.C.: Center for Air Force History, 1993.

———. *The 31 Initiatives: A Study in Air Force–Army Cooperation*. Washington, D.C.: Office of Air Force History, 1987.

de la Billière, Peter. *Storm Command: A Personal Account of the Gulf War*. New York: HarperCollins, 1992.

Dean, David J. *The Air Force Role in Low-Intensity Conflict*. Maxwell Air Force Base, Fla.: Air University Press, 1986.

Department of the Air Force. *Strategic Air Operations: Air Doctrine.* AFM 1-8. Washington, D.C.: Department of the Air Force, May 1, 1954.

Department of the Army, *FM 100-5: Operations.* Washington, D.C.: Government Printing Office, 1976.

Department of Defense. *Department of Defense Dictionary of Military and Associated Terms.* Joint Publication 1-02. Washington, D.C.: The Joint Staff, November 8, 2010, as amended through November 15, 2015.

———. "Department of Defense Press Briefing by Col. Warren via Teleconference from Baghdad, Iraq." U.S. Department of Defense news transcript, December 29, 2015.

———. "Lieutenant General John W. Hesterman III, USAF, Combined Force Air Component Commander, Holds a Defense Department News Briefing via Teleconference." U.S. Department of Defense press release, June 5, 2015.

———. "Operation Inherent Resolve: Targeted Operations against ISIL Terrorists." Department of Defense special report, November 23, 2015.

Deptula, David A. "We Can't Stop the Islamic State with a 'Desert Drizzle.'" *USA Today*, November 15, 2015.

De Young, Karen, and Greg Jaffe. "NATO Runs Short on Some Munitions in Libya." *Washington Post*, April 15, 2011.

De Young, Karen, and Missy Ryan. "As Bombing in Syria Intensifies, a Debate about the Rules of Engagement." *Washington Post*, December 22, 2015.

Doglione, John A., et al. *Airpower and the 1972 Spring Invasion.* Washington, D.C.: Government Printing Office, 1976.

Douhet, Giulio. *The Command of the Air.* Washington D.C.: Office of Air Force History, 1983.

Drea, Edward J. *McNamara, Clifford, and the Burdens of Vietnam, 1965–1969.* Washington, D.C.: Office of the Secretary of Defense, 2011.

Drew, Dennis. "Desert Storm as a Symbol: Implications of the Air War in the Desert." *Airpower Journal* 6, no. 3 (Fall 1992).

———. *Rolling Thunder 1965.* Maxwell Air Force Base, Ala.: Air University Press, 1986.

———. "Two Decades in the Air Power Wilderness: Do We Know Where We Are?" *Air University Review* 37, no. 6 (September–October 1986): 2–13.

Drozdiak, William. "Yugoslav Troops Devastated by Attack." *Washington Post*, June 9, 1999.

Drury, Richard S. *My Secret War.* Fallbrook, Calif.: Aero, 1979.

Dunstan, Simon. *The Yom Kippur War*, 2 vols. Oxford: Osprey Publishing, 2003.

Dupuy, Trevor, and Paul Martell. *Flawed Victory: Arab-Israeli Conflict and the 1982 War in Lebanon.* Fairfax, Va.: Hero Books, 1986.

Eisenhower, John S. D. *Strictly Personal.* Garden City, N.Y.: Doubleday, 1974.

Eisman, Dale. "Over Balkans, It's Beauty vs. the Beast." *Norfolk Virginian-Pilot*, April 26, 1999.

Engen, Donald D. *Wings and Warriors*. Washington, D.C.: Smithsonian Institution Press, 1997.

"Entangled: Why America Must Stay Engaged in the Middle East." *Economist*, June 6–12, 2015.

Entous, Adam, and Julian E. Barnes. "U.S. Secretly Flying Drones over Iraq." *Wall Street Journal*, June 12, 2014.

Erlanger, Steven. "Economists Find Bombing Cuts Yugoslavia's Production in Half." *New York Times*, April 30, 1999.

Eschmann, Karl J. *Linebacker: The Untold Story of the Air Raids over North Vietnam*. New York: Ballantine, 1989.

Evans, Michael. "Ground War 'Error.'" *London Times*, March 24, 2000.

———. "U.S. Troops and Helicopters Set for Ground War." *London Times*, October 11, 2001.

Fall, Bernard B. *Street without Joy: The French Debacle in Indochina*. Mechanicsburg, Pa.: Stackpole, 2005.

Farrell, Stephen, and Michael Evans. "SAS Searches bin Laden Cave System." *London Times*, December 4, 2001.

Faulkenberry, Barbara J. *Global Reach—Global Power: Air Force Strategic Vision, Past and Future*. Maxwell Air Force Base, Ala.: Air University Press, 1995.

Fick, Nathaniel. *One Bullet Away: The Making of a Marine Officer*. New York: Houghton Mifflin, 2005.

Finney, Robert T. *History of the Air Corps Tactical School, 1920–1940*. Washington, D.C.: Center for Air Force History, 1992.

Flournoy, Michele, and Richard Fontaine. *An Intensified Approach to Combatting the Islamic State*. Policy Brief. Washington, D.C.: Center for a New American Security, 2015.

Fogelman, S. "Two Years after Operation Cast Lead—Back to the Bombing of the Policemen Academy in Gaza." *Haaretz*, December 23, 2010.

Fogleman, Ronald R. "What Air Power Can Do in Bosnia." Letter to the editor, *Wall Street Journal*, October 11, 1995.

Frank, Richard B. *Downfall: The End of the Imperial Japanese Empire*. New York: Random House, 1999.

Frankum, Ronald B., Jr. *Like Rolling Thunder: The Air War in Vietnam, 1964–1975*. Lanham, Md.: Rowman & Littlefield, 2005.

Frostic, Fred. *Air Campaign against the Iraqi Army in the Kuwaiti Theater of Operations*, Report MR-357-AF. Santa Monica, Calif.: RAND, 1994.

Fulghum, David A. "Electronic Bombs Darken Belgrade." *Aviation Week and Space Technology*, May 10, 1999.

Futrell, Robert F. *The USAF in Korea, 1950–1953*. New York: Duell, Sloan & Pearce, 1961.

Garamone, Jim. "Dempsey Makes Case for Long-Term Effort to Defeat ISIL." U.S. Department of Defense news release, August 17, 2015.

Gates, Robert M. *Duty: Memoirs of a Secretary at War.* New York: Knopf, 2014.

Gelb, Leslie H., and Richard K. Betts, *The Irony of Vietnam: The System Worked.* Washington, D.C.: Brookings Institution, 1979.

Gelb, Leslie H., et al., eds. *Evolution of the War: Origins of the Insurgency, 1954-1960*, v. IV.A.5 of *United States-Vietnam Relations 1945-1967.* Washington, D.C.: Vietnam Task Force of the Office of the Secretary of Defense, January 15, 1969.

George, Alexander L. *The Chinese Communist Army in Action: The Korean War and Its Aftermath.* New York: Columbia University Press, 1967.

Gertler, Jeremiah. "Operation Odyssey Dawn [Libya]: Background and Issues for Congress." Congressional Research Service, March 28, 2011.

Giusti, Ernest H., and Kenneth W. Condit. "Marine Air Covers the Breakout." *Marine Corps Gazette* 36, no. 8 (August 1952): 20-27.

Glennon, John P., et al., eds. *National Security Policy*, vol. 19 of *Foreign Relations of the United States, 1955-1957.* Washington, D.C.: Government Printing Office, 1990.

Glosson, Buster. *War with Iraq: Critical Lessons.* Charlotte, N.C.: Glosson Family Foundation, 2003.

Golani, Motti. "Chief of Staff in Quest of a War: Moshe Dayan Leads Israel into War." *Journal of Strategic Studies* 24, no. 1 (March 2001): 49-70.

Goodwin, Doris Kearns. *Lyndon Johnson and the American Dream.* New York: Harper & Row, 1976.

Gorst, Anthony, and Lewis Johnman. *The Suez Crisis.* London: Routledge, 1997.

Graham, Bradley. "Air Power 'Effective, Successful,' Cohen Says." *Washington Post*, June 11, 1999.

Graham, Bradley, and Vernon Loe. "Cave Complexes Smashed by Bombs." *Washington Post*, October 12, 2001.

Graham, Bradley, and Dana Priest. "Allies to Begin Flying Refugees Abroad." *Washington Post*, April 5, 1999.

Grant, Rebecca. "Linebacker I." *Air Force Magazine*, June 2012, 71-74.

Granville, John M. *Summary of USAF Aircraft Losses in SEA*, Report 7409. Langley Air Force Base, Va.: Directorate of Force Development and Analysis, HQ Tactical Air Command, June 1974.

Grau, Lester W., and Jacob W. Kipp. "Maintaining Friendly Skies: Rediscovering Theater Aerospace Defense." *Aerospace Power Journal* 16, no. 2 (Summer 2002).

Gray, Colin S. *The Airpower Advantage in Future Warfare: The Need for Strategy.* Maxwell Air Force Base, Ala.: Air Research Institute, 2007.

———. *Airpower for Strategic Effect.* Maxwell Air Force Base, Ala.: Air University Press, 2012.

Greenleaf, Jason R. "The Air War in Libya." *Air and Space Power Journal* 27, no. 2 (March-April 2013).

Greer, Thomas H. *The Development of Air Doctrine in the Army Air Arm, 1917–1941*. Washington, D.C.: Office of Air Force History, 1985.

Grossman, Elaine M. "For U.S. Commander in Kosovo, Luck Played Role in Wartime Success." *Inside the Pentagon* 15, no. 36 (September 9, 1999).

Gunzinger, Mark, and John Stillion. "The Unserious Air War against ISIS." *Wall Street Journal*, October 14, 2014.

Haas, Michael E. "Jungle Jim: At the Tip of the Spear." *Air Commando Journal* 4, no. 1 (Winter–Spring 2015).

Hall, R. Cargill, ed. *Case Studies in Strategic Bombardment*. Washington, D.C.: Air Force History and Museums Program, 1999.

Hallion, Richard P. "Doctrine, Technology, and Air Warfare: A Late Twentieth-Century Perspective." *Airpower Journal* 1, no. 2 (Fall 1987): 4–27.

———. "Girding for War: Perspectives on Research, Development, Acquisition, and the Decision-Making Environment of the 1980s." *Air University Review* 37, no. 6 (September–October 1986): 46–62.

———. *The Naval Air War in Korea*. Baltimore: Nautical & Aviation Publishing, 1986.

———, ed. *Silver Wings, Golden Valor: The USAF Remembers Korea*. Washington, D.C.: Air Force History and Museums Program, 2006.

———. "A Troubling Past: Air Force Fighter Acquisition since 1945." *Airpower Journal* 9, no. 4 (Winter 1990): 4–23.

Hansell, Haywood S., Jr. *The Air Plan That Defeated Hitler*. Atlanta: Higgins-McArthur / Longino & Porter, Inc., 1972.

Hartsook, Elizabeth H. *Air Power Helps Stop the Invasion and End the War, 1972*. Washington, D.C.: U.S. Air Force, 1978.

Hassan, Mehdi. "Bomb Iran and It Will Surely Decide to Build Nuclear Arms." *Guardian*, March 26, 2012. http://www.theguardian.com/commentisfree/2012/mar/25/bomb-iran-nuclear-arms-iraq-israel.

Hebert, Adam. "Air Force Follows Roadmap in Employment of Bombers against Serbia." *Inside the Air Force*, April 2, 1999.

Herr, John K., and Edward S. Wallace. *The Story of the U.S. Cavalry, 1775–1942*. Boston: Little, Brown, 1953.

Hersh, Seymour M. *The Samson Option: Israel's Nuclear Arsenal and American Foreign Policy*. New York: Random House, 1991.

Herzog, Chaim. *The Arab-Israeli Wars*. London: Arms & Armour, 1982.

Hickey, Lawrence J., and James G. Bruce Jr. *Operation Attleboro*. K717.0413-13. Hickam Air Force Base, Hawaii: SEA Team, Project CHECO, 1967.

Hiltermann, Joost R. "Bomb Now, Die Later." *Mother Jones* 16, no. 4 (July–August 1991).

Holbrooke, Richard. *To End a War*. New York: Random House, 1998.

Holley, I. B., Jr. *Buying Aircraft: Materiel Procurement for the Army Air Forces, Special Studies, United States Army in World War II*. Washington, D.C.: Office of the Chief of Military History, Department of the Army, 1964.

Holloway, Bruce K. "Air Superiority in Tactical Air Warfare." *Air University Review* 19, no. 3 (March–April 1968).

Holloway, James L., III. *Aircraft Carriers at War: A Personal Retrospective of Korea, Vietnam, and the Soviet Confrontation.* Annapolis, Md.: Naval Institute Press, 2007.

Howard, Michael. *The Lessons of History.* New Haven, Conn.: Yale University Press, 1991.

———. "The Use and Abuse of Military History." *Journal of the Royal United Services Institute* 107, no. 625 (1962).

———. "The Use of Military History." *Shedden Papers*, Australian Defence College: Centre for Defence and Strategic Studies, January 22, 2008. http://www.defence.gov.au/ADC/Publications/Shedden/2008/Publctns_Shed Paper_050310_TheUseofMilitaryHistory.pdf.

Howze, Hamilton H. *A Cavalryman's Story.* Washington, D.C.: Smithsonian Institution Press, 1996.

Hudson, David. "President Obama: We Will Degrade and Ultimately Destroy ISIL." White House blog, September 10, 2014.

Hunt, Colin. "NATO Has Little to Show from Its Libya Intervention." *Cicero Magazine*, August 12, 2015.

Huntington, Samuel P. *Political Order in Changing Societies.* New Haven, Conn.: Yale University Press, 1968.

Hurley, Matthew M. "The BEKAA Valley Air Battle, June 1982: Lessons Mislearned?" *Air Power Journal* 3, no. 4 (Winter 1989).

Hutcheson, Keith A., and Charles T. Robertson. *Air Mobility: The Evolution of Global Reach.* Vienna, Va.: Point One, 1999.

The Insight Team of the Sunday Times. *The Yom Kippur War.* New York: ibooks, 2002.

Jackson, Robert. *Suez 1956: Operation Musketeer.* London: Ian Allen, 1980.

Jacobs, Jody, David E. Johnson, Katherine Comanor, Lewis Jamison, Leland Joe, and David Vaughn, *Enhancing Fires and Maneuver Capability through Greater Air-Ground Joint Interdependence.* Santa Monica, Calif.: RAND, 2009.

Jamieson, Perry D. *Lucrative Targets: The U.S. Air Force in the Kuwaiti Theater of Operations.* Washington, D.C.: Air Force History and Museums Program, 2001.

Joffe, Lawrence. "Obituary, Lieut-Gen Rafael Eitan." *Guardian*, November 25, 2004.

Johnson, David E. *Learning Large Lessons: The Evolving Roles of Ground Power and Air Power in the Post–Cold War Era.* Santa Monica, Calif.: RAND, 2006.

Joint Logistics Plans Committee, Office of the Joint Chiefs of Staff. *Dictionary of United States Military Terms for Joint Usage (First Revision).* Washington, D.C.: Government Printing Office, June 1950.

Kagan, Frederick W. *Finding the Target: The Transformation of American Military Policy.* New York: Encounter Books, 2006.

———. "The President and the Generals." *Weekly Standard*, December 12, 2011.

Kainikara, Sanu. *Red Air: Politics in Russian Air Power*. Boca Raton, Fla.: Universal Publishers, 2007.

Kamps, Charles Tustin. "The JCS 94-Target List: A Vietnam Myth That Still Distorts Military Thought." *Aerospace Power Journal* 15, no. 1 (Spring 2001).

Kane, Gregory C. *Air Power and Its Role in the Battles of Khe Sanh and Dien Bien Phu*. Maxwell Air Force Base, Ala.: Air University, 1997.

Kaplan, Fred. "Obama's Way: The President in Practice." *Foreign Affairs*, January–February 2016.

Keaney, Thomas A., and Eliot A. Cohen, *Gulf War Air Power Survey Summary Report*. Washington, D.C.: Government Printing Office, 1993.

Keating, Timothy J. Interview: Vice Admiral Timothy J. Keating, U.S. Navy—"This Was a Different War." U.S. Naval Institute *Proceedings* 129, no. 6/1,204 (June 2003).

Keefer, Edward C., Charles S. Sampson, and John P. Glennon, eds. *Foreign Relations of the United States, 1964–1968*. Vol. 1: *Vietnam, 1964*. Washington, D.C.: Government Printing Office, 1992.

Keegan, John. "Modern Weapons Hit War Wisdom." *Sydney Morning Herald*, June 5, 1999.

Kempster, Norman. "U.S. and Britain Strike Iraq; Impeachment Debate on Hold." *Los Angeles Times*, December 17, 1998.

Kinnard, Douglas. *The War Managers*. Hanover, N.H.: University Press of New England, 1977.

Kissinger, Henry. *Years of Upheaval*. London: Weidenfeld and Nicolson, 1982.

Knaack, Marcelle Size. *Post–World War II Fighters, 1945–1973*. Vol. 1 of *Encyclopedia of U.S. Air Force Aircraft and Missile Systems*. Washington, D.C.: Office of Air Force History, 1978.

Knights, Michael "Campaign Acceleration: How to Build on Progress and Avoid Stalemate against ISIL." *War on the Rocks* (blog), November 3, 2015. http://warontherocks.com/2015/11/campaign-acceleration-how-to-build-on-progress-and-avoid-stalemate-against-isil/.

———. *Cradle of Conflict: Iraq and the Birth of the Modern U.S. Military*. Annapolis, Md.: Naval Institute Press, 2005.

Kohn, Richard H., and Joseph P. Harahan, eds. *Air Interdiction in World War II, Korea, and Vietnam*. Washington, D.C.: Office of Air Force History, 1985.

Kopp, Carlo. "Iraqi Freedom—The Hammer and Anvil." *Australian Aviation*, May 2003, 25–35.

Korte, Gregory. "Obama Embraces Doctrine of 'Strategic Patience.'" *USA Today*, February 6, 2015.

Kulik, A. "Hezbollah and the Next War." *Strategic Review* 3, no. 10 (November 2007): 33–42.

Kuperman, Alan J. "Obama's Libya Debacle: How a Well-Meaning Intervention Ended in Failure." *Foreign Affairs*, March–April 2015.

Kyle, Keith. *Suez*. London: I. B. Tauris, 2011.

Lambert, Andrew P. N. *The Psychology of Air Power*. London: Royal United Services Institute for Defence Studies, 1994.

Lambeth, Benjamin S. "AirLand Reversal." *Air Force Magazine*, February 2014.

———. *Air Operations in Israel's War against Hezbollah: Learning from Lebanon and Getting It Right in Gaza*. Santa Monica, Calif: RAND, 2011.

———. *Air Power against Terror: America's Conduct of Operation Enduring Freedom*. Santa Monica, Calif.: RAND, 2005.

———. *American Carrier Air Power at the Dawn of a New Century*. Santa Monica, Calif.: RAND, 2005.

———. "Israel's War in Gaza: A Paradigm of Effective Military Learning and Adaptation." *International Security* 37, no. 2 (Fall 2012): 81–118.

———. "Lessons from Modern Warfare: What the Conflicts of the Post–Cold War Years Should Have Taught Us." *Strategic Studies Quarterly* 7, no. 3 (Fall 2013): 28–72.

———. "Moscow's Lessons from the 1982 Lebanon Air War." RAND Project Air Force Paper R-3000-AF. Santa Monica: RAND, September 1984.

———. *NATO's Air War for Kosovo: A Strategic and Operational Assessment*. Santa Monica, Calif.: RAND, 2001.

———. *Russia's Air Power in Crisis*. Washington, D.C.: Smithsonian Institution Press, 1999.

———. *The Transformation of American Air Power*. Ithaca, N.Y.: Cornell University Press, 2000.

———. *The Unseen War: Allied Air Power and the Takedown of Saddam Hussein*. Annapolis, Md.: Naval Institute Press, 2013.

Lamothe, Dan. "Operation against Islamic State to be Called Inherent Resolve." *Washington Post*, October 15, 2014.

Lansdown, J. R. P. *With the Carriers in Korea*. Upton, U.K.: Severnside Publishers, 1992.

Leary, William M. *Anything, Anywhere, Anytime: Combat Cargo in the Korean War*. 50th ann. comm. ed. Washington, D.C.: Defense Department, Air Force Department, 2000.

Lehman, John F., Jr. *Command of the Seas*. New York: Scribner, 1988.

Lewin, Avraham Shmuel. "Osirak Revisited." *Jewish Press*, Frontpagemag.com, December 18, 2007. http://archive.frontpagemag.com/readArticle.aspx?ARTID=29258.

Lewis, Michael. *Lt. Gen. Ned Almond, USA: A Ground Commander's Conflicting View with Airmen over CAS Doctrine and Employment*. Maxwell Air Force Base, Ala.: Air University Press, 1996.

Lewis, Richard B. H. "JFACC Problems Associated with Battlefield Preparation in Desert Storm." *Airpower Journal* 8, no. 1 (Spring 1994): 4–21.

Lizza, Ryan. "The Consequentialist: How the Arab Spring Remade Obama's Foreign Policy." *New Yorker*, May 2, 2011.

Luttwak, Edward. N. "Misreading the Lebanon War." *Jerusalem Post*, August 20, 2006.

MacFarquar, Neil. "Hafez al-Assad, Who Turned Syria into a Power in the Middle East, Dies at 69." *New York Times*, June 11, 2000.

Mak, Tim. "Exclusive: Pentagon Map Hides ISIS Gains." *Daily Beast*, April 22, 2015.

Marion, Forrest L. "First Fight: Special Tactics in Panama." *Air Commando Journal* 3, no. 3 (Fall 2014).

Marolda, Edward J., and Robert J. Schneller Jr. *Shield and Sword: The United States Navy and the Persian Gulf War*. Washington, D.C.: Navy Historical Center, Department of the Navy, 1998.

Marrett, George J. *Cheating Death: Combat Rescues in Vietnam and Laos*. Washington, D.C.: Smithsonian Books, 2003.

Marshall, Tyler. "U.S., British Pound Military Sites." *Los Angeles Times*, December 18, 1998.

———. "U.S. Rejects Calls for Efforts to Oust Hussein." *Los Angeles Times*, December 24, 1998.

Marx, Karl, and Frederick Engels. "Austria's Weakness." *New York Daily Tribune*, May 7, 1855, in *Collected Works*, vol. 14 (London: Lawrence and Wishart, 1975–1983), 689–93.

Mason, R. A. "The Air War in the Gulf." *Survival* 33, no. 3 (May–June 1991): 211–29.

———, ed. *War in the Third Dimension: Essays in Contemporary Air Power*. London: Brassey's Defence Publishers, 1986.

McCants, William. *The ISIS Apocalypse: The History, Strategy, and Doomsday Vision of the Islamic State*. New York: St. Martin's Press, 2015.

McCarthy, James R., and George B. Anderson, eds. *Linebacker II: A View from the Rock*. With Col. Robert E. Rayfield. Washington, D.C.: Government Printing Office, 1976.

McCarthy, Niall. "The Biggest Military Budgets as a Percentage of GDP." *Forbes Business*, June 25, 2015. http://www.forbes.com/sites/niallmccarthy/2015/06/25/the-biggest-military-budgets-as-a-percentage-of-gdp-infographic-2/.

McCullogh, Amy. "With the Raptors over Syria." *Air Force Magazine*, February 2016, 26–33.

McFarland, Stephen L. *America's Pursuit of Precision Bombing, 1910–1945*. Tuscaloosa, Ala.: University of Alabama Press, 1995.

McFarland, Stephen L., and Wesley Phillips Newton. *To Command the Sky: The Battle for Air Superiority over Germany, 1942–1944*. Washington, D.C.: Smithsonian Institution Press, 1991.

McNamara, Steve. "Assessing Airpower's Importance." *Armed Forces Journal International*, March 1997.

McPeak, Merrill A. "The Kosovo Result: The Facts Speak for Themselves." *Armed Forces Journal International*, September 1999.

———. *Selected Works: 1990–1994*. Maxwell Air Force Base, Ala.: Air University Press, 1995.

Mehta, Aaron. "Carter 'Prepared' to Change Rules of Engagement against ISIS." *Defense News*, November 19, 2015.

Meid, Pat, and James M. Yingling. *Operations in West Korea*. Vol. 5 of *U.S. Marine Operations in Korea, 1950–1953*. Washington, D.C.: Historical Branch, G-3, Headquarters, U.S. Marine Corps, 1972.

Meilinger, Phillip S. "Gradual Escalation: NATO's Kosovo Air Campaign, Though Decried as a Strategy, May Be the Future of War." *Armed Forces Journal International*, October 1999.

———. *10 Propositions Regarding Air Power*. Washington D.C.: Air Force History and Museums Program, 1995.

Mersky, Peter B. *U.S. Marine Corps Aviation*. Annapolis, Md.: Nautical & Aviation Publishing, 1983.

Mersky, Peter B., and Norman Polmar. *The Naval Air War in Vietnam*. Annapolis, Md.: Nautical & Aviation Publishing, 1981.

Mets, David R. *The Air Campaign*. Maxwell Air Force Base, Ala.: Air University Press, 1999.

———. *The Quest for a Surgical Strike*. Eglin Air Force Base, Fla.: Armament Division, 1987.

Meyers, Steven Lee. "Pentagon Said to Be Adding 300 Planes to Fight Serbs." *New York Times*, April 13, 1999.

Middleton, Drew. *Can America Win the Next War?* New York: Scribner's, 1975.

Mikesh, Robert C. *Flying Dragons: The South Vietnamese Air Force*. Atglen, Pa.: Schiffer, 2005.

Miller, Nathan. *The Naval Air War 1939–1945*. Annapolis, Md.: Naval Institute Press, 1991.

Miller, Ronald, and David Sawers. *The Technical Development of Modern Aviation*. New York: Praeger, 1968.

Minz, Alex. "The Military-Industrial Complex: The Israeli Case." *Journal of Strategic Studies* 6, no. 3 (September 1983): 103–27.

Modley, Rudolf, and Thomas J. Cawley, eds. *Aviation Facts and Figures, 1953*. Washington, D.C.: Lincoln Press, 1953.

Momyer, W. W. *Air Power in Three Wars: World War II, Korea, Vietnam*. Maxwell Air Force Base, Ala.: Air University Press, 1978.

Montross, Lynn, and Nicholas A. Canzona. *The Chosin Reservoir Campaign*, vol. 3 of *U.S. Marine Operations in Korea, 1950–1953*. Washington, D.C.: Historical Branch, G-3, Headquarters, U.S. Marine Corps, 1957.

Morgan, Adam. *Eating the Big Fish: How Challenger Brands Can Compete against Brand Leaders*, 2nd ed. Hoboken, N.J.: Wiley, 2009.

Morison, Samuel Eliot. *Coral Sea, Midway and Submarine Actions, May 1942–August 1942*. Boston: Little, Brown, 1955.

———. *Victory in the Pacific, 1945*. Boston: Little, Brown, 1960.

Morris, Benny. *The Birth of the Palestinian Refugee Problem*. Cambridge: Cambridge University Press, 1988.

———. *1948: A History of the First Arab-Israeli War*. New Haven, Conn.: Yale University Press, 2008.
———. *Righteous Victims: A History of the Zionist-Arab Conflict, 1881–1999*. New York: Knopf, 1999.
Moseley, T. Michael. "Coalition Forces Air Component Commander Briefing, April 5, 2003." Department of Defense news transcript, April 5, 2003.
Mowbray, James A. "Air Force Doctrine Problems: 1926–Present." *Airpower Journal* 9, no. 4 (Winter 1995).
Moyar, Mark. *Triumph Forsaken: The Vietnam War, 1954–1965*. Cambridge: Cambridge University Press, 2006.
Mueller, Karl P. "Airpower: Two Centennial Appraisals." *Strategic Studies Quarterly* 5, no. 4 (Winter 2011): 123–32.
———, ed. *Precision and Purpose: Airpower in the Libyan Civil War*. Santa Monica, Calif.: RAND, 2015.
———. "Sky King." *American Interest* 7, no. 3 (January–February 2012): 104–8.
Munro, Alan *Arab Storm: Politics and Diplomacy behind the Gulf War*. London: Tauris, 2006.
Murray, Williamson. *Strategy for Defeat: The Luftwaffe 1933–1945*. Maxwell Air Force Base, Ala.: Air University Press, 1983.
Murray, Williamson, and Robert H. Scales, *The Iraq War: A Military History*. Cambridge, Mass.: Harvard University Press, 2003.
Nakdimon, Shelomoh. *First Strike: The Exclusive Story of How Israel Foiled Iraq's Attempt to Get the Bomb*. New York: Summit Books, 1987.
Nalty, Bernard C. *The Air Force Role in Five Crises, 1958–1965: Lebanon, Taiwan, Congo, Cuba, Dominican Republic*. Washington, D.C.: USAF Historical Division Liaison Office, 1968.
———. *Air Power and the Fight for Khe Sanh*. Washington, D.C.: Office of Air Force History, 1986.
———. *Tactics and Techniques of Electronic Warfare*. Washington, D.C.: Office of Air Force History, 1977.
———, ed. *Winged Shield, Winged Sword: A History of the United States Air Force*, vol. 2: *1950–1997*. Washington, D.C.: Air Force History and Museums Program, 1997.
NATO. *Offensive Air Support*, ATP-27A. Brussels: NATO, 1975.
———. *Tactical Air Doctrine*. ATP-33. Brussels: NATO, 1976.
Naylor, Sean D. "Army Panels Warn of Technology Dependence." *Defense News*, August 31–September 1, 1998.
Nechushtan, Ido. *Flying High—The Israeli Air Force Missions and Challenges*. Tel Aviv: Ministry of Defense, 2011.
Neff, Donald. "Ike Forces Israel to End Occupation after Sinai Crisis." *Washington Report on Middle Eastern Affairs*, February–March 1996, 89–91.
———. "Israel Bombs Iraq's Osirak Nuclear Research Facility." *Washington Report on Middle Eastern Affairs*, June 1995, 81–82.

Newman, Rick, and Don Shepperd. *Bury Us Upside Down: The Misty Pilots and the Secret Battle for the Ho Chi Minh Trail*. Novato, Calif.: Presidio, 2006.

Nichols, John B., and Barrett Tillman. *On Yankee Station: The Naval Air War over Vietnam*. Annapolis, Md.: Naval Institute Press, 1987.

Nitze, Paul, Steven L. Rearden, and Ann M. Smith. *From Hiroshima to Glasnost: At the Center of Decision*. New York: Grove, 1989.

Nolan, Keith William. *Into Laos: The Story of Dewey Canyon II/Lam Son 719, Vietnam 1971*. New York: Dell, 1986.

Nordeen, Lon O. *Fighters over Israel*. New York: Orion Books, 1990.

Nordeen, Lon, and David Nicolle. *Phoenix over the Nile: A History of Egyptian Air Power 1932–1994*. Washington, D.C.: Smithsonian Institution Press, 1996.

Null, Gary. *Weapon of Denial: Air Power and the Battle for New Guinea*. Washington, D.C.: Air Force History and Museums Program, 1995.

Office of the Secretary of the Air Force. *The Air Force and U.S. National Security: Global Reach—Global Power*. Washington, D.C.: U.S. Department of the Air Force, 1991.

Olds, Robin. *Fighter Pilot: The Memoirs of Legendary Ace Robin Olds*. With Christina Olds and Ed Rasimus. New York: St. Martin's, 2010.

Olsen, John Andreas, ed. *Air Commanders*. Washington, D.C.: Potomac Books, 2012.

———, ed. *Airpower Reborn: The Strategic Concepts of John Warden and John Boyd*. Annapolis, Md.: Naval Institute Press, 2015.

———, ed. *Global Air Power*. Washington D.C.: Potomac Books, 2011.

———, ed. *A History of Air Warfare*. Washington D.C.: Potomac Books, 2010.

———. *John Warden and the Renaissance of American Air Power*. Washington, D.C.: Potomac Books, 2007.

Oren, Michael B. *Six Days of War: June 1967 and the Making of the Modern Middle East*. Oxford: Oxford University Press, 2002.

Orme, William A., and Greg Myre. "Ezer Weizman, Former President of Israel and Hero of 1967 War, Dies at 80." *New York Times*, April 25, 2005.

Owen, Robert C., ed. *Deliberate Force: A Case Study in Effective Air Campaigning*. Maxwell Air Force Base, Ala.: Air University Press, 1999.

Panetta, Leon. *Worthy Fights: A Memoir of Leadership in War and Peace*. With Jim Newton. New York: Penguin, 2014.

Pappé, Ilan. *The Ethnic Cleansing of Palestine*. Oxford: Oneworld, 2011.

Parker, Ned. "The Iraq We Left Behind: Welcome to the World's Next Failed State." *Foreign Affairs*, March–April 2012.

Parks, W. Hays. "Linebacker and the Law of War." *Air University Review* 34, no. 2 (January–February 1983): 2–30.

Perlez, Jane. "Holbrooke to Meet Milosevic in Final Peace Effort." *New York Times*, March 22, 1999.

———. "U.S. Option: Air Attacks May Prove Unpalatable." *New York Times*, March 23, 1999.

Peterson, Nolan. "Inside the U.S. Air War against ISIS." *Daily Signal*, September 28, 2015.

Pfeiffer, Jack B. *Official History of the Bay of Pigs Operation*. Vol. 1: *Air Operations, March 1960–April 1961*. McLean, Va.: Central Intelligence Agency, 1979.

———. *The Taylor Committee Investigation of the Bay of Pigs*. McLean, Va.: Central Intelligence Agency, 1984.

Phinney, Todd R. *Airpower versus Terrorism*. Maxwell Air Force Base, Ala.: Air University Press, 2007.

Pierce, Kenneth R. "The Battle of the Ia Drang Valley." *Military Review* 69, no. 1 (January 1989).

Podhoretz, Norman. *Why We Were in Vietnam*. New York: Simon and Schuster, 1983.

Pollack, Kenneth M. *Arabs at War: Military Effectiveness, 1948–1991*. Lincoln: University of Nebraska Press, Kindle eBook, 2002.

———. *The Threatening Storm: The United States and Iraq; The Crisis, the Strategy, and the Prospects after Saddam*. New York: Random House, 2002.

Polmar, Norman, and Edward J. Marolda. *Naval Air War: The Rolling Thunder Campaign*. Washington, D.C.: Naval History and Heritage Command, 2015.

Poole, Walter S. *Adapting to Flexible Response, 1960–1968*. Washington, D.C.: Office of the Secretary of Defense, 2013.

Porter, Melvin F. *The Siege at Plei Me*. K717.0413-1. Hickam Air Force Base, Hawaii: SEA Team, Project CHECO, February 24, 1966.

———. *Silver Bayonet*. K717.0413-2. Hickam Air Force Base, Hawaii: SEA Team, Project CHECO, February 28, 1966.

Powell, Colin L. *My American Journey*. With Joseph E. Persico. New York: Random House, 1995.

Putney, Diane T. *Airpower Advantage: Planning the Gulf War Air Campaign, 1989–1991*. Washington, D.C.: Air Force History and Museums Program, 1994.

Quintana, Elizabeth, and Jonathan Eyal, eds., *Inherently Unresolved: The Military Operation against ISIS*, RUSI Occasional Paper. London: Royal United Services Institute for Defence and Security Studies, October 2015.

Rearden, Steven L. *Council of War*. Washington, D.C.: National Defense University Press, 2012.

Remnick, David. "Going the Distance: On and Off the Road with Barack Obama." *New Yorker*, January 27, 2014.

Reynolds, Richard T. *Heart of the Storm: The Genesis of the Air Campaign against Iraq*. Maxwell Air Force Base, Ala.: Air University Press, 1995.

Rich, Ben R., and Leo Janos. *Skunkworks: A Personal Memoir of My Years at Lockheed*. New York: Little, Brown, 1994.

Richburg, Keith, and William Branigan. "Attacks Out of the Blue: U.S. Air Strikes on Taliban Hit Military Targets and Morale." *Washington Post*, November 18, 2001.

Richter, Paul. "B-2 Drops Its Bad PR in Air War." *Los Angeles Times*, July 8, 1999.

———. "U.S. Says Strikes Badly Disrupted Iraqi Regime." *Los Angeles Times*, January 9, 1999.
Ricks, Thomas E. *Fiasco: The American Military Adventure in Iraq.* New York: Penguin, 2006.
———. "Warplanes Begin Deploying to Gulf, Central Asia." *Washington Post*, September 20, 2001.
Ricks, Thomas E., and Vernon Loeb, "Initial Aim Is Hitting Taliban Defenses." *Washington Post*, October 8, 2001.
Ridgeway, Matthew B. *The Korean War.* Garden City, N.Y.: Doubleday, 1967.
Rochester, Stuart I., and Frederick T. Kiley, *Honor Bound.* Washington, D.C.: Office of the Secretary of Defense, 1998.
Rogers, Everett M. *Diffusion of Innovation*, 5th ed. New York: Free Press, 2003.
Romjue, John L. *From Active Defense to AirLand Battle: The Development of Army Doctrine, 1973–1982.* Fort Monroe, Va.: Historical Office, U.S. Army Training and Doctrine Command, 1984.
Rose, Gideon. "Tell Me How This One Ends." *Washington Post*, March 27, 2011.
Rowell, Ross E. "Aircraft in Bush Warfare." *Marine Corps Gazette* 14, no. 3 (September 1929).
Rowley, Ralph A. *The Air Force in Southeast Asia: FAC Operations, 1965–1970.* Washington, D.C.: Office of Air Force History, May 1975.
———. *Tactics and Techniques of Close Air Support Operations, 1961–1973.* Washington, D.C.: U.S. Air Force, February 1976.
———. *USAF FAC Operations in Southeast Asia, 1961–1965.* Washington, D.C.: U.S. Air Force, 1972.
Royal Australian Air Force, Air Power Development Centre. "The Air Power Manual." *Australian Air Publication AAP 1000-D* (September 2013).
Rubenstein, Murray, and Richard Goldman. *The Israeli Air Force Story.* London: Arms and Armour Press, 1979.
Rubin, Alissa J., Tim Arango, and Helene Cooper. "U.S. Jets and Drones Attack Militants in Iraq, Hoping to Stop Advance." *New York Times*, August 9, 2014.
Ruge, Friedrich. *Rommel in Normandy.* San Rafael, Calif.: Presidio, 1979.
Scales, Robert H., *Certain Victory: The U.S. Army in the Gulf War.* McLean, Va.: Brassey's, 1994.
Scarborough, Rowan. "Momentum for Troops Growing." *Washington Times*, April 5, 1999.
Schmitt, Eric, and Steven Lee Meyers. "NATO Said to Focus Raids on Serb Elite's Property." *New York Times*, April 19, 1999.
Schogol, Jeff. "U.S. Dropping More Bombs on Islamic State Than Ever Before." *Air Force Times*, November 25, 2015.
Schwarzkopf, H. Norman. *It Doesn't Take a Hero.* With Peter Petrie. New York: Bantam, 1992.

Secord, Richard. *Honored and Betrayed: Irangate, Covert Affairs, and the Secret War in Laos*. With Jay Wurts. New York: Wiley, 1992.

Shapira, Avraham. *The Seventh Day: Soldiers' Talk about the Six-Day War*. New York: Simon and Schuster, 1971.

Sharon, Assaf. "The Jewish Terrorists." *New York Review of Books*, September 24, 2015.

Sharp, Jeremy M. *U.S. Foreign Aid to Israel*. Washington, D.C.: Congressional Research Service, 2015.

Sharp, U. S. Grant. *Strategy for Defeat: Vietnam in Retrospect*. San Rafael, Calif.: Presidio, 1978.

Shear, Michael D. "U.S. Airstrikes on Militants in Iraq." *New York Times*, August 10, 2014.

Shultz, Richard H., Jr., and Robert L. Pfaltzgraff Jr., eds. *The Future of Air Power in the Aftermath of the Gulf War*. Maxwell Air Force Base, Ala.: Air University Press, July 1992.

Sieg, Kent, and David S. Patterson, eds. *Foreign Relations of the United States, 1964–1968*, vol. 5: *Vietnam 1967*. Washington, D.C.: Government Printing Office, 2002.

Singer, P. W., and August Cole. *Ghost Fleet: A Novel of the Next World War*. New York: Houghton Mifflin Harcourt, 2015.

Smith, Douglas V., ed. *One Hundred Years of U.S. Navy Air Power*. Annapolis, Md.: Naval Institute Press, 2010.

Smith, R. Jeffrey, and Molly Moore. "Plan for Kosovo Pullout Signed." *Washington Post*, June 10, 1999.

Sorley, Lewis. *A Better War: The Unexamined Victories and Final Tragedy of America's Last Years in Vietnam*. San Diego: Harcourt, 1999.

———. "Courage and Blood: South Vietnam's Repulse of the 1972 Easter Invasion." *Parameters* 29, no. 2 (Summer 1999): 38–56.

Staaveren, Jacob van. *Air Operations in the Taiwan Crisis of 1958*. Washington, D.C.: U.S. Air Force Historical Division Liaison Office, 1962.

———. *Gradual Failure: The Air War over North Vietnam, 1965–1966*. Washington, D.C.: Air Force History and Museums Program, 2002.

———. *Interdiction in Southern Laos, 1960–1968: The United States Air Force in Southeast Asia*. Washington, D.C.: Center for Air Force History, 1993.

Starr, Barbara. "Deny Flight Shootdown May Put USAF on the Offensive." *Jane's Defense Weekly*, June 24, 1995.

———. "NATO Strikes Strive to Stop Serb Shelling." *Jane's Defense Weekly*, September 9, 1995.

Starry, Donn A. "A Perspective on American Military Thought." *Military Review* 69, no. 7 (July 1989): 2–11.

Stein, David J. *The Development of NATO Tactical Air Doctrine*. R-3385-AF. Santa Monica, Calif.: RAND, 1987.

Stephens, Alan. *Going Solo: The Royal Australian Air Force, 1946-1971.* Canberra: Australian Government Publishing Service, 1995.

——, ed. *The War in the Air 1914-1994.* Fairbairn, Canberra: Air Power Studies Centre, 1994.

Stephens, Alan, and Stuart McKenzie. "Bolt from the Blue: The Ballistic and Cruise Missile Problem." Air Power Studies Centre Paper No. 20. Canberra: Air Power Studies Centre, 1994.

Stephens, Alan, and Brendan O'Loghlin, eds. *The Decisive Factor.* Canberra: Australian Government Publishing Service, 1990.

Stewart, James T., ed. *Airpower: The Decisive Force in Korea.* Princeton, N.J.: Van Nostrand, 1957.

Stout, Jay A. *Hammer from Above: Marine Air Combat over Iraq.* New York: Presidio, 2005.

Stumpf, Robert E. "Air War with Libya." U.S. Naval Institute *Proceedings* 112, no. 8 (August 1986).

Sullivan, William H. *Obbligato, 1939-79: Notes on a Foreign Service Career.* New York: Norton, 1984.

Summers, Harry G., Jr. *On Strategy: A Critical Analysis of the Vietnam War.* Novato, Calif.: Presidio, 1982.

Tal, David. "Symbol Not Substance? Israel's Campaign to Acquire Hawk Missiles, 1960-1962." *International History Review* 22, no. 2 (June 2000): 304-17.

Taw, Jennifer Morrison. *Operation Just Cause: Lessons for Operations Other Than War.* Santa Monica, Calif.: RAND, 1996.

Thatcher, Margaret. *The Downing Street Years.* London: HarperCollins, 1995.

Thiessen, Marc. "George W. Bush Was Right about Iraq Pullout." *Washington Post*, September 8, 2014.

Thompson, James Clay. *Rolling Thunder: Understanding Policy and Program Failure.* Chapel Hill: University of North Carolina Press, 1980.

Thompson, Warren. "Shooting Stars over Korea." *Airpower* 15, no. 2 (March 1985).

Thompson, Wayne. *To Hanoi and Back: The USAF and North Vietnam, 1966-1973.* Washington, D.C.: Smithsonian Institution Press, 2000.

Thompson, Wayne, and Bernard C. Nalty. *Within Limits: The U.S. Air Force and the Korean War.* Washington, D.C.: Air Force History and Museums Program, 1996.

Tilford, Earl H., Jr. *Setup: What the Air Force Did in Vietnam and Why?* Maxwell Air Force Base, Ala.: Air University Press, 1991.

Tillman, Barrett. *Whirlwind: The Air War against Japan, 1942-1945.* New York: Simon & Schuster, 2010.

Tín, Bùi. *Following Ho Chi Minh.* Translated by Judy Stowe and Do Van. Honolulu: University of Hawaii Press, 1995.

Tirpak, John. "Lessons from Libya." *Air Force Magazine*, December 2011, 34-38.

Tolson, John J. *Airmobility, 1961-1971.* Washington, D.C.: U.S. Army, 1973.

Trest, Warren A. *Khe Sanh.* K717.0413-35. Hickam Air Force Base, Hawaii: Directorate, Tactical Evaluation, CHECO Division, September 13, 1968.

Trotti, John. *Phantom over Vietnam.* Novato, Calif.: Presidio, 1984.

Tunner, William H., and Booton Herndon. *Over the Hump: The Story of General William H. Tunner—The Man Who Moved Anything Anywhere, Anytime.* New York: Duell, Sloan and Pearce, 1964.

UN Security Council. "Security Council Approves 'No-Fly Zone' over Libya, Authorizing All Necessary Measures to Protect Civilians, by a Vote of 10 in Favour with 5 Abstentions." SC/10200, 6498th Meeting [night]. New York: UN Department of Public Information, March 17, 2011.

UNESCO. *World Illiteracy at Mid-Century.* Switzerland: UNESCO, 1957. http://unesdoc.unesco.org/images/0000/000029/002930eo.pdf.

United Nations Environmental Programme. *Lebanon: Post-Conflict Environmental Assessment.* Nairobi, Kenya: UNEP, 2007.

United States Arms Control and Disarmament Agency. "World Military Expenditures and Arms Transfers 1972–1982." Washington, D.C., April 1984. http://www.state.gov/documents/organization/185658.pdf.

United States Marine Corps. *Small Wars Manual.* Washington, D.C.: Government Printing Office, 1940.

U.S. Air Force Historical Division (USAF HD). *United States Air Force Operations in the Korean Conflict, 25 June–1 November 1950.* Washington, D.C.: U.S. Air Force Historical Division, July 1, 1952.

U.S. Congress, Senate, Committee on Armed Services, Senate Preparedness Investigating Subcommittee. *Air War against North Vietnam,* 90th Cong., 1st sess. August 9–29, 1967.

U.S. Department of State. *The Department of State Bulletin* 68, no. 750 (January 8, 1973): 33–41.

U.S. War Department. *Final Report of Gen. John J. Pershing.* Washington, D.C.: Government Printing Office, 1919.

———. *FM 31-35: Air-Ground Operations.* Washington, D.C.: Government Printing Office, 1946.

———. *FM 100-20: Command and Employment of Air Power.* Washington, D.C.: Government Printing Office, 1943.

Varble, Derek. *The Suez Crisis 1956.* Oxford: Osprey Publishing, 2003.

Venkus, Robert E. *Raid on Qaddafi: The Story of History's Longest Fighter Mission.* New York: St. Martin's, 1992.

Vick, Alan. *Proclaiming Airpower: Air Force Narratives and American Public Opinion from 1917 to 2014.* Santa Monica, Calif.: RAND, 2015.

———. *Snakes in the Eagle's Nest: A History of Ground Attacks on Air Bases.* Santa Monica, Calif.: RAND, 1995.

Vogel, Steve, and Walter Pincus. "Al-Qaeda Complex Destroyed; Search Widens." *Washington Post,* January 15, 2002.

Vriesenga, Michael P. *From the Line in the Sand.* Maxwell Air Force Base, Ala.: Air University Press, March 1994.

Walter, William. "Operation Acid Gambit: The Rescue of Kurt Muse from Modelo Prison." *Air Commando Journal* 3, no. 3 (Fall 2014).

Warden, John A., III. *The Air Campaign: Planning for Combat.* Washington, D.C.: National Defense University Press, 1988.

Warnock, A. Timothy, ed. *Short of War: Major USAF Contingency Operations, 1947–1997.* Maxwell Air Force Base, Ala.: Air University Press / Air Force Historical Research Agency, 2000.

Watts, Barry D., and Williamson Murray. *Operations*, part 1, vol. 2, *Gulf War Air Power Survey.* Washington, D.C.: Government Printing Office, 1993.

Weinberger, Caspar W. *Fighting for Peace: 7 Critical Years in the Pentagon.* New York: Warner, 1990.

Weiner, Tim. "From President, Victory Speech and a Warning." *New York Times*, June 11, 1999.

Werrell, Kenneth P. *Archie, Flak, AAA, and SAM.* Maxwell Air Force Base, Ala.: Air University Press, 1988.

———. "Linebacker II: The Decisive Use of Air Power?" *Air University Review* 38, no. 2 (January–March 1987): 58–61.

———. *Sabres over MiG Alley: The F-86 and the Battle for Air Superiority in Korea.* Annapolis, Md.: Naval Institute Press, 2005.

Whitcomb, Darrel. "Farm Gate." *Air Force Magazine* 88, no. 12 (December 2005): 84–87.

———. *On a Steel Horse I Ride.* Maxwell Air Force Base, Ala.: Air University Press and the Air Force Research Institute, 2012.

Willmott, H. P., and Michael B. Barrett. *Clausewitz Reconsidered.* Santa Barbara, Calif.: Greenwood Publishing, 2010.

Winnefeld, James A., and Dana J. Johnson. *Joint Air Operations: Pursuit of Unity in Command and Control, 1942–1991.* Annapolis, Md.: Naval Institute Press and RAND, 1993.

The Winograd Commission Final Report, January 2008. http://www.jewishvirtual library.org/jsource/History/winograd.html.

Winograd Commission Report on the Lebanon Campaign, partial report, April 30, 2007. http://www.jewishvirtuallibrary.org/jsource/History/winograd.html.

Wise, Harold Lee. *Inside the Danger Zone: The U.S. Military in the Persian Gulf, 1987–1988.* Annapolis, Md.: Naval Institute Press, 2007.

Wolfe, Richard I., ed. *The United States Air Force Basic Documents on Roles and Missions.* Washington, D.C.: Office of Air Force History, 1987.

Wolk, Herman S. *Cataclysm: General Hap Arnold and the Defeat of Japan.* Denton: University of North Texas Press, 2010.

Woods, Kevin M., with Michael R. Pease, Mark E. Stout, Williamson Murray, and James G. Lacey. *Iraqi Perspectives Project: A View of Operation Iraqi*

Freedom from Saddam's Senior Leadership. Norfolk, Va.: Joint Center for Operational Analysis, U.S. Joint Forces Command, 2006.

Woodward, Bob. *The Commanders*. New York: Simon and Schuster, 1991.

——. *State of Denial*. New York: Simon & Schuster, 2006.

Woodward, Margaret. "Operation Odyssey Dawn—United States." *Air Power and Coercive Diplomacy*. Proceedings of the 2012 RAAF Air Power Conference, Canberra, Australia. National Convention Centre, May 10–11, 2012.

Wright, Monte D. *Most Probable Position: A History of Aerial Navigation to 1941*. Lawrence: University Press of Kansas, 1972.

Wright, Robin. "Endgame in Iraq Still Elusive Despite Strikes." *Los Angeles Times*, December 21, 1998.

——. "The War against ISIS, by the Numbers." *Wall Street Journal*, December 30, 2014.

Wright, Robin, and John Daniszewski. "Air Assault on Iraq Called Off after 4 Nights." *Los Angeles Times*, December 20, 1998.

Y'Blood, William T. *Down in the Weeds: Close Air Support in Korea*. Washington, D.C.: Air Force History and Museums Program, 2002.

Yonay, Ehud. *No Margin for Error*. New York: Pantheon, 1993.

Young, Stephen. "How North Vietnam Won the War." *Wall Street Journal*, August 3, 1995.

Zampaglione, Arturo. "Italy Blocks Stealth Fighters." *La Repubblica*, September 12, 1995.

Zenko, Micah. "Is Operation Desert Fox a Useful Comparison for Bombing Iran?" Council on Foreign Relations (blog), April 15, 2015. http://blogs.cfr.org/zenko/2015/04/15/is-operation-desert-fox-a-useful-comparison-for-bombing-iran/.

Zhang, Xiaoming. *Deng Xiaoping's Long War: The Military Conflict between China and Vietnam, 1979–1991*. Chapel Hill: University of North Carolina Press, 2015.

——. *Red Wings over the Yalu: China, the Soviet Union, and the Air War in Korea*. College Station: Texas A&M University Press, 2002.

Editor and Authors

JOHN ANDREAS OLSEN is a colonel in the Royal Norwegian Air Force currently assigned to NATO Headquarters in Brussels, a professor at the Norwegian Institute for Defence Studies, a non-resident senior fellow of the Mitchell Institute for Aerospace Studies, a fellow of the Royal Swedish Academy of War Sciences and a member of the RUSI Journal editorial board. His previous assignments include tours as director of security analyses in the Norwegian Ministry of Defence; deputy commander and chief of the North Atlantic Treaty Organization (NATO) Advisory Team at NATO Headquarters, Sarajevo; dean of the Norwegian Defence University College; and head of its division for strategic studies. Olsen is a graduate of the German Command and Staff College and has served both as liaison officer to the German Operational Command in Potsdam and as military assistant to the Norwegian Embassy in Berlin. He has a doctorate in history and international relations from De Montfort University, a master's degree in contemporary literature from the University of Warwick, and a master's degree in English from the University of Trondheim. Professor Olsen's books on airpower appear on the professional reading lists of the Royal Air Force, Royal Australian Air Force, Royal Netherlands Air Force, Royal Norwegian Air Force and the U.S. Air Force, and include *Strategic Air Power in Desert Storm* (Frank Cass, 2003), *John Warden and the Renaissance of American Air Power* (Potomac Books, 2007), *A History of Air Warfare* (Potomac Books, 2010), *Global Air Power* (Potomac Books, 2011), *Air Commanders* (Potomac Books, 2012), *Destination NATO: Defence Reform in Bosnia and Herzegovina, 2003–13* (with Rohan Maxwell, Routledge Journals, 2013), *European Air Power: Challenges and Opportunities* (Potomac Books, 2014), and *Airpower Reborn: The Strategic Concepts of John Warden and John Boyd* (Naval Institute Press, 2015).

RICHARD P. HALLION received a Ph.D. in history from the University of Maryland and completed postgraduate programs at the Federal Executive Institute and Harvard University's John F. Kennedy School of Government. He has been a founding curator at the Smithsonian Institution's National Air and Space Museum; a historian with the National Aeronautics and Space Administration and the U.S. Air Force; the Harold Keith Johnson Chair of Military History at the U.S. Army War College; Charles Lindbergh Visiting Professor at the National Air and Space Museum; a senior issues and policy analyst for the secretary of the Air Force; historian of the U.S. Air Force; a senior advisor for Air and Space Issues for the Air Force's Directorate for Security, Counterintelligence, and Special Programs; a special advisor for aerospace technology for the Air Force chief scientist; a senior advisor to the Science and Technology Policy Institute of the Institute for Defense Analyses; a Verville Fellow and research associate in aeronautics for the National Air and Space Museum; and a trustee of Florida Polytechnic University. He is a Fellow of the American Institute of Aeronautics and Astronautics, the Royal Aeronautical Society, and the Royal Historical Society, and he publishes and lectures extensively on aerospace issues. Dr. Hallion has written several books, including *Rise of the Fighter Aircraft, 1914-1918* (Nautical & Aviation Pub., 1984), *Storm over Iraq: Air Power and the Gulf War* (Smithsonian Institution Press, 1992), and *Strike from the Sky: The History of the Battlefield Air Attack, 1911-1945* (University of Alabama Press, 1998).

BENJAMIN S. LAMBETH is a nonresident Senior Fellow with the Center for Strategic and Budgetary Assessments. He assumed this position in 2011 after thirty-seven years as a senior research associate at the RAND Corporation. His areas of professional interest include strategy, defense planning, force development, air campaign assessment, and air and space doctrine, operations, and training. An internationally recognized expert on military aviation and air warfare, he has conducted research and lectured and written widely on these subjects. A civil-rated pilot, he has flown or flown in more than forty different fighter, attack, and jet trainer aircraft types with the U.S. Air Force, Navy, and Marine Corps as well as with eight foreign air forces. In December 1989 he became the first U.S. citizen to fly the Soviet MiG-29 fighter and the first Westerner invited to fly a combat aircraft of any type inside Soviet airspace since the end of World War II. In 2008 Secretary of Defense Robert Gates appointed him to serve as a member of Air University's Board of Visitors. He also serves on the editorial advisory boards of *Air and Space Power Journal* and *Strategic Studies Quarterly*. His publications include *The Transformation of American Air Power* (Cornell University Press, 2000), *NATO's Air War for Kosovo* (RAND, 2001), *Mastering the Ultimate High Ground: Next Steps in the Military Uses of Space* (RAND, 2003), *Air Power against Terror: America's Conduct of Operation Enduring Freedom* (RAND, 2005), *Air Operations in Israel's War against Hezbollah* (RAND, 2011), and *The Unseen War: Allied Air Power and the Takedown of Saddam Hussein* (Naval Institute Press, 2013).

RAPHAEL RUDNIK is a lieutenant colonel (res.) in the Israel Defense Forces and holds a Ph.D. in international relations from the Hebrew University of Jerusalem. His thesis focuses on the paradoxes of the asymmetrical armed conflicts between state and nonstate entities in the twenty-first century. He has served as a senior research fellow at the Dado Center for Interdisciplinary Military Studies in the Israel Defense Forces. He is currently visiting fellow at the Fisher Institute for Air and Space Strategic Studies and a research coordinator at the Shasha

Center for Strategic Studies at the Hebrew University of Jerusalem. Dr. Rudnik has vast military experience as a reconnaissance commander and as a strategic and operational planner at the Israel Defense Forces' Operations Directorate. He teaches strategy and operational art courses at the Israel Defense Forces. His areas of professional interest and writing include world politics, international and national security, military history, strategic and operational planning, international law, and Middle Eastern studies. His latest articles include "The Road for Legitimacy" (2013), "The Evolution of Military Operations" (2014), and "The War between Israel and the Jihad" (2015), all in Hebrew.

EPHRAIM SEGOLI is a brigadier general (res.) in the Israeli Air Force. He joined the Israel Defense Forces in 1970, served as a helicopter pilot for twenty-six years, and participated in two wars and numerous operational missions. His last active duty position (1992-95) was as commander of one of the Israeli Air Force's largest bases. Upon retiring from active service Segoli was invited by the U.S. Air University to serve as a research fellow at its School of Advanced Airpower Studies. After returning to Israel he joined a Ministry of Defense research institute that develops concepts and methodologies for operational and systemic thinking, and worked there until 2012. Segoli wrote scenarios for various experiments and war games and facilitated groups and workshops. In 2006 Segoli joined the Fisher Institute for Air and Space Strategic Studies, heading the Center for Air Power and Asymmetric Conflict. This center organizes the annual national defense conferences that discuss various airpower topics and concepts, and also conducts research. Segoli remains an active reservist, serving as an instructor in Israel Defense Forces senior schools. He holds degrees in Israeli studies and political science from the Bar-Ilan University. He also attended a squadron commander course in 1982 and a brigade commander course in 1991.

ALAN STEPHENS is a Visiting Fellow at the University of New South Wales in Canberra, Australia, and a Fellow of the Sir Richard Williams Foundation. Previously he has been a senior lecturer at University of New South Wales, an advisor on foreign affairs and defense in the Australian Federal Parliament, and a pilot in the Royal Australian Air Force, where his experience included a tour in Vietnam and command of an operational squadron. Dr. Stephens has lectured and published extensively. His books include *Making Sense of War: Strategy for the 21st Century* (Cambridge University Press, 2006), and *A Centenary History of the Royal Australian Air Force* (Oxford University Press, 2006); he also edited *The War in the Air, 1914-1994* (Air University Press, 2012). He has contributed chapters on Gen. George Kenney, the Korean War, Asian-Pacific airpower, and fifth-generation strategy to John Andreas Olsen's series of airpower books. His work has been translated into some twenty languages. In 2008 Dr. Stephens was made a member of the Order of Australia for his contribution to military history.

JOHN A. WARDEN III is an executive, strategist, planner, author, and motivational speaker whose work has had a worldwide impact in business, in the military, in government, and in education. After earning his fighter wings in 1966, he flew 250 combat missions in Vietnam. Warden held several staff and command positions, including commander of the 36th Tactical Fighter Wing at Bitburg, Germany (1986-87). While in charge of the Warfighting Concepts Division at the Pentagon he developed the "Instant Thunder" plan, which became the foundation for the Operation Desert Storm air campaign. Warden next served as the special assistant to the vice president of the United States and then as commandant of the U.S. Air Force Command and Staff College (1992-95). Colonel Warden received a bachelor's degree in national security affairs from the U.S. Air Force Academy in 1965 and a master's degree in political science from Texas Tech University in 1975. While attending the National War College (1985-86) he wrote the seminal work on modern airpower theory, *The Air Campaign* (National Defense University Press, 1988), translated into at least seven languages. Warden has published several articles, including "The Enemy as a System" (1995) and is the coauthor (with Leland A. Russell) of *Winning in Fast Time* (Venturist, 2002). He is the chairman and president of Venturist, Inc., a company he founded after leaving the Air Force. Venturist, using its Prometheus strategy process based on the concepts behind the first Gulf War, works with companies that range from very large enterprises such as Texas Instruments and McDonald's to small start-ups to help them align their resources to achieve real strategic impact.

Index

Names beginning with al and al- are alphabetized under the main element of the name. For example, al-Qaeda is alphabetized under Q.

Abbas, Mahmoud, 314
Abu Nidal terrorists, 71
Accountability, Operation (1993): concept and execution, 290–91; observations, 291–93; overview, 8–9; strategic context, 288–90
aerial refueling, 41, 94–95, 176–77, 265
aerospace industry: Egyptian, 240, 247; Israeli, 228–29, 238–39, 250, 272
aerospace technology: Desert Storm and, 93, 95; revolution in, 82, 119n265. *See also* military aerospace in U.S.; technology
Afghan Northern Alliance ground forces, 154, 155, 156
Afghanistan: Enduring Freedom and, 6, 124, 151–61; military campaigns (early twenty-first century), 298
Ahtisaari, Martti, 147
The Air Campaign (Warden), 69
Air Corps Tactical School, Maxwell Field, 16
air sanctuaries, Korean War, 34
air superiority: Korean War and, 32–34; military success and, 365–66
air supremacy: military success and, 365–66; Normandy invasion and, 20
air tasking order (ATO): First Gulf War, 87, 94; Navy and, 123n328
airborne warning and control system (AWACS): First Gulf War and, 84, 95; Panama intervention and, 80
Airbus, transport aircraft and, 25
aircraft: B-1 bomber, 138; B-2 stealth bomber, 149; B-52s, 56, 63, 64, 65–66, 149; combat vulnerabilities, Vietnam and, 70, 117n223; F-22 stealth fighters, 188, 213n159; F-51 Mustangs, Korean War and, 28; F-80 Shooting Star squadron, Korean War and, 28; F-86A Sabre jets, Korean War and, 33; long-range bombers, 17, 19–20, 28, 29, 103n35, 139–40; technology innovations vs., 352; World War II and development of, 15
aircraft carriers: Enduring Freedom, 152–53; Korean War, 42; World War II, 16, 19
Air-Land Forces Application, 69
airlift: evacuation from Panama, 78; in Howard AFB, Panama, 80–81. *See also* Berlin Airlift
Airlift Task Force, Berlin blockade and, 23
Air-Naval Gunfire Liaison Companies, Korean War and, 30
airpower: biases over, Desert Storm and, 96; COIN fighting in Iraq and Afghanistan and, 204n3; economics of, 274–75, 284n132; embedded journalists and, 163; FM 100-20 on landpower and, 18, 19, 29; future of, 10; ground forces reversed roles with, 199–201; ground troops, campaign goals and, 196–97; high-technology combat and, 201–2; as instrument of war, 361; land surface operations vs., 343–44; land-force availability and, 197–98; linking policy and, 345–48; operational and strategic relevance and, 198–99; operations, planning and executing, 348–50; surface power concept and characteristics vs., 287; tomorrow's wars and, 194–95; Trenchard's model of, 219; triumphalism, 367
airpower in action: American, NATO, and Israeli, 3–4; book synopsis, 4–10; as mode of inquiry, 2–3; overview, 1; prospects, 10
airpower profession: characteristics, 354–58; conclusion, 362–63; creativity in, 358; developing and maintaining tactical and strategic proficiency, 353; education for, 360–62; knowledge,

397

354–56; leadership in, 356–58; next fifty years, 358–60; overview, 342; reflections on, 9–10; securing support and funding, 352–53; special roles for, 345–53
Albright, Madeleine, 137, 144, 207n47
Alexander, Minter, 87
Allied Force, Operation: airpower's accomplishments, 148–50; assessing, 150–51; bombing intensifies, 147–48; execution problems, 208n67; halting start, 143–46; overview, 143; against Serbia, 6, 124
all-weather operations, Berlin blockade and, 23
Almond, Edward "Ned," 27
Alvarez, Everett, Jr., 50
Amer, Abdel Hakim, 246
America, 71, 73, 133
American and NATO airpower: airpower in tomorrow's wars and, 194–95; Allied Force, 143–51; deficient strategy and, 202–4; Deliberate Force, 130–34; Deny Flight, 127–29; Desert Fox, 134–43; Enduring Freedom, 151–61; ground forces reversed roles with, 199–201; ground troops, campaign goals and, 196–97; high-technology combat and, 201–2, 215–16n193; Inherent Resolve, 180–94; Iraqi Freedom, 161–70; land-force availability and, 197–98; Odyssey Dawn, 170–80; operational and strategic relevance and, 198–99; overview, 124–27, 204n1–2; seven lessons, 194–204, 215n180; Unified Protector, 170–80. *See also* NATO airpower; United States
Anaconda, Operation, 156–58
Anglo-American warfare, World War II and, 20
antiaircraft guns: Korean War after Sept. 1951 and, 35–36; Rolling Thunder and, 57
antiballistic missile defense, Desert Storm and, 95, 97
antiradiation ordnance, First Lebanon War and, 271
antiwar partisans. *See* peace activists
Arab League, 170–71
Arab Revolt (1916), 218

Arab-Israeli Wars: conclusion, 276–77; First, 218–24; First Lebanon War, 269–76; October War, 253–63; overview, 7–8, 217–18; Six-Day, 235–45; Suez, 225–35; al-Tuwaitha Raid, 263–69; War of Attrition, 245–52. *See also* asymmetric conflicts
Arkin, William, 139
Army Air Corps (Forces), 15, 17, 18, 21, 22–23
Arnold, H. H., 270
Arrow, Operation, 147
Arthur, Stanley, 86
Arzav, Operation, 272–74, 276
al-Assad, Bashir, 183, 193, 300
al-Assad, Hafez: death of, 300; First Lebanon War and, 272; October War and, 253, 254, 257, 258, 261; RAF training and, 241; SyAAF airpower doctrine and, 271
asymmetric conflicts: Cast Lead (2008–9), 314–20; concluding thoughts, 333–36; Days of Return (2004), 302–5; developments (2000–2004), 298–302; from First Lebanon war to, 285–88; Grapes of Wrath (1996), 293–98; IFA and, overview, 285; Operation Accountability (1993), 288–93; Pillar of Defense (2012), 321–24; Protective Edge (2014), 325–33; Second Lebanon War (2006), 305–14. *See also* Arab-Israeli Wars; Israeli Air Force
Atef, Mohammed, 154
atomic war, USAF preparation for, 42–43
Attain Document, Operation, 71–72
Austin, Lloyd, 182
Aziz, Tariq, 135

Baghdad, Iraq, 85, 89, 96, 136–37
Bailey, Lawrence R., 108n95
Baker, James, III, 141
Baldwin, Hanson, 31
Balfour, Arthur, 218
Balfour Declaration, 219, 278n2
Ball, George, 51, 53, 68
ballistic missiles, Iraq's, 85
Bar Lev Line, Israel's, 249, 254, 258
Barrel Roll program, from North Vietnam to Laos, 51–52
Bates, Lyndsi, 138
Battalion 2000, Panama, 78

Index

battle damage assessment (BDA): former Yugoslavia, 132; Iraqi Freedom, 167. *See also* body counts; casualties in action
battlefield air interdiction: erosion of basic skills after World War II and, 30; in Korean War, 27–29, 35–36, 38
Bay of Pigs crisis (1961), 43, 108n94
BDM Corporation, 55
Begin, Menachem, 264, 265
Ben Eliyahu, Eitan, 298–99
Benghazi, Libya: American diplomatic compound assault, 178–79; Arab Spring in, 170; targets, 73–74
Ben-Gurion, David, 220, 228, 234, 238
Berger, Samuel "Sandy," 142
Berlin: LaBelle discotheque bombing in, 72
Berlin Airlift: as coordinated response, 22–24; as crisis response, 239–34; observations, lessons, and reflections, 24–25
best practices, operational history and, 2
Betts, Richard, 269
Bien Hoa airbase, Vietnam, 47, 49, 51
bin Laden, Osama, 152, 155, 162
Bismarck Sea, Battle of the (1943), 18
Black September terrorist movement, 252
Blade Jewel, Operation, 78
Blue Spoon campaign, Panama, 79–80, 118n251
Bodinger, Herzl, 294–95
body counts: Vietnam War, 58, 61, 113n182. *See also* battle damage assessment; casualties in action
Boeing, 25
Boomer, Walt, 86
Bowie, Christopher, 82–83
Boxer, 28, 39
Brezhnev, Leonid, 240
Britain, 75, 229–33. *See also* NATO airpower; Royal Air Force
Britain, Battle of (1940), 17, 21
Broughton, Jacksel "Jack," 67
Brown, Harold, 53
Bùi Tín, 56–57, 64, 115n209
Bundy, McGeorge, 44, 51, 55–56
Bundy, William, 51, 53
Bush, George H. W., and administration: on airpower in Desert Storm, 93; Desert Shield and, 88; Desert Storm and, 89; Hussein's invasion of Kuwait and, 85; Noriega and, 78; Panama intervention and, 79, 80
Bush, George W., and administration: Desert Fox and, 142; Enduring Freedom and, 152; on Iraq withdrawal, 181; Iraqi Freedom and, 162, 166, 168, 169–70; troop surge in Iraq and, 126, 183

Cactus Air Force, Pacific Theater, World War II, 18
Cambodia, 45, 63. *See also* Southeast Asia
campaign, DoD definition of, 191–92
Cannon, John K., 23
Carl Vinson, 152, 153
Carter, Jimmy, 71
Cast Lead, Operation (2008–9): concept and execution, 315–20; Grapes of Wrath and, 305; observations, 320; overview, 8–9; strategic context, 314–15
Castro, Fidel, 43
casualties in action: airpower and, 353. *See also* battle damage assessment; body counts
Central Intelligence Agency (CIA), 43, 45, 47, 54–56
Chad, 71, 117n226
Charles de Gaulle (France), 173
chemical weapons, 85
Cheney, Richard, 79, 85, 88, 89, 97
Chernomyrdin, Viktor, 147
Cherokee strikes, in Korean War, 37
China, 195, 202, 365
China's People's Liberation Army, 26, 32, 37
Christian Phalangist militia, 275
Chu Lai, Vietnam, Viet Cong attacks on, 61
civil air transport, U.S. (1919–33), 14–15
Clark, J. J., 37
Clark, Mark, 34, 36, 38
Clark, Wesley, 144–45, 196
Clausewitz, Carl von, 333, 342, 343, 363
Clinton, Bill, and administration: Allied Force and, 144–45, 148; on Desert Fox, 137, 138, 139; Desert Fox and, 140–42, 206n40; Vietnam lessons and, 129
Clinton, Hillary, 179
Clodfelter, Mark, 55

close-air support (CAS): Bosnian Serbs and, 127; emergency, Anaconda and, 157–58; erosion of basic skills after World War II and, 30; Iraqi Freedom and, 167; in Korean War, 27–29, 35, 38; Push CAS, Iraqi armored advance and, 84
CNN. *See* journalists
Cohen, Eliot A., 2, 119n265
Cohen, William, 140, 144, 150
combat search and rescue (CSAR), helicopters in Vietnam and, 59
Combined Airlift Task Force, Berlin blockade and, 24
command and control: Arab, 243; Bay of Pigs, 43; Desert Fox, 136, 137; Hezbollah, 290, 292, 308–9; Iraqi, 88, 97, 167; Israeli Air Force, 224; Korean War, 27–28, 40; Rolling Thunder, 53–54; in Sicily, World War II, 19; Syrian, 273, 276; Vietnam in-country war, 59–60; Vietnam War, 67, 68–69, 100
communication procedures: Korean War and, 30; over Vietnam and Laos, 49
Composite Air Strike Forces, USAF, 44
Coningham, Arthur, 59
containment, enemy's centers of gravity and, 347
contextualization, case studies and, 3
Coral Sea, 71, 73, 74
Cordesman, Anthony, 142, 163, 185, 189, 193–94
Corley, John D. W., 209n84
counterinsurgency (COIN): post–Desert Storm, 125, 204n3; warfare, USAF and, 44
counterterrorist operations, post–Desert Storm, 125
creativity: in airpower profession, 358; in U.S. and Israel, 366
Creech, Wilbur, 83
Crist, George, 83
Cuban missile crisis (1962), 44
Curtiss, Glenn, 13

Daalder, Ivo, 178
Daniel Guggenheim Fund for the Promotion of Aeronautics (1926–30), 14
Dayan, Moshe: on Egypt's soldiers vs. officers, 255; October War and, 255;

Six-Day War and, 236, 237, 244, 245; Suez War and, 230–31
Days of Return, Operation (2004): concept and execution, 303–4; observations, 304–5; overview, 8–9; strategic context, 302–3
Dayton Peace Accords (1995), 134
de Gaulle, Charles, 248
Defensive Shield, Operation (2002), 301, 337n4
degrading capabilities: as Desert Fox strategy in Iraq, 137, 138–39; as Inherent Resolve strategy for ISIS, 184–85
Deliberate Force, Operation: achievements, 133–34; in Bosnia and Herzegovina, 6; combat highlights, 130–32; overview, 130, 205n9; precision air attacks, 132–33; against Serbia, 124
DeMarco, Anthony R., 113n182
Dempsey, Martin, 186
Deny Flight, Operation: Allied Force and, 143; limited objectives of, 6, 125; overview, 127–28; predictability and, 128–29; same mistakes after, 126
Deptula, David, 82–83, 87, 193
DePuy, William E., 63, 69, 114n189
Desert Fox, Operation: final countdown, 135; limited objectives of, 6; mission results, 138–41; overview, 134–35; strategic context, 141–42; strike operations, 136–38
Desert Shield, Operation: crises leading to, 85–86; protecting Saudi Arabia, building forces, and campaign planning, 86–89; single air commander for, 87–88
Desert Storm, Operation: modern air power and, 204n1; precision air attacks during, 6; single air commander for, 94; as twentieth-century airpower, 89–92; Vietnam memories and, 67
Desert Viper, 135, 140
Desert Viper Plus, 135
deterrence, enemy's centers of gravity and, 347
Dewey Canyon II/Lam Son 719, Operation, into Laos, 48
Dichter, Avi, 305
Diệm, Ngô Đình, 49, 50
Dignity Battalions, Panama, 78

disruptiveness of airpower, 344, 350–52
Dixon, Robert, 69
doctrinal principles: airpower forces and, 21–22; assumptions, World War II and, 17–19; Vietnam War and, 69
domino theory, 46, 108n94
Doolittle, James, 19
Doolittle raid (1942), 17
Douhet, Giulio, 236, 237–38, 243
Drea, Edward, 55–56
Dugan, Michael, 87

economic theory and practice, knowledge of, 354, 355
Eden, Anthony, 232, 233, 234
Egypt: Air Defense Command, 246, 247; aircraft engineering (early 1950s) in, 225–26; First Arab-Israeli War and, 220; Muslim Brotherhood's rise in, 321; oriental despotism in, 221–22; Ottoman Empire, Britain and, 219; Protective Edge and, 326, 329, 331; Russian military aid for, 239–40; Six-Day War and, 235; social change in, 255–56; treaty with Israel (1979), 263. *See also* Arab-Israeli Wars
Egyptian Air Academy, 226
Egyptian Air Force (EAF): learning from failure, 246–47; maintenance and leadership issues, 240–41; October War and, 260; overview, 226–27; Six-Day War and, 243–44; Suez War and, 232–33; War of Attrition and, 251–52
8th Air Force, World War II and, 19
Eisenhower, Dwight: Bay of Pigs crisis and, 43; on domino theory, 46, 108n94; New Look defense doctrine, 42; Soviet attack on combat air patrol near Vladivostok and, 34; on Suez War, 233–34
Eisenhower and its battle group, 85
Eitan, Rafael, 267, 270, 276
Eizenberg, Eyal, 305
El Dorado Canyon, Operation: Attain Document and, 71–72; as limited joint airpower, 6, 73–76; observations, lessons, and reflections, 76–77, 118n246
Elaborate Maze, 79, 118n251
Ellis, James, 150, 203

Elron Electronic Industries (Elbit Systems), 239
Enduring Freedom, Operation: Anaconda imbroglio, 156–58; on balance, 160–61; distinctive aspects, 158–59; execution problems, 159–60; as new kind of air war, 153–56, 208n77; Sept. 11 terrorist attacks and, 151–52; shaping a plan for, 152–53; against Taliban in Afghanistan, 6, 124
enemy's centers of gravity, airpower's direct strategic effect on, 347–48
Enterprise, 136, 152, 153
Eshel, Amir: on high importance targets, 334; on IAF and military decisions, 299; on "opening strike" idea, 341n79; Pillar of Defense and, 324; Protective Edge and, 332–33; on systemic change and technology, 303
Eshkol, Levi, 249
Essex-class carriers, World War II and, 19
evacuation airlift, Panama, 78
exit points, airpower professionals on, 348

Fahd, King of Saudi Arabia, 85–86
Far East Air Forces (FEAF): air pressure vs. interdiction by, 36–38; air sanctuaries in Korean War and, 34; interdiction after Sept. 1951, 35–36; Korean War and, 27, 29
Farm Gate, Vietnam, 49–50, 60
Fatah party, Hamas and, 314
Felt, Harry D., 50, 60
Fick, Nathaniel, 200
15th Air Force, World War II and, 19
5th Air Force, Korean War and, 27, 30–31, 36
First Arab-Israeli War (1948–49): commentary, 224; Israel and Trenchard model, 219–21; modern vs. archaic methods, 222–24; oriental despotism model, 221–22; overview, 7–8, 218–19
1st Cavalry Division (Air Mobile), 61
First Gulf War: crises leading to, 82–86; Desert Shield, 86–89; Desert Storm, 89–92; observations, lessons, and reflections, 92–98
First Lebanon War (1982): Arnold Doctrine and, 270–72; commentary, 276; "dislodging" the problem, 269–70; dynamic vs. inflexible, 272–74;

economics of airpower, 274–75; Hezbollah formation and, 276; overview, 7–8; Syria and indirect conflict against Israel due to, 286–87. *See also* Second Lebanon War
First Marine Air Wing, Korean War and, 27, 31
1st Special Operations Wing (SOW), Panama intervention and, 80, 81
Flaming Dart I and II, 52
Fleet Air Wings, Korean War and, 27
Flournoy, Michèle, 191
FM 100-20 (Command and Employment of Air Power), 18, 19
Fogleman, Ronald, 133–34
Ford, Gerald, 115n209
Foreign Affairs, 179
Forgan, David W., 74
Forrestal, 42
Forrestal, James, 22
forward air controllers (FACs): Korean War and, 30; in Laos, 46; Vietnam in-country war and, 59–61
Fox News. *See* journalists
France: arms embargo, Israel and, 248; El Dorado Canyon and, 74, 76; Iraqi Air Force and, 266; no-fly zone over Libya and, 170–71; Suez War and, 229–33
Franks, Tommy, 162–63, 165, 166, 167
friendlies, in Panama, dangers for, 81–82
future, postwar, establishing picture of, 345–47

Gabriel, Charles, 69
Gaddafi, Muammar: Attain Document and, 71–72; El Dorado Canyon and, 73–74, 75; Libyan resistance and, 170; NATO's war against, 6; Odyssey Dawn and, 171–73; Unified Protector against, 126–27, 173–74. *See also* Libya
Gates, Robert, 171, 183
Gaza Strip: armed Palestinian struggle in, 301; Hamas buildup after Cast Lead in, 321; Hamas in, Israeli campaigns against, 8–9, 302–5; Summer Rains and, 306; tunnels from Sinai to, 314, 315, 317–18, 319–20; tunnels to Israel from, 325–27, 330
Gelb, Leslie H., 107n91

"The General Staff Concept of Operations for the IDF" (2006), 335
Geneva Accords (1954), 46
geopolitical history, knowledge of, 354, 355
George H. W. Bush, 180
Germany, World War II air attacks on, 19–20
GHQ Air Force, U.S., 16
Giap, Vo Nguyen, 62, 63–64, 65
Global Reach—Global Power (Rice), 69, 82–83
Glosson, Buster, 87, 88, 89
Godley, G. McMurtrie, 46, 48
Goldfein, David, 193
Goldstone Commission, 320
Goldwater-Nichols Defense Reorganization Act (1986), 79, 82
Goodwin, Doris Kearns, 54
Gordon, Shmuel L., 272
graduated response, enemy's centers of gravity and, 347
Grapes of Wrath, Operation (1996): concept and execution, 294–96; observations, 296–98; overview, 8–9; strategic context, 293–94
Gray, Colin S., 2–3
Gray, George, 81
Great Aerodrome, Langley's, 13
Great Scud Hunt, Desert Storm, 91
Grimsley, William, 168
ground tactical air control parties (TACPs), Korean War and, 30

Haganah (Jewish defense organizations in Palestine), 219–20
Hagenbeck, Franklin, 156
Hallion, Richard P., 5–6
halt-phase operations, Korean War and, 41
Halutz, Dan: on asymmetric conflicts, 292, 297; on IAF and ground forces' battles, 302; IAF campaign planning and, 301; one-size-fits-all mentality and, 334; on perceptual decisions, 299; Second Lebanon War and, 305–6, 307, 312
Hamas: buildup after Cast Lead, 321; Cast Lead and, 317, 318, 319; in Gaza Strip, 8–9, 314–15; Pillar of Defense and, 322–23; Protective Edge and, 325–32, 340n71; shelling Gaza Strip Israeli settlements, 302–3; Sisi government

in Egypt and, 325; terror operations, 300
Hansell, Haywood S., 357
al-Hariri, Rafik, 306
Hariri, Sa'ad, 306
Harkins, Paul D., 60
Hart, Basil Liddell, 237
helicopters: Anaconda and, 156; combat vulnerabilities, Vietnam and, 70, 117n223; Serbia and Kosovo, 144; turboshaft-powered, Southeast Asia and, 44; Vietnam in-country war and, 59, 61–62
Herr, John K., 351
Hezbollah: accountability and, 290–91, 292; formation of, 276, 286; Grapes of Wrath and, 294–97; as Hamas model, 314; Israeli campaigns against, 8–9; Israel's withdrawal from Lebanon and, 299–300; as Lebanese military and political entity, 288–89; Lebanon and, 293; military infrastructure, 307–8; Second Lebanon War and, 306–7, 308–12; UAVs of, 365
Higgins, Gerald J., 31
high-velocity aerial rockets (HVARs), in Korean War, 28, 29
Hilsman, Roger, 108n94
history: military and geopolitical, 354–55, 360–61; as a mode of inquiry, case studies and, 3; review of, future and, 358–60
Hmong, 46, 48
Ho Chi Minh, 43
Ho Chi Minh Trail, 45–48
Holloway, Bruce K., 43
Holloway, James, 59
Hong Xuehi, 33
Hornburg, Hal, 137
Horner, Charles A. "Chuck": as Chief of CENTAF, 83; Desert Shield and, 86, 87–88, 89; Desert Storm and, 89–90, 91; on increased ISR and connectivity, 160; on Iraq's ballistic missiles, 85; on loss of integrity in Vietnam, 67; Schwarzkopf on Hussein and, 84
Howard, Michael, 194
Howard Air Force Base, Canal Zone, 78, 80–81
Howze, Hamilton, 44

"Hunter-Killer" teams, World War II and, 19
Hussein, King of Jordan, 252, 267
Hussein, Saddam: army of, 91; CENTCOM against, 83; Desert Fox against, 136–38, 139, 140, 142; hostility toward Israel, 263–64; Iraqi Freedom against, 6, 161–62, 164; Schwarzkopf on, 84; toppling of, 168–69; al-Tuwaitha Raid and, 268; UN on WMD and, 125–26, 134–35. *See also* Iraq
hydroelectric dams, North Korean, attacks on, 36–37

Ia Drang valley battle, Vietnam, 61
Idris, King of Libya, 71
Imperial Japanese Navy: aircraft carriers of, 16. *See also* Pearl Harbor
Inchon invasion, Korean War, 26, 30, 31
Independence battle group, 85
industry: investment, airpower forces and, 21–22; World War II and, 15–17. *See also* aerospace industry
Inherent Resolve, Operation: air war thus far, 184–87; assessing, 187–94; how ISIS challenge arose, 181–84; against ISIS, 126; overview, 180–81
Instant Thunder, 87
integrated air defense system (IADS): high-technology combat and, 202; Libyan, U.S. intelligence on, 172; Serbian, 128, 129, 130, 131–32; Syrian, 213n159
intelligence: actionable, Desert Storm and, 96–97; Hezbollah and, 294; for Israeli Air Force, 223
intelligence, surveillance, and reconnaissance (ISR): Allied Force and, 149; Egyptian, Six-Day War and, 242–43; Enduring Freedom, 154, 158, 160; Iraqi Freedom and, 165; land and air forces and, 200; Unified Protector, 174, 176
interdiction. *See* battlefield air interdiction
Internal Look 90, 85
International Atomic Energy Agency, 235
in-theater maintenance, Berlin blockade and, 23
Iran: Hezbollah support by, 289, 299; Iraq tanker war with, 83–84; Iraqi "flush" of aircraft to, 91; Iraqi wars with,

264–65; Israel's al-Tuwaitha raid and, 266; late-twentieth-century influence of, 300; U.S. air bases in threat ring of, 365
Iranian Revolutionary Guard, 288
Iraq: aerial reconnaissance to monitor ISIS, 212n133; Desert Shield and, 86–89; Desert Storm and, 89–92; First Arab-Israeli War and, 220; as Gulf region power, 84–85; hostility toward Israel, 263; Iran tanker war with, 83–84; Iran wars with, 264–65; military campaigns (early twenty-first century), 298; nuclear reactors of, 264, 265, 283n114; oriental despotism in, 222, 279n19; political shocks of 1950s and 1960s, 241; postcampaign stabilization in, 168–69; surge in, 126; Yazidi refugees, 180. See also Hussein, Saddam
Iraqi army, 92, 122n321
Iraqi Freedom, Operation: air offensive effects, 164; breakthrough achievements, 166–68; failure of prior resourcing, 168–69; as joint campaign, 164–65; most important takeaway, 169–70; overview, 161–62; against Saddam Hussein, 6, 124; strategy for, 203; as unseen war, 162–64
Iraqi Security Forces, 187
Iron Dome systems, IDFs: Pillar of Defense and, 321, 322, 323, 324, 325; Protective Edge and, 327–28, 330, 331
Islamic jihad, late twentieth century, 300
Islamic State in Iraq and Syria (ISIS): aerial reconnaissance of, 212n133; formation of, 126; Inherent Resolve and, 180–94; Libya after Gaddafi and, 178; rise of, 181–84; U.S. strategy and, 203–4
Islamic State of Iraq and the Levant (ISIL): NATO's war against, 6; Obama administration on, 185
Ismail Ali, Ahmed, 253–54, 255
Israel: airpower and military success of, 365; Ben Eliyahu on air force challenges, 298–99; delegated discretionary authority in, 366; GDP for defense, 274–75, 284n132; Halutz on military decision and the air force, 299; Jordan treaty with (1993), 300; nuclear research reactor, 235; nuclear weapons production by, 249; PLO attacks from Lebanon, 269–70; Rolling Thunder vs. June 1967 victory by, 58; surprise attack on Iraq's nuclear reactor, 133, 206n22; treaty with Egypt (1979), 263. See also Arab-Israeli Wars

Israel Aerospace Industries (IAI), 228–29
Israel Defense Forces (IDF): air vs. ground war and, 286, 305–6, 313; Hamas in Gaza Strip and, 315–16; Hezbollah attacks (2000), 300; IAF and, 235; Offensive Shield and, 301; in security zone, Hezbollah and, 289, 293; Suez War and, 230–31, 234. See also asymmetric conflicts
Israel Military Industries (IMI), 239
Israeli Air Force (IAF): Accountability and, 289–93; Arnold Doctrine and, 271; Cast Lead and, 316–19; contributions (1948–82), 8; damages Iraqi reactor, 264; First Arab-Israeli War and, 220–21, 222–23; First Lebanon War and, 272–74; Grapes of Wrath and, 294–98; Hezbollah and, 293–94; military campaigns (1993–2014), 8–9; October War and, 255, 258–60; Pillar of Defense and, 323, 324; post-1982 learning process, 334, 340–41n79; precursor to, 219–20; Protective Edge and, 326–29, 331, 332–33; from raiding to battlefield presence, 335; Second Lebanon War and, 309–11; selection for study, 3–4; Six-Day War and, 235, 243–44; Suez War and, 227–29, 230–33; transformation of, 236–38; al-Tuwaitha Raid and, 265–68; War of Attrition and, 251–52; war on terror conference, 301–2. See also asymmetric conflicts
Israeli Army, October War and, 259–60
Ivry, David: on airpower, 286; First Lebanon War and, 272, 273, 276; al-Tuwaitha Raid and, 267, 268
Izz ad-Din al-Qassam battalions, of Hamas, 314–15

Jabari, Ahmed, 322
Japan: Allied air attacks on, 19–20. See also Imperial Japanese Navy

Jews: Balfour's proposal for, 218. *See also* Israel
Jodice, Ralph, 177
Johnson, Dana, 76, 110n143, 117n232
Johnson, Lyndon: election of 1964 and, 51; Flaming Dart and, 52; micromanaging by staff and, 54, 55–56, 111n148; military aid to Israel and, 249; Pierce Arrow and, 50; Rolling Thunder and, 52–56, 58; Soviet weapons to Egypt and Syria and, 248; Unger on Laos and, 47; Vietnam and legacy of, 67; on Vietnam War end point, 68
joint: standard military use of term, 209n87. *See also* jointness
joint and combined warfare: Iraqi Freedom as, 162; standard military use of term, 209n87
Joint Chiefs of Staff, 43, 45, 52, 54, 55–56
joint special operations, CENTCOM and, 83
Joint Task Force, Panama, 79, 117n236
jointness: in military operations, 343–44. *See also* joint
Jordan: civil war in, 252; First Arab-Israeli War and, 220; Israel treaty with (1993), 300; military upgrades after Suez War, 241; oriental despotism in, 222, 279n19; War of Attrition and, 251
Joulwan, George, 128
journalists, 89, 90, 93, 97–98, 162–63
Joy, C. Turner, 27
Jungle Jim, Project, 44
Just Cause, Operation: observations, lessons, and reflections, 80–82, 119n257; Panama intervention and, 6, 77–80

Kamps, Charles Tustin, 111n154
Karzai, Hamid, 156
Kasserine, Battle of (1943), 18
Kay, David, 141
Keaney, Thomas A., 119n265
Kearsarge, 172, 173
Keating, Timothy, 165
Keegan, John, 196
Keightley, Charles, 230
Kelso, Frank B., 73
Kennedy, John F., 43–44, 46, 48–49, 108n94
Key West Agreement, 22

Khe Sanh, siege of, 62
Khomeini, Ayatollah, 288
Khrushchev, Nikita, 239–40
kill boxes, in Desert Storm, 89, 121–22n311
Kim Il-Sung, 31, 37, 38
Kissinger, Henry, 253
Kitty Hawk, 152
Knights, Michael, 135
Kong Le, 45–46
Korean War: air pressure to armistice, 36–38; air superiority and, 32–34; airpower in limited war, 25–26; armistice and reckoning, 38–39; challenges of, 5; halt-phase warfare, 29–31; interdiction issues, 35–36; observations, lessons, and reflections, 39–41; phases and immediate challenges of, 26–29, 102n30
Kosovo: Allied Force and, 144–46; military campaigns (end of twentieth century), 298; topography and weather, 143; UN peacekeepers in, 148. *See also* Serbia and Bosnian Serbs
Kosovo Liberation Army (KLA), 147, 148
Kuwait, 84, 89

Lambeth, Benjamin S., 6–7
land-force availability, airpower and, 197–98
Langley, Samuel, 13
Laos, 45, 51, 63. *See also* Southeast Asia
Laskov, Haim, 228
Lavon Affair, Israeli agents in Egypt and, 226
Laws of Armed Conflict, 189
leadership: airpower professionals and, 356–58. *See also* political leaders
Lebanon: Accountability and, 289–91; after Suez War, 241; civil war in, 269; First Arab-Israeli War and, 220; Hezbollah and, 293; Israeli occupation of, 275–76; Israel's withdrawal from, 299–300; as Syrian protectorate, 288; UNIFIL and end to fighting in, 287. *See also* First Lebanon War; Hezbollah; Second Lebanon War
LeMay, Curtis E., 23
Lewinsky, Monica S., 140–41
Libya: Arab Spring and, 170–71; Attain Document and, 71–72; El Dorado Canyon against, 73–76; NATO's war

against, 6; observations, lessons, and reflections, 76–77; resistance forces, 174–75; state-building in, 178; Unified Protector against, 126–27. *See also* Gaddafi, Muammar
Linebacker I, 63–65
Linebacker II, 65–66
Lister, Charles, 186
Lockheed, transport aircraft and, 25
Locklear, Samuel, 172
Loh, John "Mike," 87
low-altitude high-speed attacks, 77

MacArthur, Douglas, 27, 30–31, 39–40
main line of resistance (MLR): in Korean War, 26–27, 33; stable, UN interdiction issues along, 35–36
al-Maliki, Nouri, 182, 183
Mao Zedong, 32, 37
maps: Korean War and, 30; for Vietnam and Laos, 49
marketing, 354, 355–56, 361
Marx, Karl, 221
Mason, Richard A. "Tony," 93, 204n1
Mattis, James, 193
Mauz, Henry H., Jr., 86
Mayaguez incident (1975), 45
McConnell, John P., 52
McConnell, Mike, 96
McCutchan, Clay, 119n262
McDonnell-Douglas, transport aircraft and, 25
McNamara, Robert S., 44, 55–56, 58, 111n157
McPeak, Merrill, 89, 197
media. *See* journalists
Meir, Golda, 220, 255, 258
memoirs, Vietnam War, 67, 115–16n212
Meyer, Edward "Shy," 69
Middle East conflicts, 7–8
military aerospace in U.S.: Berlin Airlift and, 22–25; conclusions, 98–100; First Gulf War, 82–98; Just Cause in Panama, 77–82; Korean War and, 25–41; Libyan intervention, 71–77; setting the stage, 13–15; Southeast Asia, 42–71; World War II and, 15–22
Military Air Transport Service, Berlin Airlift and, 23
Military Assistance Command, Panama, 79

Military Assistance Command, Vietnam (MACV), 50, 54–56. *See also* Westmoreland, William
military history, knowledge of, 354–55
Mill Pond, Project, Laos, 46
Milošević, Slobodan: Allied Force and, 143, 144, 145, 146; Deny Flight mistakes and, 126; land-force availability and, 196, 198
Mitchell, William "Billy," 14, 351, 356
Moffett, William "Billy," 14, 15
Mollet, Guy, 233
Momyer, William W.: on airpower use, 54; on command relationships in Laos, 46–47; as Horner mentor, 83; integrating Army and Air Force and, 69; Khe Sanh siege and, 62–63; on Rolling Thunder, 52
Monk, Erika, 93
Moore, Royal N., Jr., 86
Morsi, Mohamed, 325
Moseley, T. Michael "Buzz," 166, 167, 200
Mountbatten, Louis, 233
Mubarak, Hosni, 85, 253, 263
Mule Team, Project, 49
Munro, Alan, 88
al-Musawi, Abbas, 289
Muse, Kurt, 81
Muslim Brotherhood, 321, 325

Nam Il, Korean War and, 33
napalm, 29, 33, 35–36
Nasrallah, Hassan, 289, 307
Nasser, Gamal Abdel: after Six-Day War, 245; after Suez War, 239–40; death of, 253; EAF standards and, 241; military leadership and, 246; modernizing armed services, 226; nationalist revolution and, 221; nationalizes Suez Canal, 225, 229; Sedky Mahmoud on preemptive strikes to, 242; Six-Day War and, 242–43; Suez War and, 231, 232–33, 234; War of Attrition and, 249, 250
National Advisory Committee for Aeronautics, 14
National Security Agency, Vietnam War and, 54–56
NATO airpower: Deliberate Force, 130–33; France and, 170; information sharing, 177; Libyan-related bombings

and, 72–73; maturing of, 7; selection for study, 3–4; Tactical Air Working Party, 69; Unified Protector, 173–74, 175–76; USAFE expansion, Kennedy administration and, 44. *See also* American and NATO airpower
naval action, direct strategic effects from, 346
naval airpower, Korean War and, 28–29
Naval Forces Far East (NAVFE), 27, 35–38
Nechushtan, Ido, 320, 335
Nelson, Horatio, 357
Nevo, Yak "Moked" (Focus), 238, 243
Nimrod Dancer, Operation, 78
Nitze, Paul, 111n157
Nixon, Richard M.: North Vietnam spring invasion (1972) and, 63; OPEC oil embargo and, 262–63; Paris peace talks, Vietnam War and, 65; Soviet participation in War of Attrition and, 251; Vietnamization policy of, 61; Watergate and, 66, 115n209
Noriega, Manuel, 77, 78, 79, 80
Normandy invasion, 20
North Africa, sea-air-land invasion (1942), 17–18
North Korean People's Army (NKPA) Air Force, 28, 29, 31, 37
North Vietnam: fighting to win, 68, 115n209; Joint Chiefs on air action against, 51; spring invasion (1972), 62, 63; U.S. bombing, air war in Middle East and, 250; Vietnam air war and, 45
Northern Watch, Operation, 166–67

Obama, Barack, and administration: Iraq withdrawal under, 180; Islamic State and, 126, 181–84, 192, 203–4; Libya and, 171, 179
October War (1973): commentary, 263; "evils of wanton conceit" and, 255; logistics as strategy, 262–63; North Vietnam spring invasion (1972) and, 65; overview, 7–8; social change and, 255–56; strategy for, 253–54; technology and training, 256–58; as war in two parts, 258–62
Odyssey Dawn, Operation: against Gaddafi, 126; genesis of, 171–73; overview, 170–71; in retrospect, 178–80; successes and problems, 174–77. *See also* Unified Protector, Operation
Offensive Shield, Operation (2002), 301
O'Grady, Scott, 205n5
Olmert, Ehud, 307, 315, 318
On Strategy: A Critical Analysis of the Vietnam War (Summers), 116n215
Opera, Operation, al-Tuwaitha and, 265–68
operational assumptions, World War II and, 17–19
operational history, as pedagogical tool, 2
Operations Strangle I and II (Korea), 35
OPLAN 1002-90, 85
opponent, desired postwar condition of, 346
Organization of the Petroleum Exporting Countries (OPEC), 262–63
oriental despotism, Egypt, Syria, Iraq, and, 221–22
Oslo Accords (1993), 300
Ottoman Empire, 218, 221

Pacific theater, World War II, 17–19, 20
Pahlavi, Mohammad Reza, 264
Pak Hon-Yong, 31
Palestine Flying Service, 219–20
Palestine Liberation Organization (PLO): attacking Israel from Lebanon, 269–70; First Lebanon War and, 275, 287; formation of, Suez War and, 235; hostility toward Israel, 263; October War and, 255; Six-Day War and, 245; terror strikes by, 300; War of Attrition and, 251, 252
Palestinian Authority, 300–301, 317
Palestinian Jihad, 326
Palestinian Legislative Council, 314
Palestinians: Balfour Declaration and, 278n2; First Arab-Israeli War and, 222–23, 224; Israel establishment and, 217, 220; in Lebanon, Israel attacks by, 288; Six-Day War and, 245; suicide bombings, 300
Panama intervention, Just Cause and, 6, 77–82
Panamanian Defense Force (PDF), 78–79, 80, 81
Panetta, Leon, 183
parallel war, planning and executing, 349–50

Paris Peace Accords (1973), 66, 112n173
Paris peace talks, Vietnam War and, 65
Pathet Lao, 46, 47, 108n95
Paz, Robert, 78
peace activists: Desert Storm and, 93, 97; on precision attacks, 233. *See also* protests
Peace for Galilee, Operation, 270, 285. *See also* First Lebanon War
Pearl Harbor, 16–17, 235
Peng Dehuai, 32
People's Army of Vietnam (PAVN), 47, 48, 52, 62, 63–64
People's Liberation Army Air Force, 32
Peres, Shimon, 228
Peretz, Amir, 307, 312
Perry, William, 129
Pershing, John, 14
Petraeus, David, 168
Pierce Arrow, Operation, 52
Pillar of Defense, Operation (2012): concept and execution, 322–24; observations, 324; overview, 8–9; strategic context, 321–22
Plain of Jars, Laos, 46, 47
Plei Me, Vietnam, Viet Cong attacks on, 61
Pleiku, Vietnam, Viet Cong attacks on, 52, 61
Pol Pot regime, Cambodia, 45
political leaders: airpower support and funding and, 352–53; not collaborating with airpower professionals, 348; serial vs. parallel war and, 349–50; teaching strategy to, 346–47
Pollack, Kenneth, 140, 142
Portugal, El Dorado Canyon and, 74
Powell, Colin: Desert Shield and, 87, 88; Desert Storm and, 89, 97; Hussein's invasion of Kuwait and, 85; Just Cause and, 79, 80
Prairie Fire, Attain Document and, 71–72
Prayer Book, 118n251
precision air attacks: Allied Force, 150; Cast Lead, 319; Deliberate Force, 132–33; Deny Flight, 127; Desert Storm, 6, 89–91, 92–94; Enduring Freedom, 158; ground forces roles and, 199–201; IAF battlefield presence with, 335; Inherent Resolve, 187–88; laser-guided bombs, 76–77, 131; North Vietnam spring invasion (1972) and, 64; Odyssey Dawn and Unified Protector, 175; al-Tuwaitha Raid, 267; Unified Protector, 176, 177
predictability, Deny Flight and, 128–29
preemptive strikes, 235–36, 242, 255
principles, operational history and, 2
prisoners of war (POWs), Rolling Thunder and, 58, 112n173
Protective Edge, Operation (2014): concept and execution, 327–31; observations, 331–33; overview, 8–9; strategic context, 325–27
protests: Vietnam War, 59, 67–68. *See also* peace activists
Pusan Pocket, Korea, 26, 29–30, 31
Push CAS, Horner on Iraqi armored advance and, 84

al-Qaeda: Enduring Freedom and, 124, 151–61; in Iraq, 126; Libya after Gaddafi and, 178; rebrands as ISIS, 183; Sept. 11 terrorist attacks and, 152
Quy Nhơn, 52

Rabin, Yitzhak, 289
radar: coverage, Battle of Britain and, 17, 21; coverage, Berlin Airlift and, 24; Egyptian, Six-Day War and, 243; Egypt's Air Defense Command's, 246, 247; integrated air defenses and, 70–71; joint surveillance target-attack, 95
Radford, Arthur, 34
Rafael Armament Development Authority, Israel, 239
RAND Corporation, 53–54
Ranger, 52
Rather, Dan, 80
Razon weapons, 39, 106n72
Reagan, Ronald, and administration, 71–72, 73, 75, 77, 78
reconnaissance flights, 34, 44, 49
Red Flag program (Air Force), 70
remotely piloted aircraft (RPA), 147, 149
remotely piloted vehicles (RPVs), 271–72. *See also* unmanned aerial vehicles
Renuart, Gene, 166
reporters. *See* journalists
Republican Guard, Iraq, 91, 92, 136, 137, 161–62
Rice, Donald B., 69, 82

Ricks, Thomas, 169
Ridgway, Matthew, 40
Rio Hato, Panama, F-117 strike at, 80, 81
Rogers, Bernard, 73
Rogers, Michael, 193
Rolling Thunder: aircraft and personnel losses, 58; approved target list and, 54–56; costs, 58, 112n163, 112n171, 112n173; critical shortfalls exposed by, 57; criticism of, 59; debate over, 67; effectiveness of, 56–57, 112n161; MiGs and SAMs and, 57; overview, 52–53; route packs in the North for, 54, 111n144
Rostow, Walt, 55
Royal Air Force (RAF): Arab air forces and, 223; Battle of Britain and, 17; Enduring Freedom and, 153; as example for U.S. Air Force, 21; Royal Egyptian Air Force and, 221–22; Suez War and, 230–32
Royal Australian Air Force (RAAF), 38, 59
Royal Egyptian Air Force (REAF), 221–22, 223, 226–27
Royal Iraqi Air Force (RIrAF), 222
Royal Navy, 16
Rudnik, Raphael, 8–9
Ruge, Friedrich, 20
rules of engagement (ROE): Afghanistan, 159–60; inadequate maps for Cambodia and, 49; Inherent Resolve, 188, 189–91, 192, 214n166; in Korean War, 40; North Vietnam spring invasion (1972) and, 64; Panama intervention and, 82; Rolling Thunder and, 59; strike on Libya, 74; UN on, 128; Vietnam in-country war and, 60–61
Rusk, Dean, 43
Russ, Robert, 87
Russia: high-technology combat and, 202; Syria's Assad and, 192–93. *See also* Soviet Union
Ryan, Michael, 128, 132

Sadat, Anwar, 253, 255, 258, 260, 261–62
Samuel B. Roberts, 84
sanctuaries, in Korean War, 40
Sandino war (1927–33), 14
Saratoga, 71
Sarkozy, Nicolas, 170
Saturate, Operation, 35

Saudi Arabia, 85–86, 135
Schwarzkopf, Norman: daily ATO and, 94; Desert Shield and, 86, 89; Desert Storm and, 90, 91; Desert Storm ground force estimates, 344; Glosson briefing Bush and, 88; Horner on, 83, 84; Hussein's invasion of Kuwait and, 85; target list, 87
science: investment, airpower forces and, 21–22; knowledge of, 354. *See also* technology
science fiction, education through, 361
Scowcroft, Brent, 85, 88, 89
Scud attacks: Egyptian, 261; Iraqi, 97, 264–65
Second Lebanon War (2006): concept and execution, 308–12, 338n46; observations, 313–14; overview, 8–9; strategic context, 305–8
security, day-to-day, IDF on, 285
Sedky Mahmoud, Mohamed, 242, 246
Segoli, Ephraim, 8–9
September 11, 2001, terrorist attacks, 151–52, 162
Serbia and Bosnian Serbs: Allied Force and, 143–51; Deliberate Force and, 124, 130–34; Deny Flight and, 127–29; operations against, 6
serial warfare, planning and executing, 349
7th Air Force of the Pacific Air Forces (PACAF), 46–47, 55, 62–63, 114n189
Shabak (Israel's General Security Service), 303, 305, 316
Shah of Iran, 83
Shalikashvili, John, 128
Sharon, Ariel: on Egypt's soldiers vs. officers, 246, 255; First Lebanon War and, 275; Gaza Strip and, 301, 314; on Israel's defensive barrier, 249; limits of applying force and, 276; Peace for Galilee and, 270
Sharp, Grant, 84, 120n275
Sharp, Grant, Jr., 50, 51, 55, 56, 120n275
Shelton, Hugh, 140
Shi'ites, Hezbollah and, 288, 297, 312
Shkedy, Eliezer, 304, 305, 341n79
Short, Michael, 150
Sicilian campaign, FM 100-20 tested in, 19
Sino-Japanese War (1937–45), 17
al-Sisi, Abdel Fattah, 325

Six-Day War (1967): as airpower master class, 242–44; commentary, 244–45; North Vietnam spring invasion (1972) and, 64; overview, 7–8; platforms without policies, 239–42; preemption as strategy, 235–36; swift intuition and, 236–39
Sixth Fleet, 71–72
Smart, Jacob E., 36
smart weapons, Vietnam and development of, 71
Smith, Joseph, 23
Smith, Leighton W., Jr., 150
soft power, Berlin Airlift as, 25
Solomons campaign, 17–18
Sorley, Lewis, 64
South Lebanese Army, 289
South Vietnam: cross-border assault into Laos and, 48; Vietnam air war and, 45
South Vietnam air force (VNAF), 49, 59, 60, 64
South Vietnamese army (ARVN), 49, 50
Southeast Asia: in-country war, 59–63; Laos and Ho Chi Minh Trail, 45–48; Linebacker I and II, 63–66; overview, 42–44; prequel to, 45; Rolling Thunder, 52–59; Vietnam's consequences and lessons, 66–71; war over two Vietnams, 48–52
Southern Focus, Operation, 167
Southern Watch, Operation, 135, 166–67
Souvanna Phouma, 45–46, 48, 51
Soviet Union: Berlin blockade by, 22–24; doctrinal influence of, 241–42; economic assistance to Middle East, 275; Egypt seeks military aid from, 227; erroneous intelligence for Middle East by, 242; First Lebanon War and, 273–74; Korean War divisions between Chinese, North Koreans and, 37; military aid to Middle East, 239–41, 247, 257–58, 282n94; October War and, 261–62, 262; Sadat and Egyptian ties with, 253; technology advances and, 93; War of Attrition and, 251
Spaatz, Carl, 19
space war, First Gulf War as, 95
Spain, El Dorado Canyon and, 74, 76
Spanish Civil War (1936–39), 17
Special Forces, Israeli, 290–91, 292, 293, 295

special operations forces (SOF): Afghanistan, 152; British, Odyssey Dawn and, 175; Enduring Freedom and, 158, 160–61; helicopters in Vietnam and, 59; in Panama, 81. *See also* joint special operations
Special Security Organization, Iraq, 136
Specific Gravity, Operation (2006), 309, 313
Speicher, Michael, 122n315
Stalin, Joseph, 31, 32, 37
Stark, 84
state institutions of governance, political modernization and, 168, 210n104
Stavridis, James, 178
stealth aircraft, Vietnam and development of, 71
Stephens, Alan, 7–8
Stevens, J. Christopher, 178
Stiner, Carl W., 79
strategic proficiency, developing and maintaining, 353
Stratemeyer, George E., 27, 31
Straw, Jack, 278n2
Suez Canal, 219, 225
Suez War (1956): commentary, 234–35; Egyptian Air Force, 226–27; Egyptian nationalism and, 225–26; Israeli Air Force, 227–29; overview, 7–8; politics of war and, 233–34; war as policy, 229–33
Sui-ho Dam, North Korea, 36
Sullivan, Gordon, 196–97
Sullivan, William, 46, 47, 48, 51
Summer Rains, Operation (2006), 306
Summers, Harry G., Jr., 116n215
Sunnis, Second Lebanon War and, 312
suppression of enemy air defenses (SEAD): Bosnian Serbs, 129, 132; IAF during October War and, 259; Libya, 74, 77; Serbia, 144; Southeast Asia, 66
surface-to-air missiles (SAMs): Army's Patriot, Iraq's missiles and, 85; Israeli, 238; Libyan, U.S. intelligence on, 172; Rolling Thunder and, 57; Vietnam War, 42, 56, 57, 65, 66, 70–71, 115n205
Sykes-Picot Agreement, 218, 278n2
Syria: Assad's death and, 300; defensive barrier against Israel, 270; First Arab-Israeli War and, 220; First Lebanon War and, 272–73; Hezbollah support by, 289, 299; indirect conflict

against Israel and, 286; military upgrades after Suez War, 241; October War and, 254, 258; oriental despotism in, 222, 279n19; Russia and, 192–93; troop withdrawal from Iraq and, 183; War of Attrition and, 251
Syrian Arab Air Force (SyAAF), 222, 271

tactical air control parties (TACPs): in Korean War, 30; radio-equipped, Vietnam in-country and, 59–60
tactical air control system (TACS), Vietnam in-country war and, 60
tactical proficiency, developing and maintaining, 353
TACWAR, First Gulf War and, 85
Taiwan, China and, 195
Taliban. *See* Enduring Freedom, Operation
tanker bridge, 94–95. *See also* aerial refueling
targets: Allied Force, 144, 145, 146, 147, 149; analysis, Desert Fox, 139; analysis, Desert Storm, 96; approved list, Accountability and, 291; approved list, in Vietnam, 54–56; Enduring Freedom, 153–54, 158, 159–60; in Gaza Strip, 304; against ISIS, 188–90, 192; in Libya, 73–75, 117n232, 118n237; Second Lebanon War, 311, 313–14
Task Force 60 (TF-60), 71, 73
Task Force 77 (TF-77): air pressure by, 36, 37; air war in Vietnam and, 55; CAS after Sept. 1951 and, 35; Korean War and, 27, 34; Rolling Thunder and, 53
Taylor, Maxwell, 51
technology: airpower and, 344; airpower test against, 201–2, 215–16n193; Desert Storm and, 93–94; disruptive, developing and maintaining, 350–52; education on, 361; Egyptian, October War and, 257–58; Enduring Freedom, 155; IAF's transformation and, 238–39; investment, airpower forces and, 21–22; Israeli, October War and, 256–57; knowledge of, 354, 355, 356; preparing for surprises in, 352; weaponry and, post–Desert Storm, 125; World War II and, 15–17. *See also* intelligence, surveillance, and reconnaissance; science

telecommunications, Battle of Britain and, 21
terminal attack controllers, Enduring Freedom and, 157, 158–59
terrorilla (terror and guerilla) organization, 289. *See also* Hezbollah
Tet Offensive, 62
Thatcher, Margaret, 72, 74, 75, 76, 85
Theodore Roosevelt, 130, 133, 152
13th Air Force, Korean War and, 27
31 Initiatives, 69
Thud Ridge (Broughton), 67
Thurman, Maxwell, 79
Timberlake, Edward "Ted," 28
time frame for war operations, airpower professionals on, 348
Tlass, Mustafa, 273
Tolkowsky, Dan, 228, 236
Tomahawk land-attack missiles (TLAMs), 131–32
Tonkin Gulf Resolution, 50–51
Top Gun program (Navy), 70
training, prewar, 94, 170, 226, 257
transport aircraft, 21, 23–24, 25, 41, 59
Treaty for Nuclear Non-Proliferation, Iraq and, 264
Trenchard, Hugh, 219
Trenchard's model of airpower, 219, 227, 256
Tripoli, Libya targets, 73–75, 118n237
Truman administration, Korean War and, 39
Tuesday Lunch, air war in Vietnam and, 55
Tunner, William H., 23–24
al-Tuwaitha Raid (1981): Begin Doctrine and, 263–65; commentary, 268–69; Operation Opera, 265–68; overview, 7–8
20th Air Force, Korean War and, 27
22nd Bomb Wing, Korean War and, 29

Ultra signals intelligence, World War II and, 19
Unger, Leonard, 46, 47
Unified Protector, Operation: against Gaddafi, 126–27, 173–74; overview, 170–71; in retrospect, 178–80; successes and problems, 174–77
Union of Soviet Socialist Republics (USSR). *See* Soviet Union
United Arab Republic, 239–42

United Nations: constraints on Deny Flight, 128; First Arab-Israeli War and, 224; Grapes of Wrath and, 295, 296; Hamas against Israel in Gaza Strip and, 315; Human Rights Council, 320; October War and, 262; partitioning Palestine Mandate, 220; Resolution 678 on Iraqis in Kuwait, 89; Resolution 1134 on Iraqi weapons inspections, 134–35; Resolution 1559 on Syria's withdrawal from Lebanon, 300; Resolution 1701 on Hezbollah disarmament, 310, 312; Resolution 1973 on Gaddafi, 171, 210n110; Suez War cease fire and, 234

United Nations forces: Chinese People's Volunteers in Korea and, 32; Interim Force in Lebanon, 287; Korean War and, 26, 28, 29, 30, 31; Rapid Reaction Force against Serbs, 131; South Korea's independence and, 40

United States: Accountability mediation by, 291; airpower, selection for study, 3–4; airpower and military success of, 365; airpower maturing, 7; continental, Panama intervention and, 79; delegated discretionary authority in, 366; First Lebanon War and, 274; as global airpower leader, 3; Iran's military and, 265; Israel and military support from, 248–49, 275, 277; Israel's al-Tuwaitha raid and, 266; no-fly zone over Libya and, 171–72; October War and, 259, 261–62, 262; on Suez War, 233–34. *See also under* U.S.; *specific services and operations*

unmanned aerial vehicles (UAVs): Accountability and, 290–91, 292; Cast Lead and, 319; First Lebanon War and, 286; Grapes of Wrath and, 295; IAF battlefield presence with, 335; Protective Edge and, 332. *See also* remotely piloted vehicles

Urgent Fury, Operation, 77, 80, 100

U.S. Africa Command, Odyssey Dawn and, 176

U.S. Air Force: approved target list in Vietnam and, 55–56; CENTCOM and, 83; complacency after Korea, 42; Composite Air Strike Forces, 44; El Dorado Canyon and, 77; embedded journalists and, 163; Enduring Freedom, 153; establishment of, 22; heavy bombers in Allied Force, 148–49; joint Army ground coordination in Vietnam with, 60, 63; Korean War and CAS doctrine of, 30; Korean War and emergence of, 41; Korean War reckoning, 38, 39; Laotian air war and, 47; marketing by, 356; North Korean airspace and, 31; North Vietnam spring invasion (1972) and, 63–64; Rolling Thunder and, 54, 58, 112n163; strike on Bosnian Serbs, 130–31; strike on Libya, 72, 73; as study focus, 3; Tripoli targets for, 73, 74–75, 117n232, 118n237; Vietnam in-country war and, 59; World War II and establishment of, 21

U.S. Air Forces in Europe (USAFE): Berlin blockade and, 22–23; expansion, Kennedy administration and, 44

U.S. Air National Guard, 43

U.S. Army: Anaconda and, 156–58; Desert Storm and, 92; joint Air Force ground coordination in Vietnam with, 60, 63; Korean War and CAS doctrine of, 29–30; Patriot SAM, Iraq's missiles and, 85; Tactical Mobility Requirements Board, 44; Vietnam in-country war and, 59; World War II aircraft of, 16

U.S. Army Air Service, 14–15

U.S. Carrier Air Groups, 16

U.S. Central Command (CENTCOM), 83. *See also* First Gulf War

U.S. Marine Corps: air-ground tactical air support and, 14; B-2 stealth bomber and, 149; CENTCOM and, 83; Korean War and CAS doctrine of, 29–30; Korean War reckoning, 38, 39; North Vietnam spring invasion (1972) and, 63–64; strike on Bosnian Serbs, 130–31; withdrawal down to Hungnam, Korea, 32

U.S. Navy: aircraft and submarines after World War II and, 21; approved target list in Vietnam and, 55–56; ATO system and, 123n328; B-2 stealth bomber and, 149; Benghazi targets for, 73, 74–75, 117n232; Bureau of Aeronautics, 14; CENTCOM and, 83;

El Dorado Canyon and, 77; evolving service aviation after Korea, 42; Iranian navy and, 84; Korean War reckoning, 38; Laotian air war and, 47; North Korean airspace and, 31; North Vietnam spring invasion (1972) and, 63–64; strike on Bosnian Serbs, 130–31; strike on Libya, 72; World War II aircraft of, 16
U.S. Pacific Command (PACOM), 54–56

Van Fleet, James, 37
Vang Pao, 46, 48
victory, definition, Vietnam War and, 68
victory/loss ratios, Vietnam vs. World War II and Korea, 70
Vientiane agreement (1973), 48
Viet Cong: in-country war and, 60, 61; Flaming Dart and, 52; Ho Chi Minh Trail and, 46; shelling B-57s at Bien Hoa airbase, 51; shelling near Saigon from Laos, 47; Tet Offensive and, 62
Vietnam: air war in, 50; coups and countercoups in, 51. *See also* North Vietnam; South Vietnam; Southeast Asia
Vietnam War: consequences and lessons, 66–71; Inherent Resolve compared to, 191; wars fought during, 5–6. *See also* Southeast Asia
Vietnamization policy, 61, 63
Voenno-Vozdushnye Sily (Soviet air force), 32

Wag the Dog, 140–41
war: Israel Defense Forces' definition of, 285. *See also* Arab-Israeli Wars; Southeast Asia; *specific operations*
War of Attrition (1969–70): commentary, 251–52; consolidating success, 248–49; fighting smart-attrition warfare, 249–51; learning from failure, 246–48; overview, 7–8; politics of victory and defeat and, 245–46
Warden, John A., III, 9–10, 69, 87, 96
Watergate, 66, 115n209
Watkins, James, 73
Watts, Carol, 138
weapons deficiencies, Vietnam and, 70–71

weapons of mass destruction (WMD): Hussein and UN on, 125–26, 134, 142; Iraqi Freedom and, 162; Kay interrogations on, 141; strikes on production facilities, 136
Weinberger, Caspar, 73
Weizman, Ezer, 236–37, 238, 248, 286
Westmoreland, William, 51, 54, 60, 63
Wheeler, Earle, 55, 60–61
White House. *See specific presidents*
Whitley, Al, 357
Williams, Kendra, 138
Wilson, Andrew "Sandy," 88
Wilson, Richard, 265
Winnefeld, James A., 76, 110n143, 117n232
Winograd Commission, 313
women, as fighter pilots, 138
Woodward, Bob, 269
Woodward, Margaret, 176
World War I, 13–14, 218, 219, 225, 229
World War II: airpower ascendency and, 5; airpower in context of, 15–22; doctrinal and operational assumptions, 17–19; drawdown after, 5, 26, 39; Israeli Air Force and, 220–21; maturation of U.S. airpower and, 19–20; Middle East and, 222; observations, lessons, and reflections, 20–22; Suez Canal and, 225; technical and industrial dimensions, 15–17; U.S. civil air transport and, 14–15
Wratten, William "Bill," 88
Wright Military Flyer (1908 and 1909), 13

Xiaoming Zhang, 37

Ya'alon, Moshe, 327
Yadlin, Amos, 297
Yassin, Ahmed, 301
Yeosock, John, 86
Yugoslav civil war, 124, 125, 126, 130–34. *See also* Kosovo; Serbia and Bosnian Serbs

Zakai, Shmuel, 303
Zhou Enlai, 32
Zinni, Anthony, 140
Zionist Federation of Great Britain and Ireland, 218

The Naval Institute Press is the book-publishing arm of the U.S. Naval Institute, a private, nonprofit, membership society for sea service professionals and others who share an interest in naval and maritime affairs. Established in 1873 at the U.S. Naval Academy in Annapolis, Maryland, where its offices remain today, the Naval Institute has members worldwide.

Members of the Naval Institute support the education programs of the society and receive the influential monthly magazine *Proceedings* or the colorful bimonthly magazine *Naval History* and discounts on fine nautical prints and on ship and aircraft photos. They also have access to the transcripts of the Institute's Oral History Program and get discounted admission to any of the Institute-sponsored seminars offered around the country.

The Naval Institute's book-publishing program, begun in 1898 with basic guides to naval practices, has broadened its scope to include books of more general interest. Now the Naval Institute Press publishes about seventy titles each year, ranging from how-to books on boating and navigation to battle histories, biographies, ship and aircraft guides, and novels. Institute members receive significant discounts on the Press' more than eight hundred books in print.

Full-time students are eligible for special half-price membership rates. Life memberships are also available.

For more information about Naval Institute Press books that are currently available, visit www.usni.org/press/books. To learn about joining the U.S. Naval Institute, please write to:

Member Services
U.S. Naval Institute
291 Wood Road
Annapolis, MD 21402-5034
Telephone: (800) 233-8764
Fax: (410) 571-1703
Web address: www.usni.org